Fodor's

BELIZE

WELCOME TO BELIZE

It's easy to become immersed in the natural beauty of Belize. Broadleaf canopies shelter exotic birds, and ancient Mayan ruins are wrapped in vines. Underwater caves and the chute of the Blue Hole offer some of the world's best diving, and the Belize Barrier Reef astounds snorkelers with a lavish medley of coral and fish. Belize's secluded resorts embrace these surroundings: here, you can sleep under a palm-thatched roof in a lush jungle lodge and escape to a dreamy overwater bungalow with turquoise sea views all on the same trip.

TOP REASONS TO GO

★ **Mayan Ruins:** Evidence of the ancient Mayan empire is everywhere in Belize.

★ **Snorkeling:** The Belize Barrier Reef presents amazing underwater vistas.

★ **Diving:** Reefs and atolls provide many of the world's greatest dive sites.

★ **Bird-Watching:** Belize has more than 500 species of birds, many rare or endangered.

★ **Beach Stays:** Often remote or removed, and nearly always right on the water.

★ **Jungle Lodges:** For an unforgettable close-to-nature experience in comfort.

12

TOP EXPERIENCES

Belize offers terrific experiences that should be on every traveler's list. Here are Fodor's top picks for a memorable trip.

1 Belize Barrier Reef

Widely considered one of the world's best sites for diving and snorkeling, the Belize Barrier Reef is home to more than 300 species of fish and 65 kinds of coral. It's the longest barrier reef in the Western or Northern hemispheres. *(Ch. 3, 6)*

2 Cave Tubing

Overland journeys and undersea adventures are just part of the Belize experience. Underground, you'll find subterranean rivers that provide thrilling passage through spooky caves. *(Ch. 5, 6, 7)*

3 Bird-watching

Belize's jungles teem with wild birds—nearly 600 species. Endangered beauties such as the scarlet macaw and keel-billed toucan roam freely in the country's interior. *(Ch. 4–7)*

4 Kayaking

The Belize Barrier Reef blocks big swells, so the country has some of the region's best open-water kayaking. Inland, there are rivers for all levels of paddlers. *(Ch. 3, 5, 6, 7)*

5 Jaguar Trekking

Jaguars are shy and nocturnal, so sightings are rare. But Belize has the highest concentration of them in the world. With patience and luck, you might spot one in the wild. *(Ch. 4, 5, 6)*

6 Ziplining

One of the most thrilling ways to explore Belize is from its treetops. Canopy tours zip you through a network of suspended platforms high in the trees. *(Ch. 5, 6, 7)*

7 Remote Escapes

Private islands are the stuff of dream vacations, and Belize's cayes and atolls have a number of these fantasy getaways—some with surprisingly down-to-earth prices. *(Ch. 3)*

8 Mayan Ruins

For 5,000 years the Mayans inhabited this region. Caracol and more than a dozen sites are open to visitors for climbing, exploring, and general ogling of astounding architectual ingenuity. *(Ch. 2–8)*

9 Staying at a Jungle Lodge

In Belize there's a jungle lodge for every budget, from simple cabins to the deluxe Caves Branch Lodge. Included free each night is the jungle music of birds, monkeys, and tree frogs. *(Ch. 4–7)*

10 Hummingbird Highway

A drive on this scenic roadway winds through limestone hill country, deep-green mountains, and citrus country with groves of Valencia oranges. *(Ch. 5)*

11 Actun Tunichil Muknal (ATM)

More than a cave system, ATM is a visit to a Mayan underworld filled with eerie chambers where ancient artifacts and human skeletons remain undisturbed. *(Ch. 5)*

12 Ambergris Caye/Caye Caulker

Belize's largest island and its "little sister" attract divers and beachcombers, sunbathers and snorkelers, with the most water sports, beach resorts, and restaurants in the country. *(Ch. 3)*

CONTENTS

CONTENTS

MAPS

ABOUT THIS GUIDE

Fodor's Recommendations

Everything in this guide is worth doing—we don't cover what isn't—but exceptional sights, hotels, and restaurants are recognized with additional accolades. **Fodor's**Choice★ indicates our top recommendations. Care to nominate a new place? Visit Fodors.com/contact-us.

Trip Costs

We list prices wherever possible to help you budget well. Hotel and restaurant price categories from **$** to **$$$$** are noted alongside each recommendation. For hotels, we include the lowest cost of a standard double room in high season. For restaurants, we cite the average price of a main course at dinner or, if dinner isn't served, at lunch. For attractions, we always list adult admission fees; discounts are usually available for children, students, and senior citizens.

Hotels

Our local writers vet every hotel to recommend the best overnights in each price category, from budget to expensive. Unless otherwise specified, you can expect private bath, phone, and TV in your room. For expanded hotel reviews, facilities, and deals visit Fodors.com.

Restaurants

Unless we state otherwise, restaurants are open for lunch and dinner daily. We mention dress code only when there's a specific requirement and reservations only when they're essential or not accepted. To make restaurant reservations, visit Fodors.com.

Credit Cards

The hotels and restaurants in this guide typically accept credit cards. If not, we'll say so.

Top Picks
★ **Fodor's**Choice

Listings
⊠ Address
⊠ Branch address
☎ Telephone
🖶 Fax
⊕ Website
✉ E-mail
🎫 Admission fee
☉ Open/closed times
Ⓜ Subway
✛ Directions or Map coordinates

Hotels & Restaurants
🏨 Hotel
🛏 Number of rooms
🍽 Meal plans
✗ Restaurant
🔑 Reservations
👔 Dress code
▭ No credit cards
$ Price

Other
⇨ See also
☞ Take note
⛳ Golf facilities

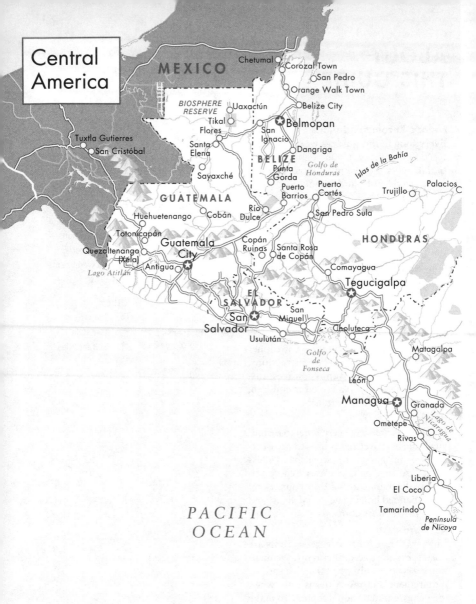

Central America

PACIFIC
OCEAN

0   100 miles

0   150 km

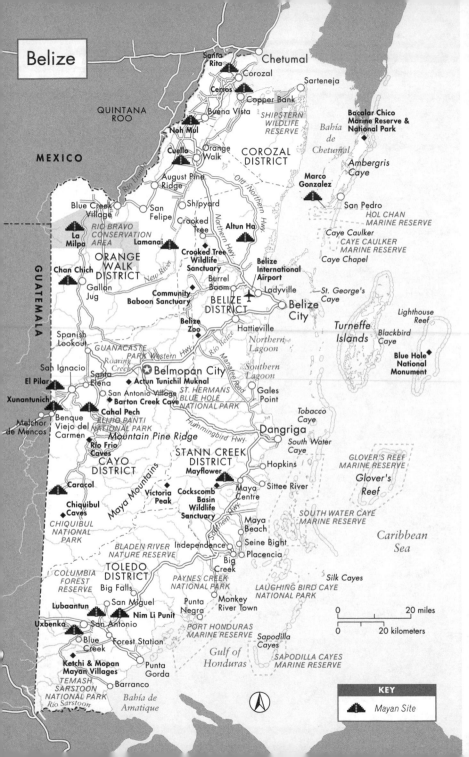

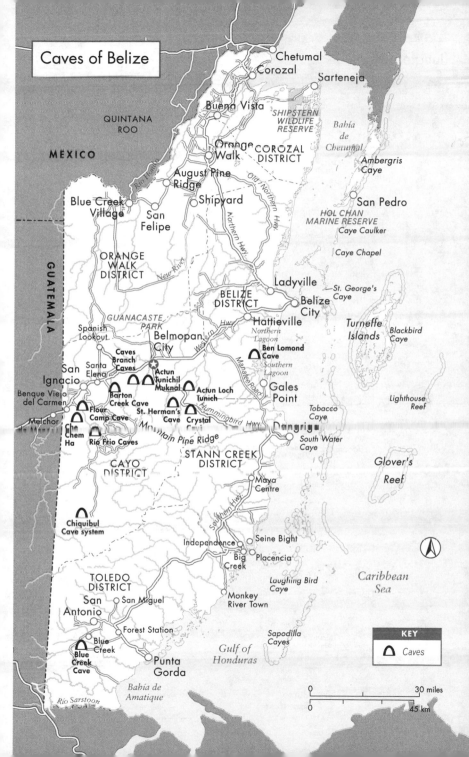

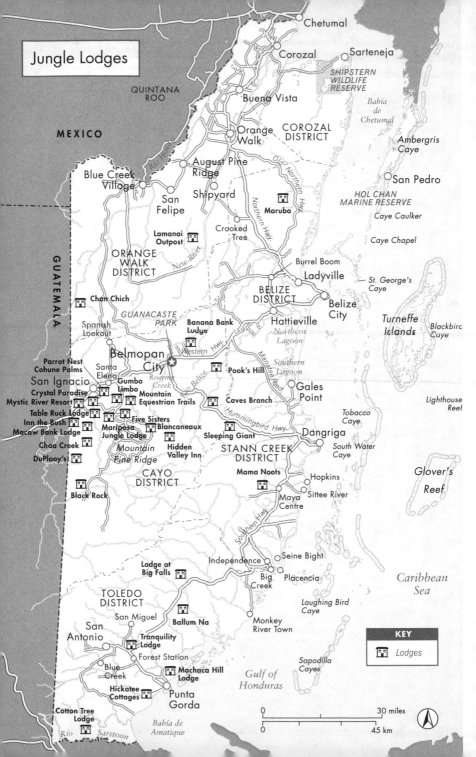

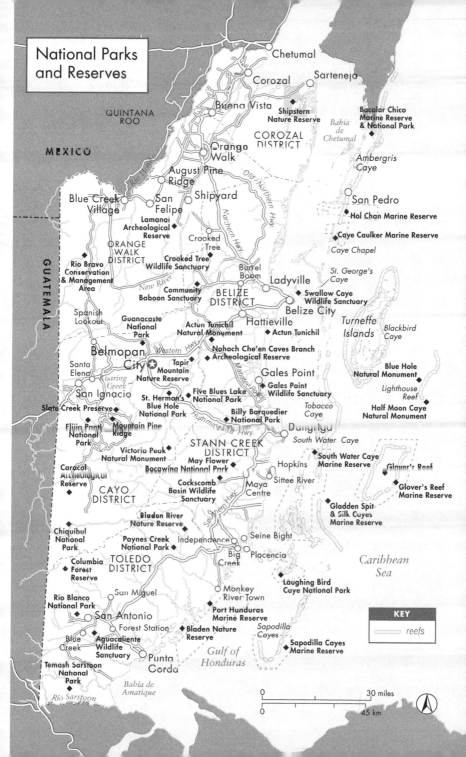

National Parks and Reserves

MEXICO

QUINTANA ROO

GUATEMALA

Chetumal
Corozal
Sarteneja
Buena Vista
Shipstern Nature Reserve
Bacalar Chico Marine Reserve & National Park
Bahía de Chetumal
COROZAL DISTRICT
Ambergris Caye
Orange Walk
August Pine Ridge
Shipyard
Blue Creek Village
San Felipe
San Pedro
Hol Chan Marine Reserve
Lamanai Archeological Reserve
Crooked Tree
Caye Caulker Marine Reserve
Caye Chapel
ORANGE WALK DISTRICT
Old Northern Hwy.
Northern Hwy.
Rio Bravo Conservation & Management Area
Crooked Tree Wildlife Sanctuary
Burrel Boom
New River
Ladyville
St. George's Caye
Community Baboon Sanctuary
BELIZE DISTRICT
Spanish Lookout
Guanacaste National Park
Actun Tunichil Natural Monument
Actun Tunichil
Swallow Caye Wildlife Sanctuary
Belize City
Hattieville
Turneffe Islands
Blackbird Caye
Belmopan City
Western Hwy.
Nohoch Che'en Caves Branch Archeological Reserve
Santa Elena
Roaring Creek
Tapir Mountain Nature Reserve
Gales Point
Gales Point Wildlife Sanctuary
Blue Hole Natural Monument
San Ignacio
Slate Creek Preserve
St. Herman's Blue Hole National Park
Five Blues Lake National Park
Billy Barquedier National Park
Tobacco Caye
Lighthouse Reef
Half Moon Caye Natural Monument
Elijin Pnnti National Park
Mountain Pine Ridge
Hummingbird Hwy.
Dangriga
South Water Caye
Victoria Peak Natural Monument
STANN CREEK DISTRICT
May Flower
Bocawina National Park
Hopkins
South Water Caye Marine Reserve
Glover's Reef
Caracol Archeological Reserve
CAYO DISTRICT
Cockscomb Basin Wildlife Sanctuary
Maya Centre
Sittee River
Glover's Reef Marine Reserve
Chiquibul National Park
Bladen River Nature Reserve
Paynes Creek National Park
Southern Hwy.
Gladden Spit & Silk Cayes Marine Reserve
Columbia Forest Reserve
TOLEDO DISTRICT
Independence
Seine Bight
Big Creek
Placencia
Caribbean Sea
Rio Blanco National Park
San Miguel
Monkey River Town
Laughing Bird Caye National Park
San Antonio
Port Hunduras Marine Reserve
Blue Creek
Forest Station
Aguacaliente Wildlife Sanctuary
Bladen Nature Reserve
Sapodilla Cayes
Punta Gorda
Temash Sarstoon National Park
Río Sarstoon
Bahía de Amatique
Gulf of Honduras
Sapodilla Cayes Marine Reserve

0 — 30 miles
0 — 45 km

KEY
reefs

EXPERIENCE BELIZE

WHAT'S WHERE

The following numbers refer to chapters.

2 Belize City. Depending on your perspective, Belize's commercial, transportation, and cultural hub is either a lively Caribbean port city of raffish charm or a crime-ridden, edgy backwater best seen through the rearview mirror.

3 The Cayes and the Atolls. Hundreds of cayes (pronounced *keys*) dot the Caribbean Sea off Belize, both inside and outside the Barrier Reef. The largest are Ambergris, Belize's most popular visitor destination, and Caulker. Farther out are three South Pacific–style atolls.

4 Northern Belize. This is the land of sugarcane and sweet, off-the-beaten-path places to visit. Corozal Town, up against the Mexican border, has a lovely bayside setting, and Sarteneja is a fishing village just waiting to be discovered.

5 The Cayo. The rolling hills of Western Belize, anchored by San Ignacio, offer outdoor activities aplenty—caving, canoeing, hiking, horseback riding, and mountain biking. Several remarkable Mayan sites also await you, including Caracol and Actun Tunichil Muknal.

6 The Southern Coast. Want beaches? The best on the mainland are on the Placencia peninsula, especially in the Maya Beach area, and in Hopkins.

7 The Deep South. Rainy and lush, beautiful and remote, Punta Gorda in far southern Belize is the jumping-off point for the unspoiled Mayan villages of Toledo District and for onward travel to Guatemala and Honduras.

8 El Petén. This part of Guatemala, easily visited from the Cayo District of Belize, is home to the most spectacular of all Mayan sites, Tikal, and the remains of many other ancient cities.

1

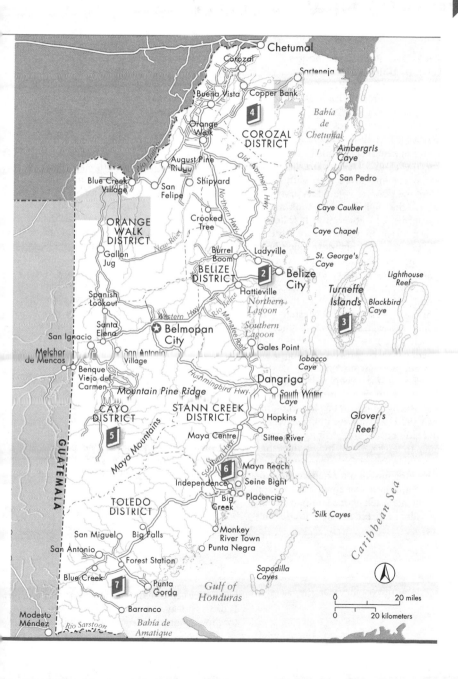

Chetumal
Corozal
Sarteneja
Buena Vista Copper Bank
Orange
Walk
COROZAL
DISTRICT
Bahía
de
Chetumal
Ambergris
Caye
4
San Pedro
August Pine
Ridge
Blue Creek   San   Shipyard
Village   Felipe
Caye Caulker
Caye Chapel
ORANGE
WALK
DISTRICT
Crooked
Tree
Gallon
Jug
Burrel
Boom   Ladyville
St. George's
Caye
Lighthouse
Reef
BELIZE
DISTRICT
2 Belize
City
Hattieville
Turneffe
Islands *Blackbird*
Caye
Spanish
Lookout
Northern
Lagoon
Southern
Lagoon
3
Santa   Western Hwy
Elena
San Ignacio
★ **Belmopan**
City
Gales Point
Iobacco
Caye
Melchor
de Mencos
Benque
Viejo del
Carmen
San Antonio
Village
Mountain Pine Ridge
Hummingbird Hwy.
Dangriga
South Water
Caye
Glover's
Reef
CAYO
DISTRICT
5
STANN CREEK
DISTRICT
Hopkins
Maya Mountains
Maya Centre
Sittee River
GUATEMALA
Maya Beach
6
Independence Seine Bight
Big   Placencia
Creek
TOLEDO
DISTRICT
Silk Cayes
Caribbean Sea
San Miguel Big Falls
San Antonio
Monkey
River Town
Punta Negra
Forest Station
Sapodilla
Cayes
Blue Creek
7
Punta
Gorda
Gulf of
Honduras
Barranco
Modesto
Méndez
Rio Sarstoon
Bahía de
Amatique

0   20 miles

0   20 kilometers

WHAT'S NEW IN BELIZE

Belize's Own Politics of Change

Like the United States, Belize held national elections in 2012, and, also like the United States, Belize re-elected its first black leader in history. Dean Barrow, a lawyer by profession, educated in Jamaica and Miami, first became prime minister in general elections in 2008. His party, the United Democratic Party (or UDP) swept into office then with about 57% of the popular vote. In its first years in office, the UDP generally took a low-key approach to governing. It followed a reform-oriented agenda in an effort to mitigate charges of high-level corruption levied against the former government. Seeking greater diversity in government, the UDP tapped Mayas and Mennonites for high office, in addition to the traditional core of Creole and Mestizo politicians. However, as the years since the 2008 election passed, Belize's UDP government has faced growing challenges and increasing popular discontent. The 2012 election against the People's United Party, the main opposition party, was much closer. Rising prices and a slow economy (when the U.S. sneezes, Belize catches a bad cold) cost Prime Minister Barrow some popularity, as has increasing crime, especially in Belize City. The government has become mired in new charges of corruption and in messy efforts to renationalize the main telephone company, Belize Telemedia Ltd., and the electric company.

Transportation Changes

Although a runway extension at Goldson International Airport near Belize City was completed years ago, anticipated new scheduled airline service, including from Europe and Canada, hasn't yet materialized. Indeed, existing airlines serving Belize, including Delta and US Airways (as of this writing set to merge with American), have cut back on service from the United States. While international service by one of Belize's two puddle jumper airlines, Maya Island Air, fizzled, the other local airline, Tropic Air, has added international service to Cancún, Mexico, San Pedro Sula, Honduras, and Flores and Guatemala City, Guatemala. Tropic also added domestic service to Belmopan and the San Ignacio/Benque Viejo area. Construction on a controversial new international airport near Placencia has essentially stopped, and it's now unclear when or even if the airport will open. The national bus network, divided into northern, western, and southern zones, with franchises often awarded on a political patronage basis, has been in a state of flux since the bankruptcy or closing of several large bus companies. A number of small regional bus lines have filled the gap, providing frequent and inexpensive, if not always comfortable, service on the main George Price Highway (formerly Western Highway), Philip Goldson Highway (formerly Northern Highway), and Southern Highway routes and elsewhere. Belize's water-taxi network has expanded, and there are now three different companies providing service between Belize City and San Pedro and Caye Caulker. Also, two water-taxi companies are now running boats between Chetumal, Mexico, and San Pedro and Caye Caulker, making it easier for those flying into Cancún to reach Belize.

WHEN TO GO

Belize, like much of Central America and the Caribbean, has two basic seasons: the rainy season and the dry season. The rainy season is roughly June through October, extending in some areas through November or even December. The dry season usually runs from December through May. However, by "dry season" Belizeans usually mean specifically the months in late winter and spring, February through May, when temperatures inland may reach 100°F. April is usually the hottest month of the year.

If you want to escape crowds and high prices and don't mind getting a little wet, visit in the rainy—or green—season. Though some restaurants may close and hotels may offer limited facilities, especially in September and October, reservations are easy to get, even at top establishments, and you'll have the Mayan ruins and beaches to yourself. And the rains, which most often come at night, do make the entire country lush and green.

The dry season can be a less attractive time for inland trips, with dusty roads and wilting vegetation, but this is a good time to visit the coast and cayes, with their cooling winds from the sea.

The busiest time in Belize is the Christmas–New Year's period, followed closely by Easter, but most hotels count the high season as mid-November through April.

Scuba enthusiasts can dive all year, but the water usually is clearest from March to June. Between November and February, cold fronts from North America can push southward, producing blustery winds known as "northers" that bring rain and rough weather and tend to churn up the sea, reducing visibility. Water temperatures, however, rarely stray far from 80°F, so many dive without a wet suit.

Climate and Hurricane Season

Belize is a small country, but there's considerable variation in climate from north to south, and also from the cayes to the mainland. Rainfall, for example, varies dramatically depending on where you are: the Deep South gets as much as 160 to 200 inches of rain each year, but the rest of the country gets a lot less, as little as 50 inches in Corozal. The cayes generally get less rain than the mainland. The rainy season doesn't mean monsoons, but rather seasonal rains that green the countryside.

Belize's Caribbean coast often gets sweltering, humid weather, especially in summer, while the Mountain Pine Ridge, with elevations up to almost 3,700 feet, is cooler and less humid. Overall, Belize's subtropical temperatures generally hover between 70°F and 85°F (21°C and 29°C).

The western Caribbean's hurricane season is from June through November. September and October are the two prime months for tropical storms and hurricanes in Belize. Over the past century, about 85% of storms to hit Belize arrived in those two months, hurricanes, however, are relatively rare.

Rainy season. The rainy season typically peaks from June through September. By November, rainfall in nearly all areas of Belize averages 8 inches or less a month. Many old Belize hands say they prefer traveling in summer or fall: prices are lower, hotel rooms are plentiful, and the landscape is lush after rains. It's also a little cooler than in the dry season months of April and May, and water visibility is usually very good.

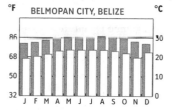

°F   BELMOPAN CITY, BELIZE   °C

QUINTESSENTIAL BELIZE

The Jewel

Belizeans frequently talk about "the Jewel." They say, "Get yourself a piece of the Jewel." Or, "When are you coming back to the Jewel?" By Jewel, they simply mean Belize. And Belize is a jewel. It's a place of incredible natural beauty, of mint-green seas and emerald-green forests, of the longest Barrier Reef in the Western or Northern hemisphere, with more kinds of birds, butterflies, flowers, and trees than in all of the United States and Canada combined. Massive ceiba trees and graceful cohune palms stand guard in rain forests where jaguars still roam free and toucans and parrots fly overhead. Rivers, bays, and lagoons are rich with hundreds of different kinds of fish. And Belizeans themselves are jewels. The country is a gumbo of cultures—African, Hispanic, Mayan, Asian, European, and Caribbean. Belize? It's a Jewel.

Passing the Time

Nearly every country claims to be full of friendly, smiling, welcoming people, but in the case of Belize it's really true. The vast majority of Belizeans are open and gracious, and they're happy, even eager, to spend a few minutes chatting with you about nothing in particular— the weather, the beautiful morning, how you're enjoying the Jewel. In most cases they don't want anything from you, except to pass the time of day. So let your guard down a little, relax, smile, and share a few rewarding moments with the shopkeeper, the waitress, the fellow you meet in the bar, or the lady you sit next to on the bus.

If you want a sense of life in Belize, familiarize yourself with some of its simple pleasures. There are a few highlights that will send you home saying, "Ah mi gat wahn gud guf taim" ("I had a good time" in Creole).

Bird-Watching

Once you see toucans at Tikal or the hard-to-find motmot in the Cayo, you too might get caught up in the excitement of searching for some of Belize's 600 species of birds. Many Belizeans know all their local birds (although the names they have for them may differ from those in your birding guide) and where the best places are to find them. Crooked Tree, Chan Chich at Gallon Jug, the New River and New River Lagoon near Lamanai, the Mountain Pine Ridge, and much of the Toledo District in the Deep South are wonderful areas for bird-watching; keep your eyes peeled to the treetops and don't forget your binoculars.

Archaeological Treasures

Though the ancient Mayan empire—which once occupied much of present-day Guatemala and extended into Belize, Mexico, Honduras, and El Salvador—began to collapse around AD 900, it still left one of the richest cultural and archaeological legacies in the world. Only a fraction of the thousands of Mayan ruins have been excavated from the jungle that over the centuries has swallowed the splendid temples and sprawling cities. Evidence of the Maya is everywhere in Belize, from the lagoon-side temples of Lamanai to the caves of Actun Tunichil Muknal. All together, Belize has more than 600 Mayan sites, most small and unexcavated, with likely hundreds or even thousands still to be discovered. A short day or overnight trip from western Belize is Tikal, arguably the most impressive of all Mayan sites, along with many other ruins in Guatemala's Petén.

IF YOU LIKE

Luxury Resorts

Deluxe duvets. 1,200-thread-count sheets. Your own villa on a private island or a jungle hideaway with fine wines and gourmet dinners. You may be traipsing around Mayan ruins or diving the Blue Hole during the day, but at night you can look forward to pampering at Belize's luxury jungle lodges and beach resorts.

■ **Azul Resort, North Ambergris Caye.** It's all top-of-the-line at this hip and exclusive beach resort. Kick back with a frozen mojito at the Rojo Lounge and Market.

■ **Blancaneaux Lodge, Mountain Pine Ridge.** Francis Ford Coppola's riverside jungle lodge hints of Beverly Hills.

■ **Cayo Espanto, near Ambergris Caye.** Really want to splurge? A stay on this small, private island will cost you, but you'll have your own butler, chef, and gorgeous views of the sea.

■ **El Secreto.** Thirteen splendid thatch villas line the beachfront, a small lagoon, and beautiful gardens at this property far enough north of San Pedro to feel like a secret island.

■ **The Lodge at Chaa Creek, Cayo.** Soak up the carefully tended landscaping, deluxe garden suites, spa, Cuban cigars, and expensive cognac.

■ **Turtle Inn, Placencia.** Francis Ford Coppola hand-picked the Balinese furniture and art in these thatch cabanas, but that's not even the best part. Just wait until you see the garden showers.

■ **The Phoenix, San Pedro.** At the site of one of the caye's oldest hotels, The Phoenix rose from the sands, offering stunning suites, convenience to all the in-town restaurants, clubs, and shops, and its own excellent restaurant.

Fishing

Some of the world's most exciting sport-fishing lies off Belize's coast and cayes. Go for the "grand slam" of tarpon, bonefish, permit, and snook on the shallow flats between the mainland and the reef. Sailfish, wahoo, marlin, and barracuda abound farther out to sea. Several specialty resorts and fishing camps, such as Turneffe Flats and El Pescador, cater to the angler, but most hotels can help you organize excellent fishing trips. You'll need a fishing license for most sportfishing in Belize (except off piers and shores); your hotel or fishing guide can arrange it for you. In some marine reserves where fishing is allowed, such as Glovers Reef Marine Reserve, usage fees are also charged.

■ **Ambergris Caye and Caye Caulker.** There's surprisingly good saltwater fishing on the northern cayes—look for bonefish, permit, and tarpon.

■ **Glover's Atoll.** Shallow tidal flats around the atoll make for plenty of bonefish; there's also permit, jack, and barracuda.

■ **Placencia.** If you don't want to pay the big bucks that the resorts charge farther north, head here. Budget hotels start around BZ$50 a night. Permit's the number one catch inside the reef, or cast a line in the lagoon or the deep sea beyond the reef.

■ **Punta Gorda.** If you're serious about fishing, this is a great place to be. There's world-famous permit fishing.

■ **Turneffe Atoll.** Bonefish, tarpon, permit, snappers, jacks, barracuda, wahoo, dorado, and billfish all ply the waters.

Caving

One of the most exciting ways to tour Belize is to head underground—there are hundreds of caves all over the country. You can canoe down subterranean rivers in some, ducking under low-hanging stalactites while keeping your eyes trained for Mayan artifacts. The easiest caves to visit are in Cayo; you don't need a guide to visit open caverns such as Rio Frio and the entrance to St. Herman's. Before you head out to cave, make sure to find out whether it's open to the public, whether you need a guide, and, if the cave has a river, whether the water level is low enough for visitors.

■ **Actun Tunichil Muknal.** Go here for amazing limestone formations, many undisturbed Mayan artifacts, and calcified human remains. It's the top caving experience in Belize.

■ **Barton Creek Cave.** Canoe about a mile on an underground river through Barton Cave, which has some Mayan artifacts and skeletal remains.

■ **Caves Branch Caves.** The Caves Branch River cave system has become a popular place for cave tubing.

■ **Che Chem Ha.** This cave, once used by the Maya for grain storage and ceremonial rituals, is on private land about 25 minutes from San Ignacio in the Vaca Plateau.

■ **Hokeb Ha.** Blue Creek Cave (as it's known in English), near Blue Creek village, is Toledo's answer to Actun Tunichil Muknal, with vaulted limestone chambers and underground waterfalls.

■ **Rio Frio Cave.** Though it's more a natural tunnel than a cave, it's still worth a visit for its large entryway and path above the Cold River.

Scuba Diving and Snorkeling

Don your scuba or snorkeling gear and soak up the cast of aquatic characters offshore and around the Barrier Reef. One moment you may come upon an enormous spotted eagle ray; the next you may find the feisty little damselfish, a bolt of blue no bigger than your little finger. Bloated blowfish hover in their holes; barracuda patrol the depths; and queen angelfish shimmy through the water with puckered lips and haughty self-assurance. Graceful sea fans and great chunks of staghorn coral add to the exhilarating underwater experience.

■ **Blue Hole.** The underwater sinkhole, one of the most famous dives in Belize, forms a perfectly round, deep blue circle.

■ **Glover's Reef.** This is probably the least visited yet arguably most pristine dive and snorkel area in Belize. You can see nurse sharks and manta rays and go wreck diving.

■ **Hol Chan Marine Reserve.** Snorkel with nurse sharks and stingrays at Shark-Ray Alley and keep your eyes peeled for moray eels in the reserve.

■ **Sapodilla Cayes.** Fringe reefs and patch reefs in shallow water around the cayes support tropical fish like spadefish and parrot fish.

■ **South Water Caye.** If you want to shore snorkel, come here. The beach is sandy, and the island is one of Belize's most beautiful.

■ **Turneffe Islands.** Mangroves line a shallow lagoon, creating a rich nursery for sea life where snorkelers and divers alike can see reef sharks, dolphins, eagle rays, moray eels, and turtles.

GREAT ITINERARIES

RUINS, RAIN FORESTS, AND REEF

Sample the best of all that Belize offers—ruins, rain forests, and reef—in only seven or eight days. If you have only five days, shave off some time in the Cayo and head to Actun Tunichil Muknal on Day 2 instead of Day 3.

Day 1: Arrival

Fly into the international airport near **Belize City** and immediately head out to the **Cayo** in Western Belize, about two hours by road from the airport. Stay at one of the superb jungle lodges, such as the Lodge at Chaa Creek, Mystic River Resort, or duPlooy's, or, for less money, Black Rock, Table Rock, or Crystal Paradise.

Logistics: The best way to see the mainland is by rental car. Pick up a car at one of the car-rental agencies in kiosks just across the main parking lot at the international airport. If you'd rather not drive, you can arrange a shuttle van, take a bus, or ask your hotel in the Cayo to pick you up. Buses don't come to the international airport—if you're taking one, you have to take a taxi into town (BZ$50). Tropic Air has service from Belize City to the Maya Flats airstrip between San Ignacio and Benque Viejo.

Day 2: Exploring the Cayo

On your first full day in Belize, get out and explore San Ignacio and the beautiful hill country around the Cayo. Among the top attractions are the small but interesting Mayan ruins at Xunantunich and Cahal Pech, Green Hills Butterfly Farm, the Rainforest Medicine Trail at Chaa Creek, and the Belize Botanical Gardens at duPlooy's. Save a little time for walking around and shopping in San Ignacio. After a full day of exploring, have cocktails and dinner at your lodge.

Logistics: You can do all the main attractions and San Ignacio in one day if you have a rental car and if you don't dawdle. Sans car, you can hire a taxi for the day, or opt for your hotel's tours.

Day 3: Actun Tunichil Muknal (ATM)

Prepare to be wowed by the ultimate cave experience. Go into the mysterious and beautiful Mayan underworld and see untouched artifacts dating back thousands of years.

Logistics: You must have a guide for ATM, so book your trip the day before with an authorized tour guide company. It's an all-day event, and you'll get wet—bring a change of clothes and wear walking shoes, not sandals. If you're badly out of shape or have mobility or claustrophobia issues, this isn't a tour for you. You have to hike several miles, swim a little, and clamber through the dark. Photography in the cave is not permitted.

Day 4: Tikal

Tikal, very simply, is the most awe-inspiring Mayan site in all of Central America, rivaling the pyramids of Egypt and the ruins of Angor Wat in Cambodia. It's well worth at least two days and nights, preferably staying in one of the three lodges at the park, but even on a day tour you'll get a sense of the majesty of this Classic-period city.

Logistics: Although you can go on your own, the easiest and most stress-free way to see Tikal is on a tour from San Ignacio—you'll leave around 6:30 am and return in the late afternoon; lunch is usually included. Overnight and multi-night tours also are available.

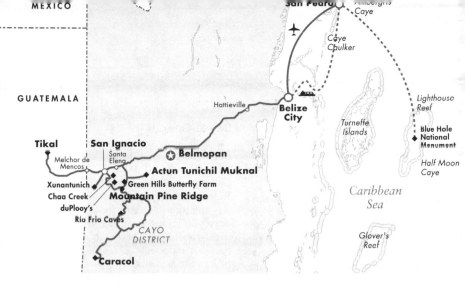

Day 5: Caracol and the Mountain Pine Ridge

A terrific day trip is to Caracol, the most important Mayan site in Belize. The trip there is part of the fun—you bump along winding roads through the Mountain Pine Ridge, past the Macal River, and through broadleaf jungle. If you've seen enough Mayan ruins, skip Caracol and spend the day exploring the Mountain Pine Ridge—there's the Rio Frio cave and numerous waterfalls. A bonus: the higher elevation here means it's cooler and less humid than other parts of Belize. If you don't mind packing and unpacking again, for your last night in Cayo consider switching to one of the four lodges in the Pine Ridge. Our favorites are Blancaneaux and Hidden Valley Inn.

Logistics: From Blancaneaux or Hidden Valley it's around a two-hour drive to Caracol, and about an hour longer from most lodges around San Ignacio. The road can be near-impassable after heavy rains, and there have been some incidents with bandits from Guatemala, so check locally for the latest conditions and cautions.

Alternative: If you tire of rain forest and ruins, and long for the sea, head a day early to San Pedro or Caye Caulker.

Day 6: San Pedro

Return to Belize City by plane, car, bus, or shuttle van. Then fly or take a water taxi to San Pedro (Ambergris Caye) for fabulous eating (our favorites include Rojo Lounge and Market at Azul Resort, El Fogon, Aji Tapa, Robin's Kitchen for low-cost local cooking, and, for breakfast with your feet in the sand, Estel's). Try to arrive early enough to do a snorkel trip to Hol Chan/Shark Ray Alley.

Alternative: San Pedro's a bustling town, so if you want a more laid-back and less-expensive experience on the water, stay on Caye Caulker instead. You still have access to the same snorkel and dive sites, with less costly hotels and restaurants.

Day 7: Blue Hole

Take a day trip to dive or snorkel the Blue Hole at Lighthouse Reef atoll. Dive boats also stop at Half Moon Caye for other dives (or snorkeling) besides the Blue Hole.

Logistics: A trip to the Blue Hole involves a full day on the water, so bring seasickness medicine, a hat, and plenty of sunscreen. Dive boats to Lighthouse leave early, usually before 7 am.

Alternative: If you're not up to the time and expense required for a trip to the Blue Hole, there's excellent diving on the Barrier Reef just a short boat ride from San Pedro or Caye Caulker.

⚠ Some dive organizations recommend a minimum 24-hour interval between a dive and a flight, so if you're flying out early the next day consider diving earlier in your trip, or snorkel instead. Also, the Blue Hole is a deep dive recommended only for more experienced divers.

Day 8: Departure
Return to Belize City by plane or water taxi for your international flight.

Logistics: Plan on arriving at least two hours ahead of your international flight. There's often a long line at check-in.

MAYAN SITES BLITZ

If you want to see the top Mayan sites in one trip, base yourself in the Cayo for a few days. If after a few days in western Belize and Guatemala you still haven't had your fill of things Mayan, you can add extensions to northern Belize and to Punta Gorda in southern Belize. *Information on tour operators and guides, and on admissions to specific sites, is in destination chapters.*

Day 1: San Ignacio
San Ignacio is an easy jumping-off spot for seeing several small but fascinating nearby ruins. If you get an early start, you can take in **Xunantunich, Cahal Pech,** and **El Pilar.** Both Cahal Pech and Xunantunich can be reached by bus (albeit with a short hike after the bus ride in both cases), but a taxi or rental car is needed to get to El Pilar. Guided tours of all these sites can be arranged in San Ignacio or at lodges and hotels in the area. (⇨ *See The Cayo, Chapter 5*)

Day 2: Caracol
Caracol, the most important Mayan site in Belize, deserves a full day. You can drive yourself—or go on a tour. There is no bus transportation in the Mountain Pine Ridge. Even if you arrive independently, you can hire a guide to show you around once you're at the site, or you can tour it on your own. There's an informative museum and visitor center. Due to a series of bandit incidents, trips to Caracol are being done in convoys, protected by Belize Defence Forces soldiers. Check locally for updates. (⇨ *See The Cayo, Chapter 5*)

Days 3 and 4: Tikal
Tikal is by far the most impressive Mayan site in the region and shouldn't be missed (check in advance about travel warnings to the area). Many operators offer day tours of Tikal from the San Ignacio area. (⇨ *See El Petén, Chapter 8*)

Tips
Altun Ha, the ruin closest to Belize City, gets crowds of cruise-ship day-trippers; try to avoid days when there are several cruise ships in port.

Before heading anywhere remote by yourself, check with the locals to find out if there have been any recent safety issues.

On your visit to Tikal, stay at one of the three lodges at the park—you'll be able to visit the ruins early in the morning or late in the afternoon, when howler monkeys and other animals are active and most day visitors have left. If you can't overnight at Tikal, do a day tour from San Ignacio; there also are daily flights from Belize City to Flores near Tikal.

Bring bug repellent. Mosquitoes are especially bad around Cerro Maya in Northern Belize and at the ruins near Punta Gorda.

FAQ'S

Is Belize a safe place to visit? The best answer is "Yes, but." Most visitors say they feel quite safe in Belize (except, they say, in some areas of Belize City especially after dark). Tourist Police patrol areas of Belize City, Placencia, Ambergris Caye, and elsewhere, and many hotels and jungle lodges have security guards. Out of the hundreds of thousands of visitors annually, the number who are victims of any kind of crime, mostly petty theft, is perhaps a few hundred. So, while this is still a developing country, enjoy yourself and follow standard travel precautions: Don't wander into areas that don't feel safe; avoid deserted beaches and streets after dark; and don't flash expensive jewelry or cash. Be aware that there have been a few carjackings and robberies on remote roads or at little-visited parks and Mayan sites; travel in a group or with a guide to less popular places.

Should I stay at an All-Inclusive? Although Belize is not an All-Inclusive kind of destination, some beach resorts and jungle lodges offer a tweaked version of the sort of all-inclusive you often find in Mexico or Jamaica: optional packages that include nearly everything, such as all meals, guided tours, and sports (fishing, diving, or snorkeling). So when is it worth your money to choose one of these over selecting room, meals, and activities à la carte?

The answer is: It depends. If you're going to a remote caye resort or jungle lodge, you may not have a choice. When you're two hours away from the nearest restaurant, you're pretty much stuck eating at your hotel. On the other hand, at a destination such as Ambergris Caye, Caye Caulker, Placencia, Hopkins, or San

Ignacio, there are many excellent restaurants to choose from. Even in less-visited areas such as Corozal and Punta Gorda, you'll find good, affordable food. It would be a shame to lock yourself into a single dining experience. A few resorts on Ambergris Caye, mainly those located on the far north end of the island (a long boat ride away from San Pedro), do offer all-inclusive or near all-inclusive packages; however, for most people, one of the main reasons for coming to Ambergris Caye is the opportunity to sample the variety of restaurants.

The main advantage of an all-inclusive or mostly inclusive package is that you don't have to worry about the details of travel planning. Once you've paid your fixed price, all you have to do is show up at the airport with your bags packed. The resort or lodge picks you up at the Belize International Airport, takes you on guided tours, provides your meals, and practically holds your hand. It's almost like being on a cruise, with few decisions to make. If you're the type of person who likes an organized travel experience, an AI or semi-AI package could be a good bet for you.

Before you book, be sure to total up the value of what you expect to get at the All-Inclusive, and compare that with what you probably would pay on an à la carte basis.

Are the beaches in Belize nice? Although there are lovely stretches of beaches, many of them are not as good for swimming or sunbathing as the wide, sandy beaches of the main Caribbean or of Mexico's Yucatán. Belizean beaches are usually narrow ribbons of sand with clear but shallow water, sea grass, and an often-mucky sea floor. The best beaches on the mainland are on the Placencia peninsula and in the Hopkins area. Ambergris Caye has some beautiful beaches, though swimming isn't always good. South Water Caye and Belize's three atolls have excellent (nearly deserted) beaches as well. Beach resorts keep their beach areas clean, but elsewhere you may see garbage on the beach, brought in by the tides from other areas and from boats.

Why are airfares to Belize so high, and how can we find cheaper flights? Belize is not a mass-market tourist destination. Air service is still limited, and service is mostly from a few hubs in the United States. Charter flights are rare, so fares tend to stay high. To find the most affordable flights, stay flexible on your dates, check the meta-fare comparison websites such as Kayak.com, avoid peak holiday travel (around Christmas and Easter), and sign up for Internet specials and email fare alerts on the airlines flying to Belize—currently United-Continental, American-US Airways, Delta, and TACA. Another option is to fly into Cancún, which usually has good air deals, bus to Chetumal at the Mexico-Belize border, and water taxi or bus from there, or alternatively fly Tropic Air from Cancun International to Belize International. The other option is the ADO express overnight service from Cancún to Corozal Town, Orange Walk Town, and Belize City.

While traveling around the country, should we rent a car, take a bus, fly, or hire a taxi? Each has advantages and disadvantages. With a rental car you go when and where you want, including remote areas that don't have air or bus service or to sites that would otherwise require an expensive guided tour. However, auto rental costs are high, and gas is around BZ$12 a gallon. Buses provide a true local experience, and fares are dirt cheap, but buses mainly run on the major roads and stop frequently to pick up and drop off passengers. Buses—usually old U.S. school buses—take up to twice as long as a private car. Flying is the fastest way to get around the country; service is frequent on most routes, and the views from low altitudes are often dramatic. The downside? Fares—especially if you're traveling with a family—can add up, and not all destinations have service. In some cases, transfers by taxi can be an option, although taxis generally are quite expensive. For most long-distance trips there are no set fares, so the rate is a matter of negotiation and can vary considerably, depending on your bargaining skills. Drivers may also ask a little more if there are three or four going together, rather than just one or two. Expect to pay around BZ$3 a mile for longer taxi trips in Belize. Shuttles are another option, especially on popular routes such as between the international airport and San Ignacio, where shared shuttles operating on a fixed schedule are BZ$70 per person and up, and private shuttles leaving anytime range from around BZ$180 to BZ$200, and up, for up to three persons.

We want to spend time at the beach and also in the jungle. Where should we go? On a first and relatively brief visit to Belize, sample the best "surf and turf" by splitting your time between one of the popular beach areas—Ambergris Caye, Caye Caulker, Hopkins, or Placencia—and the rest in the Cayo, which has the largest concentration of popular mainland activities.

TOP MAYAN SITES

The following are our picks for the most notable Mayan sites in Belize. *See the destination chapters for detailed information on the sites, including hours and admission fees.* Fees at most sites for non-Belizeans are BZ$10–BZ$20, and Actun Tunichil Muknal is BZ$50. As of this writing, a scheduled admission increase to some Mayan sites has yet to be implemented—ask locally. Admission fees are in addition to any fees for guides or tours.

Northern Belize

Altun Ha. The most visited Mayan site in Belize, though not the most impressive, is popular with cruise-ship passengers and for those staying on Ambergris Caye or Caye Caulker. It's a little more than an hour's drive north of Belize City. One of the temples at Altun Ha is prominently pictured on Belikin beer bottles.

Cerro Maya. Although the few remaining original structures here are weathered, and there's no museum or visitor center, Cerro Maya—like Tulum in the Yucatán—enjoys a glorious location right beside the water.

Chan Chich. The lodge of the same name was built literally on top of this minor ceremonial site. It can be reached by car or charter flight and is best visited in connection with a stay at the lodge.

Cuello. It's one of the oldest Mayan sites in the region, settled more than 2,500 years ago. It's on the property of a rum distillery near Orange Walk Town, and you have to get permission in advance to visit it.

Marco Gonzalez. This 2,100-year-old site on the southern end of Ambergris Caye, 5½ miles (9 km) south of San Pedro, is the first Mayan site national park on a Belize island. Today the site is mostly unexcavated, but there are plans for a new education and visitor center. Access to the site is via a rough boardwalk over mangrove swamp—bring lots of mosquito spray!

La Milpa. The third-largest Mayan site in Belize (only Caracol and Lamanai are larger), La Milpa is in the early stages of exploration and excavation. It can be visited through advance arrangement with Programme for Belize, on whose land it sits.

Lamanai. Boat your way up the New River to the shores of the New River Lagoon to see this ruin, which has the most beautiful setting of any Mayan site in Belize. You also can reach it by road from Orange Walk Town. Lamanai has a small museum and a resident troop of howler monkeys.

Santa Rita. Corozal Town is built on what was the large Mayan trading center known as Chactemal (or Chetumal, as the capital of Quintana Roo, Mexico, is known today). A part of the ruins, now called Santa Rita, is on a hill on the outskirts of Corozal. The Belize government is trying to promote Santa Rita by transforming it into the "Official Mayan Wedding Garden of Belize."

The Cayo

Actun Tunichil Muknal. "ATM," near Belmopan, provides the most rewarding Mayan cave experience in Belize, and indeed in the entire region. Many visitors say it is the highlight of all their travels in Central America. To see the cave, you have to take a 45-minute hike and a brief swim, and be a part of a guided tour. Only about 30 guides are certified to lead trips to ATM. Photography is no longer permitted.

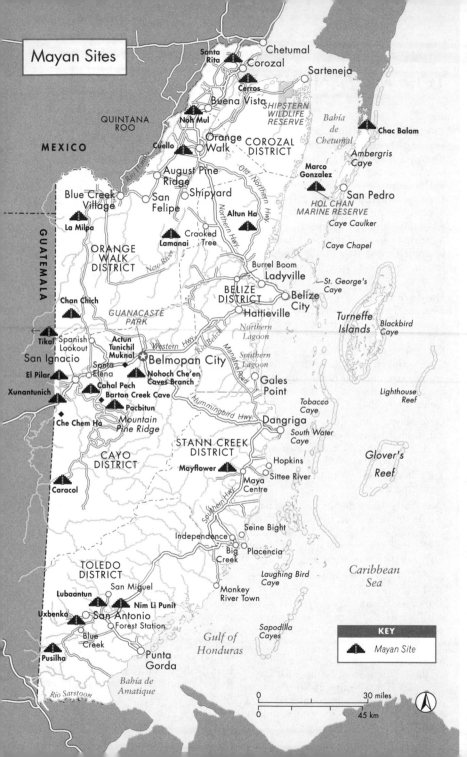

Mayan Sites

MEXICO

QUINTANA
ROO

GUATEMALA

Santa Rita
Chetumal
Corozal
Sarteneja
Cerros
Buena Vista
SHIPSTERN
WILDLIFE
RESERVE
Bahía
de
Chetumal
Noh Mul
Chac Balam
Cuello
Orange
Walk
COROZAL
DISTRICT
August Pine
Ridge
Marco
Gonzalez
Ambergris
Caye
San
Felipe
Shipyard
San Pedro
Blue Creek
Village
HOL CHAN
MARINE RESERVE
La Milpa
Altun Ha
Caye Caulker
ORANGE
WALK
DISTRICT
Crooked
Tree
Lamanai
Caye Chapel
Burrel Boom
Ladyville
St. George's
Caye
New River
BELIZE
DISTRICT
Belize
City
Chan Chich
GUANACASTE
PARK
Hattieville
Turneffe
Islands
Blackbird
Caye
Northern
Lagoon
Tikal
Spanish
Lookout
Actun
Tunichil
Muknal
Western Hwy.
Río Belize
Belmopan City
Southern
Lagoon
San Ignacio
El Pilar
Santa
Elena
Nohoch Che'en
Caves Branch
Lighthouse
Reef
Xunantunich
Cahal Pech
Barton Creek Cave
Pacbitun
Gales
Point
Tobacco
Caye
Che Chem Ha
Mountain
Pine Ridge
Hummingbird Hwy.
Dangriga
South Water
Caye
Glover's
Reef
CAYO
DISTRICT
STANN CREEK
DISTRICT
Caracol
Mayflower
Hopkins
Sittee River
Maya
Centre
Independence
Seine Bight
Caribbean
Sea
Big
Creek
Placencia
TOLEDO
DISTRICT
San Miguel
Laughing Bird
Caye
Lubaantun
Nim Li Punit
Uxbenka
San Antonio
Monkey
River Town
Sapodilla
Cayes
Blue
Creek
Forest Station
Gulf of
Honduras
Pusilha
Punta
Gorda
Bahía de
Amatique
Río Sarstoon

Northern Hwy.
Río Hondo
Old Northern Hwy.
Manatee Road
Southern Hwy.

0   30 miles
0   45 km

KEY
Mayan Site

Barton Creek Cave. You can canoe through part of this 7-mile (11-km) wet-cave system once used by the Maya for human sacrifices. It's about a half hour off the Chiquibul Road on the way to the Mountain Pine Ridge.

Cahal Pech. This small Late Classic site, with a lovely location on a hill overlooking San Ignacio, is easily accessible from town. It has a little museum.

Caracol. The largest and most significant site in Belize is a must if you're in the Cayo. It's an all-day trip from San Ignacio through the Mountain Pine Ridge, but it's well worth the time. There's a museum and visitor center, and extensive excavations have been underway for more than 30 years.

Che Chem Ha. This cave on private land south of Benque Viejo has artifacts dating back 2,000 years.

El Pilar. Set on low hills above the Mopan River at the Guatemalan border is one of the largest sites in Belize, but little of it has been excavated.

Pacbitun. Near San Antonio village on the road to the Mountain Pine Ridge, Pacbitun dates back to at least 1000 BC. It's on private land.

Xunantunich. Though it's not one of the largest sites in Belize, Xunantunich is one of the easiest and most pleasant to visit. To reach it, you cross the Mopan River on a quaint, hand-pulled ferry. There's a well-done museum and visitor center. It's off the Western Highway, west of San Ignacio.

Southern Belize

Lubaantun. Occupied for less than 200 years in the Late Classic period, Lubaantun is unusual in that no stelae were ever found here, and the precisely fitted building stones, laid without mortar, have rounded corners. The controversial "Crystal Skull" supposedly was found here. Lubaantun is near San Pedro Columbia village, about 20 miles (32 km) from Punta Gorda.

Mayflower. This Classic-period site, off the Southern Highway just south of Dangriga, is in the early stages of excavation. Waterfalls nearby make the setting appealing.

Nim Li Punit. Off the Southern Highway north of Punta Gorda is Nim Li Punit ("Big Hat" in Ketchi), a small but pretty site. There's a visitor center.

Pusilha. At a site near Aguacate Village on the Moho River is this collection of extensive but low-lying structures on a small hill. Also visible are the remains of a stone bridge. It is officially closed to the public, though you can ask locally to see it. Because of its remote location off the main highway, there aren't many visitors who make the trip out here.

El Petén, Guatemala

Tikal. Along with Copán in Honduras and Palenque in Mexico, Tikal is considered by many to be the most impressive of all Mayan sites. The Petén area is home to several other ruins, including **Nakúm, El Ceibal, Uaxactún, Yaxhá, Yaxchilán, El Zotz,** and **El Mirador.** Some, like El Mirador, are extremely remote, requiring a multiday jungle trek.

PLANNING YOUR ADVENTURE

These days more travelers than ever are seeking trips with an active or adventure component, and tour operators are responding with an ever-increasing selection of exciting itineraries. Belize, with its opportunities for many different kinds of activities, is at the leading edge of the adventure-travel trend.

In Belize you can select something easy, like cave tubing, snorkeling, fishing, horseback riding, hiking, birding, wildlife-spotting, and canoeing. Or you can go for jungle trekking, caving, windsurfing, sea kayaking, or mountain-biking expeditions that require higher degrees of physical endurance and, in some cases, considerable technical skill. You can rough it or opt for comfortable, sometimes even luxurious, accommodations; put adventure at the center of your trip or make it only a sideline; go for a multiweek package or only a day trip. Study multiple itineraries and packages to find the trip that's right for you.

Choosing a tour package carefully is always important, but it becomes even more critical when the focus is adventure or sports. When wisely chosen, special-interest vacations lead to distinctive, memorable experiences—just pack your curiosity along with the bug spray.

Belize Tourism Board. For information about a specific activity or destination within Belize, contact the Belize Tourism Board *(or see tour operators listed in the Tours section of each destination chapter)*. ⊠ *64 Regent St., Corner Regent & South Sts., Belize City* ☎ *800/624–0686, 227/2420* ⊕ *www.travelbelize.org.*

Choosing a Trip

With dozens of options for special-interest and adventure tours in Belize, including do-it-yourself or fully guided package trips, it's helpful to think about certain factors when deciding which company or package will be right for you.

■ **Are you interested in adventure travel on the sea or the mainland or both?** Belize offers two very different adventure environments: the sea and the mainland. The Caribbean, various bays and lagoons, the Barrier Reef that runs 185 miles (303 km) along the eastern coast of the country, and three South Pacific–style atolls are perfect for activities such as fishing, sailing, diving, snorkeling, and windsurfing. Inland, you can rappel hundreds of feet into a limestone sinkhole, explore an underworld labyrinth of caves full of Mayan artifacts, hike the rain forest, ride horses or bikes to remote waterfalls, or tube down underground rivers. Some travelers prefer to concentrate on either water or land activities, but you can combine the two. Just be sure to give yourself enough time.

■ **How strenuous a trip do you want?** Adventure vacations commonly are split into "soft" and "hard" adventures. Hard adventures, such as strenuous jungle treks and extended caving trips, usually require excellent physical conditioning and previous experience. Most hiking, biking, canoeing-kayaking, cave tubing, snorkeling, brief cave tours, and similar soft adventures can be enjoyed by persons of all ages who are in good health and are accustomed to a reasonable amount of exercise. A little honesty goes a long way—recognize your own level of physical fitness and discuss it with the tour operator before signing on. Keep in mind that for most of the year in Belize you'll face hot weather and high humidity, conditions that can take a lot out of you, even if you're in good shape.

■ **Would you like to pick up new skills?** Belize is a great place to pick up new skills, whether it's how to paddle a kayak, how to rappel down a cliff face, or how to dive. For example, you can take a quick resort diving course to see if you like scuba, or you can do a complete open-water certification course, usually in three to four days. Before committing to any program, do some research to confirm that the people running it are qualified. Check to see if the dive shop or resort is certified by one of the well-known international dive organizations, such as the Professional Association of Diving Instructors (PADI), the largest certification agency in the world, or National Association of Underwater Instructors (NAUI), the second largest. Among the other how-to programs or lessons offered in Belize are kayaking, horseback riding, snorkeling, kitesurfing, and windsurfing.

■ **Do you want an "off-the-shelf" tour package or do you prefer to build your own trip?** You can opt to buy a prepackaged adventure or special-interest trip, complete with full-time guides who will do everything from meeting your international flight to cooking your meals, or you can go the more independent route, arranging local guides or tour operators on a daily, or even hourly, basis. Because English is the official language in Belize and most tour operators have email and websites, it's easy to put together an adventure package à la carte. Many package tour operators also offer you the ability to combine two or more trips or to create a custom itinerary. It all comes down to whether you're happier doing it yourself or having someone else take care of all the logistics and details.

■ **How far off the beaten path do you want to go?** As one of the least densely populated countries in the hemisphere—more than two-fifths of the country is devoted to nature reserves and national parks—Belize offers many off-the-beaten-path experiences. Although many trips described here might seem to be headed into uncharted territory, tour operators carefully check each detail before an itinerary goes into a brochure. You won't usually be vying with busloads of tourists for photo ops, but you'll probably run into occasional small groups of like-minded travelers. Journeys into truly remote regions, such as Victoria Peak in the Maya Mountains, typically involve camping or the simplest of accommodations, but they reward with more abundant wildlife and locals who are less accustomed to the clicking of cameras.

■ **What sort of group is best for you?** At its best, group travel offers curious, like-minded companions with which to share the day's experiences. Do you enjoy mixing with people from similar backgrounds, or would you prefer to travel with people of different ages and backgrounds? Inquire about group size; many companies have a maximum of 10 to 16 members, but 30 or more is not unknown. The larger the group, the more time spent (or wasted) at rest stops, meals, and hotel arrivals and departures.

If groups aren't your thing, most companies will customize a trip for you. In fact, this has become a major part of many tour operators' businesses. Your itinerary can be as flexible or as rigid as you choose. Such travel offers all the conveniences of a package tour, but the "group" is composed of only you and those you've chosen as travel companions. Responding to a renewed interest in multigenerational travel, many tour operators also offer family trips, with itineraries carefully crafted to appeal both to children and adults.

Money Matters

■ **How much are you willing to spend?** Tours in Central America can be found at all price points, and Belize has an adventure for every budget. Local operators are usually the best deal. Tours that are run by as many local people and resources as possible are generally cheaper, and also give the greatest monetary benefit to the local economy. These types of tours are not always listed in guidebooks or on the Internet, so often they have to be found in person or by word of mouth. Safety and date specificity can fluctuate. Amenities such as lodging and transportation may be very basic in this category. Some agencies pay attention to the environment, whereas others do not. You really have to do your research on every operator, no matter the cost, to be sure you get what you need. When you find the right match, the payoff in terms of price and quality of experience will be worth it.

On the other end of the spectrum, the large (often international) tour agencies are generally the most expensive; however, they provide the greatest range of itinerary choices and highest quality of services. They use the best transportation, like private tour buses and boats, which rarely break down. First-rate equipment and safe, reliable guides are the norm. Dates and times are set in stone, so you can plan your trip down to the time you step in and out of the airport. Guides are certified, and well paid. When food and lodging is provided it is generally of high quality. If you are a traveler who likes to have every creature comfort provided for, look for tour operators more toward this end of the spectrum.

■ **Are there hidden costs?** Make sure you know what is and is not included in basic trip costs when comparing companies. International airfare is usually extra. Sometimes domestic flights in-country are too. Is trip insurance required, and if so, is it included? Are airport transfers included? Visa fees, if any? Departure taxes? Gratuities? Although some travelers prefer the option of an excursion or free time, many, especially those visiting a destination for the first time, want to see as much as possible. Paying extra for a number of excursions can significantly increase the total cost of the trip. Many factors affect the price, and the trip that looks cheapest in the brochure could well turn out to be the most expensive. Don't assume that roughing it will save you money, as prices rise when limited access and a lack of essential supplies on-site require costly special arrangements.

■ **TIP→** Tour prices operated by companies in Belize incur a 12.5% Goods and Services Tax. In some cases, the GST is not included in the tour prices shown (though technically it should be included).

VOLUNTEERING IN BELIZE

Want to help others less fortunate than you? Want to make the world a better place? Then you may want to investigate volunteer opportunities in Belize. There are basically three kinds of volunteer opportunities available:

Church and mission trips. This typically involves a week to several weeks of volunteer work in a medical or dental clinic, or building churches or homes, or other hands-on assistance. Usually these volunteer groups are based outside of Belize, often at a church or school or as a part of a local medical society. In most cases, volunteers pay for their own transportation to Belize, along with personal expenses in the country, but food and lodging may be provided by the mission. Your best bet is to contact your church, college, or local medical society and ask if they know of upcoming mission trips to Belize.

Independent volunteering. Find a worthwhile organization and volunteer your services. Conservation organizations, churches, libraries, medical clinics, humane societies, and schools are among those that may welcome volunteers. You typically won't receive any lodging or food in return for your volunteer activities. To arrange this kind of independent volunteer work, you usually need to be in Belize and make personal contact with the organization you are seeking to help.

Organized volunteer programs. These volunteer programs often revolve around conservation, such as working with wildlife or reef preservation. A few programs offer volunteer opportunities in education, animal care, or social work. Some programs require volunteers to pay a placement fee, which can be several hundred U.S. dollars or more, plus pay for room, board, and transportation to Belize. In other programs, volunteers do not pay a fee and they may receive food and lodging in exchange for their volunteer work, but they usually have to pay transportation and incidental expenses out of pocket. For longer-term volunteering, consider the U.S. Peace Corps, which currently has more than 30 volunteers here.

Some organizations that accept volunteers in Belize:

Belize Audubon Society (*BAS*). The Belize Audubon Society is the oldest and largest conservation group in Belize. It manages nine protected areas and parks in Belize and accepts some qualified volunteers to assist in its park management, conservation, tourism development, and other programs. The BAS usually requires a minimum three-month commitment for its overseas volunteers working inland, and one month for volunteers in the marine program. Although the BAS prefers to partner with universities to get its interns, it does also accept individual volunteer applications. The BAS does not pay for lodging or living expenses. ⊠ *12 Fort St., Fort George, Belize City* ☎ *223/5004* ⊕ *www.belizeaudubon.org.*

Belize Botanic Gardens. Belize Botanic Gardens, 45 acres of tropical gardens at duPlooy's Lodge near San Ignacio, accepts occasional interns who need to complete field work for their college degree in fields such as ethnobotany, botany, environmental science, environmental education, and tropical ecology, and also volunteers who have skills in horticulture, organic agriculture, landscape design and related fields. Volunteers pay a fee of up to US$550 a month for food and lodging. ⊠ *Big Eddy, Chial Rd., at duPlooy's Lodge, San Ignacio, Cayo* ☎ *824/3101* ⊕ *www. belizebotanic.org.*

Belize Zoo and Tropical Education Center. The Belize Zoo, one of the great conservation organizations in Central America, and the associated Tropical Education Center have a wide range of education and outreach programs. A few motivated volunteers/interns are accepted to assist Belize Zoo and TEC programs. The Zoo says it's looking for interns to help guide and teach Belizean students, to help manage the animals, and in certain professional and skill areas. Internships are usually two to four weeks in length. The zoo provides food and accommodations, but interns pay a weekly fee. To apply, at least eight weeks in advance send a letter of inquiry by mail, fax or email indicating your reasons for applying, areas of interest, education and experience, and a medical certificate from a physician with your health status. ⊠ *Mile 29, George Price Hwy., (formerly Western Hwy.), Belmopan* ☏ *822/8000* ✎ *education@belizezoo.org* ⊕ *www.belizezoo.org.*

Cornerstone Foundation. This nonprofit's programs include cultural, community service, AIDS prevention, natural healing, and community volunteer programs in Cayo District. Volunteers commit for a minimum of one week and up to three months. For longer programs, individuals pay US$385 to US$485 a month for bunk-style housing and food. Fees for one-week programs start at US$199. Volunteers at Cornerstone must have travel and basic medical insurance. ⊠ *43 Church St., San Ignacio* ☏ *824/2373* ⊕ *www. cornerstonefoundationbelize.org.*

Monkey Bay Wildlife Sanctuary. Monkey Bay is a private wildlife sanctuary and environmental education center on 1,060 acres near the Belize Zoo, with satellite campuses in the Mountain Pine Ridge and on Tobacco Caye. It has some volunteer intern opportunities in conservation and community service. Volunteers are expected to work about 30 hours a week. Monkey Bay also offers education programs on ecology, first aid, and natural history for students and others, ranging from a few days to more than a month. These education programs have various fees. In addition, Monkey Bay rents rustic accommodations to visitors. ⊠ *Mile 31.5 George Price Hwy. (formerly Western Hwy.), Belmopan* ☏ *822/8032* ⊕ *www. belizestudyabroad.net.*

Plenty International. Founded in 1974, Plenty has been working in Belize since 1990. It's currently helping the Mayan and Garifuna communities in Toledo District to develop school organic gardens, school lunches, and alternative technologies. Volunteers ideally should have gardening, farming, technical, or other skills. Contact Plenty for current needs, as programs in Belize change from year to year. There are no stipends or other payments to volunteers, and travel expenses are not paid, but in some cases volunteers may receive assistance with food and housing. ⊠ *Plenty International, Punta Gorda* ☏ *931/964–4323 U.S. number* ⊕ *www.plenty.org.*

WWOOF Belize. WWOOF is an Internet-based social networking organization that connects organic farms in some 50 countries (including Belize) with volunteers. WWOOFING in Belize allows you to trade work on an organic farm in return for room and board and in some cases a small stipend. Conditions and terms of work vary considerably from farm to farm, but keep in mind you'll usually be involved in hard physical labor for several hours a day under hot, humid, and buggy conditions. Farms usually require a minimum of one week's commitment, but some require several weeks or months. Currently there are several dozen farms in the WWOOF Belize network. To participate in WWOOF Belize, you have to join WWOOF Belize and pay a fee of US$5 for membership. Membership gives you information about farms in Belize that are looking for volunteer workers—you contact the farms. ⊕ *www.wwoof latinamerica.com.*

Ecotourism in Belize

Central America is the original ecotourism destination; as a result, you'll see the term used liberally. For lodging it can be used to describe a deluxe private cabana on a well-tended beach or a hut in the middle of nowhere with pit toilets. It may also point to environmental conservation efforts by parks or tour companies that are conscious of natural resources and their role in not depleting them. Or it may mean just the opposite. Wildlife parks, butterfly farms, rain forests, and Mayan ruins are some of the incredible eco-destinations in this area. And mountain biking, bird-watching, jungle hiking, scuba diving, cave tubing, fishing, and white-water rafting are just some of the eco-activities.

You can do your part to protect the natural heritage of Belize and the Tikal area of Guatemala by being an ecologically sensitive traveler. Where possible, choose green hotels, those that have taken care to protect the environment and that have energy-efficient cooking, lighting, and cooling systems, and that recycle and dispose of waste responsibly. Among these lodges and hotels are Hickatee Cottages near Punta Gorda; duPlooy's Lodge, Table Rock Jungle Lodge, and The Lodge at Chaa Creek near San Ignacio;

Blancaneaux Lodge in the Mountain Pine Ridge; and Hamanasi on the beach in Hopkins. Be culturally sensitive, as both countries have highly diverse populations, each with different cultural attitudes and perspectives. Also, try to do business with companies that hire local people for positions at all levels, and where possible choose local restaurants and hotels over chain properties. When diving or snorkeling, avoid touching or breaking coral, and don't take part in swim-with-dolphins or swim-with-manatees tours, as most naturalists say these programs disturb the animals. Also, use ecofriendly sunscreen. On caving or hiking trips, take nothing but photographs and leave nothing of yours behind. When visiting Mayan sites, never remove anything, not even a tiny shard of pottery.

For the most part, Belize has reaped the benefits of the growing tourism industry, drawing in much-needed capital to bolster national coffers. The costs of tourism are less obvious, however. Among other effects, indigenous communities are undermined by increasingly tourist-oriented economies—cultivating a plot of land may no longer support a family, but selling knickknacks in the streets just might. Where tourists come, expats often follow, and land, especially beachfront land, is quickly priced out of the reach of locals. There's no easy solution to this dilemma, and balancing the advantages of tourism against its drawbacks is, and will remain, a constant struggle for Belize. The long-term effects are as much dependent on the attitudes and behavior of visitors as they are on prudent national policies.

RETIRING IN BELIZE

So you fell in love with the Belize experience, outdoors and indoors, met some expats who bought their beachfront lot for a song, and want to do the same for your retirement years? Here's the scoop on what you can really expect if you decide to follow suit.

Belize can be enchanting for potential retirees. The climate is frost-free. Land and housing costs are still moderate, especially compared with already popular areas of the Caribbean. The official language is English, and the historical and legal background of the country is more comparable to that of the United States, Canada, and Great Britain than most other parts of Latin America and the Caribbean. Belize has a stable and democratic, if sometimes colorful, political tradition. Recreational activities, on land and on the water, are almost limitless.

But there are drawbacks: high costs for imported food, fuel, and household items; high import duties (up to 70% of retail value or higher on imported vehicles); crime and drug problems; culture shock for those unaccustomed to the ways of a semitropical, developing country with a true multicultural society; growing resentment of foreigners; plenty of red tape and petty corruption; increasing taxes such as the 12.5% Goods and Services Tax (GST) on everything from refrigerators to cars and restaurant meals; a 5% transfer tax on real estate purchases by foreigners, payable by the buyer (buyers of new condos or houses also pay 12.5% sales tax, the latter usually built into the sales price); and, most important for many retirees, medical care that in many cases isn't up to first-world snuff.

If retirement or relocation in Belize still sounds like a good option for you, there are three options to look into:

The Qualified Retired Persons Incentive Program. It's run by the Belize Tourism Board, and anyone at least 45 years old is eligible to participate in the program. It requires a pension, Social Security, or other provable, reliable income of at least US$2,000 a month. In return, you (and your spouse and minor children) have the right to import household goods, a car, boat, and even an airplane free of import duty. Income generated from outside Belize isn't taxed by Belize. Although as a QRP participant you can't work for pay in Belize, you can own a business and have employees who work for you. Hundreds of QRP applications have been approved since the program was started in 2001. It's a wonder that more haven't applied: 75 million baby boomers in the United States alone are expected to retire over the next 20 years. Many of them will be looking for alternatives to cold winters and high prices up north. Contact the Tourism Board for more information (⊕ *www.belizeretirement.org*).

Official Permanent Residency. For those not ready to retire, it's still possible to move to Belize, although work permits usually are difficult to obtain and salaries are a fraction of those in the United States, Canada, or Western Europe. The best option may be to invest in or start a business in Belize that employs Belizean workers, thus paving the way for a self-employment work permit and residency.

With official Permanent Residency, you can work in Belize or operate a business, just like any Belizean. You can bring in household goods duty-free. Before you can apply for residency, you need to live in Belize for a year leaving for no more than two weeks. Permanent Residency applications are handled by the Belize Immigration Department and may take a few months to a year for approval. Belize citizenship requires living in Belize for at least five years as a Permanent Resident.

Regular Tourist Permit. Many expats simply stay in Belize on a tourist permit (actually, it's a stamp in your passport). Upon entry, you receive a free visitor permit, good for up to 30 days. This permit can be renewed at any Immigration office for BZ$50 a month for up to six months. After that, renewals cost BZ$100 a month. With a tourist permit, you can't work in Belize. Renewals are never guaranteed, and the rules could change at any time.

Ambergris Caye, the Corozal Town area, Placencia and Hopkins, and Cayo have attracted the largest number of foreign residents, some full-time and others snowbirds. Ambergris Caye, the number choice for expats, has an idyllic Caribbean island atmosphere, but real estate prices here are high. Corozal Town and its environs have among Belize's lowest living costs, and Mexico is right next door. The Cayo appeals to those who want land for growing fruit trees or keeping a few horses. Placencia and Hopkins have some of the best beaches in Belize. More off-the-beaten-path areas, such as Punta Gorda area in Toledo District and parts of northeast Corozal District on the Bay of Chetumal, such as Sarteneja, are beginning to generate interest from foreigners looking for lower stress and more affordable land prices.

The best advice for anyone contemplating retiring or relocating: Try before you buy. If possible, rent an apartment or house for a few months. Be cautious about buying property. Real-estate agents generally aren't licensed or regulated, and because the pool of qualified buyers in Belize is small, it's a lot harder to sell than to buy. Bottom line: Belize isn't for everyone. The country, as seen from the perspective of a resident, isn't the same as the Belize that's experienced by vacationers.

Easy Belize, by Lan Sluder (author of *Fodor's Belize*), is a handbook for those considering retiring or relocation in Belize. The author, with more than 20 years' experience in Belize, interviewed scores of expats and retirees in Belize to help provide readers with a realistic view of the pros and cons of living here.

FLAVORS OF BELIZE

The cuisine of Belize has three major influences: first, the spicy influence of its Latin neighbors and its own multicultural population; second, the influx of tourists with discerning palates who demanded, and eventually got, a higher standard of cooking at hotels and restaurants; and, third, the availability of fish, lobster, and conch fresh from the sea.

Rice and Beans

There is no single Belizean cuisine. Belize dining, like Belize itself, grew out of a gumbo of influences—Mexican, Guatemalan, African, Caribbean, Mayan, Garífuna, English, Chinese, and American. The most Belizean of all dishes is rice and beans. Although originally considered a Creole dish, today it's eaten daily by just about everyone. Recipes vary, but most use kidney beans, garlic, coconut milk, onion, and seasonings like black pepper, salt, and thyme. The kidney beans are boiled with seasonings and a little piece of meat—salt pork, pigtail, or pieces of bacon. Then the seasoned beans are cooked together with rice. A related but different dish is beans and rice, which is stewed beans served with white rice on the side, not cooked together as in its sister dish. In many restaurants you'll have a choice of rice and beans or beans and rice. Whatever and wherever you eat, you're likely to find a bottle of **Marie Sharp's** hot sauce on the table. This proud product of Belize—it's bottled near Dangriga—comes in a spectrum of heat, from Mild to Fiery Hot to No Wimps Allowed.

Regional Specialties

Among other Creole specialties are cowfoot soup (yes, made with real cows' hooves), "boil up" (a stew of fish, potatoes, plantains, cassava and other vegetables, and eggs), and the ubiquitous "stew chicken." Many Creole dishes are cooked in coconut milk and seasoned with red or black *recado*, a paste made from annatto seeds and other spices. You'll also find many Mestizo or Latin favorites such as Belizean *escabeche* (onion soup, with lime, vinegar, and chicken), *salbutes* (fried corn tortillas with chicken and a topping of tomatoes, onions, and peppers), and the similar *garnaches* (fried tortillas with refried beans, cabbage, and cheese). Many of these homey dishes are sold at street stands, and it's usually very safe to eat at these stands. In Dangriga and Punta Gorda or other Garífuna areas, try dishes such as *sere lasus* (fish soup with plantain balls) or cassava dumplings. The Chinese influence in Belize, unfortunately, focuses on the lowest culinary common denominator. Chinese restaurants abound, but they mostly serve dishes such as cheap chop suey, with ketchup on the side. The American influence is also less than haute cuisine, having been responsible for the widespread popularity of "fry chicken" and hamburgers (usually called beefburgers in Belize).

Most local beef is grass-fed. Filets are generally the tenderest option. Belizean porks, however, are superb, and it's rare to get anything but a juicy, delicious pork chop in Belize. Chicken, the most popular meat in Belize, is also good. Most of Belize's chickens—and indeed much of other food, from eggs to cheese to vegetables—are provided by Mennonite farms in Spanish Lookout and elsewhere.

Seafood

On the coast and cayes, seafood is fresh, relatively inexpensive, and delicious. The Caribbean spiny lobster (*Panulirus argus*) is one of Belize's gourmet treats. Unlike its Maine cousin, it lacks claws, and the edible meat is in its tail. It's perfect lightly grilled and served with drawn butter, but you can also enjoy it in fritters, soups, bisques, salads, and even burgers. Lobster season runs from June 15 to February 15. Conch, in season all year except for the months of July, August, and September, also is widely served in Belize, as conch steak, fritters, and soup. In 2012, however, the conch season ended a couple of months early, due to a decline in the numbers of queen conchs. On restaurant menus you're most likely to find snapper and grouper, both tasty without being too fishy. Belizeans themselves often favor barracuda. Farm-raised tilapia is also widely available. Most shrimp are also farm-raised, from one of the large shrimp farms near Placencia or elsewhere.

Belizeans love their ceviche—raw seafood marinated in lime juice. You'll find a variety of ceviche dishes on menus everywhere—conch, shrimp, lobster, fish, and even octopus and squid. Usually the seafood is mixed with onion, hot peppers, salt, and herbs such as cilantro or *culantro* (similar to cilantro but stronger in flavor), and then "cooked" with lime or other citrus juices. It's all delicious!

Fruits and Vegetables
Belize offers a cornucopia of delicious fresh tropical fruits, although unfortunately not too much of the fruit makes its way to restaurant tables. You may have to stop at fruit stands and buy your own. In season, fruits in markets are remarkably inexpensive. For example, you can buy eight or ten bananas or a huge pineapple for BZ$1 to BZ$2. Papayas, mangoes, bananas, oranges, and watermelons are the most common fruits served usually on breakfast plates. But the markets have many other kinds of fruit: one is *craboo* or *nance*, a small yellow fruit the size of a

cherry, which ripens in July and August. They're excellent mashed and served with milk, or just eaten raw. Markets also have star fruit, soursop, breadfruit, dragon fruit, cashew fruit, and others. Among the best local markets in Belize are those in Corozal Town, Orange Walk Town, Belize City, Belmopan, San Ignacio, Dangriga, and Punta Gorda. Most operate daily, with Saturday being the busiest.

Some uncommon vegetables include *cho cho*, a mild-flavored squash also known as *mirlton* or chayote. It's often served raw in salads and also baked, fried, boiled, and stuffed. *Chaya* is a green leafy plant that is sometimes called Mayan spinach. It's often served as cooked greens or in scrambled eggs.

Beer, Wines, and Spirits
The legal drinking age in Belize is 18. Nearly all restaurants serve local brew **Belikin,** and many bars offer terrific tropical mixed drinks; a growing number offer wine. Imported liquor is expensive. Due to restrictive import laws, the beers of neighboring Mexico and Guatemala are rare, although due to Belize's membership in the Caribbean Community (CARICOM), Red Stripe and Heineken, brewed in the Caribbean, can be imported into Belize. Several Belize companies manufacture liquors, primarily rum, but also gin and vodka and a variety of local fruit wines. **Traveller's "One Barrel" Rum,** with a slight vanilla-caramel flavor, is a favorite. Imported wines are available in supermarkets and better restaurants, at about twice the price of the same wines in the United States. There are wine stores in Belize City and San Pedro. Cashew, blackberry, and other local wines are available around the country.

BELIZE CITY

By Lan Sluder

Belize City is more of a town than a city—few of the ramshackle buildings here are taller than a palm tree, and the official population within the city limits is barely over 50,000, though the metro population is near 90,000. Not far beyond the city center, streets give way to two-lane country roads where animals outnumber people. Any dining room downtown could leave the impression that everybody knows everybody else in this town, and certainly among the elite who can afford to dine out, that's probably true.

On a map Belize City appears to be an ideal base for exploring the central part of the country—it's two hours or less by car to San Ignacio, Corozal Town, Dangriga, and even less to Altun Ha, Belmopan, and the Belize Zoo. However, many old Belize hands will advise you to get out of Belize City as quickly as you can. They point to the high crime rate and to drugs and gang activity. They also note the relative lack of attractions in Belize City. There are no good beaches in or near the city, except for one man-made beach at the Old Belize facility west of town, built to attract cruise-ship visitors. Although you can sometimes spot manatees and porpoises in the harbor, and birding around the city is surprisingly good, this is not the wild rain forest visitors come to see.

All of that is true enough, and certainly any visitor to Belize City should take the usual precautions for travel in an impoverished urban area, which includes always taking a cab at night (and in rough parts of the city anytime), but Belize City does have an energy and excitement to it. There are good restaurants, including the best Chinese and Indian food in the country, a vibrant arts community, and, outside some of the rougher parts of town on the South Side, nice residential areas and a number of pleasant hotels and B&Bs. Belize City offers the most varied shopping in the country, and it's the only place to find sizeable supermarkets, department stores, and the Belizean version of big box stores. There is always some little treasure to be discovered in a shop with mostly junk. All in all, it's far more interesting than any modern mall.

Belize City also has an easygoing sociability. People meet on the street, talk, joke, laugh, and debate. Despite the Belize City streetscape's sometimes sketchy appearance, people in the shops and on the street tend to be friendly, polite, and helpful.

If you haven't spent time in Belize City, you simply won't understand Belize. Belize City is the commercial, social, sports, and cultural hub of the country. It's even the political hub, despite the fact that the capital, Belmopan, is an hour west. The current prime minister, Dean Barrow, a lawyer who came to power in 2008, former prime ministers including Said Musa, many of the other ministers, and nearly all of the country's movers and shakers live in or near Belize City.

TOP REASONS TO GO

Great Photo Ops. Belize City is highly photogenic, full of interesting faces, streets full of color, and charming old colonial houses. In short, Belize City has character.

Colonial Architecture. Belize City rewards the intrepid traveler with a surprising number of interesting sights and memorable places, among them the everyday colonial-era buildings in the Fort George and Southern Foreshore sections, where people still live and work. For the most part, buildings are wood, with tin or zinc roofs. Many are in need of a bit of repair, but they still ooze Caribbean port-of-call atmosphere.

Because You Have To. As a visitor to Belize, you'll almost certainly have to spend a little time in Belize City, whether you like it or not. The international airport is in Ladyville, at the northern edge of the metropolitan area. Belize City is the transportation hub of the country, and most flights, buses, and car rentals originate here. If you're arriving late or leaving early, you'll have to overnight in or near the city. Make the best of it. Take care, but explore and enjoy the city.

One longtime Belize resident says that despite its problems she enjoys making day trips to the city and always encourages visitors to spend some time there: "Being a landlubber, I enjoy the boats, seabirds, and smell of the salt air, and of course the Swing Bridge, watching the fishermen on fishing boats sell their fish, and seeing what fish and sea creatures are for sale in the market. When I first came here I was amazed at the fish and meat stalls, at how they were out in the open, and weren't refrigerated like back home. I think it's good for tourists to see that there are other ways of living than what they are used to. Isn't that the point of traveling?"

Still—and we can't overemphasize this—you do have to be careful, as crime is not limited just to certain areas: When you're in Belize City, bring your street smarts and exercise caution at all times.

ORIENTATION AND PLANNING

GETTING ORIENTED

If you're prepared to go beyond a cursory excursion, Belize City will repay your curiosity. There's an infectious sociability on streets like Albert and Queen, the main shopping strips. The finest British colonial houses— graceful white buildings with wraparound verandas, painted shutters, and fussy Victorian woodwork—are in the Fort George area, near the Radisson Fort George, the most pleasant part of the city for a stroll.

Fort George. The "colonial" section of Belize City is notable for its grand, if sometimes dilapidated, old 19th- and early-20th-century homes and buildings.

Marine Parade Harbor Front. Along the water near the Princess Hotel & Casino and BTL Park, there is more open, public space than there are buildings, making this a pleasant escape from the bustle of the city center.

The Commercial District. On the South Side, mainly on Albert and Regent streets, this is the commercial center of the city. Be advised, however, that it is also near some of the worst slums in Belize.

King's Park. Upscale residences line the streets near Princess Margaret Drive, about 2 miles (3 km) north of the city center.

The Northern Suburbs. Along the Philip Goldson Highway (formerly the Northern Highway) between the city center and the international airport, this is the fastest-growing part of the metropolitan area, with middle-class residential sections such as Buttonwood Bay and Belama, some of the city's stores and supermarkets, and several hotels and B&Bs.

The Western Suburbs. A few tourist attractions have popped up here, such as the Old Belize complex. This multiuse commercial and residential area along the George Price Highway (until late 2012 called the Western Highway), beginning at "Boot Hill" on Cemetery Road at the intersection of Central American Boulevard, is also on the way to the Belize Zoo, Belmopan, and Cayo.

> **TOURING TIP**
>
> If you're spending time in downtown Belize City, you may be better off without a car. Parking is limited, and leaving a car on the street overnight, especially with any valuables in it, is just asking for trouble. Streets are narrow, and many are closed for repairs, so you could find yourself lost in a maze of unmarked detours.

PLANNING

WHEN TO GO

As with the rest of Belize, the most pleasant time to visit Belize City is in the winter and early spring, December to March or April, when it's cooler and drier—similar to South Florida at that same time of year. The average high temperature in Belize City is 86.2°F, and the average low is 72.6°F. The coolest month is January, and the hottest is May. Hotel rates drop in the off-season, typically from just after Easter to U.S. Thanksgiving. September, a month marked by St. George's Caye Day (September 10) and Belize Independence Day (September 21), sees celebrations and parties; many expatriated Belizeans return home then for a visit to see family and friends. However, September is also peak time for tropical storms and hurricanes in the western Caribbean. September and October are the slowest months for tourism in Belize, and some hotels and restaurants close during this time for maintenance or to allow owners to take their own vacations.

GETTING HERE AND AROUND

AIR TRAVEL

Philip S. W. Goldson International Airport (BZE) is near Ladyville, 9 miles (14 km) north of the city. The international airport is served from U.S. gateways by American (some American flights from Miami operate as a codeshare with British Air), United, Delta, TACA, and US Airways. Tropic Air has flights between the international airport and Flores, Guatemala, gateway to Tikal, and on to Guatemala City.

2

In addition to international flights, a domestic terminal at the international airport has flights on Maya Island Air and Tropic Air to Ambergris Caye and Caye Caulker and the coastal towns of Dangriga, Placencia, and Punta Gorda. Tropic Air also has flights from the international airport to Maya Flats airstrip near San Ignacio and to Belmopan. A Maya Island flight goes to Savannah airstrip at Independence across the lagoon from Placencia.

The Belize City municipal airport, on the seafront about 1 mile (2 km) north of the city center, has domestic flights only; Maya Island Air and Tropic Air serve most of the same domestic destinations from here as from the international airport. Fares from the municipal airport are about 10% to 40% cheaper, depending on the destination, than similar flights departing from the international airport.

Contacts Maya Island Air ✉ *Muncipal Airstrip* ☎ *223/1140* ⊕ *www.mayaislandair.com.* **Tropic Air** ✉ *San Pedro* ☎ *226/2012, 800/422–3435 in U.S. or Canada* ⊕ *www.tropicair.com.*

BUS TRAVEL

TO AND FROM BELIZE CITY Belize City is the hub of the country's fairly extensive bus network, so there's service to most regions of Belize and limited service by foreign bus companies to Mexico and Guatemala. The main bus terminal on West Collet Canal Street in Belize City—still locally referred to as Novelo's, though the Novelo's bus company is no more—is used by most regional companies on the George Price Highway routes, the Goldson Highway routes, and the Hummingbird and Southern highways routes. Many of these are small, owner-operated bus lines. ⚠ **Take a cab to or from the Belize City bus terminal, as it is not in a safe area.**

From Belize City. Service on the main routes north, west, and south is frequent and inexpensive. Most of the buses are old Bluebird school buses from the U.S., with cramped seating and no air-conditioning.

The fare from Belize City to **San Ignacio** is BZ$7, and to **Corozal Town** BZ$9; express buses, when available, are BZ$2 or BZ$3 more.

The Mexican bus line ADO (⊕ *www.ado.com.mx*) runs daily express service between Cancún and Belize City, with stops at Playa del Carmen, Tulum, Corozal Town, and Orange Walk Town. The overnight service, departing from both Cancún and Belize City in the evening and arriving about eight hours later in the early morning, is handy for those flying into or out of Cancún, an option that usually offers lower fares than flying to and from the international airport near Belize City. Service is on modern Mercedes buses with air-conditioning, reclining seats, bathrooms, and videos. ADO also added Mérida–Belize City service. In Belize City, ADO uses the Novelo's terminal on West Collet Canal.

Belize Bus and Travel Guide (⊕ *belizebus.wordpress.com*) is a good site for up-to-date information on bus and other travel in Belize.

Contacts Belize City Main Bus Terminal (Locally called Novelo's) ✉ *W. Collet Canal St.*

Within Belize City. There is now limited bus service within Belize City on Lopez, Arrow Line, Haylock, Lemott, and other independent lines. Fares are BZ$1–BZ$2 depending on the route and the bus line. Again, many of the buses are old U.S. school buses, but some are modern minibuses, and the Arrow Line buses are air-conditioned. Ask locally about routes and times, as there are few if any published schedules. Also, local nonexpress regional buses will stop and drop off most anywhere in or near the city on the standard route.

CAR TRAVEL

TO AND FROM BELIZE CITY There are only two highways to Belize City: the Philip Goldson Highway, which stretches to the Mexican border, 102 miles (165 km) away, and the George Price Highway, which runs 81 miles (131 km) to Guatemala. Both are paved and in fair to good condition. Signs guide you to nearby destinations such as the Belize Zoo.

IN BELIZE CITY WITH A CAR Finding your way around the city itself can be confusing. With rare exceptions hotels in and near the city center offer mostly on-street parking, and you run the risk of a break-in if you leave the car overnight. Hotels in the suburbs north and west of the city usually have fenced or otherwise secured parking. Give your nerves a break and explore the city by taxi or on foot by day in safer sections like the Fort George area.

If you're driving between western and northern Belize, say from Belmopan to Orange Walk Town, you can take the Burrell Boom bypass around Belize City. The bypass runs between the roundabout on the George Price Highway at Hattieville at Mile 15.5 and Mile 13 of the Philip Goldson Highway. The bypass, completely paved, is about 11½ miles (18½ km) in length; it saves you about 17 miles (28 km) and about a half hour of driving time.

If you are traveling by car from Belize City to one of the northern cayes, you won't be able to take your vehicle, so you'll need a safe place to park. Shorter term parking is also available at the international airport lot for BZ$18 a night.

Contacts Edgar's Mini Storage. If you need to park your vehicle safely for a few days while you're at one of the northern cayes, one good choice is Edgar's Mini Storage, about an hour from the airport. Bring your own lock and park your car or truck in a covered storage unit, or outside in a fenced lot. Rates vary depending on the size of the vehicle. Free transport to the international airport is provided. ✉ *894 Vista del Mar, Ladyville* ☎ *602/4513* ⊕ *www.edgarsministorage.com.*

TAXI TRAVEL

Cabs cost BZ$7–BZ$10 for one person between any two points in the city, plus BZ$1 for each additional person. Outside the city, and from downtown to the suburbs, you'll be charged by distance traveled. Traveling between the international airport and any point in the city (including the businesses and hotels along the Northern Highway) is BZ$50 (for the taxi, not per person). There are no meters, so be sure to agree on a price before you leave. Authorized taxis have green license plates. You can find taxis in the Market Square area near the Swing Bridge and at the Novelo's bus terminal, or hotels will call them for you (preferred, since the hotel people know the dependable drivers). Otherwise, for pickup, call Cinderella Plaza Taxi Stand if you are in the downtown area or Belcan Taxi Stand if you are on the north end of the city.

Contacts Belcan Taxi Stand ☎ *223/2916.* **Cinderella Plaza Taxi Stand** ✉ *Freetown Rd., near Douglas Jones St.* ☎ *223/0371, 223/1612.*

WATER TRAVEL

TO AND FROM BELIZE CITY You can travel from Belize City on fast boats that hold up to 50 or 100 passengers to San Pedro (Ambergris Caye) and Caye Caulker. The boats also connect San Pedro and Caye Caulker. Caye Caulker Water Taxi boats (which also go to San Pedro) depart from the Marine Terminal at 10 North Front Street near the Swing Bridge; San Pedro Belize Express boats (which also go to Caulker) leave from the nearby Brown Sugar dock at 111 North Front Street near the Tourism Village; Water Jets International boats, also confusingly known as San Pedro Water Jets Express, leave from the Marine Terminal at 10 North Front Street.

From Belize City it's a 45-minute ride to Caye Caulker and a 75-minute trip to San Pedro. Going between Caye Caulker and San Pedro takes about 30 minutes. One-way fares between Belize City and Caye Caulker are BZ$20–BZ$24. Between Belize City and San Pedro, fares are BZ$30–BZ$35.

Each service has boats departing every couple of hours during daylight hours. Current schedules and prices are on the operators' websites, but are subject to frequent change.

The Tropic Ferry, a private service, picks you up at the international airport and transports you to a dock in Ladyville near the airport, and then on to your waterfront resort destination on Ambergris Caye. Fares are around BZ$170 per person one-way, and the whole trip takes about 90 minutes; advanced reservations required. There is no scheduled daily water-taxi service from Belize City to Placencia or other points south, nor to remote cayes. A weekly boat, Pride of Belize, stops at Dangriga enroute to Puerto Cortes, Honduras.

Contacts Caye Caulker Water Taxi Association ✉ *Marine Terminal, 10 N. Front St.* ☎ *223/5752* ⊕ *www.cayecaulkerwatertaxi.com.* **San Pedro Belize Express** ✉ *Brown Sugar Terminal, 111 N. Front St.* ☎ *223/2225* ⊕ *www.belizewatertaxi.com.* **The Tropic Ferry** ✉ *Oar House Bar Dock, 1659 Yellowtail Snapper Dr., Vista del Mar, Ladyville* ☎ *205/2100 Oar House phone – ferry has no business phone* ✎ *questions@tropicferry.com* ⊕ *www.tropicferry. com.* **Water Jets International** ✉ *Marine Terminal, 10 N. Front St.* ☎ *226/2194* ⊕ *www.sanpedrowatertaxi.com.*

EMERGENCIES

Karl Heusner Memorial, a public hospital, is the main medical center in the country. It offers generally competent and affordable care, though for serious injuries and illnesses many Belizeans who can afford it prefer to go to Miami or Houston or to Mexico or Guatemala. Belize Medical Associates and Belize Healthcare Partners are small private hospitals. Karl Heusner Memorial and Belize Medical Associates have 24-hour emergency rooms. Brodie's Pharmacy, at Market Square and on the Northern Highway, is open daily (hours vary). Belize Medical Associates Pharmacy has a pharmacist on call 24 hours.

In an emergency, dial 911. In Belize City only, for ambulance and fire, dial 90.

Hospitals Belize Healthcare Partners Limited ⊠ *Chancellor and Blue Marlin Ave.* ☎ *223/7870* ⊕ *www.belizehealthcare.com.* **Belize Medical Associates** ⊠ *5791 St. Thomas St., King's Park* ☎ *223/0303* ⊕ *www.belizemedical.com.* **Karl Heusner Memorial Hospital** ⊠ *Princess Margaret Dr.* ☎ *223/1548.*

Pharmacies Belize Medical Associates Pharmacy ⊠ *5791 St. Thomas St., King's Park* ☎ *223/0302.* **Brodie's Pharmacy** ⊠ *Regent St. at Market Sq.* ☎ *223/7070* ⊠ *Mile 2½, Goldson Hwy., formerly Northern Hwy.* ☎ *223/5587* ⊕ *www.brodiesbelize.com.*

MONEY MATTERS

U.S. dollars are accepted everywhere in Belize, but if you need to exchange another currency, you can do so at one of the five banks in Belize City: Heritage Bank, Atlantic Bank, Belize Bank, First Caribbean International Bank, and ScotiaBank. All banks in Belize City have ATMs (Belize Bank has the largest number of ATMs), and, except for ATMs of Heritage Bank, all now accept cards issued outside Belize. If your ATM card has a Visa, MasterCard, PLUS, or CIRRUS symbol, it will work in at least some Belize ATMs, and you can generally withdraw up to BZ$500 a day. You get your cash in Belize dollars only. Note that other banks you may see in Belize City are international—that is, offshore—banks that do not offer local banking services.

(See ATMs and Banks in Travel Smart for Bank addresses and phone numbers)

TOURS

From Belize City you can take day trips to Crooked Tree Wildlife Sanctuary to nearby islands, including Caulker and Ambergris cayes, either on your own or with a local tour operator. Your hotel can also arrange day trips. Keep in mind that most Belize City tour operators focus more on the cruise-ship market than on individual travelers. Some cruise-ship tour operators, while generally reputable, have no office and operate with a website and a cell phone, meeting customers at the Tourism Village.

Action Boys Belize focuses on land tours for the cruise ship market in Belize City. It offers zip-lining, cave tubing, Belize Zoo, Altun Ha, Baboon Sanctuary, and other trips. Combined zip-line and cave-tubing tours start at around BZ$170 per person. Cruise passengers are met at Tourism Village where the cruise tenders dock.

Belize Trips' Katie Valk, a transplanted New Yorker, can organize a custom trip to almost any place in the country and also to Tikal in Guatemala. With her hotel connections she can even get you a room when everything seems booked. She's also a warden for the U.S. Embassy.

CAVE TUBING

Several Belize City–based tour operators, including Action Boys Belize and Discovery Expeditions, cater to the cruise-ship day-trippers with cave tubing trips for around BZ$120–BZ$140 per person. Cave tubing and zip-line combo tours are around BZ$180–$200 per person. These tours usually include lunch.

MAYAN RUINS

Tour operators based in Belize City, including S&L Travel and Tours, Action Boys Belize, and Discovery Expeditions, which mostly cater to cruise ships, offer day trips by road, boat, or air to **Lamanai** (around BZ$200) and by road to **Altun Ha** (BZ$75–BZ$90), and also by road to **Xunantunich** and **Cahal Pech** near San Ignacio. The tours to San Ignacio (BZ$200 and up) may be combined with a stop at the Belize Zoo or cave tubing and zip-lining at Caves Branch. Discovery Expeditions, Action Boys Belize, and S&L Travel and Tours can arrange tours to **Tikal** starting at around BZ$700 per person.

Contacts Action Belize ☎ 223/2987, 888/383–6319 ⊕ www.actionbelize.com. **Action Boys Belize** ☎ 664/1975 ⊕ www.actionboysbelize.com. **Belize Trips** ☎ 223/0376, 561/210–7015 U.S. number ⊕ www.belize-trips.com. **Cave-Tubing in Belize** ☎ 605/1575 ⊕ www.cave-tubing.com. **Discovery Expeditions** ✉ 5916 Manatee Dr., Buttonwood Bay ☎ 671/0748 ⊕ www.discoverybelize.com. **S&L Travel and Tours** ✉ 91 N. Front St. ☎ 227/7593 ⊕ www.sltravelbelize.com.

VISITOR INFORMATION

Belize Tourism Board ✉ 64 Regent St. ☎ 227/2420, 800/624–0686 ⊕ www.travelbelize.org ⊗ Mon.–Thurs. 8–5, Fri. 8–4.

EXPLORING BELIZE CITY

Belize City is defined by the water around it. The main part of the city is at the end of a small peninsula, jutting out into the Caribbean Sea. Haulover Creek, an extension of the Belize River, running roughly west to east, divides the city into the North Side and the South Side. The North Side is, to generalize, more affluent than the South Side. The venerable Swing Bridge connects the two sides, although in modern times other bridges over Haulover Creek, especially the Belcan Bridge northwest of the city center, carry more traffic. At the mouth of the river, just beyond Swing Bridge, is the Belize Harbor (or Harbour, as it's written locally, in the English style).

Coming from the north, follow the Goldson Highway through several roundabouts (traffic circles) to Freetown Road and Barracks Road to reach the center. Alternatively, you can swing west on Princess Margaret Drive to Barracks Road, along the seafront. From the west, the Western Highway becomes Cemetery Road, which leads you to the center via the South Side and Orange Street. The city center itself is a confusing warren of narrow streets, many of them one-way, and many may be temporarily closed, with detours that are not well-marked or are not marked at all.

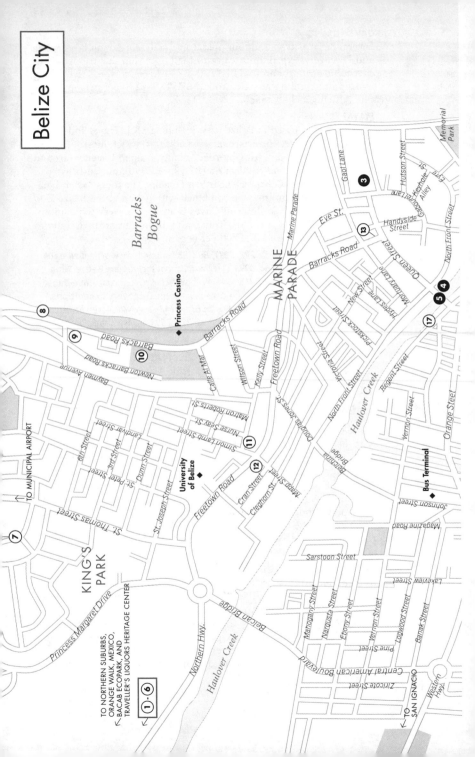

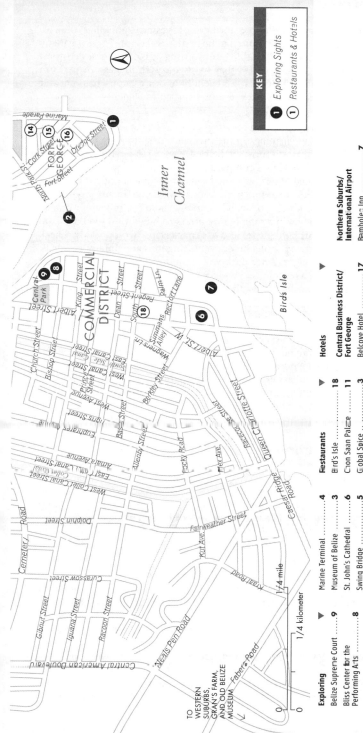

KEY

- ➊ Exploring Sights
- ① Restaurants & Hotels

Inner Channel

COMMERCIAL DISTRICT

Central Park

Bird's Isle

TO
WESTERN
SUBURBS,
GRAN'S FARM,
AND OLD BELIZE
MUSEUM

Exploring ▶

Belize Supreme Court **9**
Bliss Center for the
 Performing Arts **8**
Fort George Lighthouse
 and Bliss Memorial **1**
House of Culture **7**

Marine Terminal **4**
Museum of Belize **3**
St. John's Cathedral **6**
Swing Bridge **5**
Tourism Village **2**

Restaurants ▶

Bird's Isle **18**
Cron Saan Palace **11**
Global Spice **3**
Narie's **13**
Riverside Tavern **12**
Sahara Grill **6**
Samathi **9**

Hotels ▶

**Central Business District/
Fort George**

Belcove Hotel **17**
Chateau Caribbean **16**
The Great House **14**
Radisson Fort George **15**
Renaissance Tower **10**

**Northern Suburbs/
International Airport**

Bamboleo Inn **7**
Best Western Belize
 Biltmore Plaza **2**
D Nest Inn **4**
Global Village Hotel **5**
Hour Bar & Grill **8**
Villa Boscardi **1**

0 — 1/4 kilometer
0 — 1/4 mile

If you're staying in either the northern or western sprawling suburbs, a car is handy, as there's limited municipal bus service. There are many taxis, however, with affordable rates starting at BZ$7. It's not customary to tip taxi drivers, unless they help you with luggage or perform other services. Most drivers are friendly and are happy to point out interesting sites to visitors. A few are licensed tour guides.

SAFETY AND PRECAUTIONS

Belize City has a reputation for street crime. The government has made some progress in cleaning up the problem, despite gang activity and drugs. Crimes against tourists in Belize City are relatively rare. Still, the crime rate in Belize City is comparable to that of a distressed inner-city area in the United States, and the homicide rate is among the highest in the world. Take the same precautions you'd take in any city—don't wear expensive jewelry or watches, avoid handling money in public, and leave valuables in a safe. Ignore offers to buy drugs. On buses and in crowded areas hold purses and backpacks close to your body. Check with the staff at your hotel before venturing into any unfamiliar areas, particularly at night. After dark you should always take a taxi rather than walk even a few blocks. Avoid leaving your rental car on the street overnight. Generally the northern suburbs are safer than downtown.

FORT GEORGE

This is the most pleasant and appealing section of the city, much of it cooled by prevailing breezes from the sea. It has stately if sometimes run-down colonial buildings that escaped the hurricanes of 1931 and 1961, several embassies (though the U.S. embassy was transplanted to Belmopan in 2006), upmarket restaurants that attract the city's elite, and the city's better hotels, including the Radisson Fort George and the Great House, plus the Museum of Belize, Fort George lighthouse, and the Fort Street Tourism Village.

TOP ATTRACTIONS

FAMILY

Fodor'sChoice

★

Museum of Belize. This small but fascinating museum was the Belize City jail from 1857 to 1993. Permanent displays include ancient jade and other Mayan artifacts; medicinal, ink, and alcoholic-beverage bottles dating from the 1670s; Belize coins and colorful postage stamps; and an actual prison cell. Temporary exhibitions change periodically. ⊠ 8 Gabourel La., Belize Central Bank Compound, Fort George ☎ 223/4524 ⊕ www.nichbelize.org ☑ BZ$20 ☉ Mon.–Sat. 8–4:30.

Swing Bridge. As you might have guessed, the bridge spanning Haulover Creek in the middle of Belize City actually swings. When needed to allow a boat through or by special request of visiting dignitaries, four men hand-winch the bridge a quarter-revolution so waiting boats can continue upstream (when it was the only bridge in town, this snarled traffic for blocks). The bridge, made in England, opened in 1923; it was renovated and upgraded in 1999. It's the only one of its kind left. Before the Swing Bridge arrived, cattle were "hauled over" the creek in a barge. The bridge appears in a scene of the 1980 movie *The Dogs of War,* set in a fictitious African country but mostly filmed in Belize. ⊠ Haulover Creek where Queen and Albert Sts. meet, Fort George.

THE BEST GALLERIES IN BELIZE

BELIZE CITY
Belizean Handicraft Market Place
(formerly National Handicraft Center)
✉ S. Park ☎ 223/3627

Image Factory
✉ 1 N. Front St. ☎ 223/1149
⊕ www.imagefactorybelize.com

BELMOPAN
Art Box ✉ Mile 46, Western Hwy.
☎ 623/6129 ⊕ www.artboxbz.com

CAYE CAULKER
Caribbean Colors Art Gallery
✉ Front St. ☎ 206/0206
⊕ www.caribbean-colors.com

Cooper's Art Gallery
✉ Front St. ☎ 226/0330 ⊕ deb-biecooperart.artspan.com

DANGRIGA
Garinagu Crafts and Art Gallery
✉ 46 Oak St. at Tubroose St.
☎ 522/2596

PLACENCIA
Art 'n Soul ✉ South end of the Side-walk, Placencia village ☎ 503/3088

Spectarte ✉ Maya Beach, opposite Green Parrot ☎ 523/8019

PUNTA GORDA
Maya Bags ✉ Workshop on Airport Rd. near Tropic Air office at PG airstrip ⊕ www.mayabags.com

SAN IGNACIO
Garcia Sisters Tanah Mayan Art Museum ✉ Cristo Rey Rd., San Antonio ☎ 669/4023

Orange Gifts ✉ Mile 60, Western Hwy. ☎ 824/2341
⊕ www.orangegifts.com

SAN PEDRO, AMBERGRIS CAYE
Belizean Arts ✉ Barrier Reef Dr. at Fido's ☎ 226/3019
⊕ www.belizeanarts.com

WORTH NOTING

Belize Brewing Co. Ltd. With a virtual nationwide monopoly on beer, Bowen & Bowen's Belize Brewing Co. Ltd. is one of the country's most profitable businesses. Perfect for sipping on the beach, there are four beers to choose from: Belikin lager, with 4% alcohol; Belikin Premium, also a lager, with 5% alcohol; Lighthouse, a pale lager, with 4.2% alcohol; and Belikin Stout, a dark beer with 6% alcohol. Some cruise-ship and Belize City tours include a stop at the Bowen brewery, with a half-hour tasting of the beers. ✉ 1 King St., Belize City ☎ 227/7031 ⊕ www.bowenbz.com.

Fort George Lighthouse and Bliss Memorial. Towering over the entrance to Belize Harbor, the lighthouse stands guard on the tip of Fort George Point. It was designed and funded by one of the country's greatest bene-factors, Baron Henry Edward Ernest Victor Bliss. The English nobleman never actually set foot on the Belizean mainland, though in his yacht he visited the waters offshore. In his will he bequeathed most of his fortune to the people of Belize, and the date of his death, March 9, is celebrated as a national holiday, now officially called National Heroes and Bene-factors Day. Bliss is buried here, in a small, low mausoleum perched on the seawall, up a short run of limestone stairs. The lighthouse and mausoleum are for photo ops only—you can't enter. ✉ Marine Parade, near Radisson Fort George Hotel, Fort George 🎫 Free ⊙ 24 hours.

SOUTH SIDE COMMERCIAL DISTRICT

This area, along Albert and Regent streets, two parallel streets running north–south from Haulover Creek, is the commercial heart of the city. It has many small stores, banks, and budget hotels, along with several places of interest, including the Supreme Court, St. John's Cathedral, and the House of Culture. A third parallel street, the Southern Foreshore, hugs the waterfront along the South Side.

TOP ATTRACTIONS

Belize Supreme Court. Not the oldest building in the city but one of the most striking, the 1926 Belize Supreme Court building is patterned after its wooden predecessor, which had burned in 1918. An 1820 court building had also burned down. The current building, painted white, has filigreed iron stair and balcony rails, similar to what you might see in New Orleans (the construction company came from Louisiana), between two arms of the structure, and above the balcony a four-sided clock. This being Belize, the clock faces all seem to show different times. You can't enter the building, but it's worth admiring from the outside. ⊠ *Regent St., opposite Battlefield Park, Commercial District* ☎ *227/4387.*

House of Culture. Formerly called Government House, the city's finest colonial structure is said to have a design inspired by the illustrious British architect Sir Christopher Wren. Built in 1814, it was once the residence of the governor-general, the queen's representative in Belize. Following Hurricane Hattie in 1961, the governor and the rest of the government moved to Belmopan, and the house became a venue for social functions and a guesthouse for visiting VIPs. (Queen Elizabeth stayed here in 1985, Prince Philip in 1988.) Now it's open to the public. You can peruse its archival records, art, photographs, silver, glassware, and furniture collections, or mingle with the tropical birds that frequent the gardens. ⚠ **If going here after dark, take a cab, because it's close to some of the city's most crime-ridden areas.** ⊠ *Regent St. at Southern Foreshore, opposite St. John's Cathedral, Commercial District* ☎ *227/3050* ⊕ *www.nichbelize.org* ⊠ *BZ$10* ⊗ *Weekdays 8:30–5.*

WORTH NOTING

Bliss Center for the Performing Arts. Overlooking the harbor from the Southern Foreshore near the Supreme Court, this building houses the Institute of Creative Arts and hosts cultural and arts events throughout the year. It is a part of NICH, the National Institute of Culture and History. The Bliss Center's 600-seat theater is headquarters for the Belize International Film Festival, usually held in July. Dramas, children's festivals, dance, art displays, and other cultural and musical performances take place at various times. It also houses a small art gallery with a George Gabb sculpture, *Sleeping Giant,* which appears as the watermark on Belize five-dollar bills. ⊠ *2 Southern Foreshore, between Church and Bishop Sts., Commercial District* ☎ *227/2110* ⊕ *www.nichbelize.org.*

St. John's Cathedral. On Albert Street's south end is the oldest Anglican church in Central America and the only one outside England where kings were crowned. From 1815 to 1845, four kings of the Mosquito

Coast (a British protectorate along the coast of Honduras and Nicaragua) were crowned here. The cathedral, built of brick brought to British Honduras as ballast on English ships, is thought to be the oldest building in Belize, other than Mayan structures. Its foundation stone was laid in 1812. Inside, it has whitewashed walls and mahogany pews. The roof is constructed of local sapodilla wood, with mahogany beams. ■TIP➜ **You can combine a visit to St. John's Cathedral with a visit to the House of Culture, as they are just across the street from each other.** ⚠ **Safe to visit during day; at night take a cab.** ✉ *Albert St., at Regent St., Opposite the House of Culture, Commercial District* ☎ *227/3029* ⊕ *www. belizeanglican.org* ⊠ *Free* ⊗ *Daily 8:30–5; on Sun. times may vary.*

MARINE PARADE HARBOR FRONT

This rather nebulously defined area, which stretches from the Fort George section of Marine Parade to Barracks Road and then to the beginning of Princess Margaret Drive, could eventually be Belize City's equivalent of Havana's Malecón. Only a few years ago it was an unsightly conglomeration of old buildings and vacant lots. With cleaning up and some gentrification, the area now has several good restaurants, condominiums, a hotel-casino, and a park.

WORTH NOTING

Princess Casino. Belize City's only casino, at the Princess Hotel on the seafront, is usually bustling with local residents. It also attracts some cruise-ship passengers. There are live blackjack and poker tables, roulette wheels, and about 400 slots. The gaming and hotel complex has two movie theaters and a dance club. ✉ *Newtown Barracks, King's Park, Commercial District* ☎ *223/2670* ⊕ *www.princessbelize.com.*

WESTERN SUBURBS

For visitors, this part of the metropolitan area mostly is just a place to pass through on the way to the Cayo. However, local entrepreneurs have opened several businesses targeting cruise-ship passengers.

WORTH NOTING

FAMILY **Old Belize.** Many of the visitors here are tour groups from cruise ships, but you also can visit the museum at Old Belize on your own (it's a BZ$20 taxi ride each way from downtown Belize City). In a large warehouse-style building, exhibits are devoted to the rain forest and the Maya, Garífuna, and Creoles in Belize City, with displays on logging, chicle harvesting, and sugar production. Some of the artifacts formerly housed at the Maritime Museum at the Marine Terminal are now on display here. Also at the site of the museum are a large marina; a restaurant, TGI Crazy Gringo ($$), where you can get a decent hamburger (BZ$16) and other American-style dishes; a gift shop; and Cucumber Beach, a small man-made beach that's the only one near Belize City, a 600-foot zip line, and a waterslide. ✉ *Mile 5, George Price Hwy., formerly Western Hwy., Western Suburbs* ☎ *222/4129, 222/5588 TGI Crazy Gringo* ⊕ *www. oldbelize.com* ⊠ *BZ$10 for museum; BZ$20 for beach and waterslide; BZ$40 for beach, waterslide and zipline* ⊗ *Daily 9 am–10 pm.*

NORTHERN SUBURBS

If you're arriving by air at the international airport, you'll pass through the Northern Suburbs on your way to the city, or (unless you take the Burrell Boom bypass) on your way to points south and west.

WORTH NOTING

Traveller's Liquors Heritage Center. This museum celebrates Belize's love affair with rum and its oldest distillery, Traveller's. Although it's small, the museum is fascinating, with displays of old rum bottles and distillery equipment and the history of rum-making in Belize. You can also look through a window and see rum and other potables being made and bottled at the little factory behind the museum. Best of all, you can get samples of the various rums made by Traveller's, including its best-selling One Barrel, along with samples of more exotic drinks such as cashew wine, Rumpope (rum with eggnog), Anise & Peppermint (called A&P, it may remind you of cough syrup and is usually mixed with milk), and Craboo Liquor. The rum museum is often visited by groups from cruise ships—call ahead to schedule a visit around cruise tours. ✉ *Mile 2 1/2, Philip Goldson Hwy., formerly Northern Hwy., Northern Suburbs* ☎ *223/2855* 🌐 *www.onebarrelrum.com* 🎟 *BZ$2* ⏲ *Mon. 10–5:15, Tue.–Thurs. 9–5:15, Fri. 10–5, Sat. 10–4.*

WHERE TO EAT

Though most restaurants here cater to locals, their number and quality rival those of tourist magnet San Pedro on Ambergris Caye. The city has inexpensive dives serving "dollah chicken" (fried chicken, a local favorite, though it no longer costs just a Belize dollar), Chinese joints of 1950s vintage specializing in chow mein, and lunch spots for downtown office workers seeking Creole dishes such as cow-foot soup and rice and beans. Belize City also has upmarket restaurants serving the city's affluent elite. Only a couple of these are "dressy" (by Belize standards, this means a nice collared shirt for men and perhaps a long tropical dress for women), and reservations are rarely necessary.

A few restaurants around the Tourism Village target cruise-ship passengers, typically for lunch and drinks, but the one thing you won't find here are chain restaurants.

$$ SEAFOOD

🍴 **Bird's Isle.** This longtime local favorite is an open-air seaside bar and restaurant on the little islet at the south end of Regent Street, also called Bird's Isle. The thatched-roof spot is a great place to sip tropical drinks and eat local seafood or other dishes, away from the hustle of downtown. You'll like the prices, too. Take a taxi after dark, as the Southside area near Bird's Isle is not the best. [$] *Average main: BZ$16* ✉ *9 Albert St., at south end of Regent St., across bridge on Bird's Isle, on South Side, Commercial District* ☎ *207/2179* ⏲ *Closed Sun. dinner.*

$$ CHINESE

🍴 **Chon Saan Palace.** Locally adored for more than 35 years, Chon Saan Palace is the best Chinese restaurant in Belize City, which is otherwise full of bad Chinese eateries. It has some 200 dishes on the menu, most Cantonese-style, such as sweet-and-sour pork. We like the Chinese-style crab legs. There's a live-seafood tank with lobster and the catch of the

Made in Belize

For such a little country, some of Belize's products pack a punch. *Below is a list of possible souvenirs.*

HOT SAUCE

Marie Sharp's. One of Belize's best-known products comes from a little plant near Dangriga. This spicy sauce was originally created by Marie Sharp in her kitchen in the early 1980s. It comes in a variety of heat levels, from the moderate Mild Habanero to the fiery No Wimps Allowed, and, finally, Beware. Marie Sharp's also makes less dangerous products, such as jams, jellies, and other spices and sauces. If you call ahead, you can tour the plant on Melinda Road near Dangriga. ⊠ *Main Office, 3 Pier Rd., Dangriga* ☎ *522/2370* ⊕ *www.mariesharps-bz.com.*

RUM

Traveller's Liquors Ltd. A favorite of rum connoisseurs, One Barrel, from Traveller's Ltd., with a slight taste of vanilla and caramel, has won international tasting awards in the gold rum category. The company is run by the Perdomo family of Belize City. ☎ *223/2031* ⊕ *www.onebarrelrum.com.*

Cuellos. A good mixing white rum, and the one you'll see in most bars, is called Caribbean Rum. It is made by family-owned Cuellos distillery. ⊠ *65 Main St., Orange Walk Town* ☎ *322/2141 distillery, 322/2183 office.*

HARDWOOD FURNITURE

If the cost of shipping doesn't break your budget, the low-slung folding "clam chairs" are a favorite and made from the region's tropical hardwood.

New River Enterprises. New River Enterprises makes solid mahogany and other hardwood doors, some around BZ$2,400 plus shipping. It also makes patio furniture. ⊠ *14 Westby St., Orange Walk Town* ☎ *322/2225* ⊕ *www.newriverenterprises.com.*

Hummingbird Furnishings. Hummingbird Furnishings uses bamboo, wicker, and rattan, sometimes mixed with mahogany, for indoor and outdoor furniture. ⊠ *54 Hummingbird Hwy., Belmopan City* ☎ *822/3164* ⊕ *www.hummingbirdfurnishings.com* ⊠ *20 Coconut Dr., San Pedro* ☎ *226/2960.*

COFFEE

Gallon Jug Estates in Orange Walk District is the only commercial coffee producer in Belize (and it is small, with only about 100 acres of coffee plantings). Made with only arabica beans, Gallon Jug coffees are shade-grown and don't use pesticides, herbicides, or fungicides. Whole-bean and ground coffee, packed in colorful gold and green, can be bought all over Belize.

BEER

Belize Brewing Co. Ltd. Take a tour of the the Bowen brewery to see them brew Belikin, Belize's most popular beer, with a half-hour tasting of the varieties of brews. ⊠ *1 King St.* ☎ *227/7031* ⊕ *www.bowenbz.com.*

day, kept alive until you're ready to eat it. On Sunday, the restaurant switches gears a bit and makes sushi. [$] *Average main: BZ$18* ✉ *1 Kelly St., at Nurse Seay St., Commercial District* ☎ *223/3008*.

$ LATIN AMERICAN 🍴 **Global Spice.** We don't often include airport restaurants, but Global Spice, a no-frills restaurant near the "waving gallery" on the second floor of the main terminal, will leave you with a nice taste of Belize. Chef Jason de Ocampo has been a winner in the annual "Taste of Belize" cooking contest, which focuses on Belizean national and regional cooking. It's not a gourmet restaurant, just a good place to get that farewell plate of stew chicken with rice and beans and a cold Belikin. [$] *Average main: BZ$14* ✉ *Philip S. W. Goldson International Airport, 2nd level of main terminal, Ladyville* ☎ *225/3339*.

$$ SEAFOOD 🍴 **Hour Bar & Grill.** Created by a branch of the Barry Bowen family (owner of Belize Brewing Company), Hour Bar & Grill has quickly become a popular Belize City hang out. The food, mostly standard seafood, is only mediocre. Its greater appeal is its breezy seaside location. There's plenty of safe, guarded parking, good drinks, and, naturally, plenty of cold Belikin. It's got a lively atmosphere with lots of locals. [$] *Average main: BZ$25* ✉ *1 Princess Margaret Dr., Marine Parade Harbor Front* ☎ *223/3737* ⏲ *Closed Mon.*

$ LATIN AMERICAN 🍴 **Nerie's.** Often packed with locals, Nerie's is the vox populi of dining in Belize City. The many traditional dishes on the menu include fry jacks for breakfast and cow-foot soup for lunch. Stew chicken with rice and beans and a soft drink will set you back only about BZ$11. [$] *Average main: BZ$12* ✉ *Queen and Daly Sts., Commercial District* ☎ *223/4028* 💳 *No credit cards* [$] *Average main: BZ$12* ✉ *Douglas Jones St., Commercial District* ☎ *224/5199* 💳 *No credit cards.*

$$ AMERICAN Fodor's Choice ★ 🍴 **Riverside Tavern.** Owned and managed by the Bowen (Belikin beer) family, Riverside Tavern is one of the city's most popular and agreeable restaurants, with dependably good food, friendly service, and safe parking. The signature hamburgers, which come in several sizes from 6 oz. to enormous, are arguably the best in Belize. The Riverside has steak and prime rib dishes, from cattle from the Bowen farm at Gallon Jug. Sit inside in air-conditioned comfort, at tables set around a huge bar, or on the outside covered patio overlooking Haulover Creek. This is one of the few restaurants in Belize with a dress code—shorts aren't allowed at night. The fenced, guarded parking lot right in front of the restaurant makes it easy and safe to park for free. [$] *Average main: BZ$25* ✉ *2 Mapp St., off Freetown Rd., Commercial District* ☎ *223/5640* ⏲ *Closed Sun.*

$$ MEDITERRANEAN 🍴 **Sahara Grill.** This Mediterranean/Lebanese restaurant in the Northern Suburbs has good kebabs, kofta, falafel, and hummus, with many vegetarian options. [$] *Average main: BZ$20* ✉ *1st Floor, Vista Plaza, Mile 3, Northern Hwy., across from Belize Biltmore Plaza, Northern Suburbs* ☎ *203/3031* ⏲ *No lunch.*

$$ INDIAN 🍴 **Sumathi.** Tasty northern and southern Indian food is created at Sumathi in their authentic tandoori oven—a large clay oven with intense heat—which cooks meat and seafood quickly, leaving it crispy on the outside and juicy inside. Try the tandoori chicken, with cumin, ginger, and minty yogurt, served with *naan* (Indian flatbread). There are many vegetarian options, too. Portions are generous. Service is sometimes a

weak point. $ *Average main: BZ$22 ⊠ Off Newtown Barracks, 19 Baymen Avenue, Marine Parade Harbor Front* ☎ *223/1172* ⊗ *Open for lunch and dinner. Closed Mon.*

WHERE TO STAY

2

For expanded hotel reviews, visit Fodors.com.

Belize City has the country's largest hotels, though size is relative in Belize. The Radisson, Princess, and Biltmore Plaza each have 75 or more rooms and strive, not always successfully, for an international standard. The city also has its share of small inns and B&Bs with character, such as the Great House, D'Nest Inn, and Villa Boscardi. Although easy on the pocketbook, the city's budget hotels frequently have thin, inexpensive mattresses and scratchy sheets, and amenities such as room phones may be scarce. In Belize City safety is an issue, especially at the cheaper hotels, so be sure to check that doors and windows securely lock and that the entrance is well lighted. In the downtown areas, don't walk around after dark, even in groups; always take a taxi.

Several of the city's best hotels are in the Fort George area, but there are also good choices in the northern suburbs between downtown and the international airport. The Commercial District on the South Side (south of Swing Bridge) has a number of budget hotels.

$ ⌐⌐ **Belcove Hotel.** Right in the middle of things, the Belcove is a popular
HOTEL budget hotel just south of Swing Bridge, literally at the edge of Haulover Creek. **Pros:** good value; friendly staff; central downtown location. **Cons:** slightly funky atmosphere; you need to be very careful downtown after dark. $ *Rooms from: BZ$70* ⊠ *9 Regent St. West, just south of Swing Bridge, Commercial District* ☎ *227/3054* ⊕ *www.belcove.com* ⌐ *12 rooms, 4 with shared baths* ⦿ *No meals.*

$ ⌐⌐ **Bamboleo Inn.** New in mid-2013, this small inn in a residential area
B&B/INN of Ladyville is an appealing option for an overnight stay just five minutes from the international airport. **Pros:** new inn, attractive suites with kitchenettes; convenient to international airport; safer residential area on canal. **Cons:** not near good restaurants or other attractions. $ *Rooms from: BZ$180* ⊠ *724 Kingfish Rd., Vista Del Mar, Ladyville* ☎ *634/4429* ⊕ *www.bamboleo-inn.com* ⌐ *7 suites* ⦿ *No meals.*

$$ ⌐⌐ **Best Western Belize Biltmore Plaza.** This suburban motel, which mostly
HOTEL gets guests who don't want to stay in the downtown area, has upgraded its pool, grounds, and rooms, though it's still a little shy of luxurious. **Pros:** comfortable, secure, motel-like suburban setting; bar has good happy hour deals; deluxe rooms worth extra cost. **Cons:** not much atmosphere; a few mosquitoes around pool; so-so restaurant. $ *Rooms from: BZ$260* ⊠ *Mile 3, Goldson Hwy., Northern Suburbs* ☎ *223/2302* ⊕ *www.belizebiltmore.com* ⌐ *75 rooms.*

$ ⌐⌐ **Chateau Caribbean.** The breezy Fort George seaside location of
HOTEL this hotel is its strongest point, and some would say its only strong point. **Pros:** waterfront location; colonial atmosphere in public areas. **Cons:** shabby, worn rooms; you may see some bugs. $ *Rooms from: BZ$194* ⊠ *6 Marine Parade, Fort George* ☎ *223/0800* ⊕ *www.chateaucaribbean.com* ⌐ *20 rooms.*

CLOSE UP

Roots Belizean

If you spend time talking with Belizeans, sooner or later conversation will turn to "roots." It's not a vegetable, but a term referring to people born in Belize who share a certain set of values. Usually, but not always, it connotes ordinary folk, not wealthy Belizeans. These are Belizeans who ride the bus instead of driving a new Ford Explorer.

"Being roots Belizean is a way of life, a mind-set, and a unique set of values," says Wendy Auxillou, a Belizean who spent much of her life on Caye Caulker. Roots Belizeans enjoy the simple pleasures of life: talking with friends they run into on the streets of Belize City; skipping work or school to swim in the sea, river, or lagoon; sitting on a veranda on a hot afternoon; fishing in an old wooden skiff; raising chickens in the backyard for Sunday dinner.

Roots is also about community involvement. Children are often looked after by aunts and grannies, as well as neighbors. Misbehaving children might find themselves answering to a slew of adults in addition to their parents.

It's going to the market and eating boiled corn, *dukunu* (boiled cornbread), *garnaches* (crispy tortillas topped with beans and rice), and Belizean-style hot dogs, which are wrapped in bacon and grilled with onions. It's buying bananas 10 for a Belizean dollar. It's enjoying the smell and taste of all the local fruits, like tambran, grocea, a dozen different kinds of mangoes, sapodilla, mamie, jicama, watermelon, pineapple, guava, and papaya. It's about going to restaurants with local flavor, like Caladium in Belmopan, Nerie's or Dit's in Belize City, and Clarissa Falls in Cayo.

"It's about eating johnnycakes or plucking chickens with your neighbor, just because," says one Belizean.

Some claim that the original and perhaps only roots Belizeans are Creoles, descendents of the rough-and-ready Baymen and freed African slaves. Others argue that anybody can be a roots Belizean, that there are roots Mestizos, roots Maya, even roots Mennonites.

—Lan Sluder

$ HOTEL Fodor's Choice ★ **D'Nest Inn.** In Belama Phase 2, a safe, middle-class suburb between the international airport and downtown, D'Nest Inn is run by a charming couple, Gaby and Oty Ake. **Pros:** delightful B&B; charming and helpful hosts; delicious breakfasts included. **Cons:** only a few restaurant choices nearby. [$] *Rooms from: BZ$179* ✉ *475 Cedar St., Northern Suburbs* ✣ *From Goldson Hwy., turn west on Chetumal St. (newly resurfaced and now a divided boulevard), go about 300 yards, turn right at police station, go 1 short block and turn left, then turn right on Cedar St.* ☎ *223/5416* 🌐 *www.dnestinn.com* 🛏 *4 rooms* 🍴 *Breakfast.*

$ HOTEL **Global Village Hotel.** This Chinese-owned motel has no atmosphere and no frills, but it's clean, with modern furniture and fixtures, and a good value at around BZ$100 plus tax for a double. **Pros:** clean, barebones motel; free airport pickup and drop-off; secure parking. **Cons:** no atmosphere; mainly for an overnight en route to other locations. [$] *Rooms from: BZ$109* ✉ *Mile 8½, Goldson Hwy., just south of turnoff to international airport, Ladyville* ☎ *225/2555* 🌐 *www.globalvillage-bz.com* 🛏 *40 rooms* 🍴 *Breakfast.*

> **WORD OF MOUTH**
>
> "I loved the ferry ride from the downtown terminal to [Ambergris Caye], and I loved the plane ride back from San Pedro. A good combination of experiences (and savings)!"
>
> —sylvia3

$$$
B&B/INN

The Great House. Among Fort George's most appealing sights is the colonial facade of this large wooden house, across the street from the Radisson. **Pros:** lovely old inn; good location in Fort George. **Cons:** rooms are all upstairs and there's no elevator. [$] *Rooms from: BZ$399* ✉ *13 Cork St., Fort George* ☎ *223/3400* 🌐 *www.greathousebelize.com* 🛏 *16 rooms* 🍴 *Breakfast.*

$$$
HOTEL
Fodor's Choice ★

Radisson Fort George Hotel and Marina. This is the best international-style large hotel in the city, located in the historic Fort George section with panoramic views of the sea from rooms in the main six-story tower. **Pros:** Belize City's best large hotel, but don't expect San Francisco–level facilities; waterfront location in historic Fort George area, with marina. **Cons:** some rooms are small and could use updating. [$] *Rooms from: BZ$375* ✉ *2 Marine Parade, in Fort George area, Fort George* ☎ *223/3333, 800/967–9033 in U.S. and Canada* 🌐 *www.radissonbelize.com* 🛏 *102 rooms.*

$$$
RENTAL

Renaissance Tower. An alternative to staying in a downtown hotel is this condominium tower, with some units available on a nightly basis; the rates (around BZ$318 including tax) make it an attractive option. **Pros:** spacious, 1,064-square-foot suites with kitchens at rates the same as or lower than the better hotels. **Cons:** lacks some hotel amenities such as restaurant and pool. [$] *Rooms from: BZ$318* ✉ *8 Newtown Barracks, Marine Parade Harbor Front* ☎ *223/2614* 🌐 *www.renaissancetower.bz* 🛏 *27 2-bedroom suites* 🍴 *No meals.*

$$
B&B/INN
Fodor's Choice ★

Villa Boscardi. If you're anxious about downtown Belize City, this appealing B&B in the northern suburbs might be your cup of herbal tea. **Pros:** the Belgian-born owner is very helpful; cheerful B&B in safe area; attractive rooms. **Cons:** only a few restaurants nearby. [$] *Rooms from: BZ$203* ✉ *6043 Manatee Dr., Northern Suburbs* ✣ *Turn toward sea off Goldson Hwy. at Golding Ave., then left on 2nd lane to fifth house on right* ☎ *223/1691* 🌐 *www.villaboscardi.com* 🛏 *7 rooms* 🍴 *Breakfast.*

NIGHTLIFE AND THE ARTS

Travelers who like to use their vacations to catch up on their nightlife rather than sleep will find Belize City's scene limited at best. Although locals love to party, safety concerns keep visitors away from most night-spots except hotel bars, such as the bar at the Radisson Fort George. After dark, take a taxi, or, if driving, park in a fenced and secured lot, such as at the Riverside Tavern.

Karaoke is a craze among many Belizeans. A hugely popular, locally produced karaoke television show, *Karaoke TV*, has been running on Channel 5 in Belize City since 2001. Most of the hotel bars have karaoke nights once or twice a week. Even in Belize you'll hear tried-and-true karaoke favorites such as "Crazy" by Patsy Cline and lots of Elvis and vintage Sonny and Cher, and you'll also hear songs like "Bidi Bidi Bam Bam" by Selena and "Greatest Love of All" by Whitney Houston. Singers may go from country to Motown and hip-hop to funk and R&B to reggae, ska, and Latin soca. Belizean taste in music is nothing if not eclectic. At live music shows and clubs in Belize City you can hear an equally diverse mix of music, although rap in all its variations is as popular in Belize City as in Los Angeles.

One uniquely Belizean style of music is punta rock. It's based on the traditional punta rhythms of the Garífuna, using drums, turtle shells, and rattles. In the late 1970s Pen Cayetano, a Garífuna artist in Dangriga, began writing punta songs, updating the music with an electric guitar, keyboard, and other electronic instruments. (Cayetano now lives in Germany, although he visits Belize regularly.) Punta rock, earthy and sexy, swept Belize and later became popular in other Central American countries, a result of the export of the music by the likes of Andy Palacio, "the ambassador of punta rock," who died unexpectedly at the peak of his career in early 2008.

BARS

The bars at the upmarket hotels, particularly those at the **Princess Hotel & Casino** and at the **Radisson Fort George,** are fairly popular—and safe—places to congregate for drinks. The Bowen (Belikin beer) family-owned Riverside Tavern is a popular place to have drinks, either indoors in air-conditioned comfort or on the outside patio next to the water, as is a new bar owned by another branch of the Bowen family, Hour Bar & Grill *(see Where to Eat).*

Baymen's Tavern. This downtown bar at the Radisson Fort George is a comfortable, safe place to sip a rum and tonic, with live entertainment on weekends, usually a singer or a small band. There's also a more casual section of the bar, on an open-air deck, with views of a garden and the sea. ⊠ *Radisson Fort George Hotel, 2 Marine Parade, Fort George* ☎ *223/3333.*

Manatee Lookout. Run by a Belizean who returned home after living in Canada, Manatee Lookout, a short cab ride (around BZ$8–$10) from the airport, is a place to grab a beer and chicken wings if your flight is delayed. The bar has big windows and an open-air deck overlooking the Belize River, and you might in fact see a manatee. ⊠ *Mile 8½, Goldson Hwy., on Belize River ½ mile (1 km) south of international airport access road, Ladyville* ☎ *622/0630.*

Riverside Tavern. At the Riverside Tavern you can have drinks before dinner on the covered patio overlooking Haulover Creek or inside at the bar. Park your car safely in a fenced, guarded lot next to the tavern and restaurant. ⊠ *2 Mapp St., off Freetown Rd., Commercial District* ☎ *223/5640.*

CASINOS

Princess Hotel & Casino. The only serious gambling in town is at the Princess Hotel & Casino, which has live tables for blackjack, roulette, and poker, along with about 400 slots. Dancers from Eastern Europe and Russia put on shows, and there are free drinks and a buffet for players. It's open 365 days a year from noon to 4 am. You'll have to show your passport and register (no charge) at the reception counter before you can go in. Gamble here if you like, but we don't recommend staying at the hotel. ⊠ *Newton Barracks, Marine Parade Harbor Front* ☎ *223/0638 Casino, 223/2670 Hotel* ⊕ *www.princessbelize.com* ☉ *Daily noon–4 am.*

THEATERS

Bliss Center for the Performing Arts. The main venue for theater, dance, music, and the arts in Belize City is Bliss Center for the Performing Arts, which seats 600. It's rare to have more than one or two shows a week at the center, and most of these are local performances—a children's dance group or a young singer's debut concert. Concert organizers try to bring in performing talent from around the country, and on a Saturday night you could hear a Mayan singer from Toledo or a marimba band from Benque Viejo del Carmen. Most shows are in English, with Creole often mixed in. Ticket prices vary but typically range from BZ$10 to BZ$40. The Bliss Center is named after Baron Bliss, who died in 1926 while on his yacht off Belize City; he never set foot in Belize but donated his fortune to the country. ⊠ *2 Southern Foreshore, between Church and Bishop Sts., Commercial District* ☎ *227/2110* ⊕ *www.nichbelize.org.*

SPORTS AND THE OUTDOORS

Belize City is a jumping-off spot for trips to the cayes and to inland and coastal areas, but the city itself offers little in the way of sports and outdoor activities. There are no golf courses, public tennis courts, or other sports facilities of note around Belize City, other than a sports stadium named after the now-disgraced Olympic track star Marion Jones, a Belizean-American. Unless you're on a cruise ship or otherwise have only a short time in Belize, you'll be better off going elsewhere for your sporting activities—to the cayes and Southern Coast for snorkeling, diving, and fishing, and inland to the Cayo or Toledo for caving, cave tubing, hiking, horseback riding, canoeing, and other activities. Most of the dive, snorkel, and tour operators in Belize City do cater to the cruise-ship crowd, and prices usually are somewhat higher than you'd pay elsewhere. ⇨ *See chapters on The Cayo, Southern Coast, The Deep South, and The Cayes and Atolls, and also the Beyond Belize City section below.*

DIVING AND WATER SPORTS

Belize Dive Connection. Based in San Pedro, Ambergris Caye, and on Spanish Lookout Caye, a private island off Belize City, Belize Dive Connection also runs dive, snorkel, and some inland trips for cruise day visitors in Belize City. Belize Dive Connection can pick up cruise passengers directly from the ships docked offshore of Belize City. Dive trips to the Belize Barrier Reef, about 30–45 minutes away, cost around BZ$180–BZ$230 per person. Snorkel trips are around BZ$120–BZ$200 per person. Lower rates are available from San Pedro, which is closer to the reef. ⊠ *SunBreeze Beach Resort, San Pedro* ☎ *220/4020 office* ⊕ *www.belizediving.com.*

Sea Sports Belize. Sea Sports, with an office downtown near the cruise ship tender docks, will take you to the Barrier Reef for diving (around BZ$225) or snorkeling (BZ$190). Most of their business is with cruise ships, but they also work with visitors staying in Belize City. ⊠ *83 N. Front St.* ☎ *223/5505* ⊕ *www.seasportsbelize.com.*

FISHING

If you're a serious angler, you'll likely end up in Placencia, Punta Gorda, or even San Pedro, but you can arrange fishing charters from Belize City. Both the **Radisson Fort George** and the **Princess Hotel & Casino** have marinas, and there is also the Cucumber Marina at Old Belize, the city's best, and local fishing-guide services and lodges operate near the city. The oldest continuously operating fishing lodge, Belize River Lodge, is located near Belize City. Fishing licenses are now required for all but pier and shore fishing. Your fishing charter company can arrange them for you, at BZ$20 a day or BZ$50 a week.

Action Belize. Action Belize has 23- and 25-foot boats that will take you out on the Belize River to try your luck with snook, cubera, and tarpon. Guided fishing packages including four nights of accommodations and three days of fishing are BZ$2,578 per person, double occupancy. Day fishing trips start at BZ$250 per person. Action Belize also offers inland and sea tours for cruise ship passengers. ■ TIP→ This is not the same company as Action Boys Belize. ⊠ *Action Belize Marina, Mile 2, Goldson Hwy., formerly Northern Hwy.* ☎ *888/383–6319 in U.S., 919/250–8884 U.S. direct number* ⊕ *www.actionbelize.com.*

Belize River Lodge. Owned by Mike Heusner and Marguerite Miles, Belize River Lodge is the oldest continuously operating fishing lodge in Belize. The original lodge, basic but with air-conditioning and good food, is on the Belize River near Belize City. It also has an outpost at Long Caye near Caye Chapel for closer access to tarpon, bonefish, jacks, and barracuda inside the reef. Three-night river fishing trips with lodging, meals, guides, skiff, and transfers start at BZ$2,800 per person, based on four people; five-night trips on a 52-foot Chris Craft are BZ$5,120 per person including meals, lodging at Long Caye, guide, and tax, based on four people. ☎ *225/2002, 888/275–4843* ⊕ *www.belizeriverlodge.com.*

GOLF

There are no golf courses in Belize City, but there's a 9-hole course at Roaring River, near Belmopan a little over an hour west by car—it's fun to play, and a bargain. The Caye Chapel course, foreclosed on by its lender, has recently reopened for play, but the course has not been well-maintained, there are no facilities for club or cart rental or even to get a cold drink or snack—until the course fully reopens under new ownership, it is not recommended except for hard-core duffers who want to experience Belize's only seaside course.

Roaring River Golf Course. A little over an hour west of Belize City by car, Roaring River has a 9-hole "jungle course." Using the double tees, you can play 18 holes (par 64) totaling 3,892 yards. All greens are elevated and bunkered, and the fairways are lined with native trees. Water traps are home to crocodiles. Play 9 holes for BZ$35 or 18 holes for BZ$50. The Meating Place, a restaurant in the clubhouse with most entrées around BZ$30, is open daily for breakfast, lunch, and dinner. If you want to stay overnight and play more golf the next day, Roaring River has cottages to rent. ⊠ *Roaring River, River Lodge Rd., Belmopan City* ✛ *Turn south at Camelote Village at Mile 50¼, George Price Hwy., and follow signs to golf course* ☎ *664/5441* ⊕ *www.belizegolf.net.*

HELICOPTER TOURS

Astrum Helicopters. Astrum offers customized aerial tours of the Blue Hole, Mayan sites, the Belize Barrier Reef, and others, using five-seat Bell helicopters. It also provides helicopter transfers to upscale resorts and lodges on the cayes and inland. ⊠ *Cisco Base, Mile 3½, George Price Hwy., Formerly Western Hwy.* ☎ *222/5100, 888/278–7864* ⊕ *www.astrumhelicopters.com.*

SHOPPING

Belize City has the most varied shopping in the country. Rather than catering to leisure shoppers, most stores in Belize City cater to the local market and those from other parts of the country who need to stock up on supplies at lumberyards, home-building stores, appliance outlets, and supermarkets. Gift shops and handicraft shops are concentrated in the downtown area in and near the Tourism Village.

About a dozen cruise ships per week call on Belize City, and each time the Tourism Village shops open their doors. Wednesday is usually the biggest day of the week for cruise ships in Belize City, often with three to five in port, and Saturday is another popular day. Rarely is there a ship in port on Sunday.

Most stores in the downtown area are open Monday through Saturday from around 8 am to 6 pm. On Sunday, nearly all stores downtown are dark, although some stores in the suburbs are open Sunday afternoon.

The Queen's Square Market, with fruit, vegetable, and other food vendors, just south of the Novelo's bus terminal on West Collet Canal Street, has been renovated and also goes by the name of Michael Finnegan's Market, after a local politician.

SHOPPING CENTERS AND MALLS

Fodor's Choice **Brodies.** To stock up on picnic supplies or groceries, head to the
★ expanded, modern Brodies, a mini-department store and pharmacy as
well as a supermarket, in a safe area on the Goldson Highway. James
Brodie & Co. has been in Belize since 1887. Plenty of free, safe parking is available. There's another location on Regent Street in downtown Belize City. ⌂ *Mile 2½, Goldson Hwy., formerly Northern Hwy.,
Northern Suburbs* ☎ *223/5587* ⊕ *www.brodiesbelize.com.*

Fort Street Tourism Village. Fort Street Tourism Village (also called Fort
Point Tourism Village & Mall) is packed with day-trippers when
cruise ships are in port but is closed at other times. Tenders from the
cruise ships come in here. The Village has around 30 gift shops including MOHO chocolate shop offering free samples of organic, Belize-
made chocolates. You'll also find clean restrooms, a cybercafé, tour
kiosks, restaurants, and other services. Security is tight in the Tourism
Village, and you'll feel safe. On cruise ship days, vendors also set up
booths on streets near the Tourism Village. ⌂ *Fort George cruise-
ship docks, 8 Fort St., east of Swing Bridge, Fort George* ☎ *223/7789*
⊕ *www.tourismvillage.com.*

Mirab's. Mirab's is a department store, worth a visit if you need to pick
up something you forgot, like a flashlight or batteries. There also is a
Mirab's furniture store at Mile 1½ of the George Price Highway. ⌂ *2
Fort St. at N. Front St.* ☎ *223/2933.*

Save-U Supermarket. Save-U Supermarket is a good place for groceries,
liquor, and sundries. ⌂ *San Cas Plaza, Goldson Hwy. at Central American Blvd.* ☎ *223/1291* ⊕ *www.santiagocastillo.com.*

SPECIALTY SHOPS

Belizean Handicraft Market Place. Belizean Handicraft Market Place (formerly National Handicraft Center) has Belizean souvenir items, including hand-carved figurines, handmade furniture, pottery, and woven
baskets. The prices are about as good as you'll find anywhere in Belize,
and the sales clerks are friendly. It faces the small Memorial Park, which
commemorates the Battle of St. George's Caye and is just a short stroll
from the harbor front, the Tourism Village, and many of the hotels in
the Fort George area, including the Radisson, Chateau Caribbean, and
The Great House. ⌂ *2 S. Park St., in Fort George area across from
Memorial Park* ☎ *223/3627.*

Image Factory. The cutting edge of Belize City's art and hipster scene is at
the Image Factory. The Image Factory holds art and photography shows
and publishes books. Its gallery and shop on North Front Street sells
books, artwork, and CDs. There is free parking in a lot across North
Front Street. ⌂ *91 N. Front St.* ☎ *223/4093* ⊕ *www.imagefactorybelize.
com* ☉ *Weekdays 9–5.*

BEYOND BELIZE CITY

If you're like most visitors to Belize, you'll spend at most only a night or two, if that, in Belize City before moving on. If you're heading west to the Cayo, plan to make a stop at the wonderful Belize Zoo, about 30 miles (49 km) west of Belize City. Going north or west, you can visit the Community Baboon Sanctuary, as there is road access to Bermudian Landing, where the sanctuary is located, via either the Goldson Highway or the Price Highway. For other areas of interest, including Crooked Tree Wildlife Sanctuary and the Altun Ha Mayan site to the north, and Belmopan to the west, within an hour or so of Belize City, ⇨ *see the Northern Belize and Cayo chapters.*

BELIZE ZOO

One of the smallest, but arguably one of the best, zoos in the Americas, the Belize Zoo packs a lot into 29 acres. Containing more than 150 animals and 45 different species, all native to Belize, the zoo has self-guided tours through several Belizean ecosystems—rain forest, lagoons, and riverine forest.

FAMILY

Fodor's Choice

★

Belize Zoo. Turn a sharp corner on the jungle trail, and suddenly you're face-to-face with a jaguar, the largest cat in the Western Hemisphere. The big cat growls a deep rumbling threat. You jump back, thankful that a strong but inconspicuous fence separates you and the jaguar.

Plan for about 2 hours to see the zoo. Along with jaguars you'll see the country's four other wild cats: the puma, margay, ocelot, and jaguarundi. Perhaps the zoo's most famous resident is April, a Baird's tapir that is more than a quarter-century old. This relative of the horse and rhino is known to locals as the mountain cow, and is also Belize's national animal. At the zoo you'll also see jabiru storks, a harpy eagle, scarlet macaws, howler monkeys, crocodiles, and many snakes, including the fer-de-lance.

The zoo owes its existence to the dedication and drive of one gutsy woman, Sharon Matola. An American who came to Belize as part of a film crew, Matola stayed on to care for some of the semi-tame animals used in the production. She opened the zoo in 1983, and in 1991 it moved to its present location. She's also an active environmentalist. "The Zoo Lady" and her crusade against the Chalillo Dam is the subject of the 2008 book *The Last Flight of the Scarlet Macaw: One Woman's Fight To Save the World's Most Beautiful Bird* by *Outside* magazine writer Bruce Barcott.

Besides touring the zoo, you can stay overnight at the Belize Zoo Jungle Lodge and hike or canoe through the 84-acre Tropical Education Center. ⊠ *Mile 29, George Price Hwy., formerly Western Hwy., Belize City* ☎ *220/8004* ⊕ *www.belizezoo.org* ⊠ *BZ$30 adults, BZ$10 children* ☉ *Daily 8:30–5:30 (last admission 4:30).*

Tropical Education Center and Belize Zoo Jungle Lodge. Adjacent to the Belize Zoo is this 84-acre Tropical Education Center where you can hike or canoe. There are boardwalk trails through the savanna with wildlife viewing platforms and a deck for bird-watching. Rustic accommodations are available at the Tropical Education Center at the Belize Zoo Jungle Lodge, which include a 30-person dorm and four cabanas. Actress Cameron Diaz and the late TV animal expert Steve Irwin stayed here. Nighttime tours of the Belize Zoo are offered. ⊠ *Mile 29, George Price Hwy., formerly Western Hwy., Belize City* ☎ *822/8000* ⊕ *www.belizezoo.org.*

COMMUNITY BABOON SANCTUARY

One of Belize's most fascinating wildlife conservation projects is the Community Baboon Sanctuary, which is actually a haven for black howler monkeys (baboon is Kriol for the howler).

GETTING HERE

There are two routes to the sanctuary. If heading north on the Goldson Highway, turn west at Mile 13.2 onto the Burrell Boom Road. Go 3 miles (5 km) and turn right just beyond the new bridge over the Belize River. Signs to Bermudian Landing mark the turn. Stay on this road approximately 12 miles (20 km) to Bermudian Landing. If going west on the Western Highway, turn north on the Burrell Boom Road at a roundabout at Mile 15.5 of the Western Highway, and go 9 miles (15 km) to the new bridge over the Belize River. Just before the bridge, turn left. Signs to Bermudian Landing mark the turn. Stay on this road approximately 12 miles (20 km) to Bermudian Landing. You can also use the Burrell Boom Road as a shortcut between the Northern and Western highways, avoiding Belize City. For this shortcut, stay on the Burrell Boom Road rather than turning toward Bermudian Landing. When on the Burrell Boom Road, you may want to stop at the **Central Prison Gift Shop** at the Central Prison, on the road to Burrell Boom about 3 miles (5 km) from the Price Highway. Prisoners at the "Hattieville Ramada" make small craft items and sell them at the gift shop.

FAMILY **Community Baboon Sanctuary.** Spanning a 20-mile (32-km) stretch of the Belize River, the Baboon reserve was established in 1985 by a group of local farmers. The howler monkey—an agile bundle of black fur with a disturbing roar—was then zealously hunted throughout Central America and was facing extinction. Today the sanctuary is home, on some 200 private properties, to more than 2,000 black howler monkeys, as well as numerous species of birds and mammals. Thanks to ongoing conservation efforts countrywide, you can see the howler monkeys in a number of other areas, including at Lamanai in northern Belize, along the Macal, Mopan, and Belize rivers in western Belize, near Monkey River and around Punta Gorda in southern Belize. Exploring the Community Baboon Sanctuary is easy, thanks to about 3 miles (5 km) of trails that start near a small museum and visitor center. The admission fee includes a 45-minute guided nature tour during which you definitely will see howlers. ⊠ *Community Baboon Sanctuary, 31 miles (50 km) northwest of Belize City, Bermudian Village* ✥ *If heading north on the Northern Highway, turn west at Mile 13.2 onto the Burrell Boom Road. Go 3 miles (5 km) and turn right just beyond the new bridge over the*

Belize River. Signs to Bermudian Landing mark the turn. Stay on this road approximately 12 miles (20 km) to Bermudian Landing. If going west on the Western Highway, turn north on the Burrell Boom Road at a roundabout at Mile 15½ of the Western Highway, and go 9 miles (15 km) to the new bridge over the Belize River. Just before the bridge, turn left. Signs to Bermudian Landing mark the turn. Stay on this road approximately 12 miles (20 km) to Bermudian Landing. ☎ 249/2009 ⊕ www.howlermonkeys.org ✉ BZ$14 per person (includes admission to visitor center and a guided monkey-spotting tour); night hike BZ$24 per person ⊙ Daily 8–5.

MONKEY BAY WILDLIFE SANCTUARY

Monkey Bay is a privately owned wildlife reserve on 1,060 acres near the Belize Zoo.

FAMILY **Monkey Bay Wildlife Sanctuary.** At Monkey Bay you can canoe on the Sibun River, hike a 16-mile (31-km) nature trail along Indian Creek (only partly within Monkey Bay lands), or go bird-watching—some 250 bird species have been identified in the area. It has a natural history library with some 500 books and other reference materials, which visitors can use. The sanctuary also has educational and internship programs. Overnight accommodations for visitors are available if not occupied by students or interns, including tent camping (BZ$16 per person) and a bunkhouse (BZ$38 a person) with shared baths. Cabins are around BZ$55 to BZ$110. Meals are also available at times, if an educational group is in residence. Otherwise you'll have to make your own meals. Monkey Bay accepts short-term volunteers (minimum stay one week). Internships also are available, usually with a minimum stay of one month. Most of the reserve's facilities demonstrate high ecological awareness. Most programs are geared for overnight or multinight visits, but you can come on a day visit. Call in advance to see what activities or facilities may be available when you want to come. ✉ 31 miles (51 km) northwest of Belize City, Mile 31, George Price Hwy., formerly Western Hwy., Rural Belize District ☎ 820/3032, 770/877–2648 in the U.S. ⊕ www.belizestudyabroad.net.

WHERE TO STAY

For expanded hotel reviews, visit Fodors.com.

The most pleasant hotel near the Baboon Sanctuary is the Belizean-owned Black Orchid Resort on the Belize River. Orchid Garden Eco-Village, about halfway between Belize City and the Belize Zoo, is an option for those en route to the zoo. Or you could just stay at the Belize Zoo Jungle Lodge, part of the zoo's Tropical Education Center. Otherwise, for a broader choice of accommodations and dining, continue on to the Belmopan area.

$$$ 🏨 **Black Orchid Resort.** This Belizean-owned resort in a pleasant and
RESORT safe rural setting northwest of Belize City perches at the edge of the
Fodor'sChoice Belize River, where you can launch a canoe or kayak from the hotel's
★ dock, or just laze about the riverside swimming pool and thatch palapa.

Pros: most upscale lodging near Baboon Sanctuary; lovely riverside setting; good food; only 15 minutes from international airport. **Cons:** not directly in the Baboon Sanctuary. [$] *Rooms from: BZ$305* ✉ *2 Dawson Ln., 12 miles (20 km) from Baboon Sanctuary, Rural Belize District, Burrell Boom Village* ☎ *225/9158, 866/437–1301 in U.S. and Canada* 🌐 *www.blackorchidresort.com* 🛏 *16 rooms, 1 3-bedroom villa, 2 2-bedroom cabins* 🍴 *No meals.*

$$$$ HOTEL 🏨 **Orchid Garden Eco-Village.** A hardworking and promotion-minded couple from Taiwan runs this little hotel on the George Price Highway, heavily promoting all-inclusive packages that are handy but somewhat expensive given the location and the quality of the rooms. **Pros:** centrally located; clean rooms; tasty meals. **Cons:** not in a particularly scenic part of Belize; promotes pricey package options. [$] *Rooms from: BZ$598* ✉ *Mile 14.5, George Price Hwy., formerly Western Hwy., Belize City* ☎ *225/6991* 🌐 *www.trybelize.com* 🛏 *18 rooms* 🍴 *Multiple meal plans.*

THE CAYES
AND ATOLLS

By Lan Sluder

Imagine heading back to shore after a day of snorkeling, the white prow of your boat pointing up toward the billowing clouds, the sky's base darkening to deep lilac, spray from the green water pouring over you like warm rain. To the left, San Pedro's pastel buildings huddle among the palm trees like a detail from a Paul Klee canvas. To the right, the surf breaks in a white seam along the reef.

You can experience such adventures off the coast of Belize, where more than 400 cayes dot the Caribbean Sea like punctuation marks in a long, liquid sentence. A caye, sometimes spelled "cay" but in either case pronounced "key," is simply an island. It can be a small spit of sand, a tangled watery web of mangroves, or, as in the case of Ambergris Caye, a 25-mile-long (41-km-long) island about half the size of Barbados. (Ambergris is locally pronounced Am-BUR-griss.)

Besides being Belize's largest island, Ambergris Caye is also Belize's top visitor destination. Around half of all visitors to Belize make at least a stop at Ambergris, and many visit only this island.

Ambergris Caye is easy to get to from Belize City by water taxi or a quick commuter flight. It has the largest concentration of hotels, from budget spots to the ultra-deluxe, and the most (and some of the best) restaurants in Belize. Although the island's beaches may not compare to classically beautiful beaches of the Yucatán or the main Caribbean, Ambergris has miles and miles of beachfront on the east or Caribbean side, and the amazing Belize Barrier Reef is just a few hundred yards offshore.

Though it's developing fast, San Pedro, the only real town on Ambergris Caye, still remains mostly laid-back and low-rise. In spite of the growth in tourism, Sanpedranos remain authentically friendly and welcoming to visitors. Some of the main streets have concrete cobblestones, but most side streets are hard-packed sand. Golf carts are the main form of transportation, although the number of cars on the island continues to rise, and in some areas of downtown the traffic on the narrow streets is really bad and dangerous to pedestrians.

Caye Caulker is Ambergris Caye's sister island—smaller, less developed, and a cheaper date. Caulker, whose name derives from the Spanish word for coco plum, *hicaco*, has the kind of laid-back, sandy-street, tropical-color, low-key Caribbean charm that some travelers pay thousands to experience. Here it can be had almost for peanuts. Less than 10 miles (16 km)—about 30 minutes by boat—from San Pedro, Caye Caulker, sometimes called Caye Corker, is definitely worth a day visit.

Most of Belize's cayes are inside the Barrier Reef, which allowed them to develop undisturbed by tides and winds that would otherwise have swept them away. The vast majority of them are uninhabited but for pelicans, brown- and red-footed boobies, and some creatures curiously named wish-willies (a kind of iguana). Island names are evocative and often humorous: Wee Caye, Laughing Bird Caye, and—why ask why?—Bread and Butter Caye. Names can suggest the company you should expect: Mosquito Caye, Sandfly Caye, and Crawl Caye, which is supposedly infested with boa constrictors. Several, like Cockney Range or Baker's Rendezvous, simply express the whimsy or nostalgia of early British settlers.

Farther out to sea, between 30 miles and 45 miles (48 km and 74 km) off the coast, are Belize's atolls, Glovers (or Glover's), Lighthouse, and Turneffe, impossibly beautiful when viewed from the air. There are only four true Pacific-style atolls in the Americas, and Belize has three of them (the fourth is Chinchorro, off Mexico). At their center the water is mint green: the white sandy bottom reflects the light upward and is flecked with patches of mangrove and rust-color sediment. Around the atoll's fringe the surf breaks in a white circle before the color changes abruptly to ultramarine as the water plunges to 3,000 feet.

ORIENTATION AND PLANNING

GETTING ORIENTED

Belize's two most important cayes, Ambergris and Caulker, are both off the northern end of the country, easily reached from Belize City. Other, smaller cayes dot the Caribbean Sea off the coast all the way south to Punta Gorda. The Belize Barrier Reef runs all along most of the coast of Belize. You're closest to the reef when you're on a beach on North Ambergris Caye. As you go south, the reef is farther from shore, 20 miles (12 km) or more off the Southern Coast. The three atolls are outside the reef, as much as 45 miles (74 km) offshore.

The Cayes. Ranging from tiny stretches of sand, mangrove, and palms to large islands like Ambergris and Caulker, Belize's cayes have excellent swimming, diving, fishing, and snorkeling.

The Atolls. Ovals of coral, majestic and remote, Belize's three atolls offer some of the best diving and snorkeling in the Western Hemisphere. The catch? They're difficult and time-consuming to get to, typically requiring a two-hour boat ride on open seas.

PLANNING

WHEN TO GO

Island weather tends to be a little different from that on the mainland. The cayes are generally drier. Storm squalls come up suddenly, but just as quickly they're gone, leaving sunny skies behind. Late summer and early fall are prime tropical-storm season, a time when island residents keep a worried eye out for hurricanes; more than eight out of ten hurricanes that hit Belize arrive in either September or October. If a hurricane does threaten, the cayes are evacuated. The Christmas to Easter period, when the northern climes are cold and blustery, is the most popular time to visit the islands.

TOP REASONS TO GO

Scuba Diving. Dive destinations are often divided into reefs and atolls. Most reef diving is done on Belize's northern section, particularly off Ambergris Caye, but head to the atolls for some of the world's greatest diving opportunities.

No Shoes, No Shirt, No Problem. Unlike some parts of the mainland, the cayes are all about relaxing. "Go Slow" street signs dot the sandy roads, and you spend a lot of time lazing in hammocks or sipping beer in a beachside palapa alongside vacationing Belizeans.

Snorkeling. You don't have to don scuba gear to enjoy the colorful fish and psychedelic vistas under the surface of the sea. Some of the best

snorkeling in the Caribbean is off the coast of Belize. Jump in a boat for a short ride out to the reef or to patch coral.

Good Eats. Because they attract so many free-spending tourists, Ambergris Caye and Caye Caulker have more restaurants than anywhere else in Belize, and some of the best, too.

Beaches. While not your typical wide, sandy spreads, they're still classic postcard material, with wind-swept coco palms facing expanses of turquoise, green, and purple waters. You'll usually have a front-row seat, because most hotels in all price ranges are actually right on the beach.

GETTING HERE AND AROUND

Island hopping in the northern cayes is simple, though getting to other cayes and the atolls can be more complicated. Water taxis connect Belize City, Ambergris Caye, and Caye Caulker. There is also frequent air service between Belize City and San Pedro and Caye Caulker. For the other cayes, you're generally stuck with whatever boat transport your hotel provides. Once on the islands, you'll get around by golf cart, bike, or on foot.

AIR TRAVEL

Maya Island Airways and Tropic Air operate flights between both the international and municipal airports in Belize City and Ambergris Caye and Caye Caulker. Each airline has roughly hourly service during daylight hours to and from the cayes. One-way fares on either Tropic and Maya Island to either San Pedro or Caye Caulker for the 15- to 20-minute flight are about BZ$83 (municipal) and BZ$144 (international). To the cayes, you save more than 40% by flying from the municipal airport in Belize City rather than the international airport north of the city. The catch is that if arriving or departing internationally you have to transfer by cab between the two airports—about a 25-minute ride—and a cab is BZ$50 (for the taxi, not per-person), so unless you're in a group of three or more the extra hassle may not be worth the savings. ■TIP→ **Both airlines usually offer a 10% discount if you pay cash rather than use a credit card, and sometimes more. But you'll have to ask for the discount, which only applies in person, not online, and usually not on Saturdays.**

Contacts Maya Island Airways ⊠ *Belize City Municipal Airport, Belize City* ☎ *223/1140 for reservations* ⊕ *www.mayaislandair.com.* **Tropic Air** ⊠ *San Pedro Airstrip, San Pedro* ☎ *226/2012, 800/422–3435 in U.S.* ✐ *reservations@tropicair. com* ⊕ *www.tropicair.com.*

BOAT, FERRY, AND WATER-TAXI TRAVEL

There are no scheduled water-taxi services up and down the coast of Belize, so for example you can't hop a boat in Belize City and go down the coast to Hopkins or Placencia or to one of the southern cayes. Likewise, except from Belize City, and between busy Ambergris Caye and Caye Caulker, there is no scheduled boat service to or between Belize's cayes. There is limited water-taxi service to these northern cayes from Corozal and from Chetumal, Mexico.

Several private boats do make the run from Dangriga to Tobacco Caye for around BZ$35–BZ$50 per person one-way. They leave Dangriga around 9:30 am and return from Tobacco Caye in late morning or the afternoon. Check at the **Riverside Café** in Dangriga or ask your hotel on Tobacco Caye.

Other than that, you're generally left to your own devices for private boat transportation to the cayes. You can charter a small boat with driver—typically BZ$600 and up a day—or negotiate a one-way or round-trip price, up to BZ$800–BZ$1,500 or more one-way to the atolls. (Gas is about BZ$12 a gallon, and boats capable of handling the open water to the atolls have big dual or triple outboards.) You'll have little luck renting a powerboat on your own, as boat owners are reluctant to risk their crafts, and new laws require that you need a captain's license before you can operate a boat in Belize waters (sailing charters are excepted).

BELIZE CITY TO SAN PEDRO AND CAYE CAULKER
There are three main water-taxi companies—Caye Caulker Water Taxi Association, San Pedro Belize Express, and Water Jets International—with fast boats that hold 50 to 100 passengers, connecting Belize City with San Pedro (Ambergris Caye) and Caye Caulker. They also connect San Pedro and Caye Caulker. From Belize City it's a 45-minute ride to Caulker and 75 minutes to San Pedro. Going between Caulker and San Pedro takes about 30 minutes. There's also a new premium water taxi service, Tropic Ferry, that meets you at the international airport and takes you from its dock near the airport to your resort on Ambergris Caye.

Caye Caulker Water Taxi Association. Caye Caulker Water Taxi Association boats leave from the Marine Terminal at 10 North Front Street in Belize City. Despite the Caulker name, there are around six or seven boats per day to and from both San Pedro and Caye Caulker. On both Caye Caulker and Ambergris Caye the Water Jets International terminals are on piers on the front (sea) side of the islands. ⊠ *Marine Terminal, 12 N. Front St., near Swing Bridge, Belize City* ☎ *223/5752 in Belize City, 226/0992 in Caye Caulker* ⊕ *www.cayecaulkerwatertaxi. com* ✐ *BZ$30 one-way between Belize City and San Pedro; BZ$20 between Belize City and Caye Caulker; BZ$20 between San Pedro and Caye Caulker.*

Riverside Café. This local café on the river in Dangriga is a place to meet local boat owners and arrange transportation to Tobacco Caye. ✉ *Riverside & Oak Sts., west side of North Stann Creek River, Dangriga* ☎ *661/6390* ☾ *Daily 7 am–9 pm.*

San Pedro Belize Express Water Taxi. San Pedro Belize Express water taxis depart from the Brown Sugar terminal on North Front Street. On Caye Caulker, San Pedro Belize Express boats arrive at the pier near the basketball court on Front Street, and in San Pedro they arrive at the pier at Black Coral Street on the east (sea) side of the island. They also provide daily service between the Muelle Fiscal or municipal pier in Chetumal, Mexico, and San Pedro and Caye Caulker. ✉ *111 N. Front St., Brown Sugar Terminal, San Pedro* ☎ *223/2225 in Belize City, 226/3535 in San Pedro* ⊕ *www.belizewatertaxi.com* ✍ *BZ$20 one-way between Belize City and Caye Caulker; BZ$30 one-way between Belize City and San Pedro; BZ$20 one-way between San Pedro and Caye Caulker; BZ$75 one-way between San Pedro and Chetumal.*

SAN PEDRO TAXI

There is now limited vehicular taxi service between San Pedro Town and North Ambergris Caye, along with water-taxi service. Taxis, along with local vehicles, are permitted on the golf-cart path from 7 am to 9 pm as far north as Las Terrazas Resort, about 4 miles (6 km) from the center of San Pedro, road conditions permitting. Las Terrazas is a BZ$50 fare, including the BZ$12 vehicle fee to cross the bridge. Fares to closer hotels are less.

Tropic Ferry. The Tropic Ferry provides a premium ferry service between the international airport near Belize City and most resorts on Ambergris Caye. A ferry representative meets you at the airport for a short ride to the dock in Ladyville. It's around a 90-minute trip to your destination on Ambergris Caye. You'll get a complimentary rum punch en route. Rates for this service are somewhat higher than a flight to San Pedro. (This water taxi service is unrelated to Tropic Air, one of the domestic Belize airlines.) ✉ *1659 Yellowtail Snapper Dr., Vista del Mar, Ladyville* ☎ *631/9253* ⊕ *www.tropicferry.com* ✍ *BZ$170 per person one-way or BZ$270 round-trip between Belize international airport and your hotel on San Pedro.*

Water Jets International. Water Jets International boats, also confusingly known as San Pedro Water Jets Express, leave from the Marine Terminal at 10 North Front Street in Belize City. There are around six boats per day to and from San Pedro and Caye Caulker. On both Caye Caulker and Ambergris Caye the Water Jets International terminals are on the back (lagoon) side of the islands. They also provide daily service (sometimes every-other-day off-season) between the Muelle Fiscal or municipal pier in Chetumal, Mexico, and San Pedro and Caye Caulker. ✉ *10 N. Front St., Marine Terminal, Belize City* ☎ *226/2194* ⊕ *www.sanpedrowatertaxi.com* ✍ *One-way fares are BZ$24 between Belize City and Caye Caulker; BZ$35 between Belize City and San Pedro; BZ$24 between San Pedro and Caye Caulker; BZ$80 between San Pedro and Chetumal.*

COROZAL | **Thunderbolt.** Thunderbolt has round-trip service between Corozal Town and San Pedro Friday through Monday. (Off-season service may be reduced or eliminated.) The trip takes 90 minutes to two hours, depending on weather conditions. The boat stops in Sarteneja on demand. In Corozal, the Thunderbolt arrives and leaves at the Reunion Pier in the center of town; in San Pedro it arrives and leaves at the dock on Black Coral Street on the back side of the island near the soccer field. ⊠ *Reunion Pier, Corozal Town* ☎ *610/4475 boat captain's cell, 422/0026 landline in Corozal Town* ⌨ *DZ$45 one-way* ☉ *No service Tues.–Thurs.; service may be reduced off-season.*

UP AND DOWN AMBERGRIS CAYE | **Coastal Xpress.** Coastal Xpress provides scheduled ferry service up and down the island. It offers about a dozen daily trips between the Amigos del Mar pier in town and Pelican Reef hotel in the south, and the same number between Amigos del Mar and Blue Reef Island Resort in the north, with stops and pick-ups on demand at all private docks and hotels and restaurants. At this writing, service starts at 5:30 am and ends around 2:15 am. Coastal Xpress also offers charter boat service to other cayes and coastal locations. Ferry schedule and service is subject to change—check locally for updates. ⊠ *Amigos del Mar Pier, Beachfront, San Pedro* ☎ *226/2007* ⊕ *www.coastalxpress.com* ⌨ *BZ$8–BZ$40; weekly pass also available.*

GOLF CART TRAVEL

On Ambergris Caye and Caye Caulker there are no car rentals, but you can rent a golf cart. Most carts are gas-powered. Golf-cart rentals cost about as much as a car rental in the United States—around BZ$120 a day, or BZ$500–BZ$550 a week, plus 12.5% tax. Golf-cart-rental companies spring up like weeds, and many hotels have a few carts to rent. Compare prices and ask for discounts.

Contacts Castle Cars ⊠ *1 Barrier Reef Dr., San Pedro* ☎ *670/2624* ✉ *castle-cars@btl.net.* **Cholo's Golf Cart Rentals.** Cholo's has a fleet of more than 100 four- and six-seat rental carts, with four-seater gas cart rates BZ$120 per day or BZ$560 per week, plus 12.5% tax. ⊠ *Jewfish St. behind police and fire stations, San Pedro* ☎ *226/2406* ⊕ *www.choloscartrentals.com.* **Island Adventures Golf Cart Rentals.** Island Adventures rents four-seater gas carts for BZ$120 a day or BZ$500 per week, plus 12.5% tax. ⊠ *Coconut Dr., near airstrip, San Pedro* ☎ *226/4343* ⊕ *www.islandgolfcarts.com.* **Moncho's Cart Rentals.** Moncho's rent four-seater gas carts for BZ$146 per day or BZ$619 per week, including tax. ⊠ *11 Coconut Dr., near airstrip, San Pedro* ☎ *226/3262* ⊕ *www.sanpedrogolfcartrental.com.*

TAXI TRAVEL

Regular taxicabs are available in San Pedro and in the developed area south of town on Ambergris Caye. Most trips in and close to town are BZ$10 for up to four persons. For trips north of the bridge over Boca del Rio, cabs charge BZ$25–BZ$50, including the BZ$12 vehicle bridge fee. Currently, taxis go only as far as Las Terrazas. Have your hotel arrange for a cab, or hail one of the cabs cruising the downtown area. On Caulker there are golf-cart taxis, which charge BZ$5–BZ$10 per person for most trips.

HEALTH AND SAFETY

In San Pedro Town and nearby, the water comes from a municipal water system and is safe to drink, although most people including local residents prefer to drink bottled water. On North Ambergris, water may come from cisterns or wells. On Caye Caulker the water, sometimes from brackish shallow wells, may smell of sulfur. A new village reverse osmosis system began operation in 2011, but not everyone is on it. If in doubt, drink bottled water. On other remote cayes, the water usually comes from cisterns. Stick to the bottled stuff, unless you're assured that the water is potable. To be green, you can buy water in large one- or five-gallon bottles and refill your carry-around bottle rather than throwing away liter bottles after use; you'll save a little money, too.

In terms of crime risk, the cayes are among the safest areas of Belize. However, petty thefts—and sometimes worse—do happen. With some 20,000 people on Ambergris Caye, if you count tourists and itinerant workers, the island has the same crime problems, including rapes and murders, as any area of similar population. There are drugs, including crack cocaine, on both Caye Caulker and Ambergris Caye. Ignore any offers to buy drugs, even marijuana, which, while widely used in Belize, is still illegal, and police do make arrests for weed.

EMERGENCIES

The San Pedro Lions Poly Clinic and the public San Pedro Dr. Otto Rodriquez Poly Clinic II on Ambergris Caye have services just short of a full-scale hospital. They are open weekdays 8–8 and Saturday 8–noon. Doctors and nurses are on 24-hour call. Three or four other clinics and private medical practices, four pharmacies, a chiropractic clinic, several dentists, and a hyperbaric chamber (affiliated with many Belize dive shops) are also on the island. For serious medical emergencies, patients are usually transferred to Karl Heusner Memorial Hospital, the nation's main public referral hospital, in Belize City, or to one of the private hospitals in Belize City, Belize Medical Associates or Belize Healthcare Partners.

On Caye Caulker the Caye Caulker Health Center is usually staffed by a volunteer doctor from Cuba. For dental care or serious ailments you need to go to Belize City. There are no medical facilities on any of the other cayes, but if you have an emergency, call your embassy or contact Karl Heusner Memorial Hospital, Belize Medical Associates, or Belize Healthcare Partners.

Astrum Helicopters provides emergency airlift services.

For police emergencies, call 911. On marine radios, channel 16 is the international distress channel.

Clinics Caye Caulker Health Center ⊠ *Estrella St., Caye Caulker* ☏ *226/0166.* **San Carlos Medical Clinic, Pharmacy and Laboratory.** San Carlos Medical Clinic is a private medical clinic, pharmacy, and laboratory, operated by Dr. Giovanni Solarzano. ⊠ *Pescador Dr., San Pedro* ☏ *226/2918.* **San Pedro Dr. Otto Rodriquez Poly Clinic II.** The government clinic has three physicians, two health nurses/midwives, two practical nurses, two registered nurses, a dentist with a volunteer assistant, a lab technician, a pharmacist, an assistant pharmacist, and two caretakers, along with administrative staff. ⊠ *San Pedro Dr. Otto Rodriquez Poly Clinic, San Pedro* ☎ *226/2536* ⏱ *Weekdays 8–8; Sat. 8–noon.* **San Pedro Lions Polyclinic.** The San Pedro Lions Clinic is supported by the local Lions Club. ⊠ *Near airstrip, San Pedro* ☎ *226/4052 office number, 600/9071 for emergencies* ⏱ *Weekdays 8–8; Sat. 8–noon.* **Subaquatics of Belize.** This is the only hyperbaric chamber in Belize. The hyperbaric clinic is a part of the international SSS Recompression Chamber Network with locations also in Mexico, the Bahamas, Galapagos Islands, Thailand, and Germany. ⊠ *Near airstrip, 11 Lion St., San Pedro* ☎ *226/2051* ⊕ *www.sssnetwork.com.*

Other Emergency Contacts Astrum Helicopters ⊠ *Cisco Base, Mile 3½, George Price Hwy., formerly Western Hwy., Belize City* ☎ *222/5100, 888/278-7864 from the U.S.* ⊕ *www.astrumhelicopters.com.* **Belize Healthcare Partners** ⊠ *Corner Chancellor and Blue Marlin Aves., West Landivar, Belize City* ☎ *223/7870* ⊕ *www.belizehealthcare.com.* **Belize Medical Associates** ⊠ *5791 St. Thomas St., Kings Park, Belize City* ☎ *223/0302* ⊕ *www.belizemedical. com.* **Karl Heusner Memorial Hospital** ⊠ *Princess Margaret Dr., Belize City* ☎ *223/1548* ⊕ *www.khmh.bz.* **United States Embassy in Belize** ⊠ *Floral Park Rd., Belmopan City* ☎ *822/4011, 610/5030 after hours emergencies only* ⊕ *belize.usembassy.gov* ⏱ *Weekdays 8–noon, 1–5.*

MONEY MATTERS

Most of Belize's banks operate on Ambergris Caye: Atlantic Bank, Belize Bank, Heritage Bank, and ScotiaBank. Most are open weekdays from 8 until around 3 pm, with longer hours on Friday afternoon. A couple also are open on Saturday morning. All the local banks except Heritage Bank accept ATM cards issued outside Belize, giving cash in Belize dollars. Belize Bank alone has six ATMs around San Pedro. Still, on busy weekends some ATM machines run out of money, so don't wait until you're down to your last shilling to get cash. Cash advances on your Visa or MasterCard are also available from these banks. In addition to these commercial banks, Ambergris Caye also has offices of several international banks (offshore banks) that do not offer retail financial services to local customers. On Caye Caulker there's just one bank, Atlantic Bank, but it has two ATM machines on the island. There are no banks on any other islands.

(See ATMs and Banks in Travel Smart for Bank addresses and phone numbers)

ABOUT THE RESTAURANTS

Ambergris Caye has the biggest selection of restaurants of any destination in Belize, and among them are some of the country's best. They range from simple beach barbecue joints to upscale, sophisticated eateries, where, especially if you eat lobster, you can spend BZ$100 a person or more, including a drink or two or wine. You have a wide choice of kinds of food on Ambergris: seafood, of course, but also steak, pizza, sushi, tapas, Chinese, Italian, Thai, Mexican, and French.

Caye Caulker has a number of small bistros where fish arrives at your table fresh from the ocean, and sometimes you find yourself eating with your feet in the sand. On other islands you're usually limited to eating at your dive lodge or resort.

On both Caye Caulker and Ambergris Caye street vendors set up barbecue grills along Front Street and on the beachfront and cook chicken, fish, shrimp, and lobster. Use your own judgment, but we've found in almost all cases the food from these vendors is safe, tasty, and inexpensive.

ABOUT THE HOTELS

The more budget-oriented cayes, such as Tobacco and Caulker, have mostly small hotels and simple cabins, often built of wood and typically without any amenities beyond a fan or two, though this is changing on Caulker, which now has a number of somewhat upscale hotels. At the other end, notably on Ambergris Caye, are luxurious resorts and deluxe "condotels" (condo developments where individual owners rent their units on a daily basis through a management company) and an increasing number of vacation villas, usually rented by the week. Nearly all accommodations on Ambergris Caye have air-conditioning, and most also have swimming pools. Regardless of which caye you're staying on, lodgings have several things in common: they're small (usually fewer than 30 or 40 rooms), low-rise (nearly all have three stories or fewer), and almost always are directly on the water.

Off-season (typically May to around Thanksgiving), most island hotels, except some budget hotels, reduce rates by around 20% to 40%.

HOTEL AND RESTAURANT PRICES

Prices in the restaurant reviews are the average cost of a main course at dinner or, if dinner is not served, at lunch; taxes and service charges are generally included. Prices in the hotel reviews are the lowest cost of a standard double room in high season, excluding taxes, service charges, and meal plans (except at all-inclusives). Prices for rentals are the lowest per-night cost for a one-bedroom unit in high season.

For expanded lodging reviews and current deals, visit Fodors.com.

TOURS

From Ambergris and Caulker, and from smaller cayes with advance planning, you can do day trips to the mainland to see Mayan ruins, try cave tubing, visit the Belize Zoo, and do other activities. However, because you have to get from the islands to the mainland and then to your destination, the cost will be higher than if you did the tour from a closer point. (⇨ *Caye Caulker and Ambergris Caye sections.*)

DAY-SAILS

Contacts Raggamuffin Tours ☎ *226/0348* ⊕ *www.raggamuffintours.com.* **SEArious Adventures** ☎ *226/4202* ⊕ *www.seariousadventures.com.*

MAYAN RUINS

Tour operators on the Cayes run trips to **Lamanai** (usually a full-day trip by boat and road) and to **Altun Ha** (normally a half-day trip, although it may be longer if it includes lunch and a spa visit at Maruba Spa). You can also visit **Tikal** on an overnight trip by air to Flores, Guatemala, with a change of planes in Belize City. It's also possible to see the small, unexcavated ruins on Ambergris Caye—including Marco Gonzalez on the south end of the island, reachable by golf cart or taxi, and **Chac Balam** at Bacalar, reachable by boat.

Contacts SEAduced by Belize ☎ *226/2254* ⊕ *www.seaducedbybelize.com.*
Tanisha Eco Tours ☎ *226/2314* ⊕ *www.tanishatours.com.*

SCUBA DIVING AND SNORKELING

The largest concentration of dive-trip operators (and also snorkel-boat operators) is on Ambergris Caye. It's a short boat ride to the spur-and-groove formations along the Barrier Reef and to Hol Chan Marine Reserve. Several San Pedro operators with speedboats, including Amigos del Mar, Ecologic Divers, and Patojo's, can take you to the Blue Hole, the largest ocean sinkhole in the world. Lil' Alphonse Tours specializes only in snorkeling and does a terrific job at it. The cleverly named SEAduced and SEArious Adventures both do snorkel trips around Ambergris Caye and to Caye Caulker, along with offering mainland tours. Frenchie's and Belize Diving Services on Caye Caulker take divers to the same sites as the dive shops on Ambergris Caye, and operators such as Carlos Tours and Tsunami Adventures offer local trips.

About a dozen dive lodges and hotels are on or near Belize's atolls, including Turneffe Flats, Turneffe Island Lodge, Isla Marisol, Off the Wall Dive Center, and others. *(See Where to Stay for contact info.)*

Contacts Amigos del Mar ☎ *226/2706* ⊕ *www.amigosdive.com.* **Belize
Diving Services** ☎ *226/0143* ⊕ *www.belizedivingservices.net.* **Carlos
Tours** ☎ *226/0058.* **Ecologic Divers** ✉ *Beachfront, San Pedro* ☎ *226/4118,
800/244–7704 in U.S. and Canada* ⊕ *www.ecologicdivers.com.* **Frenchie's Diving Services** ☎ *226/0234* ⊕ *www.frenchiesdivingbelize.com.* **Patojo's Scuba
Center** ☎ *226/2283* ⊕ *www.ambergriscaye.com/tides/dive.html.* **Lil' Alphonse
Tours** ☎ *226/3136* ⊕ *www.ambergriscaye.com/alfonso.* **Red Mangrove Eco
Adventures** ☎ *607/1440* ⊕ *www.mangrovebelize.com.* **SEAduced by Belize**
☎ *226/2254* ⊕ *www.seaducedbybelize.com.* **SEArious Adventures** ☎ *226/4202.*
Tsunami Adventures ☎ *226/0160* ⊕ *www.tsunamiadventures.com.*

VISITOR INFORMATION

The best source of information on the islands is online. Operated by Marty Casado, AmbergrisCaye.com (⊕ *www.ambergriscaye.com*) is the number one source, with thousands of pages of information on San Pedro, and to a lesser extent on Caye Caulker. The Belize Tourism Board has updated its website (⊕ *www.travelbelize.org*) with more information on the cayes and atolls. The Taco Girl blog (⊕ *www.tacogirl.com*) has timely information on happenings on the island, though some of it is a little commercial. Caye Caulker's official Belize Tourist Industry Association (BTIA) website is ⊕ *www.gocayecaulker.com.* Belize First (⊕ *www.belizefirst.com*) has information and extensive free downloads on the islands. The *San Pedro
Sun* (⊕ *www.sanpedrosun.com*) newspaper publishes a free weekly tabloid-size visitor newspaper, the *San Pedro Sun Visitor Guide.*
Ambergris Today (⊕ *www.ambergristoday.com*) is an online weekly newspaper for San Pedro.

THE CAYES

ST. GEORGE'S CAYE AND OTHER CAYES NEAR BELIZE CITY

9 miles (15 km) northeast of Belize City.

Just a stone's throw from Belize City, St. George's Caye is steeped in history. The country of Belize had its origins here, as St. George's Caye held the original British settlement's first capital. In 1798 the island was the site of a decisive battle with the Spanish. Islanders had only one sloop, while the Spanish had 31 ships. Their knowledge of the sea, however, helped them to defeat the invaders in two hours. Some affluent Belize City residents weekend in their private cottages here. Although St. George's Caye has great places to dive, many serious scuba enthusiasts choose to head out to the more pristine atolls or to private cayes farther south.

Another option about 9 miles (15 km) from Belize City is Royal Palm Island Resort on Little Frenchman Caye. This caye is indeed little, but it offers modern air-conditioned accommodations in two-bedroom cottages.

GETTING HERE AND AROUND

St. George's Caye Resort and Royal Palm Island Resort will meet you at the international airport and handle your 20-minute boat transfer to the islands.

WHERE TO STAY

$$$$
ALL-INCLUSIVE

Royal Palm Island Resort. An all-inclusive option for an island vacation near Belize City is Royal Palm Island, a resort 20 minutes by boat from the mainland on Little Frenchman Caye—and it is in fact French-owned. **Pros:** relaxing getaway near Belize City; friendly service. **Cons:** not directly on reef; tiny island; expensive. $ *Rooms from: BZ$1720* ✉ *Little Frenchman Caye, 9 miles (15 km) east of Belize City* ☎ *621/4949, 888/969–7829 from U.S. and Canada* ⊕ *www.royalpalmisland.com* ⌂ *5 cottages* ⦿ *All-inclusive.*

$$$$
ALL-INCLUSIVE

St. George's Caye Resort. In colonial days St. George's Caye was a British favorite because of its proximity to Belize City, about 20 minutes by boat; more recently wealthy Belize City families weekended on the island, and today visitors favor the resort for its casual style and private island atmosphere. **Pros:** comfortable, historical setting; secluded island resort atmosphere; attractive grounds; good diving available, though not included in rates. **Cons:** not easy to visit mainland or other islands for meals or entertainment; no TV, Wi-Fi only in lodge building. $ *Rooms from: BZ$780* ☎ *220/4444, 800/813–8498 in the U.S. and Canada* ⊕ *www.belizeislandparadise.com* ⌂ *12 cabanas, 8 rooms* ⦿ *All-inclusive.*

AMBERGRIS CAYE AND SAN PEDRO

35 miles (56 km) northeast of Belize City.

At 25 miles (40 km) long and 4½ miles (7 km) wide at its widest point, Ambergris is the queen of the cayes. On early maps it was often referred to as Costa de Ambar, or the Amber Coast, a name supposedly derived from the blackish substance secreted by sperm whales—ambergris—that washes up on the beaches. Having never seen any ambergris in Belize, or a sperm whale, we're not sure we buy this explanation.

GREAT ITINERARIES

It's difficult to recommend itineraries on the cayes, because what you do and where you go depends greatly on the island where you're staying. If you're on a remote caye or atoll, your activities and itineraries are defined partly by your interests (whether it's diving, fishing, or just lazing in a hammock), and by the lodge's daily schedule (or lack of one). Your basic itinerary might go like this: dive, eat, sleep, and dive.

On the other hand, if you're on Ambergris Caye or Caye Caulker, you can set your itinerary around a wide choice of daily island activities, day trips to the mainland, snorkeling or diving on the Barrier Reef, and day trips to the atolls.

IF YOU HAVE 5 DAYS ON AMBERGRIS CAYE OR CAYE CAULKER

Spend your first full day getting to know the island. On Ambergris Caye, rent a golf cart or bike and explore the north and south ends of the caye. Have a beach picnic or enjoy one of the many good restaurants. If you're on Caulker, which is much smaller, you can explore on foot, or, if you prefer, on a bike or in a golf cart. On your second day on either caye, take a boat trip to Hol Chan Marine Reserve and Shark-Ray Alley for snorkeling, and spend the rest of the day on the beach or just hanging out in San Pedro town or Caulker village. On your third day, take a full-day dive or snorkel trip to Lighthouse Reef, with stops at the Blue Hole and Half Moon Caye. On your fourth day, if you're not planning to spend a few days on the mainland this trip, take a tour to the Lamanai Mayan ruins, which includes an exciting boat ride up the New River; or, for some pampering, take one of the combined day trips to Maruba Spa and the Altun Ha Mayan site. If you do plan a mainland stay, then use Day 4 to try windsurfing on Caye Caulker, bonefishing in the flats, or sea or lagoon kayaking. On your final day, take a relaxing daylong catamaran snorkeling trip with a beach barbecue.

IF YOU HAVE 5 DAYS ON A REMOTE CAYE OR ATOLL

On arrival, take off your shoes, take a deep breath, grab a cold drink, and relax. This is what the islands are all about, with the cooling trade winds in your hair and no decisions to make except whether you want the grilled fish or the lobster for dinner. If you're on a dive package, you typically do two to three dives a day, weather permitting. On a fishing package you'll be out on the flats or the reef all day every day. If you're not tied to a package, get up early and watch the sunrise on your first full day. Then spend the day exploring the island: go swimming, spend some time beachcombing, or snorkel off the shore. On your second day, take a dive or snorkel trip to the nearest atoll. On the third day, hire a guide and try your hand at fishing for bonefish or permit on the flats. On your fourth day, take a catamaran sail along the Barrier Reef, with stops for snorkeling and a barbecue on a deserted beach. On your final day, go kayaking around the island and relax on the beach.

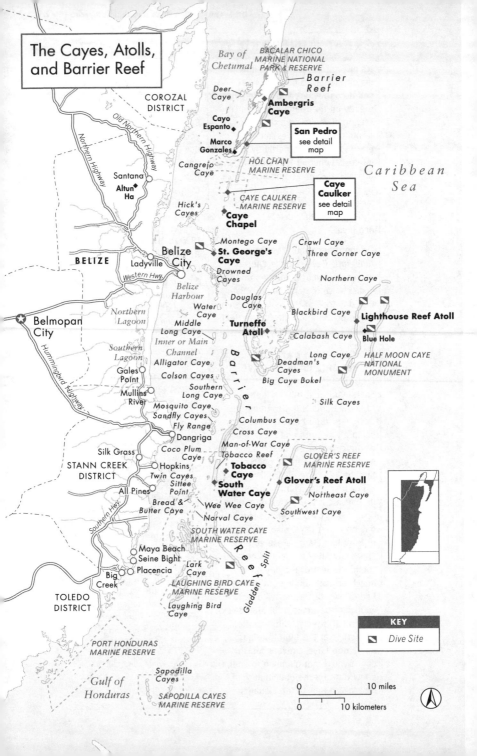

The Cayes, Atolls, and Barrier Reef

Bay of Chetumal

BACALAR CHICO MARINE NATIONAL PARK & RESERVE

Barrier Reef

COROZAL DISTRICT

Deer Caye

Ambergris Caye

Cayo Espanto

San Pedro
see detail map

Marco Gonzales

Cangrejo Caye

HOL CHAN MARINE RESERVE

Caribbean Sea

Old Northern Highway

Northern Highway

Santana

Altun Ha

Hick's Cayes

CAYE CAULKER MARINE RESERVE

Caye Caulker
see detail map

Caye Chapel

BELIZE

Ladyville

Belize City

Western Hwy.

Montego Caye

St. George's Caye

Drowned Cayes

Crawl Caye

Three Corner Caye

Northern Caye

Belize Harbour

Douglas Caye

Northern Lagoon

Water Caye

Blackbird Caye

Lighthouse Reef Atoll

Belmopan City

Middle Long Caye

Turneffe Atoll

Calabash Caye

Blue Hole

Inner or Main Channel

Southern Lagoon

Alligator Caye

Colson Cayes

Gales Point

Southern Long Caye

Long Caye

Deadman's Cayes

HALF MOON CAYE NATIONAL MONUMENT

Hummingbird Highway

Mullins River

Mosquito Caye

Big Caye Bokel

Sandfly Cayes

Fly Range

Silk Cayes

Dangriga

Columbus Caye

Silk Grass

Coco Plum Caye

Cross Caye

Man-of-War Caye

STANN CREEK DISTRICT

Hopkins

Tobacco Reef

Tobacco Caye

GLOVER'S REEF MARINE RESERVE

Twin Cayes

Sittee Point

South Water Caye

Glover's Reef Atoll

All Pines

Bread & Butter Caye

Wee Wee Caye

Northeast Caye

Southern Hwy.

Norval Caye

Southwest Caye

Maya Beach

Seine Bight

Placencia

SOUTH WATER CAYE MARINE RESERVE

Lark Caye

Big Creek

TOLEDO DISTRICT

LAUGHING BIRD CAYE MARINE RESERVE

Laughing Bird Caye

Gladden Split

PORT HONDURAS MARINE RESERVE

Gulf of Honduras

Sapodilla Cayes

SAPODILLA CAYES MARINE RESERVE

0		10 miles
0		10 kilometers

Here the reef is just a few hundred yards from shore, making access to dive sites extremely easy: the journey by boat takes as little as 10 minutes. Because Ambergris Caye is by far Belize's largest island and was the first to cater to those hoping to witness Belize's undersea world, it's generally superior in the number of dive shops, experience of dive masters, and range of equipment and facilities it offers. San Pedro has Belize's only hyperbaric chamber and an on-site doctor to tend to divers with the bends. Many dive shops are attached to hotels, where the quality of dive masters, equipment, and facilities can vary considerably.

But there's more than diving to Ambergris Caye. Today the majority of visitors to the island don't dive at all. They snorkel, fish, splash in the sea, go sailboarding, or just laze around the hotel pool until it's time to sample one of the dozens of restaurants on the island. With an island population of around 20,000, according to local observers who point to the many mainlanders who have come to the island to find work and to foreign expats who spent part of the year on the caye, or 11,510, according to the 2010 Belize Census, Ambergris and its only real town, San Pedro, remain friendly and prosperous. The caye has one of the country's highest literacy rates and an admirable level of awareness about the reef's fragility.

GETTING HERE AND AROUND
Hard-packed sand streets are giving way to the concrete cobblestones of Barrier Reef Drive, Pescador Street, Coconut Drive and other island streets, and everyone complains about the worsening car traffic in town, but the most common forms of transportation remain golf cart, bike, and foot.

TIMING
Belize's most popular destination merits a significant chunk of your vacation time. Indeed, some visitors to Belize only experience Ambergris Caye. With its many restaurants, bars, and shops, plus myriad opportunities for water sports, you can easily spend a week or more on the island without beginning to run out of things to do.

SAFETY
With rapid growth and an influx of workers from other parts of Belize and Central America, Ambergris Caye has seen an increase in all types of crime. However, nearly all visitors to Ambergris Caye say they feel perfectly safe. Use common sense and avoid walking on dark streets and deserted beaches after nightfall. Most of the larger hotels have full-time security.

WATER ACTIVITIES
CHARTERS
El Gato. A 30-foot sailing catamaran, El Gato does day cruises to Caye Caulker, with two stops for snorkeling, for BZ$130 per person (minimum three persons). Also, half-day sails to Mexico Rocks or Hol Chan, BZ$100 per person (minimum three). A sunset cruise also is BZ$100, and a sail with a beach barbecue with fresh-caught fish and lobster is BZ$160. El Gato can take a maximum of 12 persons, and usually there are just a few on board, so it's a less crowded experience than some of the other snorkel tours. The boat will pick you up at your resort. ⊠ *San Pedro* ☎ *226/2264* ⊕ *www.ambergriscaye.com/elgato.*

HISTORY

Because of their strategic locations on trade routes between the Yucatán in the north and Honduras in the south, the northern cayes, especially Ambergris Caye and Caye Caulker, were long occupied by the Maya. Then, as now, the reef and its abundance of fish provided a valuable source of seafood.

The origin of Belize's atolls remains a mystery, but evidence suggests they grew from the bottom up, as vast pagodas of coral accumulated over millions of years. The Maya were perhaps the first humans to discover the atolls, but by the time the first Spanish explorers arrived in 1508, the Mayan civilization had already mysteriously collapsed and few remained on the islands.

In the 17th century, English pirates used the cayes and atolls as a hideout, plotting their attacks on unwary ships. The most famous battle in Belize history happened on September 10, 1798, when a ragtag band of buccaneers defeated a Spanish armada at the Battle of St. George's Caye.

The economy on the islands has ebbed and flowed, as pirates were replaced by wealthy plantation owners, who were eventually usurped by lobster fishermen. The first hotel on Ambergris Caye, Holiday Hotel, opened in 1965 and soon began attracting divers. Jacques Cousteau visited the Blue Hole in 1971 and helped introduce Belize to the world. Today tourism is by far the top industry on the cayes and atolls.

FISHING

Although southern Belize, especially Placencia, is the main sportfishing center in Belize, Ambergris Caye also has good opportunities for flats, reef, and deep-sea fishing. Expect to pay about BZ$500–BZ$700 for one or two people for a day of flats fishing for bonefish, permit, or tarpon, including a guide and a boat. May to September is the best time for catching tarpon off Ambergris Caye; April to October is the best time for bonefish; and March through May is best for permit. Reef fishing for snapper, grouper, barracuda, and other reef fish runs BZ$600 or more a day, including a guide and a powerboat. Deep-sea fishing outside the reef for billfish, sailfish, wahoo, and tuna costs around BZ$1,200–BZ$1,500 a day, depending on the number in your party and the size of the boat. Although there's still a lot of confusion about it, a sportfishing license (catch and release only) is now required for fishing in Belize waters, except for fishing off piers or from shore. Licenses for visitors are BZ$20 a day or BZ$50 a week. You can buy a license online from the Belize Coastal Zone Management Authority and Institute (⊕ *www.coastalzonebelize.org*) or your fishing guide or hotel may be able to help you get it.

For fishing that's easier on the pocketbook, you can fish for snapper, barracuda, and other fish from piers and docks on the island. No license is required. Bring your own gear or buy tackle at local hardware stores and ask local anglers about bait. Small sardines work well. For fly-fishing aficionados, there's a fly-fishing shop at El Pescador *(see above).* You can also wade out in the flats near shore on North Ambergris, north of the river channel on the back (west) side, and try your luck with bonefish. Keep an eye out for the occasional crocodile. You'll catch more with a guide and boat, but fishing on your own is inexpensive fun.

Fodor's Choice ★

El Pescador. Established in 1974, El Pescador is the leading fishing lodge on Ambergris Caye, and one of the top in Belize. Located about 2 miles (3 km) north of San Pedro, it works with around 20 fishing guides. It offers bonefish, permit, and tarpon fishing packages including upscale room, meals, boat, and guide, starting at around BZ$3,550 per person, double occupancy, for three nights (two days of fishing). Rate does not include flights to Belize, fishing equipment, or tips to guides. ⊠ *El Pescador* ☎ *226/2398, 800/242–2017 in U.S. and Canada* ⊕ *www.elpescador.com.*

FISHING GUIDES

Fishing San Pedro. A fishing service run by Steve DeMaio, Fishing San Pedro works with about a half-dozen guides on the island. You call Steve, tell him what kind of fishing you want to do, and he will arrange a guide and boat for you and your party for spin or fly-fishing. Rates for a half-day of flats or reef fishing are around BZ$450 for two persons, including boat, guide, and tackle; full-day flats fishing runs around BZ$650 for two. A full day of fishing on the 38-foot *Reef Lady* is BZ$1,300 for up to six people. Tips to guides are extra. A beach barbecue with fish, lobster (in-season) and chicken is BZ$100 for the boat. ⊠ *San Pedro* ☎ *607/9967* ⊕ *www.fishingsanpedro.com.*

George Bradley. Long-time local guide George Bradley specializes in fly-fishing for bonefish. ⊠ *Pescador Dr., San Pedro* ☎ *226/2179.*

Go Fish Belize. Local fishing guide Abbie Marin arranges flats, reef, and deep sea fishing charters. A full day of fly or spin flats fishing is BZ$700 for one or two persons. ⊠ *7 Boca Del Rio Dr., San Pedro* ☎ *226/3121* ⊕ *www.gofishbelize.com.*

Pete Graniel. Local guide Captain Pedro "Pete" Graniel does both deep sea and reef trips and has a 38-foot boat, *Reel Lady*, that's good for trolling. He and the boat can be booked through Fishing San Pedro *(above).* ⊠ *Almond St., San Pedro* ☎ *226/2584, 607/9967 Fishing San Pedro.*

JET SKIS

Monkey Business Tour Shop. Monkey Business Tour Shop at Banana Beach Resort has jet ski rentals for around BZ$300 for two hours. ⊠ *Banana Beach Resort, Coconut Dr., San Pedro* ☎ *226/3890, 877/288–1011* ⊕ *www.monkeybusinesstours.com.*

SAILING CHARTERS

Belize will probably never rival the British Virgin Islands for sailing. The shallow water and hidden coral heads and tidal currents are dangerous for even those familiar with the area. When you charter a boat you have to stay inside the Barrier Reef, but there's a lot of beautiful territory to explore.

TMM Belize. TMM has about a half-dozen catamarans (38 feet–46 feet, with three to four cabins) at its small Belize base. Weeklong bareboat— sailing experience required—and captained charters are available out of San Pedro. Rates vary, depending on boat type and time of year, but range in high season from around BZ$8,400 to BZ$18,000 a week, not including provisions (available through TMM for around BZ$60 per person per day), cruising fee (BZ$20 per person), insurance fee of BZ$50 a day, and incidentals. Skippers are an additional BZ$300 per day, plus food and gratuity; cooks are BZ$220 a day, plus food and gratuity. Bareboat charters must stay inside the reef. Split among three to eight people, sailing charter prices are not as high as they sound. ⊠ *Coconut Dr., south of Wings department store across from airstrip, San Pedro* 📞 *226/3026, 800/633–0155 in U.S. and Canada* ⊕ *www. sailtmm.com* ⊙ *Office daily 8–5.*

SCUBA DIVING AND SNORKELING

Dives off Ambergris are usually single tank at depths of 50 to 80 feet, allowing about 35 minutes of bottom time. Diving trips run around BZ$90 for a single-tank dive, BZ$150 for a two-tank dive, BZ$90–BZ$110 for a one-tank night dive, BZ$450–BZ$500 for a three-tank full-day drive trip to Turneffe atoll, BZ$700–750 for day trips with three dives to Lighthouse Reef. Atoll rates include breakfast, lunch and marine reserve admission. Dive gear rental is usually extra—a full package of gear including wet suit, buoyancy compensator, regulator, mask, and fins is around BZ$60–BZ$80. Snorkeling by boat around Ambergris generally costs BZ$70–BZ$100 per person for two or three hours or BZ$140–BZ$200 for a day trip, including lunch. If you go to Hol Chan Marine Reserve there's a BZ$20 park fee, but this fee is sometimes included in the quoted rate. A snorkel trip to the Blue Hole is around BZ$450–BZ$480, including the BZ$80 Marine Reserve fee. Snorkel gear rental may be additional. Prices also may not include 12.5% tax. (Businesses are supposed to include the 12.5% GST in their quoted prices, but not all do.) Most dive shops will pick you up at your hotel or at the nearest pier.

⚠ **Be careful when snorkeling off docks and piers on Ambergris Caye. There's heavy boat traffic between the reef and shore, and boat captains may not be able to see snorkelers in the water. Several snorkelers near shore have been killed or seriously injured by boats.**

DIVE AND SNORKEL SITES

Fodor's Choice ★

Bacalar Chico Marine National Park & Reserve. Development on Ambergris continues relentlessly, but most of the far north of the island remains pristine, or close to it. At the top of the caye, butting up against Mexico, Bacalar Chico National Park and Marine Reserve spans 41 square miles (105 square km) of land, reef, and sea. Here, on 11 miles (18 km) of trails you may cross paths with whitetail deer, ocelots, saltwater crocodiles, and, according to some reports, pumas and jaguars. There are excellent diving, snorkeling, and fishing opportunities, especially off Rocky Point, and a small visitor center and museum will get you oriented. You'll need a boat and a guide to take you here, where there are some small, unexcavated Mayan ruins. Be sure to bring insect repellent. An all-day snorkel trip to Bacalar Chico from San Pedro costs around BZ$170–BZ$220 per person. Trips from Sarteneja also are offered for about the same cost. ⊠ *North end of Ambergris Caye* 🎫 *BZ$10 or BZ$30 for weekly pass.*

Fodor's Choice **Belize Barrier Reef.** The longest barrier reef in either the Western or
★ Northern hemispheres (it's just a widely accepted rumor that it's the
second-longest barrier reef in the world, after the Great Barrier Reef in
Australia), the Belize Barrier Reef is off the eastern shore of Ambergris
Caye. From the island shore, or from the air, you see the coral reef as
an almost unbroken chain of white surf. Inside the reef, the water is
clear and shallow, and the reef itself is a beautiful living wall formed
by billions of small coral polyps. Just outside the reef, the seabed drops
sharply, and from a distance the water looks dark blue or purple. The
reef is closest to shore on the far north end of Ambergris Caye. In
and around San Pedro town, the barrier reef is a few hundred yards
off the beach. ⊠ *½ mile (1 km) east of Ambergris Caye (it's closer to
shore the farther north you go on the island).*

Fodor's Choice **Hol Chan Marine Reserve.** The reef's focal point for diving and snorkel-
★ ing near Ambergris Caye and Caye Caulker is the spectacular Hol
Chan Marine Reserve (Maya for "little channel"). It's a 20-minute
boat ride from San Pedro, and about 30 minutes from Caye Caulker.
Hol Chan is a break in the reef about 100 feet wide and 20 to 35
feet deep, through which tremendous volumes of water pass with the
tides. Shark-Ray Alley, now a part of Hol Chan, is famous as a place
to swim, snorkel, and dive with sharks (nearly all are nurse sharks)
and Southern sting rays.

■ TIP➔ Especially during peak visitor periods to the cayes or when several
cruise ships are docked off Belize City, snorkel tour boats can stack up at Hol
Chan. Check locally to see when Hol Chan may be less busy, and consider
visiting in early morning before most of the tours arrive.

The expanded 21-square-mile (55-square-km) park has a miniature Blue
Hole and a 12-foot-deep cave whose entrance often attracts the fairy
hasslet, an iridescent purple and yellow fish frequently seen here. The
reserve is also home to a large moray eel population.

Varying in depth from 50 feet to 100 feet, Hol Chan's canyons lie
between buttresses of coral running perpendicular to the reef, separated by white, sandy channels. You may find tunnel-like passageways
from one canyon to the next. It's exciting to explore because as you
come over each hill you don't know what you'll see in the "valley."
Because fishing generally is off-limits here, divers and snorkelers can
see abundant marine life, including spotted eagle rays and sharks.
There are throngs of squirrelfish, butterfly fish, parrotfish, and queen
angelfish, as well as Nassau groupers, barracuda, and large shoals of
yellowtail snappers. Unfortunately, also here are lionfish, an invasive
Indo-Pacific species that is eating its way—destroying small native
fish—from Venezuela to the North Carolina coast. Altogether, more
than 160 species of fish have been identified in the marine reserve,
along with 40 species of coral, and five kinds of sponges. Hawksbill,
loggerhead, and green turtles have also been found here, along with
spotted and common dolphins, West Indian manatees, stingrays and
several species of sharks.

⚠ The currents through the reef can be strong here at times, so tell your guide if you're not a strong swimmer and ask for a snorkel vest or float. Also, although the nurse sharks are normally docile and very used to humans, they are wild creatures that on rare occasions have bitten snorkelers or divers who disturbed them. ✉ *Off southern tip of Ambergris Caye* ☎ *526/2247 Hol Chan office in San Pedro* ⊕ *www.holchanbelize.org* 🎫 *BZ$20, normally included in snorkel or dive tour charge.*

Fodor'sChoice **Shark-Ray Alley.** Shark-Ray Alley is a sandbar within Hol Chan Marine
★ Reserve where you can snorkel alongside nurse sharks (which can bite but rarely do) and stingrays (which gather here to be fed), and near even larger numbers of day-trippers from San Pedro and cruise ships. Sliding into the water is a small feat of personal bravery—the sight of sharks and rays brushing past is spectacular yet daunting. Although they shouldn't, guides touch and hold sharks and rays, and sometimes encourage visitors to pet these sea creatures (which you shouldn't do, either). The Hol Chan Marine Reserve office is on Caribena Street in San Pedro. ■TIP➜ **A night dive at Shark-Ray Alley is a special treat: bioluminescence causes the water to light up, and many nocturnal animals emerge, such as octopus and spider crab. Because of the strong current you'll need above-average swimming skills.** ✉ *Southern tip of Ambergris Caye in Hol Chan Marine Reserve* ☎ *226/2247 Hol Chan office on Caribena St. in San Pedro* ⊕ *www.holchanbelize.org* 🎫 *BZ$20 marine reserve fee included as a part of Hol Chan fee.*

DIVE   Many dive shops and resorts have diving courses. A half-day basic
SHOPS AND   familiarization course or "resort course" costs around BZ$300–
OPERATORS   BZ$350. A complete four-day PADI open-water certification course costs BZ$800–BZ$1,000. One popular variant is a referral course, where the academic and pool training is done at home, or online, but not the required dives. The cost for two days in Belize is about BZ$550–BZ$650. Prices for dive courses vary a little from island to island, generally being least expensive on Caye Caulker. However, even prices on Ambergris Caye, which tends to have higher costs for most activities, are a little lower than on the mainland.

If you're staying on Ambergris Caye, Glover's Reef is out of the question for a day trip by boat. Even with perfect weather—which it often isn't—a trip to Lighthouse Reef takes between two and three hours. Most trips to Lighthouse and the Blue Hole depart at 6 am and return at 5:30 or 6 pm, making for a long day in the sun and water. Turneffe is more accessible, though it's still a long and costly day trip, and you're unlikely to reach the atoll's southern tip, which has the best diving.

Amigos del Mar. Amigos del Mar, established in 1987, is perhaps the island's most consistently recommended dive operation. The PADI facility has a dozen dive boats and offers a range of local dives as well as trips to Turneffe Atoll and Lighthouse Reef in a fast 56-foot dive boat. Amigos charges BZ$150 per person for a local two-tank dive, not including equipment rental (if needed) or 12.5% tax, and BZ$600 for a 12-hour trip to the Blue Hole, including BZ$80 park fee and lunch but not equipment rental or tax. An open water certification

HOW TO CHOOSE A DIVE MASTER

Many dive masters in Belize are former anglers who began diving on the side and ended up doing it full-time. The best have an intimate knowledge of the reef and a superb eye for coral and marine life.

When choosing a dive master or dive shop, first check the web. Participants on forums and newsgroups such as ⊕ www.ambergriscaye.com and ⊕ www.scubaboard.com field many questions on diving and dive shops in Belize. On islands where there are multiple dive shops, spend some time talking to dive masters to see which ones make you feel most comfortable. Find out about their backgrounds and experience, as well as the actual crew that would be going out with you. Are they dive masters, instructors, or just crew? Get a sense of how the dive master feels about reef and sea life conservation.

Besides questions about costs and equipment, ask:

■ How many people, maximum, go out on your dive trips?

■ Is there a minimum number of divers before you'll make the trip?

■ What dive sites are your favorites, and why?

■ What kind of boats do you have, and how long does it take to get where we're going?

■ Who is actually in the water with the divers?

■ What kind of safety and communications equipment is on the boat?

■ What's the procedure for cancellation in case of bad weather?

■ How do you decide if you're going out or not?

If you're not comfortable with the answers, or if the dive shop just doesn't pass your sniff test, move on.

course is BZ$900. Amigos also offers snorkel and fishing trips. ✉ *On a pier off Barrier Reef Dr., near Mayan Princess Hotel, San Pedro* ☎ 226/2706, 800/882-6159 ⊕ *www.amigosdivebelize.com.*

Ecologic Divers. This PADI shop has won a good reputation for safety, service, and ecologically sound practices. Local two-tank dives go out daily at 9 and 2 and cost BZ$150, not including any equipment rental or 12.5% tax. Full-day Turneffe trips are BZ$500 including breakfast and lunch, but not 12.5% tax. ✉ *On pier at north end of San Pedro, just south of The Phoenix resort, San Pedro* ☎ 226/4118, 800/244-7774 *in U.S. and Canada* ⊕ *www.ecologicdivers.com.*

Hugh Parkey's Belize Dive Connection. The long-established Hugh Parkey's Belize Dive Connection has moved its main dive shop operation from Belize City to the dock of the SunBreeze Hotel in San Pedro. The late Hugh Parkey was a pioneer in diving in Belize, and this dive operation maintains Parkey's legacy of excellence. BDC has a 46-foot dive boat and does trips to the barrier reef as well as to Turneffe and Lighthouse atolls. Dive/hotel packages with SunBreeze are offered. ✉ *SunBreeze Hotel Pier, Beachfront, San Pedro* ☎ 220/4024 ⊕ *www. hpbelizeadventures.com.*

Lil' Alphonse Tours. Offering snorkeling only, Lil' Alphonse himself usually captains the tours, doing a fabulous job making snorkelers feel comfortable in the water. ⊠ *Coconut Dr., across street from Changes in Latitudes B&B, San Pedro* ☎ *226/3136* ⊕ *www.ambergriscaye. com/alfonso.*

Patojo's Scuba Center. Operated by Elmer "Patojo" Paz, who has nearly 20 years of diving experience, Patojo's Scuba Center at The Tides Hotel is a small dive shop with a good reputation. ⊠ *The Tides Hotel, north end of San Pedro, San Pedro* ☎ *226/2283* ⊕ *www. ambergriscaye.com/tides.*

SEAduced by Belize. This well-run snorkeling, sailing, and tour company does full-day snorkeling trips to Bacalar Chico and to Mexico Rocks and Robles Point. Trips include a lovely beach barbecue. SEAduced also does Hol Chan snorkel tours, plus mainland trips to Mayan sites and cave tubing. This locally run company offers sailing cruises as well. ⊠ *Vilma Linda Plaza, Tarpon St., San Pedro* ☎ *226/2254* ⊕ *www. seaducedbybelize.com.*

SEArious Adventures. This long-established snorkeling and sailing shop does day snorkel trips to Caye Caulker (BZ$100 plus park fees and equipment rental), along with a variety of other snorkel and sail trips. It also offers day sails and mainland tours. ⊠ *Beachfront, on dock, between Tarpon and Black Coral St., San Pedro* ☎ *226/4202* ⊕ *www. seariousadventures.com.*

White Sands Dive Shop. White Sands Dive Shop isn't at White Sands Resort but at Las Terrazas. Never mind, this PADI dive center is run by Elbert Greer, a noted diver and birder who has taught scuba in San Pedro for more than 20 years, getting some 2,500 divers certified. A daily scheduled dive and snorkel boat picks up at island resorts starting around 9 am. ⊠ *Las Terrazas, North Ambergris Caye* ☎ *226/2405* ⊕ *www.whitesandsdiveshop.com.*

DIVE BOATS If you want to hit the best dive spots in Belize and dive a lot—up to five or six dives a day—live-aboard dive boats may be your best bet. The two main international live-aboard companies serving Belize, Aggressor Fleet and Sun Dancer, have merged. Their two live-aboard boats in Belize concentrate on dives around Lighthouse Reef atoll and the Blue Hole. The boats are based at the Radisson Fort George Hotel in Belize City.

Expect to pay about US$2,300–US$2,700 per person double occupancy for six days of diving. The price includes all dives, meals, airport transfers, and stateroom accommodations on the dive boat. It doesn't include airfare to Belize, overnight stays at a hotel before or after the dive trip if necessary, tips, U.S. port fees (US$95), some alcoholic beverages, equipment rentals, Nitrox, port charges, and incidentals.

Agressor Fleet. The Agressor Fleet operates two live-aboards in Belize, the *Belize Aggressor III* and *Sun Dancer II*. Guests are met at the international airport near Belize City and are taken to the dock at the Radisson Fort George. Boats leave on Saturday evening for Lighthouse Reef, Half Moon Caye, and the Blue Hole, with as many as five or six dives each day available. They return the next Friday. The *Aggressor*

III can accommodate up to 18 passengers in nine staterooms. It's a 110-foot luxury cruiser with a hot tub and sundeck, powered by twin 500-horsepower engines. The *Sun Dancer II,* a 138-foot yacht, can accommodate up to 20 passengers in 10 staterooms. All staterooms on both live-aboards have private heads, TVs, and DVDs, plus individual climate controls. ☒ *Lighthouse Reef* ☎ *706/993–2531 U.S. office, 800/348–2628 in the U.S. and Canada, 223/0748 shore office in Belize* ✉ *info@liveaboardfleet.com* ⊕ *www.aggressor.com* ☜ *Sun Dancer II, US$2,295 to $2,495 per person; Aggressor III, US$2,495 to $2,695. Rates are plus US$95 for U.S. port fees and do not include airfare to Belize, equipment rentals, Nitrox, alcoholic beverages (except local beer), or gratuities.*

WINDSURFING AND KITESURFING

Caye Caulker is better known as a windsurfing destination, perhaps because it attracts a younger crowd than Ambergris Caye, but the winds are equally good and consistent off Ambergris Caye. February through July sees the windiest conditions, with winds 12 to 20 knots most days. Kitesurfing, combining a windsurfing-type board pulled by a large kite, is also available on Ambergris Caye.

Sailsports Belize. Sailsports Belize at Caribbean Villas offers private windsurfing instruction at around BZ$100 an hour, with equipment rental from BZ$98 a day. Kitesurfing equipment (kite and board) rentals are around BZ$164 for a full day. All rates plus 12.5% tax. Sailsports Belize also rents small catamarans and other sailboats. ☒ *Beachfront, Caribbean Villas, Seagrape Dr., San Pedro* ☎ *226/4488* ⊕ *www. sailsportsbelize.com.*

MAINLAND TOURS

You can do tours of mainland sights including Mayan ruins, the Belize Zoo, and cave tubing from San Pedro, though the cost will be higher than from the mainland. From Ambergris Caye a full-day cave-tubing trip, combined with lunch and a visit to the zoo, runs BZ$250–BZ$280. A visit to Altun Ha is BZ$150–BZ$210. Considered by many as the best San Pedro tour operator for mainland trips, Tanisha specializes in full-day Lamanai trips (around BZ$220 per person, plus 12.5% tax). The full-day Lamanai trip includes a boat ride up the New River and also includes a light breakfast, lunch, beer, rum punch, and soft drinks. Tanisha also offers cave tubing (BZ$240–BZ$350, plus tax), trips to Altun Ha (BZ$180 including tax), and other tours. SEAduced by Belize is unrivaled for its nature and kayak tours. SEAduced by Belize and SEArious Adventures both do a variety of trips, including manatee spotting, visits to Altun Ha, and others. If tour prices from San Pedro seem too high, you can take a water taxi to Belize City and rent a car or take a cab for your own DIY tour, though the hassle factor may be higher.

Contacts SEAduced by Belize ☎ *226/2254* ⊕ *www.seaducedbybelize.com.* **SEArious Adventures.** ☎ *226/420.* **Tanisha Eco Tours** ☒ *Beachfront, Boca del Rio Dr., San Pedro* ☎ *226/2314* ⊕ *www.tanishatours.com.*

WHERE TO EAT

Ambergris Caye has the largest and most diverse selection of restaurants in the country. Here you can buy cheap tacos or grilled chicken from a street vendor, eat barbecued fish on the beach, or, at the other end, dine on lobster, crab claws, and steak at upscale eateries. Even the most upmarket spots have a casual atmosphere, some with sand floors and screenless windows open to catch the breezes from the sea.

The largest concentration of restaurants is in town, but many, including some of the best on the island, are opening on the South End and on North Ambergris.

SAN PEDRO TOWN

$$$ SEAFOOD 🍴 **Blue Water Grill.** Close to the beach and perpetually busy, this restaurant's seats are on a raised, covered deck with views of the Barrier Reef a few hundred yards away. The emphasis here is on seafood such as grilled grouper or snapper, but there are good wood-fired pizzas and pastas, too. The owners run a tight ship, and by island standards the service is top-notch. The crispy coconut shrimp appetizer is our favorite. [$] *Average main: $40* ✉ *SunBreeze Beach Hotel, Coconut Dr., Beachfront* ☎ *226/3347* 🌐 *www.bluewatergrillbelize.com.*

$$$ CARIBBEAN 🍴 **Caliente.** Have a seat at Caliente and catch the sea breezes and look at the reef. You'll dig into spicy Mexican dishes with a Caribbean and Belizean twist, such as ginger rum shrimp or grilled lobster with a sauce of tomatoes, cilantro, peppers, and onions. The same owners also operate Red Ginger and Blue Water Grille. [$] *Average main: $30* ✉ *Barrier Reef Dr., in Spindrift Hotel* ☎ *226/2170* 🌐 *www.calientebelize.com* ⏲ *Closed Mon.*

$$$ SEAFOOD 🍴 **Caramba.** You'll quickly sense the frenetic energy of this noisy and often packed restaurant in the middle of town. No view, and there's nothing very fancy on the lengthy menu here—just basics like grilled or fried snapper, fried shrimp, pork chops, and Mexican fajitas and burritos—but most everything is well prepared, prices are moderate, and the service is snappy and enthusiastic. The restaurant was recently renovated. [$] *Average main: $30* ✉ *Pescador Dr.* ☎ *226/4321* ⏲ *Closed Wed.*

$ CAFÉ FAMILY Fodor's Choice ★ 🍴 **DandE's Frozen Custard & Sorbet.** Dan and Eileen (DandE) Jamison, who used to run the local weekly paper, the *San Pedro Sun*, opened this shop in 2005, and they've been serving creamy custards and cooling sorbets ever since (except for taking a little time off each summer.) For something with an island flavor, try the mango sorbet or the soursop frozen custard. The rum raisin custard is our favorite. [$] *Average main: $7* ✉ *Pescador Dr., next to Cocina Caramba* ☎ *660/5966* 🌐 *www.dande.bz* 💳 *No credit cards* ⏲ *Closed Mon. and Tues.*

$$ AMERICAN 🍴 **DJ's Seaside Bar & Restaurant.** With a menu of burgers, wings, and other American fare this casual spot near the bridge on the north end of town is designed to attract tourists and U.S. expats. If that's what you're hankering for, pull a stool up to the blue tile bar and order a mess of hot wings, a bucket of beer, and enjoy. [$] *Average main: $20* ✉ *Boca del Rio, north end of town near park* ☎ *206/2464.*

$$ **✕ El Fogon.** El Fogon serves authentic down-home Belizean cooking
LATIN AMERICAN like *chaya* tamales, gibnut, and stew chicken, in a quaint thatch build-
Fodor'sChoice ing with dirt floor. You sit at picnic tables. Food is prepared in cast
★ iron pots in a traditional fogon, a wood-burning stove. Though it's
in town just two blocks just north of the Tropic Air terminal at the
airstrip, it's a little hard to find. Ask any local where it is. $ *Average
main: $24* ✉ *North of Tropic Air terminal, 2 Trigger Fish St., near
airport, between Esmeralda and Tarpon St.* ☎ *206/2121* ▭ *No credit
cards* ☉ *Closed Sun.*

$$$ **✕ Elvi's Kitchen.** In the old days, in 1974, Elvi Staines sold burgers from
SEAFOOD the window of her house. Soon she added a few tables on the sand
under a flamboyant tree. Today, the floors are still sand, and the tree
remains (though now lifeless and cut back to fit inside the roof), but
everything else is changed. Enter through massive mahogany doors and
you'll be tended to by a staff of a couple of dozen. The burgers are still
good, but for dinner Elvi's now specializes in upmarket dishes such as
shrimp in watermelon sauce or crab claws with garlic butter. There's a
Mexican-themed night on Wednesday and a "Mayan Feast" on Friday
night. For dessert, don't pass on the coconut pie. It's all a bit touristy,
but we always enjoy Elvi's. $ *Average main: $37* ✉ *Pescador Dr., near
Ambergris St.* ☎ *226/2404* ⊕ *www.elviskitchen.com* ☉ *Closed Sun.*

$$ **✕ Estel's Dine by the Sea.** This is San Pedro's absolute best spot for a
AMERICAN hearty American-style breakfast of eggs, bacon, fried potatoes, fry jacks,
and freshly squeezed juice, or arguably the best Bloody Mary in town.
Estel's even has grits! Later in the day you can order burgers, Mexican
meals, and good seafood dishes. The little white-and-aqua building is on
the beach, as you might infer from the sandy floor and porthole-shaped
windows. Best seats for breakfast are on the terrace outside where you
can sit and watch pelicans. $ *Average main: $20* ✉ *Beachfront, Barrier
Reef Dr.* ☎ *226/2019.*

$$ **✕ Fido's Courtyard.** Sooner or later you're sure to end up at Fido's (pro-
AMERICAN nounced Fee-dough's), sipping something cold and contemplating the
sea views, under what the owners claim is the largest thatch palapa
in Belize. If not the largest in Belize, it may at least be the largest on
Ambergris Caye. This casual joint serves mediocre burgers, fish-and-
chips, tacos, and other bar food, but it's a good place to get a cold beer
and enjoy the live music most nights. $ *Average main: US$20* ✉ *Barrier
Reef Dr., Beachfront, just north of Catholic church* ☎ *226/3176.*

$$$ **✕ Red Ginger.** With its stylishly minimalist decor and ice-cold air-condi-
SEAFOOD tioning, this restaurant could be in L.A., but it's actually at The Phoenix
Fodor'sChoice resort at the north end of San Pedro. No sea views here—you gaze at
★ deep red and mocha cream walls, with brown earth-tone accents, and
tropical wild ginger plants in glass vases. After a ginger or basil mojito,
start with ceviche, your choice of grouper, or mixed shrimp and lob-
ster. Try the grilled snook with guava tamarind glaze and salsa, or the
blackened snapper. A five-course tasting menu is BZ$100 per person.
The service is a couple of notches above most other places in San Pedro.
$ *Average main: $48* ✉ *The Phoenix, Barrier Reef Dr., at north end of
town* ☎ *226/4623* ⊕ *www.redgingerbelize.com* ☉ *Closed Tues.*

3

$$$ ✕ **Wild Mango's.** Noted local chef Amy Knox made Wild Mango's one
SEAFOOD of the most interesting dining choices on the island. Many of the dishes
have a Mexican base but with Knox's sophisticated twist. She calls her
cooking "New Wave Latin"—Caribbean food infused with spicy Latin
flavors from Cuba, Argentina, and Mexico. It's good enough to have
earned her Belize Chef of the Year honors twice in the past. Start with
the Tres Amigos, three kinds of ceviche with shrimp and fish (Knox does
not use conch or lobster, because she believes it is not sustainable.) Try
the Budin Azteca, a Mexican version of lasagna, or the huge fish burri-
tos (enough for two). Seating is beach casual, with stools at tables on a
covered, open-air veranda. We especially like Wild Mango's for a casual
lunch. $ *Average main: $28* ⊠ *Beachfront, 42 Barrier Reef Dr., south
end of town just south of Ruby's Hotel* ☎ *226/2859* ⊘ *Closed Sun.*

NORTH OF SAN PEDRO

Unless you are staying near one of the North Ambergris restaurants
listed *below*, you may want to take a water taxi—the Coastal Xpress—
to these restaurants, especially after dark. Cabs from town now go as
far north on the golf-cart path as Las Terrazas Resort, though the cost
is steep (BZ$30–BZ$50 for most destinations, including the BZ$12
vehicle bridge fee). In a golf cart, the cart path is bumpy and buggy and
sometimes impassable after heavy rains.

$$$ ✕ **Aji Tapa Bar and Restaurant.** Relax in a shady seaside patio, under gumbo
SEAFOOD limbo trellises, coconut palms, and almond and sea grape trees, with views
Fodor's Choice of the barrier reef in the distance, and snack on delicious small plates of
★ barbecue shrimp, ceviche, *calamares andaluza,* and a heavenly artichoke
dip. In larger plates, try the seafood paella, which is prepared in several
varieties. If there's a downside, it's inconsistency, with the food suffering
on the few nights Chef Hugo is off. If you decide you want to stay longer,
follow the winding path through tropical gardens and cross a small bridge
over a lagoon and you'll find cute one-bedroom rental cottages. Come by
your own golf cart, cab (BZ$35 from San Pedro), or water taxi—get off
at Grand Caribe. $ *Average main: $38* ⊠ *Beachfront, North Ambergris
Caye, 2½ miles (4 km) north of town, Buena Vista Point, just north of
Grand Caribe resort* ☎ *226/4047* ⊕ *www.ajitapabar.com.*

$$ ✕ **Lazy Croc BBQ.** You'll smell the smoky aroma of barbecue well before
BARBECUE you enter this popular spot about 1½ miles (2½ km) north of the bridge.
As befits a barbecue joint, the menu is short and sweet—pulled pork,
barbecue chicken, ribs, Buffalo wings, chili, and a few other items, with
sides of coleslaw, french fries, barbecue beans, fried okra, fried pickles,
and macaroni and cheese. Barbecue platters with garlic toast and two
sides are around BZ$16 to BZ$30. Lazy Croc has very limited hours: it
is only open Thursday–Sunday 11 am–3 pm. Forget plastic—this is cash
only. And, yes, there are real crocs in the lagoon near (and even under)
the restaurant, but don't give them leftovers—feeding wild crocodiles is
illegal. Go by golf cart, cab (BZ$35 one-way from town), or water taxi
(get off at Grand Caribe). $ *Average main: $20* ⊠ *Beachfront, Buena
Vista Point, 15 Buena Vista, just north of Grand Caribe resort, North
Ambergris Caye* ⊹ *2½ miles (4 km) north of center of town and 100
yards north of Grand Caribe* ☎ *226/4015* ⊟ *No credit cards* ⊘ *Closed
Mon.–Wed. No dinner. Closes in mid-July for off-season break.*

$$$ ✕**Rendezvous Restaurant & Winery.** Belize's only Thai-French-Belizean
FRENCH restaurant combines local seafood with Thai spices and French and
Asian presentation. The menu changes frequently, with daily spe-
cials. Our favorites include pad thai and spider crabs served with
a spicy Singapore sauce. The owners, Glenn and Colleen Schweng-
inger, who have lived and worked in Thailand and Singapore, also
produce and bottle their own wines using imported grape concen-
trate. It's not bad. $ *Average main: $46 ⊠ 4 miles (6 km) north of
Sun Pedro, near Las Terrazas ☎ 226/3426 ⊕ ambergriscaye.com/
rendezvous ☉ No lunch.*

$$$ ✕**Rojo Beach Bar.** Chef Jeff Spiegel, who in a former life was a punk-
SEAFOOD rock record producer in California, leads this red-hot beach bar on
Fodor's Choice North Ambergris. Rojo Beach Bar, in a sultry open-air palapa on a
★ beautiful beach, has moved to more of a casual bar/bistro atmosphere
from a full-scale restaurant, but you can still get sophisticated snacks
like lobster pizza. The menu varies a good bit from day to day. Order
at the bar and then eat and drink at the beach or on comfy sofas in the
breezy lounge. Rojo serves killer frozen mojitos, martinis, and all kinds
of fascinating, boozy concoctions. If you feel like cooling off, there is
a swimming pool just for bar and restaurant guests. Reachable from
town by water taxi or golf cart (if it hasn't rained too much.) $ *Aver-
age main: $45 ⊠ Beachfront, North Ambergris, 5 miles (8 km) north of
town ☎ 226/4012 ⊕ www.rojolounge.com ⚓ Reservations not accepted
☉ Closed Sun. and Mon.*

SOUTH OF SAN PEDRO

$ ✕**Ali Baba.** This is the spot for takeout roast chicken, falafel, hummus,
MIDDLE EASTERN and other Middle Eastern/Lebanese dishes, at modest prices. $ *Average
main: $15 ⊠ Coconut Dr., across from Tropic Air terminal, San Pedro
☎ 226/4042 ⊕ www.aguallos.com/alibabas ⊟ No credit cards.*

$ ✕**The Baker.** Come to The Baker, in a new location and run by new
BAKERY owners, an Irish couple, for artisan breads, cookies, and pastries. The
Belizean cinnamon loaf is especially tasty, as are the cinnamon rolls,
coconut tarts, and peanut butter cookies. Try their cakes and other
desserts, too. You can buy freshly brewed coffee to go with your
breakfast pastries. $ *Average main: $8 ⊠ South of town near Marina's
grocery, Coconut Dr. (aka Seagrape Dr.), San Pedro ☎ 206/2036 ⊟ No
credit cards.*

$$$ ✕**Black Orchid.** Opened in late 2012, Black Orchid (unrelated to the
AMERICAN similarly named resort near Belize City) is a new option in upscale
dining on the island. In a raised house beside the sandy road about 2½
miles (4 km) south of town, the atmosphere is island-flavored, with a
thatch booth inside for the greeters and some Mayan-themed decor.
The luncheon choices range from beer-battered fried fish to sweet-
and-sour pork. The dinner menu includes grilled lobster (in season),
pork, and a boneless rib eye charbroiled on lava rocks and served with
mashed potatoes. For Sunday brunch try the eggs Benedict accompa-
nied by freshly made sangria. $ *Average main: $38 ⊠ S. Coconut Dr.,
about 2½ miles (4 km) south of town, San Pedro ☎ 206/2441 ⊕ www.
blackorchidrestaurant.com ☉ Closed Mon.*

3

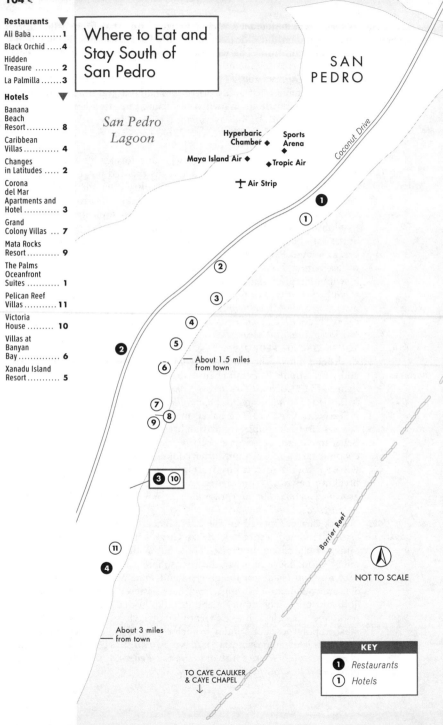

Where to Eat and Stay South of San Pedro

SAN PEDRO

San Pedro Lagoon

Coconut Drive

Hyperbaric Chamber ◆

Sports Arena ◆

Maya Island Air ◆

◆ Tropic Air

✚ Air Strip

— About 1.5 miles from town

— About 3 miles from town

Barrier Reef

NOT TO SCALE

TO CAYE CAULKER & CAYE CHAPEL
↓

KEY	
❶	*Restaurants*
①	*Hotels*

$$$ ✕ **Hidden Treasure.** Hidden away on a back street in a residential neigh-
SEAFOOD borhood south of town, at Hidden Treasure you dine romantically by
candlelight, in the sultry tropical air under a pitched roof set off by
bamboo, mahogany, and cabbage-bark wood. The signature barbe-
cue ribs are seasoned with traditional Garífuna spices and glazed with
pineapple or papaya sauce. Mojarro a la Lamanai is snapper seasoned
with Mayan spices and cooked in a banana leaf. $ *Average main: $38*
⊠ *Escalante Residential Area, 2715 Flamboyant Dr, San Pedro* ⊕ *about
1½ miles (2.4 km) south of town; go south on Coconut Dr. past Royal
Palm Villas and watch for signs* ☎ *226/4111* ⊕ *www.ambergriscaye.
com/hiddentreasure/index.html* ⊗ *No lunch.*

$$$$ ✕ **La Palmilla.** La Palmilla restaurant at Victoria House is classy without
ECLECTIC being stuffy and romantic without being precious. The setting, near
Fodor's Choice one of the Victoria House pools with views of the sea, in manicured
★ grounds, is among the most attractive in San Pedro. The restaurant
does an especially fine job with local seafood, especially grilled lobster.
Although there's a lovely indoor dining room, in good weather you
might prefer dining on the patio in the open air, with sea views and a
nice breeze from the water. $ *Average main: $55* ⊠ *Coconut Dr., at Vic-
toria House resort, San Pedro* ☎ *226/2067* ⊕ *www.victoria-house.com.*

$ ✕ **Mesa Cafe.** Mesa Cafe serves the island equivalent of fast food in a sur-
CAFÉ prisingly quiet setting. It's a great spot for an inexpensive lunch. Try the
FAMILY shrimp burger or fish tacos, and finish with craboo ice cream. $ *Average
main: $14* ⊠ *Vilma Linda Plaza, Tarpon St., San Pedro* ☎ *226/3444*
⊗ *Closed for dinner; open for breakfast and lunch daily.*

WHERE TO STAY

One of your biggest decisions in Ambergris Caye will be choosing a
place to stay. There are three basic options: in or near the town of San
Pedro, in the South Beach or South End area beyond town, or on North
Ambergris, beyond the river channel. Access to restaurants, bars, and
other activities is easiest in and around San Pedro. Accommodations
in and near town are generally simple and reasonably priced (BZ$50–
BZ$300), with a few notable upscale exceptions such as the deluxe The
Phoenix, but rooms on the main streets can be noisy from late-night
revelers and traffic.

For silence and sand, head out of town for resort-style accommoda-
tions. To get more privacy, consider the South End. Though it, too, is
developing rapidly, it's still less hectic than in town, and it's only a golf
cart or taxi ride away.

If you really want to get away, choose the more remote North Amber-
gris, which is reached mainly by water taxis and, with a recent change in
regulations, by cabs that currently go as far north as Las Terrazas Resort.

With the exception of a few budget places, nearly all the resorts on the
island are on the sea. Most are small, under 30 or 40 rooms, and nearly
all are four stories or less. Some are owner-managed. The newer resorts
and hotels are on North Ambergris Caye, of which the farthest-north
resort, Tranquility Bay, is about 12 miles (20 km) north of San Pedro,
or on the South End, where the most distant resorts are around 3 miles
(5 km) south of town.

■ TIP→ During the off-season (May–November), lodging properties often have walk-in rates that are up to a third less than advertised rates. But you'll usually have to ask for them, as otherwise you'll pay the regular rate.

CONDOTELS Besides full-service hotels and resorts, the island has condotels, which are individually owned condos managed by an on-site management company. The condo units usually are offered on a nightly basis, and in most cases the properties have full kitchens and most of the amenities of a regular hotel, except perhaps a restaurant.

VACATION HOMES Ambergris Caye has dozens of homes that can be rented on a weekly basis. These range from simple two-bedroom cottages that go for BZ$1,000–BZ$2,000 a week to luxurious four- or five-bedroom villas, which might rent for BZ$5,000–BZ$10,000 or more weekly. In many cases credit cards are not accepted. In addition to the local rental management companies listed here, also check online for Vacation Rentals By Owner (🌐 *www.vrbo.com*). VRBO lists well over 100 vacation rentals, more than any local management company.

Also on the island are clusters of upscale homes or villas that are offered for weekly, and sometimes nightly, rental. These luxury homes, often with 4,000–5,000 square feet of space or more, typically have a shared pool and other resort-like amenities. Although they usually have no restaurant, they may offer food service prepared by a chef and delivered to guests in the homes.

Caye Management. This is the island's oldest rental management company and typically has around 20 vacation homes for rent. [$] *Rooms from: $650* ✉ *Casa Coral, Barrier Reef Dr., at north end of town, San Pedro* ☎ *226/3077* 🌐 *www.cayemanagement.com* 🛏 *Around 20 vacation rental houses and suites* 💳 *No credit cards.*

TIME-SHARES Time-shares have been on the island for years. Captain Morgan's is one of them. It opened a small casino at its property in mid-2011. Reef Village, on North Ambergris just beyond the bridge, was known for its aggressive time-share touts, but in 2011 it ran into financial and management problems with its time-shares, and the future course of this development is up in the air. Fairly new to the island are upscale "fractional ownership" or "residential club" resorts, which sell longer-term memberships and rights to use the property, typically for two, four, or six months a year. One of these, Sueño del Mar, opened on North Ambergris in 2006 but shut down in 2010, leaving more than 100 owners at least temporarily out in the cold, before reopening in 2011. The moral? Think twice before putting any money in a time-share or fractional ownership scheme.

SAN PEDRO TOWN

$$ RENTAL 🏨 **Caye Casa.** This small complex on the beach at the very north end of town was designed to have a colonial atmosphere—with thatched roofs on the porches, wooden shutters, and traditional hardwood railings—but built to modern architectural standards. **Pros:** pleasant, well-designed small condo colony; quiet; beachfront spot. **Cons:** older casitas are fairly basic; pool is quite small. [$] *Rooms from: $253* ✉ *Beachfront, at north end of town, Boca del Rio Dr.* ☎ *226/2880, 800/936–3433 in U.S.* 🌐 *www.cayecasa.com* 🛏 *3 villas, 2 casitas, 2 rooms* 🍴 *No meals.*

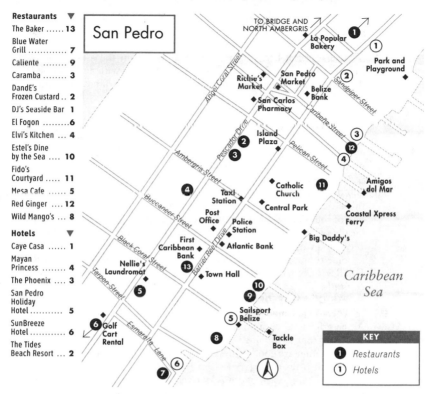

Restaurants ▼

The Baker **13**
Blue Water Grill **7**
Caliente **9**
Caramba **3**
DandE's Frozen Custard .. **2**
DJ's Seaside Bar **1**
El Fogon **6**
Elvi's Kitchen ... **4**
Estel's Dine by the Sea **10**
Fido's Courtyard **11**
Mesa Cafe **5**
Red Ginger **12**
Wild Mango's ... **8**

Hotels ▼

Caye Casa **1**
Mayan Princess **4**
The Phoenix **3**
San Pedro Holiday Hotel........... **5**
SunBreeze Hotel............ **6**
The Tides Beach Resort ... **2**

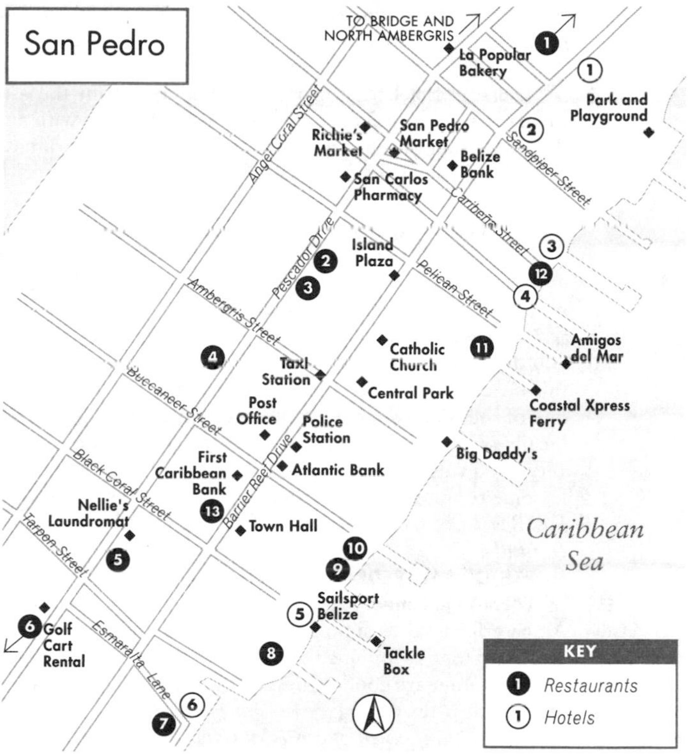
San Pedro
TO BRIDGE AND NORTH AMBERGRIS
La Popular Bakery
Park and Playground
Angel Coral Street
Richie's Market
San Pedro Market
Belize Bank
San Carlos Pharmacy
Sandpiper Street
Caribeña Street
Pescador Drive
Island Plaza
Pelican Street
Ambergris Street
Catholic Church
Amigos del Mar
Taxi Station
Central Park
Coastal Xpress Ferry
Buccaneer Street
Post Office
Police Station
Big Daddy's
Barrier Reef Drive
First Caribbean Bank
Atlantic Bank
Black Coral Street
Nellie's Laundromat
Town Hall
Caribbean Sea
Tarpon Street
Sailsport Belize
Golf Cart Rental
Esmeralda Lane
Tackle Box
KEY
Restaurants
Hotels

$$$ HOTEL

🏨 **Mayan Princess.** Sitting pretty and pink in the middle of town, this long-established seafront three-story condo hotel has rattan furniture covered with pastel-color fabrics, lacking only a pool to make it a perfect mid-level choice. **Pros:** central in-town location; pleasant one-bedroom efficiencies with sea views; near good dive shop. **Cons:** no swimming pool on-site; beach area has heavy boat and pedestrian traffic. *$ Rooms from: $345 ✉ Beachfront, Barrier Reef Dr., in center of town ☎ 226/2778, 800/850–4101 🌐 www.mayanprincesshotel.com 🛏 23 1-bedroom suites 🍴 No meals.*

$$$$ RESORT Fodor's Choice ★

🏨 **The Phoenix.** This luxury beachfront condominium resort has spacious suites, luxuriously outfitted with custom closets, cabinets, and doors in beautiful tropical hardwoods, stainless-steel kitchen appliances, washer-dryers, and original art. **Pros:** deluxe, stylish, beautifully designed condo suites; in-town's most luxurious hotel; first-rate service. **Cons:** for some it lacks a get-away-from-it-all feel. *$ Rooms from: $872 ✉ Barrier Reef Dr., beachfront, at north end of town ☎ 226/2083, 877/822–5512 in U.S. and Canada 🌐 www.thephoenixbelize.com 🛏 30 suites (not all in rental pool) 🍴 No meals.*

$$ HOTEL

🏨 **San Pedro Holiday Hotel.** Trimmed in cheery pink-and-white colors, this spic-and-span quartet of colonial-style houses on the water is near the center of San Pedro. **Pros:** central location; affordable, clean rooms; island's first hotel. **Cons:** no pool; in-town beach isn't very good for

swimming; busy town area can be noisy. [$] *Rooms from: $278* ✉ *Beachfront, Barrier Reef Dr.* ☎ *226/2014, 713/893–3825 in U.S.* 🌐 *www.sanpedroholiday.com* 🛏 *16 rooms, 1 apartment* 🍴 *No meals.*

$$$ HOTEL 🏨 **SunBreeze Hotel.** A midsize resort across from the airstrip at the town's busy southern edge (though there's no issue with aircraft noise), the waterfront SunBreeze has large rooms that surround a U-shaped, plant-filled courtyard. **Pros:** comfortable, well-run; motel-like lodging; some rooms handicap-accessible; good restaurant on-site (under separate management). **Cons:** not much of a beach; rates have crept up. [$] *Rooms from: $412* ✉ *Coconut Dr., across from Tropic Air terminal and airstrip* ☎ *226/2191, 800/688–0191 in U.S. and Canada* 🌐 *www.sunbreeze.net* 🛏 *43 rooms* 🍴 *No meals.*

$ HOTEL 🏨 **The Tides Beach Resort.** If diving is your reason for being in Belize, and you don't want to spend a ton of money, you couldn't do better than this beachfront hotel at the north end of town, owned by Patojo Paz, one of the island's most experienced dive masters, and his wife. **Pros:** locally owned beachfront hotel; respected dive shop, Patojo's, on-site; very good value. **Cons:** rooms aren't overly large; beds and furnishings in some rooms need upgrading. [$] *Rooms from: $164* ✉ *Boca del Rio Dr., Beachfront, north end of town* ☎ *226/2283* 🌐 *www.ambergriscaye.com/tides* 🛏 *12 rooms, 3 suites* 🍴 *Breakfast.*

NORTH OF SAN PEDRO

$$$ RESORT 🏨 **Ak'bol Yoga Retreat & Eco-Resort.** This hip little beach resort on North Ambergris has seven simple thatch cabanas, some with sea views, around a natural stone swimming pool. **Pros:** cool, small, laid-back resort; rooms and restaurant are good values. **Cons:** you may feel like an outcast if you can't do downward dog. [$] *Rooms from: BZ$336* ✉ *North Ambergris, 1¾ miles (3 km) north of center of town* ☎ *226/2073* 🌐 *www.akbol.com* 🛏 *7 cabanas, 30 rooms with shared baths* 🍴 *No meals.*

$$$$ RESORT Fodor's Choice ★ 🏨 **Azul Resort.** This small resort has two-level, 3,000-square-foot, two-bedroom villas on 10 private acres of beachfront. **Pros:** amazing private beachfront villas with every luxury; five-star service. **Cons:** not for those on a budget. [$] *Rooms from: BZ$1199* ✉ *North Ambergris, 5 miles (8 km) north of San Pedro* ☎ *226/4012* 🌐 *www.azulbelize.com* 🛏 *2 beach houses* 🍴 *No meals.*

$$$ RESORT FAMILY 🏨 **Belizean Shores.** If you're looking for a peaceful resort setting at competitive prices, this older beachfront condotel on North Ambergris with one-bedroom units is a good choice. **Pros:** comfortable condos; great pool; lots of on-site sports activities. **Cons:** beach swimming not that great; getting into town requires a boat ride or long golf cart ride; some units need updating and refurbishing. [$] *Rooms from: BZ$375* ✉ *3½ miles (6 km) north of San Pedro* ☎ *226/4478, 800/319–9026 in U.S. and Canada* 🌐 *www.belizeanshores.com* 🛏 *48 suites* 🍴 *No meals.*

$$$$ RESORT FAMILY 🏨 **Coco Beach Resort.** Coco Beach Resort is one of the top-end condotels on the island, with spacious one- and two-bedroom suites and large rooms on an attractive stretch of beach about 3½ miles (6 km) north of San Pedro. **Pros:** big, beautiful suites; gorgeous swimming pools; nice beach. **Cons:** food service is limited and gets mixed reviews; getting to town requires a boat ride; no breakfast served on-site—you have to walk up to Belizean Shores for your morning meal; no elevators,

and upper level suites require walking a lot of steps. $ *Rooms from: BZ$780* ⊠ *Beachfront, 4 miles (7 km) north of San Pedro* ☏ *877/744–3028 in U.S. and Canada, 226/4840* ⊕ *www.cocobeachbelize.com* ➴ *45 1- and 2-bedroom condo suites, 17 rooms* ⦿| *No meals.*

$$$
RESORT
FAMILY

⛺ **Cocotal Inn & Cabanas.** If you're looking for a small, homey spot on the beach, Cocotal could be it. **Pros:** friendly, small resort on the beach; pool; affordable rates. **Cons:** no restaurant on-site. $ *Rooms from: BZ$305* ⊠ *North Ambergris, 2½ miles (4 km) north of the center of town, San Pedro* ☏ *226/2097* ⊕ *www.cocotalbelize.com* ➴ *1 casita, 2 cabanas, 1 1-bedroom suite, 1 2-bedroom suite* ⦿| *No meals.*

$$$$
RESORT
Fodor's Choice
★

⛺ **El Pescador.** Nearly every hotel on Ambergris Caye claims that it can arrange fishing trips, but this resort really has the best angling resources, plus beautiful suites and grounds as well. **Pros:** this is the place for saltwater anglers, but it's a good choice even if you don't fish; top-notch service. **Cons:** rooms in original lodge are not as spacious as they could be; not inexpensive. $ *Rooms from: BZ$600* ⊠ *2½ miles (4 km) north of San Pedro* ☏ *226/2398, 800/242–2017 in U.S. and Canada* ⊕ *www.elpescador.com* ➴ *13 rooms, 8 villas* ⦿| *Multiple meal plans.*

$$$$
RESORT
Fodor's Choice
★

⛺ **El Secreto.** Opened in 2012, El Secreto is a beachfront resort with 13 stunning thatch villas—some beachfront, others around a small lagoon or in gardens—that is so appealing you may not even notice how remote the location is. **Pros:** like being on a private island; stunning large cabanas; excellent staff and service. **Cons:** you're in a remote area and miss a lot of the great restaurants and nightlife of San Pedro; very expensive; be prepared for some bugs. $ *Rooms from: BZ$1428* ⊠ *11 miles (18 km) north of San Pedro, Beachfront, Ambergris Caye* ☏ *236/5111, 800/479–5037* ⊕ *www.elsecretobelize.com* ➴ *13 villas* ⦿| *Multiple meal plans.*

$$$$
RENTAL
Fodor's Choice
★

⛺ **Grand Caribe Resort and Condominiums.** Set in an arc on a 5-acre beachfront site, Grand Caribe's 72 super-luxury condos, in eight four-story, red-tiled-roof clusters, face the sea and a 500-foot stretch of sandy beach. **Pros:** super-luxury condos, all with views of the sea; short hike, golf cart ride, or taxi ride to restaurants and to town. **Cons:** pricey but worth it if you want the best; taxi to town is BZ$35. $ *Rooms from: BZ$1069* ⊠ *Tres Cocos area of North Ambergris, 1¼ miles (2 km) north of bridge* ☏ *226/4726, 800/488–5903 from U.S. or Canada* ⊕ *www.grandcaribe.com* ➴ *72 condominium suites* ⦿| *No meals.*

$$$$
RENTAL

⛺ **La Perla del Caribe.** Twelve deluxe villas (eight for rental) command the beachfront about 6 miles (10 km) north of town. **Pros:** very upscale villas with every amenity; lovely beach. **Cons:** expensive; somewhat remote; no on-site restaurant. $ *Rooms from: BZ$1140* ⊠ *North Ambergris, 6 miles (10 km) north of San Pedro, Beachfront* ☏ *226/5888, 866/290–6341 in U.S. and Canada* ⊕ *www.laperladelcaribe.com* ➴ *8 rental villas.*

$$$$
RENTAL
Fodor's Choice
★

⛺ **Las Terrazas.** Las Terrazas luxury condos have 9-foot ceilings, travertine tile floors, fully equipped kitchens with Brazilian granite countertops, cable TV, and high-speed Internet. **Pros:** luxury condos on over 500 feet of beachfront; elegant interior design; good on-site dive shop. **Cons:** not inexpensive, especially for larger units. $ *Rooms from: BZ$664* ⊠ *North Ambergris, 4 miles (6½ km) north of town, Beachfront* ☏ *226/4249, 800/447–1553 in U.S. and Canada* ⊕ *www.lasterrazasresort.com* ➴ *39 condo suites (39 additional units planned)* ⦿| *Multiple meal plans.*

$$$$
RESORT
Fodor's Choice
★

Matachica Resort & Spa. Thatch casitas in shades of mango, banana, and blueberry offset by brilliant white sand give this deluxe beachfront resort a Gauguin-like quality. **Pros:** charming collection of casitas on the beach; friendly staff and good management; postcard-pretty beach. **Cons:** restaurant and bar prices are steep; air-conditioning in some units doesn't quite do the job. $ *Rooms from: BZ$663 ⊠ 5 miles (8 km) north of San Pedro, Beachfront ☎ 226/5010, 223/0002 reservations line ⊕ www.matachica.com ⊅ 21 casitas, 2 2-bedroom villas, 1 3-bedroom house ⦿ Multiple meal plans.*

$$$$
RENTAL
Fodor's Choice
★

Seascape Villas. Six posh homes spread across 4 beachfront acres are among the island's most exclusive properties. **Pros:** deluxe private villas; sophisticated designs; stunning sea views. **Cons:** no restaurant on-site. $ *Rooms from: BZ$1035 ⊠ North Ambergris, 3½ miles (6 km) north of San Pedro, Beachfront ☎ 226/2119, 888/753–5164 ⊕ www. seascapebelize.com ⊅ 6 beach houses.*

SOUTH OF SAN PEDRO

$$
RESORT

Banana Beach Resort. Original management has reclaimed Banana Beach, bringing it back to the casual, friendly, well-run, beachfront resort that it was for many years. **Pros:** recovering under original management; good value; friendly staff. **Cons:** some furnishings are a little dated; beach has a seawall. $ *Rooms from: BZ$262 ⊠ Coconut Dr., 1½ miles (2½ km) south of San Pedro, San Pedro ☎ 226/3890, 877/288–1011 in U.S. and Canada ⊕ www.bananabeach.com ⊅ 28 rooms, 43 suites ⦿ Breakfast.*

$$
RESORT
FAMILY

Caribbean Villas. It may not be as flashy as some of the newer resorts on the island, but Caribbean Villas, with its 2½ acres of gardens, a bird sanctuary, and lovely quiet beachfront, is a pleasant, affordable, and low-key alternative to the glitzier developments. **Pros:** haven of quiet in developed area; good value: good beach. **Cons:** no full-service restaurant; some units could use updating. $ *Rooms from: BZ$231 ⊠ Seagrape Dr., 1 mile (1½ km) south of town, San Pedro ☎ 226/2715, 866/290–6341 in U.S. and Canada ⊕ www.caribbeanvillashotel.com ⊅ 5 rooms, 9 suites ⦿ No meals.*

$$
B&B/INN

Changes In Latitudes. A new owner has done good things with the first true B&B in San Pedro, adding new mattresses, a fridge in every room, new air-conditioners, and doing some refurbishing. **Pros:** good value; cheerful B&B atmosphere. **Cons:** smallish rooms; not on water; close to busy street. $ *Rooms from: BZ$251 ⊠ 36 Coconut Dr., ¼ mile (½ km) south of San Pedro ☎☎ 226/2986 ⊕ www.ambergriscaye.com/latitudes ⊅ 6 rooms ⦿ Breakfast.*

$
HOTEL

Corona del Mar Apartments and Hotel. One of the best values on the island, the beachfront Corona del Mar with new pool has affordable rooms and ocean-view apartment suites with kitchens. **Pros:** top value; pleasant sea-front rooms; new pool; friendly staff. **Cons:** not fancy; included breakfast is quite modest. $ *Rooms from: BZ$196 ⊠ Coconut Dr., 1 mile (1½ km) south of town ☎ 226/2055, 800/520–8110 in U.S. and Canada ⊕ www. coronadelmarhotel.com ⊅ 12 rooms, 4 suites, 1 cottage ⦿ Breakfast.*

$$$$
RENTAL

Grand Colony Villas. These are some of the more upscale condos on the island: two- and three-bedroom, two-bath apartments, ranging from 1,100 to more than 1,900 square feet, with tall ceilings, marble or hardwood floors, mahogany doors and cabinets, and luxurious furnishings.

3

NAVIGATING AMBERGRIS CAYE

Since places around here lack proper addresses, here's a list of hotels and restaurants in this area from north to south.

- Tranquility Bay Resort
- El Secreto
- Portofino
- La Perla del Caribe
- Matachica and Mambo
- Azul Resort and Rojo Bar
- Rendezvous
- Las Terrazas
- Seascape Villas
- Belizean Shores
- Coco Beach
- Capricorn
- El Pescador
- Aji
- Lazy Croc
- Grand Caribe
- Ak'bol
- Cocotal
- Palapa Bar

Pros: deluxe condo villas; beautifully finished and furnished; on a lovely beach. **Cons:** spendy; no restaurant on-site. [$] *Rooms from: BZ$1088* ✉ *Coconut Dr., 1½ miles (3 km) south of town, San Pedro* ☎ *226/3739, 866/620–9521 in U.S. and Canada* 🌐 *www.grandcolonyvillas.com* 🛏 *21 condo apartments* 🍴 *No meals.*

$$$ RESORT 🏨 **Mata Rocks Resort.** The squeaky-clean rooms at this intimate, mid-level hotel right on a nice stretch of beach, about a 30-minute walk or 10-minute bike ride from town, have sea views and breezes. **Pros:** small beachside resort; good value. **Cons:** no restaurant on-site. [$] *Rooms from: BZ$316* ✉ *Coconut Dr., 1½ miles (2½ km) south of town, San Pedro* ☎ *226/2336, 888/628–2757 in U.S. and Canada* 🌐 *www.matarocks.com* 🛏 *17 rooms* 🍴 *Breakfast.*

$$$ RENTAL 🏨 **The Palms Oceanfront Suites.** Stay here for the sea views, beachside vibe, and ultra-convenient location near town. **Pros:** comfortable beachfront apartments; convenient location near town; good management; next to best in-town beach. **Cons:** small, shaded pool; not as upscale as some of the island's new luxe condo developments; no fitness room or bar/restaurant on-site; rates have crept up. [$] *Rooms from: BZ$485* ✉ *Coconut Dr., at south edge of town, San Pedro* ☎ *226/3322* 🌐 *www.belizepalms.com* 🛏 *8 2-bedroom apartments, 5 1-bedroom apartments* 🍴 *No meals.*

$$$$ RENTAL Fodor's Choice ★ 🏨 **Pelican Reef Villas.** While listening to the pool's trickling turquoise waterfall, it's easy to believe you've stumbled upon a hidden tropical treasure; however, the faux cave is a swim-up bar, and Pelican Reef is only a little south (2½ miles or 4 km) of San Pedro's bustle. **Pros:** well-run condo colony in quiet south-end location; luxurious accommodations; friendly staff; good beach area. **Cons:** no full-service restaurant on-site; at the far south end of most current development on the island; a lot of steps to climb to upper-level units. [$] *Rooms from: BZ$804* ✉ *Coconut Dr., 2½ miles (4 km) south of town, San Pedro* ☎ *226/2352, 281/394–3739 U.S. reservations number* 🌐 *www.pelicanreefvillas.com* 🛏 *24 condo apartments* 🍴 *Breakfast.*

$$$
RESORT
Fodor'sChoice
★

Victoria House. With its bougain-villea-filled gardens, this property about 2 miles (3 km) south of San Pedro has the style and seclusion of a dignitary's residence, if the dignitary lived on a stunning beach, loved good food and drink, and preferred to walk around barefoot. $ *Rooms from: BZ$478* ⊠ *Coconut Dr., 2 miles (3 km) south of town* ☎ *226/2067, 800/247–5159 in U.S. and Canada, 713/344–2340 U.S. number* ⊕ *www.victoria-house.com* ⌨ *14 rooms, 4 casitas, 3 suites, 8 villas* ⦿ *Multiple meal plans.*

$$$$
RENTAL

Villas at Banyan Bay. If you enjoy little luxuries like a whirlpool bath in your room, this red tile–roofed complex about 1½ miles (2½ km) south of town may suit you splendidly. **Pros:** well-maintained two- and three-bedroom condos, ideal for families or two couples; one of island's best beaches. **Cons:** restaurant is expensive; tribulations of bank foreclosure and operation by various hired hands has taken its toll. $ *Rooms from: BZ$600* ⊠ *Beachfront, Coconut Dr., 1½ miles (2½ km) south of town, San Pedro* ☎ *226/3739, 866/352–1163 in U.S.* ⊕ *www.banyanbay.com* ⌨ *42 suites* ⦿ *No meals.*

$$$
RESORT
Fodor'sChoice
★

Xanadu Island Resort. Billed as the "world's first monolithic dome resort," Xanadu has thatch-roof domes, creating a beach resort that can withstand winds up to 300 mph while providing a delightful seafront vacation. **Pros:** friendly management; attractive suites; tropically perfect pool; convenient location. **Cons:** seawall at beach; no restaurant or bar on-site. $ *Rooms from: BZ$468* ⊠ *Sea Grape Dr., 1 mile (1½ km) south of town, San Pedro* ☎ *226/2814, 866/351–4752* ⊕ *www.xanaduresort-belize.com* ⌨ *19 suites* ⦿ *No meals.*

CAYO ESPANTO

$$$$
ALL-INCLUSIVE
Fodor'sChoice
★

Cayo Espanto. A group of seven deluxe beachfront villas is all there is on the small private island in the bay on the backside of Ambergris Caye, and the entire island staff is dedicated to giving you a memorable experience. **Pros:** over-the-top luxury and service; beautiful views; your every wish is yours immediately (for a price, of course). **Cons:** island is on the back side of Ambergris Caye, not on the main Caribbean Sea. $ *Rooms from: BZ$3883* ⊠ *3 miles (5 km) west of Ambergris Caye, Cayo Espanto* ☎ *888/861–4282, 910/323–8355 in U.S.* ⊕ *www.aprivateisland.com* ⌨ *7 villas* ⦿ *All-inclusive.*

NIGHTLIFE

San Pedro has the most active nightlife scene in Belize, but, still, don't expect Miami's South Beach. A few in-town spots such as Fido's have live music. At Jaguar's Temple nightclub, the action starts after 10 or 11 and often goes until almost daybreak. (Be careful going back to your hotel in the middle of the night after sampling rums—take a taxi if possible.) There are plenty of spots just to have a cold one, including some classic beach and pier bars like BC's, Tackle Box, Wet Willy's, and Palapa Bar, or tonier spots like Rojo Bar. There's a small casino at Captain Morgan's on North Ambergris. Many hotels have bars that mostly draw their own guests, but anyone, staying there or not, is welcome. Among the better resort bars are those at Victoria House, Banana Beach Resort, Spindrift (with a hilarious betting game on Thursday involving live chickens and where they poop), Pedro's Hotel, Mata Rocks (which has a classic small thatch beach bar), Matachica, and Ramon's Village. Karaoke is big in Belize, and some bars and clubs in San Pedro have karaoke nights, which are as much for locals as visitors. In late January and early February, singer Jerry Jeff Walker holds "Camp Belize," two weeklong events in San Pedro during which Walker puts on shows for his loyal fans.

BARS AND CLUBS

BC's Beach Bar. BC's Beach Bar is a popular seafront bar and hangout at the south edge of town. ⊠ *Beachfront, just south of SunBreeze Hotel, San Pedro* ☎ *226/3289.*

Fido's. Under a giant seaside thatch palapa, Fido's is usually jumping and has live music some nights starting around 9 pm. Truth be known, Fido's is a living on its reputation a bit. Bar food now is so-so, service can be spotty, but the beer is cold, and the setting is still fun. ⊠ *Barrier Reef Dr., San Pedro* ☎ *226/2056* ⊕ *www.fidosbelize.com.*

Jaguar's Temple. Jaguar's Temple is San Pedro's largest dance club. You can party here on weekends until the wee hours. ⊠ *Barrier Reef Dr. and Pelican St., across from Central Park, San Pedro* ☎ *226/4077* ⊕ *www.jaguarstempleclub.com* ☉ *Thurs.–Sat. 9 pm–4 am.*

Palapa Bar and Grill. The setting and festive atmosphere at this popular thatch-roof bar at the end of a pier are what draw the crowds here, not the food (although the sandwiches, burgers, and seafood aren't bad for bar food). The breezy two-story palapa at the end of a pier, about ¼ mile (1 km) north of the bridge, has stunning views of the sea and reef by day; by night, the colorful bar lighting lends a festive air. Bring a bathing suit and jump in the sea beside the pier (there are handy inner tubes). The Palapa doesn't rock all night, though—it usually closes around 9 pm. ⊠ *Beachfront, North Ambergris* ☎ *226/2528* ⊕ *www.palapabarandgrill.com* ☉ *Daily 10–9.*

Pedro's Sports Bar & Pizzeria. If you're up for a cold drink and pizza and watching sports on large-screen TVs, Pedro's is your spot. It attracts mostly expats and visitors. There are poker games some nights, and karaoke on Thursday. The decor runs to walls covered with hundreds of Jägermeister bottles. ⊠ *Seagrape Dr., south of town, San Pedro* ☎ *226/3825, 206/2198* ⊕ *www.pedroshotel.com.*

Road Kill Bar. This popular roadside bar serves a wide variety of beers (for Belize) and, despite the name, also grills a good hamburger. Karaoke on Wednesday nights. ⊠ *Coconut Dr., about ¼ mile (½ km) from south edge of town, San Pedro, San Pedro* ☉ *Daily 4 pm–midnight.*

Rojo Beach Bar. This stunning beachfront bar on North Ambergris is a sophisticated, yet casual, romantic place to sip a Shark Bite (light rum, coconut rum, Meyer's rum, mango juice and pineapple juice) or a frozen mojito. Great pizzas and light meals. ⊠ *5 miles (8 km) north of town, Beachfront, North Ambergris Caye* 📞 *226/4012* ⊕ *www.rojolounge. com* 🕐 *Tues.–Sat.*

Tackle Box Bar & Grill. The motto of this burgers-and-beer waterfront spot is "Lunch all day—party all night." The Tackle Box, on a pier in the middle of town, is one of the island's most popular bars, attracting as many as 500 patrons on weekends. Pub fare such as wings and burgers is served. ⊠ *Beachfront on pier, San Pedro* 📞 *226/4313* ⊕ *www. tackleboxbarandgrill.com* 🕐 *Closed Mon.*

Wahoo's Lounge. On the odd side of the nightlife spectrum is the Chicken Drop, held on Thursday nights at Wahoo's Lounge (formerly Pier Lounge) beachfront at the Spindrift Hotel. Bet on a numbered square, and if the chicken poops on your square, you win the pot, which can get up to around BZ$1,000. ⊠ *At Spindrift Hotel, Beachfront, Barrier Reef Dr., near Buccaneer St., San Pedro* 📞 *226/2002* 🕐 *Daily noon–midnight; chicken drop starts around 6 pm Thurs.*

Wet Willy's Cantina. Wet Willy's is a wood-paneled, thatch-roof bar at the end of a 340-foot pier at the north end of town. There's indoor and outdoor seating, with live music some nights. Under new management in 2012, the boathouse bar began focusing more on food, offering smoked barbecue chicken, pork, and other meats. ⊠ *At Wet Willy's pier, Beachfront, Boca del Rio area, San Pedro* 📞 *226/4136* ⊕ *www.wetwillysbelize.com* 🕐 *Bar open daily 11 am–midnight; food service Tues.–Sat. 11:30–9.*

CASINO

Captain Morgan's Retreat Casino. The small casino at Captain Morgan's Retreat, a time-share resort, is billed as "Las Vegas–style" with about 40 slot and video poker machines, live table games, poker tournaments, and a full bar. It's currently the only true casino on the island. ⊠ *3 miles (5 km) north of the bridge, Captain Morgan's Retreat, North Ambergris Caye* 📞 *226/2207, 888/653 in U.S. and Canada* ⊕ *www. captainmorgans.com.*

MOVIE THEATER

Paradise Theater. The Paradise Theater is part of the troubled Reef Village condo and timeshare development, though it is now under new management. Here you can watch first-run or near-first-run movies in air-conditioned comfort and with Dolby 5.1 sound for as little as BZ$5. The theater, which has 300- and 150-seat rooms, is also used for live shows. If you're thirsty, there's a bar. ■**TIP→ If you're staying in town or south and don't want to pay the BZ$10 fee to take your golf cart across the bridge, you can park it on the south side of the bridge and walk over (no toll for pedestrians), as the theater is a just a few hundred feet from the bridge.** ⊠ *Golf cart path, North Ambergris, just across the bridge near the Reef Village development, San Pedro* 📞 *636/8123.*

SHOPPING

Barrier Reef Drive, formerly sandy Front Street, but sadly now paved with concrete cobblestones, is San Pedro's Street of Shopping Dreams—it's lined with souvenir shops complemented by restaurants, small hotels, banks, and other anchors of tourist life on the island. Stores with more local appeal are on Pescador Drive (Middle Street) and Angel Coral Street (Back Street), especially at the north end of town. Barrier Reef Drive is closed to golf carts and vehicles on weekends, starting around 6 pm Friday, and local vendors set up shop selling locally made jewelry and wood carvings (they're also out during the week in high season). Except for these items, few are made on the island. Most of the souvenir shops sell crafts from Guatemala and Mexico, along with carved wood and slate from the mainland.

Belizean hot sauces, such as Marie Sharp's and Gallon Jug's Lissette Sauce, along with local rums, make good souvenirs; they're cheaper in grocery stores (try Pescador Drive and Angel Coral Street) than in gift shops. To avoid worsening the plight of endangered sea life, avoid buying souvenirs made from black coral or turtle shell.

Vendors on the beach occasionally try to sell you carvings, jewelry, Guatemalan fabrics, and sometimes drugs, but they're not pushy.

Belizean Arts. The first art gallery in Belize, established more than 20 years ago by Londoner Lyndsey Hackston, Belizean Arts today has the largest selection of art by Belizeans and Belize residents of any gallery in the country, with paintings by Walter Castillo, Pen Cayetano, Nelson Young, Leo Vasquez, Piva, Eduardo García, Curvin Mitchell, Jorge Landero, and others. The gallery also carries art by Cuban and other Caribbean artists, along with ceramics, jewelry, and other crafts. ⊠ *Fido's Courtyard, Barrier Reef Dr., San Pedro* ☎ *226/3019* ⊕ *www.belizeanarts.com.*

D & G Fine Jewelry and Art. This long-established shop crafts locally made jewelry. We encourage you not to buy items made of black coral, because it is highly endangered. ⊠ *Across from Super Buy grocery, 17 Angel Coral St., aka Back St., San Pedro* ☎ *226/2069* ⊕ *ambergriscaye. com/DandG.*

Graniel's Dreamland Construction & Cabinet Shop. Graniel's Dreamland, the showroom for Armando Graniel's beautiful carpentry, has high-quality wood chairs, tables, and other furniture and furnishings, made from Belizean tropical hardwoods, some of which the shop will break down and package for carrying back on the airplane or for shipping. ⊠ *Pescador Dr., San Pedro* ☎ *226/2938* ⊕ *www.granielsdreamlandbelize.com.*

Island Supermarket. Island Supermarket has the largest selection of groceries, liquor, and beer, along with hot sauces and other Belizean-produced items, though it's not the cheapest place in San Pedro. Grocery prices in San Pedro generally are 20% to 75% higher than in supermarkets in the United States, except for a few items, such as rum, produced in Belize, and Island Supermarket's prices are high even by San Pedro standards. ⊠ *Coconut Dr., south of town, across from Bowen & Bowen Belikin distributors, San Pedro* ☎ *226/2972.*

Marina's Store. Marina's Store about 1 mile (1½ km) south of town has good prices for groceries but only a small selection. ✉ *Seagrape Dr., about 1 mile (1½ km) south of town, San Pedro* ☎ *226/3647.*

Mata Grande Grocery. This little grocery serves residents and condo guests on North Ambergris. You can order and pay online, and Mata Grande will deliver groceries to your vacation home rental or condo north of the Boca del Rio bridge. ✉ *4½ miles (7½ km) north of the bridge, North Ambergris* ☎ *629/7411* ⊕ *www.matagrandegrocery.com.*

San Pedro Supermarket. One of the less expensive places to buy groceries is San Pedro Supermarket. ✉ *Lagoon St., at traffic circle at north end of town off Pescador Dr., San Pedro* ☎ *226/3446.*

Super Buy. Many local residents buy their groceries at Super Buy, because of lower prices. ✉ *Angel Coral St., aka Back St., San Pedro* ☎ *226/4667.*

Toucan Gift Shops. For gaudy geegaws and unabashedly touristy souvenirs, the Toucan Gift Shops, including Toucan Too, all sporting the bright green, yellow, and red Toucan logo, are hard to miss. ✉ *Barrier Reef Dr., San Pedro* ☎ *226/3263.*

Wine De Vine. Wine De Vine has the best selection of wines on the island, many from Chile and Argentina, and imported cheeses, at prices (due to import taxes) roughly double the cost in the United States. ✉ *Coconut Dr., next to Island Supermarket, San Pedro* ☎ *226/3430* ⊕ *www.winedevine.com* ⊘ *Closed Sun.*

SPORTS AND THE OUTDOORS
TENNIS
The San Pedro Family Fitness Club. The San Pedro Family Fitness Club has two hard-surfaced outdoor tennis courts, along with a large swimming pool and a fully equipped air-conditioned gym open to the public. Day, weekly, and monthly passes available. ✉ *½ mile (1 km) south of town, San Pedro* ✛ *From town, go south on Coconut Dr. until you reach Crazy Canucks and Road Kill bars, at corner of Coconut and Hurricane Sts. Turn west toward lagoon. Go 3 blocks to Fitness Club.* ☎ *226/4749* ⊕ *www.sanpedrofitness.com.*

CAYE CAULKER

5 miles (8 km) south of Ambergris Caye, 18 miles (29 km) northeast of Belize City.

A half-hour away from San Pedro by water taxi and sharing essentially the same reef and sea ecosystems, Caye Caulker is very different from its big sister island, Ambergris Caye. It's smaller (with a population of around 1,500), less developed, way more relaxed, and less expensive.

Caye Caulker has long been a stop on the Central America backpacker trail, and it remains Belize's most popular budget destination, although more upscale lodgings are opening and the island now has several condo developments. Still, flowers outnumber cars 1,000 to 1 (golf carts, bicycles, and bare feet are the preferred means of transportation).

As you might guess from all the "no shirt, no shoes, no problem" signs at the bars, the living is relatively easy here. This is the kind of place where many of the listings in the telephone directory give addresses like "near football field." However, Caye Corker, as it's sometimes called in Belize (or Cayo Hicaco in Spanish, a reference to the coco plums on the island), isn't immune to change. Many hotels have added air-conditioning, and the island now has cybercafés and several upmarket restaurants and fairly upscale hotels. Still, Caye Caulker remains the epitome of laid-back, and as development continues at a fevered pace on neighboring Ambergris Caye, Caulker's simpler charms exercise even more appeal to those who seek an affordable and relaxing island experience.

For those used to researching and booking everything online, here's a caution about Caye Caulker: As is common with budget destinations, some of the tour operators and cheaper lodging choices on Caulker don't have websites. In fact, some tour operators work from a spot on the beach and have only a cell phone, if that. Those that are online often have websites that are done on the cheap, with poor graphics and servers that are down intermittently. Consider it part of the charm of Caye Caulker.

GETTING HERE AND AROUND

Other than a few emergency vehicles and several private cars, there are few cars on Caye Caulker. Most locals and visitors get around the island's sand streets on foot, although you can rent a golf cart or bike. (Golf-cart taxis charge around BZ$5–BZ$10 per person to most destinations in the village.)

Like Ambergris Caye, Caye Caulker can be used as a base for exploring part of the mainland. It's only about 45 minutes by water taxi, or 15 minutes by air, to Belize City. Two water-taxi companies now offer daily service between Caye Caulker and Chetumal, Mexico. Tours run from Caulker to the Mayan ruins at Lamanai and Altun Ha, and other tours go to the Belize Zoo and to the Caves Branch River for cave tubing.

Caye Caulker is a fairly small island, only 5 miles (8 km) long and a little over 1 mile (2 km) wide at the widest point—most of the island is only a few hundred feet wide. The island itself is divided by "the Split," a small channel of water separating the north area and the south area. The area north of the Split is mostly mangroves and lagoons, accessible only by boat, while the only village occupies most of the area south of the Split. From the Split to the airstrip, which is at the south end of the island, is about a mile (2 km). Directions in the village usually use the main public pier or dock, where you come in on the Caye Caulker Water Taxi boat, as the reference point. (To confuse things, another water taxis comes into a different pier near the original public pier.) Things are either north of the main pier or south of the main public pier. The village has only three main streets: Front, Middle, and Back running north and south; Back Street just runs on the south side of the village. These are the names everyone uses, but maps may give different names: Hicaco Avenue for Middle Street,

Avenida Lagosta for Middle Street, and Avenida Mangle for Back Street. The east-west street between the public pier and the lagoon-side dock is called Center Street or Dock Street or Calle al Sol (sometimes Calle del Sol).

All the streets on the island are hard-packed sand. On the east side you can also walk along the beachfront. Generally, the north end of the village bustles more than the south end, which is primarily residential, and it also is home to the airstrip.

TIMING

Caye Caulker's low-key charms take a while to fully appreciate. Stay here a day, and you'll complain that there's nothing to do. Stay a week, and you'll probably tell everyone how much you hate overdeveloped islands like Ambergris.

SAFETY

Several high-profile muggings, rapes, and stabbing of visitors have brought Caulker unwanted attention. Despite these crimes, and the general disreputable vibe of some Rasta-phonians who hang out at bars or call out to passing tourists, Caye Caulker remains one of the safest places in Belize. Just don't bring the barfly back to your room or wander around dark alleys at night. Also, keep your camera, wallet, and other possessions close to you, especially in cheaper hotels.

WATER ACTIVITIES AND TOURS

When you see the waves breaking on the Barrier Reef just a few hundred yards from the shore, boats full of eager snorkelers and divers, and the colorful sails of windsurfers dashing back and forth in front of the island, you know you've come to a good place for water sports and activities. You can dive, snorkel, and fish the same areas of the sea and reef as you can from San Pedro, but usually for a little less dough. One area where Caulker suffers by comparison with its neighboring island is in the quality of its beaches. Caulker's beaches, though periodically nourished by dredging to replenish the sand, are modest at best, mostly narrow ribbons of sand with shallow water near the shore and, in places, a mucky sea bottom and lots of sea grass. You can, however, have an enjoyable swim at "the Split," a channel originally cut through the island by Hurricane Hattie in 1961 and expanded over the years, at the north end of the village, or from the end of piers.

FISHING

Caye Caulker was a fishing village before it was a visitor destination. From Caulker you can fly-fish for bonefish or permit in the grass flats behind the island, troll for barracuda or grouper inside the reef, or charter a boat to take you to blue water outside the reef for deep-sea fishing. Ambergris Caye offers more options for chartering boats for deep-sea fishing than Caye Caulker. For a guide and boat for flats and reef fishing, you'll pay around BZ$600–BZ$700 a day for one or two people. If you're a do-it-yourself type, you can fish off the piers or in the flats. Anglers Abroad has a small fly-fishing and tackle shop where you can rent fishing gear, if you didn't bring your own. Blue marlin weighing more than 400 pounds have been caught beyond the reef off Caye Caulker, along with big sailfish, pompano, and kingfish. If you can find a charter on Caulker for blue-water deep-sea fishing, you'll pay BZ$1,000–BZ$1,200 and up for a full day's fishing for up to four people. Remember, you now need a fishing license to fish in Belize waters, except from shore or piers. Your guide or hotel can help you get a license.

CHARTERS, LESSONS, AND EQUIPMENT
Fodor'sChoice
★

Anglers Abroad. Haywood Curry, a transplanted Texan, and his crew run all types of fishing trips, starting with half-day trips at around BZ$500 for two persons and, "for the adventurous" two- or three-day camping and fishing expeditions, with camping on a remote caye. Anglers Abroad, associated with Seadreams Hotel, also has a fly-fishing and tackle shop. ⊠ *At Seadreams Hotel near the Split, Hattie St.* ☎ *226/0303* ⊕ *www.anglersabroad.com.*

Porfelio "Piggy" Guzman. Porfelio "Piggy" Guzman is one of the best-known fishing guides on the island, and he may charge a little more than others. ⊠ *Calle Almendro* ☎ *226/0152.*

Tsunami Adventures. Tsunami Adventures offers reef and flats fishing trips starting at BZ$500 for a half day for two persons, including boat and guide, or BZ$700 for a full day, both inclusive of tax. Your guide will be a local fisherman, Rolly Rosado. ⊠ *Front St.* ☎ *226/0462* ⊕ *www. tsunamiadventures.com.*

MANATEE SPOTTING

Several operators do boat trips to see West Indian manatees. The 9,000-acre Swallow Caye Wildlife Sanctuary, established in 2002 in great part due to the efforts of Chocolate Heredia, who sadly passed away in 2013, and his wife Annie Seashore, is home to many of these endangered mammals. It's just 10 minutes by boat from Caye Caulker. It's illegal in Belize to get into the water with the gentle sea cows, but a few tour operators unfortunately do permit it. Half-day tours typically cost around BZ$75–BZ$100 per person, including the BZ$10 sanctuary admission fee. Some stop at Goff's Caye, which has excellent snorkeling.

CHARTERS, LESSONS, AND EQUIPMENT
Fodor'sChoice
★

Carlos Tours. Carlos Tours, one of the most recommended tour operators on Caye Caulker, runs snorkeling trips with stops at some of the best snorkel spots near Caye Caulker, and also at Hol Chan Marine Reserve and other places, along with manatee-spotting tours. Prices vary according to the destination but range from around BZ$80 to BZ$175 per person. ⊠ *Front St., at Calle del Sol* ☎ *226/0058* ✍ *carlosayala10@hotmail.com.*

Red Mangrove Eco Adventures. Red Mangrove Eco Adventures offers "ecologically sensitive" manatee-watching tours—no swimming with the manatees. It also offers other sea and inland tours. ⊠ *Front St.* ☎ *226/0669, 607/1440* ⊕ *www.mangrovebelize.com.*

SAILING

A few small sailboats offer sailing and snorkeling trips to nearby areas. One company, Raggamuffin Tours, also offers multiday combination sailing, snorkeling, and camping trips to Placencia.

Blackhawk Sailing. Formerly Seahawk Sailing, Blackhawk Sailing offers snorkeling, overnight camping, and charter trips on a 30-foot sailboat captained by "Big Steve." ⊠ *Front St., next to De Real Macaw* ☎ *607/0323* ⊕ *www.blackhawksailingtours.com.*

Raggamuffin Tours. Raggamuffin Tours has day sails and sunset and moonlight sails. A full-day snorkeling tour is BZ$140 including marine reserve fees, full lunch, and snorkel gear. Two-night/three-day camping and sailing trips to Placencia, with nights at Tobacco Caye and Ranguana Caye, are BZ$700 per person one-way. These normally depart Caye Caulker twice a week, on Tuesday and Friday, weather permitting. Rates at Christmas/New Years are higher. ⊠ *Front St., north of main public pier, near Split* ☎ *226/0348* ⊕ *www. raggamuffintours.com.*

SCUBA DIVING AND SNORKELING

Hol Chan Marine Reserve at the southern tip of Ambergris Caye *(⇨ see Ambergris Caye section, above)* is a popular destination for snorkel and dive trips from Caye Caulker. At Hol Chan you can swim with nurse sharks and stingrays and see hundreds of tropical fish, some quite large due to the no-fishing restrictions in the reserve. On the way, your boat may be followed by a pod of frolicking dolphins, and you may spot sea turtles or even a manatee. Larger boats from Caulker also go to Lighthouse Reef, including the Blue Hole, and Turneffe atolls.

The Caye Caulker Marine Reserve north and east of Caye Caulker, with its coral canyons, is a favorite of divers, especially for night dives. Caulker has its own mini version of San Pedro's Shark-Ray Alley, called Shark-Ray Village.

A plethora of dive and snorkel operators offer reef tours (some of them are "cowboys"—unaffiliated and unreliable—so make sure you use a reputable company). Plan on spending about BZ$40–BZ$60 for a snorkel trip around the island or BZ$70–BZ$100 for a six-hour snorkel trip to Hol Chan Marine Reserve.

Local two-tank reef dives typically run about BZ$150, and those to Hol Chan or other nearby areas cost about BZ$160–BZ$180. Day trips to Lighthouse or Turneffe atoll, with three dives, cost around BZ$250–BZ$300. If you stop at Half Moon Caye, there's an additional BZ$80 park fee. At Hol Chan, the park fee is BZ$20, and at Caye Caulker Marine Reserve, BZ$10. These park fees, which apply for divers and snorkelers, are sometimes not included in the quoted prices for dive and snorkel trips. The 12.5% Goods and Services Tax (GST) may—or may not—be included in the price you're quoted. Ask, to be sure.

Anwar Tours. Anwar Tours, operated by brothers Erico and Javier Novelo, runs snorkel trips to see manatees at Swallow Caye, with a visit at St. Georges Caye, and stops at three other good snorkel sites. Rate for this full-day trip is BZ$170. A night snorkel trip is BZ$100, and other snorkel tour rates start at BZ$50. Anwar, like other tour operators, provides various snorkel and land tour options, depending on demand. Stops and length of trips vary depending on weather and sea conditions. ⊠ *Hicaco Ave.* ☎ *226/0327* ⊕ *www.anwartours.page.tl.*

3

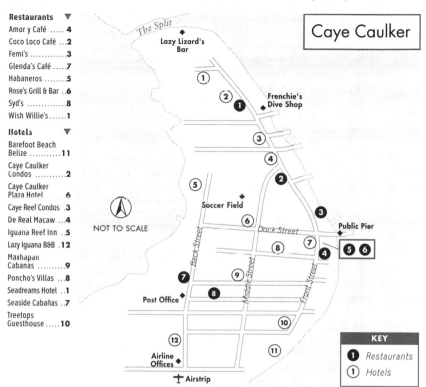

Belize Diving Services. Established in 1978, Belize Diving Services has been around long enough to know the best spots. They train around 500 divers every year, with a full open water course running around BZ$800. A two-tank local reef dive is BZ$170, and a one-tank BZ$90, not including gear rental, 12.5% tax, and BZ$10 reserve admission fee. A two-tank Turneffe North (not Elbow) trip is BZ$220 plus tax and gear rental. A full-day Blue Hole/Lighthouse Reef trip is BZ$450 plus tax and gear rental, but does include lunch. ✉ *Chapoose St., near soccer field and Iguana Reef Inn* ☎ *226/0143* ⊕ *www.belizedivingservices.net.*

Frenchie's Diving Services. If you're looking for someone to take you out to the reef for diving, or to the Blue Hole, Frenchie's Diving Services is a respected local operator. Frenchie's leaves early for the Blue Hole, to try to be the first boat there. The three-dive, full-day trip, including gear, breakfast, lunch, BZ$80 park fee, and 12.5% tax is BZ$450 per person for divers, and BZ$249 for those snorkeling only. Three dives at Turneffe Elbow are BZ$337 including lunch. Half-day reef two-tank diving trips are around BZ$230, including tax and marine reserve fee. Four-day open water certifications courses run BZ$800. If visiting in high season, best book ahead because Frenchie's is popular. Blue Hole trips are scheduled every other day. ✉ *Beachfront off Front St., on dock north of main public pier* ☎ *226/0234* ⊕ *www.frenchiesdivingbelize.com.*

Raggamuffin Tours. Go out for a snorkel on a sailboat with Raggamuffin Tours, which goes to Hol Chan for around BZ$140 for a full-day snorkel trip, including the park entrance fee, lunch, and booze. ✉ *Front St.* ☎ *226/0348* 🌐 *www.raggamuffintours.com.*

WINDSURFING AND KITESURFING

With brisk easterly winds most of the year, Caye Caulker is one of Belize's premier centers for windsurfing. The island gets winds over 12 knots most days from November to July. The best windsurfing is in the morning and afternoon, with lulls around midday. In the late winter and spring, winds frequently hit 20 knots or more.

CHARTERS, LESSONS, AND EQUIPMENT

KiteXplorer. KiteXplorer offers beginning and advanced kitesurfing lessons. A three-hour introduction to kitesurfing costs BZ$360 including equipment and insurance. A basic course over three or four days is BZ$960. If you already are an inexperienced kitesurfer, supervised equipment rental is BZ$90 an hour. KiteXplorer also sells equipment. ✉ *Beachfront* ☎ *635/4967* 🌐 *www.kitexplorer.com.*

WHERE TO EAT

Once your dining choice on Caulker was fish, fish, or fish, but now you can also enjoy Italian, Mexican, and Chinese, as well as wonderful fresh conch and lobster and, of course, fish. Several restaurants serve wholesome natural foods and vegetarian dishes. Prices for meals here are generally lower than on other islands, and even a lobster dinner is usually less than BZ$45. The cheapest way to eat on the island is to buy grilled fish, chicken, lobster, and other items from the folks with barbecue grills who set up along Front Street and elsewhere. Though you should use good judgment, the food is almost always well prepared and safe to eat. Locals also sell meat pies, tacos, tamales, cakes, and other homemade items at very low prices. Do what local people do and buy your snacks and some of your meals from these street vendors.

$ CAFÉ

🍴 **Amor y Café.** This is the best spot on Caye Caulker for a warm smile, coffee (including espresso and lattes), and breakfast. Sit on the front porch, do some people-watching on Front Street, and try the fruit with granola and homemade yogurt, or the yummy fresh-baked breads. [$] *Average main: BZ$12* ✉ *15 Front St., 1 block south of main pier* ☎ *610/2397* 💳 *No credit cards* 🕒 *Closed Mon.*

$ CAFÉ

🍴 **Coco Loco Café in Caribbean Colors.** For a good cup of coffee, a really good cup of coffee, this little café cum art gallery and gift shop in the heart of Front Street is the place to go. It's owned by an expat artist, Lee Vanderwalker, who has lived on the island for many years. The café, called Coco Loco, also serves a few breakfast items such as bagels (rare in Belize) and pancakes, but coffee is the thing. [$] *Average main: BZ$10* ✉ *Front St.* ☎ *668/7205* 🌐 *www.caribbean-colors.com* 🕒 *Closed Thurs. No dinner.*

$$ SEAFOOD

🍴 **Femi's.** Popular with younger travelers, Femi's is on the beach, with no walls to spoil the view. Frankly, the view is better than the food, but try the Mexican dishes at lunch, or the smoothies any time. In the evening, Femi's is more of a bar. [$] *Average main: BZ$16* ✉ *Beachfront, just south of the main public pier, Beachfront* ☎ *622/3469.*

$
CAFÉ
FAMILY

🍴 **Glenda's Café.** The menu here is on a chalkboard, short and sweet, and you place your order at the window. At breakfast, when this café is most popular, you can get a hearty breakfast of eggs, bacon, beans, homemade cinnamon roll (only BZ$1) or johnnycakes and fresh orange juice for a pittance. It opens at 7 am daily except Sunday (though sometimes it's closed on other days, because this is Caye Caulker) and get there early to get a cinnamon bun. [$] *Average main: BZ$8* ✉ *Back St., north of post office* ☎ *226/0148* 💳 *No credit cards* 🕒 *Closed Sun. No dinner.*

$$$
SEAFOOD
Fodor's Choice ★

🍴 **Habaneros.** The most expensive dining spot on Caye Caulker, Haberneros is also a place that tends to generate mixed reactions: One diner goes ga-ga over the coconut encrusted snapper with mixed fruits and loves the dramatic lighting, while another guest sniffs at the combination of pork topped with crab and thinks the restaurant is too dark. Chef-owner Darren Casson hits for the fences with some of his dishes, and he doesn't always connect, with too many competing flavors and over-the-top presentations, but for a splurge on Caye Caulker this is your most interesting, if conflicted, choice. Just be aware that with drinks, appetizers, dessert, tip, and taxes (Haberneros doesn't include the 12.5% GST in the menu price), you'll face a hefty check, at least for Caye Caulker. And you could be one of those who just don't care for Habaneros. [$] *Average main: BZ$40* ✉ *Front St., due west from main public pier* ☎ *226/0487* 🕒 *Dinner only; closed Thurs.*

$$$
SEAFOOD
Fodor's Choice ★

🍴 **Rose's Grill & Bar.** This little restaurant has some of the best word of mouth on the island, and the tables on the porch and inside are often packed. The specialty is seafood, and it's all fresh. As you arrive you pick out your snapper, grouper, barracuda, lobster, or other seafood from the fresh selection displayed, and then it's grilled in front of the restaurant. If we had a gripe, it would be that the seafood is more expensive than most on the island, but it's sure tasty! [$] *Average main: BZ$35* ✉ *Calle del Sol (Center St.) at Front St., behind Habaneros* ☎ *226/0407* 🌐 *www.rosesgrillandbar.com* 🕒 *No lunch May–Oct.*

$$$
ITALIAN
Fodor's Choice ★

🍴 **Sandros Piccola Cucina.** After being closed for a while, Sandros has reopened in a new location to almost unanimously rave reviews. At dinner, you'll love their honest, authentic Italian food such as carbonara spaghetti, lasagna, seafood ravioli, and lobster linguini with a choice of sauces. The Italian owner is friendly and gregarious, and as you enter you can watch the food being prepared in the open kitchen, though the seating is in a garden patio. There's a limited wine list. [$] *Average main: BZ$26* ✉ *Pasero St., short distance from Atlantic Bank* 📧 *sandros.belize@gmail.com* 💳 *No credit cards* 🕒 *Closed Wed.*

$
LATIN AMERICAN
FAMILY

🍴 **Syd's.** If you ask a local resident for a restaurant recommendation, chances are you'll get a vote for Syd's, in an old white frame house on Middle Street. It serves Belizean favorites like beans and rice, stew chicken, *garnaches,* and tostadas, along with (in-season) lobster and conch at prices lower than you'll pay at most other eateries. The fried chicken here is the absolute best on the island, and a bargain for a big serving with sides for less than BZ$10. [$] *Average main: BZ$14* ✉ *Middle St. at Aventurera St.* ☎ *226/0294* 🕒 *Closed Sun.*

3

$$ SEAFOOD 🍴 **Wish Willie's.** At Wish Willie's you eat on picnic tables in the sandy backyard of the owner, Maurice Moore, and he will tell you what's on the menu for the day. It may be fresh fish, lobster, or chicken. In most cases, the prices are very low, and the rum drinks cost less than almost anywhere else on the island. You may have to share a table with other guests, and the service is sometimes slow, but keep in mind the money you're saving and the good time you're having! [$] *Average main: BZ$18* ✉ *Park St., off Front St. due west of Frenchies* ☎ *660/7194* 💳 *No credit cards* 🕒 *Usually closed Sep.–Oct.*

WHERE TO STAY

Caye Caulker has more than 40 hotels, mostly small places with just a few rooms. The older budget hotels are mostly clapboard, with fans but no air-conditioning, and usually without TV or room phones. If they're not on the water where they can catch the prevailing sea breezes, they are often burning hot during the day. Hotels built in the last decade or so are generally constructed of concrete, and most newer properties have air-conditioning. There are only a handful of swimming pools on the island.

$ HOTEL 🏨 **Barefoot Beach Belize.** This little seafront hotel, about a 10 to 15-minute walk to the main part of the village, has three basic rooms and a suite set in a pastel blue, concrete building with pink and yellow trim, along with three cottages. **Pros:** choice of accommodations; pier is nice spot to enjoy the water. **Cons:** short walk or bike ride from the south to main restaurant area; some units need upgrading; no pool. [$] *Rooms from: BZ$150* ✉ *Beachfront, south of main public pier* ☎ *226/0205* 🌐 *www.barefootbeachbelize.com* 🛏 *3 rooms, 1 suite, 3 cottages* 🍽 *No meals.*

$$ RENTAL 🏨 **Caye Caulker Condos.** If you want a full kitchen to prepare some of your own meals, these moderately priced condos with all the mod-cons including a pool are a good choice. **Pros:** pleasant small apartments with kitchens; good location near water and most restaurants; swimming pool; good value. **Cons:** units are not particularly large. [$] *Rooms from: BZ$216* ✉ *Front St., Corner of Calle Almendro, near Split* ☎ *226/0072* 🌐 *www.cayecaulkercondos.com* 🛏 *8 apartments* 🍽 *No meals.*

$ HOTEL 🏨 **Caye Caulker Plaza Hotel.** This 32-room, three-story hotel is an attractive option for modern and moderate-cost accommodations in the center of the island, if you don't need to be on the water. **Pros:** modern hotel in the center of the village; clean rooms with A/C. **Cons:** not on beach; no pool; rates have increased; not any local atmosphere. [$] *Rooms from: BZ$175* ✉ *Middle St. at Calle del Sol* ☎ *226/0780* 🌐 *www.cayecaulkerplazahotel.com* 🛏 *32 rooms* 🍽 *No meals.*

$$$ RENTAL FAMILY Fodor's Choice ★ 🏨 **Caye Reef Condos.** Caye Reef Condos are among the most upmarket and spacious digs on the island, especially for families or couples traveling together. **Pros:** upscale condo apartments; lots and lots of space; pool; convenient location. **Cons:** some furnishings are looking a little worn; prices are high for Caulker. [$] *Rooms from: BZ$436* ✉ *Front St. at Park St., near Split* ☎ *226/0381* 🌐 *www.cayereef.com* 🛏 *6 2-bedroom condo apartments; some can be rented as 1-bedroom* 🍽 *No meals.*

3

$ **De Real Macaw.** De Real Macaw has a desirable location in the heart
HOTEL   of the Front Street activities, across the street from the water and a
short walk to the Split, and the prices are right. **Pros:** clean and well-run; good location near water and most restaurants. **Cons:** not many
frills; some units not air-conditioned. *$ Rooms from: BZ$109 ⌧ Front
St., corner of Crocodile St., north of main public pier ☎226/0459
⊕ www.derealmacaw.biz ⤳6 rooms, 2 suites, 1 2-bedroom condo, 1
house ¶⃝ No meals.*

$$$ **Iguana Reef Inn.** One of Caye Caulker's most upscale lodgings, Iguana
HOTEL   Reef has just about everything but a concierge. **Pros:** attractive, well-designed lodging, with pool. **Cons:** on back side of island. *$ Rooms
Fodor's Choice   from: BZ$305 ⌧ Near north end of Middle St., next to soccer field
★   ☎ 226/0213 ⊕ www.iguanareefinn.com ⤳ 12 1-bedroom suites and 1
2-bedroom penthouse suite ¶⃝ Breakfast.*

$$ **Lazy Iguana B&B.** This comfortable B&B is one of the tallest structures
B&B/INN   on the island, providing stunning views of the sunset from the fourth-level rooftop terrace. **Pros:** laid-back, nicely furnished B&B; big home-made breakfast. **Cons:** not on sea; back-of-island location
is 10-minute walk to main restaurant area. *$ Rooms from: BZ$207
⌧ Alamina Dr., on back side of island near airstrip ☎226/0350 ⊕ www.
lazyiguana.net ⤳ 4 rooms ¶⃝ Breakfast.*

$ **Maxhapan Cabañas.** This little spot is in the center of the village and
HOTEL   not on the water, but it makes up for it by being neat and clean and a
fine value, and set in a small, shady, sandy garden. **Pros:** inexpensive,
clean rooms. **Cons:** not on the water. *$ Rooms from: BZ$140 ⌧ 55
Av. Pueblo Nuevo, in center of village south of the main public pier
☎226/0118 ⤳ 3 rooms.*

$ **Pancho's Villas.** Cutesy name aside, Pancho's Villas offers six attrac-
RENTAL   tive, modern one-bedroom suites in a lemon-yellow three-story build-ing. **Pros:** pleasant one-bedroom suites. **Cons:** not on beach. *$ Rooms
from: BZ$142 ⌧ Pasero St., between Front and Middle Sts. ☎226/0304
⊕ www.panchosvillasbelize.com ⤳6 suites ¶⃝ No meals.*

$$ **Seadreams Hotel.** Seadreams is ideal for those who like to fish or
B&B/INN   enjoy taking in beautiful sunsets from a private pier on the lagoon.
Fodor's Choice   **Pros:** convenient location near the Split; ideal for anglers; private pier
★   on lagoon. **Cons:** not on beach. *$ Rooms from: BZ$230 ⌧ Hattie St.,
near the Split ☎ 630/1008 ⊕ www.seadreamsbelize.com ⤳ 5 rooms, 3
apartments ¶⃝ Breakfast.*

$$ **Seaside Cabañas.** If your Belizean dreams include lounging poolside
RESORT   just steps from the sea, Belikin in hand, get thee to Seaside, a delightful
Fodor's Choice   beachfront inn with one of the few hotel swimming pools on the island.
★   **Pros:** a top choice on the island; pool; prime location. **Cons:** beach swim-ming in front of hotel is not good. *$ Rooms from: BZ$251 ⌧ Front and
Dock Sts., at main public pier ☎ 226/0498 ⊕ www.seasidecabanas.com
⤳ 16 rooms, 1 suite ¶⃝ No meals.*

$ **Treetops Guesthouse.** Austrian-born owner Doris Creasey brings inter-
B&B/INN   national flair and Teutonic cleanliness to this three-story colonial-style
Fodor's Choice   guesthouse with four rooms and two suites, set back a ways from the
★   sea, which is so well run and such a good value that it's almost always
full. **Pros:** meticulously clean and well run; quiet location near the

water; excellent value. **Cons:** some guests complain about fairly strict rules. $ *Rooms from: BZ$135* ✉ *Beachfront, Playa Asunción, south of main public pier* ☎ *226/0240* 🌐 *www.treetopsbelize.com* 🛏 *4 rooms, 2 with shared bath, 2 suites* 🍴 *No meals.*

VACATION HOME RENTALS

A handful of privately owned homes are available for rent on the island, either daily or by the week. Expect to pay around BZ$100–BZ$200 a night or BZ$800–BZ$2,000 a week. In most cases, credit cards are not accepted.

Caye Caulker Rentals (🌐 *www.cayecaulkerrentals.com* ☎ *630–1008*) is the largest vacation home rental source on the island. It manages about 20 cottages from BZ$130 a night, plus 9% tax. Small beachfront houses start at around BZ$1,300 a week.

NIGHTLIFE

You don't come to Caye Caulker for the hot nightlife, but the island does have its share of laid-back bars. The most famous is the Lazy Lizard at the Split. The Lizard has done some renovation recently and serves bar food as well as beer and booze.

I&I Reggae Bar. Knock back a Belikin or two to the beat of reggae music at I&I Reggae Bar. Swings hang from the ceiling, replacing bar stools, on the first floor, and the top floor has hammocks and a thatch roof. The second floor is for dancing, with a live DJ. There's really nothing else like this three-story bar in Belize. There is a small cover charge (around BZ$3) some nights. ✉ *Middle St. at Luciano Reyes St.* ✣ *South of public pier. Go south on Front St. to dead end, then turn right.* ☎ *660/2205* 🕒 *Daily 4 pm–1 am.*

Lazy Lizard. "Sunny place for shady people" is the slogan of the Lazy Lizard. During the day you can swim at the Split and then cool off with some Belikins (BZ$20 for a bucket of six) on the barstools at the Lizard, which sits right at the edge of the water at the northernmost tip of the village. Sunsets are amazing here. After dark there's a spotlight pointed into the water, so you can see fish, small sharks, and occasionally even a crocodile swimming around. Lazy Lizard is usually open late. Don't expect clean bathrooms, seating or delicious bar snacks, but because of the location this is by far the most popular hangout on the island. ✉ *At the Split* ☎ *623/1454.*

SHOPPING

You won't find nearly as many shops here as in San Pedro, but there are a few standout stores to poke around in for some interesting souvenirs. Every day vendors set up on a section of Front Street north of the main public pier, selling crafts and souvenirs. A few vendors along Front Street can be pretty aggressive—ignore them and buy from someone else.

Caribbean Colors. Caribbean Colors has colorful watercolors and silk screenings by the owner, Lee Vanderwalker, along with handmade jewelry, scarves, and art by other artists. A small café, Coco Loco, in the gallery serves great coffee and some breakfast/lunch items. ✉ *Front St., just south of main public pier* ☎ *226/0206, 877/809–1659* 🌐 *www.cafepress.com/caribbeancolors.*

Chan's. Chan's is the largest grocery in the village. Pick up your basic groceries and Marie Sharp's hot sauce here. ⌧ *Middle St. at Calle del Sol* ☎ *226/0165.*

Cooper's Art Gallery. Cooper's Art Gallery has paintings and prints by Walter Castillo, Nelson Young, and other Central American artists, along with pieces by owner Debbie Cooper. ⌧ *Front St., north of main public pier* ☎ *226/0330* ⊕ *www.debbiecooper.artspan.com.*

SOUTHERN CAYES

3

GETTING HERE AND AROUND

The southern cayes are specks of land spread out over hundreds of square miles of sea. There is no scheduled air or boat service to any of these islands. In the case of Tobacco Caye, private boats leave Dangriga daily around 9 to 9:30 am. To other cayes and atolls you'll have to arrange transportation with the lodges or resorts on the islands, or charter your own boat at high cost.

TIMING

Because of the difficulty and expense of getting to the islands, most resorts have minimum-stay requirements, sometimes as little as three days but often a week. Bring several beach novels, and be prepared to enjoy a quiet vacation filled with salty adventures on and under the sea.

TOBACCO CAYE

11 miles (18 km) southeast of Dangriga.

Tobacco Caye is at the northern tip of the South Water Caye Marine Reserve, a 62-square-mile (160-square-km) reserve that's popular for diving and fishing and has some of the most beautiful islands in Belize. Visitors to the South Water Caye Marine Reserve pay BZ$10 a day for up to three days, or BZ$30 a week, park fee. Rangers come around and collect it from guests at the Tobacco Caye hotels.

The island has no shops or restaurants, except those at the hotels, and just a couple of bars, but there is one small dive shop. Boats leave from the Riverside Café in Dangriga for the 40-minute, BZ$40–BZ$50 trip to Tobacco Caye. Get to the Riverside by 9 am; most boats leave around 9:30 (though at busy times such as Easter they come and go all day long). You can get information on the boats, as well as breakfast, at the Riverside Café. ⇨ *See Southern Coast chapter.*

If you don't want to pay a lot for your place in the sun, Tobacco Caye may be for you. It's a tiny island—barely 4 acres, and a walk around the entire caye takes 10 minutes—but it's right on the reef, so you can wade in and snorkel all you want. Though the snorkeling off the caye is not as good as in some other areas of Belize (some of the coral is dead and most of the fish are small), you can see spotted eagle rays, moray eels, octopuses, and other sea life.

WHERE TO STAY

All the accommodations are budget places, basically simple wood cabins, some not much larger than sheds. Since a half-dozen hotels vie for space, the islet seems even smaller than it is. Periodically the hotels get blown away by storms but are rebuilt, usually a little better than they were before. Unfortunately, garbage tends to pile up on the island, and the hotels don't always use the most ecologically sound methods for disposing of it.

Though rates have increased, most prices remain affordably low, around BZ$100–BZ$150 a day per person, including meals.

⚠ **Hotels can be casual about reservations. After making reservations months in advance, you may arrive to find that your reservation has been lost and the hotel is fully occupied.** Fortunately, it's usually easy to find a room in another hotel.

$$
HOTEL
⌂ **Tobacco Caye Lodge.** This cluster of pastel blue cabins is a few feet from the turquoise sea. **Pros:** most "upscale" of Tobacco Caye hotels; friendly staff. **Cons:** still pretty basic, just slightly above backpacker level. $ *Rooms from: BZ$220* ✉ *Tobacco Caye Lodge* ☎ *532/2033* ⊕ *www.tclodgebelize.com* ⏍ *6 cabins* ⓧ *No meals.*

$
RENTAL
⌂ **Tobacco Caye Paradise Cabins.** Whether it's paradise or not depends on your expectations, but if what you're seeking is a little shack built partly over the water, backed by cocopalms, with snorkeling and swimming right out your door, at an affordable price, this could be it. **Pros:** huts on the beach with meals at modest prices; snorkeling is 15 feet away; friendly staff; good value. **Cons:** very basic rooms; past time for repairs. $ *Rooms from: BZ$100* ✉ *Tobacco Caye Paradise* ☎ *532/5101* ⊕ *www.tobaccocayeparadisecabin.com* ⏍ *6 cabins, 3 rooms with shared baths* ⓧ *Multiple meal plans.*

THATCH CAYE
WHERE TO STAY

$$$$
RESORT
⌂ **Thatch Caye.** Thatch Caye is all about you and your private island vacation, so you can head out for a day of fishing, diving, sea kayaking, or snorkeling and return to supremely comfortable accommodations. **Pros:** beautiful private island with congenial hosts; plenty of marine activities; attractive cabanas directly on the water. **Cons:** limited snorkeling off beach; not on reef; no air-conditioning; no pool. $ *Rooms from: BZ$702* ✉ *Part of the Coco Plum Caye group, 9 miles (15 km) or about 25 minutes by boat from Dangriga, Thatch Caye* ☎ *800/435–3145 in U.S. and Canada* ⊕ *www.thatchcayebelize.com* ⏍ *11 cabanas, 1 family villa* ⓧ *All meals.*

COCO PLUM CAYE
WHERE TO STAY

$$$$
ALL-INCLUSIVE
Fodor's Choice
★
⌂ **Coco Plum Island Resort.** It all comes down to this: Relax in a hammock on the veranda of your cottage, sip a cold drink, and gaze at the Caribbean at this all-inclusive private island resort off Dangriga. **Pros:** air-conditioned cabins on tranquil small island; friendly staff; excellent service. **Cons:** only fair snorkeling off beach; not on reef. $ *Rooms from: BZ$1120* ✉ *Coco Plum Caye, 8 miles (13 km) from Dangriga, Coco Plum* ☎ *522/2200, 800/763–7360 U.S. reservations number* ⊕ *www.cocoplumcay.com* ⏍ *14 cottages, 1 3-bedroom villa* ⓧ *All-inclusive.*

SOUTH WATER CAYE

Fodor's Choice
★

14 miles (23 km) southeast of Dangriga.

This is one of our favorite underrated spots in Belize. The 15-acre South Water Caye has good off-the-beaten-reef diving and snorkeling in a stunning tropical setting, and the beach at the southern end of the island is one of Belize's sandy beauties. The reef is only a short swim from shore. The downside of the small caye? The sand flies here can be a nuisance, and there aren't any facilities other than those at the island's two resorts and the International Zoological Expeditions' student dorm.

WHERE TO STAY

$$$$
RESORT

Blue Marlin Lodge. A good, though pricey, base for fishing, snorkeling, and diving trips, this Belizean-owned resort at the north end of beautiful Southwater Caye is only 50 yards from the reef. **Pros:** Belizean-owned; great snorkeling and diving nearby; friendly staff. **Cons:** some rooms need upgrades; expensive. $ *Rooms from: BZ$990 ⊠ South Water Caye* ☎ *522/2243, 800/798–1558 in U.S. and Canada* ⊕ *www. bluemarlinlodge.com* ⌁ *8 cottages, 6 rooms.*

$$$$
RESORT

Pelican Beach Resort South Water Caye. Steps from one of Belize's best beaches, where you can swim, snorkel, and dive from shore, and fish to your heart's content, is this former convent turned peaceful island retreat on 3½ seaside acres. **Pros:** on great little beach, with snorkeling from shore; tasty Belizean food; comfortable, eco-friendly no-frills accommodations. **Cons:** you have to make your own entertainment. $ *Rooms from: BZ$649 ⊠ South Water Caye* ☎ *522/2044* ⊕ *www.pelicanbeachbelize.com* ⌁ *5 rooms, 4 cottages, 1 student dorm* ⍾ *All meals.*

SOUTHERN CAYES OFF PLACENCIA AND SOUTHERN COAST

8–18 miles (13–30 km) east of Placencia.

A few miles off the coast of southern Stann Creek District are several small islands with equally small tourism operations. If Placencia and Hopkins aren't far enough away from civilization for you, consider an overnight or longer visit to one of these quiet little paradises surrounded by fish. French Louie Caye is one of them, a private two-acre island with a nice coral sand beach. You can do a day trip here from Placencia, or stay for longer periods in basic cabins. Hatchet Caye and Whipray Caye are two other islands off Placencia with small lodges.

WHERE TO STAY

$$$$
RENTAL

French Louie Caye. Rent your own private island 8 miles (13 km) from Placencia with a lovely coral sand beach and a reef for snorkeling and fishing, and enjoy lobster and fish freshly prepared by your own cook. **Pros:** beautiful 2-acre private island; lovely coral sand beach; delicious fresh seafood and other meals prepared to your order. **Cons:** simple accommodations; no longer inexpensive. $ *Rooms from: BZ$840 ⊠ French Louie Caye, 8 miles (13 km) east of Placencia, Placencia* ☎ *523/3636, 800/886–4265 in U.S.* ⊕ *www.frenchlouiecaye.com* ⌁ *1 cabin* ⍾ *All meals.*

$$$$ RESORT 🏨 **Hatchet Caye.** On a private island about 17 miles (28 km) east of Placencia, Hatchet Caye offers an unspoiled, remote getaway for honeymooners, divers, or just anyone wanting a complete escape. **Pros:** modern, upscale resort in remote area; very good food; on-site PADI shop offers good diving and snorkeling nearby; friendly staff. **Cons:** small island with no shops or choice of restaurants; we've heard some complaints about the suite unit, which unlike the cabanas doesn't have much of a sea view. [$] *Rooms from: BZ$595* ✉ *Hatchet Caye, Hatchet Caye* ☎ *533/4446 reservations number* 🌐 *www.hatchetcaye.com* 🛏 *7 rooms in duplex cottages, 1 suite, 1 1-bedroom house* 🕒 *Closed Oct.* 🍴 *Multiple meal plans.*

$$$$ ALL-INCLUSIVE 🏨 **Whipray Caye Lodge.** Whipray Caye (also called Whippari Caye) lures anglers with some of the best permit and bonefish fishing in Central America, and owner Julian Cabral (who claims he is descended from a pirate who stopped off in Belize in the 17th century) is a top-flight fishing guide and fly fisherman. **Pros:** good choice for hard-core anglers. **Cons:** basic accommodations; very expensive. [$] *Rooms from: BZ$2155* ✉ *Whipray Caye, island 9 miles (15 km) from Placencia village, Whipray Caye* ☎ *610/1068* 🌐 *www.whipraycayelodge.com* 🛏 *4 rooms in 2 cottages* 🍴 *All-inclusive.*

THE ATOLLS

There are only four atolls in the Western Hemisphere, and three of them are off Belize (the fourth is Chinchorro Reef, off Mexico's Yucatán). Belize's atolls—Turneffe, Lighthouse, and Glover's—are oval-shape masses of coral. A few small islands, some sandy and others mostly mangrove, rise up along the atolls' encircling coral arms. Within the coral walls are central lagoons, with shallow water 10 to 30 feet deep. Outside the walls, the ocean falls off sharply to 1,000 feet or more, deeper than any diver can go.

Unlike the more common Pacific atolls, which were formed from underwater volcanoes, the Caribbean atolls began forming millions of years ago, atop giant tectonic faults. As giant limestone blocks slowly settled, they provided platforms for coral growth.

Because of their remoteness (they're 25 miles [40 km] to 50 miles [80 km] from the mainland) and because most of the islands at the atolls are small, the atolls have remained nearly pristine. Only a few small dive and fishing resorts are here, and the serious divers and anglers who favor the area know that they have some of the best diving and fishing in the Caribbean, if not the world. The atolls are also wonderful for beachcombing, relaxing, and snorkeling—just bring plenty of books, as there are no shops or restaurants other than at the hotels. Of course, paradise has its price: most of the atoll resorts are very, very expensive and have minimum-stay requirements. You can buy a small new compact car for the cost of bringing your family for a week to most of these atoll lodges. While there are good reasons why remote fishing and diving lodges on the cayes must charge a small fortune just to break even, the high rates are one prominent reason Belize is considered a high-cost vacation destination.

GETTING HERE AND AROUND

Getting to the atolls usually requires a long boat ride, sometimes rough enough to bring on *mal de mer*. You'll need to take one of the scheduled boats provided by your lodge or ride out on a dive or snorkel boat with a group; otherwise, you'll likely pay BZ$800–BZ$2,000 or more to charter a boat one-way. Remember, there are no commercial services at the atolls, except those associated with an island dive or fishing lodge. To charter a boat, check with a lodge on the atoll where you wish to go, or ask locally at docks in Belize City, San Pedro, Dangriga, Hopkins, or Placencia.

Dive shops and sailing charters in San Pedro, Caye Caulker, Placencia, and Hopkins make regular trips to the atolls, and may take additional passengers, for a fee, if space is available. ⇨ *See Dive sections of the pertinent destination chapter for contact information on dive shops.*

TIMING

Because of the difficulty and expense of getting to the atolls, most resorts have minimum-stay requirements, sometimes as little as three days but more often a week. There's nothing to do on the atolls except dive, snorkel, fish, eat, sleep, and drink. If you don't like sea sports, or if you do but hit consecutive days of bad weather, you may be bored out of your gourd.

TURNEFFE ATOLL

25 miles (40 km) east of Belize City.

The largest of the three atolls, Turneffe, is the closest to Belize City. It's one of the best spots for diving, thanks to several steep drop-offs. Only an hour from Lighthouse Reef and 45 minutes from the northern edge of Glover's Reef, Turneffe is a good base for exploring all the atolls.

The best-known attraction, and probably Belize's most exciting wall dive, is the **Elbow,** at Turneffe's southernmost tip. You may encounter eagle rays swimming nearby. As many as 50 might flutter together forming a rippling herd. Elbow is generally considered an advanced dive because of the strong currents, which sweep you toward the deep water beyond the reef.

Though it's most famous for its spectacular wall dives, the atoll has dives for every level. The leeward side, where the reef is wide and gently sloping, is good for shallower dives and snorkeling; you'll see large concentrations of tube sponges, soft corals such as forked sea feathers and sea fans, and plenty of fish. Also on the atoll's western side is the wreck of the *Sayonara*. No doubloons to scoop up here—it was a small passenger and cargo boat that sank in 1985—but it's good for wreck dive practice.

Fishing here, as at all of the atolls, is world-class. You can fly-fish for bonefish and permit in the grassy flats, or go after migratory tarpon from May to September in the channels and lagoons of the atoll. Jack, barracuda, and snappers lurk in the mangrove-lined bays and shorelines. Billfish, sailfish, and other big creatures are in the blue water around the atoll.

WHERE TO STAY

$$$$ RESORT Fodor's Choice ★ **Turneffe Flats.** The sound of the surf is the only thing you'll hear at these smart, white with blue trim, red-roofed beachfront air-conditioned cabins. **Pros:** quality fishing lodge; beautiful atoll scenery; diving and just plain relaxing available. **Cons:** comes at a price. [$] *Rooms from: BZ$1038* ✉ *Turneffe Flats Lodge, Turneffe Atoll* ☎ *232/9022, 888/512–8812* 🌐 *www.tflats.com* 🛏 *8 cottages, 2 3-bedroom villas* 🍴 *Multiple meal plans.*

$$$$ ALL-INCLUSIVE Fodor's Choice ★ **Turneffe Island Resort.** White dive tanks serving as fence posts and a rusty anchor from an 18th-century British warship set the tone at this remote upscale resort offering fishing, diving, beachcombing, and more, including a spa. **Pros:** beautiful atoll setting near great diving and snorkeling; delicious and varied meals. **Cons:** very expensive. [$] *Rooms from: BZ$1333* ✉ *Coco Tree Caye* ☎ *532/2990, 800/874–0118* 🌐 *www.turnefferesort.com* 🛏 *12 rooms, 8 cabanas* 🕒 *Closed Sept. and Oct.* 🍴 *All-inclusive.*

LIGHTHOUSE REEF ATOLL, THE BLUE HOLE, AND HALF MOON CAYE

50 miles (80 km) east of Belize City.

If Robinson Crusoe had been a man of means, he would have repaired here for a break from his desert island.

Lighthouse Reef is about 18 miles (29 km) long and less than 1 mile (2 km) wide and is surrounded by a seemingly endless stretch of coral. Here you'll find two of the country's best dives.

At this writing, visiting Lighthouse Reef is best done as a side trip from Ambergris Caye, Caye Caulker, or another location in northern Belize. The marine reserve fee here is a steep BZ$80 per person.

TOP ATTRACTIONS

Fodor's Choice ★ **Blue Hole.** From the air, the Blue Hole, a breathtaking vertical chute that drops several hundred feet through the reef, looks like a dark blue eye in the center of the shallow lagoon. The Blue Hole was first dived by Jacques Cousteau in 1970 and has since become a diver's pilgrimage site. Just over 1,000 feet wide at the surface and dropping almost vertically to a depth of 412 feet, the Blue Hole is like swimming down a mineshaft, but a mineshaft with hammerhead sharks. This excitement is reflected in the thousands of stickers and tee-shirts reading, "I Dived the Blue Hole." ✉ *Lighthouse Reef, Blue Hole.*

Half Moon Caye. The best diving on Lighthouse Reef is at Half Moon Caye Wall, a classic wall dive. Half Moon Caye begins at 35 feet and drops almost vertically to blue infinity. Floating out over the edge is a bit like free-fall parachuting. Magnificent spurs of coral jut out to the seaward side, looking like small tunnels; they're fascinating to explore and invariably full of fish. An exceptionally varied marine life hovers around this caye. On the gently sloping sand flats behind the coral spurs, a vast colony of garden eels stirs, their heads protruding from the sand like periscopes. Spotted eagle rays, sea turtles, and other underwater wonders frequent the drop-off. The island named

Half Moon Caye is managed by the Belize Audubon Society. It is famous for its colony of red-footed booby birds that numbers about 4,000. ⊠ *Lighthouse Reef, Half Moon Caye* ⊕ *www.belizeaudubon. org* ⊡ *BZ$80.*

Half Moon Caye National Monument. Belize's easternmost island offers one of Belize's greatest wildlife encounters, although it's difficult to reach and lacks accommodations other than camping. Part of the Lighthouse Reef system, Half Moon Caye owes its protected status to the presence of the red-footed booby. The bird is here in such numbers that it's hard to believe it has only one other nesting ground in the entire Caribbean (on Tobago Island, off the coast of Venezuela). Some 4,000 of these birds hang their hats on Half Moon Caye, along with iguanas, lizards, and loggerhead turtles. The entire 40-acre island is a nature reserve, so you can explore the beaches or head into the bush on the narrow nature trail. Above the trees at the island's center is a small viewing platform—at the top you're suddenly in a sea of birds that will doubtless remind you of a certain Alfred Hitchcock movie. Several dive operators and resorts arrange day trips and overnight camping trips to Half Moon Caye. Managed by the Belize Audubon Society, the park fee here is a steep BZ$80 per person. ⊠ *Half Moon Caye National Monument* ⊕ *www.belizeaudubon.org* ⊡ *BZ$80.*

3

GLOVER'S REEF ATOLL

Fodor's Choice
★ *70 miles (113 km) southeast of Belize City.*

Named after the pirate John Glover, this coral necklace strung around an 80-square-mile (208-square-km) lagoon is the southernmost of Belize's three atolls. There are five islands at the atoll. Visitors to Glover's Reef are charged a BZ$20 park fee (BZ$25 for fly-fishing).

WORTH NOTING

Emerald Forest Reef. Although most of the best dive sites are along the Glover's Atoll's southeastern side, this is the exception. It's named for its matter of huge green elkhorn coral. Because the reef's most exciting part is only 25 feet down, it's excellent for novice divers. ⊠ *Glover's Reef.*

Long Caye Wall. This is an exciting wall at Glover's Atoll with a dramatic drop-off hundreds of feet down. It's a good place to spot turtles, rays, and barracuda. ⊠ *Glover's Reef.*

Southwest Caye Wall. Southwest Caye Wall is an underwater cliff that falls quickly to 130 feet. It's briefly interrupted by a narrow shelf, then continues its near-vertical descent to 350 feet. This dive gives you the exhilaration of flying in blue space, so it's easy to lose track of how deep you are going. Both ascent and descent require careful monitoring. ⊠ *Glover's Reef.*

Kayaking is another popular sport here; you can paddle out to the atoll's many patch reefs for snorkeling. Most hotels rent kayaks.

WHERE TO STAY

$$$$ RESORT 🏨 **Isla Marisol.** At Isla Marisol, almost 40 miles (67 km) off Belize's coast at Glover's Reef, after a good night's sleep in an air-conditioned cabana, and a breakfast of mango and johnnycake, you can dive "The Pinnacles," where coral heads rise 40 feet from the ocean floor. **Pros:** Belizean-owned and run; beautiful setting; great diving; you can see whale sharks in the late spring. **Cons:** prices aren't a bargain; sand flies sometimes are troublesome. [$] *Rooms from: BZ$1326* ✉ *Southwest Caye, Isla Marisol* ☎ *855/350–1569 in U.S. and Canada* 🌐 *www.islamarisolresort.com* 🛏 *10 cabins, 1 2-bedroom house* 🍴 *Some meals.*

$$$$ RESORT 🏨 **Off the Wall Dive Center & Resort.** Though this lodge on Glover's Atoll focuses on diving, there's excellent snorkeling and fishing as well. **Pros:** competitive price (for an atoll lodge in Belize); easy access to great diving; very knowledgeable dive staff. **Cons:** modest accommodations; bugs can be a nuisance. [$] *Rooms from: BZ$860* ✉ *Off the Wall Dive Center, Long Caye, Glover's Reef Atoll* ☎ *532/2929* 🌐 *www.offthewallbelize.com* 🛏 *5 cabanas* 🍴 *All meals.*

NORTHERN BELIZE

By Lan Sluder

Razzmatazz and bling are in short supply in northern Belize. Here you'll find more orange groves than beach bars, more sugarcane than sugary sand, and more farms than restaurants. Yet if you're willing to give in to the area's easygoing terms and slow down to explore back roads and poke around small towns and villages, this northern country will win a place in your traveler's heart. You'll discover some of Belize's most interesting Mayan sites, several outstanding jungle lodges, and a sprinkling of small, inexpensive inns with big personalities.

Northern Belize includes the northern part of Belize District and all of Orange Walk and Corozal districts. Altogether, this area covers about 2,800 square miles (7,250 square km) and has a population of around 90,000. The landscape is mostly flat, with mangrove swamps on the coast giving way to savanna inland. Scrub bush is much more common than broadleaf jungle, although to the northwest near the Guatemala border are large, wild tracts of land with some of the world's few remaining old-growth mahogany trees. The region has many cattle ranches, citrus groves, sugarcane fields, and, in a few areas, marijuana fields.

The only sizable towns in the region are Orange Walk, about 53 miles (87 km) north of Belize City, with about 14,000 residents, and the slightly smaller Corozal, with a population of around 10,000, 85 miles (139 km) north of Belize City. Both are on the Philip Goldson Highway, formerly the Northern Highway, a paved two-lane road that runs 95 miles (156 km) from Belize City up the center of the region, ending at the Mexican border.

Northern Belize gets less rain than anywhere else in the country (roughly 50 inches annually in Corozal), a fact that's reflected in the sunny disposition of the local population, mostly Maya and Mestizos. Both Orange Walk and Corozal towns have a Mexican ambience, with central plazas serving as the focus of the downtown areas. Most locals speak Spanish as a first language, though most also know some English, and many speak both Spanish and English fluently. Offering little in the way of tourism facilities itself, Orange Walk Town is a jumping-off point for trips to Lamanai and other Mayan ruins, to Mennonite farmlands, and to several well-regarded jungle lodges in wild, remote areas. Corozal Town, next door to Chetumal, Mexico, is a place to slow down, relax, and enjoy the laid-back atmosphere of a charming small town on the beautiful Corozal Bay (or, as Mexico calls it, Chetumal Bay).

If you tire of small-town pleasures, the Belize side of the Mexican border has three casinos, including one called Las Vegas that claims to be the largest casino in Central America, and a duty-free zone (though the shopping here is mostly for cheap clothing and appliances, with little of interest to international visitors). Corozal has begun to draw foreign expats looking for inexpensive real estate and proximity to Chetumal, the Quintana Roo Mexican state capital, whose metropolitan population is nearly as large as that of the entire country of Belize. Chetumal offers urban conveniences that Belize doesn't, including a modern shopping mall, fast food, a multiplex cinema, and big-box stores including Walmart and Sam's Club. Sarteneja Village, in the far northeastern part of Corozal District, about 35 miles (57 km) from Corozal Town, is a still undiscovered fishing village at the edge of the sea, near the Shipstern Wildlife Reserve. On the way are several pristine lagoons, including the lovely Progresso Lagoon.

ORIENTATION AND PLANNING

GETTING ORIENTED

The Philip Goldson Highway, a paved two-lane road, renamed in 2012 for a prominent politician (the international airport is also named for him), is the transportation spine of the region, running about 95 miles (156 km) from Belize City to the Mexican border at Chetumal, passing the two main towns in northern Belize, Orange Walk and Corozal. A bypass around Orange Walk provides a way to avoid the congested downtown.

Branching off the Goldson Highway are a number of tertiary roads, mostly unpaved, including the road to Crooked Tree Wildlife Sanctuary; the Old Northern Highway that leads to the Altun Ha ruins and Maruba Lodge and Spa; a road to Shipyard, a Mennonite settlement, which also connects with roads to the Lamanai ruins and to La Milpa ruins and Chan Chich Lodge at Gallon Jug; the San Estevan Road that is a route to Progresso, Copper Bank, and the Cerros Maya ruins, or, via a different branch, to Sarteneja. An additional section of the San Estevan Road from Orange Walk to Progresso was scheduled to be paved in 2012, but as of mid-2013 that is still pending. Another route, unpaved, to Sarteneja runs from Corozal Town and requires crossing the New River and the mouth of Laguna Seca on hand-pulled auto ferries.

Crooked Tree Wildlife Sanctuary. A paradise for birders, this wildlife sanctuary is an "inland island" surrounded by a chain of lagoons, in total covering about 3,000 acres. Traveling by canoe among countless birds, you're likely to see iguanas, crocodiles, coatis, and turtles.

Altun Ha. Easy to get to from the Northern Cayes or Belize City, Altun Ha is the most visited Mayan ruin in Belize. After the ruins, treat yourself to a cold drink or mud bath at nearby Maruba Resort Jungle Spa.

Northwest Orange Walk District. A fascinating combination of Mennonite farm country, wild jungle, and Mayan sites including Lamanai, La Milpa, and Chan Chich, this remote part of Belize is anchored by two remarkable jungle lodges, Chan Chich Lodge and Lamanai Outpost.

Sadly, and almost unbelievably, one of the largest Mayan temples in Belize, Nohmul on private lands near Orange Walk Town, in mid-2013 was bulldozed by a contractor for use as roadfill.

Corozal Bay. It's so low-key you may doze off occasionally, but for relaxation at modest cost you can't find a better spot than the shores of Corozal Bay. Copper Bank and Sarteneja are especially laid-back. Corozal Town is an expat magnet.

PLANNING

WHEN TO GO

Corozal Town and the rest of northern Belize get about the same amount of rain as Atlanta, Georgia, so even the "rainy season"—generally June to November—here is not to be feared. It's hot and humid for much of the year, except in waterfront areas where prevailing breezes mitigate the heat. December to April is usually the most pleasant time, with weather similar to that of south Florida. In winter, cold fronts from the north occasionally bring rain and chilly weather, and when the temperature drops to the low 60s, locals wear sweaters and sleep under extra blankets.

GETTING HERE AND AROUND

AIR TRAVEL

Corozal Town has flights only to and from San Pedro (Ambergris Caye). Tropic Air and Maya Island Air each fly four to six times daily between Ambergris Caye and the airstrip at Corozal, about 2 miles (3 km) south of town off the Goldson Highway. The journey takes 20 minutes and costs around BZ$100 one-way. From Corozal, there's no direct service to Belize City or other destinations in Belize. Charter service is available to Chan Chich Lodge and the Indian Church/Lamanai area.

Contacts Maya Island Air ⊠ *Corozal Air Strip, Ranchito* 🖀 *422/0711 Corozal Airstrip, Ranchito, 223/1140 Belize City* ⊕ *www.mayaislandair.com.* **Tropic Air** ⊠ *Corozal Air Strip, Ranchito* 🖀 *226/2012 San Pedro main office, 800/422–3435 in U.S., 444/0210 Corozal Airstrip, Ranchito Village* ⊕ *www.tropicair.com.*

BOAT AND WATER-TAXI TRAVEL

Ferry from Corozal. An old, hand-pulled sugar barge ferries passengers and cars across the New River from just south of Corozal Town to the road to Copper Bank, Cerros, and the Shipstern peninsula. The ferry is free from 6 am to 9 pm daily. ✢ *To get to the ferry from Corozal, take the Northern Highway south toward Orange Walk Town and look for the ferry sign. Turn left and follow the unpaved road to the ferry landing.*

Ferry between Copper Bank and Sarteneja. A second, hand-pulled auto ferry has been added between Copper Bank and Sarteneja, at the mouth of Laguna Seca. ✢ *From Copper Bank, follow the ferry signs. Near Chunox, at a T-intersection, turn left and follow the unpaved road 20 miles (32 km) to Sarteneja.*

Water Taxi between Corozal Town and Ambergris Caye. A daily water taxi operates between Corozal Town and Ambergris Caye, with a stop on demand at Sarteneja. The *Thunderbolt* departs from Corozal at the pier near Reunion Park behind Corozal House of Culture at 7 am and also goes from a pier on the back side of San Pedro near the soccer field to

TOP REASONS TO GO

Mayan Sites: Several of the most interesting Mayan sites in the region are in northern Belize. These include Altun Ha, Lamanai, and Cerros. Altun Ha gets the most visitors of any Mayan site in Belize, and Lamanai, on the New River Lagoon, and Cerros, on Corozal Bay, are notable because of their beautiful locations.

Wild, Open Spaces: This part of Belize has some of the country's wildest tracts of land. The quarter-million acres of Rio Bravo Conservation and Management Area host only a few thousand visitors each year. Although people are scarce, Rio Bravo teems with wildlife. Other large tracts of land include the Gallon Jug lands, 130,000 privately owned acres around Chan Chich Lodge. The Shipstern Reserve is a 22,000-acre expanse of swamps, lagoons, and forests on the Sarteneja peninsula. Huge numbers of birds nest at the Crooked Tree Wildlife Sanctuary.

Jungle Lodges: Northern Belize is home to several first-rate lodges, including Chan Chich Lodge, a paradise for birders and the place where you're most likely to spot the jaguar in the wild. Lamanai Outpost, on the New River Lagoon, is a center for crocodile research.

4

Corozal at 3 pm. Fare is BZ$45 one-way. The trip usually takes nearly two hours but may be longer if there's a stop at Sarteneja, or if the weather is bad. Off-season, service is sometimes reduced and occasionally is discontinued altogether.

Chetumal to San Pedro and Caye Caulker. Two similarly named Belize-based water-taxi companies, San Pedro Belize Express and San Pedro Water Jets Express, provide service direct from Chetumal, Mexico, to San Pedro and Caye Caulker. In addition to water taxi charges, leaving Chetumal you pay a US$5 port fee and 295 Mexican peso (about US$24) tourist tax if you cannot prove you have paid it earlier, for example with your air ticket to Mexico; leaving San Pedro or Caulker you pay BZ$37.50 Belize unit fee plus US$5/BZ$10 port fee.

San Pedro Belize Express. The San Pedro Belize Express departs from the Muelle Fiscal in Chetumal, Mexico, at 3 pm. It returns from Caye Caulker (the pier on Front St. near the basketball court) at 7 am and from San Pedro (pier on beachfront, near Tackle Box Bar & Grill) at 7:30 am. The advertised rates are US$37.50 (BZ$75) between Chetumal and San Pedro, and US$40 (BZ$80) between Chetumal and Caye Caulker. The water taxi takes about 90 minutes between Chetumal and San Pedro and 2 hours between Chetumal and Caye Caulker. If you are buying your ticket in Chetumal— the ticket office is near the entrance to the pier—you may be able to negotiate a lower price than the advertised rate. Off-season (summer/early fall) service may be reduced. ⊠ *Beachfront at Tacklebox Bar & Grill, San Pedro Town* ☎ *226/3535 in San Pedro, 521/983–832–1648 in Mexico* ⊕ *www.belizewatertaxi.com.*

San Pedro Water Jets Express. The San Pedro Water Jets Express boat departs leaves Chetumal, Mexico, from the Muelle Fiscal (Municipal Pier) daily at 3 pm, arriving at the pier on the back side of San Pedro near the soccer field. The boat continues on to Caye Caulker. From Caye Caulker to Chetumal, the boat departs daily at 7:30 am; from San Pedro to Chetumal, the boat departs daily at 8 am. The advertised rate is US$40 (BZ$80) between San Pedro and Chetumal, and US$45 (BZ$90) to or from Caye Caulker. This water taxi takes about 90 minutes between Chetumal and San Pedro and 2 hours between Chetumal and Caye Caulker. If you are buying your ticket in Chetumal—ticket offices are near the entrance to the pier—you may be able to negotiate a lower price than the advertised rate. In low season (summer/early fall) service may be reduced. ⊠ *San Pedro Water Jets Express, San Pedro Town* ☎ *226/2194 in San Pedro* ⊕ *www.sanpedrowatertaxi.com.*

BUS TRAVEL AND SHUTTLE SERVICE

Buses between Belize City and Corozal run about every half hour during daylight hours in both directions, and some of these continue on to Chetumal, Mexico.

Several small bus lines, including Belize Bus Owners Cooperative (BBOC), Chell, Morales, Russell, Tillett, T-Line, Frazer, Valencia, J&J, and others, make the 3- to 3½-hour journey between Belize City and Corozal Town, with service by one line or another approximately every half hour during the day.

Northbound buses from Belize City. Northbound buses depart beginning at 5:30 am, with the last departure around 7:30 pm.

Southbound buses from Corozal. Southbound buses begin at 3:45 am, with the last departure at 7:30 pm.

The cost between Belize City and Corozal is about BZ$9 or BZ$10, or BZ$12 for express service; the cost between Belize City and Orange Walk Town is around BZ$5. Some buses continue on to the Nuevo Mercado (New Market) bus terminal in Chetumal, Mexico. Fare is around BZ$3 between Chetumal and Corozal. As of this writing, none of the Belize buses arrive at or depart from the main bus station in Chetumal, the ADO terminal.

Any non-express bus will stop and pick up almost anywhere along the highway.

■TIP→ Bus service to the villages and other sites off the Goldson Highway is limited, so to reach them you're best off with a rental car or a guided tour. There is some bus service on the Old Northern Highway and from Orange Walk to Sarteneja. Bus franchises and routes in Belize, which are controlled by the government, are in a state of flux. Ask locally for updates on bus lines, routes, and fares. The Belize Bus Blog (⊕ *www.belizebus.wordpress.com*) is a good source of information on buses and other transportation in Belize.

To Guatemala. In addition to regular buses, a Guatemalan tourism bus operator, San Juan Travel Services, operates a daily bus from the main Chetumal ADO bus terminal, currently leaving at 5 am and going all the way to Flores, Guatemala, near Tikal, with a stop at the Marine Terminal in Belize City. The three-hour trip to Belize City costs BZ$20; it's a total of about eight hours and BZ$70 from Chetumal to Flores.

Two shuttle services based in Corozal Town, Belize VIP Transfers and George and Esther Moralez Travel, provide inexpensive and handy transportation across the border between Corozal and Chetumal. These services, which cost BZ$60–BZ$70 one-way for up to three or four people, make crossing the border easy and hassle free.

The transfer services also provide shuttles to and from Cancún and other destinations in the Yucatán and in Belize. To or from Cancún, you'll pay around BZ$800 for up to four persons.

Contacts Belize VIP Transfers (Henry Menzies) ✉ *Caribbean Village, South End, Corozal* ☎ *422/2725* ⊕ *www.belizetransfers.com.* **George & Esther Moralez Travel Service** ✉ *3 Blue Bird St., Corozal Town* ☎ *604/5789* ⊕ *www.gettransfers.com.*

CAR TRAVEL

Corozal is the last stop on the Goldson Highway before you hit Mexico. The 95-mile (153-km) journey from Belize City will probably take about two hours, unless you're slowed by sugarcane trucks. The Goldson Highway is a two-lane paved road in fairly good condition. Other roads, including the Old Northern Highway, roads to Lamanai, Río Bravo, and Gallon Jug, and the road to Sarteneja are mostly unpaved. Because tour and long-distance taxi prices are high, especially if you're traveling with family or in a group, you likely will save money by renting a car.

Car-rental agencies in Belize City will usually deliver vehicles to Corozal and Orange Walk, but there will be a drop fee, starting at around BZ$150. Two small local car-rental agencies, Corozal Cars and Belize VIP Service, have a few cars to rent, at rates starting around BZ$140 a day, plus tax.

Contacts Belize VIP Service ✉ *Caribbean Village, South End, Corozal* ☎ *422/2725* ⊕ *www.belizetransfers.com.* **Corozal Cars** ✉ *Mile 85, Philip Goldson Hwy., formerly Northern Hwy., Corozal* ☎ *422/3339* ⊕ *www.corozalcars.com.*

TAXI TRAVEL

To get around Corozal, call the Taxi Association or ask your hotel to arrange for transportation. Fares to most destinations in town are low, at BZ$10 or less, but rates to points outside town can be expensive; agree on a price beforehand. Likewise, in Orange Walk call the Taxi Association or ask your hotel to arrange a taxi.

Contacts Taxi Association in Corozal ✉ *1st St. South, Corozal* ☎ *422/2035.* **Taxi Association in Orange Walk** ✉ *Queen Victoria Ave., Orange Walk Town* ☎ *322/2560.*

EMERGENCIES

For dental and medical care, many of Corozal's residents go to Chetumal, Mexico. In Corozal, visit Bethesda Medical Centre if you need medical care. Bethesda is associated with InterAmerican Medical University, a small offshore med school. The Corozal Hospital, with only limited facilities, is on the Goldson Highway. In Orange Walk, the Northern Regional Hospital doesn't look very appealing, but it provides emergency and other services. Consider going to Belize City or Chetumal for medical and dental care, if possible.

Emergency Contacts Bethesda Medical Centre ⊠ *Mile 85.5, Goldson Hwy., Corozal* ☎ *422/3000.* **Corozal Community Hospital** ⊠ *Philip Goldson Hwy., Corozal* ☎ *422/2076.* **Northern Regional Hospital** ⊠ *Northern Hwy., Orange Walk* ☎ *322/2752.*

MONEY MATTERS

Although American dollars are accepted everywhere in Corozal and Orange Walk, money changers at the Mexico border and in Corozal Town exchange Belize dollars for U.S. and Mexican currency, usually at better rates than in banks. The four banks in Corozal—Atlantic Bank, Belize Bank, Heritage Bank, and ScotiaBank—have ATMs, and three (all accept Heritage) accept ATM cards issued outside Belize. Look for ATM machines that display the Cirrus or Plus network logos. Orange Walk Town also has branches of Atlantic Bank, Heritage Bank, and ScotiaBank; Atlantic and ScotiaBank have ATMs that accept foreign ATM cards. There are no banks in Sarteneja or the Copper Bank area, or around Altun Ha or near the jungle lodges in remote areas of Orange Walk District. *(See ATMs and Banks in Travel Smart for Bank contact information)*

ABOUT THE RESTAURANTS

With the exception of dining rooms at upscale jungle lodges, where four-course dinners can run BZ$70 or more, restaurants are almost invariably small, inexpensive, family-run places, serving simple meals such as stew chicken with rice and beans. Here, you'll rarely pay more than BZ$25 for dinner, and frequently much less. If there's a predominant culinary influence, it's Mexican, and many restaurants serve tacos, tamales, *garnaches* (small, fried corn tortillas with beans, cabbage, and cheese piled on them), and soups such as *escabeche* (onion soup with chicken). A few places, mostly in Corozal Town, cater to tourists and expats with burgers and steaks. For a quick snack, restaurants on the second floor of the Corozal market sell inexpensive breakfast and lunch items (usually closed Sunday). You can also buy delicious local fruits and vegetables at the market—a huge papaya, two lovely mangoes, and a bunch of bananas cost as little as BZ$2.50 or BZ$3.

ABOUT THE HOTELS

As with restaurants, most hotels in northern Belize are small, family-run spots. In Corozal and Orange Walk towns, hotels are modest affairs with room rates generally under BZ$150–BZ$200 for a double, a fraction of the cost of hotels in San Pedro or other more popular parts of Belize. Generally, the hotels are clean, well maintained, and offer a homey atmosphere. They have private baths and plenty of hot and cold water, and most also have air-conditioning. Hotels and lodges in Crooked Tree, Sarteneja, and Copper Bank are also small and inexpensive; some have air-conditioning. The jungle lodges near Lamanai, Gallon Jug, and Altun Ha, however, are a different story. Several of these, including Chan Chich Lodge, Maruba Jungle Lodge and Spa, and Lamanai Outpost Lodge, are upscale accommodations, with gorgeous settings in the jungle or on a lagoon and prices to match, typically BZ$500 or more for a double in-season; meals and tours are extra. These lodges also offer all-inclusive and other package options that may go for BZ$1,000 and more.

GREAT ITINERARIES

IF YOU HAVE 3 TO 5 DAYS IN NORTHERN BELIZE

If you are starting in Belize City, rent a car and drive to Crooked Tree Wildlife Sanctuary, which has great birding and offers the chance to see the jabiru stork, the largest flying bird in the Americas. Spend a few hours here, canoeing on the lagoon and hiking trails. If you have an interest in birding, you'll want to overnight here at one of the simple lagoon-side lodges, such as Bird's Eye View Lodge or Crooked Tree Lodge. Otherwise, you could drive on to Maruba, an upscale jungle lodge and spa. The drive from Crooked Tree takes about 45 minutes. While you're at Maruba, visit the Altun Ha Mayan site, which you can see in a couple of hours. On the second day, drive to Corozal Town, about 1½ hours from Maruba or Crooked Tree. Base here in Corozal Town for two days, at one of the small hotels on Corozal Bay such as Almond Tree Hotel Resort or Tony's Inn and Beach

Resort, making day trips by boat to Lamanai and Cerros ruins (or you can drive). If you have additional days in the north, you can add a visit to Sarteneja or cross the border into Chetumal, Mexico. Alternatively, after the first night in Crooked Tree or at Maruba, drive to the Lamanai Mayan site and spend the night there at Lamanai Outpost Lodge on the New River Lagoon, or, for a different experience, proceed to Blue Creek Village, a Mennonite area, and spend the night at Hillside B&B, or at La Milpa Field Station. Then, continue on through Programme for Belize lands to Chan Chich Lodge and spend the rest of your time in northern Belize at this amazing jungle lodge. If money isn't much of an object and you want one of the best jungle lodge experiences in Central America, then ditch the car and fly from Belize City to Chan Chich, where you can spend all your time looking for jaguars and listening to the howler monkeys.

HOTEL AND RESTAURANT PRICES

Prices in the restaurant reviews are the average cost of a main course at dinner or, if dinner is not served, at lunch; taxes and service charges are generally included. Prices in the hotel reviews are the lowest cost of a standard double room in high season, excluding taxes, service charges, and meal plans (except at all-inclusives). Prices for rentals are the lowest per-night cost for a one-bedroom unit in high season.

For expanded lodging reviews and current deals, visit Fodors.com.

SAFETY

Corozal is one of Belize's safer areas, but petty theft and burglaries aren't uncommon, so use common sense when traveling through the area. Both Corozal Town and Orange Walk Town have some crack cocaine users. Often, they stand on the street with a pigtail bucket (a 5-gallon bucket) of water and try to earn money by washing car windshields—ignore them if you can.

TOURS

SEEING THE RUINS

Your hotel in Orange Walk Town or Corozal Town can arrange tours to **Lamanai, Cerros,** and other sites, starting at around BZ$80 per person. In Orange Walk, Reyes & Sons River Tours, Beyond Touring, and J.

Avila & Sons run boat trips (around BZ$80 per person, plus BZ$10 admission fee) up the New River to Lamanai and can help arrange other tours and trips. In Corozal Town, Belize VIP Transfers *(see Bus Travel)* can arrange tours of Cerros, Santa Rita and elsewhere.

Contacts Beyond Touring ⊠ *Tower Bridge, Goldson Hwy., at New River, Orange Walk Town* ☎ *954/415–2897 in the U.S.* ⊕ *www.beyondtouring. com.* **J. Avila & Sons River Tours** ⊠ *42 Riverside St., Orange Walk Town* ☎ *322/0419.* **Reyes & Sons River Tours** ⊠ *Tower Hill Bridge, Orange Walk Town* ☎ *322/3327.*

SNORKELING

From Sarteneja, Sarteneja Adventure Tours can take you to Bacalar Chico Marine Reserve and National Park off North Ambergris Caye. Rates are BZ$170 per person for a full-day snorkel tour, including guide, park admission, snorkeling gear, and lunch.

Contact Sarteneja Adventure Tours ⊠ *N. Front St., Sarteneja* ☎ *621/833⁵.*

VISITOR INFORMATION

An excellent source of general information on northern Belize is the website Northern Belize, ⊕ *www.northernbelize.com.* For information about Corozal, check ⊕ *www.corozal.com.* Local information on Orange Walk managed by the Orange Walk Town Council is at ⊕ *www.owtc.bz.*

The Corozal House of Culture *(see Exploring Corozal Town)* houses a museum devoted to the history of Corozal Town and northern Belize, and a visitor information center.

CROOKED TREE WILDLIFE SANCTUARY

33 miles (54 km) northwest of Belize City.

Crooked Tree Wildlife Sanctuary is one of Belize's top birding spots. The 16,400-acre sanctuary includes more than 3,000 acres of lagoons, swamp, and marsh, surrounding what is essentially an inland island. Traveling by canoe, you're likely to see iguanas, crocodiles, coatis, and turtles. The sanctuary's most prestigious visitors, however, are the jabiru storks, which usually visit between November and May. With a wing-span up to 12 feet, the jabiru is the largest flying bird in the Americas. ■**TIP**➔ For birders the best time to come is in the dry season, roughly from February to late May, when lowered water levels cause birds to group together to find water and food, making them easy to spot. Birding is good year-round, however, and the area is more scenic when the lagoons are full. Snowy egrets, snail kites, ospreys, and black-collared hawks, as well as two types of duck—Muscovy and black-bellied whistling—and all five species of kingfishers native to Belize can be spotted. Even on a short, one- to three-hour tour, you're likely to see 20 to 40 species of birds. South of Crooked Tree, on Sapodilla Lagoon and accessible by boat, is a small Mayan site, Chau Hiix.

GETTING HERE AND AROUND

An easy 25-minute drive north from the international airport takes you to the entrance road to Crooked Tree Wildlife Sanctuary at Mile 30.8 of the Goldson Highway. From there it's another 2 miles (3 km) on an unpaved

LOCAL FOOD FESTIVALS

Belizeans love to party, and festivals celebrating lobster, chocolate, cashews, and other local foods give them—and you—the chance to join in the fun. Here are some of the food festivals in Belize. Note that dates can change from year to year.

Cashew Festival, Crooked Tree in early May. Crooked Tree village is named for the cashew tree that often grows in a serpentine fashion, curling and growing sideways as well as up. The yellow cashew fruit, which tastes a little like mango and smells like grapes, ripens in late spring, and the Crooked Tree Festival celebrates the cashew in all its forms: fruit, nut, juice, jam, and wine.

Chocolate Festival of Belize, Toledo in late May. Toledo's increasingly popular tribute to local cacao celebrates the home of chocolate in Belize, with tours of small chocolate factories in Punta Gorda and nearby, visits to organic cacao farms, and local music and dances. Belikin beer even brews a special chocolate stout for the occasion.

Hopkins Mango Festival and Cultural Jam in late May or early June. New in 2011, the Hopkins Mango Fest is devoted to the sweet, juicy mango, spiced by local Garifuna culture. Events include a Garifuna drumming competition, along with bicycle and canoe races.

Placencia LobsterFest in late June. Belize's biggest and best salute to the spiny lobster is held in Placencia village, usually on the last weekend in June. Booths sell local lobster grilled, fried, curried, and in fritters, and there's music, dancing, and lots of Belikin. LobsterFests also are held, typically in late June or early July, in San Pedro and Caye Caulker.

causeway to the sanctuary visitor center and Crooked Tree village. If you don't have a rental car, any of the frequent non-express buses going north to Orange Walk or Corozal will drop you at the entrance road, but you'll have to hike across the causeway to the village (or arrange a pickup by your Crooked Tree hotel). Jex buses leave from the corner of Regent Street West and West Canal Street in Belize City and go directly to the village, currently three times daily except Sunday (BZ$4).

TIMING

One full day is enough to do a canoe trip on the lagoon, hike local trails, and see the small Creole village. But if you're a birder, you'll want at least another day.

Bus Info Jex and Sons Bus Service ✉ *Crooked Tree Village* ☎ *225/7017.*

EXPLORING

Crooked Tree Village. One of Belize's oldest inland villages, established some 300 years ago, Crooked Tree is at the reserve's center. With a population of about 900, most of Creole origin, the community has a church, school, and one of the surest signs of a former British territory: a cricket pitch. There are many large cashew trees around the village, the serpentine growth pattern of which gave the village its name. The cashews are highly fragrant when in bloom in January and February, and when the cashew fruit ripen to a golden yellow color in May and June, they taste something like mango and smell like sweet grapes. The cashew nuts require roasting to make them edible. Villagers make and sell cashew wine. A Cashew Festival is held annually in early May. ✉ *Off Philip Goldson Hwy. (formerly Northern Hwy.), Crooked Tree* ☎ *223/5004* 🌐 *www.belizeaudubon.org.*

CROOKED TREE GUIDES

For an introduction to the sanctuary, and for a guide, visit the Crooked Tree Visitor Center at the end of the causeway. The visitor center can put you in touch with all the best local guides. Expect to pay about BZ$20–BZ$30 an hour for guide services, more if you're going by boat or horseback.

Crooked Tree Visitor Center. At the Crooked Tree Visitor Center at the end of the causeway where you pay your BZ$8 sanctuary admission fee, you can arrange a guided tour of the sanctuary or rent a canoe (around BZ$10–$20 per person per hour) for a do-it-yourself trip. The sanctuary is managed by the Belize Audubon Society. You can also walk through the village and hike birding trails around the area. If you'd prefer to go by horseback, you'll pay around BZ$30 an hour. The visitor center has a free village and trail map. If you're staying overnight, your hotel can arrange canoe or bike rentals and set up tours and trips. Although tours can run at any time, the best time is early in the morning, when birds are most active. ✉ *Crooked Tree Sanctuary Visitor Center, Crooked Tree Village* ☎ *223/5004 Belize Audubon Society* 🌐 *www.belizeaudubon.org* 🎟 *BZ$8* ⏲ *Daily 8–4.*

WHERE TO STAY

$ B&B/INN 🏨 **Bird's Eye View Lodge.** Many of the 20 spic-and-span rooms, all with air-conditioning and all recently refurbished, at this modern concrete hotel have views of the lagoon. **Pros:** on shores of Crooked Tree Lagoon; delicious meals made with local ingredients; breezy second-floor patio with great lagoon views. **Cons:** undistinguished, blocky buildings; no-frills guestrooms. [$] *Rooms from: BZ$167* ✉ *Bird's Eye View Lodge, on lagoon, Crooked Tree* ☎ *203/2040* 🌐 *www.birdseyeviewbelize.com* 🛏 *20 rooms* 🍴 *Multiple meal plans.*

$ B&B/INN FAMILY Fodor's Choice ★ 🏨 **Crooked Tree Lodge.** Owned by a British-Belizean couple on the site of the old Paradise Lodge, this lodge has six comfy hardwood cottages on a gorgeous 11½-acre site on the shores of the Crooked Tree Lagoon. **Pros:** wonderful lagoon-side location; friendly hosts; good food. **Cons:** no air-conditioning. [$] *Rooms from: BZ$131* ✉ *Crooked Tree Lodge, on Crooked Tree Lagoon, Crooked Tree* ☎ *626/3820* 🌐 *www.crookedtreelodgebelize.com* 🛏 *5 cabanas and 1 2-bedroom cottage* 🍴 *Multiple meal plans.*

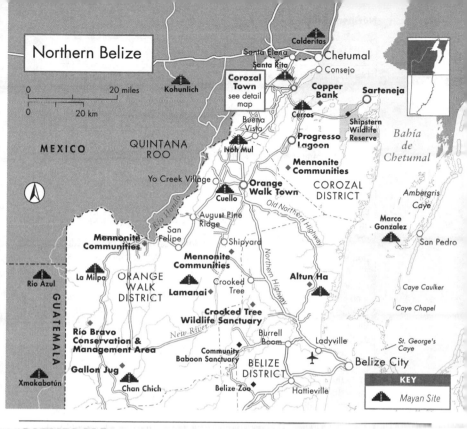

Northern Belize

0 _____ 20 miles
0 _____ 20 km

MEXICO

QUINTANA
ROO

Calderitas

Santa Elena
Santa Rita
Chetumal
Consejo

Corozal
Town
see detail
map

Copper
Bank

Sarteneja

Kohunlich

Cerros

Buena
Vista

Shipstern
Wildlife
Reserve

Bahía
de
Chetumal

Noh Mul

Progresso
Lagoon

Mennonite
Communities

COROZAL
DISTRICT

Yo Creek Village

Orange
Walk Town

Old Northern Highway

Ambergris
Caye

Cuello

August Pine
Ridge

San
Felipe

Shipyard

Marco
Gonzalez

San Pedro

Mennonite
Communities

Mennonite
Communities

Northern Highway

Caye Caulker

La Milpa

ORANGE
WALK
DISTRICT

Lamanai

Crooked
Tree

Altun Ha

Caye Chapel

Rio Azul

GUATEMALA

Crooked Tree
Wildlife Sanctuary

New River

Burrell
Boom

Ladyville

St. George's
Caye

Rio Bravo
Conservation &
Management Area

Community
Baboon Sanctuary

BELIZE
DISTRICT

Belize City

Gallon Jug

Xmakabatún

Chan Chich

Belize Zoo

Hattieville

KEY

Mayan Site

ALTUN HA

28 miles (45 km) north of Belize City.

If you've never experienced an ancient Mayan city, make a trip to Altun Ha, which is a modern translation in Mayan of the name "Rockstone Pond," a nearby village. It's not Belize's most dramatic site—Caracol and Lamanai vie for that award—but it's one of the most accessible and most thoroughly excavated. The first inhabitants settled before 300 BC, and their descendants finally abandoned the site after AD 1000. At its height during the Classic period the city was home to 10,000 people.

GETTING HERE AND AROUND

Altun Ha is easily visited on your own—if you have a car. From Belize City, drive north on the Goldson Highway to Mile 18.9; turn right on the *Old* Northern Highway and go 10½ miles (17 km). The Old Northern Highway is a mix of gravel areas, broken pavement, and paved sections. The turnoff from the Old Northern Highway to Altun Ha, on the left, is well marked. If coming from Corozal or Orange Walk, you can also enter the Old Northern Highway at Mile 49 of the Goldson Highway. There's limited bus service from Belize City to Maskall Village near Altun Ha.

NORTHERN BELIZE HISTORY

The Maya settled this area thousands of years before the time of Christ. Cuello, near Orange Walk Town, dates from 2500 BC, making it one of the earliest known Mayan sites in all of Mesoamerica (the region between central Mexico and northwest Costa Rica). In the Pre-Classic period (2500 BC–AD 300) the Maya expanded across northern Belize, establishing important communities and trading posts at Santa Rita, Cerros, Lamanai, and elsewhere.

During the Classic period (AD 300–AD 900), Santa Rita, Lamanai, Altun Ha, and other cities flourished. To feed large populations perhaps totaling several hundred thousand, the Maya developed sophisticated agricultural systems, with raised, irrigated fields along the New River and other river bottoms. After the mysterious collapse of the Mayan civilization by the 10th century AD, the region's cities went into decline, but the Maya continued to live in smaller communities and rural areas around the many lagoons in northern Belize, trading with other settlements in Belize and in Mexico. Lamanai, perched at the edge of the New River Lagoon, was continuously occupied for almost three millennia, until late in the 17th century.

The Spanish first set foot in these parts in the early 1500s, and Spanish missionaries made their way up the New River to establish churches in Mayan settlements in the 16th and 17th centuries. You can see the remains of a Spanish church at the entrance of Lamanai near Indian Church Village. About this same time, small groups of shipwrecked British sailors established settlements in Belize but the Battle of St. George's Caye in 1789 effectively put an end to Spanish control in Belize.

In the second half of the 19th century, the so-called Caste Wars (1847–1904), pitting Maya insurgents against Mestizo and European settlers in Mexico's Yucatán, had an important impact on northern Belize. Refugees from the bloody wars moved south from Mexico, settling in Corozal Town, Orange Walk Town, Sarteneja, and also on Ambergris Caye and Caye Caulker.

Today more than 40,000 acres of sugarcane are harvested by some 4,000 small farmers in northern Belize. Mennonites, who came to the Blue Creek, Shipyard, and Little Belize areas in the late 1950s, have contributed greatly to agriculture in the region, producing rice, corn, chickens, milk, cheese, and beans. And tourism, foreign retirement communities, and casino gaming are becoming important, especially in northern Corozal District.

TIMING
You can see Altun Ha in a couple of hours. If you add lunch and a spa treatment at the nearby Maruba Resort Jungle Spa, you'll spend most of the day in the area.

SAFETY AND PRECAUTIONS
Marijuana is illegally grown in remote areas off the Old Northern Highway. Avoid hiking off trail, where you might accidentally stumble on someone's weed plantation.

EXPLORING

FAMILY **Altun Ha.** A team from the Royal Ontario Museum first excavated Altun Ha in the early 1960s and found 250 structures spread over more than 1,000 square yards. At Plaza B, in the Temple of the Masonry Altars, archaeologists unearthed the grandest and most valuable piece of Mayan art ever discovered—the head of the sun god Kinich Ahau. Weighing nearly 10 pounds, it was carved from a solid block of green jade. The head is kept in a solid steel vault in the Central Bank of Belize, though it is occasionally displayed at the Museum of Belize. The jade head appears on all denominations of Belize currency. If the Masonry Altars temple looks familiar to you, it's because an illustration of the Masonry Altars structure appears on Belikin beer bottles. Because the Altun Ha site is small, it's not necessary to have a tour guide, but licensed guides may offer their services when you arrive.

Tours from Belize City, Orange Walk, and Crooked Tree also are options. Altun Ha is a regular stop on cruise ship excursions, and on days when several ships are in port in Belize City, typically midweek, Altun Ha may be overrun with cruise passengers. Several tour operators in San Pedro and Caye Caulker also offer day trips to Altun Ha, often combined with lunch at the nearby Maruba Resort Jungle Spa. Most of these tours from the cayes are by boat, landing at Bomba Village. From here, a van makes the short ride to Altun Ha. If traveling independently or on a tour that includes it, you can stop at Maruba Resort Jungle Spa for a drink, lunch, or a spa treatment *(see Where to Stay).* ✉ *Rockstone Pond Rd., off Old Northern Hwy., Maskall Village* ✣ *From Belize City, take Northern Hwy. north to Mile 18.9. Turn right (east) on Old Northern Hwy., which is only partly paved, and go 14 miles (23 km) to signed entrance road at Rockstone Pond Rd. to Altun Ha on left. Follow this paved road 2 miles (3 km) to visitor center.* ☎ *822/2106 NICH/Belize Institute of Archeology* 🌐 *www.nich.org* 🎫 *BZ$10* 🕒 *Daily 8–5.*

WHERE TO STAY

$$$ RESORT 🏨 **Maruba Resort Jungle Spa.** Maruba definitely delivers an exotic experience in a jungle setting, complete with 24-hour electricity, air-conditioned cabanas, fresh flowers in the rooms, high-thread-count sheets, and, in some suites, hot tubs. **Pros:** remote; some find it sexy and hip. **Cons:** some find it outlandish; can be buggy; not in a particularly scenic area of Belize. [$] *Rooms from: BZ$436* ✉ *Mile 40.5 Old Northern Hwy., 10 miles (17 km) north of Altun Ha, Maskall Village* ☎ *225/5555* 🌐 *www.maruba-belize.com* 🛏 *8 rooms, 10 suites* 🍴 *Multiple meal plans.*

NORTHWEST ORANGE WALK DISTRICT

This district borders both Mexico and Guatemala, and holds four areas well worth the time it takes to visit them: Lamanai Archeological Reserve, at the edge of the New River Lagoon; the Mennonite communities of Blue Creek and Shipyard; the 260,000-plus acres of the Río Bravo Conservation Area; and Gallon Jug lands, 130,000 acres in which the remarkable Chan Chich Lodge nestles.

These areas, especially Río Bravo and Gallon Jug, are best visited on an overnight or multi-night stay. You can visit Lamanai on a day trip by boat or road from Orange Walk Town (and guided day tours are also available from Belize City, San Pedro, and Caye Caulker), though it's well worth at least an overnight stay. If you're staying in Blue Creek, you can go to Río Bravo, Lamanai, and even Gallon Jug and Chan Chich on a day trip, but the poor roads will slow you down, and you'll have little time to explore. Both the Gallon Jug and Programme for Belize (Río Bravo) lands are private, with gated entrances, so you'll need advance permission to visit.

ORANGE WALK TOWN

52 miles (85 km) north of Belize City.

Orange Walk Town is barely on the radar of visitors, except as a jumping-off point for boat trips to Lamanai, road trips to Gallon Jug and Río Bravo, or as a place to gas up en route from Corozal to Belize City. Though its population of around 14,000, mostly Mestizos, makes it the fifth-largest urban center in Belize (after Belize City, San Pedro, Belmopan City, and San Ignacio), it's more like a "county seat" in an agricultural area than a city. In this case, it's county seat of Belize's sugarcane region, and you'll see big tractors and trucks hauling sugarcane to the Tower Hill refinery. Happily, a bypass around Orange Walk Town has reduced through traffic.

The town's atmosphere will remind you a little of Mexico, with signs in Spanish, a central plaza, and sun-baked stores set close to the streets. The plaza, near the Orange Walk Town Hall, has a small market (daily except Sunday and holidays) with fruits, vegetables, and inexpensive local foods for sale. This was once the site of Fort Cairns, which dates to the Caste Wars of the 19th century.

GETTING HERE AND AROUND

Orange Walk Town is about midway between Belize City and Corozal Town, a drive of an hour or so from either one. Most buses on the busy Goldson Highway route will drop you in Orange Walk Town. There is no scheduled air service.

TIMING

The only reason most visitors stop at Orange Walk Town is to take a day trip to Lamanai, up the New River. An excellent restaurant, Nahil Mayab, makes a stopover in Orange Walk more pleasant.

SAFETY AND PRECAUTIONS

While generally safe, Orange Walk Town does have its share of crack problems, and the cheap bars can get rough on weekend nights.

EXPLORING

FAMILY **Las Banquitas House of Culture.** This small museum—the name refers to the little benches in a nearby riverside park—presents changing exhibitions on Orange Walk District history and culture. Among the permanent displays are artifacts from Lamanai and Cuello. A restaurant, Paniscea, is located under the House of Culture. Las Banquitas is one of four House of Culture museums; the other three are in Belize City, Corozal Town, and Benque Viejo. These museums are operated by NICH, the National Institute of Culture and History. ✉ *Main and Bautista Sts.* ☎ *822/3302 NICH* 🌐 *www.nichbelize.org* 🎟 *Free, some exhibits have small fees* ⏲ *Weekdays 8:30–4:30.*

WHERE TO EAT

$$ LATIN AMERICAN 🍴 **El Establo Bar & Grill.** This friendly, family-run eatery is at the edge of town near the northern end of the Orange Walk bypass. The dining room has a rustic charm, with displays of antiques, old farm implements, and old photographs. It's a good place to stop for lunch or dinner on a trip between Belize City and Corozal Town. Enjoy local dishes such as cow-foot soup, *escabeche* (fried fish), *relleno negro* (black turkey stew), and, of course, rice and beans. [$] *Average main: BZ$15* ✉ *Orange Walk Bypass, near Philip Goldson Hwy.* ☎ *322/0094* 🌐 *www.aguallos.com/elestablo* ⏲ *No dinner Sun.*

$$ LATIN AMERICAN Fodor's Choice ★ 🍴 **Nahil Mayab.** Orange Walk Town may be the last place you'd expect to find an upscale restaurant like this, with its Maya-inspired decor, well-prepared food, and extra-friendly servers. Nonetheless, it opened here, on a corner behind the Shell station, in December 2008 to rave reviews and has enjoyed steady business since. Sit in the tropical gardens in the back, or in air-conditioned comfort in the main dining room, and enjoy a cold drink and a delicious shrimp or conch ceviche appetizer. For a main course try the lobster fajitas (in season) or one of the Yucatán-inspired dishes such as hor'och, corn balls cooked in black beans and served with stew chicken. [$] *Average main: BZ$25* ✉ *Guadeloupe and Santa Ana Sts., 2 blocks behind Shell Station on Belize-Corozal Rd. (Goldson Hwy.)* ☎ *322/0831* 🌐 *www.nahilmayab.com* ⏲ *Closed Sun. No dinner Mon.*

$$ INTERNATIONAL 🍴 **Paniscea Restaurant.** Paniscea is a relatively new dining option in Orange Walk Town, and a good one if you want more than rice and beans. It's in an open-air setting under Las Banquitas House of Culture (for which it also serves as an event center), overlooking the New River. Try the pork chops or one of the pasta dishes. Beware: mosquitoes come out in force around dusk—the management provides bug spray. Open for dinner, but lunch or breakfast can be arranged with advance reservations. [$] *Average main: BZ$20* ✉ *Main St.* ☎ *623/7200.*

WHERE TO STAY

$ HOTEL Fodor's Choice ★ 🏨 **Hotel de la Fuente.** Orlando de la Fuente's place is a step up from other hotels in Orange Walk Town, and the low rates, for the standard rooms with air-conditioning complimentary Wi-Fi, fridge, cable TV, and continental breakfast, put it among the best values in northern Belize. **Pros:** excellent value; attractive and modern rooms; central location. **Cons:** no pool. [$] *Rooms from: BZ$70* ✉ *14 Main St.* ☎ *322/2290* 🌐 *www.hoteldelafuente.com* 🛏 *20 rooms, 2 suites.*

CLOSE UP

What's in a Name?

The name *Belize* is a conundrum. According to *Encyclopaedia Britannica*, it derives from *belix*, an ancient Mayan word meaning "muddy water." Anyone who's seen the Belize River swollen by heavy rains can vouch for this description. Others trace the name's origin to the French word *balise* (beacon), but no one can explain why a French word would have caught on in a region once dominated by the English (Belize was known as British Honduras). Perhaps nothing more than a drinker's tale, another theory connects Belize to the Mayan word *belikin* (road to the east), which also happens to be the name of the national beer. A few even think the name may have come from Angola in West Africa, where some of the slaves who were brought to the West Indies and then to Belize originated, and where today there is a town called Belize. Some say Belize is a corruption of Wallace, the name of a Scottish buccaneer who founded a colony in 1620; still others say the pirate wasn't Wallace but Willis, that he wasn't Scottish but English, and that he founded a colony not in 1620, but in 1638.

There was indeed a pirate named Wallace, a onetime lieutenant of Sir Walter Raleigh's who later served as Tortuga's governor. Perhaps it was liquor or lucre that turned him into a pirate, but at some point in the early-to-mid-1600s he and 80 fellow renegades washed up near St. George's Caye. They settled in and lived for years off the illicit booty of cloak-and-dagger raids on passing ships. In 1798 a fleet of 31 Spanish ships came to exterminate what had now blossomed into an upstart little colony. Residents had a total of one sloop, some fishing boats, and seven rafts, but their maritime knowledge enabled them to defeat the invaders in two hours. That was the last Spanish attempt to forcibly dislodge the settlement, though bitter wrangles over British Honduras's right to exist continued for nearly a century.

We may never know whether Wallace and Willis were one and the same, but what's in a name, anyway? Grab a Belikin and come up with a few theories of your own.

$ **Lamanai Riverside Retreat.** It's many miles from the Lamanai ruins, but
B&B/INN   this hotel with just three cabins and a restaurant is pleasantly set right beside the New River, the water route to the famous Mayan ruins. **Pros:** relaxing riverside setting; friendly owners; open-air riverside dining. **Cons:** it's a short hike into town; pesky mosquitoes at times. $ *Rooms from: BZ$109 ⊠ Lamanai Alley ☎ 302/3955 ⇱ 3 cabanas.*

$ **St. Christopher's Hotel.** On a quiet street near the Banquitos House
HOTEL   of Culture and backing up on the New River, this family-run hotel has simple but clean rooms, with tile floors and brightly colored bedspreads, at reasonable rates. **Pros:** unpretentious, family-run hotel; central location near market and the river; a good value. **Cons:** no-frills rooms. $ *Rooms from: BZ$65 ⊠ 10 Main St. ☎ 302/1064 ⊕ www. stchristophershotelbze.com ⇱ 25 rooms.*

LAMANAI

About 2½ hrs northwest of Belize City, or 24 miles (39 km) south of Orange Walk Town.

Lamanai ("submerged crocodile" in Yucatec Maya) is Belize's longest-occupied Mayan site, inhabited until well after Christopher Columbus discovered the New World in 1492. In fact archaeologists have found signs of continuous occupation from 1500 BC until AD 1700.

GETTING HERE AND AROUND

There are several ways to get here. One option is to drive on the mostly unpaved road from Orange Walk Town. Turn west off the Goldson Highway (also known in Orange Walk Town as Queen Victoria Avenue or Belize-Corozal Road) at the Orange Walk fire station. From here go to Yo Creek, then southwest to San Felipe Village, a total of 24 miles (39 km). In San Felipe, go straight for another 12 miles (19 km) to reach the ruins. Another route by road is via Shipyard—the unpaved road to Shipyard is just south of Orange Walk. The best way to approach the ruins, however, is by boat, which takes about an hour and a half from Orange Walk. Boats leave around 9 am from the Tower Hill bridge over the New River on the Goldson Highway, about 6 miles (10 km) south of Orange Walk, and from a dock in town. The cost is BZ$80–BZ$90 per person. If you are staying at Lamanai Outpost, the lodge has its own boats to take you up the river, departing from a dock just southwest of the dock where the other boats depart. Some hotels in Orange Walk Town arrange Lamanai tours, with pickup and drop-off at the hotel, also for around BZ$80–BZ$100 per person. You can also take a 15-minute charter plane trip from Belize City, around BZ$500–BZ$800 depending on the number of persons.

TIMING

Most people visit Lamanai as a day trip, but to see the ruins and explore the New River Lagoon, you'll want to overnight at least, and preferably stay two to three nights.

EXPLORING

Fodor's Choice **Lamanai.** What makes Lamanai so special is its setting on the west bank ★ of a beautiful 28-mile-long (45-km) lagoon, one of only two waterside Mayan sites in Belize (the other is Cerros, near Corozal Town). Nearly 400 species of birds have been spotted in the area and a troop of howler monkeys visits the archaeological site regularly.

For nearly 3,000 years Lamanai's residents carried on a lifestyle that passed from one generation to the next, until the Spanish missionaries arrived. You can still see the ruins of the missionaries' church near the village of Indian Church. The same village also has an abandoned 19th-century sugar mill. With its immense drive wheel and steam engine—on which you can still read the name of the manufacturer, Leeds Foundry of New Orleans—swathed in strangler vines and creepers, it's a haunting sight. In all, 50 to 60 Mayan structures are spread over this 950-acre archaeological reserve. The most impressive is the largest Pre Classic structure in Belize—a massive, stepped temple built into the hillside overlooking the New River Lagoon. Many structures at Lamanai have only been superficially excavated. Trees and vines grow from the tops of temples, and the sides of one pyramid are covered with vegetation. On the grounds you'll find a visitor center with educational displays on the site, and pottery, carvings, and small statues, some dating back 2,500 years. Local villagers from the Indian Church Village Artisans Center set up small stands on the grounds to sell handmade carvings, jewelry, and other crafts, along with T-shirts and snacks. Many visitors enjoy Lamanai not only for the stunning setting on the New River Lagoon, but also for the boat ride up the New River, where you are likely to see many birds, along with howler monkeys and crocodiles. ✉ *Near Indian Church Village, Orange Walk District* 🎫 *BZ$10* 🕐 *Daily 8–5.*

WORD OF MOUTH

"Lamanai Outpost: We loved the boat trip to get there, the daily activities and the property, the beautiful sunsets and sunrises. Do not miss the sunset cocktail cruise and the spotlight safari, both big highlights of our trip. The ruins were interesting, but the troop of howler monkeys made our day."
—xyz99

WHERE TO STAY

$$$$ B&B/INN Fodor's Choice ★ 🏨 **Lamanai Outpost Lodge.** Perched on a low hillside on the New River Lagoon within walking distance of the Lamanai ruins, this eco-lodge's well-designed thatch cabanas sit amid lovely gardens and have porches with lagoon views. **Pros:** gorgeous setting on the New River Lagoon; easy access to Lamanai ruins; good tours. **Cons:** high rates; getting here requires a boat or plane ride, or a long drive; lodge's airboats are very noisy. [$] *Rooms from: BZ$1460* ✉ *Near Indian Church Village, Orange Walk District* ☎ *235/2441, 888/733–7864 U.S. reservation office* 🌐 *www.lamanai.com* 🛏 *20 cabanas* 🍴 *Multiple meal plans.*

MENNONITE COMMUNITIES

2½ hrs northwest of Belize City.

The Mennonite religion emerged in Holland during the Protestant Reformation in the 16th century. These Anabaptists (so called for the practice of baptizing adults) first moved to Germanic lands—many in Belize still speak Low German, which combines elements of German and Dutch—and then to Prussia, the United States (mainly Pennsylvania), and Manitoba, Canada. In the 1950s some 3,000 Mennonites emigrated to Belize, where they established communities in the Orange Walk and Cayo districts. Today there are an estimated 12,000 Mennonites in Belize.

The Blue Creek Mennonite community is predominantly progressive, which means the Mennonites accept modern conveniences such as automobiles and electricity. Near the Linda Vista shopping center is a small bed-and-breakfast where you can stay and learn a little about Mennonite life in Belize.

Both Little Belize and Shipyard are primarily farming areas, and have no hotels or tourist facilities, but the unexpected sight, on dusty rural roads, of pale-skin folks in old-fashioned dress—the women in long plaid dresses and the men with suspenders and straw hats—in horse-pulled buggies will remind you of how diverse Belizean culture really is.

GETTING HERE AND AROUND

The progressive Blue Creek Mennonite community is about midway between Orange Walk Town and Chan Chich Lodge—it's 33 miles (54 km) from Orange Walk Town via Yo Creek, August Pine Ridge, and San Felipe, and 36 miles (59 km) from Chan Chich. About 6 miles (10 km) beyond Blue Creek, you'll enter the Río Bravo reserve managed by Programme for Belize. Shipyard is accessed via an unpaved road that turns west off the Northern Highway just south of Orange Walk Town. Little Belize is visited by driving northeast from Orange Walk Town via San Estevan. Keep in mind that Shipyard and Little Belize are conservative Mennonite communities; they shun the use of cars and motorized farm equipment.

TIMING

Unless you have a particular interest in Mennonite culture or farming methods, you'll probably just drive through the Mennonite communities in Northern Belize, as there are no specific tourist sites or activities. With rare exceptions, Mennonites aren't much involved in tourism development.

WHERE TO STAY

$ B&B/INN **Hillside Bed and Breakfast.** After Mennonites John and Judy Klassen finished raising their 10 children, they opened this small B&B in Blue Creek, a progressive Mennonite community. **Pros:** beautiful vistas over Blue Creek; great way to get to know a little of the Mennonite community. **Cons:** basic, motel-like rooms; cabanas require a steep climb; B&B accessible only if you have your own transport. [$] *Rooms from: BZ$135* ✉ *Main Rd., Orange Walk District, Blue Creek Village* ☎ *323/0155* 🛏 *5 rooms, 2 cabanas* 💳 *No credit cards* 🍴 *Breakfast.*

RÍO BRAVO CONSERVATION AND MANAGEMENT AREA

2½ hrs west of Belize City.

Created with the help of distinguished British naturalist Gerald Durrell, the Río Bravo Conservation & Management Area spans 260,000 acres near where Belize, Guatemala, and Mexico meet. The four-hour drive from Belize City takes you through wildlands where you may encounter a troupe of spider monkeys, wildcats, flocks of ocellated turkeys, a dense shower of butterflies—anything but another vehicle.

GETTING HERE AND AROUND

By car from Belize City or Corozal Town, drive to Orange Walk Town, going into town rather than taking the bypass. Turn west at the crossroads near the Orange Walk fire station toward Yo Creek. Continue on through Yo Creek, following the road that turns sharply south and goes through San Lazaro, Trinidad, and August Pine Ridge villages. At San Felipe, 24 miles (40 km) from Orange Walk Town, the road turns sharply to the west (right) at a soccer field. Follow this road for about 7 miles (12 km) to the Río Bravo bridge and into Programme for Belize lands. If you don't have your own car, contact Programme for Belize and ask if they can arrange transportation for you from Orange Walk Town, Belize City, or elsewhere.

Contact **Programme for Belize.** Programme for Belize is a conservation-oriented, private nongovernmental organization that manages 260,000 acres in Orange Walk District (Río Bravo Conservation & Management Area) and operates two remote lodges (La Milpa and Hillbank). ✉ *Programme for Belize, Orange Walk* ☎ *277/5616* ⊕ *www.pfbelize.org.*

TIMING

If you decide to visit this remote part of Belize, you'll want to spend a minimum of two days, and preferably longer, so you can explore the jungle, La Milpa, and nearby Mestizo villages.

SAFETY AND PRECAUTIONS

Once away from the Field Station grounds, you're in the bush. Keep a wary eye out for poisonous snakes, scorpions, stinging insects, and other denizens of the wild.

EXPLORING

Río Bravo Conservation & Management Area. Managed by Belize City–based Programme for Belize, a not-for-profit organization whose mission is the wise use and conservation of Belize's natural resources, the Río Bravo Conservation Area contains some 400 species of birds, 70 species of mammals, and 200 types of trees. About half of Río Bravo is managed as a nature reserve, and the rest is managed to generate income, from forestry and other activities, including tourism. Programme for Belize is actively involved in research and conservation programs to protect endangered species including the Yellow Headed Parrot.

Within the reserve's borders are more than 60 Mayan sites; many have yet to be explored. The most important is **La Milpa,** Belize's largest site beside Caracol and Lamanai. At its height between AD 400 and 830, La Milpa was home to almost 50,000 people. The suburbs of this city spread out some 3 miles (5 km) from the city center, and the entire city encompassed some 30 square miles (78 square km) in area. So far, archaeologists have discovered 20 large courtyards and 19 stelae.

Visiting Río Bravo, like the other areas of northwestern Orange Walk, is best done in a four-wheel-drive vehicle. You must make arrangements to visit in advance with **Programme for Belize** *(see above),* as the entire Río Bravo conservation area is managed by this private, nonprofit organization, and the main road through its lands is gated. You also need advance reservations to stay at La Milpa Field Station *(see below).* Staying overnight or longer at this field station is the best way to see Río Bravo, but you can visit it briefly on a day trip. Another field station, at Hill Bank, primarily serves as a research base for sustainable forest management but visitors with an interest in forest research can be accommodated in two cabanas and a dorm that sleeps six. Contact Programme for Belize *(see above)* for information.

Guides and information are available at La Milpa Field Station. Chan Chich Lodge, Lamanai Outpost Lodge, and other hotels also can arrange visits with guides to La Milpa and the Río Bravo Conservation & Management Area. ✉ *Rio Bravo Conservation and Management Area, Orange Walk* ☎ *227/5616 Programme for Belize* ⊕ *www.pfbelize.org.*

WHERE TO STAY

$$ 🏨 **La Milpa Field Station.** About 3 miles (5 km) from La Milpa Mayan
RENTAL site, this field station is a combination lodge and exotic summer camp.
Pros: you'll feel like an archaeologist here; quiet and remote setting sur-
rounded only by nature; dining room serves filling Belizean dishes. **Cons:**
accommodations are very basic; not easy to get to. $ *Rooms from:*
BZ$208 ✉ *Programme for Belize, 1 Eyre St., Belize City* ☎ *227/5616*
⊕ *www.pfbelize.org* ⤷ *8 rooms in 4 cabins, 1 dormitory (30 beds)*
¶○¶ *Multiple meal plans.*

GALLON JUG

4

3½ hrs west of Belize City.
The 130,000 acres of Gallon Jug Estates, owned by the family of the
late Sir Barry Bowen, is home to old-growth mahogany trees and many
other tropical hardwoods along with more than 350 species of birds
and many mammals and reptiles.

GETTING HERE AND AROUND

The easiest and fastest way to get here is by charter airplane (about
BZ$800 for two people to Gallon Jug Estates' own 3,000-foot air-
strip). Javier Flying Service in Belize City has three- and five-passenger
Cessna airplanes, and charter flights are also available through Maya
Island Air and Tropic Air. Chan Chich will arrange the flights for you.
With advance permission, you can also drive to Chan Chich, about 3½
hours from Belize City. Follow the route to Río Bravo *(see above)* and
continue on through Programme for Belize lands to the Cedar Crossing
gatehouse and into Gallon Jug lands. It's a long but beautiful drive, and
you're almost certain to see a considerable amount of wildlife along
the dirt road. Chan Chich offers a transfer by road from Belize City for
around BZ$650 for two persons.

Contacts Javier Flying Service ✉ *Municipal Airport, Belize City* ☎ *824/0460*
⊕ *www.javiersflyingservice.com.*

TIMING

You'll want to spend at least two to three days at Chan Chich, longer
if you have a keen interest in birding or wildlife spotting.

SAFETY AND PRECAUTIONS

Despite its remote location, Chan Chich is one of the safest places in Belize.

EXPLORING

Gallon Jug. A working farm that produces coffee and raises cattle, cacao,
and corn, Gallon Jug Estates is the only truly commercial coffee opera-
tion in Belize. Elevations in Belize are too low to grow high-quality
Arabica coffees that thrive at over 4,000 feet. Gallon Jug Estates also
produces hot sauces and delicious mango jams, which sell in Belize
and elsewhere. Tours of the coffee plantings and the production facil-
ity, along with other farm tours, can be arranged through Chan Chich
Lodge. Jaguar sightings are fairly common around the Chan Chich
Lodge, averaging around one a week. You're likely to see toucans, many
different hummingbirds, and flocks of parrots. Chan Chich, one of the
best jungle lodges in Central America, is the only place to stay in the

area. It's possible to visit on a day trip from La Milpa Field Station, Blue Creek Village, or even Lamanai or Orange Walk Town, but you need your own transportation and advance permission to come on the gated, private Gallon Jug lands. ⌧ *Gallon Jug* ⊕ *www.chanchich.com.*

WHERE TO STAY

$$$$
ALL-INCLUSIVE
Fodor'sChoice
★

Chan Chich Lodge. Arguably the best lodge in Belize and one of the top lodges in all of Central America, Chan Chich is set in a remote, beautiful area literally on top of a Mayan ruin, with 12 rustic yet comfortable cabanas. **Pros:** some of the best birding and wildlife spotting in Belize; so safe you don't lock your cabana's door; magnificent setting within a Mayan site; understated but eminently comfortable accommodations. **Cons:** somewhat difficult to get to; definitely splurge prices. $ *Rooms from: BZ$1450* ⌧ *Chan Chich Lodge, Gallon Jug* ☎ *223/4419, 800/343–8009 in U.S.* ⊕ *www.chanchich.com* ⌁ *12 cabanas, 1 2-bedroom villa* ◎| *All-inclusive.*

COROZAL BAY

Corozal Bay, or Chetumal Bay as it's called on most maps, has tropically green and turquoise waters. It provides a beautiful waterside setting for Corozal Town and a number of villages along the north side of Corozal District. Tarpon, bonefish, permit, and other game fish are not hard to find. The drawback is that there are few natural beaches in Corozal District, although some hotels have trucked in sand to build human-assisted beach areas. Also, there's no good snorkeling or diving locally, and the Belize Barrier Reef is several long hours away by boat. However, the Mexican border and the outskirts of the city of Chetumal are only 9 miles (14½ km) away. Chetumal, capital of Quintana Roo state, with a modern mall, big-box stores such as Walmart and Sam's Warehouse, and air-conditioned multiplex movie theaters, provides a bustling counterpoint to small, easygoing Corozal.

At the border, the Commercial Free Zone (usually called the Corozal Free Zone, though that's not its official name) promises duty-free goods and cheap gas. The reality is a little less appealing. Most of the duty-free items are cheap trinkets from China and Taiwan, and the gasoline, while one-third cheaper than in Belize, is more expensive than in Mexico. Plus, to sample the questionable enticements of the Free Zone, visitors have to formally exit Belize, paying exit taxes and fees totaling BZ$37.50 per person.

Casinos have sprung up on the Belize side of the border, at the edge of the Commercial Free Zone. There are three casinos: the **Princess Casino,** the larger **Royal Princess Casino** (both associated with the Princess Hotel & Casino in Belize City), and the largest of the three, the **Las Vegas Casino.** The Las Vegas casino has 54,000 square feet of gaming area, making it, according to management, the largest in Central America. In addition to more than 300 slot machines, plus blackjack, roulette, and poker, the casino has gaming areas designed to appeal to visitors from Asia, with Pai Gow, mah-jongg, and other games. There's also a private club area for high rollers from Mexico and elsewhere. The casinos are busy on weekends, but the crowds thin out during the week.

COROZAL TOWN

95 miles (153 km) north of Belize City.

Settled by refugees from the Yucatán during the 19th-century Caste Wars, Corozal is the last town before Río Hondo, the river separating Belize from Mexico. Though thoroughly ignored by today's travelers, this friendly town is great for a few days of easy living. It's hard not to fall into the laid-back lifestyle here—a sign at the entrance of a local grocery used to advertise "Strong rum, 55 Belize dollars a gallon."

English is the official language in Corozal, but Spanish is just as common here. The town was largely rebuilt after Hurricane Janet nearly destroyed it in 1955. Many houses are clapboard, built on wooden piles, and other houses are simple concrete-block structures, though the growing clan of expats is putting up new houses that wouldn't look out of place in Florida. One of the few remaining 19th-century colonial-era buildings is a portion of the old fort in the center of town, now the Corozal House of Culture.

GETTING HERE AND AROUND

Corozal Town is the last stop on the Goldson Highway before the Mexico border. There's frequent bus service from early morning to early evening on the Goldson Highway from Belize City. Maya Island Air and Tropic Air have a total of around 10 daily flights to San Pedro, Ambergris Caye (a couple of flights stop in Sarteneja on demand), but no other scheduled air service. A daily water taxi operated by San Pedro-Belize Express Water Taxi runs between Corozal Town and San Pedro with a stop on demand at Sarteneja.

Contacts Maya Island Air ☎ 223/1140 ⊕ www.mayaislandair.com.
Tropic Air ✉ San Pedro Airstrip, San Pedro ☎ 226/2012 ⊕ www.tropicair.com.

TIMING

Although from your base in Corozal Town you can make day trips to the ruins at Cerros and Lamanai, the main activity for visitors in Corozal is simply relaxing and hanging out.

SAFETY AND PRECAUTIONS

Corozal Town and the rural parts of the district are among the safer places in Belize, but crack cocaine has made its ugly appearance here (police seem oddly unable to find and close down the crack houses), which is one reason petty thefts are an issue.

ADO Bus Line. ADO is the main bus line providing service between Cancún/Playa del Carmen and Chetumal. It also also has express service between Belize City and Cancún, with stops in Corozal, Orange Walk Town, Chetumal, and elsewhere. ✉ *ADO Bus Terminal, Av. Insurgentes and Av. Belice, Chetumal, Quintana Roo, Mexico* ☎ *800/009–9090* ⊕ *www.ado.com.mx.*

EXPLORING

Commercial Free Zone. About 300 wholesale and retail companies are located in the Corozal Commercial Free Zone/Zona Libre Belice on the Belize side of the Belize-Mexico border. Visitors may find some bargains on clothing and household items imported from Asia, along with discounted gasoline and liquor, though the retail stores target Mexicans rather than U.S. or other international tourists. Three casinos also target the Mexican market, especially on weekends. Visitors going from Belize to the Free Zone must may the BZ$37.50 exit fee, which cuts into any savings on gas or merchandise, and pay duties on goods (especially liquor) brought back into Belize. ☒ *1 Freedom Ave., Belize-Mexico Border, Corozal* ☎ *423/7010* ⊕ *www.belize corozalfreezone.com.*

Corozal House of Culture. The old Corozal Cultural Centre was completely renovated and reopened in 2012 as the Corozal House of Culture. Located in one of the oldest buildings in northern Belize (other than ancient Mayan structures), the House of Culture was built in 1886. It's operated by the National Institute of History and Culture (NICH) as an art gallery, museum devoted to the history of Corozal Town and northern Belize, and visitor information center. NICH operates three other Culture museums in Belize City, Orange Walk Town, and Benque Viejo. ☒ *1st Ave., near Corozal Bay* ☎ *422/0071* ⊕ *www.nichbelize.org* ☉ *Weekdays 8–5.*

Corozal Town Hall. The history of Corozal, including a graphic portrayal of the brutality of colonial rule on the indigenous people, is depicted in a strikingly beautiful mural by Manuel Villamor Reyes on the wall of the Corozal Town Hall. ☒ *1st St. South* ☎ *422/2072* ☒ *Free* ☉ *Weekdays 9–noon and 1–5.*

Gabrielle Hoare Market. This market on 6th Avenue has stalls selling a good selection of local fruits and vegetables. ☒ *6th Ave.* ☉ *Mon.–Sat. 6:30–5:30, Sun. 6:30–3.*

Santa Rita. Not far from Corozal are several Mayan sites. The closest, Santa Rita, is a short walk from the town's center. It's on a low hill across from the Coca-Cola plant at the north end of town. Only a few of its structures have been excavated, so it takes some imagination to picture this settlement, founded around 1500 BC, as one of the district's major trading centers. The government of Belize in 2012 designated Santa Rita as an official "Wedding Gardens of Belize," and there are plans for facilities for weddings. In December 2012, a reenactment of the wedding of Tzazil-Ha, a Mayan princess, and Gonzalo Guerrero, a Spanish conquistador, was held here. At this writing the Belize Institute of Archeology has plans to build a visitor center. ☒ *Santa Rita, near Corozal Hospital and Coca-Cola plant* ☒ *Free.*

HOT PROPERTY

Corozal District has become a hot spot for expats seeking property for retirement and snowbirds looking for a vacation home. Several hundred foreign expats live in Corozal District, and the numbers are growing. They're attracted by the home prices—a two-bedroom, modern home in a nice area near the water can go for less than US$150,000, though you can always pay more. An expat "friendship luncheon" is held the second Tuesday of every month at 1:30 pm at the Purple Toucan Restaurant and Bar, 7th Avenue South in Corozal Town. Newcomers and wannabes welcome.

WHERE TO EAT

$$ ✕**Corozo Blue's.** A new addition to Corozal, this eatery in a pleasant
PIZZA   stone building on the bay at the South End serves excellent wood-fired
Fodor's Choice   pizza, burgers, sandwiches, and ceviche, plus a few traditional Belizean dishes like rice and beans. By Corozal standards, prices are on the
★   high side, but the atmosphere, bayside setting, and friendly staff make
it well worth a visit. $ *Average main: BZ$25* ✉ *Goldson Hwy., South End* ☎ *422/0090* ⊕ *corozoblues.com.*

$ ✕**Miss June's Kitchen.** The best breakfast in Corozal is served by Miss
ECLECTIC   June at her home. There is seating for only about a dozen guests in an
open-air patio. Everything is homemade, freshly prepared, and served
by Miss June and her family. You can have a delicious breakfast of an
omelette, peppery sausage, fried potatoes and freshly squeezed orange
juice with whole wheat bread for about BZ$10. Lunch featuring conch
and other local dishes is available, but breakfast is the stand-out. $ *Average main: BZ$12* ✉ *3rd Street S* ☎ *422/2559* ⊗ *Closed Sun. No dinner.*

$ ✕**Patty's Bistro.** Patty's Bistro (sometimes spelled Patti's) serves some
LATIN AMERICAN   of the best food in town, the service is sprightly and friendly, the
atmosphere is no-frills, and prices are low. For a local treat, try the
hearty conch soup. $ *Average main: BZ$12* ✉ *2nd St. N.* ☎ *402/0174* ⊗ *Closed Sun.*

$ ✕**Venke's Kabob Corner.** For takeout curries and other Indian food at
INDIAN   modest prices, Venke's is the spot. It's run by an Indian who formerly
was a chef at the Las Vegas Casino in the Free Zone in Belize and at a
leading Belize City Indian restaurant. As for atmosphere, Venke's has
none, but the delicious curries come in servings big enough for two,
with rice and tortillas on the side. Also try the excellent chicken tikka
masala. $ *Average main: BZ$15* ✉ *5th Ave. South, across from Immigration office* ☎ *402/0536* ▭ *No credit cards.*

WHERE TO STAY

$ ▦ **Almond Tree Hotel Resort.** Directly on the bay just south of town,
RESORT   Almond Tree Hotel Resort raises the bar on Corozal Town lodging.
Fodor's Choice   **Pros:** nicest accommodations in town; attractively designed rooms;
★   swimming pool; bayside setting with views. **Cons:** on the South End, a
bit away from the main part of town; limited dining options at resort
but good restaurants nearby. $ *Rooms from: BZ$185* ✉ *425 Bayshore Dr., South End* ☎ *628/9224* ⊕ *www.almondtreeresort.com* ⌕ *5 rooms, 3 suites* ◎| *No meals.*

$ ▦ **CasaBlanca by the Sea.** In a quiet village, with views of Chetumal across
B&B/INN   Corozal Bay, this is a fine place to get away and catch up on your reading, but be aware that the location is off-the-beaten path, and there's not
much to do around the hotel. **Pros:** charming bayside setting; great place
to get away; quiet and rarely busy. **Cons:** taxi or your own transportation
required to visit town; no pool or real beach; bay swimming is only
so-so. $ *Rooms from: BZ$155* ✉ *8 miles (18 km) northeast of Corozal Town, next to customs office in Consejo Village, Consejo* ✛ *From Corozal Town, take 4th Ave. North, which becomes unpaved Consejo Rd. Stay on Consejo Rd. 7 miles (10 km), through Consejo village. CasaBlanca is at end of road on bay, next to customs office* ☎ *423/1018* ⊕ *www.casablancabelize.com* ⌕ *7 rooms, 3 suites* ◎| *No meals.*

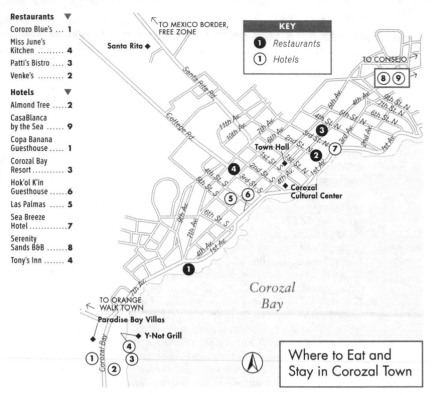

Restaurants ▼

Corozo Blue's ... 1
Miss June's Kitchen 4
Patti's Bistro 3
Venke's 2

Hotels ▼

Almond Tree 2
CasaBlanca by the Sea 9
Copa Banana Guesthouse 1
Corozal Bay Resort........... 3
Hok'ol K'in Guesthouse......6
Las Palmas 5
Sea Breeze Hotel.............7
Serenity Sands B&B 8
Tony's Inn 4

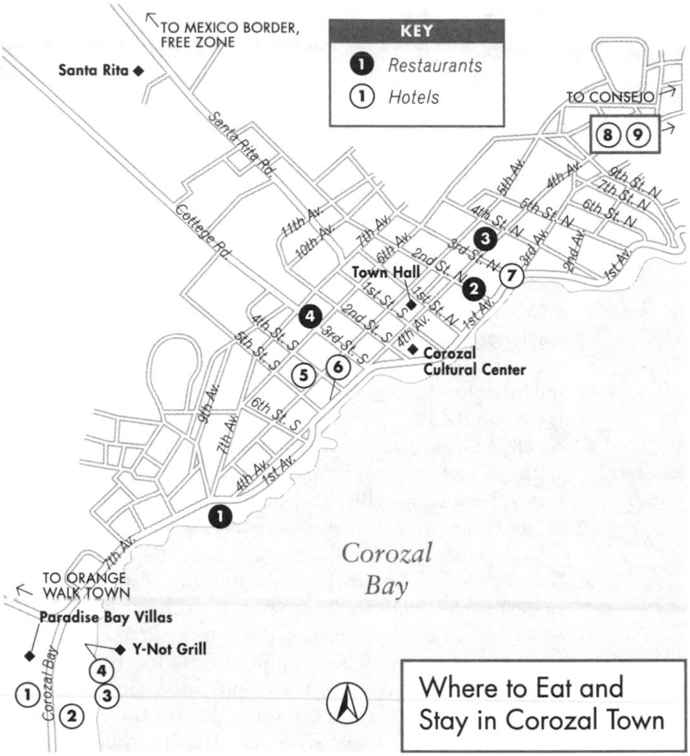
TO MEXICO BORDER, FREE ZONE
Santa Rita
KEY
Restaurants
Hotels
TO CONSEJO
Santa Rita Rd.
Cottage Rd.
11th Av.
10th Av.
7th Av.
6th Av.
5th Av.
4th Av.
3rd Av.
2nd Av.
1st Av.
9th St. N
7th St. N
6th St. N
5th St. N
4th St. N
3rd St. N
2nd St. N
1st St. N
1st St. S
2nd St. S
3rd St. S
4th St. S
5th St. S
6th St. S
Town Hall
Corozal Cultural Center
9th Av.
Corozal Bay
TO ORANGE WALK TOWN
Paradise Bay Villas
Y-Not Grill
Where to Eat and Stay in Corozal Town

$ B&B/INN 🏨 **Copa Banana Guesthouse.** This homelike inn, painted banana yellow, has five sunny suites with air-conditioning and cable TV carved out of two houses across the street from Corozal Bay. **Pros:** handy to have kitchen privileges; tastefully decorated; close to bay. **Cons:** bike ride or long walk to heart of town. *[$] Rooms from: BZ$120 ✉ 409 Bay Shore Dr. ☎ 422/0284 🌐 www.copabanana.bz 🛏 5 rooms, 1 apartment 🍴 No meals.*

$ RESORT 🏨 **Corozal Bay Resort.** This casual bayside resort has value-priced thatch cabanas in pastel colors on Corozal Bay, with all the modern conveniences. **Pros:** nice tropical feel to thatch cabanas; without A/C, price is a real value; breezy bayside setting. **Cons:** beach has seawall, no bar or restaurant (breakfast is available). *[$] Rooms from: BZ$55 ✉ Almond Dr., off Goldson Hwy. at South End, on bay ☎ 422/2416 🌐 www.corozalbay.biz 🛏 10 cabanas 🍴 Multiple meal plans.*

$ HOTEL 🏨 **Hok'ol K'in Guest House.** Yucatec Maya for "coming of the rising sun," Hok'ol K'in, founded by an American Peace Corps veteran and now operated by Belizeans, is a friendly small budget hotel on the Corozal bayfront. **Pros:** breezy bayfront location within walking distance of most shops and restaurants; friendly management; some handicap-accessible rooms. **Cons:** no-frills rooms. *[$] Rooms from: BZ$104 ✉ 89 4th Ave. ☎ 422/3329 🌐 www.corozal.net 🛏 10 rooms and 1 2-bedroom apartment 🍴 No meals.*

$ **Las Palmas.** Totally renovated and rebuilt, this whole property is
HOTEL   upmarket but still a good value. **Pros:** handy central location in town;
good value. **Cons:** not on the water; limited secure parking. $ *Rooms
from: BZ$98* ✉ *123 5th Ave.* ☎ *422/0196* ⊕ *www.laspalmashotelbelize.
com* ⇨ *20 rooms.*

$ **Sea Breeze Hotel.** Run by a Welshman who lived for years in Antigua,
B&B/INN   Guatemala, the Sea Breeze is a top budget choice in Corozal. **Pros:** good
value in a budget hotel; convivial owner; cheapest breakfasts in town.
Cons: rooms are simple; those without A/C can be hot. $ *Rooms from:
BZ$55* ✉ *23 1st Ave.* ☎ *422/3051* ⊕ *www.theseabreezehotel.com* ⇨ *7
rooms* ❍| *Breakfast.*

$ **Serenity Sands B&B.** This upscale, eco-oriented B&B is hidden away
B&B/INN   off the Consejo Road north of Corozal Town, with four tastefully
Fodor'sChoice   decorated rooms on the second floor with private balconies overlook-
★   ing gardens, Belizean art, and locally made hardwood furniture. **Pros:**
beautiful rooms; family-friendly; eco-oriented management. **Cons:** in
an out-of-the-way location, best visited with a rental car; not directly
on the water. $ *Rooms from: BZ$185* ✉ *Mile 3, Consejo Rd.* ✢ *From
Corozal Town, take 4th Ave. North, which becomes unpaved Consejo
Rd. Stay on Consejo Rd. 3 miles (5 km). Turn right at Serenity Sands
sign. Follow Serenity Rd. ¾ mile (1.2 km); turn at first right and follow
this road turning left, then right until you reach Serenity Sands B&B*
☎ *669/2394* ⊕ *www.serenitysands.com* ⇨ *4 rooms and 1 2-bedroom
house* ❍| *Breakfast.*

$$ **Tony's Inn and Beach Resort.** One of the oldest hotels and restaurants
HOTEL   in northern Belize, Tony's Inn is still going strong, with spacious, newly
Fodor'sChoice   refurbished rooms and a popular bayside restaurant and bar, all on
★   beautifully landscaped grounds. **Pros:** attractive renovated rooms;
breezy bayside setting with landscaped grounds; excellent open-air
restaurant, safe guarded parking. **Cons:** currently there is no swim-
ming pool, but one is planned. $ *Rooms from: BZ$225* ✉ *South End
☎ *422/2055* ⊕ *www.tonysinn.com* ⇨ *24 rooms* ❍| *No meals.*

COPPER BANK

12 miles (20 km) southeast of Corozal Town.

Copper Bank is a tidy and small (population around 500) Mestizo fish-
ing village on Corozal Bay. The village is something of a footnote to the
nearby Mayan site, Cerros.

GETTING HERE AND AROUND

One way to get here is by boat from Corozal, which costs around
BZ$80–BZ$160 for up to four people. You can also drive from Corozal
Town, crossing the New River on the hand-pulled ferry. To get to the
ferry from Corozal, take the Northern Highway south toward Orange
Walk Town (watch for ferry sign). Turn left and follow this unpaved
road for 2½ miles (4 km) to the ferry landing. After crossing the river,
drive on to a T-intersection and turn left for Copper Bank. The trip from
Corozal Town to Copper Bank takes about a half hour, but longer after
heavy rains, as the dirt road can become very bad. As you enter Copper
Bank, watch for signs directing you to "Cerros Maya."

TIMING

Most visitors do only a day trip to see the Cerros ruins, although if you want a quiet, off-the-main-path place to finish writing that novel, you won't find a better place than Cerros Beach Resort.

EXPLORING

Cerros. Like the Tulum site in Mexico, Cerros (also referred to as Cerro Maya, or Mayan Hill in Spanish) is unusual in that it's directly on the water. Unlike Tulum, however, there is no development around it, and at times you can have the place all to yourself. With a beautiful setting on a peninsula jutting into Corozal Bay, near the mouth of the New River, the late Pre-Classic center dates to 2000 BC and includes a ball court, several tombs, and a large temple. Altogether, there are some 170 structures, many just mounds of stone and earth, on 52 acres. Bring plenty of bug spray—mosquitoes can be fierce here. **■ TIP→ The easiest way to get to Cerros is to charter a boat in Corozal Town, for a 15-minute ride across the bay.** ✉ *2½ miles (4 km) north of Copper Bank* ✥ *Follow signs from the south end of Corozal Town and cross the New River on the Pueblo Nuevo hand-cranked ferry. At the T-intersection, go left to Copper Bank Village and follow signs west on unpaved roads to Cerros.* 🎟 *BZ$10* ⏲ *Daily 8–5.*

WHERE TO STAY

$ RESORT 🏨 **Cerros Beach Resort.** Cerros Beach Resort is an off-the-grid option for good food and simple lodging on Corozal Bay, near the Cerros ruins. **Pros:** low-key, crowd-free small resort on the bay; tasty food; good value. **Cons:** mosquitoes sometimes can be pesky. [$] *Rooms from: BZ$131* ✉ *Cerros Beach Resort* ✥ *Near Cerros Maya site on north side of Cerros peninsula; entering Copper Bank village, watch for signs to Cerros Beach Resort. The resort will arrange for a pickup by boat from Consejo or Corozal Town for parties of 5 or more.* ☎ *623/9763* 🌐 *www.cerrosbeachresort.com* 🛏 *4 cabanas* ⏲ *Restaurant closed Mon.*

$ HOTEL 🏨 **Copper Bank Inn.** If you want to get away from it all at modest cost, Copper Bank Inn, a white, two-story, 10,000-square-foot house with a small bar and restaurant, is a good choice. **Pros:** quiet get-away; swimming pool; low rates. **Cons:** off-the-beaten path. [$] *Rooms from: BZ$64* ✉ *Copper Bank Village* ☎ *662/5281* 🌐 *www.copperbankinn.com* 🛏 *10 rooms.*

$$ B&B/INN 🏨 **Crimson Orchid B&B.** An unexpected addition to Orchid Bay real estate development is this stylish three-level, nine-room B&B, which opened in late 2012. **Pros:** newest and nicest accommodations in the Cerros-Sarteneja area; reasonable prices; authentic English breakfast. **Cons:** unusual location in area that gets few tourists; no pool yet (one is planned). [$] *Rooms from: BZ$218* ✉ *Pescadores Park, off Sarteneja Rd., at Orchid Bay development* ☎ *669/5076* 🛏 *9 rooms* 🍴 *Breakfast.*

SARTENEJA

40 miles (67 km) from Corozal Town.

The bay setting of the Mestizo and Creole community of Sarteneja makes it one of the most relaxed and appealing destinations in Belize. It's also the largest fishing village in Belize. You can swim in the bay here, though in many places the bottom is gunky.

Lobster fishing and pineapple farming are the town's two main industries, and Sarteneja is also a center for building wooden boats. Most residents speak Spanish as a first language, but many also speak English.

Visitors and real-estate buyers are beginning to discover Sarteneja, and while tourism services are still minimalist, several small guesthouses are now open, and there are a few places to get a simple, inexpensive bite to eat.

GETTING HERE AND AROUND

Driving to Sarteneja from Corozal Town takes about 1½ hours via the New River ferry and a second, bay-side ferry across Laguna Seca. The road is unpaved and can be very muddy after heavy rains. You also can drive to Sarteneja from Orange Walk Town, a trip of about 40 miles (67 km) and 1½ hours. There are several Sarteneja Bus Line buses a day, except Sunday, from Belize City via Orange Walk Town. The trip from Belize City takes 3½ to 4 hours and costs BZ$10.

The daily water taxi between Corozal Town and San Pedro will drop you at Sarteneja on request. You also can hire a private boat in Corozal to take you and your party to Sarteneja.

Sarteneja has an airstrip, with flights on Tropic Air from San Pedro to Corozal Town stopping at Sarteneja on demand.

TIMING

Once you visit Shipstern and take a splash in the sea, you've just about exhausted all there is to do in Sarteneja. So bring several good books and enjoy the slow-paced village life.

EXPLORING

Shipstern Wildlife Reserve. About 3½ miles (6 km) west of Sarteneja on the road to Orange Walk or Corozal is the Shipstern Wildlife Reserve. You pass the entrance and visitor center as you come into Sarteneja. The 31 square miles (81 square km) of tropical forest forming the reserve are, like the Crooked Tree Wildlife Sanctuary, a paradise for bird-watchers. Currently, Shipstern is owned and operated by a Swiss conservationist nongovernmental organization, but it is slated to become a Belize national park. More than 300 species of birds have been identified here. Look for egrets (there are 13 species), American coots, keel-billed toucans, flycatchers, warblers, and several species of parrots. Mammals are in healthy supply as well, including pumas, jaguars, and raccoons. The butterfly farm next to the visitor center is now a small education area, and butterflies are being repopulated. Nearby, a small museum at Mahogany Park focuses on the history and uses of this beautiful tropical hardwood. There is a botanical trail leading from the visitor center, with the names of many plants and trees identified on small signs. Admission, a visit to the butterfly center, and a one-hour guided tour of the botanical trail is BZ$10 per person. You can add a tour of the Mahogany Park for BZ$5. Other tours are available, including one to the lagoon at Xo-Pol to see crocodiles. Bring plenty of bug juice. For tour information, stop at the Shipstern visitor center. ✉ *Shipstern Wildlife Reserve, Chunox-Sarteneja Rd., near Sarteneja village* ☎ *621/8336 Sarteneja Tour Guide Association* 🎟 *BZ$10* 🕒 *Daily 8–5.*

WHERE TO EAT

$ MEXICAN FAMILY 🍴 **Liz Fast Food.** Some of the tastiest and certainly the cheapest food in Sarteneja is at this little restaurant, hardly more than a glorified street stall. Liz Perez and her sister prepare and serve delicious, inexpensive tacos, *salbutes*, and *garnaches* for breakfast, lunch, and dinner. At lunch, locals stop by for spicy Buffalo chicken wings. It's hard to spend more than BZ$5 here for a filling meal. [$] *Average main: BZ$3* ✉ *Primitivo Aragon Ave., opposite the old church* 💳 *No credit cards.*

$ SEAFOOD 🍴 **Ritchie's Place.** This no-frills, family-run restaurant serves the freshest seafood in Sarteneja, from a whole fried snapper (BZ$15) to fish empanadas to conch and lobster in season. Owner Ritchie Cruz lives next door to his restaurant, which is just a few tables on a screened porch. Even a hungry family of four will find it difficult to spend more than BZ$50 for dinner unless you buy specials such as lobster. [$] *Average main: BZ$10* ✉ *Ritchie's Place, Front St., near public pier* ☎ *423/2031* 💳 *No credit cards.*

WHERE TO STAY

$ B&B/INN 🏨 **Candelie's Sunset Cabañas.** Our picks for the best, and best-value, lodging in Sarteneja are the two seaside cottages at Candelie's. **Pros:** spacious private cottages; lovely waterside location; good value; friendly manager. **Cons:** mattresses are a little thin. [$] *Rooms from: BZ$120* ✉ *On waterfront at west end of village, N. Front St.* ☎ *423/2005* 📧 *candeliescabanas@yahoo.com* 🛏 *2 cottages* 💳 *No credit cards* 🍽 *No meals.*

$ B&B/INN 🏨 **Fernando's Seaside Guesthouse.** Lounge on the second-floor veranda of this small waterfront guesthouse and watch the fishing boats anchored just a few hundred feet away. **Pros:** seaside location; water views from the second-floor porch. **Cons:** rooms at back lack a sea view and can be hot. [$] *Rooms from: BZ$65* ✉ *North Front St.* ☎ *423/2085* 🛏 *4 rooms.*

5

THE CAYO

By Lan Sluder

When the first jungle lodges opened in the early 1980s in the Cayo, few thought this wild area would become a tourist magnet. The mountainous region was too remote. Roads were bad. Restaurants were few. What would visitors do, besides visit cattle ranches and orange groves? After three decades of thoughtful development, and remarkable growth in lodging, restaurants, and other infrastructure, more than half of those touring Belize visit the Cayo during their trip, making this the country's second most popular destination after Ambergris Caye.

You'll be lured by the rugged beauty of the region, with its jagged limestone hills, low green mountains where tapirs, peccaries, and jaguars still roam free, and its boulder-strewn rivers and creeks. You'll also appreciate its diversity, in a compact and accessible package. Even on a short stay, you can canoe or kayak rivers, hike remote mountain trails, visit a Mayan ruin, explore underground cave systems, go birding or wildlife-spotting, shop at a busy local market, chill out at a sidewalk café, and dine in style at a good restaurant or by lamplight at a jungle lodge.

You'll know when you've entered the Cayo a few miles east of Belmopan. Running along the Belize River for miles (though it's usually not visible from the road), the Western Highway then winds out of the valley and heads into a series of sharp bends. In a few minutes you'll see cattle grazing on steep hillsides and horses flicking their tails. The Creole people who live along the coast give way to Maya and Mestizos; English is replaced by Spanish as the predominant language (though English is also widely spoken). The lost world of the Maya comes alive through majestic, haunting ruins. And the Indiana Jones in you can hike through the jungle, ride horseback, canoe down the Macal or Mopan River, and explore incredible caves such as Actun Tunichil Muknal, which some call the highlight of their entire Central American experience.

The best of Cayo is mostly found in its scenic outdoors—nearly two-thirds of the district is in national parks and forest reserves. But you should also take time to appreciate its towns and villages. Belmopan, once just a sleepy village, is in the middle of a boom, with new government and residential construction fueled by real-estate speculation. These days, it's officially known as Belmopan City, one of only two such official government destinations, the other of course being Belize City. San Ignacio is a thriving little town, its downtown area usually busy with locals come to buy supplies and backpackers looking to book tours or grab a bite and a Belikin at one of San Ignacio's many inexpensive eateries. The village of San Antonio is predominantly Mayan. Benque

TOP REASONS TO GO

National Parks and Reserves.
About 60% of the Cayo District is
national parks and reserves. Good
news If you like hiking, birding,
wildlife-spotting, canoeing, or
engaging in other outdoor activities.

Caves. Although there are caves
in Toledo and elsewhere in Belize,
the Cayo has the biggest and
most exciting ones. Actun Tunichil
Muknal is the top caving experience
in Belize.

Mayan Sites. The Cayo is home
to the largest and most important Mayan site in Belize; Caracol
has more than 35,000 buildings,
though so far only a handful have
been excavated. Cayo also has the
most easily accessible Mayan sites
in the country, Cahal Pech and

Xunantunich, along with dozens of
smaller ones.

Jungle Lodges. With more than
30 jungle lodges, the Cayo has far
more than all the other districts of
Belize combined. There's a lodge
for every budget, from bare-bones
cabins along the Mopan River to
ultradeluxe villas on the Macal River
and in the Mountain Pine Ridge.

Mountains. The Mountain Pine
Ridge's 2,000–3,500 foot mountains,
with their waterfalls, caves, and
rivers, provide a welcome respite
from the heat and humidity of
lowland Belize, though most of it
is not broad-leaf jungle but piney
woods not too different from the
Southern Appalachians in Alabama
or Georgia.

Viejo del Carmen, just 2 miles (3 km) from the border, feels more Guatemalan than Belizean, and Spanish Lookout, the Mennonite center, with
its well-kept farms and no-nonsense farm-supply and general stores,
could as well be in the U.S. Midwest.

El Cayo is Spanish for "the caye" or key. Local residents still call San
Ignacio Town "El Cayo," or just "Cayo," which can potentially create
some confusion for outsiders. The name is thought to have originally
referred to the small island formed where the Macal and Mopan rivers
meet at San Ignacio.

ORIENTATION AND PLANNING

GETTING ORIENTED

The Cayo's main connection to the coast is the George Price Highway
(formerly Western Highway), a paved two-lane road running 78 miles
(128 km) between Belize City and the Guatemala border. The highway
is in generally good condition, but shoulders are narrow, and parts
of the highway can be extremely slick after rains. Scores of people
have died in traffic accidents on the highway in recent years. Secondary
roads, mostly unpaved and sometimes difficult to drive on, branch off
the Western Highway, leading to small villages and to the Mountain
Pine Ridge, the Spanish Lookout Mennonite area, and various jungle
lodges. The Mountain Pine Ridge is crisscrossed by an extensive network of gravel and dirt roads, some formerly logging trails.

At Belmopan the paved Hummingbird Highway is Belize's most scenic road, cutting 54 miles (90 km) southeast through the Maya Mountains to Dangriga, passing Five Blues Lake and Blue Hole national parks. Mile markers on the Hummingbird start in Dangriga and increase as they go to Belmopan.

Belmopan City. While hardly a tourism hot spot, Belmopan is Belize's newest city (in Belize the government designates urban areas as cities, towns, or villages) with a growing number of restaurants and hotels. The U.S. Embassy has a US$50 million compound here, and around Belmopan are several excellent jungle lodges.

San Ignacio. The hub of western Belize, San Ignacio is a bustling little town. Here you can arrange tours (often at lower prices than from jungle lodges), shop at the local market, and get a good meal, whether you're hungry for Indian, Italian, Chinese, Belizean, or even Sri Lankan.

Benque Viejo. The last town in Belize before you reach Guatamala, Benque Viejo has modest art and cultural attractions worth checking out, as well as a Mayan burial cave.

Mountain Pine Ridge. The largest forest reserve in Belize, the Mountain Pine Ridge covers almost 300 square miles (777 square km). Criss-crossed by old logging roads and small rivers, and dotted with water-falls, the Mountain Pine Ridge—at elevations up to almost 3,400 feet, and noticeably cooler than other parts of Cayo—is the gateway to the Chiquibul wilderness and to Caracol.

Caracol. The largest and most important Mayan site in Belize, Caracol rivals Tikal in Guatemala in historical importance and archaeological interest.

PLANNING

WHEN TO GO
The best time to visit the Cayo is late fall and winter, when temperatures generally are moderate. During the peak of the dry season, March to May or early June, at the lower elevations around San Ignacio and Belmopan daytime temperatures can reach 100°F, though it does cool off at night. Seasonal rains usually reach the Cayo in early June. In summer, after the rains begin, temperatures moderate a little, but humidity increases. Year-round the Mountain Pine Ridge is noticeably cooler and less humid than anywhere else in Belize, and at times in winter it can be downright chilly; lodges in the Pine Ridge have fireplaces.

GETTING HERE AND AROUND
AIR TRAVEL
Most people bound for the Cayo fly into Belize City. Tropic Air now has flights to Maya Flats airstrip on the Chial Road between San Ignacio and Benque Viejo. For charter flights, there also is an airstrip near San Ignacio at Central Farm. Blancaneaux Lodge and Hidden Valley Inn in the Mountain Pine Ridge have their own private airstrips and helipads.

Maya Flats Airstrip (MYF). This newly opened small airport is on the Chial Road off the Benque Viejo Road (aka George Price Highway) about midway between San Ignacio and Benque Viejo del Carmen. Currently it is served only by Tropic Air and used by some private aircraft. ⊠ *Maya Flats Airstrip, Chial Rd., San Ignacio.*

Tropic Air ⊠ *Maya Flats Airstrip, Chial Rd., San Ignacio* ☏ *226/2012 in Belize, 800/422–3435 from U.S. and Canada* ⊕ *www.tropicair.com.*

BUS TRAVEL

A number of bus lines provide frequent service—about once every half hour during daylight and early evening hours—between Belize City and Cayo, with a stop in Belmopan. Among small bus companies authorized to operate on the George Price Highway are BBOC, D and E, Guerra's Bus Service, Middleton's, Shaw Bus, and Westline. James Line runs from Belize City to Belmopan, and then down the Hummingbird and Southern highways to Dangriga and Punta Gorda. Westbound buses depart from Belize City about every half hour beginning at around 5am, with the last departures at 9 or 9:30 pm.

The cost between Belize City and San Ignacio is BZ$7 on a local, and BZ$9 on an express if you can find one. From Belize City regular buses are about BZ$5 to Belmopan and BZ$8 to Benque Viejo. Buses are typically old U.S. school buses and are not air-conditioned. Most buses from Belize City leave from what is still called the Novelo's terminal on West Collet Canal Street, even though the Novelo's bus line is defunct. Look for any bus with "Cayo" or "Benque" on the front. There is a bus station in the center Belmopan, while buses stop at a new parking area next to the Cayo Welcome Center on Savannah Avenue in the center of San Ignacio. The Belize Bus Blog (⊕ *www.belizebus.wordpress.com*) has helpful information on bus travel.

Welcome Center Bus Area. Next to the new Cayo Welcome Center in downtown San Ignacio is the pick-up and drop-off area for buses arriving and departing San Ignacio. This is not an actual bus terminal, but it's where all the buses on the George Price Highway now stop in downtown San Ignacio. ⊠ *Savannah St., next to Cayo Welcome Center, San Ignacio.*

CAR TRAVEL

Other than the two-lane George Price Highway most roads in the Cayo are unpaved and dusty in the dry season, muddy in the rainy season. To get to the Cayo, simply follow the Price Highway west from Belize City. Watch out for "sleeping policemen" (speed bumps) near villages along the route. ⚠ **Be especially careful when driving the Price Highway. Most of the road lacks shoulders, and the surface can be extremely slick when wet. Horrific auto accidents occur frequently on this highway, which is long overdue for major upgrading.** If you didn't rent a car in Belize City, you can rent one in San Ignacio. Of the handful of car-rental companies in San Ignacio, Cayo Auto Rentals is usually the cheapest, with vehicles from around BZ$90 a day plus tax.

Rental Information Cayo Auto Rentals ⊠ *81 Benque Viejo Rd., George Price Hwy., San Ignacio* ☏ *824/2222* ⊕ *www.cayoautorentals.com.* **Flames Auto Rental** ⊠ *Joseph Andrews Dr., San Ignacio* ☏ *824/3198* ⊕ *www.flamesautorentals.com.* **Matus Car Rental** ⊠ *18 Benque Viejo Rd., George Price Hwy., San Ignacio* ☏ *824/2005* ⊕ *www.matuscarrental.com.*

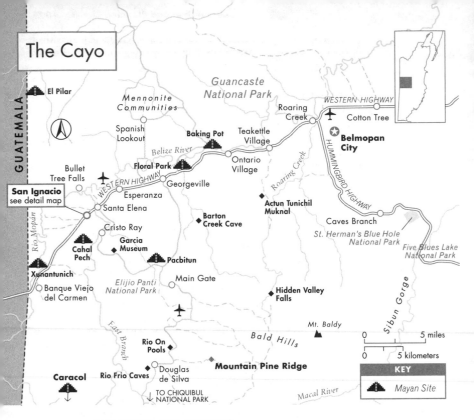

The Cayo

GUATEMALA

El Pilar

Mennonite Communities

Guancaste National Park

WESTERN HIGHWAY

Roaring Creek

Cotton Tree

Spanish Lookout

Baking Pot

Teakettle Village

Belize River

Belmopan City

HUMMINGBIRD HIGHWAY

Bullet Tree Falls

Floral Park

Ontario Village

Roaring Creek

San Ignacio see detail map

WESTERN HIGHWAY

Georgeville

Esperanza

Santa Elena

Actun Tunichil Muknal

Caves Branch

Rio Mopan

Cristo Ray

Barton Creek Cave

St. Herman's Blue Hole National Park

Five Blues Lake National Park

Garcia Museum

Cahal Pech

Pacbitun

Xunantunich

Banque Viejo del Carmen

Elijio Panti National Park

Main Gate

Hidden Valley Falls

Sibun Gorge

East Branch

Mt. Baldy

Bald Hills

0   5 miles

0   5 kilometers

Rio On Pools

Rio Frio Caves

Douglas de Silva

Mountain Pine Ridge

Macal River

KEY

Caracol

TO CHIQUIBUL NATIONAL PARK

Mayan Site

TAXI TRAVEL AND SHUTTLES

Taxis are plentiful in and around San Ignacio, but they're expensive if you're going to a remote lodge. For example, a taxi from San Ignacio to one of the Mountain Pine Ridge lodges is likely to be BZ$100–BZ$150, and to one of the lodges west of San Ignacio on the Macal River, about BZ$50–BZ$80 (rates are negotiable). Taxis within San Ignacio shouldn't be more than BZ$6 to most points and around BZ$15 to Bullet Tree. Collective taxis (they pick up as many passengers as possible) run to the Guatemala border for BZ$5 or less. Colectivos to Bullet Tree are BZ$2. You can find taxis at Market Square in the middle of town, near Burns Avenue, or call **Cayo Taxi Association** (☎ 824/2196) or **Savannah Taxi** Association (☎ 824/2155), or have your hotel call a taxi.

Many Cayo hotels and lodges provide van transportation from the international airport and other points in Belize City for about BZ$200–BZ$300 for up to four people one way. Several operators run shuttle vans between Belize City and San Ignacio for around BZ$70–BZ$100 per person. Among those currently offering shuttles are William's Shuttle, Belize Shuttles and Transfers, and Discounted Belize Shuttles and Tours. Of these, we highly recommend William's Shuttle. Dutch expat William Hofman is reliable, friendly, and knowledgeable; he charges around BZ$90 per person for two between Belize City and San Ignacio, or BZ$70 per person for three or more. Belize Shuttles and Transfers has both on-demand and fixed-time shuttle trips, the fixed-time shuttles to San Ignacio from either Belize City airport costing BZ$70 per person, plus 12.5% tax. Discounted Shuttles charges BZ$70 per person for two people from the international airport to Belmopan and BZ$90 per person to San Ignacio; these rates include tax.

A taxi from the International airport near Belize City to San Ignacio will cost around BZ$180–BZ$250 (for the cab, not per person), depending on your bargaining ability.

Shuttle Vans Belize Shuttles and Transfers ⊠ *Philip Goldson International Airport, Ladyville* ☎ *631/1749, 757/383–8024 U.S. number* ⊕ *www.belizeshuttlesandtransfers.com.* **Discounted Belize Shuttles and Tours** ⊠ *Philip Goldson International Airport, Ladyville* ☎ *620/1474* ⊕ *www.discounted belizeshuttlesandtours.com.* **William's Shuttle** ⊠ *Parrot Nest Lodge, Bullet Tree Falls* ☎ *620/3055* ⊕ *www.parrot-nest.com/belize-shuttle.html.*

EMERGENCIES

In case of emergency, there's the private Seventh Day Adventist hospital La Loma Luz, in Santa Elena, east of San Ignacio, as well as the public hospital, San Ignacio Hospital, in a new facility west of town on Bullet Tree Road. Belmopan is home to the Western Regional Hospital, and there is a sizeable government clinic in Benque Viejo, along with small clinics in several villages.

For police and fire, dial 911.

Hospitals La Loma Luz Hospital ⊠ *George Price Hwy., formerly Western Hwy., Santa Elena* ☎ *804/2985* ⊕ *www.lalomaluz.org.* **San Ignacio Hospital** ⊠ *Bullet Tree Rd., San Ignacio* ☎ *824/2066.* **Police** ⊠ *San Ignacio* ☎ *911, 824/2022.* **Western Regional Hospital** ⊠ *North Ring Rd., Belmopan* ☎ *822/2263* ⊕ *www.whr.health.gov.bz.*

MONEY MATTERS

Although U.S. dollars are accepted everywhere, you can exchange money at the border crossing near Benque Viejo. Money changers at the border often give slightly better rates. Banks in San Ignacio include Atlantic Bank, Belize Bank, and ScotiaBank. They are all downtown on Burns Avenue. Belmopan has branches of all five of Belize's retail banks—Atlantic Bank, Belize Bank, First Caribbean International Bank, Heritage Bank, and ScotiaBank. ScotiaBank also has an office in Spanish Lookout. All these bank offices have ATMs, and all but Heritage Bank accept ATM cards issued outside Belize.

(See ATMs and Banks in Travel Smart for Bank addresses and phone numbers)

BUDGETING YOUR TRIP

Here is a range of rates you can expect to pay for selected trips. These charges are per person and usually include transportation, lunch (on full-day trips), and, in the case of river trips, drop-off and pickup. Admission to Mayan sites (usually BZ$10–BZ$20, except about US$20 at Tikal), border fees (BZ$37.50 to go from Belize to Guatemala), may or may not be included—you should ask. Gratuities for guides are almost always extra. On some day trips, such as to Tikal or Caracol, there's often a flat fee for one to three or four persons, so the more going together, the cheaper. Keep in mind that, especially off-season, rates for some of these tours may be negotiable.

- Guided nature walk, at lodge: BZ$20–BZ$60
- Morning birding walk, at lodge: BZ$10–BZ$30 (sometimes free)
- Day tour to Tikal: BZ$250–BZ$500 (cheaper for larger parties)
- Overnight trip to Tikal: BZ$400–BZ$900
- Day trip to Caracol: BZ$180–BZ$300 (cheaper for larger parties)
- Half-day tour of Xunantunich: BZ$40–BZ$100
- Mountain Pine Ridge tour: BZ$100–BZ$250
- Actun Tunichil Muknal: BZ$180–BZ$260
- Barton Creek Cave with canoe: BZ$75–BZ$160
- Self-guided canoe or kayak trip on Macal or Mopan rivers: BZ$50–BZ$70
- Half-day horseback riding: BZ$60–BZ$140
- Mountain bike rental: BZ$25–BZ$70 a day (complimentary at some lodges)
- Overnight camping trip, with guide: BZ$300 or more per night for up to three persons, plus supplies

HEALTH

While the Cayo normally has relatively few mosquitoes, thanks to the porous limestone terrain that doesn't allow water to stand in puddles, there are occasional outbreaks of dengue fever. Dengue, which causes flu-like symptoms, and, in more serious cases, death from internal bleeding, is transmitted by the bite of *Aedes aegypti* and *Aedes albopictus* mosquitoes. These species are most active in the early morning and late afternoon. Travelers, especially during the rainy season, should consider using insect repellent with DEET. There is no preventative medicine for dengue.

Health standards in the Cayo are high. The water in San Ignacio and Santa Elena comes from a treated municipal system, so it's safe to drink, though many people prefer the taste of bottled water. Resorts in the region have their own safe water systems.

ABOUT THE RESTAURANTS

San Ignacio is the culinary center of the Cayo, with some two-dozen restaurants. Most are small spots with only a few tables. Restaurants offer Indian, French, German, and even Sri Lankan fare as well as burritos and beans. Prices, designed to appeal to the budget and mid-level travelers who stay in town, rarely rise above the moderate level. At the jungle lodges outside San Ignacio prices are much higher. Some lodges charge BZ$65–BZ$80, or more, for dinner.

ABOUT THE HOTELS

In the Cayo you have two very different choices in accommodations: jungle lodges and regular hotels. Jungle lodges, regardless of price or amenities, offer a close-to-nature experience, typically next to a river or in a remote mountain setting. Many lodges house their guests in thatch cabanas patterned after traditional Mayan houses. At the top end, lodges such as Blancaneaux Lodge and The Lodge at Chaa Creek deliver a truly deluxe experience, with designer toiletries, imported mattresses, and decor that wouldn't be out of place in *Architectural Digest*. At the other end, some budget lodges have outdoor bathrooms and thin foam mattresses. In between are a number of mid-level lodges providing an off-the-beaten-path experience at moderate prices.

Whereas the district's lodges are back-a-bush (a Belizean expression for "out in the jungle"), the Cayo's hotels are in towns or along the Western Highway. The area's least expensive hotels are clustered in downtown San Ignacio, one of the backpacker centers of Belize. Hotels in and around Belmopan are a little more expensive because they cater to people in the capital on government business. Whether hotel or jungle lodge, most properties in the Cayo are small, typically run by the owners.

Generally, inexpensive hotels and lodges maintain the same rate year-round, though some may discount a little in the off-season (generally mid-April to early December). More expensive places have off-season rates 20% to 40% less than high season.

HOTEL AND RESTAURANT PRICES

Prices in the restaurant reviews are the average cost of a main course at dinner or, if dinner is not served, at lunch; taxes and service charges are generally included. Prices in the hotel reviews are the lowest cost of a standard double room in high season, excluding taxes, service charges, and meal plans (except at all-inclusives). Prices for rentals are the lowest per-night cost for a one-bedroom unit in high season.

For expanded lodging reviews and current deals, visit Fodors.com.

TOURS

ADVENTURE

Green Dragon Adventure Travel. Associated with the Belize Jungle Dome hotel near Belmopan, Green Dragon Adventure Travel offers 3- to 14-day tours of Belize. Among them are four- and five-day adventure tours of Cayo, incorporating visits to Mayan ruins and caves, with activities including hiking, river kayaking, and horseback riding. Rates for these Cayo tours are US$1,195 to US$1,639 per person, not including airfare to Belize. ⊠ *Banana Bank, Belmopan* ☎ *822/2124* ⊕ *www.greendragonbelize.com.*

MOUNTAIN BIKING

Ceiba International. Ceiba International has a seven-day mountain biking tour in Belize for US$1,995 per person, not including airfare to Belize. After a night in Belize City the tour begins in the Mountain Pine Ridge, then moves on to the Macal River Valley near San Ignacio and then to the area around Pook's Hill Lodge. You stay in comfortable, upscale hotels and lodges, with no camping. ⊠ *Flagstaff, Arizona, USA* ☎ *800/217–1060 in U.S. and Canada, 928/527–0171 U.S. number* ⊕ *www.ceibainternational.com.*

SEEING THE RUINS

San Ignacio makes a good jumping-off spot to see Tikal, either on a day trip or overnight. It's also a good base for visiting Mayan sites in the Cayo, including **Caracol, Xunantunich, Cahal Pech,** and **El Pilar.** It's also a base for visiting Actun Tunichil Muknal, the amazing caves that introduces you to the Maya Underworld.

Belize Magnificent Mayan Tours. Run by local tour guide Albert Williams, Belize Magnificent Mayan Tours (or BZM Tours for short) does tours to Caracol, Tikal, Xunantunich, and elsewhere. Day tours to Mayan sites range from around BZ$140 per person for Cahal Pech to BZ$910 for trips to the ruins near Punta Gorda in the far south. BZM Tours also has package tours, such as a three-night/four-day package that includes pick-up at the international airport and tours of Xunantunich, Cahal Pech, and Chechem Ha Cave, with extras such as a visit to the Belize Zoo and river canoeing. ⊠ *3 Burns Ave., San Ignacio* ☏ *621/0312* ✐ *albert@bzmtours.com* ⊕ *www.bzmtours.com.*

PACZ Tours. PACZ specializes in tours to the spooky, wonderful Actun Tunichil Muknal near Belmopan (BZ$220 for a day tour, and BZ$560 for an overnight trip) with its Mayan relics but also other Mayan tours, including ones to Tikal and Caracol. The day tour to Tikal is BZ$290 and includes transportation from downtown San Ignacio, lunch, border fees, admission to Tikal and guides. The full-day Caracol tour is BZ$220 and includes transportation from downtown San Ignacio, admission fees, guide, lunch and stops at some sites in the Mountain Pine Ridge including Rio On and Rio Frio cave. ⊠ *30 Burns Ave., San Ignacio* ☏ *824/0536, 604/6921 cell phone, after 8 pm* ⊕ *www.pacztours.net.*

VISITOR INFORMATION

A new BZ$4 million welcome center in the heart of San Ignacio opened in mid-2013, and it's a beauty. The Cayo Welcome Center *(see Exploring in San Ignacio)* has a visitor information center and displays of Maya artifacts dug up from under Burns Avenue and elsewhere.

The Belize Tourism Board website, ⊕ *www.travelbelize.org,* has some information on visiting the Cayo. Eva's restaurant, when run by Englishman Bob Jones and his wife, was known for many years as the place to get the latest news and gossip about Cayo. Jones is now associated with PACZ Tours. Eva's is now under new management and is a ghost of its former self.

The Cayo Star, a weekly tabloid newspaper, has news about the Cayo and particularly about San Ignacio. It's available online at ⊕ *www.belizenews.com* and elsewhere. San Ignacio Town (⊕ *www.sanignaciotown.com*), though a commercial site, has considerable information on the Cayo. Best of Cayo (⊕ *www.bestofcayo.com*) offers opinionated recommendations of the best places to stay, eat, shop, and drink in San Ignacio. Belmopan City Online (⊕ *www.belmopancityonline.com*) has tourism information on the Belmopan area, along with local news of the capital city. For information on how Belize is governed, visit the National Assembly of Belize website (⊕ *www.nationalassembly.gov.bz*)—the site also explains how you can request a visit to the legislative assembly.

GREAT ITINERARIES

IF YOU HAVE 3 DAYS IN THE CAYO

Upon arrival at the international airport, immediately head to the Cayo by rental car, bus, or shuttle van. If you have time, stop en route at the Belize Zoo. Stay at one of the jungle lodges around San Ignacio if it's within your budget. On your first full day in the Cayo, explore the area around San Ignacio, visiting the Xunantunich and Cahal Pech Mayan ruins (both have visitor centers, and the one at Xunantunich is new in 2013), the Belize Botanic Gardens on the grounds of duPlooy's Lodge, and Green Hills Butterfly Farm. Assuming you have the energy, walk the Rainforest Medicine Trail and spend a few minutes at the Natural History Center, both at The Lodge at Chaa Creek. On the second day, if you're not planning to move on to Tikal in Guatemala after your stay in the Cayo, at least take a day tour there. Guided tours from San Ignacio usually include van transportation to the Tikal park, a local guide at the site, and lunch. Alternatively, if you're heading to Tikal later, take a day trip to Caracol in the Mountain Pine Ridge. Bring a picnic lunch and make stops at Río On pools, the Río Frio cave, and

a waterfall, such as Five Sisters on the grounds of Gaia Lodge, or Big Rock Waterfall nearby. On your final day, take a full-day guided tour of Actun Tunichil Muknal. Have dinner at a restaurant in San Ignacio.

IF YOU HAVE 5 DAYS IN THE CAYO

Rent a car at the international airport and drive to a jungle lodge near Belmopan. If you have time, stop en route at the Belize Zoo and do a quick driving tour of the capital. On your first full day, go cave tubing and take a zip-line canopy tour at Nohoch Che'en Caves Branch Archeological Reserve, also called Jaguar Paw after a now-closed jungle lodge at the site. Alternatively, for a more strenuous day, take a trip with Caves Branch Adventure Camp, or do its cave-tubing trip. End your day with dinner at your lodge and a night wildlife-spotting tour. On your second day, drive down the Hummingbird Highway and take a dip in the inland Blue Hole. Also, visit St. Herman's Cave, or go horseback riding at Banana Bank Lodge near Belmopan. On the third day, move on to a jungle lodge near San Ignacio or in the Mountain Pine Ridge and follow the three-day itinerary.

BELMOPAN CITY

50 miles (80 km) southwest of Belize City.

It used to be said that the best way to see Belize's capital, which was moved here from Belize City in 1970, was through the rearview mirror as you head toward San Ignacio or south down the Hummingbird. It's still mostly a dreary cluster of concrete office buildings plunked in the middle of nowhere, surrounded by residential areas that may remind you of a central Florida town, proving that cities can't be created overnight. However, with the opening of the main campus of the University of Belize in Belmopan in 2002, the relocation of several embassies (including the U.S. embassy) from Belize City to Belmopan, and new

BUTTERFLY MIGRATIONS

Belize is on the flyway for Sulphur and other butterfly migrations from the U.S. and Canada to and through Central America. The summer migration usually starts in June and can last for several weeks. Among the species of butterflies migrating at this time are Cloudless Sulphur (*Phoebis sennae*), Orange Banded Sulphur (*Phoebis philea*), Ruddy Daggerwing (*Phoebis philea*), Great Southern White (*Ascia monuste*), and Giant Swallowtail (*Heraclides cresphontes*), among many others.

Monarchs (*Danaus plexippus*) usually migrate south to and through Belize in the late fall, and northward in the early spring. (Monarchs are believed to be the only species that migrate both north and south.) Butterfly and moth expert Jan Meerman at Green Hills Butterfly Farm estimates that as many as two million butterflies and moths migrate through Belize in a single day during migration season.

commercial activity around the capital, Belmopan—finally—is showing signs of life. The population has grown to more than 18,000. Commercial and retail activities are booming, and there's a minor real-estate gold rush going on. Despite all this, however, except for a brief ride around the city to see the government buildings and perhaps a stop for lunch or to shop the local market, we recommend that you spend your time at nearby sites rather than in the city itself.

GETTING HERE AND AROUND

Belmopan is about 48 miles (79 km) on the George Price Highway from Belize City. By car, it takes about an hour. As you approach the turnoff to Belmopan from the east, Guanacaste National Park is on your right. Turn south at Mile 47.4 on the Hummingbird Highway. In about 1¼ miles (2 km) you'll come to the main entrance road to Belmopan City. Turn left and soon you come to the Ring Road, a two-lane road that circles the city and provides access to the streets inside the ring. The jungle lodges near Belmopan are located either off the Price or Hummingbird highways.

TIMING

The highlights of Belmopan City itself can easily be seen in a couple of hours. If you're staying at a jungle lodge nearby, you can easily spend two to three days exploring the wider area, or longer, if you want to see the San Ignacio area while basing here.

EXPLORING THE BELMOPAN CITY AREA

At the edge of Belmopan City is **Guanacaste**, Belize's smallest national park. The **Belize Zoo** (⇨ *See Chapter 2*), one of the country's top sights, is only a half hour east of Belmopan via the Price Highway. **Actun Tunichil Muknal**, the cave that many view as one of the top sights and experiences in the region, is not far from Belmopan, off Mile 52.5 of the Price Highway. Neither is the **Nohoch Che'en Caves Branch** archeological park, accessible on a paved road off the Price Highway at Mile 37, with its exhilarating cave tubing. Belmopan is also the gateway to the **Hummingbird Highway,** Belize's most scenic roadway and home to the inland **Blue Hole** and **Five Blues Lake.** If you have an interest in Belizean history and politics, the **George Price Centre for Peace and Development** is a museum, library, and cultural center focused on Belize's Founding Father and first prime minister.

TOP ATTRACTIONS

Hummingbird Highway. Hands down, Hummingbird Highway is the most scenic roadway in Belize. The Hummingbird, a paved two-lane road, runs 54½ miles (91 km) from the junction of the George Price Highway (formerly Western Highway) at Belmopan to Dangriga. Technically, only the first 32 miles (53 km) is the Hummingbird—the rest is the Stann Creek District Highway, but most people ignore that distinction. As measured from Belmopan at the junction of the Western Highway—the road has a few milepost signs running north from Dangriga, but we'll ignore them—the Hummingbird first winds through limestone hill country, passing St. Herman's Cave (Mile 12.2) and the inland Blue Hole (Mile 13.1). It then starts rising steeply, with the Maya Mountains on the west or right side, past St. Margaret's village and Five Blue Lake (Mile 23). The views, of green mountains studded with cohune palms and tropical hardwoods, are incredible. At the Hummingbird Gap (Mile 26, elevation near 1,000 feet, with mountains nearby over 3,000 feet), you're at the crest of the highway and now begin to drop down toward the Caribbean Sea. At Middlesex village (Mile 32), technically the road becomes the Stann Creek District Highway and you're in Stann Creek District. Now you're in citrus country, with groves of grapefruit and Valencia oranges. Near Steadfast village (watch for signs around Mile 37) there's the 1,500-acre Billy Barquedier National Park, where you can hike (guide required) to waterfalls. At Mile 48.7 you pass the turn-off to the Southern Highway and at Mile 54.5 you enter Dangriga, with the sea just ahead. ■TIP→ If driving keep a watch for "sleeping policemen," speed bumps to slow down traffic near villages. Most are signed, but a few are not. Also, gas up in Belmopan, as there are no service stations until you approach Dangriga. ⌂ *Belmopan to Dangriga, Hummingbird Hwy.*

FAMILY **St. Herman's Blue Hole National Park.** Less than a half hour south of Belmopan, the 575-acre St. Herman's Blue Hole National Park has a natural turquoise pool surrounded by mosses and lush vegetation, wonderful for a cool dip. The "inland Blue Hole" is actually part of an underground river system. On the other side of the hill is St. Herman's Cave, once inhabited by the Maya. There's a separate entrance to St. Herman's. A path leads up from the highway, but it's quite steep and difficult to climb unless the ground is dry. To explore St. Herman's cave beyond the first 300 yards or so, you must be accompanied by a guide (available at the park), and no more than five people can enter the cave at one time. With a guide, you also can explore part of another cave system here, the Crystal Cave (sometimes called the Crystalline Cave), which stretches for miles; the additional cost is BZ$20 per person for a two-hour guided tour. The main park visitor center is 12½ miles (20½ km) from Belmopan. St. Herman's Blue Hole National Park is managed by the Belize Audubon Society. ⌂ *Mile 42.5, Hummingbird Hwy.* ☎ *223/5004 Belize Audubon Society* ⊕ *www.belizeaudubon.org* ⌂ *BZ$10* ☉ *Daily 8–4:30.*

WORTH NOTING

George Price Centre for Peace and Development. A permanent exhibit at this cultural center, library, and museum follows the life story of the Right Honorable George Price as he led the British colony to independence. Born in 1919 in Belize City, George Price was Belize's first and longest-serving prime minister. The "George Washington of Belize" is widely respected for his incorruptible dedication to the welfare of Belize and Belizeans. There's a sizeable library of books on human rights, peace, and national development, and the center hosts art shows, concerts, and film screenings. George Price passed away September 19, 2011, at age 92, just two days short of the 30th anniversary of Belize's independence. ⊠ *Price Centre Rd.* ☎ *822/1054* ⊕ *www.gpcbelize.com* ✉ *Free* ⊙ *Mon.–Thu. 9–6, Fri. 9–5, Sun. 9–noon, closed Sat.*

Guanacaste National Park. Worth a quick visit on the way in or out of Belmopan is Belize's smallest nature reserve, Guanacaste National Park, named for the huge guanacaste trees that grow here. Also called monkey's ear trees because of their oddly shaped seedpods, the trees tower more than 100 feet. (Unfortunately, the park's tallest guanacaste tree had to be cut down in 2006, due to safety concerns that it might fall.) The 50-acre park, managed by the Belize Audubon Society, has a rich population of tropical birds, including smoky brown woodpeckers, black-headed trogons, red-lored parrots, and white-breasted wood wrens. You can take one of the eight daily hourly tours, or you can wander around on your own. After, cool off with a refreshing plunge in the Belize River; there's also a small picnic area. ⊠ *Mile 47.7, George Price Hwy., formerly Western Hwy.* ☎ *223/5004 Belize Audubon Society in Belize City* ⊕ *www.belizeaudubon.org* ✉ *BZ$5* ⊙ *Daily 8:30–4:30; tours every hr. 8:30–3:30.*

A WACKY TALE

Five Blues Lake National Park. At the 4,000-acre Five Blues Lake National Park, until 2006 you were able to hike 3 miles (5 km) of trails, explore several caves, and canoe and swim in a 10-acre lake with five shades of blue. The lake was a cenote, a collapsed cave in the limestone. In July 2006, despite heavy rains, the water level in the lake began to recede. On July 20, 2006, local residents heard a strange noise "as if the lake were moaning." A giant whirlpool formed, and most of the water in the lake was sucked into the ground. Many of the fish died, and the lake looked like a dry pit. Researchers believe that a sediment "plug" dissolved and the lake drained, like water from a bathtub, into underground sinkholes and caves. The lake has since refilled with water, but the park isn't what it was before 2006. The park entrance is about 3½ miles (5¾ km) from the Hummingbird Highway, via a narrow and very rough dirt road. Bikes can be rented in St. Margaret's village, from which village volunteers manage the park, and homestays and overnight camping in the village also can be arranged. ⊠ *At end of Lagoon Rd., off Mile 32, Hummingbird Hwy., St. Margaret's Village.*

CAYO HISTORY

The Maya began settling the Belize River Valley of the Cayo some 4,000 years ago. At the height of the Maya civilization, AD 300 to 900, Caracol, El Pilar, Xunantunich, Cahal Pech, and other cities and ceremonial centers in what is now the Cayo were likely home to several hundred thousand people, several times the population of the district today.

Spanish missionaries first arrived in the area in the early 17th century, but they had a difficult time converting the independent-minded Maya, some of whom were forcibly removed to the Petén in Guatemala.

The first significant Spanish and British settlements were logwood and mahogany logging camps. The town of San Ignacio and its adjoining sister town, Santa Elena, were established later in the 1860s. Though only about 70 miles (115 km) from Belize City, San Ignacio remained fairly isolated until recent times, because getting to the coast by horseback through the bush could take three days or longer. What was then the Western Highway was paved in the 1980s, making it easier to get here. The first jungle lodges began operation, and tourism now vies with agriculture as the main industry.

5

WHERE TO EAT

In addition to the restaurants listed here, the food and produce stalls at the Belmopan market (**Market Square,** open Monday–Saturday, off Bliss Parade next to the bus terminal on Constitution Drive) are good places to buy tasty Belizean produce, snacks, and fruit at inexpensive prices—for example, you can get eight or ten bananas for BZ$1. If you can't wait to get to Belmopan to eat, near the Belize Zoo is a well-known roadside eatery where you can grab a good burger and a cold beer, **Cheers** (✉ *Mile 31, Western Hwy.* ☎ *822–8014*).

$$ LATIN AMERICAN

🍴 **Caladium.** In business since 1984, the Caladium is one of the oldest businesses in this young capital. Most Belizeans know it, since it's next to the bus station at Market Square. Here you'll find many of the country's favorites on the menu, including fried chicken, tender barbecued pork ribs, traditional rice and beans with chicken, beef, or pork, and conch soup. It's authentic, clean, affordable, well-run, and air-conditioned. [$] *Average main: BZ$16* ✉ *Market Sq.* ☎ *822/2754* ⏲ *Closed Sun.*

$$ ECLECTIC
Fodor's Choice ★

🍴 **Corkers Restaurant and Bar.** Next door to the Hibiscus Hotel, Corkers is run by the husband-and-wife team of Geoff Hatto-Hembling and Sam Buxton from the U.K. To catch any breezes, sit in the covered, open-air patio, or you can dine inside in the cozy air-conditioned dining room. The menu is eclectic, ranging from classic English fish and chips to a grilled American cheeseburger with fries to Indian curries, plus pasta, steak, pork ribs, fried chicken, and a nice variety of salads. Drink prices are reasonable, with half price cocktails at an extended happy hour 4 to 10 pm Thursday through Saturday. [$] *Average main: BZ$20* ✉ *Corkers, Hibiscus Plaza* ☎ *822/0400* 🌐 *www.corkersbelize.com* ⏲ *Closed Sun.*

WHERE TO STAY

$ **Banana Bank Lodge.** Set on the banks of the Belize River, this jungle
B&B/INN   lodge is a good spot for families, especially for those who like to ride
FAMILY   horses. **Pros:** good choice for families and horse lovers; lodge has
a swimming pool; guests and owners mingle at meals. **Cons:** pesky
mosquitoes and other bugs; some object to the lodge's caged birds and
animals; quality and condition of less-expensive rooms may not meet
your standards. $ Rooms from: BZ$164 ⊠ Banana Bank Ranch ✛ By
boat: across the Belize River, turn north at Mile 47 of the George Price
Hwy. Continue to a split in the road and keep right. At the next sharp
turn, keep right and continue ½ mile (1 km) to the end of the road,
park, and bang the gong to summon a boat from Banana Bank. By
road: from the Price Hwy., turn north at Mile 46.9 and cross bridge
over Belize River. Follow gravel/dirt road 3 miles (5 km) to Banana
Bank sign. Turn right and follow dirt road for 2 miles (3 km) to
lodge ☎ 832/2020 ⊕ www.bananabank.com ⤳ 10 rooms, 5 cabanas,
3 suites ⎮⊙⎮ Multiple meal plans.

$$ **Belize Jungle Dome.** This well-appointed small inn near the Belize
RESORT   River has four attractively furnished small suites, with tile floors, lots of
windows, and an uncluttered look. **Pros:** intimate upscale accommoda-
tions in a lovely setting; large selection of tours; access to hiking trails,
horseback riding, and other facilities at nearby Banana Bank Lodge.
Cons: stairs to some rooms and the café may be a problem for guests
with mobility limitations. $ Rooms from: BZ$207 ⊠ Banana Bank, off
Mile 47, George Price Hwy. ✛ From George Price Hwy. turn north at
Mile 46.9 and cross bridge over Belize River. Follow gravel/dirt road
3 miles (5 km) until you see Banana Bank sign. Turn right and follow
dirt road 2 miles (3 km). Belize Jungle Lodge is on the right just before
Banana Bank Lodge ☎ 822/2124 ⊕ www.belizejungledome.com ⤳ 1
room, 4 suites, 1 3-bedroom house ⎮⊙⎮ No meals.

$$$ **Caves Branch Adventure Co. & Jungle Camp.** This adventure lodge has
RESORT   recently gone upscale, adding hillside "treehouse suites" 20 feet above
FAMILY   the ground, a multilevel swimming pool with Jacuzzi, and a botani-
Fodor's Choice   cal garden featuring orchids and bromeliads. **Pros:** some of the best
★   adventure tours in Belize; lush jungle setting; swimming pool and
botanical garden. **Cons:** in dry weather the river often goes completely dry; no longer a cheap date. $ Rooms from: BZ$368 ⊠ Mile
42½, Hummingbird Hwy., 12 miles (19½ km) south of Belmopan
☎ 610/3451, 866/357–2698 ⊕ www.cavesbranch.com ⤳ 10 tree
houses, 4 suites, 5 bungalows, 10 cabanas ⎮⊙⎮ Multiple meal plans.

$ **Hibiscus Hotel.** If you want to sleep well literally and figuratively, try
HOTEL   the Hibiscus Hotel, where one-half of the profit from your stay goes
to the bird rescue and rehab program at Belize Bird Rescue near Belmopan. **Pros:** central location; good value; free Wi-Fi; some of their
profits go to funding bird conservation efforts in Belize; next door to
good restaurant. **Cons:** no pool; basic rooms. $ Rooms from: BZ$120
⊠ Hibiscus Plaza, Melhado Parade ☎ 822/0400 ⊕ www.hibiscusbelize.
com ⤳ 6 rooms.

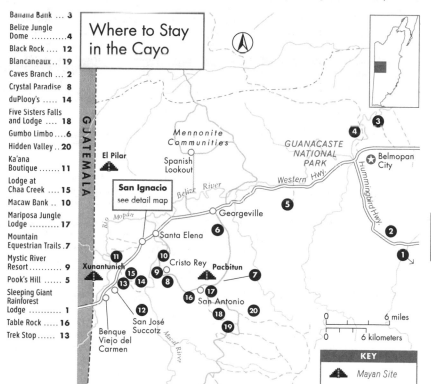

Where to Stay in the Cayo

KEY

🔺 Mayan Site

$$$
B&B/INN
Fodor's Choice
★

Pook's Hill. When the lamps are lighted each night on the polished rosewood veranda, this low-key, remote jungle lodge is one of the most pleasant places in the Cayo. **Pros:** well-managed jungle lodge in true jungle setting; on doorstep of Actun Tunichil Muknal; bar and dining room are conducive to guest interaction. **Cons:** insects can be a nuisance; with meals and tours lodge is not inexpensive. [$] *Rooms from: BZ$436 ⊠ Pook's Hill, Off Mile 52.5 of George Price Hwy. ⊕ At Mile 52.5 of George Price Hwy., at Teakettle village, head south on unpaved track for 5 miles (8 km) ☎ 832/2017 ⊕ www.pookshillbelize.com ⋟ 11 cabanas ⎥◯⎟ No meals.*

$$$
RESORT
Fodor's Choice
★

Sleeping Giant Rainforest Lodge. This new lodge, just off the Hummingbird Highway near the Sibun River, offers luxury in a remote rainforest setting. **Pros:** air-conditioned luxury accommodations in the foothills of the Maya Mountains; attractive grounds bordered by Sibun River; good food. **Cons:** presently caters to many groups; casitas are somewhat pricey. [$] *Rooms from: BZ$320 ⊠ Mile 36½, Hummingbird Hwy. ☎ 822/3851 in Belize, 888/332–4268 U.S. and Canada, 610/2635 cell phone at lodge ⊕ www.sleepinggianthelize. com ⋟ 4 rooms in lodge, 3 casitas, 2 units in a 2-bedroom house ⎥◯⎟ Multiple meal plans.*

$ B&B/INN [icon] **Twin Palms B&B.** This unpretentious, pleasant B&B in Belmopan offers affordable, comfortable rooms with TV, fan, fridge, plus the bonus of a small swimming pool. **Pros:** comfortable; genial hosts; has swimming pool; reasonable rates. **Cons:** no air-conditioning. [$] *Rooms from: BZ$120* ✉ *8 Trio St., off Hummingbird Hwy., Belmopan* ✣ *From Hummingbird Hwy. at Belmopan look for Uno gas station. Entrance to Trio St. is across the highway. Look for Twin Palms sign* ☎ *822/0176* 🌐 *www.belmopanbedandbreakfast.com* 🛏 *6 rooms* 🍴 *Breakfast.*

SPORTS AND THE OUTDOORS

Belmopan and San Ignacio offer a similar lineup of outdoor activities, and since they're only about 20 miles (33 km) apart, even if you are staying in San Ignacio you can enjoy the activities near Belmopan.

BIRDING

Although there's good birding in many areas around Belmopan, Pook's Hill Lodge *(⇨ see review in Where to Stay)*, 5½ miles (9 km) off the Western Highway at Mile 52.5, is in a league of its own. The birding list from Pook's Hill includes the Mealy Parrot, Spectacled Owl, Aztec Parakeet, and Keel-billed Toucan.

CANOEING AND KAYAKING

The Belize River, wide and mostly gentle (Class I–II) offers good canoeing and kayaking. It was once used by loggers to transport mahogany to Belize City and hosts the annual La Ruta Maya Mountains to the Sea Canoe Race. The multiday race is held in March during the Baron Bliss holiday. You can also canoe or kayak portions of the Caves Branch River (also Class I–II). Many hotels and lodges arrange canoe or kayak trips, including **Caves Branch Adventure Co. & Jungle Lodge** (☎ *822/2800*), off the Hummingbird Highway. Full-day canoe or kayak trips start at around BZ$120 per person.

CANOPY TOURS

You may feel a little like Tarzan as you dangle 80 feet above the jungle floor, suspended by a harness, moving from one suspended platform to another.

Jaguar Paw Zipline. Jaguar Paw has eight zip line platforms set 100 to 250 feet apart. At the last platform you have to rappel to the ground. There's a 240-pound weight limit. Zip line tours often are combined with cave tubing in the Caves Branch River. *(⇨ See Nohoch Che'en Caves Branch Archeological Reserve.)* The cost for the zip line is around BZ$120–BZ$200, depending on the tour and whether lunch and transportation are included. ✉ *Off Mile 37, George Price Hwy.* ☎ *223/4438, 877/424–8552 in U.S. and Canada* 🌐 *www.chukkacaribbean.com.*

CAVING

The area around Belmopan, with its karst limestone topography, is a paradise for cavers.

Fodor's Choice ★ **Actun Tunichil Muknal.** The Actun Tunichil Muknal (ATM) cave system runs some 3 mile (5 km) through the limestone of Cayo, just a few miles from Belmopan. ATM is the resting place of the Crystal Maiden, a Maya girl who was sacrificed here, along with at least 13 others, including seven children, hundreds of years ago. If you visit Actun Tunichil Muknal ("Cave of the Stone Sepulcher" in the Mayan language), you will experience what many say are the most awesome sights in all of Central America. You'll see amazing limestone formations, thousand-year-old human calcified skulls and skeletons, and many Mayan artifacts including well-preserved pottery. As long as you are in adequate physical condition— you have to hike almost an hour, swim in neck-deep water, and clamber through dark, claustrophobic underground chambers—this is

sure to be the most memorable tour you'll take in Belize. Cameras are banned from the cave, and the tour is not suitable for young children.

■TIP→ Although you can drive on your own to the staging area for ATM, you must have a licensed guide to visit it, as you'll be up close and personal with priceless Maya artifacts. It's easiest to do an all-day tour from San Ignacio or Belmopan. These tours run around BZ$200–$240, including lunch and the government admission fee. ⊠ *Off Mile 52.5, George Price Hwy., road entrance at junction of Price Hwy. and Teakettle Village* 🕾 *822/3302 National Institute of Culture & History (NICH)* 🎫 *BZ$.50, plus required guide fee* ☉ *Daily 8–4:30.*

St. Herman's Blue Hole National Park. At St. Herman's Blue Hole National Park *(⇨ see review)*, at Mile 42 of the Hummingbird Highway, there are two large caves, St. Herman's and the Crystal Cave. Both require a guide to explore (guides are available at the national park visitor center), though you can go without a guide into the first 300 yards of St. Herman's. ⊠ *Mile 42, Hummingbird Hwy.* ⊕ *www.belizeaudubon. org* 🎫 *BZ$10.*

CAVE TUBING

An activity you'll find in few places outside Belize is cave tubing. You drift down a river, usually the Caves Branch River in the Cayo District, in a large rubber inner tube. At certain points the river goes underground, and you float through eerie underground cave systems, some with Mayan artifacts still in place. The only light is from headlamps.

In the last decade since Jaguar Paw Lodge (now no longer operating as a lodge) and Caves Branch Adventure Co. & Jungle Lodge (🕾 *673/3454, 866/357–2698* ⊕ *www.cavesbranch.com*) first introduced it, cave tubing has become one of the most popular soft-adventure activities in Belize. It's the number one mainland shore excursion of cruise-ship passengers, and on days when several large ships are docked in Belize City you should expect inner-tube traffic jams.

Caves Branch River has two main entry points: near the former **Jaguar Paw Lodge** (✉ *Off Mile 37 of Western Hwy.*), at **Nohoch Che'en Caves Branch Archeological Reserve,** and near **Caves Branch Adventure Co. & Jungle Lodge** (✉ *Off Hummingbird Hwy.* ☎ *822/2800*). The Jaguar Paw access attracts more people, and when several cruise ships are in port at Belize City the river here can be jammed. There's a parking area about ½ mile (1 km) from Jaguar Paw, and here you'll find a number of independent tour guides for cave-tubing tours, which vary in length, generally costing from BZ$50 to BZ$70. Cave-tubing tours from Belize City, Belmopan, and San Ignacio, including transportation and perhaps lunch, cost more, generally BZ$120–BZ$180. ⇨ *See Tours in Belize City and the San Ignacio section of this chapter.* Cave-tubing trips from Caves Branch Lodge are longer, require more hiking, and cost more. For example, the "River of Caves" trip, through 7 miles (12 km) of underground caves, takes much of a day and costs BZ$190 per person.

Cave tubing is subject to changes in the river levels. In the dry season (February–May or June), the river levels are often too low for cave tubing. Also, after heavy rains, the water level in the river may be too high to safely float through caves, so in the rainy season (June–November) cave-tubing trips may occasionally be canceled. Always call ahead to check if tours are operating.

Nohoch Che'en Caves Branch Archeological Reserve. Nohoch Che'en Caves Branch (sometimes still referred to as Jaguar Paw) is the most-visited archeological site in Belize, mainly because of the number of cruise ship daytrippers who come here. However, that doesn't diminish the grandeur—and just plain fun—you'll experience when you float on inner tubes in the Caves Branch River through caves that the ancient Maya held sacred. Many Belize City, Belmopan, and San Ignacio tour companies offer cave tubing tours that include transportation, equipment, and a guide, typically for a charge of BZ$150 to $250 per person (more expensive tours include the zip line), although you can drive to the park and do cave tubing on your own with a guide for lower cost. The site, now fairly commercial with a large paved parking lot, changing rooms, concession stands, bar, and shops, is at the end of a paved road off Mile 37 of the George Price Highway, near Jaguar Paw (which is no longer operating as a hotel). Tour operators at the site including Caves Branch Outpost (⊕ *www.cavesbranchoutpost.com* ☎ *671–0987*) provide guides and equipment, and independent guides wait to offer tours. With an independent guide you'll pay around BZ$50 to BZ$80, depending on how many caves you want to go float through. Tours start with a 30-minute hike to the cave entrance, and then you float back to a point near the parking lot. There is also a zip line at this site. Cave tubing is not recommended for young children—some operators have a 12-year-old age requirement. At times during the rainy season water may be too high for safe tubing. There is a weight limit for the zip line. ✉ *Nohoch Che'en Caves Branch, off Mile 37, George Price Hwy. (formerly Western Hwy.), Frank's Eddy Village* ✛ *From Belize City, follow the George Price Hwy. to Mile 37. Turn south (left) on a paved road and follow about 6 miles (10 km) to Nohoch Che'en Caves Branch Archeological Reserve parking lot* ☎ *226/2882* ⊕ *www.nichbelize.org* 🎟 *BZ$20.*

GOLF

Roaring River Golf Course. The only public golf course on the mainland is Roaring River Golf Course. This 9-hole, 1,933-yard, par-32 jungle course (watch out for the crocs in the water traps) with double tees that let you play 3,892 yards at par 64, was the pet project of an expat South African, Paul Martin, who found himself with some extra time and a lot of heavy earth-moving equipment on his hands. Before long, he'd carved out the greens and bunkered fairways. It's not Pebble Beach, but it's fun, and affordable, too, as fees are only BZ$35 for 9 holes or BZ$50 for 18 holes. After a round of golf, you can sip a Belikin at the clubhouse. Roaring River Golf Course also has air-conditioned cottages for rent, and a restaurant, The Meating Place, for guests and groups. ✉ *Off Mile 50¼, George Price Hwy., near Camalote village* ✛ *Turn south at Camalote village at Mile 50¼ of Price Hwy. and follow signs* ☎ *820/2031* ⊕ *www.belizegolf.net.*

HORSEBACK RIDING

Banana Bank Lodge & Jungle Horseback Adventures. The largest equestrian operator in this part of Belize is Banana Bank Lodge, off the George Price Highway near Belmopan. Run by John Carr, a former Montana cowboy and rodeo rider, Banana Bank has more than 90 horses, mostly quarter horses, a large round-pen riding arena, stables, and miles of jungle trails on a 4,000-acre ranch. They offer occasional agricultural tours that introduce visiting farmers or others interested in agriculture to Mennonite and other farm operations in Belize. A two- to three-hour ride costs BZ$120, and a five-hour ride is BZ$180. Night rides are available also (BZ$120) as are horseback riding vacation packages. ✉ *Banana Bank* ☎ *832/2020* ⊕ *www.bananabank.com.*

SHOPPING

Art Box. Art Box has one of the largest selections of arts and crafts in Belize, including hand-crafted gift items, books, jewelry, tons of souvenirs, and more. Upstairs is a gallery featuring Belizean artists including Carolyn Carr. ✉ *Mile 46, George Price Hwy., formerly Western Hwy.* ☎ *623/6129* ⊕ *www.artboxbz.com* ⊗ *Mon.–Sat. 8–6.*

Hummingbird Furnishings. Hummingbird Furnishings uses bamboo, wicker, and rattan, sometimes mixed with mahogany, for indoor and outdoor furniture. ✉ *54 Hummingbird Hwy., Belmopan City* ☎ *822/3164* ⊕ *www.hummingbirdfurnishings.com* ✉ *20 Coconut Dr., San Pedro* ☎ *226/2960.*

SAN IGNACIO AND ENVIRONS

23 miles (37 km) southwest of Belmopan.

When you see the Hawksworth Bridge, built in 1949 and the only public suspension bridge in Belize, you'll know you've arrived at San Ignacio, the hub of the Cayo district. San Ignacio, with its twin town Santa Elena just to the east, is an excellent base for exploring western Belize. Nearby are three Mayan ruins, as well as national parks and a cluster of butterfly farms.

With its well-preserved wooden structures, San Ignacio is a Belizean town where you might want to linger. Evenings are comfortable and usually mosquito-free, and the colonial-era streets are lined with funky bars and restaurants. It's worth coming at sunset to listen to the eerily beautiful sounds of the grackles, the iridescent black birds that seem to like the town.

GETTING HERE AND AROUND

San Ignacio is less than two hours by car on the Western Highway from Belize City. Coming into San Ignacio is a little confusing. As you go through the "twin town" of Santa Elena and head into San Ignacio, you'll see the Hawksworth Bridge straight ahead. The bridge is one way coming from the west but this is not well marked; those coming from the east and unfamiliar with the area often try to drive across the bridge the wrong way. A sign noting a detour has been erected, directing vehicles to another bridge.

To keep from running afoul of traffic rules, turn right before the Hawksworth Bridge, following the detour to what is called the "lower bridge" or "low lying bridge." Cross this and follow Savannah Avenue around the sports stadium and, if you're lucky, you'll soon end up back on Price Highway just to the west of San Ignacio. Alternatively, after you cross the river, you can turn left and follow Savannah Avenue past the new Cayo Welcome Center to central San Ignacio. A part of Burns Avenue, the main street in town, is now closed to vehicles and has been turned into a small pedestrian mall. From San Ignacio, the George Price Highway continues on about 9 miles (15 km) to the Guatemala border. This stretch is locally known as the Benque Road.

TIMING

San Ignacio and the jungle lodges around it are used by many visitors to explore western Belize, which easily takes a week or more if you want to see it all.

SAFETY AND PRECAUTIONS

On several occasions in the past decade, armed bandits from nearby Guatemala robbed tourists around San Ignacio. At this writing, the U.S. Embassy had issued a warning about highway banditry on unpaved roads near the Guatemala border, and trips to Caracol may be made only in convoys accompanied by Belize Defence Forces soldiers. Ask locally about any recent incidents before starting road trips to remote areas. However, most visitors say they feel quite safe. As a visitor, you're unlikely to encounter any problems.

EXPLORING

TOP ATTRACTIONS

Fodor's Choice ★ Most tours to **Actun Tunichil Muknal** leave from San Ignacio, although this amazing cave is actually near Belmopan. (⇨ *See Belmopan section above for information.*)

FAMILY
Fodor's Choice ★ **Belize Botanic Gardens.** The life's work of Ken duPlooy, an ornithologist who died in 2001, the personable Judy duPlooy, and their family, is the 45-acre Belize Botanic Gardens. It's an extensive collection of hundreds

of trees, plants, and flowers from all over Central America. Enlightening tours of the gardens, set on a bank of the Macal River at duPlooy's Jungle Lodge, are given by local guides who can tell you the names of the plants in Maya, Spanish, and English as well as explain their varied medicinal uses. An orchid house holds the duPlooys' collection of more than 100 orchid species, and there also is a palm exhibit. The gardens and duPlooy's Lodge in general offer great birding. On some days duPlooy's runs shuttles from San Ignacio. The BZ$70 per person fee (minimum two persons) from San Ignacio includes the round trip shuttle and admission. Call for information and schedule. A day at the gardens, including shuttle, guided tour, and lunch is BZ$100 per person. A taxi from San Ignacio will likely cost at least BZ$50–$60 one-way. The Botanic Gardens also runs gardening programs for Belize residents and internship and volunteer programs. ⊠ *Chial Rd.* ✛ *From San Ignacio, head 4¾ miles (7½ km) west on Benque Rd., turn left on the unpaved Chial Rd. and go about 5 miles (8 km) to duPlooy's Jungle Lodge* ☎ *834/4800* ⊕ *www.belizebotanic.org* ☞ *BZ$15 self-guided tour; BZ$30 guided tour* ☉ *Daily 7–4; guided tours daily 7–3.*

Cayo Welcome Center. Opened in mid-2013, the Cayo Welcome Center is the largest and most appealing tourism information center in the country. According to the Belize Tourism Board, the BZ$4 million Welcome Center was established in San Ignacio because Cayo's archeological sites and rainforest jungle lodges are getting increasing numbers of visitors. Besides friendly staff who provide information on tours, lodging, restaurants, and sightseeing, the Center has exhibits of Mayan artifacts found buried under San Ignacio's Burns Avenue, along with contemporary art and cultural displays. Buses on the George Price Highway route drop off and pick up passengers in a waiting area adjoining the center, and those arriving by car can park in a secure lot next door (BZ$2 fee for two hours). Food stalls and an upscale restaurant, Fuego, are in the Center complex, and there is easy access to the pedestrian-only section of Burns Avenue, with its tour guide offices, restaurants, bars, banks, shops, and hotels. The Cayo Welcome Center also functions as a community center, with free movies and musical concerts by local bands some nights. ⊠ *Savannah St., across from the market* ☎ *623/3918, 800/624–0686 Belize Tourism Board* ⊕ *www.travelbelize.org.*

WORTH NOTING

FAMILY **Cahal Pech.** Just at the western edge of San Ignacio, on a tall hill, is a small, intriguing Mayan site, the unfortunately named Cahal Pech ("Place of the Ticks"). You probably won't be bothered by ticks now, however. It was occupied from around 1200 BC to around AD 900. At its peak, in AD 600, Cahal Pech was a medium-size settlement of perhaps 10,000 people with some three dozen structures huddled around seven plazas. It's thought that it functioned as a guard post, watching over the nearby confluence of the Mopan and Macal rivers. It may be somewhat less compelling than the area's other ruins, but it's no less mysterious, given that these structures mark the presence of a civilization we know so little about. Look for answers at the small visitor center and museum. ⊠ *Cahal Pech Hill* ☎ *822/2016 Belize Institute of Archeology* ⊕ *www.nichbelize.org* ☞ *BZ$10* ☉ *Daily 8–5.*

FAMILY **Chaa Creek Natural History Centre & Blue Morpho Butterfly Farm.** The Natural History Centre at The Lodge at Chaa Creek has a small library and lots of displays on everything from butterflies to snakes (pickled in jars). Outside is a screened-in Blue Morpho butterfly-breeding center. If you haven't encountered Blue Morphos in the wild, you can see them up close here and even peer at their slumbering pupae, which resemble jade earrings. Once you're inside the double doors, the electric blue beauties, which look boringly brown when their wings are closed, flit about or remain perfectly still, sometimes on your shoulder or head, and open and close their wings to a rhythm akin to inhaling and exhaling. Tours are led by a team of naturalists. You can combine a visit here with one to the Rainforest Medicine Trail (⇨ *see below*). ⊠ *The Lodge at Chaa Creek, Chial Rd.* ☎ *834/4010* ⊕ *www.chaacreek.com* 🖃 *BZ$10 self-guided tour; BZ$20 combined with self-guided Rainforest Medicine Trail tour; all free to Chaa Creek guests* ☉ *Daily 9–4.*

El Pilar. El Pilar, near the border of Belize and Guatemala, is still being excavated under the direction of Anabel Ford, a professor at the University of California at Santa Barbara, and the MesoAmerican Research Center. El Pilar is three times larger than Xunantunich, but because it's at the end of a 7-mile (12 km) rough dirt road, it gets only a few hundred visitors a year. Excavations of Mayan ruins have traditionally concentrated on public buildings, but at El Pilar the emphasis has been on reconstructing domestic architecture—everything from houses to gardens with crops used by the Maya. El Pilar, occupied from 800 BC to AD 1000, at its peak may have had a population of 20,000. Several well-marked trails take you around the site. Because the structures haven't been stripped of vegetation, you may feel like you're walking through a series of shady orchards. ■ **TIP→ Don't forget binoculars: In the 5,000-acre nature reserve there's terrific bird-watching.** Behind the main plaza, a lookout grants a spectacular view across the jungle to El Pilar's sister city, Pilar Poniente, on the Guatemalan border. There is a visitor center, the Be Pukte Cultural Center of Amigos de El Pilar, in Bullet Tree Falls (usually open daily 9–5), where you can get information on the site and pay the admission fee. Note that several incidents of robbery have occurred at or near El Pilar. You may want to visit this site on a tour, available from several tour operators in San Ignacio including duPlooy's and Crystal Paradise/Birding in Paradise. ⊠ *7 miles (12 km) northwest of Bullet Tree Falls, off Bullet Tree Rd., Bullet Tree Falls* ✢ *Take the Bullet Tree Road in San Ignacio to Bullet Tree Falls. In Bullet Tree Falls, just before the bridge over the Mopan River on the left you will see the Be Pukte Cultural Center of the Amigos de El Pilar. To go on to El Pilar, cross the Mopan River Bridge and you will see signs to the El Pilar Road.* ☎ *822/2106 NICH Institute of Archeology in Belmopan* ⊕ *www.nichbelize.org* 🖃 *BZ$10* ☉ *Daily 8–5.*

FAMILY **Rainforest Medicine Trail.** The Rainforest Medicine Trail at The Lodge at Chaa Creek, originally developed by natural medicine guru Rosita Arvigo, gives you a quick introduction to traditional Mayan medicine. The trail takes you on a short, self-guided walk through the rain forest, giving you a chance to study the symbiotic nature of its plant life. Learn about the healing properties of such indigenous plants as red gumbo-limbo and see some endangered medicinal plants. The shop here sells Mayan medicinal products like Belly Be Good and Flu Away. ✉ *The Lodge at Chaa Creek, Chial Rd.* ☎ *834/4010 Chaa Creek front desk* ⊕ *www.chaacreek.com* 🖂 *BZ$10 self-guided tour; BZ$20 guided tour. BZ$20 for self-guided tour including Natural History Centre and Blue Morpho Breeding Center; all free to Chaa Creek guests* ⊗ *Daily 9–4.*

San Ignacio Market. On Saturday morning, San Ignacio Market comes alive with farmers selling local fruits and vegetables. Vendors also hawk crafts, clothing, and household goods. Some vendors show up on other days as well, but Saturday has by far the largest market. A smaller vegetable and fruit market is open weekdays near Burns Avenue, closer to town. ✉ *Savannah St., across from soccer stadium* ⊗ *Sat. 6 am–noon; other days limited number of vendors 6 am–noon.*

Spanish Lookout. The hilltop community of Spanish Lookout, population 2,500, about 5 miles (8 km) north of the George Price Highway, is one of the centers of Belize's 11,000-strong Mennonite community, of which nearly 3,000 are in Cayo District. The easiest access to Spanish Lookout is via the paved Route 30 at Mile 57½ of the Price Highway. The village's blond-haired, blue-eyed residents may seem out of place in this tropical country, but they're responsible for much of the construction, manufacturing, and agriculture in Belize. They built many of Belize's resorts, and most of the chickens, eggs, cheese, and milk you'll consume during your stay come from their farms. Many of the small wooden houses that you see all over Belize are Mennonite pre-fabs built in Spanish Lookout. In conservative communities, women dress in cotton frocks and head scarves, and the men don straw hats, suspenders, and dark trousers. Some still travel in horse-drawn buggies, though most Mennonites around Spanish Lookout have embraced pickup trucks and modern farming equipment. The cafés and small shopping centers in Spanish Lookout offer a unique opportunity to mingle with these sometimes world-wary people, but they don't appreciate being gawked at or photographed any more than you do. Stores in Spanish Lookout are modern and well-stocked, the farms wouldn't look out of place in the U.S. Midwest, and many of the roads are paved (the Mennonites do their own road paving). Oil in commercial quantities was discovered in Spanish Lookout in 2005, and several wells now pump several thousand barrels of black gold daily. ✉ *Spanish Lookout.*

FAMILY **Tropical Wings.** Besides thoughtful displays on the Cayo flora and fauna, Tropical Wings, a little nature center, raises about 20 species of butterfly including the Blue Morpho, Owl, Giant Swallowtail, and Monarch varieties. The facility, at The Trek Stop (⇨ *see review*), also has a small restaurant and gift shop, along with cabins. ✉ *Mile 71.5, George Price Hwy. (aka Benque Rd.), 6 miles (10 km) west of San Ignacio, San José Succotz* ☎ *823/2265* ⊕ *www.thetrekstop.com/tropwings.htm* 🖂 *BZ$6 adults, BZ$3 children 12 and under* ⊗ *Daily 9–5.*

5

WHERE TO EAT

Besides the restaurants listed here, most of the jungle lodges in the Cayo have their own restaurants. Those at Table Rock Lodge, Mystic River Lodge, The Lodge at Chaa Creek, and duPlooy's Lodge are especially good. Nearer town, the restaurants at Ka'ana Boutique Resort and San Ignacio Resort Hotel also are noteworthy. On the other end of the price scale, street vendors set up barbecue grills and food stalls on the Price Highway just east of the Hawksworth Bridge in Santa Elena, and you can get big plates of food for little money.

$$ LATIN AMERICAN 🍴 **Erva's.** Nothing fancy here, just downhome Belizean dishes at moderate prices, and that's exactly why it's popular. Go for the traditional beans and rice dishes or Belizean *escabeche* (onion soup with chicken and lime); the ceviche is good, too. If you're in the mood for something else, you can get a pizza or fish. The waiters are extra-friendly. It's a couple of blocks off the main drag, so it's quieter and more relaxing here, whether you dine on the veranda or inside in the homey dining room. [$] *Average main: BZ$16* ✉ *4 Far West St.* ☎ *824/2821* 🕒 *Closed Sun.*

$$ LATIN AMERICAN 🍴 **Flayva's Bar & Grill.** Generous portions of Belizean dishes are what Flayva's (the local way of saying "flavors") is known for, and it's also the name of the owner's pet parrot. On the pedestrian-only section of Burns Avenue, with some seating outside, Flayva has good traditional breakfasts (served all day) with fryjacks and big breakfast burritos. At lunch and dinner we suggest the shrimp dishes, such as curried shrimp or mango shrimp. Occasionally service can be slow. There's a DJ some nights. [$] *Average main: BZ$16* ✉ *22 Burns St., San Ignacio* ☎ *804/804–2267* 🌐 *www.flayvasbarandgrill.com.*

$$ LATIN AMERICAN Fodor's Choice ★ 🍴 **Fuego Bar & Grill.** Inside the Cayo Welcome Center, Fuego Bar & Grill is the most upscale and attractive restaurant in downtown San Ignacio. With its farm-to-table philosophy, Fuego—which was opened by Ian Lizerraga of Ka'ana Resort—uses produce and meats from the San Ignacio market across the street and from local farms. Chef Jesse Mas creates intriguing combinations such as grilled pork chops glazed with coffee and molasses, served with plantains and green beans. The drinks are interesting, too, such as a chocolate martini and beer with cucumber juice, lime, and salt on the rim. You'll need reservations on weekend nights. A photo gallery highlights local foods. There's outdoor dining and live music some nights. [$] *Average main: BZ$25* ✉ *Cayo Welcome Center, near Savannah St.* ☎ *824/3663* 🕒 *No lunch. Closed Sun. and Mon.*

$ LATIN AMERICAN FAMILY 🍴 **Hode's Place Bar & Grill.** Popular for cold beers, karaoke, and billiards, Hodes is often the busiest place in town. It has a large shaded patio next to a citrus grove, and with swings, slides, and an ice-cream bar (cones BZ$2), Hode's is bigger than it looks from the outside. They serve good food in large portions at moderate prices. The Belizean *escabeche* (onion and chicken soup with lime juice) is terrific, and the fried chicken with french fries is some of the best in Cayo. [$] *Average main: BZ$14* ✉ *Savannah St., across from sports stadium* ☎ *804/2522.*

$$
ECLECTIC
Fodor's Choice
★

× **Ko-Ox Han-Nah.** From the Maya language Ko-Ox Han-Nah roughly translates to "let's go eat." It's far from fancy—you eat on simple tables in what is essentially a large open-front building on busy Burns Avenue—but service is cheerful, and the food is inexpensive and well-prepared. Much of the food is raised on the farm of the Zimbabwe-born owner. In addition to the usual Belizean beans-and-rice dishes, Ko-Ox Han-Nah serves fusion food influenced by Mexican, Southeast Asian, and North and South Indian cooking, with salads, sandwiches, burritos, Burmese dishes, Cambodian and Korean chicken dishes, and Indian lamb curries. $ *Average main: BZ$16* ✉ *5 Burns Ave.* ☎ *824/3014.*

$$
PIZZA

× **Mr. Greedy's Pizzeria.** In the heart of downtown in the pedestrian mall, Mr. Greedy's is the best place in Cayo for pizza by the slice or whole. Enjoy the pizza or some decent Buffalo wings and subs on their covered, street-side deck. In the afternoons, a cheap happy hour (BZ$2 rum and cokes) draws a crowd. Mr. Greedy's is open for breakfast, but there's better fare at lunch or dinner . There's free Wi-Fi, too. $ *Average main: BZ$16* ✉ *39 Burns Ave., across from Venus Hotel* ☎ *804/4688.*

$$
LATIN AMERICAN

× **Sanny's Grill.** With sizzling spices, this restaurant transforms basics like chicken or pork chops beyond standard fare. Try the pork chops in brandy-mustard sauce, the coconut chicken, or the grilled fish with coriander. Eat in the casual dining room or out on the covered deck, with views through the vines and flowers. In a residential area off Benque Road, the place can be hard to find, especially after dark. Consider taking a taxi. $ *Average main: BZ$24* ✉ *Pelican Ln., heading west of San Ignacio on Benque Rd., look for sign on right* ☎ *824/2988* ☺ *No lunch.*

$$
INDIAN

× **Serendib.** What's a Sri Lankan restaurant doing here? The original Ceylonese owner and his wife came to Belize with the British Army, and like many other *squadies* (enlisted men), decided to stay on and open a business. Over the years, the menu here has migrated more to Belizean, Chinese, and American dishes such as rice and beans, burgers, grilled fish, and fried chicken. The new owners are a Belizean-American couple, but you can still get authentic Sri Lankan curries (you choose the heat level) and a choice of teas. The conversion of part of Burns Avenue to a pedestrian mall has given Serendib an appealing location, and there's outdoor dining in a patio out back. $ *Average main: BZ$20* ✉ *27 Burns Ave.* ☎ *824/2302* ☺ *Closed Sun.*

WHERE TO STAY

SAN IGNACIO

Hotels in downtown San Ignacio are all budget to moderate spots. On the western edge of town, with hotels such as the San Ignacio Resort Hotel and Ka'ana, lodgings become more upscale. The lodges along the Mopan River, a dark jade–colored river that winds into Belize from Guatemala, tend to be in the budget to moderate range. Most lodges on the Macal River, such as The Lodge at Chaa Creek and duPlooy's Lodge, are upmarket, though there are some exceptions. A number of lodges, including Mystic River, Inn the Bush, Table Rock, and Mariposa have opened on the Cristo Rey Road en route to the Mountain Pine Ridge, most with access to the Macal River.

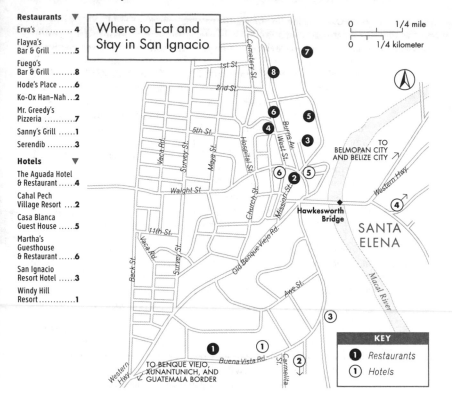

Restaurants ▼

Erva's 4
Flayva's Bar & Grill 5
Fuego's Bar & Grill 8
Hode's Place 6
Ko-Ox Han-Nah ... 2
Mr. Greedy's Pizzeria 7
Sanny's Grill 1
Serendib 3

Hotels ▼

The Aguada Hotel & Restaurant 4
Cahal Pech Village Resort 2
Casa Blanca Guest House 5
Martha's Guesthouse & Restaurant 6
San Ignacio Resort Hotel 3
Windy Hill Resort 1

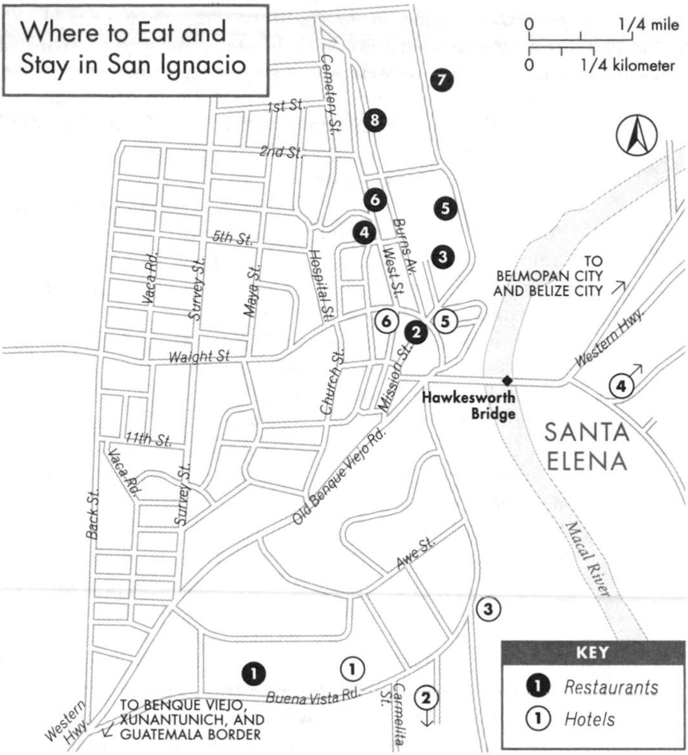

$ HOTEL 🏨 **Aguada Hotel & Restaurant.** Frugal travelers jump at the opportunity to stay in this tidy, attractive, and inexpensive hotel with air-conditioned rooms and saltwater swimming pool in Santa Elena, the low-key town adjoining San Ignacio. **Pros:** clean, inexpensive rooms with air-conditioning; one of the few budget hotels with a pool. **Cons:** location is a bus or short taxi ride away from downtown San Ignacio; traffic near the hotel may increase when the new San Ignacio bridge opens. [$] *Rooms from: BZ$90* ✉ *La Loma Luz, Off George Price Hwy. across from La Loma Luz hospital, Santa Elena* ☎ *804/3609* 🌐 *www.aguadabelize.com* 🛏 *25 rooms.*

$ RESORT 🏨 **Cahal Pech Village Resort.** Once you make it up the steep hill, you'll enjoy the best views in Cayo at this hotel at the western edge of San Ignacio, near the Cahal Pech Mayan site. **Pros:** great views; enticing pool; good value. **Cons:** some rooms and cabanas are a bit dowdy and need upgrading; limestone dirt road up to hotel is very steep, especially if you're walking. [$] *Rooms from: BZ$180* ✉ *1 mile (2 km) west of town, off George Price Hwy., Cahal Pech Rd., Cahal Pech Hill* ☎ *824/3740, 239/494–3281 U.S. number* 🌐 *www.cahalpech.com* 🛏 *16 rooms, 6 suites, 25 cabanas* 🍴 *No meals.*

$ HOTEL 🏨 **Casa Blanca Guest House.** Though it's in the center of San Ignacio, on bustling Burns Avenue, this small hotel is an oasis of peace and one of Belize's top budget choices. **Pros:** central downtown location;

extremely clean, appealing rooms; good value. **Cons:** limited parking nearby. [$] *Rooms from: BZ$45* ✉ *10 Burns Ave.* ☎ *824/2080* 🌐 *www.casablancaguesthouse.com* 🛏 *9 rooms* 🍴 *No meals.*

$ B&B/INN **Martha's Guesthouse and Restaurant.** With clean rooms, a good restaurant, handy laundry, and convenient tours, Martha's provides just about everything you need right in the heart of downtown San Ignacio. **Pros:** handy downtown location. **Cons:** can be noisy; rates are higher than most other downtown hotels. [$] *Rooms from: BZ$153* ✉ *10 West St.* ☎ *804/3647* 🌐 *www.marthasbelize.com* 🛏 *16 rooms, 7 with shared baths, 1 suite* 🍴 *No meals.*

$$$ RESORT Fodor's Choice ★ **San Ignacio Resort Hotel.** Queen Elizabeth II once stayed at this highly elegant, comfortable resort with rooms that have verandas facing a lovely hillside. **Pros:** safe, comfortable choice at the edge of town; good restaurant and bar. **Cons:** a little pricey for what you get. [$] *Rooms from: BZ$435* ✉ *18 Buena Vista Rd.* ☎ *824/2034, 855/488–2624 in U.S. and Canada* 🌐 *www.sanignaciobelize.com* 🛏 *24 rooms, 2 suites* 🍴 *No meals.*

$$ RESORT **Windy Hill Resort.** The cabanas at this lodge on the George Price Highway about 2 miles (3 km) west of San Ignacio all have private verandas and are perched on a low hill across the landscaped grounds. **Pros:** handy roadside location; offers many tours; pleasant cabins on hillside. **Cons:** not a jungle lodge; meals somewhat pricey. [$] *Rooms from: BZ$220* ✉ *1 mile (1½ km) west of San Ignacio, George Price Hwy. (aka Benque Rd.)* ☎ *824/2017, 800/946–3995 in U.S. and Canada* 🌐 *www.windyhillresort.com* 🛏 *16 cabanas and 9 rooms* 🍴 *Multiple meal plans.*

ALONG THE MOPAN RIVER

$ RESORT FAMILY **Clarissa Falls Resort.** The low gurgle of nearby Mopan River rapids is the first and last sound of the day at Clarissa Falls Resort. **Pros:** quiet, pastoral riverside setting; good food; you'll want to hug the owner. **Cons:** resort is on a ranch and not in a true jungle setting. [$] *Rooms from: BZ$150* ✉ *Mile 70, George Price Hwy. (aka Benque Hwy.), 5½ miles (9 km) west of San Ignacio, San Ignacio* ☎ *824/3916* 🛏 *11 cabanas, 1 bunkhouse with 10 beds, camping* 🍴 *No meals.*

$$$$ RESORT Fodor's Choice ★ **Ka'ana Boutique Resort and Spa.** Ka'ana brings a welcome level of luxury to San Ignacio with tranquil gardens, a wine cellar, and spacious rooms outfitted with 500-count cotton sheets, iPod docks, high-end toiletries, and flat-screen TVs. **Pros:** terrifically comfortable beds; convivial staff; luxury amenities; good bar and restaurant. **Cons:** not a true jungle lodge; pricey. [$] *Rooms from: BZ$550* ✉ *Mile 69¼, George Price Hwy. (aka Benque Rd.), San Ignacio* ☎ *824/3350, 305/735–2553 U.S. number* 🌐 *www.kaanabelize.com* 🛏 *5 rooms, 8 suites, 2 villas* 🍴 *No meals.*

$$$ RESORT **Mahogany Hall Boutique Resort.** An upmarket alternative to fancy jungle lodges is this resort in, of all places, Bullet Tree Falls, on the banks of the Mopan River. **Pros:** gorgeous suites; lovely views of the Mopan River; super comfortable beds. **Cons:** somewhat unusual location—neither a jungle lodge nor in-town hotel; room rates have a 5% "administrative fee." [$] *Rooms from: BZ$372* ✉ *Paslow Falls Rd., Bullet Tree Falls* ☎ *884/4047* 🌐 *www.mahoganyhallbelize.com* 🛏 *3 rooms and 5 suites* 🍴 *No meals.*

5

$ 🏠**Parrot Nest.** If ever since you were a kid you've wanted to sleep in a
HOTEL tree house by a river, this is your chance. **Pros:** rustic but cute cabanas
and tree houses; good value; helpful, friendly owners. **Cons:** you're not
really in the jungle here; cabanas are small. $ *Rooms from: BZ$107
⊠ Off Bullet Tree Rd., on Mopan River, Bullet Tree Falls* 🕾 *820/4058
⊕ www.parrot-nest.com* 🛏 *2 tree houses, 7 cabanas, some with shared
baths* 🍽 *No meals.*

ALONG THE MACAL RIVER

$$ 🏠**Black Rock River Lodge.** Some 800 feet above limestone cliffs and the
RESORT Macal River gorge, Black Rock has one of the most beautiful settings
of any lodge in the country. **Pros:** remote, beautiful setting; eco-con-
scious management. **Cons:** you're stuck here for somewhat pricey meals
and tours unless you have a four-wheel drive vehicle. $ *Rooms from:
BZ$229* ⊠ *On Macal River, 13 miles (22 km) upriver from San Igna-
cio, San Ignacio* 🕾 *834/4038* ⊕ *www.blackrocklodge.com* 🛏 *13 cabins*
🍽 *No meals.*

$$$ 🏠**duPlooy's Lodge.** High above a bend in the Macal River called Big
RESORT Eddy is this remarkable, relaxing lodge whose grounds include the
FAMILY 45-acre Belize Botanic Gardens. **Pros:** variety of lodging choices; excellent food; botanic gardens on-site; first-rate birding; eco-conscious management. **Cons:** costs for meals, transfers, and tours add up. $ *Rooms
from: BZ$464* ⊠ *Chial Rd., San Ignacio* ✛ *From San Ignacio head
4¾ miles (7½ km) west on George Price Hwy (also called Benque
Rd.), turn left on Chial Rd., and go about 5 miles (8 km) to duPlooy's*
🕾 *824/3101, 512/243–5285 U.S. number* ⊕ *www.duplooys.com* 🛏 *3
houses, 4 cabins, 3 suites, 11 rooms* 🍽 *Breakfast.*

$$$$ 🏠**The Lodge at Chaa Creek.** This was the first true jungle lodge in the
B&B/INN Cayo, and owners Mick and Lucy Fleming (he's from England, she's
Fodor'sChoice from the U.S.) have spent three decades polishing The Lodge at Chaa
★ Creek to a fine, rich patina, while adding new features like a gorgeous
bi-level swimming pool and appealing tree house Jacuzzi suites. **Pros:**
stunningly landscaped grounds; excellent staff and service; lovely
cabanas and suites; gorgeous pool; green and socially conscious owners. **Cons:** lodging and meal prices, except at the safari camp, may strain
your budget. $ *Rooms from: BZ$798* ⊠ *Chial Rd., San Ignacio* ✛ *From
San Ignacio go 4¾ miles (7½ km) west on Benque Rd., aka George
Price Hwy., turn left on Chial Rd. and go about 4½ miles (7 km). Follow signs to Chaa Creek* 🕾 *824/2037 local reservations, 877/709–8708
⊕ www.chaacreek.com* 🛏 *14 rooms in duplex cottages, 6 suites, 4 villas, 10 casitas, 1 2-bedroom suite* 🍽 *Breakfast.*

SPORTS AND THE OUTDOORS

San Ignacio is the center for touring in western Belize. Just walk along
busy Burns Avenue and you'll see signs for all kinds of tours and find
the offices of several tour operators. Individual tour guides, who by law
must be Belizean citizens and be licensed by the government, may work
for tour operators, for a lodge or hotel, or they may freelance on their
own. Some hang out at restaurants in town, especially those on busy
Burns Avenue, and post notices at bulletin boards in downtown hotels

and restaurants. PACZ Tours and others have offices downtown. You can compare prices and sign up for the next day's tours. Obviously, the more layers of costs involved, the higher the price for you, but on the other hand larger operators and hotel tour companies have more resources, and they have their long-term reputations to protect, so they may be more reliable. Tours from lodges usually are more costly than if booked with an independent tour operator. Also, some lodges try to sell packages of tours rather than individual ones.

Most jungle lodges offer a full range of day trips, using either their own guides or working with independent guides and tour companies. The largest lodge-affiliated tour operations are Chaa Creek Expeditions and Windy Hill Tour Company, but Crystal Paradise, duPlooy's, Maya Mountain, Cahal Pech Village, San Ignacio Resort Hotel, and other hotels and lodges also do many tours and trips.

If you have a rental car, you can visit all of the Mayan sites in the Cayo on your own, along with other attractions such as the butterfly farms, the Belize Botanic Gardens, Rainforest Medicine Trail, and many of the attractions in the Mountain Pine Ridge. However, for most caving tours, notably Actun Tunichil Muknal, you'll need a guide, and for canoe and kayak trips, you'll need drop-off and pickup. Local guides also are critical for nature hikes and birding trips, as many of these guides have remarkable local knowledge and ability to spot things you probably wouldn't see otherwise.

BIRDING

The area around San Ignacio is good for birding because it contains such a variety of habitats—river valleys, foothills, lagoons, agricultural areas, and broadleaf jungle—each of which attracts different types of birds. For example, Aguacate Lagoon near Spanish Lookout attracts waterbirds such as night herons, neotropic cormorants, and whistling ducks. Open land and pastures are good for spotting laughing falcons, vermillion flycatchers, eastern meadowlarks, and white-tailed kites.

There's good birding on the grounds of most of the lodges along the Mopan and Macal rivers, including **Chaa Creek, duPlooy's, Crystal Paradise,** and **Clarissa Falls.** In addition, local guides and tour companies run birding trips.

Paradise Expeditions. Paradise Expeditions, based in Cayo and connected with Crystal Paradise Lodge, has five- to eleven-night birding trips to various parts of Belize, starting at BZ$2,500 per person for a five-night, six-day birding trip in Central Belize, and ranging up to around BZ$3,000 per person for an 11-night expedition. ✉ *Crystal Paradise, Cristo Rey Rd. (P. O. Box 106)* ☎ *610/5593* ✆ *info@birdinginbelize. com* ⊕ *www.birdinginbelize.com.*

CANOEING AND KAYAKING

The Cayo's rivers, especially the Mopan and Macal, make it an excellent place for canoeing and kayaking. Most of the larger resorts, like **Chaa Creek** and **duPlooy's,** have canoes or inflatable kayaks. Generally you put in the Macal and paddle and float down to the Hawksworth Bridge at San Ignacio, a trip that takes two or three hours depending on your starting point. You'll pay about BZ$50 per person for canoe rental and pickup. You'll see iguanas and birdlife on the banks, and if you dip in for a swim, don't be surprised if tiny (toothless) fish school around you to figure out whether you're food.

Do exercise caution. You won't believe how fast the rivers, especially the Macal, can rise after a heavy rain. Following rains in the Mountain Pine Ridge, it can reach a dangerous flood stage in just a few minutes. Also, in the past there have been a few rare incidents of visitors in canoes being stopped and robbed on the Macal. Watch weather forecasts, and ask locally about safety on the rivers.

River Rat. River Rat arranges canoeing and kayaking trips, both for beginners and experienced river runners, as well as tours to Caracol, ATM, El Pilar, and elsewhere. ☎ 628/6033 ⊕ *www.riverratbelize.com.*

CAVING

Fodor's Choice
★ Over the millennia, as dozens of swift-flowing rivers bored through the soft limestone, the Maya Mountains became pitted with miles of caves. The Maya used them as burial sites, and, according to one theory, as subterranean waterways that linked the Cayo with communities as far north as the Yucatán. Previously, the caves fell into a 1,000-year slumber, disturbed only by the nightly flutter of bats. In recent years, the caves have been rediscovered by spelunkers.

Caves Branch Adventure Co. & Jungle Camp. First on the scene was Ian Anderson of Caves Branch Adventure Co. & Jungle Camp. He and his friendly staff of trained guides run exhilarating adventure-theme caving, tubing, and hiking trips from an upscale jungle camp just south of Belmopan. (⇨ *See Belmopan lodging.)* They also run day and overnight kayaking trips in the Cayo District. ⊠ *12 miles (19½ km) south of Belmopan, Mile 42½, Hummingbird Hwy., Belmopan* ☎ *610/3451, 866/357–2698* ⊕ *www.cavesbranch.com.*

PACZ Tours. Arguably the best Actun Tunichil Muknal tour operator, PACZ has been operated by Emilo Awe since 1998, with help by Bob Jones, formerly of Eva's, and about eight tour guides. The ATM tour costs around BZ$220 from downtown San Ignacio—including lunch and ATM admission, if you book directly with PACZ. Your hotel or lodge can arrange an ATM or other caving trip but may add an additional fee. ⊠ *30 Burns Ave.* ☎ *824/0536* ⊕ *www.pacztours.net.*

HIKING

Most of the lodges have hiking trails. **Black Rock River Lodge, Chaa Creek, Maya Mountain, Crystal Paradise,** and **duPlooy's** all have especially good areas for hiking. If you want even more wide-open spaces, head to the Mountain Pine Ridge, which offers hundreds of miles of hiking trails, mostly old logging roads. (⇨ *See Mountain Pine Ridge, below.)* For more adventurous hikes and overnight treks, you'll want to go with a guide. (⇨ *See also Caves Branch Adventure Co. & Jungle Camp listing above for another great guide.)*

Maya Guide Adventures. Marcos Cucul and son Francis, who run Maya Guide Adventures, are Ket'chi Mayans who are trained in cave and wilderness rescue. They can take you on overnight caving and kayaking trips, or guide you in Elijio Panti National Park, with trips starting at BZ$700 per person (minimum two persons). For the Maya Guide Adventures trips you must be physically fit. ⊠ *Yaxche Jungle Camp, Belmopan* ☎ *600/3116* ⊕ *www.mayaguide.bz.*

HORSEBACK RIDING

The Lodge at Chaa Creek. The Lodge at Chaa Creek has a stable of riding horses. Two- to three-hour guided horseback trips, with morning or afternoon options, cost BZ$90 per person, plus 12.5% tax. Rides cover about 5 miles (8 km). A horseback tour to Chaa Creek's Maya organic farm also is BZ$90. ⊠ *Chial Rd.* ☎ *824/2037, 877/709–8708 in U.S. and Canada* ⊕ *www.chaacreek.com.*

Mountain Equestrian Trails. When it comes to horseback-riding adventures, whether on the old logging roads of the Mountain Pine Ridge or on trails in the Slate Creek Preserve, the local experts are found at Mountain Equestrian Trails. Full-day rides range from BZ$166 to BZ$180. Five-night riding packages including accommodations are BZ$4,880 double in-season. ⊠ *Mile 8, Mountain Pine Ridge Rd., aka Georgeville Rd.* ☎ *669/1124, 800/838–3918* ⊕ *www.metbelize.com.*

SHOPPING

Arts & Crafts of Central America. In town, Arts & Crafts of Central America has a small selection of quality crafts at competitive prices. ⊠ *24 Burns Ave.* ☎ *824/3734.*

Celina's Superstore. The friendliest little grocery in Cayo is Celina's Superstore, which has almost anything you'll need, including groceries, picnic supplies, toiletries, snacks, booze, and more. ⊠ *43 Burns Ave.* ☎ *824/2247.*

Orange Gifts. Orange Gifts has one of the best selections of Belizean and Guatemalan crafts in Belize. It has an especially good selection of wood items from tropical hardwoods, including bowls, small pieces of furniture, and carvings. There's also a small restaurant and guesthouse here. ⊠ *Mile 60, George Price Hwy., east of San Ignacio* ☎ *824/3296* ⊕ *www.orangegifts.com.*

BENQUE VIEJO

7 miles (11 km) southwest of San Ignacio

Old Bank, or Benque Viejo in Spanish, is the last town in Belize before you reach Guatemala. Modest in size and population (about 9,000), Benque is low-key in other ways, too, but the little House of Culture is worth a stop, and neighboring San José Succotz village is home to the Xunantunich Mayan site. The Poustinia Land Art Park is perhaps the most unusual element of Belize's art scene.

EXPLORING

TOP ATTRACTIONS

FAMILY **Xunantunich.** Xunantunich, pronounced *shoo-nan-too-nitch,* is one of the most accessible Mayan sites in Belize, located on a hilltop site above the Mopan River west of San Ignacio. You take a hand-pulled ferry across the river (it carries pedestrians and a car or two), near the village of San José Succotz. As you hike or drive through the profusion of maidenhair ferns to the ruins, you may encounter numerous butterflies flitting through the air. A magnificent avenue of cohune palms announces your arrival at an important ceremonial center from the Mayan Classic Period. Xunantunich means "stone maiden." The structures here, in six plazas with more than two-dozen buildings, date from 200 to 900 A.D. El Castillo, the massive 120-foot-high main pyramid, still the second-tallest structure in Belize after Caana at Caracol, was built on a leveled hilltop. The pyramid has a spectacular 360-degree panorama of the Mopan River valley into Guatemala. On the eastern wall is a reproduction of one of the finest Mayan sculptures in Belize, a frieze decorated with jaguar heads, human faces, and abstract geometric patterns telling the story of the Moon's affair with Morning Light. Drinks and snacks are available at a visitor center and museum (opened in 2013) that explains the history of the site. ⊠ *Near San José Succotz Village, 6½ miles (11 km) southwest of San Ignacio, George Price Hwy. (Benque Rd.), San José Succotz* ☎ *822/2106 Institute of Archeology, NICH, Belmopan* ⊕ *www.nichbelize.org* 🖃 *BZ$10* ☉ *Daily 8–5.*

WORTH NOTING

Actun Chechem Ha. On private land, Actun Chechem Ha, which means "Cave of the Poisonwood Water," is a Mayan burial cave with artifacts that date back three millennia. There are many pots and a stela used for ceremonial purposes. This cave may have the largest collection of Mayan pottery in one place anywhere in Belize, possibly the world. To examine the pottery, you'll have to climb ladders, and getting to the cave requires a 35- to 45-minute walk, mostly uphill. The cave is on private property, and the landowner's family sometimes gives tours. Tour companies, with registered guides, also visit here from San Ignacio and Belmopan, charging from BZ$150 per person. ■TIP➜ Belize Magnificant Tours in San Ignacio, which charges BZ$190 per person, is one recommended tour company for this trip. Due to the hike to the cave entrance and climbing in the cave, you need to be reasonably physically fit to visit Chechem Ha. ⊠ *10 miles (17 km) south of Benque Viejo, Mile 7, Hydro Rd., near Vaca Falls, Benque Viejo del Carmen* ☎ *653/0799* 🖃 *Tours to Chechem Ha including transportation from San Ignacio or your lodge, lunch, admission fee, and sometimes swimming at Vaca Falls are around BZ$150–$200 per person* ☉ *By appointment.*

Benque House of Culture. The mission of Benque House of Culture, one of five government-sponsored houses of culture in Belize (others are in Belize City, Orange Walk Town, Corozal Town, and San Ignacio/Santa Elena), is "promoting beauty and goodness." Who could argue with that? Housed in the former Benque police station, this little museum has displays on the history of Benque Viejo, which celebrated its centennial in 2004, and also offers classes for local schoolchildren and their teachers. ✉ *64 Joseph St., 7 miles (11½ km) west of San Ignacio, Benque Viejo del Carmen* ☎ *823/2697* 🌐 *www.nich.org* 🎟 *By donation* ⏲ *Weekdays 9–4.*

Poustinia Land Art Park. One of the most unusual and least-known attractions in Belize, Poustinia Land Art Park is a collection of about 30 original works by artists from a dozen countries, including Belize, Norway, Guayana, Brazil, Guatemala, and England, scattered about some 60 acres of a former cattle ranch. It's owned by an architect, who calls Poustinia an "environmental project." *Poustinia* is Russian for "desert of the soul." Among the works of outdoor art, which some would call funky and others fascinating, are "Downtown," by Venezuelan artist Manuel Piney, and "Returned Parquet," a reference to Belize's colonial history in mahogany parquet flooring by Tim Davies, a British artist. Nature is slowly taking over the art works, which apparently is part of the plan. Getting around the park, which is open by appointment only, requires sometimes strenuous hiking. Bring insect repellent. Make arrangements to visit the park and for a tour guide at the Benque House of Culture in Benque Viejo. Two simple cabins at the site may be available for rent "to artists and short-term visitors" for around BZ$80 per night, and camping is BZ$10 per night. Birding is good on the site. ✉ *2½ miles (5 km) south of Benque Viejo, 8 miles (13 km) southwest of San Ignacio, Mile 2½, Hydro Rd., Benque Viejo del Carmen* ☎ *822/3532 Park information, 823/2697 Benque House of Culture* 🎟 *BZ$20* ⏲ *By appointment.*

5

WHERE TO EAT

$ LATIN AMERICAN Fodor's Choice ★

🍴 **Benny's Kitchen.** This little open-air restaurant near Xunantunich has won many fans who come for hearty Mayan, Mestizo, and Creole dishes at rock bottom prices. You'll find mostly locals here, many from San Ignacio, Benque Viejo, and other parts of Cayo District. Most items on the menu are BZ$12 or less, including *chilimole* (chicken with mole sauce), cow-foot soup, Belizean *escabeche*, and stew pork with rice, beans, and plantains. You can make a meal of the Mestizo appetizers including *salbutes*, tostadas, and empanadas, most under BZ$1 each. The classic Mayan *pibil* (pork cooked in an underground oven) is sometimes on the menu. The banana and mango *licuados* (milk shakes) are delicious, and you can also enjoy the official national drinks of Belize: Belikin and Fanta. [$] *Average main: BZ$10* ✉ *Across Benque Rd., (George Price Hwy.) from ferry to Xunantunich, San José Succotz* ✥ *Turn south just west of Xunantunich ferry and follow signs about three blocks; most streets in Succcotz don't have names, so if you miss it, ask locally* ☎ *823/2541.*

WHERE TO STAY

$ RENTAL **The Trek Stop.** After a day spent out and about, a cold Belikin and filling Mexican and Belizean dishes await you at this cluster of neat-as-a-pin cabins on a hilltop near Xunantunich ruins. **Pros:** top value for the money; friendly local management. **Cons:** just a couple steps up from camping; location means you'll have to take a bus or taxi to most sights, except Xunantunich. [$] *Rooms from: BZ$52* ✉ *6 miles (9 km) west of San Ignacio, George Price Hwy. (aka Benque Rd.), near Xunantunich, San José Succotz* ☎ *823/2265* 🌐 *www.thetrekstop.com* 🛏 *9 cabins, 7 with shared bath* 🍴 *No meals.*

MOUNTAIN PINE RIDGE

17 miles (27 km) south of San Ignacio.

The best way to describe Mountain Pine Ridge is to paraphrase Winston Churchill: it's a puzzle wrapped in an enigma. Instead of the tropical vegetation you'd expect to find, two-thirds of this large reserve is pine forest, mainly Honduras Pines. Most pines are young, due to losses from wildfires and beetle infestations. Old logging roads cut through red clay, giving the region an uncanny resemblance to northern Georgia in the U.S. Sinkholes, caves, and waterfalls are common in limestone areas. With elevations up to 3,335 feet, winter temperatures can drop into decidedly untropical low 40s, yet exotic wildlife abound, including orange-breasted falcons, toucans, tapirs, jaguars, and crocodiles.

GETTING HERE AND AROUND

From the Western Highway, there are two routes into the Mountain Pine Ridge, both just east of San Ignacio: the Mountain Pine Ridge Road (also sometimes called the Chiquibul Road or the Georgeville Road), at Georgeville at Mile 61.6 of the Western Highway; and the Cristo Rey Road, with the turnoff at Mile 66.5 of the Western Highway. From the Western Highway, the entrance to the Mountain Pine Ridge is 10.2 miles (17 km) via the Mountain Pine Ridge Road and 14.8 miles (25 km) via the Cristo Rey Road. Both roads cut through limestone and are rough, but currently the Georgeville Road is rougher.

Heading southeast from San Ignacio on the Cristo Rey Road, a little beyond San Antonio, the Cristo Rey Road meets the Mountain Pine Ridge Road coming from Georgeville. Turn right to go into the Mountain Pine Ridge. After 2½ miles (4 km) a guard at a gatehouse will record your name, destination, and license-plate number. The main road through the Mountain Pine Ridge is a dirt road that can become almost impassable after heavy rains.

There is no public bus transportation into the Mountain Pine Ridge. Charter flights from Belize City can fly into private airstrips at Blancaneaux Lodge and Hidden Valley Inn. Tropic Air offers service to Hidden Valley Inn on demand.

Entrance into the Mountain Pine Ridge is free, though there is a nominal charge collected if you go to the viewing area for Thousand Foot Falls.

TIMING

You could spend a week or longer exploring the streams, waterfalls, and distant trails of the Mountain Pine Ridge.

SAFETY AND PRECAUTIONS

The Mountain Pine Ridge is a remote and lightly populated area. Occasionally, bandits have taken advantage of this to stop and rob visitors, and some Guatemalan squatters have tried to move across the border in search of free land, prompting run-ins with Belize authorities. Currently, Belize Defence Forces soldiers accompany vehicles to Caracol. However, the main danger to most visitors is not bandits but getting lost on a hiking trail or old logging road, or being stung by a scorpion.

EXPLORING

TOP ATTRACTIONS

FAMILY **Green Hills Butterfly Ranch and Botanical Collections.** Green Hills is the largest and best of Belize's butterfly farms open to the public, with about 30 native species in a huge flight area on display at any given time. (Some 90 species have been raised at the farm.) Jan Meerman, who has published a book on Belize's butterflies and moths, runs the place with Dutch partner Tineke Boomsma and other staff. The staff speak English, Spanish, Dutch, Yucatec Maya, and Creole. On the 100-acre grounds also are many flowers, including passion flowers, bromeliads, heliconias, and orchids. Birding is good here as well. Bring lunch and eat it on the Green Hills picnic area. A cave, Pempem ("butterfly" in the Yucatec Maya language) is on the grounds but is not open to the public. ⊠ *Mile 8, Mountain Pine Ridge Rd. (aka Chiquibul Rd.), El Progresso/7 Mile* ☎ *834/4017* ⊕ *green-hills.net/Protected_area.htm* ☞ *Guided tour BZ$20 adults, BZ$10 children under 10* ⊙ *Daily 8–4, last tour 3:30.*

Mountain Pine Ridge Forest Reserve. This reserve is a highlight of any journey to Belize and an adventure to reach and explore, although the scenery may remind you more of the piney woods of the far southern Appalachians than of tropical jungle. The Mountain Pine Ridge Forest Reserve is in the high country of Belize—low mountains and rolling hills are covered in part by vast pine forests and crisscrossed with old logging roads. Waterfalls and streams abound, and there are accessible caves, such as Rio Frio. The higher elevations, up to near 3,400 feet, provide cooler temperatures and outstanding views. The best way to see this area, which covers more than 106,000 acres, is on a mountain bike, a horse, or your own feet, not bouncing around in an SUV. But it's not bad from an SUV, either, which you'll need to get you through the Pine Ridge to the Chiquibul wilderness and the magnifent ruins of Caracol. Aside from the Honduras pines, 80% of which were damaged in recent years by the Southern pine beetle but are now recovering, you'll see lilac-color mimosa, Saint-John's-wort, and occasionally a garish red flower appropriately known as hotlips. Look out for the craboo, a wild tree whose berries are used in a brandylike liqueur believed to have aphrodisiacal properties. Birds love this fruit, so any craboo is a good place to spot orioles and woodpeckers. You may not see them, but the Pine Ridge is home to many of Belize's large mammals, including tapirs, cougars, jaguars, and ocelots. In the streams are a few Morelet's crocodiles. Admission is free, but check in at the entrance gate (if you are asked for a "contribution" entering or leaving, politely decline as it's just a scam). ⊠ *Mountain Pine Ridge, San Antonio.*

WORTH NOTING

Barton Creek Cave. This wet cave in a remote area off the Mountain Pine Ridge Road offers a canoeing adventure in Xibalba (the Mayan underworld). You'll float through part of a long underground chamber—the cave is nearly 5 miles (8 km) long. You'll see Mayan ceramics along with ancient calcified skeletal remains and skulls. You can go on a tour from San Ignacio or from your lodge. PACZ Tours, for example, offers a six-hour tour, including lunch and admission to the cave, for BZ$170 plus tax per person, and Chaa Creek offers a half-day tour for two to four persons for BZ$310 plus tax. You can also drive to the cave yourself, rent a boat and gear, and hire a guide from Mike's Place near the cave. There also is a zip line at Mike's Place. Getting to the cave is an adventure in itself, requiring a long drive on very rough roads. Part of the road and the cave itself may be inaccessible after hard rains. Be careful in the cave—one visitor drowned in a boating accident here in 2011. Though more expensive, we recommend you go with a reputable tour company with an experienced tour guide and reliable, well-maintained equipment such as float vests. ⊠ *Barton Creek Cave, Upper Barton Creek* ✛ *Turn at Mile 62 of the George Price Hwy. (formerly Western Hwy.) onto Mountain Pine Ridge Rd. aka Georgeville Rd. or Chiquibul Rd. Go about 3 miles (5 km) and, at Cool Shade, turn left. Go 4 miles (6 km) on a rough, unpaved road through Lower Barton Creek Mennonite community to Upper Barton Creek and the cave. Watch for signs for Barton Creek Outpost, Mike's Place, and the cave* ☎ *822/2106 Institute of Archeology* ⊕ *www.nichbelize.org* ☞ *BZ$10.*

Chalillo Lake. Chalillo Lake was created in late 2005 by the controversial damming of the Macal River for an electric power plant owned by the Canadian power company, Fortis. Since then, two other dams have been completed. The original 150-foot-high dam with a span width of 420 feet, along with its sisters, destroyed a habitat for endangered species such as the scarlet macaw and was opposed by environmentalists in Belize and around the world. How many unexplored Mayan sites were flooded is anyone's guess. The lake extends some 12 miles (20 km) along the Macal and Raspacula river valleys. The dams are still controversial, and some in Cayo and elsewhere blame the dams for deteriorating water quality in the Macal and sediment in the river, along with loss of wildlife habitat. At present the reservoir has limited recreational uses of interest to visitors. However, some lodges in Cayo are now developing boat trips on the lake. For example, Hidden Valley Inn, in association with EcoQuest Expeditions, has a tour that includes a motorized skiff tour of Chalillo Lake and the Raspaculo and Upper Macal rivers. ⇨ *The Lodge at Chaa Creek also is developing a*

pontoon boat trip on the lake. In 2011, the Belize government rena-
tionalized the Fortis-owned Belize Electricity Ltd. power company.
⊠ *Chalillo Dam Reservoir.*

Elijio Panti National Park (*Noj K'a'ax Meen Elijio Panti National Park*).
Named after the famed Guatemala-born herbal healer who died in
1996 at the age of 106, Elijio Panti National Park is the latest addition to Belize's extensive national parks system. It spans about 16,000
acres around the villages of San Antonio, Cristo Rey, and El Progreso
into the Mountain Pine Ridge. In the park are Sakt'aj waterfalls and
two dry caves known as Offering and Cormorant. The hope is that
with no hunting in this park, more birds and wildlife will return to
western Belize. At this writing, a visitor center with a natural healing
medicine trail near the village of San Antonio is under construction.
Currently you must be accompanied by a licensed tour guide to enter
the park. For information on the park and how to visit it, check with
tour guides in San Ignacio or ask at the Garcia Sister's gift shop at
the Tanah Art Museum in San Antonio village. ⊠ *Off Cristo Rey*
Rd., San Antonio ☎ *651/3750 San Antonio Women's Group—local*
information on park, guides, rental cabin in park, 664/5318 Belize
Development Foundation, Belmopan ⊕ *www.elijiopantinationalpark.*
com 🎟 *BZ$10.*

Thousand Foot Falls (*Hidden Valley Falls*). Inside the Mountain Pine
Ridge Forest Reserve, Thousand Foot Falls actually drops nearly
1,600 feet, making it the highest waterfall in Central America. A thin
plume of spray plummets over the edge of a rock face into a seemingly bottomless gorge below. The catch is that the viewing area,
where there is a shelter with some benches and a public restroom,
is some distance from the falls. Many visitors find the narrow falls
unimpressive from this vantage point. To climb closer requires a major
commitment: a steep climb down and up the side of the mountain is
several hours. ⊠ *Mountain Pine Ridge, 1000 Foot Falls* ✛ *From the*
Mountain Pine Ridge gate, go 2 miles (3 km) and turn left toward
Hidden Valley Inn. Go 4 miles (6 km) to the falls observation area.
It's well-signed. 🎟 *BZ$4* ☉ *Daily 7–5.*

FAMILY **Río Frio Caves.** Río Frio Caves are only a few miles by car down a steep
track, but ecologically speaking, these caves are in a different world.
In the course of a few hundred yards, you drop from pine savanna to
tropical forest. Nothing in Belize illustrates its extraordinary geological
diversity as clearly as this startling transition. A river runs right through
the center of the main cave—actually it's more of a tunnel, open at
both ends—and, over the centuries, has carved the rock into fantastic
shapes. Swallows fill the place, and at night ocelots and margays pad
silently across the cold floor in search of slumbering prey. Seen from
the dark interior, the light-filled world outside seems more intense and
beautiful than ever. About a mile away (2 km) are the Cuevas Gemelas
(Twin Caves), best seen with a guide. Due to occasional bandit activity
in the area, at times a Belize Defence Forces escort is required to visit
the Río Frio Caves—if driving on your own, ask at your hotel or at the
Douglas de Silva forestry station, where private vehicles meet up with
a Defence Force escort.

At the **Río On,** just north of the Río Frio Caves, you can sunbathe on flat granite boulders or dunk yourself into crystal-clear pools and waterfalls. ✉ *Mountain Pine Ridge* ✥ *From the entrance gate of the Mountain Pine Ridge, go 14 miles (23 km). Turn right Douglas de Silva forestry station at Río Frio sign and drive 5 miles (8 km) to the caves.* 🎟 *Free.*

WHERE TO STAY

NEAR MOUNTAIN PINE RIDGE

In addition to the lodges in the Mountain Pine Ridge itself, which include the top-end Blancaneaux Lodge and Hidden Valley Inn, along with the moderate Five Sisters Lodge, several jungle lodges, some recently opened and all in the moderate price category, are on the two roads leading to the Mountain Pine Ridge—the Chiquibul Road from Georgeville (also called the Mountain Pine Ridge Road or the Georgeville Road) and the Cristo Rey Road from Santa Elena. Of the lodges en route to the Mountain Pine Ridge, Table Rock Lodge, Mystic River Lodge, Macaw Bank Lodge, Inn the Bush, and Crystal Paradise Resort are on the Macal River, while Mariposa Jungle Lodge, Gumbo Limbo Village Resort, and Mountain Equestrian Trails are not.

$ HOTEL 🏨 **Crystal Paradise Resort.** This jungle lodge is operated by the Tut (pronounced *Toot*) family—Mom and Dad Tut and their 10 (!) children. **Pros:** Belizean-owned; good guided tours. **Cons:** no-frills rooms and cabanas. [$] *Rooms from: BZ$164* ✉ *Cristo Rey Rd., Cristo Rey Village* ☎ *820/4014* 🌐 *www.crystalparadise.com* 🛏 *14 cabanas, 1 cottage, 2 rooms* 🍴 *Multiple meal plans.*

$$ HOTEL 🏨 **Gumbo Limbo Jungle Resort.** Well-priced, with a lovely hilltop setting, and amenities such as a pool, this small lodge is an attractive option just 2 miles (3 km) from the George Price Highway at Georgeville. **Pros:** attractive cottage accommodations; lovely views from hilltop setting; swimming pool. **Cons:** steep hill on dirt access road is a doozy. [$] *Rooms from: BZ$294* ✉ *Mile 2, Mountain Pine Ridge Rd. (aka Chiquibul Rd. or Georgeville Rd.), Georgeville* ☎ *650/3112* 🌐 *www.gumbolimboresort.com* 🛏 *4 cottages.*

$$ B&B/INN 🏨 **Inn the Bush.** With only three cabanas, every guest gets personal attention at this small ecolodge where you can lounge in a four-poster king bed and then jump in the pool for a refreshing swim. **Pros:** small ecolodge with personal service; reasonable rates; swimming pool; peace and quiet. **Cons:** access road is rough. [$] *Rooms from: BZ$273* ✉ *Mile 6, Cristo Rey Rd., Macaw Bank, off Cristo Rey Rd., Cristo Rey Village* ☎ *670/6364* 🌐 *www.innthebushbelize.com* 🛏 *3 cabanas* 🍴 *No meals.*

$$$ B&B/INN 🏨 **Macaw Bank Lodge.** This small, laid-back ecolodge on 50 acres adjoining the Macal River is for travelers seeking a no-frills spot where you can hear the jungle hum outside your doorstep and where the air bristles with the promise of bird and animal sightings. **Pros:** laid-back ecolodge with moderate rates. **Cons:** a bit of a hike to the river for swimming. [$] *Rooms from: BZ$338* ✉ *Cristo Rey Rd., Cristo Rey Village* ☎ *665/7241* 🌐 *www.macawbankjunglelodge.com* 🛏 *5 cottages* 🍴 *No meals.*

$$$$ RESORT **Mariposa Jungle Lodge.** This small, intimate lodge has six well-designed cabanas set in the shade on a low hill, with pimento walls, thatch roofs, and furniture handmade at the lodge and elsewhere in Belize. **Pros:** personalized service; attractive cabanas; swimming pool. **Cons:** bumpy 30-minute drive from San Ignacio; lodging, meals, tours, and transfers rates are a little spendy. [$] *Rooms from: BZ$536* ✉ *Cristo Rey Rd., near junction with Mountain Pine Ridge Rd., San Antonio Village* ☎ *670/2113, 304/244–2136 in U.S.* 🌐 *www.mariposajunglelodge.com* 🛏 *6 cabanas* 🍴 *No meals.*

$$ HOTEL **Mountain Equestrian Trails.** MET, as most people call it, is one of Belize's top equestrian spots. **Pros:** equestrian charm abounds; other activities include caving and birding; reasonable prices for cabanas. **Cons:** facilities a bit too rustic for some. [$] *Rooms from: BZ$288* ✉ *Mile 8, Mountain Pine Ridge Rd. (aka Chiquibul Rd. or Georgeville Rd.)* ☎ *669/1124, 800/838–3918 U.S. reservations* 🌐 *www.metbelize.com* 🛏 *10 cabanas* 🍴 *Multiple meal plans.*

$$$$ RESORT Fodor's Choice ★ **Mystic River Resort.** Operated by a French-American couple formerly of Ambergris Caye, this jungle resort on the Macal River is a step up in luxury, service, and dining from run-of-the-mill lodges. **Pros:** stylishly decorated cottages all with views and fireplaces; excellent food; friendly owners and staff. **Cons:** a little pricey. [$] *Rooms from: BZ$661* ✉ *Mile 6, Cristo Rey Rd., San Antonio Village* ☎ *834/4100* 🌐 *www.mysticriverbelize.com* 🛏 *6 cottages* 🍴 *No meals.*

$$$ B&B/INN FAMILY Fodor's Choice ★ **Table Rock Lodge.** At this intimate, jungle eco-spot cobblestone walkways and thick awnings of foliage gracefully blend into a jungle setting, perched just above the Macal River. **Pros:** low-key, relaxing, off-the-beaten-path ecolodge; good value; wonderful food. **Cons:** it's a bumpy 20-minute ride to San Ignacio. [$] *Rooms from: BZ$345* ✉ *Cristo Rey Rd., San Antonio Village* ☎ *834/4040* 🌐 *www.tablerockbelize.com* 🛏 *5 cabanas.*

MOUNTAIN PINE RIDGE

$$$$ RESORT Fodor's Choice ★ **Blancaneaux Lodge.** As you sweep down Blancaneaux's hibiscus- and palm-lined drive, past the big swimming pool, you may get a whiff of Beverly Hills, and indeed the lodge is owned by film director Francis Ford Coppola. **Pros:** fabulous grounds; deluxe cabanas and villas; wonderful food and service. **Cons:** many steep steps may pose problems for the infirm or elderly; very expensive. [$] *Rooms from: BZ$807* ✣ *Turn right at Blancaneaux sign 4½ miles (7½ km) from Mountain Pine Ridge entrance gate* ☎ *824/4912 concierge at lodge, 800/746–3743 in U.S. and Canada* 🌐 *www.blancaneaux.com* 🛏 *10 cabanas, 7 villas, 1 house* 🍴 *Breakfast.*

$$$ RESORT **Gaia Riverlodge.** Perched on a steep hill above the Five Sisters waterfalls this laid-back lodge is romantic and stylish. **Pros:** appealing small lodge; a little less expensive than other lodges in the Mountain Pine Ridge. **Cons:** some standard cabanas don't have much of a view. [$] *Rooms from: BZ$417* ✣ *From the main Mountain Pine Ridge Rd., turn right at Blancaneaux and Five Sisters signs 1½ miles (7½ km) from Pine Ridge entrance gate. Continue past Blancaneaux airstrip about 1 mile (2 km).* ☎ *834/4024* 🌐 *www.gaiariverlodge.com* 🛏 *16 cabanas* 🍴 *Multiple meal plans.*

5

$$$$ B&B/INN Fodor's Choice ★ [🏨] **Hidden Valley Inn & Reserve.** Owned by a prominent Belize City family, the Roes, Hidden Valley Inn sits on 7,200 acres and has more than a dozen waterfalls, at least two private caves, and 90 miles (150 km) of hiking and mountain biking trails. **Pros:** charming lodge atmosphere; wonderful waterfalls; excellent birding, stunning pool. **Cons:** meals are pricey; loss of many mature pines due to the pine beetle means it can be hot and dry on the trails. [$] *Rooms from: BZ$583* ✣ *From main Mountain Pine Ridge Rd., turn left at Hidden Valley Inn sign 3¾ miles (6¼ km) from Pine Ridge entrance gate* ☎ *822/3320, 866/443–3364 in U.S. and Canada* 🌐 *www.hiddenvalleyinn.com* 🛏 *12 cottages* 🍴 *Multiple meal plans.*

SPORTS AND THE OUTDOORS

BIRDING

Birding is great in the Mountain Pine Ridge, and, surprisingly, it's even better now that many of the pines were felled by the southern pine beetle. Without the tall pines, it's much easier to spot orange-breasted falcons, blue crown motmots, white king vultures, stygian owls, and other rare birds. Some of the best birding is at **Hidden Valley Inn**, a destination for numerous birding tours, and open only to guests.

CAVING

Easily accessible in the Cayo is the Río Frio Cave (⇨ *see above*). You can also do trips to Barton Creek Cave, about 8 miles (13 km) northwest of Mountain Pine Ridge entrance gate, off Mountain Pine Ridge Road, and to Actun Tunichil Muknal from Mountain Pine Ridge. Hidden Valley Inn has two caves open only to guests of the inn.

HIKING

With its karst limestone terrain, extensive network of old logging trails and roads, and cooler temperatures, the Mountain Pine Ridge is ideal for hiking. All of the lodges here have miles of marked trails. You can also hike along the roads (mostly gravel or dirt), as there are very few cars in the Pine Ridge. Most people find this more pleasant than trying to fight their way through the bush. The mountain area around Baldy Beacon, the highest point in the Pine Ridge at around 3,335 feet, is especially beautiful; it may remind you of part of the Highlands of Scotland.

All of the Mountain Pine Ridge and Chichibul Wilderness is lightly populated, and some of the residents, such as unemployed squatters who have moved into this remote area, may not always have your best interests at heart. Cell phones don't usually work here, although there has been talk of installing some cell-phone towers as a security measure. Lodges such as Hidden Valley Inn provide radio phones to guests who are hiking. Always leave word with a responsible party about your hiking plans and time of expected return. Carry plenty of water, food, a compass, and basic medical supplies, especially on long hikes to remote areas. You may want to hire a guide.

CLOSE UP

A Crime of Flowers

A rather plain-looking palm leaf has become a big-money target for poachers in Belize—and a huge problem for the Forestry Department. The leaves in question, xate (pronounced sha-tay), are widely used in the floral industry because they stay fresh-looking for 45 to 60 days after harvest. They come from three *Chamaedorea* palm species: *C. elegans,* known as parlor palm; *C. oblongata,* called xate macho; and *C. ernesti-augustii,* or fishtail. The latter is the most sought-after, fetching up to US$1 at its final destination, though poachers get only a fraction of that.

Xate grows wild in Belize, and also in parts of Guatemala and Mexico. Guatemalan xate collectors, called *xateros,* have stripped much of their own El Petén jungles and have now moved on to Belize, crossing the border into the Chiquibul and other remote areas. Xateros earn more collecting xate than working at regular jobs, if they can even find work in the economically depressed rural areas of El Petén. Not surprisingly, Belizeans are increasingly joining the ranks of xate poachers. The harvesters sweep through the jungle, removing the palm leaves with a pocketknife or machete. Each palm plant produces two to five usable leaves.

Unfortunately, the poachers do more than just collect xate. They sometimes stumble across Mayan sites and loot them for priceless artifacts. Some trap toucans, parrots, and the endangered scarlet macaw for sale on the black market, and they hunt wild animals, including protected tapirs, for food. The Belize Forestry Department has reported significant depletion of native wildlife in areas with large numbers of xate collectors. In a few cases, xateros have been implicated in robberies or in attacks on researchers and on Belize Defence Forces soldiers. With little chance of getting caught and only modest fines if they are, xate poachers are working at minimal risk.

What can you do to reduce the damage done by illegal xate collectors? First, avoid buying flower arrangements that contain xate, unless you're sure that the xate was harvested legally. You can also support an effort by the Natural History Museum in London, in cooperation with the Belize Ministry of Natural Resources and the Belize Botanic Gardens at duPlooy's Lodge near San Ignacio to encourage sustainable, organic growing of xate by Belizean farmers.

—Lan Sluder

HORSEBACK RIDING
In this remote area with virtually no vehicular traffic and many old logging roads, horseback riding is excellent. **Blancaneaux Lodge** and **Hidden Valley Inn** offer horseback riding, and Mountain Equestrian Trails *(see listing in San Ignacio)* runs horseback tours into the Pine Ridge.

MOUNTAIN BIKING
Mountain Pine Ridge has the best mountain biking in Belize on hundreds of miles of remote logging roads. Mountain biking is especially good on the 90 miles (150 km) of private hiking and mountain biking trails at Hidden Valley Inn. Blancaneaux and Hidden Valley Inn provide complimentary mountain bikes to guests. The Lodge at Chaa Creek also offers mountain biking.

ZIP-LINING

FAMILY **Calico Jack's Jungle Canopy & Zip Line.** Calico Jack's zip line is over a half mile (1 km) long. The "Ultimo Explorer" zip line tour has 9 runs on 15 platforms over 2,700 ft. There also are five caves on the grounds, two open for exploring with a guide. Calico Jack's Village has cabanas moved from its original location on the Placencia peninsula, and a restaurant called One-Eyed Jack's. ⊠ *Off Mile 7, Mountain Pine Ridge Rd., El Progreso/7 Mile* ☎ *832/2478* ⊕ *www.calicojacksvillage.com.*

SHOPPING

Tanah Art Museum. The village of San Antonio, on the way to the Mountain Pine Ridge reserve, is home to the Garcia sisters' Tanah Art Museum and gift shop, run by four sisters with clever hands and great business acumen. Look for their eye-catching slate carvings. The huge slate top of the bar at Blancaneaux Lodge was carved by the Garcia sisters. Maria Garcia, who is usually at the shop, has been a driving force behind the nearby Elijio Panti National Park. ⊠ *Cristo Rey Rd., San Antonio* ☎ *669/4023* ⊕ *www.awrem.com/tanah/museum.html.*

CARACOL

55 miles (98 km) south of San Ignacio

Caracol (Spanish for "snail") is the most spectacular Mayan site in Belize, as well as one of the most impressive in Central America. It was once home to as many as 200,000 people (almost two-thirds the population of modern-day Belize).

GETTING HERE AND AROUND

Caracol is about 55 miles (92 km) from San Ignacio, and about 35–40 miles (57–66 km) from the major lodges in the Mountain Pine Ridge. Because roads are mostly unpaved and often in poor condition, cars or tour vans take 1½ to 2 hours from the Pine Ridge lodges and about 2½ to 3 hours from San Ignacio, sometimes longer after heavy rains.

Advance permission to visit Caracol is no longer required. Although only about a 10-mile (17-km) section of the road to Caracol from San Ignacio is paved, once into the Mountain Pine Ridge the road is generally in good shape, except after heavy rains. The Belize government has plans to eventually pave the entire road to Caracol.

SAFETY AND PRECAUTIONS

Occasional holdups of tourists by armed gangs believed to be from Guatemala occurred here over the past several years. For caution's sake, trips to Caracol are now in a group convoy, protected by Belize Defence Forces troops. The meet-up point is Augustine De Silva village, a few miles into the Pine Ridge. As off-putting as that may seem, Caracol is well worth seeing. The robbery incidents have occurred only rarely, and not a single one has taken place with the Belize Defence Forces on hand. The tour operators to Caracol know the ropes, and will work to make sure your trip to Caracol is rewarding and safe.

TIMING

You can't overnight at Caracol, except occasionally on very expensive overnight tours by local hotels such as Ka'ana Boutique Resort in San Ignacio, so you have to visit on a day trip. You can see the excavated area of Caracol in a few hours.

TOURS

Most visitors to Caracol come as part of a tour group from San Ignacio, or from one of the lodges in the Mountain Pine Ridge. Full-day tours from San Ignacio, which often include a picnic lunch and stops at Río Frio Cave, Río On, and other sights in the Mountain Pine Ridge, cost from about BZ$140 to BZ$220 per person, including the BZ$20 admission fee to Caracol, depending on what is included and the number of people going. Tours from independent operators generally cost less than those from lodges. Lodges in the Mountain Pine Ridge charge around BZ$200–BZ$250 per person for tours to Caracol, including tax.

Because of its remote location, Caracol gets only about 12,000 visitors a year. That's about one-tenth the number who visit Altun Ha, one-fifth the number who visit Xunantunich, and a smaller fraction of the number who see Tikal. Thus, you're in exclusive company, and on some slow days you may be one of only a handful of people at the site. Excavations by a team from the University of Central Florida usually are carried out in the winter, typically January through March.

EXPLORING

Fodor's Choice
★
Caracol. Caracol was a metropolis with five plazas and 32 large structures covering almost a square mile. In AD 650, the urban area of Caracol had a radius of approximately 6 miles (10 km) around the site's center. It covered an area larger than present-day Belize City. Altogether it is believed there are some 35,000 buildings at the site, though only a handful of them have been excavated. Excavations at Caracol are being carried on by Diane and Arlen Chase of the University of Central Florida. The latest excavations are in an area approximately 500 yards southeast of Caracol's central plaza. Once Caracol has been fully excavated it may dwarf even the great city of Tikal, which is a few dozen miles away (as the toucan flies) in Guatemala. The evidence suggests that Caracol won a crushing victory over Tikal in the mid-6th century, a theory that Guatemalan scholars haven't quite accepted. Until a group of *chicleros* (collectors of gum base) stumbled on the site in 1936, Caracol was buried under the jungle of the remote Vaca Plateau. It's hard to believe it could have been lost for centuries, as the great pyramid of Caana, at nearly 140 feet, is still Belize's tallest structure.

The main excavated sections are in four groups, denoted on archaeological maps as A, B, C, and D groups. The most impressive structures are the B Group at the northeast end of the excavated plaza. This includes Caana (sometimes spelled Ca'ana or Ka'ana), or "Sky Palace," listed as Structure B19-2nd, along with a ball court, water reservoir, and several large courtyards. Caana remains the tallest structure in Belize. The A Group, on the west side of the plaza, contains a temple, ball court, and a residential area for the elite. The Temple of the Wooden Lintel (Structure A6) is one of the oldest and longest-used buildings at Caracol, dating back to 300 BC. It was still in use in AD 1100. To the northwest of the A Group is the Northwest Acropolis, primarily a residential area. The third major plaza forming the core of the site is at the point where a causeway enters the "downtown" part of Caracol. The D Group is a group of structures at the South Acropolis.

Near the entrance to Caracol is a small but interesting visitor center. If you have driven here on your own (with a Belize Defence Forces escort, used as insurance against the very rare chance of bandits) instead of with a tour, a guide usually can be hired at the site, but you can also walk around on your own. Seeing all of the excavated area involves several hours of hiking around the site. Wear sturdy shoes and bring insect repellent. Also, watch for anthill mounds and, rarely, snakes. This part of the Chiquibul Forest Reserve is a good place for birding and wildlife spotting. Around the ruins are troops of howler monkeys and flocks of oscellated turkeys, and you may also see deer, coatimundis, foxes, and other wildlife at the site or on the way. ⊠ *Caracol, Chiquibul* ✛ *From Mountain Pine Forest Ridge reserve entrance, head south 14 miles (23 km) to village of Douglas DiSilva (where you can meet up with a Belize Defence Forces escort), turn left and go 36 miles (58 km)* ⊕ *www.caracol.org* ▧ *BZ$20* ☺ *Daily 8–5.*

6

THE SOUTHERN
COAST

By Lan Sluder

As always in Belize, the transition from one landscape to another is swift and startling. As you approach the Hummingbird Highway's end in coastal Dangriga, the lush, mountainous terrain of the north gives way to flat plains bristling with orange trees. Farther south, the Stann Creek Valley is where bananas, the nation's first bumper crop, and most other fruits are grown. Equally noticeable is the cultural segue: whereas San Ignacio has a Spanish air, the Southern Coast is strongly Afro-Caribbean.

The Southern Coast isn't so much a melting pot as a tropical stew full of different flavors. A seaside Garífuna village recalls Senegal, while just down the road a Creole village evokes the Caribbean. Inland, Maya live much as they have for thousands of years next door to Mestizos from Guatemala and Honduras who've come to work the banana plantations or citrus groves. Sprinkled in are expats from the northern climes, looking for a retirement home or trying to make a buck in tourism.

Tourist dollars, the staple of contemporary Belize, have largely bypassed Dangriga to land in Hopkins, and, even more tellingly, in Placencia, the region's most striking destination. Just a decade or so ago there were only three small resorts on the peninsula north of Placencia Village. Now there are more than 20, stretching up to the village of Seine Bight, Maya Beach, and beyond. Despite the global recession, plans are in the works for new condos and hotels, although some of these developments were stalled by a shortage of financing and a scarcity of buyers. A few shut down, victims of the real-estate bust, or are rotting away in the tropical humidity. Still, owners of small beach resorts and inns are cashing in, selling out to developers, who are in turn combining several small tracts into one, hoping to put together larger residential or resort projects.

With the paving of the Placencia road now completed, with the on-again, off-again construction of a new international airport going on just north of the peninsula, and with talk of a new cruise-ship port on a caye off Placencia, or even in Placencia village, many believe that the tipping point for the Placencia peninsula has been reached and that the new wave of resorts and residential developments will be larger, more upscale, and more multinational. Local residents appear divided about the dramatic changes coming to the peninsula. Some embrace the development in hopes of a better economic future; others bitterly oppose it, citing the impact on the narrow peninsula's fragile ecosystems. With the exception of a few shop owners and some guides, most Placencia residents appear to oppose the coming of mass cruise-ship tourism to the fragile peninsula, but powerful political and economic forces in the country appear to be ready to bring cruise ships to this part of Belize soon.

The surfacing of the Southern Highway from Dangriga all the way to Punta Gorda has made the region much more accessible. Off the main highway, however, most roads consist of red dirt and potholes. The road that once was the worst in the region, the dirt track from the Southern Highway to Placencia Village, has been transformed, thanks to a loan from the Caribbean Development Bank, into a smooth, paved, two-lane thoroughfare. The repaving of the Hopkins Road has been scheduled to begin by 2014.

Real-estate sales are a driving force in Placencia, Hopkins, and elsewhere along the coast. The lure is the beaches. The Southern Coast has the best beaches on the mainland, although as elsewhere inside the protecting Barrier Reef, the low wave action means the beaches are narrow and there's usually sea grass in the water close to shore. (Sea grass—not seaweed, which is an algae—may be a nuisance for swimmers, but it's a vital part of the coastal ecosystem, acting as a nursery for sea life.) Much of the seafront land has been divided into lots awaiting development; if things continue at this pace, the area will one day rival Ambergris Caye as Belize's top beach destination. Indeed, at the Belize Tourism Board annual awards ceremonies in 2013, for the first time ever most of the national tourism honors for best hotels, restaurants, guides, and tourism staff went to the Placencia peninsula instead of San Pedro.

ORIENTATION AND PLANNING

GETTING ORIENTED

From the north, two roads lead from the George Price Highway (formerly Western Highway) to the Southern Coast: the Hummingbird Highway from Belmopan, and the Coastal Road from La Democracia. The Hummingbird is paved, and the most scenic drive in all of Belize. The Coastal Road is unpaved, dusty or muddy, depending on the amount of rain. Despite the name, it does not hug the coast; in fact you never glimpse the sea from it. The loose gravel roadway is an accident waiting to happen. In short, if you're driving, take the Hummingbird.

Off the spine of the Southern Highway, various shorter roads lead to villages on the coast and inland: from the highway it's about 4 miles (7 km) on a partly paved road to Hopkins (the road is supposed to be surfaced soon); 25 miles (42 km) to Placencia Village, nicely paved all the way; and 5 miles (8 km) to Big Creek/Independence on a paved road.

Gales Point and Dangriga. Gales Point is a small Creole village, with a beautiful waterside setting, known for the manatees in nearby lagoons. Dangriga is the largest Garífuna settlement in Belize, and a jumping-off spot for several offshore cayes. However, neither Gales Point nor Dangriga is a tourism center.

TOP REASONS TO GO

Beaches. The mainland's best beaches are on the Placencia peninsula and around Hopkins. Although they're narrow ribbons of khaki rather than wide swaths of talcum-powder sand, they're ideal for lazing in a hammock under a coco palm. And you don't have to fight the crowds for a spot—at least not yet.

Jaguars. The world's first and only jaguar preserve is the Cockscomb Basin Wildlife Sanctuary. Chances are you won't actually see one of these big, beautiful cats in the wild, as they roam the high bush mainly

at night, but you may see tracks or hear a low growl in the darkness.

Water Sports. Anglers won't be disappointed by the bonefish, tarpon, and other sportfishing. The Barrier Reef here is generally 15 miles (25 km) or more off the coast, so it's a long trip out, even with the fast boats the dive shops use. However, there are patch reefs around closer islands, with excellent snorkeling. Serious divers will find two of Belize's three atolls, Turneffe and Glover's, within reach. In a charter sailboat you can island-hop in the protected waters inside the reef.

Hopkins. The most accessible and friendliest Garífuna village in Belize, Hopkins has good beaches and a growing tourism industry. It's similar to what Placencia was like 15 years ago.

Placencia Peninsula. This peninsula has the best beaches on the mainland. With the paving of the Placencia road, real-estate development and tourism are taking off, bringing more high-quality accommodations and dining, along with problems associated with development.

PLANNING

WHEN TO GO

The weather on the Southern Coast is similar to that in central and northern Belize, only a little wetter. On average, for example, the Cayo District has rain, or at least a shower, on 125 days a year, while in Stann Creek District there's some rain on 183 days—usually thanks to late fall and winter cold fronts or summer tropical fronts passing through. These showers are generally followed by sunshine. Summer daytime temperatures along the coast reach the high 80s, occasionally the 90s. Humidity is high most of the year, typically 80% or more.

GETTING HERE AND AROUND

AIR TRAVEL

You'll arrive fresher if you fly. From Belize City (both international and municipal airports) there are frequent flights to Dangriga and Placencia on Maya Island Air and Tropic Air. There are more than 20 flights daily between Belize City and Placencia, and more than a dozen to Dangriga. You'll generally fly in small turbine or prop aircraft, such as the 13-passenger Cessna Caravan C208. Fares to Placencia are BZ$180– BZ$197 one-way from the Belize City municipal airport, BZ$213–BZ$233 from the international airport; to Dangriga, fares are BZ$91–BZ$106 from municipal, BZ$144–BZ$160 from international.

Contacts Maya Island Air ⊠ *Placencia airstrip, Placencia* ☎ *523/3443 in Placencia, 223/1140 in Belize City* ⊕ *www.mayaislandair.com.*
Tropic Air ⊠ *Placencia airstrip, Placencia* ☎ *523/3410 in Placencia, 226/2012 in Belize City, 800/422-3435 in the U.S.* ⊕ *www.tropicair.com.*

BOAT AND FERRY TRAVEL

There is a well-established water taxi, a small boat named the *Hokey Pokey,* between Placencia Village and Independence, a village on the west side of Placencia Lagoon. Fare is BZ$10 one-way. Currently there are seven trips each way daily, with reduced service on Sunday. Schedules for the boat are set to coincide with James Bus Line stops in Independence, so you can make connections to Punta Gorda to the south, or Dangriga, Belmopan, and Belize City to the north.

From Placencia, a weekly boat, the *D'Express,* runs to Puerto Cortes, Honduras, on Friday, with a stop in Big Creek across the lagoon to clear immigration and customs. It departs from the Shell Dock at Placencia village (note that the service station is no longer a Shell station, and as of this writing is closed). In Puerto Cortes, the boat arrives at the Muelle de Mariscos, next to Delfin restaurant and returns from Puerto Cortes on Monday morning. Fare is BZ$120 one-way. Get information from the Placencia Tourism Center in Placencia village.

Happy Go Luckie Tours in Hopkins has a water taxi service from Hopkins to Dangriga (BZ$50), Tobacco Caye (BZ$50), Placencia (BZ$100) and a few other destinations. Prices are based on a minimum of three persons. There is no fixed schedule; passengers must book trips in advance.

Contacts D' Express ⊠ *at end of Main St., Placencia* ☎ *523/4045 in Placencia* ⊕ *www.belizeferry.com.* **Happy Go Luckie Tours** ⊠ *Hopkins* ☎ *635/0967* ⊕ *www.hgltours.com.* **Hokey Pokey** ⊠ *Placencia MnM Dock, Placencia* ☎ *523/2376* ⊕ *www.aguallos.com/hokeypokey* ☑ *BZ$10.* **Pride of Belize** ⊠ *Belize City* ☎ *600/3259* ⊕ *www.prideofbelize.com.*

BUS TRAVEL

In the south, James Bus Line runs from Belize City via Belmopan to Dangriga and Independence and then Punta Gorda. Schedules are subject to change, but James Bus Line has about 10 buses daily. Ritchie's Bus Line also has three to four buses daily each way between Dangriga and Placencia, with reduced service on Sunday. Fares from Belize City are around BZ$15 to Dangriga (BZ$10 between Dangriga and Placencia). With connections, the trip from Belize City to Dangriga and Hopkins is three to five hours; Placencia is around five to six hours or more, depending on the number of stops and connections. Buses are usually old U.S. school buses or ancient Greyhound buses, are often crowded, and don't have air-conditioning or restrooms. The James Bus Line buses generally are in the best condition.

Contacts James Bus Line ⊠ *7 King St., Punta Gorda* ☎ *702/2049.*
Ritchie's Bus Line. Tickets sold at Placencia Tourism office, or flag down the bus and pay conductor. ⊠ *Ritchie's Bus Service, Main Rd., Placencia* ☎ *523/3806* ⊕ *www.ritchiesbusservice.com.*

CAR TRAVEL

To get to Placencia, head southeast from Belmopan on the Hummingbird Highway. The highway is one of Belize's better roads, as well as its most scenic. On your right rise the jungle-covered Maya Mountains, largely free of signs of human habitation except for the occasional field of corn or beans. As you approach Dangriga you'll see large citrus groves.

Several small local outfits, including Barefoot Services, rent cars in Placencia. Some also rent golf carts, which can be driven on the roads. Budget, based in Belize City, has a branch in Placencia. Car rental rates in Placencia start at around BZ$160 per day, plus tax.

Contacts Barefoot Services ⊠ *Caribbean Travel and Tours Office, Main St., Placencia* ☎ *523/3066, 629/9602* ⊕ *www.barefootservicesbelize.com* ⊙ *Closed Sat.* **Budget** ⊠ *Live Oak Plaza, south of airstrip, Placencia* ☎ *223/2435 in Belize City, 523/3068 in Placencia* ✍ *reservations@budget-belize.com* ⊕ *www.budget-belize.com.*

TAXI TRAVEL

If you need a ride to the airport in Dangriga, have your hotel call a taxi. The fare from downtown Dangriga to the airstrip at the town's north end is about BZ$6–BZ$8. From Dangriga to Hopkins the fare is around BZ$100–BZ$120. Taxis are expensive in Placencia, given the relatively short distances involved and the fact that the road is now paved. Fares within Placencia village are BZ$6 for one or two persons and BZ$6 each for three or more. From the village to the airstrip the fare is BZ$12 for one or two persons, and BZ$6 each for three or more. It's BZ$22 for one or two persons between Placencia village and Seine Bight, and BZ$8 each for three or more. Between Placencia village and the north end of the peninsula, where The Placencia condotel is, it's BZ$50 one-way for one to three persons and BZ$15 per person for four or more, and BZ$40 one-way between Placencia village and Maya Beach for one to three persons and BZ$15 per person for four or more. Your hotel can arrange a taxi for you, or call Radiance Ritchie.

Contacts Radiance Ritchie ⊠ *Placencia Rd., Placencia* ☎ *523/3321.*

EMERGENCIES

Placencia has a small medical clinic with a physician and nurse. Seine Bight, Hopkins, and Independence also have medical clinics. For more serious medical attention you should go to the Southern Regional Hospital in Dangriga or one of the hospitals in Belize City. The Belize Emergency Response Team, based in Belize City, provides ambulance and air transport all over the country. Wallen's Market has a small pharmacy. Dial 911 in case of emergency.

Hospitals Belize Emergency Response Team ⊠ *1675 Sunrise Ave., Coral Grove Area, Belize City* ☎ *223/3292, 610/3890* ⊕ *www.bertbelize.org.* **Placencia Medical Clinic** ⊠ *In center of village, near primary school, Placencia* ☎ *523/3326.* **Southern Regional Hospital** ⊠ *Stann Creek District Hwy., Dangriga* ☎ *522/2078* ⊕ *www.shr.health.gov.bz.* **Wallen's Market and Pharmacy** ⊠ *Main Rd., Placencia* ☎ *523/3128.*

MONEY MATTERS

There are three banks in Placencia. Atlantic Bank has an office on the road just north of Placencia Village, as well as a second ATM in Placencia Village, and ScotiaBank is also in the village. Belize Bank has an office at Placencia Point. All three banks have ATMs that accept foreign-issued cards.

Belize Bank in Dangriga accepts foreign-issued ATM cards. First Caribbean International Bank in Dangriga has an ATM that accepts foreign cards. Belize Bank now has an ATM in Hopkins, but not a full-service branch. *(See ATMs and Banks in Travel Smart for Bank contact information)*

ABOUT THE RESTAURANTS

Broiled, grilled, fried, sautéed, cooked in lime juice as ceviche, or barbecued on the beach: any way you eat it, seafood is the life-stuff on the Southern Coast. Restaurants serve fish, lobster, conch, and shrimp, often fresh from the boat, or, in the case of shrimp, straight from the shrimp farms near Placencia.

Expect mostly small, locally owned restaurants; some breezy beachside joints with sand floors, others wood shacks. Placencia has by far the largest number of eateries, with Hopkins a distant second. Chef Rob's is Hopkins' best restaurant. Some of the upscale restaurants are in resorts, such as Inn at Robert's Grove and Turtle Inn. The Bistro at Maya Beach Hotel is one of the country's best restaurants. And it's worth making a trip to Placencia just to sample the incredible gelato at Tutti-Frutti.

Off-season, especially in late summer and early fall, restaurants in Placencia and Hopkins may close for a few weeks, and on any day the owners may decide to close early if there are no customers, so call ahead. It's also a good idea to make reservations so the cooks will have enough food on hand.

ABOUT THE HOTELS

There are two kinds of lodging to choose from on the Southern Coast: small, basic hotels, often Belizean-owned, and upscale beach resorts, usually owned and operated by Americans or Canadians. The small hotels are clustered in Placencia Village, Hopkins village, and in Dangriga town. The beach resorts are on the Placencia peninsula north of Placencia Village and also near Hopkins. Several of these resorts, including Hamanasi in Hopkins, are among the best hotels in Belize. There also are some vacation rental houses near Hopkins and on the Placencia peninsula.

At least a dozen condo developments have opened, are under construction, or are in the planning stages on Placencia peninsula and near Hopkins. Only time will tell whether all these plans will fully materialize (one large condo development, Bella Maya, on the Placencia peninsula, closed, but in mid-2013 reopened under different management) or whether supply will outstrip demand, but it's clear that this area has reached the point where, sooner or later, development by large international companies is inevitable.

HOTEL AND RESTAURANT PRICES

Prices in the restaurant reviews are the average cost of a main course at dinner or, if dinner is not served, at lunch; taxes and service charges are generally included. Prices in the hotel reviews are the lowest cost of a standard double room in high season, excluding taxes, service charges, and meal plans (except at all-inclusives). Prices for rentals are the lowest per-night cost for a one-bedroom unit in high season.

For expanded lodging reviews and current deals, visit Fodors.com.

TOURS

Altogether, Placencia has about 80 licensed tour guides. Most of the guides, except the fishing guides, work on a contract basis for resorts or tour operators. These tour guides and operators offer dive and snorkel trips to Laughing Bird or other cayes and to the Barrier Reef, wildlife tours to Monkey River, birding tours to Red Bank, hiking trips to Cockscomb Basin Wildlife Sanctuary, excursions to Mayan ruins, and other tours.

The larger resorts on the peninsula, including Inn at Robert's Grove, Chabil Mar, Turtle Inn, and others, offer a variety of tours and trips, using tour guides they have come to trust. ⇨ *See Where to Eat and Stay sections for contact information.*

To book tours and trips, check with your hotel or walk along the sidewalk in Placencia Village, where several of the tour operators have small shops. Also check with the Belize Tourism Industry Association (BTIA) visitor information office, which publishes a monthly tabloid and online newspaper, Placencia Breeze. The BTIA's friendly staff can advise you on tours. You'll probably pay a little less by booking in the village instead of at your hotel, but the savings may not be worth the effort.

ADVENTURE TOURS AND MULTISPORT

Toadal Adventures Belize. Dave Vernon's Toadal Adventure provides topnotch multiday sea and river expedition kayak trips in southern Belize. Toadal Adventures can customize trips to your specific schedule and interests. Dave and Deb Vernon also operate a budget guesthouse, Deb & Dave's Last Resort, and a more upscale lodging, The North, in Placencia village. ⊠ *Point Placencia, near sidewalk, Placencia* ☎ *523/3207* ⊕ *www.placencia.com/Members/Toadaladventure.html.*

BOATING, SAILING, AND WATER SPORTS

Five- or six-hour snorkeling trips inside the reef, to Laughing Bird Caye and other snorkel spots, are around BZ$125–BZ$150, while a full-day snorkel trip might run BZ$140–BZ$160. Half-day boat trips to Monkey River are around BZ$120, while a boat excursion on the Placencia Lagoon to look for manatees is around BZ$80–BZ$100. Full-day Cockscomb day trips run about BZ$150–BZ$170. Most full-day trips include a picnic lunch. If you're going to an area with an admission fee, such as Cockscomb, often the fee is additional.

Belize Sailing Charters. Belize Sailing Charters has day sails on catamarans from Placencia. Several boats, including *El Gato* and *Winnie Estelle*, do day trips out of San Pedro. Sailboat owners tend to be free spirits who may pick up and sail to another port at the drop of a yachting cap, so check locally to see what boats are still sailing.

About once a month, Belize Sailing Charters offers a nine-night private catamaran sail from Placencia to the Rio Dulce in Guatemala, with a visit by land to Tikal, for around BZ$20,000 for two persons. ⊠ *Main St., Point Peninsula, Placencia* ☎ *523/3138, 505/717–7301 U.S. number* ⊕ *www.belizesailingcharters.com.*

Joy Tours. Joy Tours offers a wide range of land and sea tours. Sea tours include whale shark trips, fishing, diving, kayaking, and snorkeling. Land tours include hiking in Cockscomb and other destinations near Placencia. ⊠ *Placencia* ☎ *253/3325* ⊕ *www.belizewithjoy.com.*

Splash Dive Center. Splash Dive Center offers dive and snorkel trips, including late spring and early summer whale shark trips. It won the 2013 Belize Tourism Award for "Best Tour Operator." ⊠ *Splash Dive Center, Placencia* ☎ *523/3058* ⊕ *www.splashbelize.com.*

Sunsail. Clearwater, Florida–based international charter company Sunsail offers sail charters from Placencia, operating out of the same marina as TUI Travel sister company The Moorings at Laru Beya Resort. Weeklong Sunsail bareboat charters are around BZ$6,000 to $14,000, depending on number of sailors, size of boat, and time of year. ⊠ *Laru Beya Marina, Placencia* ☎ *877/651–5610 In the U.S. and Canada, 523/4057* ⊕ *www.sunsail.com.*

MAYAN RUINS

Day trips to **Nim Li Punit** and **Lubaantun Mayan** sites near Punta Gorda cost around BZ$160–BZ$190 per person, while day trips to the **Mayflower** ruins and waterfalls run about BZ$120. *(See also Ocean Motion in Placencia Village.)*

Destinations Belize. Owner Mary Toy, a former attorney in the U.S., has been offering tours in the Placencia area since 1998. Destinations Belize is especially strong in arranging guided fishing trips, but it also offers land and sea tours of all kinds. In addition, Mary Toy can help with overall Belize trip planning, including booking hotels and transportation. Toy has been a leader of the Peninsula Citizens for Sustainable Development, an organization dedicated to responsible and well-planned development in the Placencia area. ⊠ *Placencia* ☎ *253/4018, 610/718* ⊕ *www.destinationsbelize.com.*

VISITOR INFORMATION

The Placencia office of the Belize Tourism Industry Association is now in a new location behind Re/Max Real Estate on the Main St. The BTIA publishes the *Placencia Breeze,* an informative monthly newspaper, and has a very helpful website listing all accommodations, restaurants, and bars, ⊕ *www.placencia.com.* Another helpful site on Placencia is put together by local resident Mary Toy, ⊕ *www.destinationsbelize.com.* Hopkins has several interesting websites put together by local residents, including ⊕ *www.hopkinsbelize.com* and ⊕ *www.cometohopkins.com.*

Information Belize Tourism Industry Association. The Belize Tourism Industry Association (BTIA) office, also known as the Placencia Tourism Center, in Placencia village offers friendly and helpful information about lodging, tours, transportation, restaurants and other visitor information. In 2013, the office moved to a new location behind Re/Max Property Center on Main Street. The BTIA publishes the informative monthly tabloid newspaper, *Placencia Breeze,* which is also available online on the Placencia BTIA's website. ⊠ *Main St., Behind Re/Max Property Center, Placencia* ☎ *523/4045* ⊕ *www.placencia.com.*

FROM GALES POINT TO PLACENCIA

Thanks to its good beaches, the Southern Coast—the area from Gales Point to Placencia—is the up-and-coming part of Belize, with a growing number of resorts and restaurants, especially in Hopkins and Placencia.

DANGRIGA

99 miles (160 km) southeast of Belmopan.

With a population of around 9,000, Dangriga is the largest town in the south and the home of the Garífuna or Black Caribs, as they're also known (though some view the latter term as a remnant of colonialism). Strictly speaking the plural is Garinagu, but Garifunas also is used. There's not much to keep you in Dangriga. Though the town is on the coast, there are no good beaches, no truly first-class hotels, few restaurants, and, except for a small museum on Garífuna culture in the outskirts of town, not much to see. Rickety clapboard houses on stilts and small shops line the downtown streets, and the town has a kind of end-of-the-road feel. Dangriga isn't really dangerous, and in fact it's friendlier than it first seems, though it has a rough vibe, a little like Belize City, that's off-putting for many visitors.

Each year, on November 19 and the days around it, the town cuts loose with a week of Carnival-style celebrations. Garífuna drumming, costumed Jonkunu dancers, punta music, and a good bit of drinking make up the festivities of Garífuna Settlement Day, when these proud people celebrate their arrival in Belize and remember their roots.

GETTING HERE AND AROUND

You can arrive in Dangriga by car, bus, or airplane. The Hummingbird, Belize's most scenic highway, runs 54 miles (89 km) from Belmopan to Dangriga. As it approaches Dangriga, it technically becomes the Stann Creek District Highway, but most people simply refer to the entire road as the Hummingbird Highway. James Line and other bus lines have frequent service during the day from Belize City via Belmopan to Dangriga. The bus station in Dangriga is seven blocks south of town on the main road. By air, Maya Island and Tropic together have around a dozen flights daily from the international and municipal airports in Belize City. The airstrip is at the north edge of town.

Contacts James Bus Line ✉ *7 King St., Punta Gorda* ☎ *722/2265* ⊕ *www.pgbelize.com/jamesbusline.*

TIMING

Candidly, Dangriga isn't exactly a mecca for tourists. (Some hotels have Dangriga mailing addresses, even though they're physically located in Hopkins or on an offshore caye or elsewhere.) Unless you have a special interest in Garífuna culture, need to overnight there on your way to Tobacco Caye, Southwater Caye, or another offshore caye, or simply have a yen to visit quirky, Graham Greene-ish spots, you'll probably spend only a few hours in Dangriga, if that. We do note that the best french fries we've ever had in Belize are at the Pelican Beach Hotel in Dangriga, the best hotel in town.

GREAT ITINERARIES

IF YOU HAVE 3 DAYS ON THE SOUTHERN COAST

Base yourself in Placencia. On your first full day, walk the Sidewalk in Placencia Village, hear the latest gossip, and get to know a little of village life. Hang out on the beach at your hotel and get on Belize time, then have drinks and dinner in the village, perhaps at Rumfish y Vino, Secret Garden, or La Dolce Vita. If you still have energy, have some Belikins at the Barefoot Bar or Tipsy Tuna. On your second day,

take a snorkel trip to Laughing Bird Caye or another snorkel area, or, if you dive, do a full-day dive trip to Turneffe or Glover's atoll. On your final day, drive or take a guided tour to Cockscomb Basin Wildlife Sanctuary. Be sure to stop at the Maya Centre craft cooperative for gift shopping. If there's time, also visit the Mayflower/Bocawina National Park, with its Mayan sites and waterfalls. End the day with dinner at the Bistro at Maya Beach Hotel.

SAFETY AND PRECAUTIONS

Visitors may get hassled a little on the streets of Dangriga, and care should be exercised if walking around town after dark.

EXPLORING

TOP ATTRACTIONS

FAMILY

Fodor's Choice

★

Gulisi Garífuna Museum. Named after a Garífuna heroine who came to Belize with her 13 children and founded the village of Punta Negra in Toledo District, this museum has a number of displays on Garífuna history and life. Exhibits cover the Garífuna migration from Africa to St. Vincent, then to Roatan and Belize. Another exhibit is on Thomas Vincent Ramos, a visionary Garífuna leader who, in 1941, established the first Garífuna Settlement Day. Other displays are on Garífuna food, clothing, medicinal plants, and music and dance. The museum also has rotating displays of paintings by Garífuna artists including Pen Cayetano. ⊠ *Chulubadiwa Park, Stann Creek Valley Rd., about 2 miles (3 km) from Dangriga* ☎ *699/0639* ⊕ *www.ngcbelize.org* ⊠ *BZ$10* ⊗ *Weekdays 10–5, Sat. 8–noon.*

Mayflower Bocawina National Park. Declared a national park in 2001, Mayflower Bocawina has some small Mayan ruins, lovely waterfalls, and good hiking on more than 7,000 acres. A private lodge, Mama Noots *(see Where to Stay)*, is in the park and has lodging, food and drink, and a zip line. The park has three minor Mayan ceremonial sites: Mayflower, T'au Witz, and Maintzunum, near Silk Grass Creek. Nearby are the three waterfalls: Bocawina Falls, Three Sisters Falls, and Antelope Falls. Access to Mayflower is easiest from Hopkins, about 20 minutes by car. However, tours are offered from Placencia and Dangriga as well as from Hopkins. The entrance to the park is about 4½ miles (7½ km) on a dirt road off the Southern Highway. From the visitor center, to get to Bocawina and Three Sisters Falls, which are close together, it's an easy hike of about 1¼ miles (2 km) on the marked Bocawina Falls trail. The trail to Antelope Falls, about 1¾ miles (3 km), is somewhat more difficult due to some steep sections that can be slick after rain. Maps of

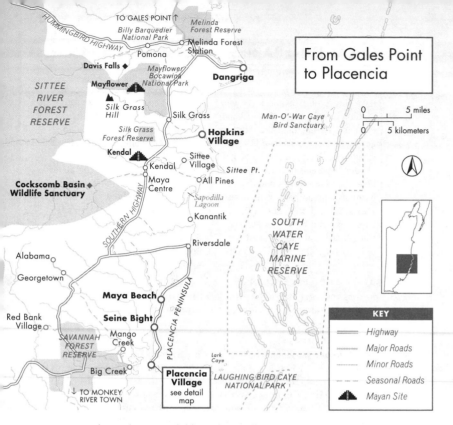

From Gales Point to Placencia

TO GALES POINT ↑
Billy Barquedier National Park
Melinda Forest Reserve
Melinda Forest Station
Pomona
Davis Falls ◆
Mayflower Bocawina National Park
Mayflower ▲
Dangriga
SITTEE RIVER FOREST RESERVE
Silk Grass Hill
Silk Grass
Silk Grass Forest Reserve
Hopkins Village
Man-O'-War Caye Bird Sanctuary
Kendal
Kendal
Sittee Village
Sittee Pt.
Maya Centre
All Pines
Cockscomb Basin ◆ Wildlife Sanctuary
Sapodilla Lagoon
Kanantik
SOUTH WATER CAYE MARINE RESERVE
Riversdale
Alabama
Georgetown
Maya Beach
Seine Bight
Red Bank Village
Mango Creek
SAVANNAH FOREST RESERVE
Big Creek
Lark Caye
Placencia Village see detail map
LAUGHING BIRD CAYE NATIONAL PARK
↓ TO MONKEY RIVER TOWN

HUMMINGBIRD HIGHWAY
SOUTHERN HIGHWAY
PLACENCIA PENINSULA

0 — 5 miles
0 — 5 kilometers

KEY
Highway
Major Roads
Minor Roads
Seasonal Roads
▲ Mayan Site

the trails are available at the small visitor center. So far, little excavation has been conducted at the Mayan sites, but the parklike setting at the base of the Maya Mountains is beautiful. ⊠ *Off Mile 6, Southern Hwy.* ✚ *From Mile 6 on Southern Hwy, go west 4½ miles (7½ km) west on dirt road to park visitor center* ☐ *BZ$10* ⊙ *Daily 8–4.*

Southern Lagoon. One of the most beautiful lagoons in Belize, Southern Lagoon, is about 25 miles (41 km) north of Dangriga—a 45-minute car ride. This lagoon is home to many West Indian manatees, and on beaches nearby, hawksbill turtles nest May to October. The Northern and Western lagoons also are in this area. ⊠ *Southern Lagoon, Gales Point* ✚ *From Dangriga, drive west on the Stann Creek Hwy./Hummingbird Hwy. to Melinda; turn right on the unpaved Coastal Hwy. and go about 12 miles (20 km) to the turn-off for Gales Point and follow 2½ miles (4 km) to the lagoon and Gales Point village.*

WORTH NOTING

Billy Barquedier National Park. Billy Barquedier National Park is a 1,500-acre park along the Hummingbird Highway in Stann Creek District. Established in 2001, the park is still in its infancy. Although it offers no spectacular sights, it does have primitive hiking trails and the Barquedier Waterfall (locally sometimes called Bac-a-Der Waterfall). It's part of a community comanagement program for parks and reserves, in this case with the Steadfast Tourist and Conservation group of Steadfast village, along with the Belize Forestry Department. It's best to enter the park via the northern entrance at Mile 16½ of the Hummingbird Highway. Entrance fee to the park is BZ$8, and a 3-hour guided tour to the falls by Holistic Eco Tours is BZ$120 for up to four persons. Camping is available in the park for BZ$20 per person, plus the park entrance fee. ⊠ *Main entrance, Mile 16½, Hummingbird Hwy., Steadfast Village* ☎ *603/0863 for park caretaker and Holistic Eco Tours guide* ⊕ *billybarquediernp.webs.com* ⬚ *BZ$8* ☉ *Daily 9–4:30.*

Davis Falls. Getting to Davis Falls requires a four-wheel-drive vehicle or tractor and wagon plus an arduous 2 miles (3 km) hike, but the falls here are about 500 feet high and are the second highest in the country (after Thousand-Foot Falls in the Mountain Pine Ridge), and the natural pool at the base of the falls is 75 feet deep. The swimming is wonderful, and the undisturbed forest around the falls is great for a picnic or enjoying nature. Before going to Davis Falls, stop at the Citrus Products of Belize plant (Mile 14.5 of Hummingbird Highway/Stann Creek District Highway), for information and to pay your admission fee. Tours of Davis Falls are offered by several tour guides including Holistic Eco Tours at Steadfast village. (⇨ *Billy Barquedier National Park.*) ⊠ *Mile 14.5, Hummingbird Hwy.* ☎ *603/2339 for Holistic Eco Tours* ⬚ *BZ$10* ☉ *Daily 9–4:30.*

Gales Point. The small Creole village of Gales Point, population about 500, has an idyllic setting on the Southern Lagoon. The lagoon and nearby waters are home to many manatees. Gales Point is home to several drum makers, including Boombay Andrewin, who gives Creole-style drumming lessons (about BZ$16 an hour). You can drive to Gales Point, and tours are available from Dangriga and Hopkins. ⊠ *Gales Point* ✢ *To Gales Point: From Dangriga, go northwest on Hummingbird Hwy. 8½ miles (14 km) to village of Melinda; turn right on Manatee Hwy. (Coastal Rd) and follow 13 miles (21 km) to turnoff, a sharp right turn. This dirt road to Gales Point Village runs about 2½ miles (4 km) until it ends at lagoon and Manatee Lodge* ☎ *209/8031 community phone for Gales Point.*

Marie Sharp's Factory. You can visit the source of one of Belize's few well-known exports, Marie Sharp's Hot Sauce, made in about 10 different heat levels from Mild to Beware. The small factory, with about 25 workers, established and still run by Marie Sharp and family, is open to interested visitors weekdays, but for a tour it's best to call in advance. Besides the factory tour, you can also see the entire selection of products manufactured by Marie Sharp, and most are offered for sale. Marie Sharp's main office is in Dangriga (⊠ *3 Pier Rd.* ☎ *522–2370*), where there also is a small shop. Her products are sold in nearly every grocery in Belize and are on tables in most restaurants in Belize. ⊠ *1 Melinda Rd., 8 miles (13 km) west of Dangriga, Stann Creek Valley* ☎ *520/2087* ⊕ *www.mariesharps-bz.com* ⬚ *Free.*

HISTORY

As elsewhere in Belize, the Maya were here first. They had settlements in what is now Stann Creek District at least from the Early Classic period (around AD 300) until the Post-Classic period (about AD 1200). However, this part of Belize did not have the large Mayan cities that existed elsewhere. Few of the known Mayan sites in the area have been extensively excavated, but they appear to have been small ceremonial centers.

In the 1600s, small numbers of English, some of whom were pirates, settled on the Placencia peninsula, though most eventually left the area. Creoles from Jamaica came to Stann Creek in the 1700s, mainly to work in logging, and, later, in fishing. In the next century English traders and farmers arrived in what is now Dangriga. They called their coastal trading posts "stands," which was corrupted to "stann." Hence the name Stann Creek. On November 19, 1823, a group of Garinagu from the Bay Islands of Honduras, former African slaves who had intermarried with Carib Indians in the southern Caribbean, arrived at the mouth of the Stann Creek River, at what was then called Stann Creek Town. This date is still celebrated in Belize as Garífuna Settlement Day. Later, the name of Stann Creek Town (but not the district) was changed to Dangriga, which means "sweet water" in the Garífuna language.

In the late 1800s several families, originally from Scotland, Portugal, Honduras, and elsewhere, arrived in Placencia. The names of these families—Garbutt, Leslie, Westby, and Cabral—are still common on the peninsula. In the 19th and early 20th centuries the fertile soils of the coastal plain were found to be ideal for growing bananas and citrus, and soon agriculture became the most important industry in the region. The first railroad in Belize, the Stann Creek Railway, built by the United Fruit Company to transport bananas, started operation around World War I. The railroad closed in the 1950s.

The first small tourist resorts were developed on the Placencia peninsula in the 1960s and '70s, but the bad roads and lack of infrastructure meant that few visitors got this far south. The first fishing cooperative was established in Placencia in 1962. Although fishing is still a way of life for a few people on the coast, the big money now is real-estate development and tourism. Shrimp farming, once an up-and-coming industry around Placencia, has run into problems due to competition from Asia, and several Belize shrimp farms have closed.

Hurricane Iris in 2001 devastated much of the Southern Coast south of Maya Beach, Tropical Storm Arthur in 2008 caused extensive flooding, and a minor earthquake in 2009 damaged some homes in Placencia and Monkey River, but the area has bounced back stronger than ever, and you will see few signs of the natural disasters.

WHERE TO EAT

$ LATIN AMERICAN 🍴 **King Burger.** Formerly called Burger King, but a far cry from the U.S. chain of the same name, this is one of the best places in Dangriga to get an honest plate of chicken and rice and beans. Prepared by the Cuban owner, the fresh fish is good, and, yes, so are the hamburgers. Everything's affordable, too. No alcohol served, but you can BYOB (Bring Your Own Belikin). [$] *Average main: BZ$12* ✉ *135 Commerce St., on Dangriga's main street just north of the bridge on the North Stann Creek River* ☎ *522/2476* 💳 *No credit cards* 🕒 *Closed Sun.*

$ LATIN AMERICAN 🍴 **Riverside Café.** The Creole and Garífuna dishes here are hearty and tasty, prepared fresh by Maudeline Westby. The restaurant is often busy with fishermen and the guys who run boats out to Tobacco Caye and other offshore cayes. If you're going to the islands you can arrange transportation while sipping a beer or having breakfast or a plate of rice and beans. [$] *Average main: BZ$12* ✉ *Riverside and Oak Sts., on west side of North Stann Creek river* ☎ *661/6390* 💳 *No credit cards.*

WHERE TO STAY

DANGRIGA

$$ HOTEL 🏨 **Pelican Beach Resort.** This waterfront hotel on the north end of Dangriga, near the airstrip, is the best the town has to offer. **Pros:** charming colonial-era main building; breezy seaside location; the best lodging in Dangriga. **Cons:** not the beach of your dreams. [$] *Rooms from: BZ$247* ✉ *Scotchman Town, North End* ☎ *522/2044* 🌐 *www.pelicanbeachbelize.com* 🛏 *20 rooms.*

NEAR DANGRIGA

$ B&B/INN 🏨 **Mama Noots Eco Resort.** Being environmentally conscious doesn't have to come at the expense of comfort or adventure at this newly reopened lodge in Mayflower Bocawina National Park, with renovated rooms and its own zip line. **Pros:** hard-to-beat location in national park; lots of wildlife and birds; on-site zip line. **Cons:** you may need lots of bug spray; park admission fee not waived for guests. [$] *Rooms from: BZ$175* ✉ *Mayflower Bocawina National Park, near Mayflower archaeological site, 5 miles (8 km) off Mile 6, Southern Hwy.* ☎ *670/8019* 🌐 *www.mamanootsbelize.com* 🛏 *6 standard rooms, 3 casita rooms, 4 deluxe rooms* 🍽 *No meals.*

$$ B&B/INN 🏨 **Manatee Lodge.** This colonial-era lodge, just feet from the Southern Lagoon and surrounded by flowers, has a stunning setting, though the facilities do not live up to its location. **Pros:** beautiful waterside setting; interesting colonial atmosphere. **Cons:** off-the-beaten-path location; lodge would benefit from updating and upgrades. [$] *Rooms from: BZ$210* ✉ *Manatee Lodge, on Southern Lagoon, Gales Point* ☎ *532/2400* 🌐 *www.manateelodge.com* 🛏 *8 rooms.*

SHOPPING

Dangriga has some interesting, offbeat shopping, notably for Garífuna arts and crafts. Collectors may want to spend a day looking for items that are rarely available outside Belize and in some cases may not be available elsewhere in Belize. Austin Rodriquez sells his handmade drums here. Noted Garífuna artist Pen Cayetano has a studio and gallery. Garífuna cultural expert Frank Swaso has a gallery selling local drums, dolls, masks, and wood carvings.

Austin Rodriguez Drums. Visit this small seafront thatched shed for locally made drums. Ask locally for directions to the shop. Rodriguez's drums also are sold at Lebeha Drumming School in Hopkins village *(see Worth Noting in Hopkins Village, below)*. ⊠ *Seafront at North Stann Creek River* ☎ *502/3752.*

Garinagu Crafts Gallery. This small gallery sells Garífuna drums, masks, wood carvings and other locally made items. In the gallery is a small museum on Garífuna life. ⊠ *46 Oak St. at Tubroose St.* ☎ *522/2596.*

Pen Cayetano Studio Gallery. Punta rocker and internationally known Garífuna artist Pen Cayetano displays his bold, colorful paintings at his studio and gallery at his home in Dangriga. Work by his wife, Ingrid Cayetano, and daughter, Mali, are also displayed. The house, built around 1900 and totally redone by Cayetano, alone is worth a visit, as it is one of the most interesting old buildings in Dangriga. ⊠ *3 Aranda Crescent at Gallery St.* ☎ *628/6807* 🖅 *BZ$5* ☉ *Closed at lunch time and on Mon.*

HOPKINS VILLAGE

10 miles (17 km) south of Dangriga on the Southern Hwy., then 2 miles (3 km) east on a partially paved road.

Hopkins is an intriguing Garífuna coastal village of about 1,500 people, halfway between Dangriga and Placencia. Garífuna culture is more accessible here than in Dangriga. Hopkins has the same toast-color beaches as those in Placencia, and a number of new resorts have opened to take advantage of them. Americans, Canadians, and Europeans are snapping up beachfront land here at prices a bit lower than in Placencia or on Ambergris Caye, but so far only a few vacation homes and condos have been built. If there's a downside to the area, it's the biting sand flies, which can be vicious at times.

GETTING HERE AND AROUND

The turnoff to Hopkins from the Southern Highway is 10 miles (16 km) south of the junction of the Hummingbird and Southern highways. The Hopkins Road is rutted and potholed. Plans have been announced to redo and pave the Hopkins Road, with completion by late 2014. A longer, but less potholed, route to Hopkins is via the Sittee River Road, 2½ miles (4 km) farther south on the Southern Highway. Buses on the Southern Highway will drop you at the entrance road to Hopkins, and a few stop in Hopkins itself. Hopkins has no air service. You can fly to Dangriga and take a taxi to Hopkins (about BZ$100–BZ$120), if your hotel doesn't provide a shuttle.

Contacts James Bus Line ⊠ *7 King St., Punta Gorda* ☎ *722/2049, 664/2185.*

TIMING

The highlights of Hopkins can be seen in much less than a day, but if this is your beach destination, you can profitably spend several days, or longer, here enjoying activities on the water.

WORTH NOTING

Lebeha Drumming Center. In Hopkins you can watch local Garífuna boys hone their drumming skills at the Lebeha Drumming Center. *Lebeha* means "the end" in the Garífuna language, a reference to the school's location at a small guesthouse with a bar, budget rooms, and cabins. Visitors are welcome. The drums, mostly made by a noted drum maker in Dangriga, Austin Rodriquez, are of mahogany or mayflower wood, with deerskin on the drumhead. Other instruments include *shakas*, or shakers, calabash gourds filled with fruit seeds and turtle shells. The drumming goes on nightly, though most activity is on weekends. Donations are accepted. You can take drumming lessons and purchase a CD of Lebeha drumming. ⊠ *Lebeha Drumming, Main Rd., near north end of village* ☎ *665/9305* ⊕ *www.lebeha.com.*

WHERE TO EAT

$$$
MEDITERRANEAN
Fodor's Choice
★
✕ **Barracuda Bar & Grill.** Owners Tony and Angela Marsico traded running a restaurant in Alaska for operating a beachside bistro in Belize. They've turned this restaurant, part of Beaches and Dreams Seafront Inn, into one of the best eateries on the Southern Coast, with delicious dishes like fresh grilled snapper and smoked chicken or ribs. Catch the sea breezes on the covered, open-air deck while you munch a handmade pizza or enjoy a burger. The restaurant usually closes for a few weeks off-season. $ *Average main: BZ$45* ⊠ *Sittee Point* ☎ *523/7259* ⊕ *www.beachesanddreams.com.*

$$$
CARIBBEAN
Fodor's Choice
★
✕ **Chef Rob's Gourmet Cafe.** You'll recognize this restaurant by the big sign out front made from one side of a red 1964 Peugeot 404, but inside the restaurant at Parrot Cove Lodge, Chef Rob Pronk's eclectic Caribbean-style, locally sourced food is surprisingly contemporary. And delicious. You can order a four-course meal (soup, salad, entrée, and dessert) from the prix fixe menu or order à la carte). The menu changes daily, but the entrée might be lobster, fresh fish, or ribs, all presented creatively and with interesting sauces. The restaurant is on the beach at Parrot Cove Resort, which Rob and his wife Corrie Pronk also manage. Chef Rob says he plans to add some of his "Love on the Rocks" dishes from a second location in Hopkins. At Love on the Rocks, you cook your own food on a hot lava rock, a concept the chef introduced in Belize years ago at the Radisson Fort George Hotel restaurant in Belize City. In-season, you'll likely need reservations. $ *Average main: BZ$50* ⊠ *Beachside, False Sittee Point, at Parrot Cove Resort* ☎ *670/0445, 523/7225 Parrot Cove* ⊕ *www.parrotcovelodge.com* ⚫ *Reservations essential.*

$$
PIZZA
✕ **Driftwood Beach Bar and Pizza Shack.** Driftwood arguably has the best pizza in Southern Belize, served up by outgoing British American owners in a friendly, casual atmosphere in a beachfront thatch palapa. Try the Driftwood combo pizza, with red sauce, pepperoni, Italian sausage, peppers, onion, mushrooms, and black olives (in three sizes). If pizza isn't your thing, go for the catch of the day or one of the pasta dishes. Plenty of cold beer and rum at reasonable prices. There's usually a beach BBQ on Sunday afternoons. If you're driving, be careful where you park, as it's easy to get bogged down in the soft sand if you don't have four-wheel drive. $ *Average main: BZ$25* ⊠ *North end of Hopkins* ☎ *667/4072* ⊕ *www.driftwoodpizza.com* ☺ *Closed Wed.*

The Garífuna Struggle

Perhaps the most unusual of the ethnic groups calling Belize home, the Garífuna have a story that is both bizarre and moving, an odyssey of exile and dispossession in the wake of the confusion wrought in the New World by the Old. The Garífuna are descended from a group of Nigerian slaves who were shipwrecked on the island of St. Vincent in 1635. The Caribs, St. Vincent's indigenous population, fiercely resisted the outsiders at first, but they eventually overcame their distrust.

In the eyes of the British colonial authorities, the new ethnic group that developed after years of intermarriage was an illegitimate and troublesome presence. Worse still, the Garífuna sided with, and were succored by, the French. After nearly two centuries of guerrilla warfare, the British decided that the best way to solve the problem

was to deport them en masse. After a circuitous and tragic journey across the Caribbean, during which thousands perished of disease and hunger, some of the exiles arrived in Belize.

That the Garífuna have preserved their cultural identity testifies to Belize's extraordinary ability to encourage diversity. They have their own religion, a potent mix of ancestor worship and Catholicism; their own language, which, like Carib, has separate male and female dialects; their own music, a percussion-oriented sound known as punta rock; and their own social structure, which dissuades young people from marrying outside their community. In writer Marcella Lewis, universally known as Auntie Madé, the Garífuna also had their own poet laureate. In 2002 the United Nations designated the Garífuna as a World Heritage culture.

$
LATIN AMERICAN
✕ **Innies Restaurant.** At Innies, as at most local restaurants in Hopkins, you're eating in a spot that was once somebody's house or back porch. Here, you can dine inside, or outside and get the full flavor of village life. The food is authentic (though some dishes cater to the taste of tourists), delicious, and inexpensive. You'll find the staff very friendly. Traditional Garífuna dishes such as *hudut* (fish cooked in coconut milk and served with mashed plantains) and *ereba* (grated cassava bread) with *bundiga* (a gravy of grated plantains and coconut) are available, but less exotic dishes like fried chicken and rice and beans with stew chicken are also served. $ *Average main: BZ$12* ⊠ *South end of village, Front St.* ☎ *503/7333* ▭ *No credit cards.*

$
SEAFOOD
✕ **King Cassava Cultural Restaurant and Bar.** With its sand floors King Kassava may not look like much, but when the rum and beer start flowing, the drums start drumming, and the action at the pool table in the back room gets hot, this is the place to be in Hopkins. The food here is just so-so, but the beer is cold and patrons are convivial. Seating is inside and on the covered open-air patio. $ *Average main: BZ$14* ⊠ *Main T-intersection entering village, Junction of Main St. and Hopkins Rd.* ☎ *503/7305* ▭ *No credit cards* ☾ *Closed Mon.*

$
CAFÉ
✕ **Thongs.** This European-run coffee shop and bistro has good coffee, well-prepared breakfast omelets, and satisfying smoothies. For lunch, try the salads. It's open for dinner on weekends only. Thongs is small

but stylish, with Belizean wood carvings and paintings on the walls. The prime tables on the front patio fill up quickly. Free Wi-Fi and helpful, friendly owners. [$] *Average main: BZ$14* ✉ *South of main T-intersection, High St.* ☎ *622/0110* ⏲ *Closed Mon.–Tues. No dinner Wed., Thurs., and Sun.*

WHERE TO STAY

In addition to the resorts and hotels listed *(see below)*, Hopkins has about 20 small guesthouses, mostly run by local villagers but also by some expats who have found that the easygoing Hopkins life suits them. Typically just two or three rooms are built next to the home of the owner, who has an eye to tapping the growing tourism market in Hopkins. Most don't look like much from the outside, but have the necessities including electricity and, usually, private baths. Among the better ones are **Wabien Guest House** (☎ *523/7010*), **Seagull's Nest Guest House** (☎ *522/0600*), **Whistling Seas Vacation Inn** (☎ *608/0016*), **Ransoms Seaside Gardens** (☎ *No phone*), and **Laruni Cabins** (☎ *523/7026*). Rates in most cases are less than BZ$100 for a double, with the least expensive ones, usually a block or two back from the water, costing less than BZ$50 for a double. At these guesthouses it's usually not necessary to make reservations. When you arrive in the village, just walk around until you find one that suits you.

6

$ B&B/INN 🏨 **All Seasons Guest House.** The small but immaculate rooms in this European-style guesthouse with a garden and sunny patio aren't directly on the beach, but the atmosphere, friendly management, and reasonable prices make this an appealing choice nonetheless. **Pros:** pleasant, very clean rooms; lovely garden. **Cons:** rooms in main house not directly on the sea. [$] *Rooms from: BZ$107* ✉ *All Seasons Guest House* ☎ *523/7209* 🌐 *www.allseasonsbelize.com* 🛏 *4 rooms, 3 apartments, 1 cabana.*

$$$$ RESORT 🏨 **Almond Beach Resort & Spa.** Variety is the spice of beach life here, with an assortment of rooms, suites, and villas, some of which can be combined into uber-suites, including a 5,500 square foot family suite. **Pros:** variety of accommodations; spa; full-service resort. **Cons:** not inexpensive. [$] *Rooms from: BZ$632* ✉ *Almond Beach* ☎ *822/3851, 866/624–1516 in U.S. and Canada* 🌐 *www.almondbeachbelize.com* 🛏 *13 rooms, 6 suites, 1 casita* 🍴 *No meals.*

$$ B&B/INN 🏨 **Beaches and Dreams Seafront Inn.** Refugees from Alaska's harsh winters purchased this small beachfront inn, turning it into a popular kick-back beach spot. **Pros:** kick-off-your-shoes atmosphere; steps from the sea; good restaurant. **Cons:** inn offers comfort, not luxury; restaurant rates not cheap. [$] *Rooms from: BZ$300* ✉ *Sittee Point* ☎ *523/7259* 🌐 *www.beachesanddreams.com* 🛏 *5 rooms* 🍴 *Breakfast.*

$$$$ RESORT 🏨 **Belizean Dreams.** This collection of seaside condos is among the most upmarket accommodation choices on the Southern Coast. **Pros:** deluxe condo apartments; units can be combined and configured to meet your needs; friendly service. **Cons:** pool is small; some units have a minimum stay. [$] *Rooms from: BZ$590* ✉ *Hopkins* ☎ *523/7271, 800/456–7150 in U.S. and Canada* 🌐 *www.belizeandreams.com* 🛏 *9 3-bedroom villas (available as 1-, 2-, or 3-bedroom units)* 🍴 *Multiple meal plans.*

$$$$ RESORT Fodor's Choice ★ 🏨 **Hamanasi.** With beautifully landscaped grounds, top-notch accommodations, and an excellent dive program, Hamanasi (Garífuna for "almond") is among Belize's very best beach and dive resorts. **Pros:** well-run resort; deluxe lodging in beautiful beachside setting; high-quality dive trips and inland tours. **Cons:** expensive restaurant; pricey accommodations (but worth it); diving requires a long boat trip to the reef or atolls. [$] *Rooms from: BZ$796* ✉ *Hamanasi, Sittee River Rd.* ☎ *533/7073, 877/552–3483 in U.S.* 🌐 *www.hamanasi.com* 🛏 *10 beachfront rooms, 2 suites, 8 tree houses, 5 deluxe tree houses* 🍴 *Breakfast.*

$ B&B/INN 🏨 **Hopkins Inn.** Greg and Rita Duke are helpful hosts at their little beachfront cottage colony in Hopkins, featuring four cozy cabins with tile floors, ceilings paneled in local hardwoods, fridges, fans, and porches with sea views. **Pros:** on the beach; helpful owners. **Cons:** you may be awakened by the sound of roosters. [$] *Rooms from: BZ$150* ✉ *Hopkins* ☎ *533/7283* 🌐 *www.hopkinsinn.com* 🛏 *4 cottages* 🍴 *Breakfast.*

$$$$ HOTEL 🏨 **Jaguar Reef Lodge.** Jaguar Reef Lodge, the original upscale resort in Hopkins, has been operating for more than 20 years. **Pros:** attractive and well-kept grounds; lovely beachside location. **Cons:** operation has gone through several major changes in recent years, but seems to be back on keel now. [$] *Rooms from: BZ$540* ✉ *Jaguar Reef Resort, Sittee River Rd.* ☎ *731/1132, 888/731–1132 in U.S. and Canada* 🌐 *www.jaguarreef.com* 🛏 *20 units.*

$ B&B/INN 🏨 **Jungle Jeanie by the Sea.** Although not actually in the jungle, this group of seven pleasant wood cabanas on stilts is on about 2 acres of beachfront nicely shaded by coconut palms. **Pros:** comfortable cabanas; lovely stretch of beach; laidback, quiet location south of Hopkins village. **Cons:** short hike to other resorts or to in-town restaurants and bars; don't expect luxury. [$] *Rooms from: BZ$120* ✉ *Sittee River Rd.* ☎ *533/7047* 🌐 *www.junglebythesea.com* 🛏 *7 cabanas* 🍴 *No meals.*

$$$ B&B/INN 🏨 **Parrot Cove Lodge.** This small beachfront resort with rooms in earth tones arranged around a courtyard with a pool, is an attractive option if you don't need all the amenities of the larger resorts but want an excellent restaurant. [$] *Rooms from: BZ$342* ✉ *Sittee Point, 1 mile (1½ km) south of Hopkins* ☎ *523/7225, 877/207–7139 in U.S. and Canada* 🌐 *www.parrotcovelodge.com* 🛏 *5 rooms, 1 suite, 2 2-bedroom apartments* 🍴 *No meals.*

$ B&B/INN 🏨 **Tipple Tree Beya Hotel.** This tiny beachfront guesthouse in the heart of Hopkins village, in business since 1998, provides a comfortable, no-frills alternative to the coast's upmarket resorts. **Pros:** steps from the water; hammocks on the porch. **Cons:** basic, not overly large rooms; can be hot in summer. [$] *Rooms from: BZ$83* ☎ *533/7006* 🌐 *www.tippletree.com* 🛏 *4 rooms, 1 with shared bath, 1 cabin.*

SPORTS AND THE OUTDOORS

BIRD-WATCHING

Cockscomb Basin Wildlife Sanctuary has excellent birding, with some 300 species identified in the reserve. You can also sometimes see the jabiru stork, the largest flying bird in the Western Hemisphere, in the marsh areas just to the west of Hopkins Village. Keep an eye out as you drive into the village from the Southern Highway. North of Hopkins is Fresh Water Creek Lagoon, and south of the village is Anderson Lagoon.

Development, Belize-Style

"People are building $500,000 houses on $5,000 roads!" This is the sentiment of many who watch in amazement as huge condos and luxury houses sprout up along narrow, muddy golf-cart trails. In some areas huge 4,000- to 6,000-square-foot homes are being built where there is no municipal water or sewage system, and in more remote parts of the country no electricity or telephone. One stretch of road on the Placencia peninsula is now sprinkled with massive McMansions, gated communities, and condo projects, built on filled land next to the lagoon.

Belize's lack of infrastructure is nothing new. As late as the 1980s open sewers were common all over Belize City. Even today, in some rural villages, especially in Toledo District, telephone service is a rare commodity, and drinking water comes from a community well. With the unemployment rate in Belize in the low double digits, and with good, high paying jobs scarce, many hope that the new housing boom will provide a needed economic boost and sustainable job growth. But environmentalists are taking a darker view.

In the Hopkins area, near Sittee Point, environmentalists worry that some of the tallest mangroves in the Western Hemisphere will fall prey to developers. It is illegal to remove endangered mangroves in Belize without a government permit, but this rule, like many other environmental protections, is often ignored. It isn't unusual for homeowners and developers with waterfront property to simply tear out these precious trees and deal with possible fines later.

Belize effectively has no zoning or comprehensive land-use planning, though there is now a countrywide building code that applies to individual buildings and houses. Environmental regulations, while strict in theory—every development is required to have a formal Environmental Impact Plan approved by the national government—often fail in practice. Protective regulations and permit procedures are circumvented, flouted, or just plain ignored. Government officials, whose resources are stretched thin, often can't provide oversight on development projects. According to environmentalists, some government officials are corrupt; they believe that developers can do what they like, if the price is right.

Economic growth, the environment, and the housing boom in Belize are complex, with parties facing off on a multitude of issues. Who knows if everyone will ever see eye to eye?

–Lan Sluder

These lagoons and mangrove swamps are home to many waterbirds, including herons and egrets. A kayak trip on the Sittee River should reward you with kingfishers, toucans, and various flycatchers. About 30 minutes by boat off Hopkins is Man-o-War Caye, a bird sanctuary that has one of the largest colonies of frigate birds in the Caribbean, more than 300 nesting birds. **Hamanasi, Jaguar Reef,** and other hotels arrange bird-watching trips. Costs for guided birding tours run from BZ$50 to BZ$200 per person, depending on where you go and the length of time.

CANOEING AND KAYAKING

When kayaking or canoeing on the Sittee River, you can see many birds and, possibly, manatees and crocodiles. Manatees and porpoises are often spotted in the sea just off the Hopkins shore. If you go on a tour with a licensed guide from a local lodge, expect to pay BZ$100–BZ$150 per person. Several hotels in Hopkins, including **Tipple Tree Beya Hotel, Hopkins Inn, Jungle by the Sea,** and **All Seasons Guest House,** rent kayaks, canoes, and other water equipment by the hour or day. Although it's possible to do sea kayaking from Hopkins, often the water is choppy. Long sea-kayaking trips should be tried only by experienced kayakers, preferably with a guide.

> ### DISTANCES
>
> Hopkins is less than 10 minutes by road (rough and potholed) from the paved Southern Highway and is ideally situated for a variety of outdoor adventures, both land and sea. Here's the distance from Hopkins to selected points of interest:
>
> ■ Belize Barrier Reef: 10 miles (17 km)
>
> ■ Cockscomb Basin Wildlife Sanctuary: 10 miles (17 km)
>
> ■ Glover's and Turneffe atolls: 25 miles (42 km)
>
> ■ Mayflower Bocawina National Park: 15 miles (25 km)

CAVING

Caving tours from Hopkins typically go to St. Herman's Cave and the Crystal Cave at Blue Hole National Park on the Hummingbird Highway. Cost is around BZ$120–BZ$150 per person.

DIVING

Diving off Hopkins is very good to terrific. The Barrier Reef is closer here—about 10 miles (17 km) from shore—than it is farther south. Diving also is fairly costly here. Half-day, two-tank dive trips to the South Water Caye Marine Reserve are around BZ$200–BZ$280, not including regulator, BCD, wet suit, and other equipment rental, which can add BZ$50. Dive shops with fast boats can also take you all the way to the atolls—Turneffe, Glover's, and even Lighthouse. These atoll trips generally start early in the morning, at 6 or 7 am, and last all day. Costs for three-tank atoll dives are around BZ$380–BZ$400 for Glover's and Turneffe, and BZ$580 for Lighthouse and the Blue Hole. In late spring, when whale sharks typically show up, local dive shops offer dives to see the Belizean behemoths at Gladden Spit Marine Reserve for around BZ$400. Marine park fees (sometimes included in dive trip charges) are BZ$10 each for South Water and Glover's marine reserves, and BZ$20 for Gladden Spit.

Hamanasi. One of the best diving operations in Southern Belize is at Hamanasi. They have three large, well-equipped dive boats, including a 45-ft. boat with three 200-horsepower outboard engines. ☎ *533/7073* ⊕ *www.hamanasi.com.*

HIKING

Most hiking trips go to Cockscomb Basin Wildlife Sanctuary, where there are a dozen short hiking trails near the visitor center. Full-day trips to Cockscomb generally cost about BZ$120–BZ$150 per person from Hopkins and can be booked through your hotel. If you're a glutton for punishment, you can go on a guided hike to Victoria Peak, the second-highest mountain peak in Belize. The 40-mile (67-km) hike from the visitor center at Cockscomb Basin Wildlife Sanctuary to the top entails inclines of 45 to 60 degrees. Most of these trips require three to five days up and back and cost in the range of BZ$600–BZ$800 per person (minimum of two people). One guide who will take you on jungle tours is **Marcos Cucul** (⊕ *www.mayaguide.bz*). He is a jungle survival guide who is a member of the Belize National Cave and Wilderness Rescue Team.

HORSEBACK RIDING

Local lodges arrange horseback-riding trips, working with ranches near Belmopan and Dangriga. A full-day horseback trip, including transportation to the ranch and lunch, is around BZ$150 per person.

MANATEE-WATCHING TOURS

Local lodges offer trips to Gales Point and the Southern Lagoon to try to spot Antillean manatees, a subspecies of West Indian manatees. These large aquatic mammals—adults weigh 800 to 1,200 pounds—are related to elephants. They're found in shallow waters in lagoons, rivers, estuaries, and coastal areas in much of Belize, and are especially common in the lagoons around Gales Point. These gentle herbivores can live 60 years or longer. The cost of manatee-spotting trips varies, but is around BZ$150 per person. Under Belize government guidelines, you're not permitted to feed manatees, to swim with them, or to approach a manatee with a calf.

SNORKELING

Snorkeling off Hopkins is excellent, though expensive compared with the Northern Cayes. Half-day snorkeling trips from Hopkins to the Belize Barrier Reef, usually a pristine section of it in the South Water Caye Marine Reserve, cost from BZ$150 to BZ$230 per person. These snorkel trips are at least twice as pricey as those to Hol Chan from Ambergris Caye or Caye Caulker, partly because the trip out and back to snorkel sites here is longer, and also because there's less competition to hold prices down. Full-day whale-shark snorkeling trips (usually whale sharks are best seen in late spring and early summer around the time of a full moon) are about BZ$350–BZ$400.

WINDSURFING

Windsurfing is a growing sport in Hopkins, as the wind is a fairly consistent 10 to 15 knots, except in August and September, when it sometimes goes calm. The best winds are in April and May.

Windschief. Windschief rents well-maintained windsurfing equipment for BZ$20 for the first hour, then BZ$10 for additional hours, or BZ$60 a day. Private lessons are BZ$60 an hour. Windschief also has beach cabanas from BZ$60 a night double, and a bar. ☎ 668/6087 ⊕ *www.windsurfing-belize.com*.

SHOPPING

Shopping is limited in Hopkins, where the local "shopping center" is a small clapboard house. Locals traditionally make much of what they use in daily life, from cassava graters to fishing canoes and paddles, and drums and *shakas* (shakers made from a calabash gourd filled with seeds). Around the village, you'll see individuals selling carvings and other local handicrafts made from shells and coconuts. Also, several small shops or stands, including **Wood Work Shop, Kulcha Gift Shop,** and **Tribal Arts,** few of which have phones, sell locally made crafts. You can bargain for the best price, but remember that there are few jobs around Hopkins and that these craftspeople are trying to earn money to help feed their families.

COCKSCOMB BASIN WILDLIFE SANCTUARY

10 miles (17 km) southwest of Hopkins Village.

The mighty jaguar, once the undisputed king of the Central and South American jungles, is now endangered. But it has a haven in the Cockscomb Basin Wildlife Sanctuary, which covers 128,000 acres of lush rain forest in the Cockscomb Range of the Maya Mountains. With the Bladen Nature Reserve to the south, the jaguars have a continuous corridor of about 250,000 acres. Thanks to these reserves, as well as other protected areas around the country, Belize has the highest concentration of jaguars in the world.

GETTING HERE AND AROUND

Maya Centre, at the entrance of the road to Cockscomb, is at Mile 15 of the Southern Highway. You can drive here, or any local bus on the Southern Highway will drop you. From Maya Centre it's 6 miles (10 km) to the park. You can drive, hike (about two hours), or take a local taxi (about BZ$30 one-way). Admission to the sanctuary is BZ$10, and is collected at the crafts shop at Maya Centre.

TIMING

Most visitors come to Cockscomb only on a day visit. However, for the best chance to see wildlife and even a jaguar, a stay of several nights is best.

EXPLORING

FAMILY

Fodor's Choice

★

Cockscomb Basin Wildlife Sanctuary. Some visitors to Cockscomb are disappointed that they don't see jaguars and that wildlife doesn't jump out from behind trees to astound them as they hike the trails. The experience at Cockscomb is indeed a low-key one, and seeing wildlife requires patience and luck. You'll have the best chance of seeing wild animals, perhaps even a jaguar or one of the other large cats, if you stay overnight, preferably for several nights, in the sanctuary. You may also have better luck if you go for an extended hike with a guide. Several nearby lodges, such as Hamanasi, offer night hikes to Cockscomb, departing around dusk and returning around 9 pm.

Cockscomb Basin has native wildlife aside from the jaguars. You might see other cats—pumas, margays, and ocelots—plus coatis, kinkajous, deer, peccaries, and, last but not least, tapirs. Also known as the mountain cow, this shy, curious creature appears to be half horse, half hippo, with a bit of cow and elephant thrown in. Nearly 300 species of birds have been identified in the Cockscomb Basin, including the keel-billed toucan, the king vulture, several hawk species, and the scarlet macaw.

Within the reserve is Belize's best-maintained system of jungle and mountain trails, most of which lead to at least one outstanding swimming hole. The sanctuary also has spectacular views of Victoria Peak and the Cockscomb Range. Bring serious bug spray with you—the reserve swarms with mosquitoes and tiny biting flies called no-see-ums—and wear long-sleeve shirts and long pants. The best times to hike anywhere in Belize are early morning, late afternoon, and early evening, when temperatures are lower and more animals are on the prowl.

You have to check in at a thatch building at Maya Centre on the Southern Highway before proceeding several miles to the visitor center. In the same building is an excellent gift shop selling baskets, wood and fabric crafts, and slate carvings by local Maya craftspeople, at good prices. Buying crafts at this shop, which is run as a co-op by local residents, generally gets more of the money into local hands than if you buy from a commercial gift shop. At Maya Centre there is also a small butterfly farm.

The road from Maya Centre to the Cockscomb ranger station and visitor center winds 6 miles (10 km) through dense vegetation—splendid cahune palms, purple mimosas, orchids, and big-leaf plantains—and as you go higher the marvelous sound of tropical birds, often resembling strange windup toys, grows stronger and stronger. This is definitely four-wheel-drive terrain. You may have to ford several small creeks as well as negotiate deep, muddy ruts. At the end, in a clearing with hibiscus and bougainvillea bushes, you'll find a little office, where you can buy maps of the nature trails, along with restrooms, several picnic tables, cabins, and a campground. The Belize Audubon Society manages the Cockscomb and can assist in making reservations for the simple accommodations in the sanctuary.

Altogether there are some 20 miles (33 km) of marked trails. Walking along these 12 nature trails is a good way to get to know the region. Most are loops of ½–1½ miles (1–2 km), so you can do several in a day. The most strenuous trail takes you up a steep hill; from the top is a magnificent view of the entire Cockscomb Basin. Longer hikes, such as to Victoria Peak, require a guide and several days of strenuous walking.

Hotels and tour operators and guides in Hopkins, Placencia, and Dangriga offer tours to Cockscomb; Hopkins is closest to the sanctuary. ✉ *Outside Maya Centre, off Southern Hwy., Maya Centre* ☎ *227/7369, 223/5004 Belize Audubon Society in Belize City* ⊕ *www.belizeaudubon. org* 🎫 *BZ$10* ☼ *Daily 8–4:30.*

WHERE TO STAY

Although most visitors come to Cockscomb on day trips and stay in Hopkins, Placencia, or Dangriga, you can camp at one of three campgrounds in the reserve for BZ$10 per night per person, or for a little more money you can stay in rooms in a dormitory with solar-generated electricity starting at BZ$40 per person. Also, a small house and three cabins, each with private bath, can accommodate up to four or six people (BZ$106–BZ$150 per house/cabin). An old, primitive cabin with 10 bunk beds is around BZ$16 per person. There's a communal kitchen for cooking—bring your own food and water. No fishing or hunting is allowed in the reserve, and pets are prohibited. Book in Belize City through the **Belize Audubon Society** (☎ *223/5004* ⊕ *www. belizeaudubon.org*).

$ 🏠 **Tutzil Nah Cottages.** Gregorio Chun
RENTAL   and his family, Mopan Maya people who've lived in this area for many generations, provide affordable accommodations in simple thatch cabanas. **Pros:** near Maya Centre; owners highly knowledgeable about Cockscomb; interesting tours available. **Cons:** very basic accommodations; furnishings and beds need repairs and upgrading. $ Rooms from: BZ$50 ⊠ Near Maya Centre, Mile 13½, Southern Hwy., Maya Centre 🕿 533/7045 ⊕ www.maya center.com 🛏 2 cabanas, 1 with share bath.

JAGUARS
Jaguars are shy, nocturnal animals that prefer to keep their distance from humans, so the chances of viewing one in the wild are slim. The jaguar, or *el tigre*, as it's known in Spanish, is a supremely independent creature that shuns even its own kind. Except during a brief mating period and the six months the female spends with her cubs before turning them loose, jaguars roam the rain forest alone.

PLACENCIA PENINSULA

28 miles (47 km) south of Dangriga by road.

The Placencia peninsula is fast becoming one of the major visitor destinations in Belize, one that may eventually rival Ambergris Caye as the most popular resort area in the country. It's one 16-mile- (26-km-) long peninsula, with three different but complementary areas: Northern Peninsula/Maya Beach, Seine Bight, and Placencia Village.

The former dirt track that ran 25 miles (41 km) from the Southern Highway to the tiny community of Riversdale and then down the peninsula to Placencia Village has been paved, and the road is now in excellent condition (beware the speed bumps, however). Beginning at Riversdale, at the elbow where the actual peninsula joins the mainland, you'll get a quick glimpse through mangroves of the startlingly blue Caribbean. As you go south, the Placencia Lagoon is on your right, and behind it in the distance rise the low Maya Mountains, the Cockscomb Range ruffling the tropical sky with its jagged peaks. On your left, a few hundred feet away, beyond the remaining mangroves and a narrow band of beach, is the Caribbean Sea. A broken line of uninhabited cayes grazes the horizon.

The northern end of the peninsula from Riversdale south to Maya Beach once had just a few small seaside houses, and Maya Beach was a sleepy beach community. Now the towering five-story buildings of the Copal Beach condominium development, currently under construction, rise up out of the flat peninsula land. "For Sale" signs dot the roadside, supersize beach- and lagoon-side mansions are going up at The Placencia Residences and elsewhere, and several new condominium communities and resorts are open or planned (though some are struggling to find buyers). These new resorts and condo developments join a small group of laid-back seaside hotels and cabins. The beaches toward the upper end of the peninsula are some of the best on mainland Belize, and more restaurants and shops are starting to open here. One of the best restaurants in all of Belize, the Bistro at Maya Beach Hotel, is usually packed. There's now even a small bowling alley in Maya Beach, Jaguar Lanes.

Roughly midway down the peninsula is the Garífuna village of Seine Bight, struggling to adapt to change. At both the north and south ends of the village upscale resorts and condo developments have sprung up to take advantage of the appealing beaches.

On a sheltered half-moon bay at the southern tip of the peninsula is Placencia Village. Founded by pirates, and long a Creole village, the community is now inhabited by an extraordinary mélange of people, local and expatriate. Most of the hotels in the village are modest, and the shops have tiny selections. Never mind, once you arrive you'll probably just want to lie in a hammock with a good book, perhaps getting up long enough to cool off in the gentle waves or to sip a Belikin at one of the village saloons.

From anywhere on the Placencia peninsula you can dive along the reef, swim in the warm sea water, look for scarlet macaws in Red Bank Village to the southwest (between December and February), explore the Mayan ruins at Mayflower and hike to the waterfalls there, or, on a full day trip, travel to the Mayan sites at Lubaantun and Nim Li Punit near Punta Gorda, or treat yourself to some of the best sportfishing in the country.

GETTING HERE AND AROUND

Both Tropic Air and Maya Island Air fly from Belize City to Placencia, usually with a quick stop in Dangriga, and also from Punta Gorda. The airstrip is about 2 miles (3 km) north of the center of Placencia Village. A so-called international airport has been under construction for years about 2 miles (3 km) northwest of the Placencia peninsula, though in mid-2013 construction on the airport had slowed to a standstill. Details on when and if the airport will open or the flights it will have are, as of this writing, only speculative.

By road, from the Southern Highway at Mile 22.2, it's about 8¼ miles (14 km) to Riversdale, 15¼ miles (26 km) to Maya Beach, 19 miles (31 km) to Seine Bight, and 25 miles (41 km) to Placencia Village. The road is completely paved. Ritchie's Bus Line has buses between Dangriga and Placencia three or four times a day.

Since there's no point-to-point bus service on the peninsula, and taxis are expensive (BZ$50 one-way between Placencia Village and The Placencia hotel area at the northern end of the peninsula), a rental car can be handy. If you haven't rented one in Belize City, you can rent one locally. Currently there are several car-rental agencies on the peninsula, plus a branch of Belize City's Budget agency. Expect to pay BZ$160 and up per day for a rental.

Contacts Barefoot Services. Barefoot rents cars, trucks, SUVs, motorscooters, and golf carts. Car rentals start at BZ$150 a day plus 15% tax and service fee. The company also will deliver vehicles to Dangriga, Hopkins, and Punta Gorda. ✉ *Main St., Placencia* ☎ *523/3066* ⊕ *www.barefootservicesbelize.com* ☺ *Closed Sat.*

TIMING

It takes but a couple of days to explore all of the Placencia peninsula. How long you spend here depends on how much beach and water-sports time you want. Many visitors stay a week or longer, and some end up buying a lot or a house with the intention of retiring here permanently.

SAFETY AND PRECAUTIONS

The influx of construction workers to the peninsula, some from Guatemala and Honduras, has somewhat changed the security situation here. Petty thefts and break-ins are more common. However, overall the Placencia peninsula is safe.

NORTHERN PENINSULA AND MAYA BEACH

36 miles (61 km) south of Dangriga by road.

Some of the best beaches on the Placencia peninsula—and therefore on mainland Belize—are at the northern end of the peninsula and the Maya Beach areas. The light khaki-color sand is soft, the surf is gentle, and, while the Barrier Reef is miles off the coast here as it is elsewhere in this part of Belize, there is good snorkeling a short kayak ride away, around False Caye just east of Maya Beach.

GETTING HERE AND AROUND

From the Southern Highway you go about 8¼ miles (14 km) east to Riversdale, where the Placencia peninsula formally meets the mainland. From there, head south through the northern end of the peninsula 7 miles (12 km) to Maya Beach.

WHERE TO EAT

$$ SEAFOOD

🍴 **Mango's of Maya Beach.** Frank Da Silva, long-time chef at the award-winning restaurant at Inn at Robert's Grove, took over Mango's, raising this casual beachside, three-story thatch-roofed eatery and bar to a new level. The chef brought with him some of his favorites from Robert's Grove, such as conch fritters with chipotle mayonnaise. Many of the dishes are bar snacks, such as fajitas, peel-and-eat shrimp, or chicken wings. You can also sip a beer, enjoy the sea view and breezes from the water, and feast on bigger dishes like filet mignon or baby back ribs. Open 11 am to midnight daily except Monday. [$] *Average main: BZ$24* ✉ *Maya Beach, Placencia Rd.* ☎ *523/8102* ⏲ *Closed Mon.*

$$$ SEAFOOD Fodor's Choice ★

🍴 **Maya Beach Hotel Bistro.** Before ending up on the Placencia peninsula, Maya Beach Bistro owners John and Ellen Lee (he's Australian, she's American) traveled the world and worked in 20 countries. They obviously figured out what travelers love, because their bistro by the beach is one of our favorite restaurants in all of Belize. It won "Restaurant of the Year" honors for the last two years from the Belize Tourism Board. The Bistro has been expanded to provide more beachside seating. The setting, in a covered patio by the swimming pool with breezes from the sea, which is just a few yards away, is everything you come to the Caribbean to enjoy. The menu changes regularly, but among the standards you'll go gaga over are nut-encrusted snapper and cocoa-dusted pork chop on a risotto cake. There also are nightly seafood specials. The Bistro has a selection of small plates and appetizers including fish cakes, coconut shrimp, and honey-coconut ribs. No matter what you choose, you'll find the flavors and presentation interesting and creatively inspired. At breakfast, don't miss the fresh-baked cinnamon roll—it's big enough for Godzilla. $ *Average main: BZ$42* ⊠ *Maya Beach Bistro, Maya Beach Hotel* ☎ *533/8040* ⊕ *www.mayabeachhotel.com* ⌂ *Reservations essential.*

WHERE TO STAY

$$ 🏠 **Barnacle Bill's Beach Bungalows.** "Barnacle Bill" Taylor, known as the wit of Maya Beach, and wife Adriane rent a pair of wooden Mennonite bungalows set among palm trees on a lovely beach about 80 feet from the sea; each cottage is on stilts and has a private bath and a kitchen where you can prepare your own meals. **Pros:** friendly spot; helpful owners; nice place just to relax. **Cons:** don't expect luxury. $ *Rooms from: BZ$251* ⊠ *23 Maya Beach Way* ☎ *533/8110* ⊕ *www. barnaclebills-belize.com* ⇨ *2 cottages* ⏿⊙ *No meals.*

B&B/INN

$$$ 🏠 **Green Parrot Beach Houses.** This resort has Mennonite-built cottages, some showing their age, along a nice stretch of beach, each with a kitchenette and dining area. **Pros:** good option for families; pleasant beach area. **Cons:** no swimming pool; time to upgrade and renovate lodging facilities. $ *Rooms from: BZ$405* ⊠ *No. 1 Maya Beach, 4 miles (6½ km) north of Seine Bight* ☎ *533/8188* ⊕ *www.greenparrot-belize.com* ⇨ *6 cabins, 2 cabanas* ⏿⊙ *Breakfast.*

B&B/INN

$$ 🏠 **Maya Beach Hotel.** This is the kind of small, unpretentious beachfront hotel that many come to Belize to enjoy, but few actually find. **Pros:** like a small Caribbean beach hotel should be; good value; excellent restaurant. **Cons:** rooms are only a couple of steps up from basic; Wi-Fi is a little spotty. $ *Rooms from: BZ$238* ⊠ *Maya Beach* ☎ *533/8040* ⊕ *www. mayabeachhotel.com* ⇨ *5 rooms, 3 apartments, 2 cottages* ⏿⊙ *No meals.*

B&B/INN
Fodor's Choice
★

$$$ 🏠 **The Placencia.** Transplant an upscale, gated Florida condo community to Belize, and you might end up with something like The Placencia, with tennis courts, an upscale restaurant, and the nation's largest swimming pool. **Pros:** beautiful beach; huge pool; attractive condos. **Cons:** meal plans are pricey; rarely many guests; expensive cab ride to Placencia village; high-rise condos and McMansions out of character with rest of peninsula. $ *Rooms from: BZ$426* ⊠ *Northern end of Placencia peninsula, Placencia* ☎ *533/4117, 800/810–8567 In U.S. and Canada* ⊕ *www. theplacencia.com* ⇨ *92 condo apartments* ⏿⊙ *Multiple meal plans.*

RESORT

$$ 🏠 **Singing Sands.** The six wood-and-thatch cabanas here, recently redone with polished hardwood floors, are nicely decorated and attractively priced. **Pros:** small, owner-run beach hotel; pleasant cottages; good restaurant; reasonable prices. **Cons:** smallish rooms. $ *Rooms from: BZ$251* ⊠ *714 Maya Beach Rd., 6 miles (10 km) north of airstrip* ☎ *533/3022, 888/201–6425 In U.S. and Canada* ⊕ *www.singingsands. com* ⇨ *6 cabanas, 4 apartments* ⏿⊙ *No meals.*

B&B/INN

SHOPPING

Spectarte Art and Garden Gallery. You won't find tacky souvenirs here. Instead, you'll see unusual pottery, weavings, carvings, paintings, and home furnishings. Many of the items are of Maya origin, gathered on field trips to remote areas of Toledo. This is one of the country's best art and home-furnishings galleries. ⊠ *100 Embarcadero Rd., directly across road from Green Parrot* ☎ *533/8019* ⊕ *www.spectarte.com* ⊗ *Closed Tues. and Wed.*

6

SEINE BIGHT

47 miles (77 km) south of Dangriga.

Like Placencia, its Creole neighbor to the south, Seine Bight is a small coastal fishing village. It may not be for long, though, as Placencia's resorts are stretching north to and through this Garífuna community, one of six predominantly Garífuna centers in Belize. The beach, especially south of Seine Bight, is excellent, though near the village garbage sometimes mars the view. Hotels do rake and clean their beachfronts, and several community cleanups have been organized in an effort to solve this problem. All the businesses catering to tourists are along the paved main road (actually, it's the only road) that leads south to Placencia Village. The name Seine Bight derives from a type of net, called a seine, used by local fishermen. Bight means an indentation or inward bend in the coastline.

GETTING HERE AND AROUND

By road, Seine Bight is around 19 miles (31 km) from the Southern Highway. By air, you'll fly into the Placencia airstrip.

TIMING

You can explore Seine Bight in a few hours at most. How long you stay depends on how much beach and water time you want. Many visitors stay a week or more.

WHERE TO EAT

$$$ AUSTRIAN 🍴 **Danube.** Wiener schnitzel and Fleischfondue in Placencia? If you have a yen for something different, most of the Austrian and other dishes are very good, if a bit pricey. Danube has a pleasant, relaxed atmosphere with art on the walls by the co-owner, Simone Gareis, and a screened porch for outdoor dining. [$] *Average main: BZ$42* ✉ *On main road 2½ miles (4 km) north of the Placencia airstrip, Placencia Rd.* ☎ *610/0132* ⏲ *No lunch. Closed Sun. and Mon.*

WHERE TO STAY

$$$ RESORT 🏨 **The Inn at Robert's Grove.** Robert's Grove is one of the most complete resorts in Belize with kayaks, windsurfers, small sailboats, a nicely equipped gym, and boats for diving with whale sharks. **Pros:** complete resort facilities; lovely seaside rooms and suites; lots of tours and on-site activities. **Cons:** nothing particularly exotic here; expensive; tennis no longer offered. [$] *Rooms from: BZ$452* ✉ *½ mile (1 km) south of Seine Bight, Placencia Rd., Placencia* ☎ *523/3565, 800/565–9757 in U.S. and Canada* 🌐 *www.robertsgrove.com* 🛏 *20 rooms, 32 suites* 🍽 *Multiple meal plans.*

$$$ RENTAL Fodor's Choice ★ 🏨 **Laru Beya Villas.** Laru Beya, a condo colony whose name means "on the beach" in the Garífuna language, sits on 7 beachfront acres, with well-priced rooms and suites that are bright and sunny. **Pros:** well-designed rooms and suites; a good value. **Cons:** minigolf course needs maintenance. [$] *Rooms from: BZ$333* ✉ *½ mile (1 km) south of Seine Bight, south of Robert's Grove* ☎ *523/3476, 800/890–8010 in U.S. and Canada* 🌐 *www.larubeya.com* 🛏 *30 units* 🍽 *Multiple meal plans.*

$$$ RENTAL 🏨 **Maine Stay Cabanas.** These well-designed cabanas on a 400-foot stretch of beautiful beach are ideal for families and for longer stays. **Pros:** attractive and comfortable suites, in either two-bedroom or one-bedroom configuratoins; ideal for families and for longer stays. **Cons:**

no restaurant on-site; no pool. [$] *Rooms from: BZ$497* ✉ *Placencia Rd.* ☎ *523/3507, 877/458–7581* 🌐 *www.traversbelize.com* 🛏 *3 cabanas (1- and 2-bedroom)* 🍴 *No meals.*

SHOPPING

Lola's Art. Painter and writer Lola Delgado moved to Seine Bight from Belize City in the late 1980s. Her workshop, Lola's Art, displays her bold, cheerful acrylic paintings of local women and scenes (BZ$100 and up). She also sells hand-painted cards, painted gourd masks, and some of her husband's wood carvings. Espresso and pastries are available. The workshop is up a flight of steps in a tiny wooden house off the main street, behind the football field. ☎ *601/1913, 523/3342* 🌐 *www.lolasartinbelize.blogspot.com.*

PLACENCIA VILLAGE

5 miles (8 km) south of Seine Bight, 52 miles (85 km) south of Dangriga.

Placencia Village is a mini, downscale version of Key West, laid-back, hip, and full of atmospheric watering holes. At the end of the road, the village is the main residential center on the peninsula, with a population of around 800, predominantly Creoles. It is also the peninsula's commercial hub—if you can call a small village a hub—with a half-dozen grocery stores, a couple of hardware stores, and the majority of the region's restaurants and bars. Traffic on the Main Road (also called Main Street, and farther north Placencia Road) through the village is surprisingly heavy, and parking can be problematic. Most of the hotels in the village proper are budget spots, but just north of the village, between it and the airport, are several upscale beach resorts and condo developments.

Sometimes billed as the world's narrowest street, a single concrete path through the village called the Sidewalk is just wide enough for two people. Setting off purposefully from the southern end of the village near the harbor, the path meanders through everyone's backyard. It passes wooden cottages on stilts overrun with bougainvillea and festooned with laundry, along with a few shops and tour offices, and then, as if it had forgotten where it was headed in the first place, peters out abruptly in a little clearing. Paved sidewalks and dirt paths run between the Sidewalk and the Main Road through Placencia Village. Stroll along the Sidewalk, and you've seen the village. If you don't mind its being a little rough around the edges, you'll be utterly enchanted by this rustic village, where the palm trees rustle, the waves lap the shore, and no one is in a hurry.

Along the Sidewalk and the Main Road are most of the village's guesthouses and cafés, which serve rice and beans, burgers, and seafood.

In 2013, a large new dock complex was completed at the foot of the village, just off the Sidewalk and near the end of the main road. At this writing it's still unclear how exactly the dock will be used. Powerful political and economic interests have long pushed for a cruise ship terminal in southern Belize, either on the Placencia peninsula or on a caye off the coast. Polls and straw votes show that a large majority of local residents oppose large-scale cruise ship tourism in the area, but as of this writing nothing has been officially decided.

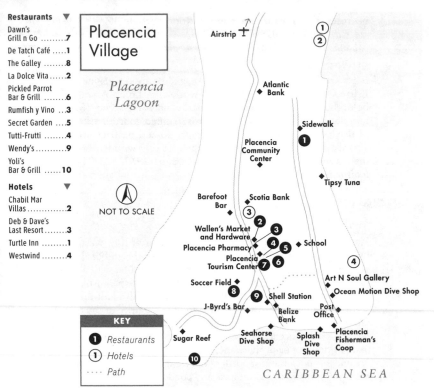

GETTING HERE AND AROUND

By road, Placencia Village is around 25 miles (41 km) from the Southern Highway. By air, you'll fly into the Placencia airstrip. From the airstrip to the village is a BZ$12 taxi ride for up to two people, BZ$6 each for three or more. You can also get here by boat, the Hokey Pokey, from Independence/Mango Creek across the Placencia Lagoon, BZ$10. There are several Ritchie buses a day to Placencia Village from Dangriga.

Contacts Hokey Pokey ⊠ *Main Street at MnM Dock* ☎ *523/4045 Placencia Tourism Center.*

TIMING

Placencia Village is small and can be seen in a day or less. How long you choose to stay depends on how much relaxing and beach and water time you desire. Many visitors stay a week or longer.

SAFETY

Most visitors say they feel safe on the Placencia peninsula. However, petty theft is a perennial problem, especially in Placencia Village. Quite a few budget travelers report thefts from their hotel rooms. A few Placencia hotels, and most of the more upscale resorts up the peninsula, have security guards. Note that at night the village and its beachfront are not well lighted.

WHERE TO EAT

$$ CARIBBEAN FAMILY

🍴 **Dawn's Grill 'n Go.** Friendly service, local atmosphere, good food simply prepared, modest prices, ice-cold beer—what more could you want? Dawn's Grill 'n Go is in a small no-frills building with screened windows (no a/c) on the main street in Placencia village. For breakfast, try an omelet with local sausage; for lunch, we like the fish tacos; and for dinner go for the grilled or fried chicken. [$] *Average main: BZ$20* ✉ *Main St., next to BTL office* ☎ *523/4079* 💳 *No credit cards* 🕒 *Closed Sun.*

$$ SEAFOOD

🍴 **De Tatch Café.** This open-air bar and restaurant near the sea with a "tatch" (thatch) roof long has been one of the most popular hangouts in the village. Try the huge shrimp burrito and wash it down with a few cold Belikins. If you go fishing and catch something, the restaurant will prepare it for you. Breakfasts are good here, too. [$] *Average main: BZ$18* ✉ *In village near Seaspray Hotel* ☎ *503/3385* 🕒 *Closed Wed.*

$$ SEAFOOD

🍴 **The Galley.** One of Placencia's oldest restaurants is making a comeback under new management (though the manager is part of the original family of owners). Located in an old building behind the football (soccer) pitch in Placencia village—the local team, the Placencia Assassins, play here—The Galley serves seafood such as fried shrimp and garlic conch, along with pizza and other dishes. It's one of a few places in the area where you can still get a seaweed shake, which is, well, an acquired taste. [$] *Average main: BZ$25* ✉ *Behind soccer field* ☎ *523/3133* 🕒 *Closed Sun.*

$$$ ITALIAN Fodor's Choice ★

🍴 **La Dolce Vita.** In a slightly Fellini-esque setting, upstairs over Wallen's Store, La Dolce Vita brings authentic antipasti, bruschetta, and pasta dishes to Placencia. The spaghetti carbonara, with the owner's own home-smoked bacon, is amazing. Try the signature penne dolce vita with a shrimp and zucchini sauce or the linguini with calamari, octopus, squid, and shrimp. Most dishes are in large portions. The Rome-born chef-owner, Simone DeAngelis, imports Italian pastas, olive oils, and wines to make sure everything is top quality. With opera music playing softly in the background, it's like being in a small, family-run restaurant in Italy. [$] *Average main: BZ$28* ✉ *Main Street, above Wallen's Store* ☎ *523/3115* 🌐 *www.ladolcevitaplacencia.com* 🕒 *No lunch.*

$$ AMERICAN

🍴 **Pickled Parrot Bar & Grill.** This long-established feet-in-the-sand restaurant and bar with a thatch roof is in the heart of Placencia village. Try the Philly cheesesteak or the burgers. The bar's mascot is a friendly three-legged border collie. [$] *Average main: BZ$20* ✉ *Off main road, behind Wallen's Market* ☎ *636/7068* 💳 *No credit cards* 🕒 *Closed Tues.*

$$$ SEAFOOD

🍴 **Rumfish y Vino.** This hip spot run by transplanted New Yorkers, in a breezy second-floor location near Tutti-Frutti, is a good place to have drinks, tapas, interesting seafood creations, and Italian pasta. Try the small plates of Thai shrimp cakes or *pescado relleño* (red snapper stuffed with shrimp). Bigger dishes include fish stew and several pasta and seafood dishes. There's a good selection of Italian and California wines. [$] *Average main: BZ$27* ✉ *Placencia Village Square, off Main St., near Tutti-Frutti* ☎ *523/3293* 🌐 *www.rumfishyvino.com* 🕒 *No lunch.*

6

$$$ ECLECTIC Fodor's Choice ★ 🍴 **Secret Garden Restaurant.** What was once Placencia's first coffeehouse has gone upmarket under new management, serving sophisticated international meals at dinner in an open-air, palm-lined, romantically lighted garden. Enjoy the friendly service and an eclectic mix of dishes including ceviche, jerk chicken, black bean soup, and bacon-wrapped steak. The chef can do vegan and gluten-free dishes. Save room for the delicious key lime pie, the best in Placencia. [$] *Average main: BZ$34* ✉ *In village, behind Wallen's store* ☎ *523/3420* 🌐 *www.secretgardenplacencia.com* 🕒 *No lunch.*

$ CAFÉ Fodor's Choice ★ 🍴 **Tutti-Frutti.** Authentic, Italian-style gelato is the thing here, and it's absolutely delicious, the equal of any you'll find in New York, Buenos Aires, or even Rome. Try the tropical fruit flavors, such as banana, lime, coconut, papaya, and mango, or an unusual flavor such as sugar corn, all created from natural ingredients by Italian owner Tiziana Del Col. Beware: You may become addicted and return day after day to sample new flavors. [$] *Average main: BZ$8* ✉ *Main Square, Main Rd.* 💳 *No credit cards* 🕒 *Often closed at the end of summer.*

$$ SEAFOOD 🍴 **Wendy's.** No, not that Wendy's. This Wendy's is a local restaurant operated by Wendy Lemus. It moved to a new location in an attractive new building, and unfortunately prices have increased, while the service has decreased. However, the grilled fish is still fresh and delicious, and there are many dishes to choose from, including creole items like cowfoot's soup for lunch on Friday and mestizo dishes like escabeche with fresh flour tortillas. You can dine inside (but there's no a/c) or outside on the porch. [$] *Average main: BZ$20* ✉ *Main St.* ☎ *523/3335* 🌐 *www.wendyscuisine.com.*

$ BARBECUE 🍴 **Yoli's Bar & Grill.** The best sea views in the village are from your table at Yoli's. Built on a pier jutting out into the Placencia Harbor, Yoli's attracts a sizeable crowd at night. It's also a pleasant place to sip a Belikin and enjoy the sea breezes during the day. This is more a bar than a restaurant, but you can get some basic food cooked at Merlene's restaurant nearby and brought out to the pier. There's usually a BBQ on Sundays. [$] *Average main: BZ$14* ✉ *Harborfront in Bakader area* ☎ *523/3183.*

WHERE TO STAY

$$$$ RENTAL Fodor's Choice ★ 🏨 **Chabil Mar.** Chabil Mar means "beautiful sea" in Ket'chi Mayan, and the sea and almost 400 feet of beach are indeed gorgeous at this gated luxury condo resort. **Pros:** beautiful grounds; luxurious condos; lovely stretch of beach; every comfort and convenience at hand. **Cons:** expensive, but worth it. [$] *Rooms from: BZ$714* ✉ *Main road north of Placencia Village, 2284 Placencia Rd., Placencia* ☎ *523/3606, 866/417–2377 in U.S. and Canada* 🌐 *www.chabilmarvillas.com* 🛏 *19 villas* 🍽 *Multiple meal plans.*

$ B&B/INN 🏨 **Deb & Dave's Last Resort.** This simple budget spot in Placencia Village is owned by Deb and Dave Vernon, and while it's nothing fancy, the rooms are spotless, and it's set in pleasant gardens. **Pros:** good value in budget accommodations; clean; well-run. **Cons:** not directly on the beach. [$] *Rooms from: BZ$55* ✉ *Back Rd., near Tipsy Tuna* ☎ *523/3207* 🛏 *4 rooms with shared baths* 🍽 *No meals.*

$$$$ **Turtle Inn.** Francis Ford Coppola's second hotel in Belize is if noth-
RESORT ing else exotic, with the furnishings, art, and most of the construction
materials bought in Bali by the film director and his wife. **Pros:** exotic
Balinese furnishings; delightful outdoor showers; beautiful seaside setting. **Cons:** no a/c; food and drinks are surprisingly expensive; some
maintenance needed. [$] *Rooms from: BZ$1068* ⊠ *Placencia Rd., 2
miles (3 km) north of Placencia village* ☎ *824/4912, 800/746–3743
in U.S. and Canada* ⊕ *www.coppolaresorts.com* ⤴ *25 thatch villas*
|◎| *Breakfast*

$ **Westwind.** A favorite with anglers and beachcombers, this is a
HOTEL dependable, no-frills spot to rest your head. **Pros:** what a beachcomber
looks for; friendly and secure. **Cons:** not for the luxury-minded.
[$] *Rooms from: BZ$148* ⊠ *Beachfront, near middle of Placencia Village* ☎ *523/3255* ⊕ *www.westwindhotel.com* ⤴ *12 rooms, 1 suite, 1
house* |◎| *No meals.*

VILLAS AND RENTALS

In addition to hotels and beach resorts, Placencia has a growing number of vacation rentals, and apartments that are available on a weekly,
sometimes daily, basis. Many are listed by their owners on the Vacation
Rental by Owner website, ⊕ *www.VRBO.com.*

Sandhill Ltd. This quality real estate management company in Placencia
offers about a dozen houses, apartments and other vacation rentals.
[$] *Rooms from: BZ$300* ⊠ *Placencia* ☎ *523/3061* ⊕ *www.silbelize.com*
⤴ *12 houses and apartments* |◎| *No meals.*

SHOPPING

The highlight of shopping on the Placencia peninsula is going to the
grocery store, and the largest (Wallen's Market and Top Value) are
about the size of convenience stores, so you get the picture. The larger
resorts, including Inn at Robert's Grove and Turtle Inn, do have gift
shops. In Placencia Village a few small gift shops and arts-and-craft
galleries are on the Sidewalk

Art 'n Soul Gallery. This little gallery on the south end of the Sidewalk
has paintings by owner Greta Leslie, along with work by other Belizean
artists and some jewelry, too. ⊠ *South end of the Sidewalk* ☎ *503/3088.*

Sunova Beach Gift Shop. This spot sells T-shirts, wood carvings, and local
art. ⊠ *On sidewalk near Tipsy Tuna* ☎ *523/4060.*

Wallen's Market & Pharmacy. The oldest grocery in Placencia, though no
longer the largest (Top Value grocery at the north end of the village is
the largest), Wallen's Market has the basics, and it's even air-conditioned. Wallen's also has a pharmacy and hardware store. ⊠ *Main St.,
across from soccer field* ☎ *523/3128* ⊙ *Daily 9–5.*

NIGHTLIFE

Nightlife in Placencia is generally limited to drinking at a handful of
local bars, of which Barefoot and Tipsy Tuna are perhaps the most
popular. You can hear live music on weekends at Barefoot, Tipsy Tuna,
and J-Byrds.

Barefoot Beach Bar. This roadside bar is always busy. Expect lots of rum drinks and plenty of cold beer, along with bar food. There's live music Wednesday through Saturday nights. At this writing Barefoot is reportedly moving to a new development near its present location in the village sometime in 2014. ⊠ *Main St., next to MnM Dock* ☎ *523/3515* ⊙ *Daily 11 am–midnight.*

The Flying Pig. This roadside sports bar serves ribs, burgers, pizza, and other bar food, along with quantities of Belikin. TFP features local musicians at open mic nights. ⊠ *Placencia Rd., ½ mile (1 km) north of airstrip, Placencia* ☎ *602/6391.*

J-Byrds Bar. J-Byrds Bar attracts a fairly hard-drinking crowd, and there's live music on Friday nights. ⊠ *Near docks, Placencia Village* ☎ *523/3412* ⊙ *10 am–midnight.*

Tipsy Tuna. The popular Tipsy Tuna has an inside sports bar and an open-air beach bar. There's live music some weekend nights, and you can always shoot pool or watch sports on a big-screen TV. Fill up on bar snacks like burgers, fajitas, tacos, and shrimp baskets. There's karaoke some nights and Garífuna drumming occasionally. ☎ *523/3089* ⊙ *Sun.– Wed. 11:30 am–midnight; Thurs.–Sat. 11:30 am–2 am.*

SPORTS AND THE OUTDOORS

BOWLING

FAMILY **Jaguar Lanes.** About the last place you'd expect to find a bowling alley is Maya Beach, but Jaguar Lanes is here, and it's fun! This little four-lane alley, air-conditioned, with jaguar murals on the walls and pine ceilings, has everything your lanes back home have, except you have to keep score on paper. Games are BZ$6, and shoe rental BZ$2.50. ⊠ *Maya Beach* ☎ *664/2583* ⊙ *Closed Thurs.*

FISHING

The fly-fishing on the flats off the cayes east of the Placencia peninsula is some of Belize's best. This is one of the top areas in the world for permit. The area from Dangriga south to Gladden Caye is called "Permit Alley," and the mangrove lagoons off Punta Ycacos and other points south of Placencia are also terrific permit fisheries. You'll encounter plentiful tarpon—they flurry 10 deep in the water at times—as well as snook. You can also catch king mackerel, barracuda, wahoo, and cubera snapper. However, a lingering impact of Hurricane Iris in 2001 is that there are no longer as many good bonefish flats close to shore at Placencia. Bonefish are still around, but they're now several miles away, off the cayes.

GUIDES

Most of the better hotels also can arrange guides, many of whom pair with specific hotels. Fishing guides in Placencia are down-to-earth, self-taught guys who have fished these waters for years. They use small skiffs called *pangas*. For more information and help matching a local guide to your specific needs, get in touch with **Mary Toy at Destinations Belize** (☎ *523/4018* ⊕ *www.destinationsbelize.com*). You may want to talk with **Wayne Castellanos** (☎ *634/2852*), considered one of the best fishing guides in the area. **Wyatt Cabral** (☎ 523/3534 ⊕ *www.wyattsfishing.com*) is native of Placencia who is considered another one of the best fly-fishing guides. Another well-known fly-fishing guide is **Julian Cabral** (☎ 610/1068).

Expect to pay around BZ$500–BZ$750 for a full day of fly-fishing, spin casting, or trolling. That includes your guide, boat, and lunch. If you're on a budget, you can rent a canoe and try fishing the Placencia lagoon on your own, where you may catch snook, barracuda, and possibly other fish.

GEAR

The guides usually provide trolling gear for free, but they charge about BZ$40 a day for light spin-casting tackle gear, and you may be happier with your own spinning gear. If you're serious about fly-fishing, of course you'll want to bring your own gear. Don't forget to bring polarized sunglasses, a good fishing hat, insect repellent, lots of sunscreen and lip salve, and, if you're wading, thick-soled flats boots.

SAILING

The Moorings. Based at Laru Beya Marina along with sister charter company Sunsail, The Moorings offers bareboat and captained monohull and catamaran charters, with a week's bareboat sailing going for around BZ$9,000–BZ$16,000. ⊠ *Laru Beya Marina, Laru Beya Resort, Placencia* ☎ *523/3206, 888/952–8420 in U.S. and Canada* ⊕ *www.moorings.com.*

SCUBA DIVING

This far south, the reef is as much as 20 miles (33 km) offshore, necessitating boat rides of 45 minutes to nearly two hours to reach dive sites. Because this part of the reef has fewer cuts and channels, it's also more difficult to get out to the seaward side, where you'll find the best diving. As a result, most of the diving in this region is done from offshore cayes, which are surrounded by small reefs, usually with gently sloping drop-offs of about 80–100 feet. This isn't the place for spectacular wall dives—you're better off staying in the north or heading out to the atolls. Near Moho Caye, southeast of Placencia, you'll find brilliant red-and-yellow corals and sponges that rarely appear elsewhere in Belize.

Two marine reserves off Placencia are popular snorkeling and diving spots. Laughing Bird Caye, Belize's smallest marine reserve, about 13 miles (22 km) off Placencia, is a popular spot for snorkeling. Whale sharks, *Rhincodon typus,* gentle giants of the sea, appear off Placencia in the Gladden Spit area, part of the Gladden Spit and Silk Cayes Marine Reserves 26 miles (43 km) east of Placencia, in late spring and early summer. You can snorkel or dive with them on day trips (around BZ$180–BZ$200 for snorkel trips, BZ$330–BZ$370 for dives) from Placencia. The best time to see whale sharks is three or four days before and after a full moon, March through June. Admission fee to each of these marine reserves is BZ$20; the admission typically is included in the dive or snorkel shop fee.

Diving costs a little more in Placencia than most other places in Belize, in part due to the distance to the reef and the atolls. Full-day trips to the reef, including two-tank dive, all gear, and lunch, run BZ$190–BZ$260 per person. Two- and three-tank dive trips to Glover's Atoll are around BZ$300–BZ$450. Snorkeling trips start at around BZ$80–BZ$130, and a snorkeling tour to Glover's Atoll is around BZ$175–BZ$220.

GUIDES

Most of the larger resorts, like the Inn at Robert's Grove and Turtle Inn, have dive shops and also offer snorkel trips. Avadon Divers and the Splash Dive Center are considered two of the best dive shops in the region.

Avadon Divers. Avadon Divers, which won a recent Belize Tourism Board award for "Best Tour Operator of the Year," is generally considered one of the best dive operations in southern Belize. Besides diving and snorkeling on the reef and atolls, including whale shark trips in late spring and early summer, Avadon also does kayaking and fishing trips along with tours on the mainland to Mayan sites, nature preserves, and zip lines. ⊠ *Placencia Rd., just south of airstrip, Placencia* ☎ *503/3377, 888/509–5617 in U.S.* ⊕ *www.avadondiversbelize.com.*

Ocean Motion. For snorkeling trips check with Ocean Motion, on the Sidewalk in the heart of Placencia Village. A full-day snorkeling trip to Laughing Bird Caye is BZ$130 per person and a day trip to Ranguana Caye is BZ$150. Rates include taxes, snorkel gear, and a lunch grilled on a caye. Ocean Motion also does mainland trips to Monkey River, Mayan sites near Punta Gorda, and to other destinations. ⊠ *Placencia* ☎ *523/3363* ⊕ *www.oceanmotionplacencia.com.*

THE DEEP
SOUTH

By Lan Sluder

Toledo District in the Deep South has Belize's only extensive, genuine rain forest, and its canopy of trees conceals a plethora of wildlife, including jaguars, margays, tapirs, and loads of tropical birds. The area's rich Mayan heritage is just being unearthed, with archaeologists at work at Pusilha, Nim Li Punit, Uxbenká, and elsewhere. Contemporary Maya—mainly Mopan and Ket'chi (other transliterations into English include Kekchi, Kekche, Q'eqchi', and others)—still live in villages around the district, as they have for centuries, along with the Garífuna, Creoles, East Indians, and others who constitute the Toledo population of about 31,000.

Lush, green, tropical Toledo also calls to chocolate lovers, as it's home to hundreds of small cacao growers. Cadbury's Green & Black gets some of its organic chocolate for Maya Gold chocolate bars from Toledo, and several small Belizean chocolate makers, including Cotton Tree, Goss, Ixcacao, Belcampo, and Kakaw, create gourmet chocolate from organic Toledo cacao beans. In 2007 a cacao festival was organized, and it continues annually as the Chocolate Festival of Belize, held on Commonwealth Day weekend in late May (dates vary—see ⊕ *www. chocolatefestivalofbelize.com*).

Toledo also has rice plantations, citrus orchards, and stands of mangos, pineapples, bananas, and coconuts, so you'll never go hungry here.

For many years, ill-maintained roads, spotty communications, and the country's highest annual rainfall—as much as 180 to 200 inches—kept Belize's southernmost region off-limits to all but the most adventurous of travelers. The precipitation hasn't changed, but with improvements to the Southern Highway—beautifully paved the entire way from Dangriga to Punta Gorda—and the opening of new lodges and hotels, the riches of Toledo District are finally becoming accessible. The San Antonio Road, from the area called "The Dump" on the Southern Highway to the Guatemala border, is currently being paved. When the road is completed, and an anticipated customs and immigration facility constructed, likely by late 2014 or early 2015, it's expected that a new, legal land border crossing between Belize and Guatemala will further open the Deep South to tourism and development.

Local residents are split on the wisdom of this. Some say it will mean not only more tourism dollars but also new Guatemalan markets for Toledo farm products. Others worry that the new border crossing will create new problems for Toledo.

Other areas of Belize (not to mention Guatemala and Honduras) may have more spectacular ruins than Toledo, but where the Deep South shines is in its contemporary Mayan culture. Dozens of Mopan and Ket'chi villages exist much as they have for centuries, as do the Garífuna villages of Punta Negra and Barranco and the town of Punta Gorda (PG). You can visit some of the villages and even stay awhile in guesthouses or homestay programs. If don't have time to do an overnight, you can participate in a new, one-day Maya learning experience tour in local homes in Big Falls village.

Don't expect to come to Toledo and lounge on the sand. The area doesn't have good beaches except for a few accessible only by boat. The coastal waters of the Gulf of Honduras are often muddy from silt deposited by numerous rivers flowing from the Maya Mountains. What *can* you expect? Exceptional fishing (Toledo has one of the world's best permit fisheries) and cayes off the coast that are well worth exploring. The closest are the Snake Cayes; farther out are the Sapodilla Cayes, the largest of which is Hunting Caye, with a horseshoe-shape bay at the caye's eastern end with beaches of white coral where turtles nest in late summer. The downside is that visits to the cayes and to inland sites usually require expensive tours, as distances are considerable, and public transportation is limited. The completion of the new road to Guatemala in 2014–15 should make trips and tours to many inland sites easier and, perhaps, cheaper.

ORIENTATION AND PLANNING

7

GETTING ORIENTED

The main road to the Deep South is the paved Southern Highway, which runs 100 miles (164 km) from the intersection of the Hummingbird Highway/Stann Creek District Highway to Punta Gorda (PG).

As you travel south on the Southern Highway, the Great Southern Pine Ridge is on your right, starting at about Mile 55. Farther in the distance are the Maya Mountains. On your left (though not visible from the highway) is the Caribbean Sea, and farther south, beyond Punta Negra, the Gulf of Honduras.

Branching off the Southern Highway are mostly unpaved roads, some barely more than muddy trails that lead to small villages. The San Antonio Road from the Southern Highway about 14 miles (23 km) north of PG is currently being paved and extended to the Guatemala border, where an official border crossing is expected to be established. Completion date is uncertain but should be by late 2014 or early 2015.

Punta Gorda. Many of the handful of restaurants and shops in PG open and close at the whim of their owners, and therein lies some of the charm of this little town. It's a sleepy, friendly, overgrown village with a beautiful setting on the bay.

The Maya Heartland. Nothing in Belize is quite like the Maya Heartland, where contemporary Mayan villages sit next to ancient ruins. Here also you'll see verdant rain forests, rice plantations, and cacao farms.

PLANNING

WHEN TO GO
June through September is the peak of the rainy season in Toledo, and when we say rainy we mean it—sometimes up to a foot of precipitation a day. Unless you love a good thunderstorm, come between December and early May, when most of Toledo gets only about an inch of rain a week.

GETTING HERE AND AROUND

AIR TRAVEL
Maya Island Air and Tropic Air fly south to Punta Gorda from both the municipal (BZ$231–BZ$260 one-way) and international (BZ$276–BZ$306 one-way) airports in Belize City, typically with stops at Dangriga and Placencia. Depending on stops, flights take from 1 to 1½ hours. There are four or five flights daily to PG on each airline. The Punta Gorda airstrip is on the town's west side; from the town's main square, walk four blocks west on Prince Street.

Contacts Maya Island Air ✉ *Punta Gorda Airstrip, Punta Gorda* ☎ *722/2856 in PG, 233/1140 in Belize City* ⊕ *www.mayaislandair.com.* **Tropic Air** ✉ *Punta Gorda Airstrip, Prince St., Punta Gorda* ☎ *722/2008 in PG, 226/2012 in San Pedro (main office), 800/422–3435 in U.S.* ⊕ *www.tropicair.com.*

BOAT TRAVEL
Requena's, the most reliable operator, provides daily boats departing at 9 am from the docks on Front Street, Punta Gorda, to Puerto Barrios, Guatemala. The trip takes about an hour and can be rough. The fare is BZ$40 one-way. Requena's returns to PG at 2 pm. Two other water-taxi services, Pichilingo and Marisol, run boats for around BZ$50 one-way. The Pichilingo boat departs from PG at 2 pm and Marisol at 4 pm. From Puerto Barrios, Pichilingo departs at 10 am and Marisol at 1 pm. Memo runs a daily boat from PG to Livingston, Guatemala at 1 pm and returns daily at 3 pm (fare BZ$50 one-way). On Tuesday and Friday only, Asugena has service at 10 am from PG to Livingston, and from Livingston to PG at 7 am.

These boats are small open boats for pedestrians only; there is no auto ferry between Guatemala and Punta Gorda. You must pay a BZ$37.50 exit fee when departing from PG to Guatemala and about a US$10 exit fee when departing from Guatemala for Belize.

Contact Requena's Charter Service ✉ *12 Front St., Punta Gorda* ☎ *722/2070* ⊕ *www.belizenet.com/requena.*

BUS TRAVEL
James Bus Lines dominates the route between PG and points north. Currently there are nine daily local bus departures from PG to Belize City, and one express Monday through Saturday with limited stops. The first bus is at 3:50 am and the last one at 3:50 pm. Eight local and two express James Line buses come from what is still called the Novelo's bus station in Belize City (Novelo's bus company no longer exists) to Punta Gorda daily, beginning at 5:15 am with the last bus at 3:45 pm. It's a six- to seven-hour trip to or from Belize City via Belmopan, Dangriga, and Independence, depending on whether it's

TOP REASONS TO GO

Rain Forests. The greenest, lushest jungles in Belize are in Toledo, fed by heavy rains and temperatures that stay mostly above 70°F. Red ginger, bright yellow-and-orange lobster claw, masses of pink on mayflower trees, and orchids of all colors splash the emerald-green landscape. Scarlet-rumped tanagers, black-headed trogans, green king-fishers, and roseate spoonbills join hundreds of other birds in the rain-forest cacophony.

Outpost Atmosphere. Punta Gorda has that end-of-the-road feel, as if it's the last outpost on Earth. Yes, the Southern Highway does end

here—but it's more than that. Here you get the feeling that even in today's world of 7 billion people there are still places where you could, if you needed to, hide out for a while and not be found.

Fishing. Among serious anglers, Southern Belize has a reputation for having one of the world's great permit fisheries, and for its large populations of tarpon and bonefish. The flats off Punta Ycacos are prime permit and bonefish grounds, and freshwater lagoons near Punta Negra hold snook, small tarpon, and other fish.

an express or local bus. Between Belize City and PG, fare is around BZ$22 for local and BZ$24 for express. Most buses are old U.S. Bluebird school buses—they're usually crowded, cramped, and have no air-conditioning. If you have the budget, fly. Any non-express bus will pick up and drop you anywhere along the route.

Off the Southern Highway in Toledo public transportation is limited. On market days (generally Monday, Wednesday, Friday, and Saturday) buses leave the main plaza in PG around noon. Buses, mostly old American school buses operated by local entrepreneurs, go to different villages, returning on market days very early in the morning. There's no published schedule—you have to ask locally. Fares are modest, BZ$2–BZ$5. As of this writing, buses from PG serve the villages of Aguacate, Barranco, Big Falls, Crique Sarco, Dolores, Golden Stream, Indian Creek, Jalacte, Laguna, Medina, San Antonio, San Benito Poite, San Jose, San Miquel, San Pedro Columbia, Santa Ana, San Vicente, Pueblo Viejo, and Silver Creek. As the construction of the San Antonio Road from the Southern Highway to the Guatemala border near Jalacte nears completion, bus service to some of these villages should increase.

Contact James Bus Line ✉ *7 King St., Punta Gorda* ☎ *702/2049, 722/2625.*

CAR TRAVEL

The paving of the Hummingbird and Southern highways has made the journey to Punta Gorda much shorter and more pleasant. The drive from Belize City to PG can be done in around four hours, all on paved roads. Off the Southern Highway most Toledo roads, except-ing the new San Antonio Road, are unpaved. In dry weather they're bumpy yet passable, but after heavy rains the dirt roads can turn into quagmires even for four-wheel-drive vehicles. Most tertiary roads are not well marked, so you may have to stop frequently for directions. Despite this, expensive taxis and infrequent bus service to and from the Mayan villages and elsewhere in Toledo are arguments for renting a car. There are no major car-rental companies in Punta Gorda. Your best option is to rent at the international airport in Belize City, where there are about 10 rental car companies, or in Placencia, especially if you're staying there on your way south. Bruno Kuppinger at SunCreek Lodge about 14 miles (22½ km) northwest of Punta Gorda has a few cars available to rent. Belize City–based Budget has a satellite office in Placencia and charges BZ$250 to drop a rental car from its Placencia fleet in PG. Barefoot Services in Placencia also will bring a vehicle to PG for a similar drop fee.

Barefoot Services. Barefoot Services will deliver rental cars to Punta Gorda and elsewhere in Toledo. A one-time drop fee applies. Check with Barefoot for current drop rate. Weekly rentals are around BZ$375 to $425, plus 12.5% tax and 2.5% service fee. ⊠ *Main St., Placencia* ☎ *629/9602* ⊕ *www.barefootservicesbelize.com* ☉ *Sun.–Fri. 7–5:30. Closed Sat.*

Budget Belize. This satellite office of Budget's main offices at the Belize international airport and on the Philip Goldson Highway in Belize City will deliver a vehicle to Punta Gorda for a one-time drop fee of BZ$250. High-season rates are around BZ$450 to $570 a week, plus 12.5% tax. ⊠ *Live Oaks Plaza, South of Placencia airstrip, Placencia* ☎ *523/3068, 800/284–4387 toll-free number outside Belize* ⊕ *www.budget-belize. com* ☉ *Weekdays 8–5, Sat. 8–1.*

Sun Creek Lodge. Bruno Kuppinger at Sun Creek Lodge, about 14 miles (22½ km) northwest of Punta Gorda, usually has a few cars to rent. Call ahead to confirm. ⊠ *Off Southern Hwy., San Marcos* ☎ *604/2124* ⊕ *www.suncreeklodge.de.*

TAXI TRAVEL

Taxis in the Deep South are available mostly in PG. Your hotel can call one for you. Any trip within PG should cost around BZ$7, with additional charges for extra stops. You can also hire a taxi to take you to nearby villages, but negotiate the rate in advance; it could be anywhere from BZ$20 to BZ$150, or more, depending on the destination. If you want a car and driver, a taxi likely will charge you around BZ$300 a day.

EMERGENCIES

Hospital Punta Gorda Hospital ⊠ *Main St. at south end of town, Punta Gorda* ☎ *722/2026.*

MONEY MATTERS

The only banks in Punta Gorda are Belize Bank and ScotiaBank. Both have ATMs that accept foreign-issued ATM cards (on the PLUS, CIRRUS, and Visa Electron systems). *(See ATMs and Banks in Travel Smart for Bank contact information).*

SAFETY

Punta Gorda is generally a safe, friendly town. Indeed, Toledo District has the lowest murder rate in Belize, and one of the lowest rates of other serious crimes. With normal precautions you should have no problem walking around, even after dark. The nearby Mayan villages are also relatively free of crime. Guatemala's Caribbean coast, just a short boat ride away, has a reputation for lawlessness, which can occasionally spill over into Toledo.

ABOUT THE RESTAURANTS

With relatively few tourists coming to the region, and most local residents unable to afford to eat out regularly, restaurants in Toledo often are here today and gone tomorrow. Even those that stick around often open and close at the whim of the owner or the cook. Those that do make it are usually basic spots serving local fish and staples like stew chicken with beans and rice. Prices are low—you'll rarely pay more than BZ$30 for dinner, unless you're eating at an expensive lodge such as Belcampo. Nearly all Toledo restaurants are in PG.

ABOUT THE HOTELS

The entire Toledo District has only about 30 hotels, most of them in and around Punta Gorda. Most are small and owner-run. You can usually show up without reservations and look for a place that suits you. Clean, basic rooms are under BZ$100, and for BZ$150–BZ$200 you can stay at a charming small inn. Several jungle lodges have rates of BZ$300–BZ$500 or more, and Belcampo is among the most expensive lodges in the entire country.

HOTEL AND RESTAURANT PRICES

Prices in the restaurant reviews are the average cost of a main course at dinner or, if dinner is not served, at lunch; taxes and service charges are generally included. Prices in the hotel reviews are the lowest cost of a standard double room in high season, excluding taxes, service charges, and meal plans (except at all-inclusives). Prices for rentals are the lowest per-night cost for a one bedroom unit in high season.

For expanded lodging reviews and current deals, visit Fodors.com.

TOURS

Bruno Kuppinger Tours. Among other things, Bruno Kuppinger specializes in adventure tours, most definitely not for couch potatoes, including the Maya Divide hiking trip and trips to Doyle's Delight, the highest peak in Belize. ✉ *Sun Creek Lodge, off Mile 86, Southern Hwy., San Marcos* ☎ *604/2124* ⊕ *www.suncreeklodge.de.*

Toledo Tour Guides Association. Members of the Toledo Tour Guides Association must be Belizean citizens, go through a training course, and pass a government tour guide test. These accredited guides work for local hotels and tour operators, as well as independently. The Association is based at the Visitor Information Centre at BTIA (Belize Tourism Industry Association). ✉ *46 Front St., Punta Gorda* ☎ *637/2000*

7

BOATING, FISHING, AND SAILING

Blue Belize Tours and Charters. Blue Belize Tours and Charters, run by fishing and tour guide Dan Castellanos, can arrange sea and inland tours and trips. Full-day fishing tours run around BZ$610 for two persons, with additional guests around BZ$50 each. Prices include boat, guide, taxes, marine reserve fees, lunch, snacks, and drinks. ⊠ *139 Front St., Punta Gorda* ☎ *722/2678* ⊕ *www.bluebelize.com.*

Garbutt's Marine. Garbutt's Marine on Joe Taylor Creek offers dependable snorkeling and dive trips to the Snake and Sapodilla cayes and to Port Honduras Marine Reserve, along with fishing trips. Garbutt's also has cabins to rent. ⊠ *Joe Taylor Creek, Punta Gorda* ☎ *722/0070, 604/3584* ⊕ *www.garbuttsfishinglodge.com.*

CULTURAL TOURS AND HOMESTAYS

A few programs offer the chance to live with the modern-day Maya or Garífuna at a homestay or village guesthouse program. You can also spend several days learning how to process cacao or learning to cook Belizean—including Mayan—recipes. Cotton Tree Lodge has a chocolate making program in connection with Sustainable Harvest International (⊕ *www.sustainableharvest.org*), which teaches farmers to grow food on a sustainable basis. Belcampo Lodge has programs for guests on making chocolate, rum, jams and jellies, and coffee.

Homestay and village guesthouse programs are in Toledo District near Punta Gorda. They are very inexpensive, but keep in mind that accommodations and meals are extremely basic; lodging usually lacks electricity and running water. If you'd rather invest less time but still enjoy a Mayan village learning experience, try a day of learning about Mayan crafts, cuisine, and culture in the village of Big Falls, through the Living Maya Experience. To learn more about the Garífuna culture, investigate the Warasa Garífuna Drum School, which approaches the Garífuna experience through drumming, drum making, and dance.

Barranco Village Tour. For a tour of the Garífuna village of Barranco, where famed Belize musician Andy Palacio was born and now is buried, check with tour guide Alvin Loredo, reachable by the community telephone in the Barranco. Two-hour tours of the little village (population has now dropped to under 200) include Palacio's burial site, a visit to the Garífuna dabuyaba temple, the tiny House of Culture museum, and a lunch of Garífuna food. Cost is around BZ$15, including admission to the House of Culture but not lunch. You'll have to get to Barranco on your own, by rental car, taxi, boat, or tour. You can combine a tour of Barranco with a visit to the nearby 42,000-acre Temash-Sarstoon Wildlife Sanctuary. ⊠ *Barranco* ✛ *Drive on the Southern Highway north to Jacintoville; turn west on the dirt road via San Felipe and Santa Ana to Barranco and go 9 miles (15 km). Figure a little over an hour from Punta Gorda, depending on road conditions.* ☎ *709/2010 Barranco community telephone.*

Cotton Tree Lodge. In Toledo, Cotton Tree Lodge's Chocolate Week program, held on two different weeks in the spring, lets you "work your way through the entire practical process from scratch, starting with the cacao fruit on the tree and ending with the chocolate in your mouth." ⊠ *Moho River, San Felipe* ☎ *670/0557, 866/480–4534 in U.S.* ⊕ *www.cottontreelodge.com.*

German Sho. German Sho runs a homestay program in Nah Luum Cah Mopan village. The accommodations are extremely simple—you may share a room with the family in a small thatch building with dirt floor. ⊠ *Nah Luum Cah* ☎ *664/9419* ✎ *quichpan_luum@yahoo.ca.*

Living Maya Experience. Learn about Kek'chi crafts, culture, and cuisine in a hands-on private experience in the homes of participating villages in Big Falls. You could be involved in anything from building a traditional thatch house to making corn tortillas. Call in advance for what's available, times, and charges, or ask at your hotel or the BTIA Visitor Information Centre in Punta Gorda to help arrange the Living Maya trip. Any non-express James Line bus will drop you off and pick you up at at Big Falls village (watch for Las Faldes restaurant on the Southern Highway) near the Living Maya Experience homes. Costs vary depending on which learning experiences you choose and the length of them, but most are under BZ$40. ⊠ *Southern Hwy., Big Falls* ☎ *627/7408 Anita Cal, 632/4585 Marta Chiac* ✎ *livingmaya-experience@gmail.com.*

Maya Center Women's Group. Homestays at Maya Center at the entrance to the Cockscomb Wildlife Sanctuary can be arranged through the Maya Center Women's Group, a group of about 50 Mopan women who have banded together to sell handicrafts. Two people pay a total of BZ$82 a day, including lodging and meals, plus a one-time BZ$20 registration fee. ⊠ *Southern Hwy., Maya Center, Cockscomb Wildlife Sanctuary* ☎ *603/9256.*

Toledo Cacao Growers Association. During the Chocolate Festival in May, and by advance arrangement at other times, the Toledo Cacao Growers Association (TCGA), which represents more than 1,100 small organic cacao growers in southern Belize, offers tours of working cacao farms. 🖂 *Main St., Punta Gorda* ☎ *722/2992* ⊕ *www.tcgabelize.com.*

Toledo Ecotourism Association (T.E.A.). The T.E.A. program allows visitors to participate in the village life of the Maya while maintaining some personal privacy. You stay in small guesthouses in one of nine Mopan and Kek'chi Mayan villages in Toledo District, including San Antonio, San Miguel, and Blue Creek. Barranco, a predominantly Garífuna village, also has a guesthouse. The guesthouses are very simple, with traditional thatch roofs and outdoor latrines. There is no running water or electricity in the guesthouses. You take meals in the homes of villagers and participate in the routines of village life. The program, endorsed by the Belize Tourism Board, is a collective owned by more than 200 members and is designed to promote cultural exchange. The cost is around BZ$84 a day for two, including meals. ☎ *722/2531* ✎ *teabelize@yahoo.com.*

Warasa Garifuna Drum School. Experience Garifuna culture through drumming, drum making, and dance. Ray McDonald gives private lessons in a thatch house in the Garifuna community of PG, with lessons starting at BZ$25 an hour. Call to arrange lessons or demonstrations, or you can do so through your hotel or the BTIA Visitor Information Centre on Front Street in PG. ⊠ *West St. and Cemetery Ln., Punta Gorda* ☎ *632/7701 Ray McDonald* ⊕ *www.warasadrumschool.com.*

MULTISPORT AND ADVENTURE

Big Falls Extreme Adventures. Big Falls Extreme Adventures offers zip-lining, river tubing, and hiking. Zip-lining and river tubing are BZ$80 each, and if you do both the combination rate is BZ$100. Food is available at Las Faldas restaurant; lunch is BZ$20. ⊠ *Southern Hwy., Big Falls* ☎ *634/6979* ⊕ *www.bigfallsextremeadventures.com.*

Romero's Charter and Tours. Romero's Charters and Tours, although not a tour operator, has a driver service with vans and other vehicles that can take you to any of the inland destinations. ⊠ *Forest Home* ☎ *722/2625* ✎ *rcharters@btl.net.*

TIDE Tours. TIDE Tours, a subsidiary of the Toledo Institute for Development and Environment, a nonprofit organization promoting ecotourism in Toledo, does not itself run tours but instead acts as a clearinghouse for several good tour operators. It can arrange fishing, kayaking, snorkeling to the Sapodilla and Snake cayes, as well as cultural tours, caving, and trips to Mayan ruins. Full-day snorkeling trips cost around BZ$160 per person for four persons, plus 12.5% tax and BZ$10 per person marine reserve entry fee. The cost includes lunch and snorkel equipment. ⊠ *41 Front St., Punta Gorda* ☎ *722/2129* ⊕ *www.tidetours.org.*

SEEING THE RUINS

Tour operators in Punta Gorda and nearby focus on trips by road to the ruins of **Lubaantun, Nim Li Punit,** and, less commonly, **Pusilha.** These tours usually include visits to modern Mayan villages near Punta Gorda.

VISITOR INFORMATION

The office of the Belize Tourism Industry Association (BTIA), in an octagonal building on Front Street near the water-taxi dock, is open weekdays 8–4, and Saturday 8–11:30.

Information Belize Tourism Information Center ⊠ *Toledo Tourism Information Centre, 46 Front St., Punta Gorda* ☎ *722/2531* ✎ *btiatoledo@btl.net* ⊙ *Weekdays 8-4, Sat. 8–11:30.*

PUNTA GORDA

102 miles (164 km) south of Placencia.

Most journeys south begin in the region's administrative center, Punta Gorda. PG (as it's affectionately known) isn't your typical tourist destination. Though it has a wonderful setting on the Gulf of Honduras, it has no real beaches. There are few shops of interest to visitors, a few simple restaurants, and little nightlife. Don't expect many tourist services.

So why, you ask, come to PG? First, simply because it isn't on the main tourist track. The accoutrements of mass tourism are still, refreshingly, missing here. Schoolchildren may wave at you, and residents will strike up a conversation. Toledo has stunning natural attractions, too, such as clean rivers for swimming and cave systems with Mayan artifacts that rival those in the Cayo District. Also, with several new or upgraded hotels to choose from, it's a comfortable base from which to visit surrounding Mayan villages, offshore cayes, and the high bush of the Deep South.

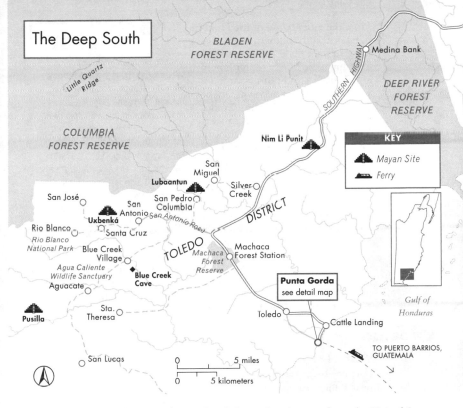

The Deep South

BLADEN
FOREST RESERVE

Medina Bank

Little Quartz Ridge

SOUTHERN HIGHWAY

DEEP RIVER
FOREST
RESERVE

COLUMBIA
FOREST RESERVE

Nim Li Punit

San
Miguel

Lubaantun

Silver
Creek

San José

San Pedro
Columbia

San
Antonio

San Antonio Road

DISTRICT

TOLEDO

Uxbenká

Rio Blanco

Santa Cruz

Rio Blanco
National Park

Blue Creek
Village

Machaca
Forest
Reserve

Machaca
Forest Station

Agua Caliente
Wildlife Sanctuary

**Blue Creek
Cave**

Aguacate

Punta Gorda
see detail map

Gulf of
Honduras

Pusilla

Sta.
Theresa

Toledo

Cattle Landing

TO PUERTO BARRIOS,
GUATEMALA

San Lucas

0   5 miles

0   5 kilometers

KEY

Mayan Site

Ferry

Settled in 1867 by ex-Confederate immigrants from the United States and later a magnet for religious missionaries, Punta Gorda once had 12 sugar estates, each with its own mill, but the sugar industry in Toledo has been replaced by rice farming, citrus groves, and small cacao plantations. After World War II, Great Britain built an important military base here, but when that closed in 1994 the linchpin of the local economy was yanked out. With some increase in tourist dollars and foreigners' growing interest in real estate here, PG is starting to pick up again, but hasn't lost its frontier atmosphere.

GETTING HERE AND AROUND

To best see the sights of Toledo, you'll need a rental car. Otherwise you'll be stuck paying high tour rates or waiting hours for infrequent bus service. If you've flown or bused in to PG, rent a car from Bruno Kuppinger at Sun Creek Lodge (he'll deliver to PG), or have a vehicle delivered to you from Budget or Barefoot in Placencia. If you'd like a knowledgeable local guide to ride with you in your rental car, Celiano Pop charges around BZ$80 a day. With a day's notice he can show you the villages and even arrange a traditional Mayan lunch for BZ$6 in one of the villages.

From the intersection of the Hummingbird and Southern highways it's a straight shot 100 miles (164 km) down the Southern, with only a well-marked right turn near Independence to slow you down. On the Southern Highway about 20 miles (33 km) north of Punta Gorda, at about Mile 83, you'll come to an intersection. If you turn left you'll stay on the Southern Highway to PG; if you bear right onto the San Antonio Road, you'll go comfortably to Lubaantun, San Antonio Village, and other Mayan villages and, by 2014–15, the Guatemala border. Assuming that you continue

> **TO MARKET, TO MARKET**
>
> On market days—Monday, Wednesday, Friday, and Saturday, with Wednesday and Saturday usually being the largest—the town comes to life with vendors from nearby Mayan villages and even from Guatemala. They pack the downtown market area with colorful fruit and vegetable stands. Fresh fish also is sold in a building at the market, daily except Sunday, and for a small fee you can have your fish cleaned.

on the Southern Highway, at about Mile 95 you have two options for reaching downtown PG. You can turn right on the mostly unpaved Saddleback Road and go 5 miles (8 km). To enter from the prettier Bay of Honduras side, as most visitors do, stay straight on the paved Southern Highway and go the same distance.

EXPLORING

WORTH NOTING

Belcampo Lodge Farm and Agritourism Center. Belcampo, the luxury lodge near Punta Gorda, has begun an agritourism program that involves teaching guests about the production of four important Belize products grown locally: chocolate, from organic cacao; rum, from local sugarcane; jams and jellies, from local fruits; and coffee, from beans produced, prepared, and roasted locally. In addition to its upscale jungle lodge, Belcampo has a 3,000-acre farm with agritourism center and 15,000-acre nature preserve near the lodge in Toledo. Programs, lengths, and costs vary. Check with the lodge to see what is offered at the time you expect to be there. ⊠ *Belcampo Lodge, Big Hill Farm Rd., Machaca Hill* ☎ *722/0050* ⊕ *www.belcampoinc.com.*

FAMILY **Cotton Tree Chocolates.** From cacao beans to final candy bars, you can see how chocolate is made at Cotton Tree Chocolates, a small chocolate factory on Front Street. It is associated with Cotton Tree Lodge. You'll get a short guided tour of the chocolate-making process and you can buy bars of delicious milk or dark chocolate. Cotton Tree Lodge also offers guests a program on sustainable cacao growing, producing, and harvesting through Sustainable Harvests International. ⊠ *2 Front St.* ☎ *670/0557* ⊕ *www.cottontreechocolate.com* ⊠ *Free* ☉ *Weekdays 8–noon and 1:30–5; Sat. 8–noon.*

FAMILY **Golden Stream Spice Farm and Botanical Gardens.** See exotic spices such as cardamom, vanilla, nutmeg, clove, cinnamon, and sandalwood growing at this spice farm just off the Southern Highway at Golden Stream. Currently, only black pepper is grown in enough quantity (about 2,000 pounds of peppercorns per year) for commercial sales in Belize, but plans are to expand other spice production for domestic and, eventually, international sales. The spice farm is part of a 500-acre tract now producing mostly citrus, owned by Dr. Thomas Matthew, an Indian-born U.S. physician, and his wife, Tessie Matthew. Visitors are given a guided tour of the farm on a cart with seats pulled by a tracked tractor. Tours generally start every hour on the hour from 8 to 4, but it's advisable to call ahead. ⊠ *Southern Hwy., Golden Stream* ☎ *732/4014* ⊕ *www.belizespicefarm.com* ⌑ *BZ$20* ⊙ *Tours for up to 6 persons on the hour daily 8–4.*

SPORTS AND THE OUTDOORS

Punta Gorda and Toledo offer great opportunities for outdoor activities—fishing, diving, snorkeling, sea and river kayaking, and caving. The problem has been that due to so few visitors to the Deep South and the limited number of tour operators, visitors often arrived to find that few tours were actually available on a given day, or if they were running, tended to cost much more than in other parts of Belize. An attempt to schedule tours to always run on specific days—for example, to Port Honduras Marine Reserve for snorkeling on Monday and to Blue Creek for caving on Tuesday—has fizzled out. Still, with tourism slowly increasing, more tours are being offered, and most prices are reasonable, given the high cost for gasoline and supplies. Try to go with a group of four to six, as many tours have a price based on a group of up to six people, not per person.

Among the most popular tours are those to the Snake Cayes. An all-day trip of snorkeling, fishing, and beach bumming costs around BZ$600 for up to four people, plus the BZ$10 per person Port Honduras Reserve entrance fee. Another popular tour combines Blue Creek caves and Agua Caliente Wildlife Sanctuary; it's around BZ$130 per person, with a minimum of two people. Tours to Lubaantun, often in combination with a visit to Rio Blanco National Park and its waterfall, are around BZ$130 a person (two-person minimum).

FAMILY **Agua Caliente Wildlife Sanctuary.** Hot springs, freshwater lagoons, caves, and hiking trails dot the 5,500-acre Agua Caliente Wildlife Sanctuary. The sanctuary is known for its water birds, including ibises, herons, egrets, woodstorks, and kingfishers. A half-mile boardwalk gives access to the visitor center. A local guide is recommended. During the dry season you can hike under the forest canopy and through wetlands to the warm springs at the base of the Agua Caliente hills. During the rainy season, canoes are available for hire. ⊠ *About 13 miles (21 km) west of Punta Gorda* ⊕ *From Punta Gorda, take Southern Hwy. 10 miles (16 km) north. Turn left on Laguna Rd. and go 3 miles (5 km). The trail to the wildlife sanctuary begins in Laguna village.*

FAMILY **Bladen Forest Reserve.** Ever been freshwater snorkeling? Check out the Bladen River in the Bladen Forest Reserve. The river snakes through the reserve, allowing for excellent kayaking, canoeing, swimming, and, yes, freshwater snorkeling. The 100,000-acre Bladen Forest Reserve is comanaged by the Belize Forestry Department and the

HISTORY

The Maya, mostly a group called the Manche Chol Maya, established sizable ceremonial centers and midsize cities in Toledo beginning almost 2,000 years ago. Uxbenká is one of the oldest centers, dating to AD 200. In the Classic period, Lubaantun, which flourished in the 8th and 9th centuries, is thought to have been the administrative center of the region, but for reasons still unclear it was abandoned not long after this. In southern Belize as elsewhere in Mesoamerica, the Mayan civilization began a long, slow decline a little more than 1,000 years ago.

Spanish conquistadors, including Hemán Cortés himself in 1525, came through southern Belize in the early 16th century, but the Maya resisted Spain's and, later, Britain's attempts to control and tax them.

The British, who arrived as loggers, tried to put the Maya in "reservations," and eventually, in the 18th and 19th centuries, moved nearly the entire Manche Chol population to the highlands of Guatemala.

In the late 19th century, groups of Mopan and Ket'chi Maya began moving into southern Belize from Guatemala, establishing more than 50 villages around Toledo. Around the same time, Garífuna from Honduras settled in Punta Gorda, Barranco, and Punta Negra.

Southern Belize, with its rain and remoteness from Belize City, has languished economically for most of the 20th century. The paved Southern Highway and planned new road from Guatemala may help boost tourism and development in the region in coming years.

Ya'axché Conservation Trust. Bladen is the centerpiece of the Maya Mountain Corridor, creating a crucial link in the last remaining large, intact block of forest in the region. Additional parts of this corridor are protected by the Cockscomb Basin Wildlife Sanctuary, the Columbia River Forest Reserve, and the Chiquibul National Park and Forest Reserve, all bordering Bladen. Tours of the Bladen Reserve also are given by interns from a private reserve managed by the Belize Foundation for Research and Environmental Education (BFREE). Camping and simple bunkhouse accommodations are available at BFREE for around BZ$80–BZ$120 per person per day, meals included. Additional charges may apply for transportation, canoe rental, laundry, and other services. ⊠ *Bladen Nature Reserve* ☎ *614/3896 for BFREE, 722/0108 for Ya'axché Conservation Trust* ⊕ *www.bfreebz.org and www.yaaxche.org.*

Columbia Forest Reserve. One of the largest undisturbed tropical rain forest areas in Central America is the Columbia Forest Reserve. It's in a remote area north of San José Village. The karst terrain—an area of irregular limestone in which erosion has produced sinkholes, fissures, and underground streams and caves—is difficult to navigate, so the only way to see this area is with a guide and with advance permission from the Belize Forestry Department. It has extremely diverse ecosystems because the elevation ranges from about 1,000 to over 3,000 feet, with sinkholes as deep as 800 feet. You'll find areas of true "high bush" here: old-growth tropical forest with parts that have never been logged at all. Much of the rich flora and fauna of this area has yet to be documented. For example, one brief 12-day expedition turned up 15 species of ferns never found before in Belize, along with several new species of palms, vines, and orchids. Check with the Toledo Tour Guide Association at the BTIA visitor information office in Punta Gorda to find a guide to take you to this remote reserve. ⊠ *Columbia Forest Reserve, north of San José village, San José* ☎ *637/2000 Toledo Tour Guide Association.*

FAMILY **Rio Blanco National Park.** This is a tiny national park (105 acres) with a big waterfall. The Rio Blanco waterfall splashes over rough limestone boulders into a deep pool, which you can jump into for a refreshing swim. You reach the waterfall after hiking a well-marked trail. Upstream a short distance from the falls is a nice area for a picnic, shaded by trees and flowering bushes. The park is managed by residents of nearby Mayan villages including Santa Elena, Santa Cruz, Golden Stream, and Pueblo Viejo. ⊠ *Rio Blanco National Park, off San Antonio Rd., Santa Cruz* ✛ *30 miles (49 km) northwest of Punta Gorda between Santa Cruz and Santa Elena villages, off San Antonio Road to Jalacte—watch for signs.*

FAMILY **Sarstoon-Temash National Park.** One of the wildest and most remote areas of Belize is the Sarstoon-Temash National Park, between the Temash and Sarstoon rivers in the far south of Toledo District on the border of Guatemala. Red mangroves grow along the river banks; animals and birds rarely seen in other parts of Belize, including white-faced capuchin monkeys, can be spotted here, along with jaguars (if you're lucky), ocelots, and tapirs, along with more than 200 species of birds. The only way to see this 42,000-acre area is with a guide by boat. Contact the Sarstoon and Temash Institute for Indigenous Management (SATIIM) for a guide, or check with the BTIA office on Front Street in PG, home to the Toledo Tour Guide Association. SATIIM, among other things, is involved in efforts to oppose oil and gas exploration in the Sarstoon-Temash. ⊠ *About 13 miles (21 km) south of Punta Gorda by boat* ☎ *722/0103* ⊕ *www.satiim.org. bz* ⊠ *BZ$20.*

FISHING

For bonefish and tarpon, head to the estuary flats in the Port Honduras marine reserve at the end of the Río Grande, or go northward to Punta Ycacos. In the Marine Reserve, anglers pay a one-day park fee of BZ$20, or BZ$60 for three to seven days. There is no fee for the Punta Ycacos, unless you fish in the Port Honduras reserve. For a full day of fly-fishing with a local guide and boat, you'll pay around BZ$550–BZ$650 for two anglers.

Blue Belize Tours and Charters. Blue Belize Tours is operated by Dan Castellanos, an experienced local fisherman and licensed guide. Fishing trips include spincasting, trolling, and catch-and-release fly-fishing, for around BZ$720 a day for up to four persons, depending on the type of fishing. ⊠ *139 Front St.* ☎ *722/2678* ⊕ *www.bluebelize.com.*

TIDE Tours. TIDE Tours has trained more than 60 tour guides in Toledo. TIDE can arrange fly-fishing guides for bonefish or permit in Payne's Creek National Park and Port Honduras Marine Reserve, from around BZ$900 per day for two persons, not including 12.5% tax or reserve entry fees. ⊠ *Mile 1, San Antonio Rd.* ☎ *722/2274* ⊕ *www.tidebelize.org.*

HIKING

"Ranger patrol hikes" are organized by the Ya'axché Conservation Trust, a nongovernmental organization that among other things manages the 15,000-acre Golden Stream corridor preserve north of Punta Gorda. These hikes start at the field station at Golden Stream, with a climb of the fire tower for a bird's-eye view of the area, and then "ranger work" such as wildlife logs, patrols, and biodiversity transects. This is something of an adventure in an area not normally accessible to visitors. Check with Hickatee Cottages (☎ *662/4475* ⊕ *www.hickatee. com*) for details.

SCUBA DIVING

This far south the reef has pretty much broken up, but individual cayes have their own small reef systems. The best of the bunch is at the Sapodilla Cayes, seven cayes with great wall dives. Lime Caye here has camping, and Hunting Caye has a lighthouse. The only drawback is that because they're 40 miles (64 km) off the coast, a day's dive trip costs around BZ$300 per person or more, depending on how many people go. The Snake Cayes, with several notable dive sites, are closer in, about 18 miles (30 km) northeast of Punta Gorda. The four Snakes—East, West, South, and Middle—are so named because of boa constrictors that once lived there.

Reef Conservation International. Reef Conservation International operates marine conservation trips in the Sapodilla Cayes Marine Reserve. You can stay there, at the ReefCI based on Tom Owens Caye, in basic accommodations—there's Internet but no hot water. You'll get plenty of snorkeling and diving, but you can also assist marine biologists and other ReefCI staff in monitoring and preserving the reef. Four-night packages including diving, dive equipment, lodging, and meals start at BZ$2,390 per person, not including air fare to Belize or transfers to PG. ⊠ *Tom Owens Caye, Sapodilla Cayes* ☎ *629/4266* ⊕ *www.reefci.com.*

SNORKELING

The turquoise waters lapping up the shores of the usually deserted white-sand beach on Snake Caye are good for snorkeling, as are the Sapodilla Cayes at the southern end of the Belize Barrier Reef.

Blue Belize Tours and Charters. Guide Dan Castellanos of Blue Belize Tours has full-day snorkeling tours to the Snake (BZ$500) or Sapodilla (BZ$650) cayes, for two persons, with additional persons BZ$50 each. Keep in mind that travel time by boat to the Sapodilla Cayes is about 2 hours, and 45 minutes to the Snake Cayes—with gas at around BZ$12 gallon, that's one reason for the high costs. Prices include all taxes, marine reserve fees, lunch, drinks, snacks and snorkel gear. Blue Belize also does fishing trips to Port Honduras reserve and elsewhere, along with other fishing and marine tours. ⊠ *139 Front St.* ☎ *722/2678* ⊕ *www.bluebelize.com.*

Garbutt's Marine. Garbutt's Marine offers all-day diving and snorkeling trips to the Snake Cayes and the Sapodilla Cayes, along with overnight stays at Lime Caye. The three Garbutt's brothers, Scully, Oliver, and Eworth, also do guided fishing trips. ✉ *Joe Taylor Creek* ☎ *722/0072* 🌐 *www.garbuttsfishinglodge.com.*

WHERE TO EAT

$$ LATIN AMERICAN Fodor's Choice ★

🍴 **Asha's Culture Kitchen.** In a rustic wood shack built right over the water, Asha's has the best views of any restaurant in Punta Gorda. From the main dining room or the breezy deck you can look across the Gulf of Honduras to Guatemala. Asha's chef-owner Ashton Martin specializes in fresh seafood served Creole-style, such as fried conch with mashed potatoes or grilled snapper with plantains and beans and rice. The menu, on a chalkboard with the day's fare marked with checks, changes daily. As items are sold out, the check marks are erased, so come early for the best selection. On Sundays, Creole drummers and other musicians provide live entertainment. [$] *Average main: BZ$20* ✉ *80 Front St.* ☎ *632/8025* 💳 *No credit cards* 🕒 *No lunch.*

$$ VEGETARIAN

🍴 **Gomier's Restaurant and Soy Centre.** This is one of the best restaurants in Punta Gorda—when and if it's open. Posted hours don't necessarily mean anything. Gomier's opens when the friendly St. Lucia–born owner, Ingnatius "Gomier" Longville, feels like cooking. When it is open, Gomier's does excellent vegetarian meals, from organic ingredients grown locally by the owner, along with some seafood. Go with the vegetarian dish of the day, which could be stir-fried tofu or vegan spaghetti. Fresh seafood dishes, such as shrimp curry, sometimes are available. Prices are very reasonable. The owner also offers tofu making and cooking classes. [$] *Average main: BZ$15* ✉ *Alejandro Vernon St., behind "Welcome to Punta Gorda" sign on Front St.* ☎ *722/2929* 💳 *No credit cards* 🕒 *Closed 3 pm to 5 pm. Closed Sun. Hours can vary.*

$ LATIN AMERICAN

🍴 **Grace's.** An established spot, Grace's has genuine value and serves a hearty plate of beans and rice and other Belizean staples. Get a seat near the entrance and eye the town's street life. This is a good place for a full breakfast of eggs, bacon, fry jacks (a Belizean version of a sopaipilla), and, of course, beans. For lunch and dinner you can always get chicken, but you can usually get fresh fish, too, plus pizza, chow mein, hamburgers, and several dozen other dishes. [$] *Average main: BZ$14* ✉ *21 Main St.* ☎ *702/2414.*

$$ SEAFOOD

🍴 **Mangrove Inn at Casa Bonita.** No pretense here—instead, you're seated on the second floor veranda of the chef-owner's house across the street from the water in the Cattle Landing of Punta Gorda. Iconie Williams cooks different dishes every evening, but you'll usually have a choice of seafood (snapper, snook, or shrimp) or a hearty dish like lasagna. It's all delicious and inexpensive. Because it's a little away from the main downtown area, most guests are local residents or expats, not tourists. [$] *Average main: BZ$16* ✉ *Front St., Cattle Landing area* ☎ *623/0497* 💳 *No credit cards* 🕒 *No lunch.*

Where to Eat
and Stay in
Punta Gorda

TO SAN ANTONIO

Airstrip

Gulf of
Honduras

Bus
Terminal

KEY

❶ *Restaurants*

① *Hotels*

NOT TO SCALE

$$ ✕**Marian's Bayview Restaurant.** On the third level of a nondescript
INDIAN   concrete building, with a thatch roof palapa, Marian's has little
atmosphere—though there is indeed a view of the bay—but the Indian
and Belizean food is inexpensive and well-prepared. Marian usually
cooks only two or three dishes each meal, and you choose among them.
It might be a freshly caught snapper seasoned with a blend of Belizean
and East Indian spices, an Indian curry, or a plate of Belizean beans
and rice. Limited selection, but you can't go wrong. ⓢ *Average main:
BZ$18* ✉ *76 Front St.* ☎ *722/0129.*

$ ✕**Snack Shack.** Burritos are the thing here, and in fact usually just about
LATIN AMERICAN   the only thing, except for smoothies, shakes, coffee, and the occasional
daily special. You get a selection of fillings and type of flour tortilla. The
huge breakfast burrito easily serves two. It's mostly a take-out spot, but
there are a few tables on the patio for open-air dining, though the view
is only of the Belize Telemedia parking lot. ⓢ *Average main: BZ$10*
✉ *Main St., in BTL parking lot* ☎ *702/0020* ▭ *No credit cards* ☉ *No
dinner. Closed Sun.*

WHERE TO STAY

$
HOTEL

☷ **Beya Suites.** From the verandas on the second- or third-floor rooftop terrace of this bright pink, waterfront hotel (*beya* means beachfront in the Garífuna language) within walking distance of downtown Punta Gorda, you have expansive views of the water. **Pros:** views of the water; Belizean-owned. **Cons:** most units are not really suites. $ *Rooms from: BZ$164* ✉ *6 Front St.* ☎ *722/2188* ⊕ *www.beyasuites.com* ⤴ *8 rooms, 2 suites* ⍥ *No meals.*

$
B&B/INN

☷ **Blue Belize Guest House.** At this pleasant small spot overlooking the water, you can settle in and do your own thing in one of the five attractive self-catering flats, with kitchens or kitchenettes, spacious bedrooms, TVs with DVD players, and verandas with hammocks. **Pros:** spacious self-catering apartments; reasonable rates; breezy waterfront location. **Cons:** no a/c. $ *Rooms from: BZ$164* ✉ *139 Front St.* ☎ *722/2678* ⊕ *www.bluebelize.com* ⤴ *4 1-bedroom apartments, 1 2-bedroom apartment* ⍥ *Breakfast.*

$
B&B/INN
Fodor'sChoice
★

☷ **Coral House Inn.** Americans Rick and Darla Mallory renovated this 1938 British colonial–era house and turned it into one of the most pleasant small guesthouses in the country, with breezy views of the Bay of Honduras. **Pros:** one of the best small inns in Belize; most comfort amenities provided, from a/c to pool to wireless; reasonable prices. **Cons:** no restaurant, so you'll have to go out for dinner. $ *Rooms from: BZ$196* ✉ *P.O. Box 53, 151 Main St.* ☎ *722/2878* ⊕ *www.coralhouseinn.net* ⤴ *4 rooms, 1 suite, 1 rental house.*

$
B&B/INN
Fodor'sChoice
★

☷ **Hickatee Cottages.** A charming and enthusiastic young British couple, Ian and Kate Morton, run this delightful small lodge with lovely Caribbean-style cottages with zinc roofs and private verandas, nestled in lush foliage where you'll hear howler monkeys and see a wide variety of birds. **Pros:** lovely cottages; some of the best food in Toledo; helpful, friendly owners; excellent value. **Cons:** a longish hike or bike ride from town; no air-conditioning. $ *Rooms from: BZ$164* ✉ *Ex-Servicemen Rd., about 1 mile (1½ km) from PG* ✢ *Coming into PG on the bayside, follow Front St. into town, past the Uno gas station (formerly Texaco), through the market area, and then turn right immediately past St. Peter Claver church. Take the next left onto Main St. and continue past the hospital; bear right where the road becomes Cemetery La. Follow Cemetery La. for 3 blocks and, when you reach the small children's playground, turn "half-left" onto Ex-Servicemen Rd. (also known as Boom Creek Rd.) Go 1 mile (1½ km) farther to Hickatee Cottages, on left.* ☎ *662/4475* ✎ *cottages@hickatee.com* ⊕ *www.hickatee.com* ⤴ *4 rooms, 2 suites* ⍥ *Breakfast.*

$$
B&B/INN

☷ **Sea Front Inn.** With its pitched roofs and stone-and-wood facade, this four-story hotel overlooking the Gulf of Honduras may remind you of a Swiss ski lodge in a tropical setting. **Pros:** appealing waterfront location; one-of-a-kind rooms. **Cons:** upper-story rooms require climbing a lot of steps; prices are a little higher than similar accommodations in Punta Gorda. $ *Rooms from: BZ$260* ✉ *4 Front St.* ☎ *722/2300* ⊕ *seafrontinn.com* ⤴ *12 rooms, 2 suites, 5 1-bedroom apartments, 1 2-bedroom apartment.*

7

$$ B&B/INN Fodor's Choice ★ 🏨 **Sirmoor Hill Farm Bed and Breakfast.** In a restored 100-year-old colonial home on a 775-acre farm near Punta Gorda, this B&B is among the most appealing small lodgings in Belize. **Pros:** gorgeous rural setting; beautifully restored colonial home; swimming pool. **Cons:** not much privacy; more like visiting friends' home. [$] *Rooms from: BZ$240* ✉ *New Road, near Belize Defence Forces camp* ☎ *722/0052* 🌐 *www.sirmoorhillfarm.com* 🛏 *2 rooms with shared bath* 🍴 *Breakfast.*

$ B&B/INN 🏨 **Tate's Guest House.** If you don't demand luxury, you couldn't find a nicer spot in Punta Gorda. **Pros:** clean accommodations at near backpacker rates. **Cons:** few frills. [$] *Rooms from: BZ$80* ✉ *34 Jose Maria Nunez* ☎ *722/0147* 🛏 *5 rooms* 💳 *No credit cards* 🍴 *No meals.*

SHOPPING

Maya Bags. Maya Bags employs about 90 Mayan women from eight local villages to sew handbags, purses, fitness bags, and travel bags, which are sold in a fair trade shop in Punta Gorda near the airstrip and, on a larger scale, to stores in the U.S. and elsewhere. ✉ *Airport St., near Punta Gorda airstrip* ☎ *722/2175* 🌐 *www.mayabags.org.*

THE MAYAN HEARTLAND

Drive a few miles out of town, and you find yourself in the heartland of the Mayan people. Half the population of Toledo is Maya, a far higher proportion than in any other region. The Toledo Maya Cultural Council has created an ambitious network of Mayan-run guesthouses, and in 1995 it initiated the Mayan Mapping Project. By collating oral history and evidence of ancient Mayan settlements, the project hopes to secure rights to land that the Maya have occupied for centuries, but that the Belizean government has ceded to multinational logging companies. There's also a separate, privately run Mayan homestay program, where you stay in local homes rather than in guesthouses. *See Where to Stay, below, for information on these two programs.*

Several notable jungle lodges also are in the Mayan Heartland, including Belcampo Lodge, The Lodge at Big Falls, Cotton Tree Lodge, and The Farm Inn. However, the largest and most ambitious group of lodges, Belize Lodge and Excursions, run by an American, was closed in 2012 after Ya'aché Conservation Trust rangers found one of two captive jaguars at Indian Creek dead of starvation, and a second captive jaguar near death in an emaciated condition. Local villagers working at the lodges complained they had not been paid for months. Later in 2012, much of one of the BL&E lodges burned down, allegedly by angry local villagers.

The Maya divide into two groups: Mopan Maya and Ket'chi-speaking peoples from the Guatemalan highlands. Most of the latter are recent arrivals, refugees from repression and overpopulation. Each group tends to keep to itself, living in separate villages and preserving unique traditions. Among the Ket'chi villages in Toledo are Crique Sarco, San Vincente, San Miquel, Laguna, San Pedro Columbia, Santa Teresa, Sunday Wood, Mabelha, and Corazon. Mopan Maya villages include San Antonio, Pueblo Viejo, and San José.

GETTING HERE AND AROUND

Since bus service to rural villages is limited at best, a car is almost a necessity unless you want to take guided tours.

TIMING

You can see the highlights in a day or two, but to explore the region thoroughly takes longer. Distances are not great, but most roads are poor to terrible, and it takes time just to get around the district.

HEALTH AND SAFETY

Malaria is a problem in rural areas of Toledo. If you're going to spend any time in the bush, discuss with your physician whether to use chloroquine or other malaria prophylaxis. In rural areas the water is often from community wells; you should drink bottled water. Otherwise, the Mayan Heartland is very safe.

EXPLORING

MAYAN VILLAGES

Blue Creek. Don't miss Blue Creek, a beautiful stretch of river dotted with turquoise swimming holes. A path up the riverbank leads to dramatic caves. The entrance to Hokeb Ha Cave is fairly easy to explore on your own (although you should be a strong swimmer), but others require a guide or a tour. International Zoological Expeditions, a Connecticut-based student travel and research organization, has established a jungle lodge at Blue Creek, with six rustic cabanas and a restaurant. To visit this part of Blue Creek, you need an okay from the **IZE Blue Creek Rainforest Lodge** (☎ *508/655–1461 in the U.S.* ✉ *info@IZE-Belize.com*). TIDE Tours and other tour operators offer trips to Blue Creek, providing lights and other necessary equipment. Don't swim in the river at night—a highly venemous snake called the fer-de-lance likes to take nocturnal dips. ✉ *Blue Creek Cave, Blue Creek Village* ✛ *If going on your own from PG, drive north on the Southern Hwy. to the area called The Dump and turn west on the San Antonio Rd. (currently being paved). Drive to the village of Mafredi and turn left toward Blue Creek. Go about 9 miles (15 km) to the entrance to the Blue Creek research station.*

San Antonio. The Mopan Maya village of San Antonio, a market town 35 miles (56 km) west of Punta Gorda, is Toledo's second-largest town, with a population of more than 2,000. It was settled by people from the Guatemalan village of San Luis, who revere their former patron saint. The village church, built of stones carted from surrounding Mayan ruins, has a stained-glass window donated by another city with a connection to the saint: St. Louis, Missouri. The people of San Antonio haven't forgotten their ancient heritage: Each June 13, they take to the streets for a festival that dates back to pre-Columbian times. At this writing the road to San Antonio is being paved past San Antonio all the way to the Guatemala border, with completion expected in 2014 or 2015. ✉ *San Antonio village, San Antonio* ✛ *Drive north on the Southern Hwy. to the Dump, and turn left and follow the San Antonio Rd. to San Antonio village.*

7

San Pedro Columbia. The Ket'chi Maya village of San Pedro Columbia is a cheerful cluster of brightly painted buildings and thatch houses off the San Antonio Road. ⊠ *San Pedro Columbia* ✚ *From PG, drive north on the Southern Hwy. to the Dump, and turn west on the San Antonio Rd. Just before the village of San Antonio, turn right on a dirt track (watch for a sign) to San Pedro Columbia.*

GARÍFUNA VILLAGE

Barranco. Although the Maya are by far the largest population in rural Toledo, this is also a home to the Garífuna. Barranco, a small village of fewer than 200 people about an hour by road from Punta Gorda, is the best-known Garífuna center in Toledo. The village, the southernmost coastal village in Belize, has electricity and a community phone, one or two shops, a bar, a police station, a health clinic, and a school. It was the birthplace of Andy Palacio, the Punta rock musician with a worldwide following, who died in 2008 at age 46. Palacio is buried in Barranco, and you can visit his grave. A guided village tour takes a couple of hours and includes, in addition to a visit to the Palacio gravesite, stops at the Dabuyaba (Garífuna temple), the House of Culture, and a cassava factory, all providing lots of information on the local culture. Lunch in a local home is also possible. A good guide is Alvin Loredo (reach him on the Barranco community telephone, ☎ *709/2010*), who charges around BZ$10 per person per hour. TIDE, Blue Belize Tours and Charters, and other tour operators also offer tours to Barranco. ⊠ *Barranco* ✚ *From PG, drive north to Jacinto village (watch for the water tower) and turn west on the dirt road to San Felipe, Santa Ana, and Barranco villages. It's about 9 miles (15 km) on the dirt road to Barranco, but it may take you as long as 45 minutes after you leave the Southern Hwy.* ☎ *709/2010 Barranco community telephone.*

MAYAN RUINS

FAMILY **Lubaantun.** Lubaantun, which lies beyond the village of San Pedro Columbia, is a Late Classic site discovered in 1924 by German archaeologist Thomas Gann, who gave it a name meaning "place of fallen stones." Lubaantun must have been an awe-inspiring sight: on top of a conical hill, with views to the sea in one direction and the Maya Mountains in the other, its stepped layers of white-plaster stone would have towered above the jungle like a wedding cake. No one knows exactly what function the structures served, but the wealth of miniature masks and whistles found suggests it was a center of ceramic production. The trio of ball courts and the central plaza with tiered seating for 10,000 spectators seems like a Mayan Madison Square Garden. There's a small visitor center at the site. In the last century Lubaantun became the scene of what is allegedly the biggest hoax in modern archaeology. After it was excavated in the 1920s, a British adventurer named F. A. Mitchell-Hedges claimed to have stumbled on what became known as the Crystal Skull. Mitchell-Hedges described the incident in a potboiler, *Danger, My Ally*, in 1951. According to the book, the Crystal Skull was found under an altar at Lubaantun by his daughter Anna. Mitchell-Hedges portrayed himself as a serious archaeologist and explorer: in truth, he was a magazine hack who was later exposed in England as an adventurer. The Crystal Skull made good copy; also known as the Skull of Doom, it was supposedly used by Mayan high priests to zap anyone they didn't care for. Mitchell-Hedges claimed it was 3,600 years old and had taken 150 years to fashion by rubbing a block of pure rock crystal with sand. A similar skull, in the possession of the British Museum, shows signs of having been manufactured with a dentist's drill. However, some archeologists believe the crystal skull may be authentic, possibly of Aztec origin. Anna Mitchell-Hedges, who died in 2007, adamantly refused to allow the Crystal Skull to be tested and denied all requests by the Belizean government to return it. It is now owned by her caregiver, Bill Homann. Most tour operators in PG can arrange trips to Lubaantun, or you can visit by rental car. ✉ *20 miles (33 km) northwest of Punta Gorda, about 1 mile (1½ km) from village of San Pedro Columbia, Lubaantun, San Pedro Columbia* 🌐 *www.nichbelize.org* 🎫 *BZ$10* 🕒 *Daily 8–5.*

FAMILY **Nim Li Punit.** Nim Li Punit, a Late Classic site discovered in 1976, has 26 unearthed stelae, including one, Stela 14, that is 30 feet tall—the largest ever found in Belize and the second largest found anywhere in the Mayan world. Nim Li Punit, which means "Big Hat" in the Ket'chi Mayan (sometimes referred to as Kek'chi) language, is named for the elaborate headgear of a ruler pictured on Stela 14. Shady trees cool you off as you walk around the fairly small site (you can see it all in an hour or so). Stop by the informative visitor center on the premises to learn more about the site. Nim Li Punit is near the Ket'chi village of Indian Creek, and children (and some adults) from the village usually come over and offer jewelry and crafts for sale. ✉ *27 miles (44 km) northwest of Punta Gorda* ☎ *822/2106 Institute of Archeology* 🌐 *www.nichbelize.org* 🎫 *BZ$10* 🕒 *Daily 8–5.*

7

FAMILY **Uxbenká.** Uxbenká, or "ancient place," is on the eastern edge of Santa Cruz Village, about 3 miles (5 km) west of San Antonio. This small ceremonial site has a main plaza with six structures, and a series of smaller plazas. More than 20 stelae have been found here, six of them carved. This site is not officially open to visitors, but if you ask a villager in Santa Cruz, you can probably get an informal guided tour, or go with a TIDE or other tour from PG (about BZ$200), which also includes a visit to the nearby Yok Balum cave. ✉ *Uxbenká, Santa Cruz* ✥ *From PG, drive north on the Southern Hwy. to the Dump and turn west on the San Antonio Rd. Drive past San Antonio village about 3 miles (5 km) to Santa Cruz village.* 🌐 *www.nichbelize.org* 🎫 *BZ$5 donation.*

WHERE TO EAT

$ LATIN AMERICAN 🍴 **Coleman's Café.** This longtime local favorite serves simple but tasty Belizean dishes such as stew chicken or pork with beans and rice. Sit at tables with oilcloth tablecloths under a covered patio, open to the breezes, and enjoy genuine Belizean hospitality at lunch and dinner. Some days Coleman's has a buffet of Belizean foods at lunch. [$] *Average main: BZ$12* ✉ *Big Falls Village, near rice mill, Main St., Big Falls* ☎ *720/2017* 💳 *No credit cards.*

WHERE TO STAY

VILLAGE HOMESTAYS

Village Homestay Network. The Village Homestay Network arranges for visitors to stay with one of about 15 or 20 Mayan families in one of three Toledo villages: Aguacate, Na Luum Cah, and San Jose. You sleep in a hammock in a traditional thatch hut with dirt floor, help with daily activities such as making tortillas (women) or working on a milpa (men), and eat meals with the host family. Bathrooms are outhouses, and you bathe in a river. Yvonne Villoria of Dem Dats Doin' (☎ 722/2470) runs the one in Aguacate and can refer you to organizers in other villages, or contact the Belize Tourism Board in Belize City or the BTIA office on Front Street in Punta Gorda. Rates are inexpensive at around BZ$45 per person per night for lodging and meals daily plus a one-time administrative fee of BZ$10 per person. The difference between this and the T.E.A. program is that with T.E.A. you stay in a village guesthouse, and with the Homestay program you stay in a local home. ✉ *BTIA Office, 46 Front St., Punta Gorda* ☎ *722/2470 for Aguacate village.*

$$$$ ALL-INCLUSIVE 🏨 **Belcampo Lodge.** New owners have moved this former fishing lodge far up the scale of luxury, renovating the main lodge, adding a gorgeous spa, and redoing the cottages. **Pros:** great views of jungle and the distant sea from hilltop location; incredible spa; the top lodge option near PG. **Cons:** very pricey and, some would say, overpriced; food, drink, and service not yet up to the prices charged. [$] *Rooms from: BZ$1384* ✉ *5 miles (8 km) north of Punta Gorda, Big Hill Farm Rd., Machaca Hill, Punta Gorda* ☎ *722/0050* 🌐 *www.belcampobz.com* 🛏 *12 cottages* 🍴 *All-inclusive.*

$$$ B&B/INN 🏨 **Cotton Tree Lodge.** This jungle lodge is named after the silk cotton tree (also called the kapok or ceiba), a giant specimen of which stands near the main lodge building, and, fittingly, the lodge strives to provide a silky-smooth experience for guests. **Pros:** stunning riverside setting, complete with rope swing to play Tarzan in the river; lots of activities. **Cons:** sometimes buggy; no a/c. [$] *Rooms from: BZ$390* ✉ *Moho River, near San Felipe village, San Felipe* ☎ *670/0557, 212/529–8622 in U.S.* 🌐 *www.cottontreelodge.com* 🛏 *5 rooms and 11 cabanas* 🍴 *Some meals.*

$ B&B/INN FAMILY 🏨 **The Farm Inn.** On a 52-acre working farm near San Antonio village, this newly opened lodge has a half-dozen nicely designed rooms and suites for a romantic getaway, along with an open air restaurant and bar serving an interesting fusian of African and Belizean food. **Pros:** quiet, natural setting near traditional Mayan villages; friendly international management; reasonable prices. **Cons:** a little off the beaten path. [$] *Rooms from: BZ$174* ✉ *San Antonio Rd., San Antonio* ✢ *From PG, drive north on the Southern Hwy. to the Dump, turn left on the San Antonio Rd. Drive to San Antonio village, and continue about 2 miles (3 km). Watch for The Farm Inn sign on right. Turn right and follow drive a few hundred yards to the lodge* ☎ *732/4781* 🌐 *www.thefarminnbelize.com* 🛏 *2 rooms, 2 suites, 2 cabanas* 🍴 *Breakfast.*

$$$$ **HOTEL** **The Lodge at Big Falls.** Relax beside a meandering jungle river, listen to otters splash, and admire colorful tropical birds and butterflies at this small lodge on 30 placid acres beside the Rio Grande River. **Pros:** it's fun to tube or swim in the river; excellent birding; good food. **Cons:** meals are pricey. [$] *Rooms from: BZ$501* ✉ *Off Mile 79, Southern Hwy., Rio Grande River, Big Falls* ☎ *732/4444* 🌐 *www.thelodgeatbigfalls.com* 🛏 *8 cabanas* 🍴 *No meals.*

$ **B&B/INN** **T.E.A** (*Toledo Ecotourism Association*). The Toledo Ecotourism Association arranges stays in one of several participating Mayan and Ket'chi villages, including San Jose, Santa Elena, San Antonio, San Miguel, and Laguna. [$] *Rooms from: BZ$170* ✉ *BTIA Office, 46 Front St., Punta Gorda* ☎ *722/2129* 📧 *reservations@teabelize.org* 🌐 *www.teabelize.org* 🛏 *5 village guesthouses* 💳 *No credit cards* 🍴 *All meals.*

$$ **HOTEL** **Tranquility Lodge.** This small lodge is indeed in a tranquil setting in Jacintoville, about 9 miles (15 km) north of Punta Gorda, yet with easy access to the Southern Highway. **Pros:** tranquil rural setting; upgraded rooms; good creek swimming. **Cons:** not near restaurants and bars. [$] *Rooms from: BZ$262* ✉ *San Felipe/Barranco Rd., Jacintoville* ✣ *About 9 miles (15 km) north of Punta Gorda, turn west off the Southern Hwy. onto the San Felipe/Barranco Rd. Go a few hundred feet and turn right at the first side road, a palm-lined dirt road to the lodge.* ☎ *800/819–9088 in U.S., 677/9921* 🌐 *www.tranquility-lodge.com* 🛏 *4 rooms, 2 casitas* 🍴 *No meals.*

SIDE TRIP TO GUATEMALA

El Petén with Tikal and other Mayan Sites

Updated by
Lan Sluder

The jungles of El Petén, Guatemala, were once the heart-land of the Mayan civilization. The sprawling empire—including parts of present-day Mexico, Belize, Honduras, and El Salvador—was made up of a network of cities that held hundreds of thousands of people, but a millennium ago this fascinating civilization went into a mysterious decline and soon virtually disappeared. The temples that dominated the horizon were swallowed up by the jungle.

Today ancient ruins seem to just crop up from El Petén's landscape. In comparison with the rest of Guatemala, which has 15 million people in an area the size of Tennessee, El Petén is relatively sparsely populated, although this is changing. Fifty years ago El Petén had fewer than 20,000 residents. Due to massive immigration from other areas of Guatemala, El Petén now has more than half a million people (almost twice the population of the entire country of Belize). Still, nature reigns supreme, with vines and other plants quickly covering everything that stands still a little too long. Whatever your primary interest—archaeology, history, birding, biking—you'll find plenty to do and see in this remote region.

Four-wheel-drive vehicles are required to get to many of the archaeological sites (but not to Tikal), while others, such as those in the Mirador Basin, are reachable only by boat or on foot. The difficulty doesn't just enhance the adventure, it gives you time to take in the exotic scenery and rare tropical flora and fauna that are with you all the way.

If you drive instead of fly from Belize, you'll notice the difference in Guatemala the instant you cross the border. Except in some hotels and other tourist businesses, Spanish replaces English. Prices for meals and lodging are considerably lower. Starting at the border, bribes and petty corruption are a way of life. Although poverty is much in evidence in some areas of this part of Guatemala, there are pockets of prosperity, too. Most major roads in the Petén are now beautifully paved, and the towns of Flores and Santa Elena bustle with activity.

The Petén may be vast and remote, but the traveler's focus takes in a far more limited area. Ruins dot the entire region, but excavation has begun on only a few of them. In the center of the region on Lago Petén Itzá sits Flores, its administrative center, and its twin town of Santa Elena, the site of the regional airport. Northeast are the famed ruins of Tikal.

HISTORY

At its peak, the Mayan civilization developed one of the earliest forms of writing, the first mathematical system to use zero, complex astronomical calculations, advanced agricultural systems, and an inscrutable belief system. It was during this zenith that spectacular cities such as Tikal were built. At its peak in AD 750 the Petén had millions of people and was one of the most densely populated areas in the world. By the time the Europeans arrived, however, the Mayan civilization had already mysteriously collapsed.

Until the 1960s the Petén region was a desolate place. This all changed when the Guatemalan government began offering small tracts of land in El Petén for US$25 to anyone willing to settle it. The landless moved in droves, and today the population is more than 500,000—a 25-fold increase in around 50 years.

Unemployment in El Petén is high, and tourism—mostly associated with Tikal and other Mayan sites—is the main industry. Many make ends meet through subsistence farming, logging, hunting for *xate* (palm leaves used in the floral industry) in the wild, and marijuana cultivation. Exploration for oil is underway in a few areas as well.

A new and disturbing industry has also come to the region: the running and smuggling of hard drugs, with the violence and brutality that often accompanies it. Drug cartels, including Los Zetas, under continuing pressure from the Mexican government, have moved some of their operations to El Petén. Beginning in late 2010 there was a wave of violence associated with these drug runners: In October 2010 a large group of armed men attacked a Guatemalan army outpost between Flores and Tikal, resulting in four deaths. Then, in May 2011 more than two-dozen farm workers in La Libertad southwest of Flores were murdered and decapitated, allegedly by members of the Zetas cartel. Also in 2011, several Guatemalan government officials were kidnapped or killed in the Petén. Since then, incidents around Tikal have been few, and the rate of major crimes has declined all over Guatemala, but in this poor country violence is never far under the surface.

8

ORIENTATION AND PLANNING

GETTING ORIENTED

The Petén is rugged country where major roads are few. But because there are only two airports—one in Guatemala City, the other in Flores—you're forced to do most of your travel by land. Many of the roads in El Petén are still unpaved, the exceptions being the road from Santa Elena–Flores to Tikal, the road from Río Dulce in the south to Santa Elena–Flores, most of the road from the Belize border to the crossroad junction to Tikal and Flores, and a few others.

Tikal. Arguably the most impressive of all Mayan sites, and rivaling even Machu Picchu in Peru and Angkor Wat in Cambodia in its ancient splendor, Tikal is a must-see, if only on a day trip from Belize.

Tikal Environs. Set at the end of a causeway in Lake Petén, the town of Flores is a charming and walkable small town, with almost a Mediterranean air. The village of El Remate, closer to Tikal and on the lake, is another pleasant and low-key base for exploring the region.

Other Mayan Sites in El Petén. El Mirador, about 80 miles (133 km) north of Flores near the Mexican border, is a huge site, but at present getting there requires a multiday, 45-mile (75-km) trek from the village of

Carmelita. The complexes of El Zotz, Nakúm, and Uaxactún are scattered around Tikal. Poor roads and possible bandit incidents limit the number of visitors. Farther removed, southwest of Flores, off the road to Cobá in Las Verapaces, are the town of Sayaxché and its nearby Ceibal ruins, along with several other Mayan sites including Aguateca. Closest to Belize, around an hour's drive from the Belize-Guatemala border, is Yaxhá, reachable by all-weather roads from Melchor de Mencos, Flores, El Remate, and elsewhere in the region. Yaxhá is the second-most visited Mayan site in El Petén, after Tikal, though you may see only a handful of other visitors there. Many tour companies in Flores and El Remate, and a few in San Ignacio, offer tours of Yaxhá and the beautiful lakes near it.

PLANNING

WHEN TO GO

It's warm here year-round. The rainy season is May to November. Occasional showers are a possibility the rest of the year, but shouldn't interfere with your plans. March and April are the hottest months, with December and January a few degrees cooler than the rest of the year. July and August see an influx of visitors during prime North American and European vacation time. Also prime visitor times around Tikal are Easter week and Christmas/New Year.

GETTING HERE AND AROUND
AIR TRAVEL

Aeropuerto Internacional Santa Elena (FRS), or the Mundo Maya International Airport, often just referred to as the Flores airport, is less than ½ mile (1 km) outside the town of Flores. This is a modern small airport with a 10,000-foot runway, able to handle all but the largest jets. Taxis and shuttles meet every plane and charge about 20 quetzales to take you into Flores. The airport has service to and from Belize City, Guatemala City, and, in the past, Cancún and the United States. However, Continental no longer has nonstop service from the U.S. to Flores.

Tropic Air offers twice-daily flights, one in the morning and one in midafternoon, between the international airport in Belize City and Flores. Fares are US$224 or BZ$448 round trip, not including international air exit taxes and fees from Belize (US$39.25 or BZ$78.50) and US$33 from Guatemala. Tropic Air's Flores flights also have continuing service between Flores and Guatemala City, some on a code-share with Guatemala airline TAG. Note that the baggage weight limit on TAG is 20 pounds. Tropic Air allows two checked bags, each of up to 33 pounds.

TACA and TAG operate flights between Guatemala City and Santa Elena–Flores that take less than an hour and cost from around US$140 each way or US$240 round trip on TACA and usually slightly less on TAG.

Contacts TACA ☎ *800/400–8222 in U.S., 502/2470–8222 in Guatemala* ⊕ *www.taca.com.* **TAG** ☎ *502/2380–9494 in Guatemala* ⊕ *www.tag.com.gt.* **Tropic Air** ☎ *800/422–3435 in U.S. and Canada, 501/226–2012 in Belize* ⊕ *www.tropicair.com.*

TOP REASONS TO GO

TIKAL

Tikal is usually ranked as the most impressive of all Mayan sites. Although Caracol and other Mayan sites in Belize are magnificent, none truly rivals Tikal in visual impact. You'll never forget the jungle setting, rich with wildlife and birds.

OTHER MAYAN RUINS

Tikal is the best known, but hardly the only important Mayan site in El Petén. El Mirador was a giant city-state, likely larger than Tikal, and in the Mirador Basin are the remains of at least four other centers, including Nakbé, El Tintal, Xulnal, and Wakná. The Guatemalan government has grandiose plans to make Mirador a tourist attraction that would rival Tikal, if not outdo it. Other Mayan sites in El Petén include Yaxhá, Nakúm, Uaxactún, Aguateca, Dos Pilas, and El Zotz.

LOW PRICES

In comparison with Belize, the Petén is rife with travel bargains. Overall, price levels in Guatemala for hotels, meals, and tours are a third to half less than in Belize.

FLORES AND PETÉN ITZÁ

The island town of Flores, separated from the grungier Santa Elena by a causeway across part of Lake Petén Itzá, has a charming European feel, with red-roof houses and cobblestone streets.

SHOPPING FOR HANDICRAFTS

The indigenous population creates countless kinds of handicrafts. There's an open-air market in Santa Elena, and Flores has a number of little shops. The village of El Remate is known for its unique wood carvings, and the gritty border town of Melchor also has a few shops catering to tourists.

8

BUS TRAVEL

Fuente del Norte. Fuente del Norte offers tourist buses daily between the Marine Terminal in Belize City and the main bus terminal in Santa Elena near Flores. Generally, the Fuente del Norte buses are nicer than those of its competitors on the Belize Santa route, and have air conditioning. Fuente del Norte also has overnight pullman service between Santa Elena and Guatemala City. ⊠ *Terminal de Buses, Santa Elena* ☎ *502/7947–7070 in Guatemala* ⊕ *www.grupofuentedelnorte.com.*

Línea Dorada. Línea Dorada has daily tourist bus service from the Marine Terminal in Belize City to the bus terminal in Santa Elena and usually continues the short distance to Flores island. The line also has service between Flores and Guatemala City. ⊠ *Terminal de Buses, Santa Elena* ☎ *502/5983–1163 in Santa Elena, Guatemala* ⊕ *lineadorada.info.*

San Juan Travel. San Juan Travel, a travel agency, tour operator, and shuttle service, has long had a mixed reputation, especially for service. It runs a daily tourist bus from Chetumal, Mexico, to the Marine Terminal in Belize City, and then continuing on to its private terminal in Santa Elena. It also has shuttles between Flores and Tikal park. ⊠ *6 Avenida, Santa Elena* ☎ *502/7926–0042 in Guatemala, 501/223–1200 Mundo Maya Travel at Brown Sugar Terminal in Belize.*

Numerous local chicken buses and minibuses run roughly hourly during the day between Melchor de Mencos at the Belize border and Santa Elena–Flores. The minibuses are usually packed, but cost only Q30 (around US$4). They won't take you all the way to Tikal, however; for that, you must get off in Ixlú (also known as El Cruce, the crossroads), and change buses. A minibus to Tikal from Ixlú is around Q20 or US$2.50. If you are just staying in El Remate you can hike the mile (2 km) or so, or take a taxi.

When leaving Belize by land, there's a US$18.75 exit fee, and a Q20 entrance fee to Guatemala. This entrance fee isn't really official, but most people pay it rather than dispute it. Returning to Belize by land there is no exit fee from Guatemala, though occasionally a border official will ask for Q10 or 20, and there is no entrance fee for Belize.

The 42-mile (70-km) paved route between Santa Elena–Flores and Tikal is served by scheduled minibus shuttles, operated by San Juan Travel and other companies. They cost around Q55 one way. The trip takes a little over an hour.

CAR TRAVEL

Main roads in El Petén, such as between Flores/Santa Elena and Tikal, are paved and in very good shape. The road from the Belize border toward Tikal and Flores has some short unpaved sections in the first few miles but is otherwise paved and the entire road is usually in good condition. Secondary roads, however, often are in poor repair and not well marked. Some roads are impassable during the rainy season, so check with the tourist office before heading out on seldom traveled roads, such as those to the more remote ruins surrounding Tikal. A four-wheel-drive vehicle, *doble-tracción,* is highly recommended.

From the Belize border it's about 62 miles (100 km) by road to Tikal, and from the Belize border to Flores it's slightly longer (70 miles or 112 km). This road, except for some dusty streets in the scruffy Guatemalan border town of Melchor de Mencos, is in good condition and nearly all paved. At El Cruce, also known as Ixlú, the road splits, turning north to Tikal and southwest to Santa Elena and Flores. Both roads are nicely paved. If, instead of going on to Tikal, you turn northwest near the village of El Remate, the road (mostly unpaved) takes you around the north side of Lake Petén Itzá, passing the villages of San José and San Andrés, and eventually ends up back around the lake at the town of San Benito, adjoining Santa Elena. Driving, by car or van, the trip to Tikal from the Belize border is roughly 1½ hours, depending on road and weather conditions.

If you're not booked on a tour, you can get around El Petén by renting a four-wheel-drive vehicle. Several major rental agencies, including Hertz, have offices at Aeropuerto Internacional Santa Elena, now officially known as Mundo Maya International Airport. Tabarini is a local company that usually has a good selection at competitive prices. Rates start at around US$40 a day for a compact car, or US$60–$70 a day for a four-wheel drive SUV. You need a valid driver's license from your own country to drive in Guatemala. Crystal Auto Rental in Belize City, Belize's largest rental company, and several rental agencies in San Ignacio permit vehicles to be taken into Guatemala (usually the El Petén/Tikal area only). Crystal requires a two-working-day notice to get paperwork ready if you are taking the vehicle into Guatemala. Keep in mind that Belize liability insurance is not valid in Guatemala, and at present there is no place at the border to buy Guatemala insurance, so you'll have to arrange that in advance. Ask your rental company for options. Car rentals in Belize usually are more expensive than in Guatemala.

Local Agencies Hertz. Hertz also has vehicles for rent at the Hotel Camino Real Tikal. ⊠ *Mundo Maya Airport, Santa Elena, 11 Av. 0-11 Zona 2, Santa Elena* ☎ *502/7926-0415 Hertz in Santa Elena, 800/654-3001 Hertz international rentals* ⊕ *rentautos.com.gt.* **Tabarini** ⊠ *Mundo Maya International Airport, Santa Elena* ☎ *502/7926-0253 in Santa Elena, 502/2322-5088 in Guatemala City* ⊕ *www.tabarini.com.*

TAXI TRAVEL

After you cross the border from Belize into Melchor de Mencos, you can hire a private taxi to take you and your party direct to Tikal or, if you prefer, to Flores. You'll usually pay Q350–Q550 (US$45–US$70) for the taxi, not per person, depending on your bargaining ability. A group taxi van for up to five persons from the border direct to Tikal is usually around US$65, or US$13 per person. A taxi to El Remate from the border will be less, as little as Q200 (US$25). Taxis from the Santa Elena–Flores airport to Tikal are around Q350–Q400 (US$45–US$50). A taxi from the Santa Elena airport into Flores is Q20 (about US$2.50) or Q10 per person, whichever is greater. A tuk-tuk (motorcycle rickshaw) ride from the Santa Elena bus terminal to Flores will be around Q5–Q10.

EMERGENCIES

El Petén's only public hospital is in San Benito, a suburb of Santa Elena. There also are two small private hospitals in the Petén, including Shalom in San Benito, operated by a U.S. religious group. Medical facilities in El Petén are not as modern as in much of the rest of the country. If you're really sick, consider getting on the next plane to Guatemala City. Centro Médico Maya in Santa Elena has physicians on staff, though little or no English is spoken. Asistur, a tourist assistance service overseen by INGUAT, can help you locate English-speaking physicians and arrange an ambulance—dial 1500 anywhere in Guatemala, 24 hours a day.

Contact Emergency Services Police ☎ *502/7926-1365, 110 police emergency, 120 police emergency.* **Centro Médico Maya** ⊠ *4 Av., 2 Av y 4 Calle, Zona 1, Santa Elena* ☎ *502/7926-0180.* **Hospital Nacional** ⊠ *San Benito* ☎ *502/7926-1333.* **Hospital Shalom** ⊠ *Km 7, San Jose Rd., San Benito* ☎ *330/477-0184 U.S. phone* ⊕ *www.newcovenantworldmissions.org.*

Pharmacy Farmacia Nueva ⊠ *Av. Santa Ana, Flores* ☎ *502/7926-1387.*

MONEY MATTERS

The exchange rate between the U.S. dollar and the Guatemalan quetzal floats—that is, it changes depending on market conditions. As of this writing, the Guatemalan quetzal is roughly Q7.8 to US$1, but at most hotels and shops in El Petén you'll get a little less.

BORDER FORMALITIES

The Belize border is about 9 miles (15 km) from San Ignacio, just west of the town of Benque Viejo del Carmen. Belize has built a new customs-and-immigration building at the border. Border crossings here are usually quick and easy.

Buses in Belize on the Goldson Highway don't go all the way to the border. The western route ends at the town of Benque Viejo, about 1 mile (2 km) from the border. You can take a taxi from Benque to the border, or you can take a taxi from San Ignacio to the border. Upon arrival at the border, you'll be approached on the Belize side by money changers asking if you want to exchange U.S. or Belize dollars for Guatemalan quetzales. Another group will approach you on the Guatemala side. The rate given by money changers may be a little less than you'll get at an ATM or bank, but you may want to exchange enough at least for your first day in Guatemala. You'll usually get better rates on the Guatemala side.

Belize formalities include paying your US$18.75 (BZ$37.50) exit fee.

Guatemala border officials usually will ask for a Q20 (US$2.50) entrance fee at this border. Even if this is not an official fee, Guatemalan border officers make it seem so, stamping your passport and checking their computer, and most visitors pay the small amount rather than making a fuss. Most visitors to Guatemala, including citizens of the United States, Canada, and European Union, do not need visas, and passports are normally stamped with a permit to enter for up to 90 days.

Melchor de Mencos is a scruffy border town with mostly unpaved streets. Shops on the main drag sell Guatemalan crafts. Some of the basic hotels in town are actually brothels.

There's no safe long-term parking at the Belize border, so if you are driving a rental car you should arrange to park it elsewhere. If you are traveling by rental car into Guatemala, be sure your vehicle paperwork is in order and allow extra time for the border crossing; arrange auto liability insurance in advance.

Although U.S. dollars are seldom refused in Guatemala, using quetzales will make transactions easier and less confusing. You can exchange U.S. dollars at any bank and in high-end hotels. If you need to exchange money, do so before heading off on your jungle adventure. Note that since 2009 Guatemala has a new Q200 note; previously, the largest denomination was Q100.

There are several banks in Santa Elena, but few anywhere else in the region, and none at Tikal park. Those on Calle 4, Santa Elena's main street, have ATMs that work with foreign ATM cards with Master-Card or Visa logos on the PLUS or CIRRUS systems. In Guatemala Visa debit cards are more widely used in ATMs than are MasterCard debit cards. Several gas stations between Santa Elena and Ixlú also have bank ATMs. In Flores there is an ATM next to Hotel Petén on Calle 30 de Junio. Banrural has an office in Flores but no ATM there. There is a bank office, Banquetzal, at the Flores airport that will exchange money, and also an ATM. Note that ATM scams in

Guatemala are common, though more so in Guatemala City, Antigua, and elsewhere than in the Santa Elena/Flores area. Thieves use electronic devices to capture your PIN number and then steal your ATM card to empty your bank account. ⚠ **The U.S. State Department states on its Guatemala travel website, "We strongly encourage you not to use ATMs."**

Banks Banrural ✉ *4 Calle at 3 Av., Santa Elena* ☎ *502/7926–1002* ⊕ *www.banrural.com.gt.* **Banco Industrial** ✉ *4 Calle, Santa Elena* ☎ *502/7926–0281* ⊕ *www.bi.com.gt.*

HEALTH

If you've been traveling in Belize, where you can generally drink the water and usually eat even street food with no problem, Guatemala's health and hygiene standards come as an unpleasant surprise. Tap water is rarely potable, and even better restaurants may not pass a health inspection. To prevent traveler's diarrhea, drink only bottled water and avoid raw vegetables—on their own or in salads—unless you know they've been thoroughly washed and disinfected. Be wary of strawberries and other unpeeled fruits. Heat stroke is another risk, but one that can easily be avoided. The best way to avoid it is to do as the locals do (wake early and retire at midday for a siesta) and drink lots of water.

United States Embassy ✉ *Av. La Reforma 7–01, Zona 10, Zona 10, Guatemala City* ☎ *502/2326–4000 in Guatemala City, 502/2331–2354 for after-hours emergency assistance* ⊕ *guatemala.usembassy.gov* ☉ *Mon.–Thurs. 8–5, Fri. 8–12:30.*

SAFETY

Most crimes directed at tourists in El Petén have been pickpocketings, muggings, and thefts from cars. However, there have been a number of incidents over the years involving armed groups stopping buses, vans, and private cars, both at Tikal park and on the road from Tikal to the Belize border.

In mid-2011 the U.S. Embassy in Belize "strongly recommended against" travel to Flores and Tikal. For several months some tour operators in San Ignacio and elsewhere in Cayo District suspended doing tours to Tikal, but as of this writing they have resumed to also, and there haven't been any major recent incidents. ⚠ **Tourists have not been specifically targeted, but due to the threat of drug cartel–related violence in El Petén you should check the current U.S. State Department travel advisories and ask locally before traveling to Tikal, Flores, and environs.**

In late 2012, INGUAT reintroduced voluntary "caravans"—security guards to accompany vans and other vehicles—between Mundo Maya International Airport and Tikal, leaving the airport around 9 am and returning at 4 pm. If staying in the Flores area, check locally to see if these security caravans are still operating, and the times.

In town, keep your camera in a secure bag, don't wear flashy jewelry or watches, and don't handle money in public. Hire taxis only from official stands at the airport, outside hotels, and at major intersections. If you can avoid it, don't drive after sunset. One common ploy used by highway robbers is to construct a roadblock, such as logs strewn across the road, and then hide nearby. When unsuspecting motorists get out of their cars to remove the obstruction, they are waylaid. ⚠ **If you come upon a deserted roadblock, don't stop. Turn around.**

8

The increase in adoption of Guatemalan children has caused some people—particularly rural villagers—to fear that children will be abducted by foreigners. Limit your interaction with children you do not know, and be discreet when taking photographs.

For police emergencies anywhere in Guatemala, dial 110 or 120 (the equivalent of 911 in the U.S. or Belize).

ABOUT THE RESTAURANTS

In El Petén you have a couple of choices for dining: *comedores,* which are small eateries along the lines of a U.S. café or diner, with simple and inexpensive local food; and restaurants, that, in general, are a little nicer and serve a wider selection of food, often with an international or American flavor. Restaurants are mostly in Flores and other towns. Elsewhere you'll probably eat in hotel or lodge dining rooms.

Some restaurants serve wild game, or *comida silvestre.* Although often delicious, the game has usually been taken illegally. You might see *venado* (venison), *coche del monte* (mountain cow or tapir), and *tepezcuintle* (paca, a large rodent) on the menu.

ABOUT THE HOTELS

El Petén now has a wide range of lodging options, from suites at luxurious lakeside resorts to stark rooms in budget hotels. The island town of Flores has many lodging choices, though most are mediocre at best; the number of hotels there keeps prices competitive. At busy times, such as Easter and Christmas, Flores hotels likely will be fully booked. The hotels in the much larger Santa Elena, the gateway to Flores, are generally larger and more upscale than the places in Flores, but with less atmosphere. El Remate, about 22 miles (35 km) from Flores on the road to Tikal, is a pleasant alternative, with several excellent small, mostly inexpensive hotels. At Tikal itself are three lodges that have the great advantage of being right at the park, although you are paying rather high rates (for Guatemala) for the in-park location rather than for service or amenities. On the north side of Lago de Petén Itzá are several hotels, including a couple of the most upscale in the region: Francis Ford Coppola's La Lancha, and the largest resort hotel in the area, Hotel Camino Real Tikal.

HOTEL AND RESTAURANT PRICES

Prices in the restaurant reviews are the average cost of a main course at dinner or, if dinner is not served, at lunch; taxes and service charges are generally included. Prices in the hotel reviews are the lowest cost of a standard double room in high season, excluding taxes, service charges, and meal plans (except at all-inclusives). Prices for rentals are the lowest per-night cost for a one-bedroom unit in high season.

For expanded lodging reviews and current deals, visit Fodors.com.

Many hotels in El Petén have high and low seasons. They charge higher rates during the dry season, December through April, especially at the peak times of Christmas and Easter, and sometimes also during the July to August vacation season. Advance reservations are a good idea during these periods, especially at Tikal park lodges.

TOURS

U.S.-based tour and travel agency with an office in Flores, Martsam Travel, run by Lileana and Benedicto Grijalva, offers many different types of tours in the area. The Mayan Adventure, associated with Café Yaxhá in Flores, offers excellent tours to popular destinations such as Tikal and Yaxhá, as well as to more remote and difficult sites such as El Zotz. The long-established La Casa de Don David, a small inn in El Remate, arranges well-run trips to Tikal and Yaxhá, along with horse-riding and birding tours. Tip tour guides about 10% of the tour price. Note that for long treks to remote sites such as El Mirador you may have to pay extra for an English-speaking guide.

Contacts Martsam Travel ⊠ *Calle 30 de Junio, lobby of Capitán Tortuga, Flores* ☎ *502/7926–0346 in Flores, 866/832–2776 in U.S. and Canada* ⊕ *www.martsam.com.*

Many tour operators in the San Ignacio, Belize, area operate day and overnight or multi-night Tikal tours. You'll pay more in Belize than in Guatemala, but you reduce the hassle factor—you'll probably be picked up at your Cayo hotel, whisked across the border, provided with a guide to Tikal, and fed lunch (hotel accommodations are arranged if you're staying overnight). You'll typically pay US$125–US$225 (BZ$250–BZ$450) per person for a day tour to Tikal from San Ignacio, and US$250–US$400 (BZ$500–BZ$800) for an all-inclusive overnight trip with lodging in the park, meals, transport, tax, fees, and guide. When comparing tour costs, check to see if border fees and Tikal admission are included. If you want an easy ride to Tikal without the formality of a tour, some tour operators in San Ignacio will allow you to go along in their vans, on a space-available basis, to Tikal for a modest fee, typically BZ$50–BZ$80 one-way. *See the Cayo chapter for more information.*

The Mayan Adventure. Run by the owners of Café Yaxhá, Anne Weirauch and Dieter Richter, The Mayan Adventure folks do excellent tours to popular destinations such as Tikal and Yaxhá. Their Yaxhá-La Blanca all-day tour ranges from US$45 for five persons to US$90 per person for two persons, plus US$11 per-person admission fees. They can also handle more adventurous trips such as a three-day hike to El Zotz (US$155 per person if there are four persons, with an extra charge for an English-speaking guide). ⊠ *Avenida 15 de Septiembre, Flores* ☎ *502/5830–2060* ⊕ *www.the-mayan-adventure.com.*

VISITOR INFORMATION

Arcas, which returns illegally captured animals to the wild, is a great resource on the flora and fauna of El Petén. The staff at INGUAT, Guatemala's tourism promotion agency, is courteous, professional, and knowledgeable. INGUAT has an information desk at the Mundo Maya International Airport in Santa Elena. CINCAP (Centro de Información sobre de Naturaleza, Cultura y Artesanías), which for years provided helpful visitor information in Flores, closed its museum and information center and is now just a gift shop. The owners of Café Arqueológico Yaxhá in Flores are very knowledgeable about the area, as are David and Rosita Kuhn, owners of La Case de Don David in El Remate. Both Café Yaxha and La Case de Don David also function as unofficial visitor information centers.

Contacts ARCAS. ARCAS is a non-profit Guatemalan NGO formed in 1989 to rehabilitate injured wildlife. Today, its rescue center near Flores is one of the largest in the world, annually helping up to 600 wild animals, of up to 40 different species. ⊠ Barrio La Ermita, 6 miles (10 km) east of Santa Elena, San Benito ☎ 502/5208–0968 Dr. Fernando Martinez (Rescue Center Director) ⊕ www.arcasguatemala.com. **INGUAT** ⊠ Mundo Maya International Airport, Santa Elena ☎ 502/7926–0533 ⊕ www.visitguatemala.com.

TIKAL

22 miles (35 km) north of El Remate, 42 miles (68 km) northeast of Flores.

Fodor's Choice ★ Tikal is one of the most popular tourist attractions in Central America— and with good reason. Smack in the middle of the 222-square-mile (575-square-km) Parque Nacional Tikal, the towering temples are ringed on all sides by miles of virgin forest. The area around the ruins is great for checking out creatures that spend their entire lives hundreds of feet above the forest floor in the dense canopy of trees. Colorful birds like yellow toucans and scarlet macaws are common sights.

GETTING HERE AND AROUND

If you're in Belize City, take the Fuente del Norte, Linea Dorada, or San Juan Travel bus from the Marine Terminal to Flores/Santa Elena. From the San Ignacio area cross the border (take a taxi to the border and walk across, or take a bus to Benque Viejo and a taxi from there to the border as buses don't run the last 1 mile (2 km) from Benque to the border) and then go by taxi or group van to Tikal. You can also take an escorted tour from San Ignacio, or fly Tropic Air from the international airport in Belize City. Tropic has flights twice daily to Mundo Maya International Airport in Santa Elena, near Flores.

TIMING

You can visit Tikal, a UNESCO World Heritage site, on a full-day trip from the San Ignacio, Belize, area and get a good sense of its grandeur. Depending on your schedule, you may choose to spend the night either at Tikal park so you can see the ruins in the morning (a must for birders), or in Flores, El Remate, or elsewhere along the shores of Lake Petén Itzá. You can easily spend two days, or longer, exploring the ruins. You may want to hire a guide for your first day, then wander about on your own on the second. If you have additional time, consider an extension in El Petén. The town of Flores, with its lakeside bistros and cobblestone streets, merits at least a half-day stroll, and, better yet, an overnight, so you can enjoy a good meal and drinks with views of the lake.

SAFETY AND PRECAUTIONS

Taxis and tourist buses are sometimes magnets to bandits in El Petén. Taxi drivers taking passengers from the Belize border to Flores or Tikal often remove taxi insignia from their vehicles before leaving the border. The bandits take passengers' valuables; occasionally passengers have been

Tikal and the Mayan Sites

Biosphere Reserve
El Mirador
Dos Lagunas
Río Azul National Park
seasonally inundated

Carmelita
Uaxactún
Tikal see detail map

seasonally inundated
Río San Pedro
EL PETÉN
Tikal National Park
Nakúm

El Zotz
Pesco
Biotopo Cerro Cahuí
Benque Viejo del Carmen

La Pava Nueva
North Shore, Lake Petén Itzá
Yaxhá
Melchor de Mencos

San José
San Andrés
Lake Yaxha
El Remate

Lake Petén Itza
Flores see detail map

Airport
San Benito
Santa Elena

La Libertad
Santa Ana
Río Mopán

GUATEMALA
Santa Ana Vieja

Río Usumacinta
Río de la Pasión
Sayaxché
Dolores

MEXICO
Dos Pilas
Ceibal
Río Machaquilá

Río Lacantún
seasonally inundated

Poptún

0 — 1/2 mi
0 — 1/2 km
Aguateca
TO RÍO DULCE

KEY
Mayan Site

BELIZE

assaulted. Keep in mind, however, that some 300,000 international visitors come to Tikal every year, and the vast majority of them have no problems with crime. Of course, tourists cause problems for Guatemala, too. During the frenzy associated the Mayan Long Count Calendar predicting that the world would end on December 21, 2012, end-of-the-world parties held on that day drew more than 7,000 people to Tikal, some of whom violated rules, climbed Temple II, and did irreparable damage to it.

EXPLORING

Tikal. Although the region was home to Mayan communities as early as 600 BC, Tikal itself wasn't established until sometime around 200 BC. One of the first structures to be built here was a version of the North Acropolis. Others were added at a dizzying pace for the next three centuries. By AD 100 impressive structures like the Great Plaza had already been built. But even though it was a powerful city in its own right, Tikal was still ruled by the northern city of El Mirador. It wasn't until the arrival of a powerful dynasty around AD 300 that Tikal arrogated itself to full power. King Great Jaguar Paw sired a lineage that would build Tikal into a city rivaling any of its time. It's estimated that by AD 500 the city covered more than 18 square miles (47 square km) and had a population of close to 100,000.

The great temples that still tower above the jungle were at that time covered with stucco and painted with bright reds and greens, and the priests used them for elaborate ceremonies meant to please the gods and assure prosperity for the city. What makes these structures even more impressive is that the Maya had no metal tools to aid in construction, had no beasts of burden to carry heavy loads, and never used wheels for anything except children's toys. Of course, as a hierarchical culture they had a slave class, and the land was rich in obsidian, a volcanic glass that could be fashioned into razor-sharp tools.

By the 6th century Tikal governed a large part of the Mayan world, thanks to a leader called Caan Chac (Stormy Sky), who took the throne around AD 426. Under Caan Chac, Tikal became an aggressive military and commercial center that dominated the surrounding communities with a power never before seen in Mesoamerica. The swamps protected the city from attack and allowed troops to spot any approaching enemy. Intensive agriculture in the *bajos* (lowlands) provided food for the huge population. A valuable obsidian trade sprang up, aided by the city's strategic position near two rivers.

Tikal thrived for more than a millennium, forming strong ties with two powerful centers: Kaminal Juyu, in the Guatemalan highlands, and Teotihuacán, in Mexico City. The city entered a golden age when Ah-Cacao (Lord Chocolate) ascended the throne in AD 682. It was Ah-Cacao and his successors who commissioned the construction of the majority of the city's most important temples. Continuing the tradition of great structures, Ah-Cacao's son commissioned Temple I, which he dedicated to his father, who is buried beneath it. He also ordered the construction of Temple IV, the tallest temple at Tikal. By the time of his death in 768 Tikal was at the peak of its power. It would remain so until its mysterious abandonment around AD 900.

For almost 1,000 years Tikal remained engulfed by the jungle. The conquistadors who came here searching for gold and silver must have passed right by the overgrown ruins, mistaking them for rocky hills. The native Peténeros certainly knew of the ancient city's existence, but no one else ventured near until 1848, when the Guatemalan government dispatched archaeologists to the region. Tikal started to receive international attention in 1877, when Dr. Gustav Bernoulli commissioned locals to remove the carved wooden lintels from across the doorways of Temples I and IV. These were sent to a museum in Basel, Switzerland.

In 1881 and 1882 English archaeologist Alfred Percival Maudslay made the first map showing the architectural features of this vast city. As he began to unearth the major temples, he recorded his work in dramatic photographs—you can see copies in the museum at Tikal. His work was continued by Teobert Maler, who came in 1895 and 1904. Both Maler and Maudslay have causeways named in their honor. In 1951 the Guatemalan air force cleared an airstrip near the ruins to improve access for large-scale archaeological work. Today, after more than 150 years of digging, researchers say that Tikal includes some 3,000 significant buildings. Countless more are still covered by the jungle. ⊠ *Parque Nacional Tikal* ⊕ *www.tikalpark.com* ⊠ *Q150* ⊗ *Daily 6–6.*

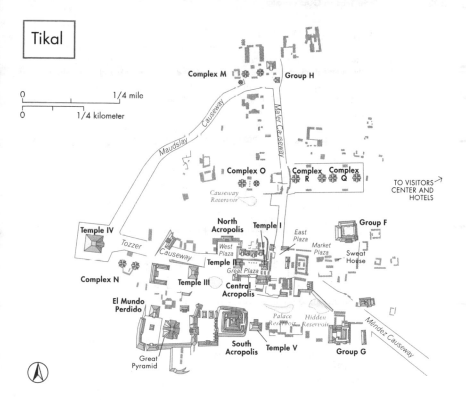

Tikal

0   1/4 mile

0   1/4 kilometer

Complex M   Group H

Complex O

Complex R   Complex Q

Causeway Reservoir

TO VISITORS CENTER AND HOTELS

Temple IV

North Acropolis   Temple I

East Plaza

Group F

Tozzer Causeway

West Plaza

Market Plaza

Sweat House

Complex N

Temple III

Temple II

Great Plaza

Central Acropolis

El Mundo Perdido

Palace Reservoir   Hidden Reservoir

Méndez Causeway

Great Pyramid

South Acropolis   Temple V

Group G

TIKAL WITH A GUIDE

Guides make the visit more interesting, though don't believe everything they tell you, as some guides have their own pet theories on the decline of the Maya or other subjects that they love to expound to tourists. Near the parking lot at Tikal is an information kiosk where you can hire guides. Rates are somewhat negotiable, but expect to pay about Q400 (a little over US$50) for a tour for up to four or five people. In a large group you may pay as little as Q60 (US$8) per person. Groups are not supposed to exceed 20 people. If you're staying more than one day, consider hiring a guide for the first day, and then wandering on your own after that. You can buy a map of the park near the visitor's center for Q20. Note that many but not all guides speak English. Roxy Ortiz is perhaps the most recommended guide at the park. An archaeologist, she is highly knowledgeable. She works out of the Tikal Inn at the park.

TIKAL ON YOUR OWN

Wear comfortable shoes and bring water—you'll be walking about 6 miles (10 km) if you intend to see the whole site. As you enter Tikal, keep to the middle trail. You'll soon arrive at the ancient city's center, filled with awe-inspiring temples and intricate acropolises. The pyramid that you approach from behind is **Temple I,** known as the Temple of the Great Jaguar because of the feline represented on one of its carved

TIKAL EXPLORING TIPS

Regular admission to Tikal is Q150 (a little less than US$20 at current conversion rates). Visitors generally are not allowed inside the ruins outside of opening hours of 6 am to 6 pm daily. The exception is that visitors staying at one of the three park lodges or camping at the park may visit the park at sunrise and sunset, between 4 am and 8 am or between 6 pm and 8 pm, but only with a certified guide. The cost is Q275 (around US$35) including Q100 special admission fee and a three-hour tour of the major temples. This admission fee is only for the duration of the tour and doesn't allow you to stay in the park after the tour, so if you want to see more you have to also purchase a regular admission for Q150. The rules about these sunrise and sunset tours change from time to time—ask park rangers or official guides about the current policy. If you are able to see sunrise in the park, perhaps the best place to see it is at the top of Temple IV.

Even if you don't take one of the extra-cost sunrise or sunset tours, if you stay at one of the three lodges on the grounds you get a jump-start on the day-tour visitors and have the advantage of being here late in the afternoon, after most everyone else has left.

We do hear tales of visitors sneaking in at night or slipping guards bribes to pass, but we strongly advise against that. The trails are not lit, and climbing the pyramids is risky in the dark. There's also a slight chance of robbery.

As of this writing, officials allow an admission ticket to the park purchased after 4 pm to be used the next day without an additional charge, but you usually have to request this at the time you purchase the ticket. If you arrive late in the afternoon and plan to return to the park the next day, or are staying at a lodge in the park overnight, be sure to ask the ranger to stamp your ticket with the next day's date.

If you have only one day or less at the park, try to see the highlights: Temples IV and V, both of which can be climbed, the Great Plaza, Mundo Perdido, and the Plaza of the Seven Temples.

lintels. It's in what is referred to as the **Great Plaza, or Gran Plaza,** one of the most beautiful and dramatic in Tikal. The Great Plaza was built around AD 700 by Ah-Cacao, one of the wealthiest rulers of his time. His tomb, comparable in magnitude to that of Pa Cal at the ruins of Palenque in southern Mexico, was discovered beneath the Temple of the Great Jaguar in the 1960s. The theory is that his queen is buried beneath **Temple II,** called the Temple of the Masks for the decorations on its facade. It's a twin of the Temple of the Great Jaguar. In fact, construction of matching pyramids distinguishes Tikal from other Mayan sites.

The **North Acropolis,** to the west of Ah-Cacao's temple, is a mind-boggling conglomeration of temples built over layers and layers of previous construction. Excavations have revealed that the base of this structure is more than 2,000 years old. Be sure to see the stone mask of the rain god at Temple 33. The **Central Acropolis,** south of the Great Plaza, is an immense series of structures assumed to have served as administrative centers.

If you climb to the top of one of the pyramids, you'll see the gray roof combs of others rising above the rain forest's canopy but still trapped within it. **Temple V,** to the south, underwent a US$3 million restoration project and is now open to the public. **Temple IV,** to the west, is the tallest known structure built by the Maya. Although the climb to the top is difficult, the view is unforgettable.

To the southwest of the plaza lies the **South Acropolis,** which hasn't been reconstructed, and a 105-foot-high pyramid, similar in construction to those at Teotihuacán. A few jungle trails offer a chance to see spider monkeys and other wildlife. Outside the park, a somewhat overgrown trail halfway down the old airplane runway on the left leads to the remnants of old rubber-tappers' camps and is a good spot for bird-watching.

At park headquarters are two small archaeological museums that display Mayan artifacts. They are a good resource for information on the enigmatic rise and fall of the Mayan people, though little information is in English.

Museo Lítico or Stelae Museum. Museo Lítico or Stelae Museum has stelae found at Tikal and interesting photos from early archaeological excavations. ⊠ *Near visitor center* 🖃 *Q10 ($1.20)* ☾ *Weekdays 9–5, weekends 9–4.*

Museo Tikal (*Tikal Sylvannus G. Morley Museum*). Museo Tikal has a replica of Ha Sawa Chaan K'awil's burial chamber and some ceramics and bones from the actual tomb (the jade, however, is a replica). ⊠ *Near visitor center* 🖃 *Free with ticket (Q10) to Museo Lítico* ☾ *Weekdays 9–5, weekends 9–4.*

WHERE TO STAY

There are three hotels on the park grounds: Tikal Inn, Jungle Lodge, and Jaguar Inn. At all of these you pay for the park location rather than amenities and great service. Electric power is from generators, which at two of the lodges, Tikal Inn and Jungle Lodge, operate only for a few hours in the morning and again for a few hours in the evening; at the Jaguar Inn, the generator (usually) runs for 24 hours. Batteries may provide limited lighting throughout the night. Bring a flashlight! None of the hotels at the park has air-conditioning. Since the hotels here have a captive audience, service is not always as friendly or helpful as it could be, and at busy times reservations are sometimes "lost," even if you have a confirming email. Camping is also available, at the park campsite (US$7 for a tent or very basic cabin shelter) or at the Jaguar Inn. Several *comedores* are at the entrance to the park, Imperio Maya and Comedore Tikal currently being the best. Expect to pay around Q60 for a meal and a beer or other drink. You can also get snacks and drinks from vendors in the parking lot (but not in the park itself) and at the hotels. All the hotels have room-only rates, but if you are booking through a travel agent or sometimes even through the hotel you may be required to take a package that includes meals and perhaps a Tikal tour. The restaurant at Jaguar Inn currently is the best of the lodge eateries.

$$$
HOTEL
🏨 **Jaguar Inn.** This small hotel has the feel of a backpacker's place, but it's in the park, which is what is important to most travelers. **Pros:** conveniently in the park; 24-hour electricity; camping available. **Cons:** basic rooms somewhat jammed together; no swimming pool; pricey for what you get. 💲 *Rooms from: Q625* ✉ *Parque Nacional Tikal, Jaguar Inn* ☎ *502/7926–0002 reservations, 502/7783–3647 front desk* ⊕ *www.jaguartikal.com* 🛏 *13 rooms in cabins, 1 dorm, camping* 🍽 *No meals.*

$$
B&B/INN
🏨 **Jungle Lodge.** Built almost 60 years ago to house archaeologists working at Tikal, this lodge has 36 spacious bungalows with double beds. **Pros:** clean and adequate accommodations; swimming pool. **Cons:** you are paying for location; food is mediocre; standard rooms are small. 💲 *Rooms from: Q510* ✉ *Parque Nacional Tikal, Jungle Lodge* ☎ *502/2477–0570* ⊕ *www.junglelodgetikal.com* 🛏 *12 rooms with shared baths, 36 bungalows, 2 junior suites* 🍽 *Breakfast.*

$$$
B&B/INN
🏨 **Tikal Inn.** Tikal Inn is our pick for the best of the three lodges at the park. **Pros:** good location in the park; swimming pool; decent service; the best of a mediocre bunch. **Cons:** rooms can be hot since there is no power for fans at night; limited hot water and electricity. 💲 *Rooms from: Q705* ✉ *Parque Nacional Tikal, Tikal Inn* ☎ *502/3038–9373 reservations* ✎ *tikalinn@gmail.com* ⊕ *www.tikalinn.com* 🛏 *18 rooms and junior suites, 18 bungalows* 🍽 *Some meals.*

TIKAL ENVIRONS

Flores, a charming small town in Lake Petén Itzá connected to the mainland by a causeway, is the main point of interest beyond Tikal. Stay in a small inn or hotel, eat at lakeside bistros, and explore the cobblestone streets on foot. Santa Elena, at the entrance to Flores, is a bustling commercial center but is far less frequented by tourists. El Remate, a village on the shore of the lake, has a number of small, mostly budget or moderately priced, hotels and is a handy, low-key jumping-off point for Tikal if you don't stay in the park.

FLORES

133 miles (206 km) north of Río Dulce, 38 miles (61 km) northeast of Sayaxché.

The red-roof town of Flores, on an island surrounded by the waters of Lago Petén Itzá, is on the site of the ancient city of Tatyasal. This was the region's last unconquered outpost of Mayan civilization, until finally falling to the Spanish in 1697. The conquerors destroyed the city's huge pyramids.

Today the capital of the department of Petén is a pleasant place to explore, with its narrow streets lined with thick-walled buildings painted pink, blue, and purple. Flowering plants droop over balconies, and there's a central square presided over by a colonial church. In recent years, many of the streets in Flores, especially those at the edge of the lake, have been repaired and resurfaced with cobblestones, making strolling around more pleasant.

Sadly, many of the hotels in Flores are also pedestrian, rarely rising above mediocrity. Flores is crying out for a truly special small inn, one that's as charming as the town itself.

Connected to the mainland by a bridge and causeway—don't be put off by the Burger King at the entrance to the causeway, or the new Mundo Maya International Mall shopping center there—Flores serves as a base for travelers to El Petén. It's also the center of many nongovernmental organizations working for the preservation of the Mayan Biosphere, an endangered area covering nearly all of northern Petén. Flores is also one of the last remaining vestiges of the Itzá, the people who built Mexico's monumental Chichén Itzá.

> **WORD OF MOUTH**
>
> "Tikal Inn is my favorite hotel in the park and I recommend staying in the park so you can do a sunrise tour; you can't do those from El Remate or Flores. Roxy Ortiz picked me up at the airport in Flores night before . . . then headed out for a visit to Uaxactún. We visited Tikal for sunset and sunrise, then headed to Yaxhá on our way to Belize where we spent a few days together caving."
>
> —hopefulist

WHERE TO EAT

$ LATIN AMERICAN

🍴 **Café Arqueológico Yaxha.** This restaurant combines a cultural and educational experience with good food, and you can often get more information here about the region than from INGUAT. German architect Dieter Richter, who has worked on projects at Yaxha and Naranjo, started this café. You can browse a collection of books, photos, maps, and other information about the Mayan world while you enjoy a hamburguesa or a Mayan dish such as *Pollo Xni Pec* (chicken in a chili sauce served with rice and yucca). Most main dishes are Q50 to Q80. You can also book tours to Yaxha and elsewhere. [$] *Average main: Q60* ✉ *Av. 15 de Septiembre* ☎ *502/5830–2060* 🌐 *www.cafeyaxha.com.*

$$ PIZZA FAMILY

🍴 **Capitán Tortuga.** The large, cartoonlike Capitán Turtle sign may fool you into thinking this restaurant is just for kids, but the grilled meats, pizza, tacos and burritos, and other options make this one of Flores' better choices for a meal with a view. The *pinchos* (grilled kebabs) are cooked on an open barbecue, sending enticing aromas throughout the restaurant. There's a nice patio out back, which offers tremendous sunset views of the lake. [$] *Average main: Q100* ✉ *Calle 30 de Junio and Callejón San Pedrito* ☎ *502/7867–5089* 🌐 *www.capitantortuga.com.*

$ CAFÉ

🍴 **Cool Beans/El Café Chilero.** Sit in a leafy garden and sip a latte or lemonade at this cool coffeehouse. You can eat breakfast for under Q40, and light meals and beer are served the rest of the day. Free Wi-Fi. [$] *Average main: Q60* ✉ *Calle 15 de Septiembre* ☎ *502/5571–9240* ⏲ *Closed Tues.*

$$ ITALIAN Fodor's Choice ★

🍴 **Il Terrazo.** Il Terrazo arguably is currently the best restaurant in Flores. Certainly the location is among the best in town. The restaurant, on a second floor terrace (as the name suggests), has wonderful views over the lake. The owners offer an eclectic mix of Italian and other dishes, and it's also a good place for a drink. [$] *Average main: Q80* ✉ *Calle Union* ☎ *502/7867–5479* ⏲ *Closed Sun.*

8

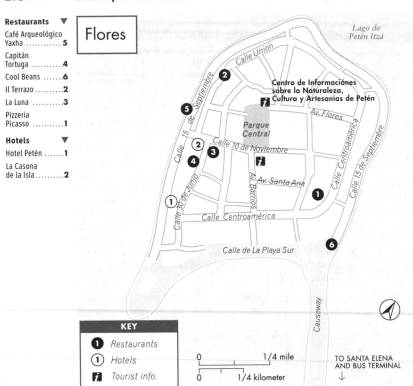

$$$ **✗La Luna.** With its homemade paper lamp shades illuminating lovely
ECLECTIC blue walls, La Luna inspires romance on any moonlit night. But you
can just as easily fall in love with what we think is the most creative
restaurant in town when you stop in for a delicious lunch or dinner.
Choose from inventive dishes, including wonderful vegetarian options
like the stuffed squash in white sauce. The fish dishes are always good.
Many people drop by for a drink at the bar. All it lacks is a view of the
lake. $ *Average main: Q120* ⊠ *Calle 30 de Junio, corner Calle 10 de
Noviembre* ☎ *502/7926–3346.*

$$ **✗Pizzeria Picasso.** If you find yourself returning to Pizzeria Picasso, it's
PIZZA because the brick-oven pizza is hot and delicious. The decor, featuring
a print of Picasso's *Guernica,* is another draw. If you're not in the mood
for pizza, there is a variety of pastas as well. Save room for cheesecake
or tiramisu and a cup of steaming cappuccino. $ *Average main: Q80*
⊠ *Calle 15 de Septiembre at Calle Centroamérica* ☎ *502/7926–0673*
☉ *Closed Mon.*

WHERE TO STAY

$$ **▦Hotel Petén.** An arabesque plunge pool graces the central courtyard of
HOTEL this classic lodging, believed to be the oldest hotel in Flores (of course
this means only a little more than 50 years, when Flores became a visi-
tor destination due to Tikal). **Pros:** classic hotel with great views of

the lake from some balcony rooms. **Cons:** four flights of stairs to get to top-floor rooms. $ *Rooms from: Q407* ✉ *Calle 30 de Junio, off Calle Centroamerica* ☎ *502/2366–2841* ✎ *reservaciones@hotelesdepeten. com* ⊕ *www.hotelesdepeten.com* ⇆ *21 rooms* ⫣ *No meals.*

$$ ⫣ La Casona de la Isla. La Casona de la Isla is a lakeside hotel in Flores, one of the top hotels on an island without many great hotels, and it has comfortable but unremarkable rooms with air-conditioning, Wi-Fi, and cable TV. **Pros:** modern conveniences like a/c, cable, and Wi-Fi; lake views from some rooms, especially on upper floors; swimming pool; friendly staff. **Cons:** don't expect real luxury (here or anywhere in Flores). $ *Rooms from: Q460* ✉ *Calle 30 de Junio* ☎ *502/2366–2841* ⇆ *26 rooms* ⫣ *Some meals.*

HOTEL

> **WATCH FOR THE ANIMALS!**
>
> Obey Tikal's 45 kph (27 mph) speed limit; it's designed to give you time to stop for animals that cross the road within the confines of the park. Be particularly careful of the raccoon-like coatimundi that locals call a *pizote*, which scurries with abandon across the road. At the park entrance a guard gives you a time-stamped ticket to be collected by another guard when you arrive at the visitor center. If you cover the 9-mile (15-km) distance in less than 20 minutes, you'll be deemed to have been speeding and possibly fined.

NIGHTLIFE

Flores has a number of bars and restaurants where you can enjoy drinks with a view, although on weekdays the town tends to close up early. Il Terrazo, an excellent restaurant, has a second-level bar with good drinks and with equally fine views of the lake. Flores nightlife gets more active on weekends, and locals tends to hang out at the cantinas on the Playa Sur area near the Gran Hotel de la Isla.

Il Terrazo. The thatch roof second-floor terrace with beautiful lake views is a good place to have a drink in the evening, with soft music from the sound system playing in the background. Come early for the happy hour. ✉ *Calle Unión* ☎ *502/7867–5479.*

La Luna. For an evening drink, the artsy La Luna has a pleasant atmosphere, but there is no lake view. ✉ *Calle 30 de Junio* ☎ *502/7926–3346.*

SPORTS AND THE OUTDOORS
BOATING

Boat trips on Lake Petén Itzá can be arranged through most hotels in Flores or by haggling with boat owners who congregate behind the Hotel Santana. Tours (Q80–Q160) often include a stop at Paraíso Escondido, a small mainland park northwest of Flores.

SANTA ELENA

¼ mile (½ km) south of Flores.

Although it lacks the charms of neighboring Flores, gritty Santa Elena is pretty much unavoidable. Most services that you'll need for your trip to El Petén, from currency exchange to gas stations, are offered here. Mundo Maya International Mall, a new shopping center near the

8

causeway to Flores, has a large grocery store and other shops. There are also more upscale hotels here than in Flores. Most are focused on tour groups and business people.

GETTING HERE AND AROUND
Tuk-tuks—the motorized three-wheeled taxi rickshaws manufactured in Asia—ply the streets of Flores and, to a lesser degree, Santa Elena. Most trips are Q20 or less.

TIMING
Santa Elena is a place to sleep in a decent hotel, get money from an ATM, and buy picnic supplies. There's little to see in Santa Elena itself. At most, you'll use it as a base for exploring other parts of El Petén, so how long you stay here depends on your exploration plans.

SAFETY AND PRECAUTIONS
Some gas stations in Santa Elena have guards armed with shotguns 24 hours a day, so that should tell you something. The better hotels are quite safe, however, and most visitors never experience any crime.

WHERE TO STAY

$$$$
HOTEL
Hotel La Casona del Lago. Santa Elena's spiffiest hotel sits on the lakeshore and has splendid views of Flores across the water, especially from the top-floor restaurant and bar. **Pros:** short walk or tuk-tuk ride across causeway to Flores; views of Flores and the lake; pool; good hotel restaurant. **Cons:** rooms on street side can be noisy; gets a good deal of group business; expensive (for this part of Guatemala). $ *Rooms from: Q783* ⊠ *Calle Litoral* ☎ *502/7952–8700* ⊕ *www. hotelesdepeten.com* ⤶ *33 rooms.*

$$$$
HOTEL
Petén Espléndido. You're not in Flores, but the views of that pretty island from your private balcony may be the next best thing to being there. **Pros:** close to mall; perhaps has the only hotel elevator in the Petén; nice views of Flores; easy access by foot or tuk-tuk to Flores. **Cons:** smallish rooms; ready for updating; somewhat overpriced. $ *Rooms from: Q925* ⊠ *1 Calle, 5-01, Zona 1, near foot of causeway leading to Flores* ☎ *502/7926–0880* ⊕ *www.petenesplendido.com* ⤶ *62 rooms.*

$$$$
HOTEL
Villa Maya. You could lie in bed and count the birds flying by your window at these modern villas at Lake Petenchel, east of Santa Elena, part of a small group of villa-type hotels around Guatemala. **Pros:** beautiful lake views; quiet and peaceful setting. **Cons:** not convenient to a selection of restaurants and shopping; bugs can be bothersome. $ *Rooms from: Q815* ⊠ *5 miles (8 km) east of Santa Elena, Laguna Petenchel* ☎ *502/7931–8350 hotel, 502/2223–5000 in Guatemala City* ⊕ *www.villasdeguatemala.com* ⤶ *56 rooms in 10 villas* ❘⊘❘ *No meals.*

SPORTS AND THE OUTDOORS
There are several caves in the hills behind Santa Elena with interesting stalactite and stalagmite formations and subterranean rivers. The easiest to visit is Actun Kan, just south of town.

FAMILY
Ixpanpajul Parque Natural. Ixpanpajul Parque Natural is a private nature reserve sitting on a large stand of primary rain forest. Hiking the suspended bridges of the skyway will give you a bird's-eye view of the indigenous flora and fauna that make the rain forest the most biodiverse

ecosystem on the planet. The park also offers myriad adventure opportunities, from nighttime ATV tours to horseback rides to mountain-bike excursions. A three-hour Tarzán Canopy Tour (zip line) costs Q235 or US$30. There is camping, and rental cabanas are available. A restaurant has specials that average around Q70. ✉ *Km 468, Ruta a Santa Elena, 6 miles (10 km) south of Santa Elena between Santa Elena and Tikal Park* ☎ *502/2336–0576, 502/4062–9812 phone in park* ⊕ *www.ixpanpajul.com* ⊙ *Daily 7–6.*

EL REMATE

18½ miles (30 km) northeast of Flores.

A mellow little town on the eastern shore of Lago Petén Itzá, El Remate is known for its wood carvings, made by families that have dedicated themselves to this craft for generations. Just west of El Remate is the Biotopo Cerro Cahuí, and you can rent a canoe or kayak (around Q10 or US$1.20 an hour) at El Remate to explore the lake. Because it's less than one hour from both Tikal and Yaxhá, El Remate makes a good base for exploring the area, and there are a growing number of small inns, hotels, and restaurants to choose from, many with views of the lake.

EXPLORING

Biotopo Cerro Cahuí. With around 1,500 acres of rainforest, Biotopo Cerro Cahuí near El Remate is one of the most accessible wildlife reserves in El Petén. It protects a portion of a mountain that extends to the eastern edge of Lago Petén Itzá, so there are plenty of opportunities for hiking. Two well-maintained trails put you in proximity of birds like ocellated turkeys, toucans, and parrots. As for mammals, look up to spot the long-armed spider monkeys or down to see squat rodents called *tepezcuintles.* Tzu'unte, a 4-mile (6-km) trail, leads to two lookouts with views of nearby lakes. The upper lookout, Mirador Moreletii, is known by locals as Crocodile Hill, because from the other side of the lake it looks like the eye of a half-submerged crocodile. Los Ujuxtes, a 2-mile (5-km) trail, offers a panoramic view of three lakes. Both hikes begin at a ranger station, where English-speaking guides are sporadically available. Some robberies and attacks on tourists have taken place in the reserve, so ask locally in El Remate about safety conditions before you explore on your own. ✉ *West of El Remate* 🎫 *Q30* ⊙ *Daily 7–5.*

GETTING HERE AND AROUND

El Remate, near the El Cruce or Ixlú crossroads, is about an hour by car from the Belize border and about a half hour from Flores.

TIMING

Most visitors use El Remate as a base for visits to Tikal and other nearby Mayan sites, so the length of stay depends on how much time you want to spend seeing ruins.

WHERE TO STAY

$$

HOTEL

La Casa de Don David. Don David Kuhn has lived in the area for 40 years and is a great source of Tikal travel tips, and his hotel near El Remate, while not the most deluxe in the area, offers a lot for the visitor. **Pros:** knowledgeable hosts; attractive grounds; good restaurant. **Cons:**

8

not a lot of frills. $ *Rooms from: Q360* ⊠ *On road to Biotopo Cerro Cahuí, near El Remate* ☎ *502/5306–2190, 502/5949–2164* ⊕ *www. lacasadedondavid.com* ⤳ *13 rooms* ⦿ *Some meals.*

$ ⛨ **La Mansión del Pájaro Serpiente.** Perched on a hillside in El Remate, La
HOTEL   Mansión del Pájaro Serpiente has some of the prettiest accommodations in El Petén. **Pros:** pretty little cabins set on a hillside; lake views (though it's not directly on the lake); lovely grounds; swimming pool. **Cons:** not for visitors who can't walk up and down steep hills. $ *Rooms from: Q345* ⊠ *On main hwy. south of El Remate* ☎ *502/5967–9816 in English or Spanish* ✍ *tikalnancy@hotmail.com* ⊕ *www.30minutesfromtikal. com* ⤳ *11 rooms* ▭ *No credit cards.*

SPORTS AND THE OUTDOORS

FAMILY   **Tikal Canopy Tour.** The fun folks at Tikal Canopy Tour have expeditions that take you to the true heart of the rain forest—not on ground level, but more than 100 feet up in the air. There are now two zip lines, one with nine and one with 10 platforms. On either canopy tour you may see monkeys and or other wildlife. Each zip line costs US$30 or Q235 per person. Prices include transport from El Remate or Tikal Park (from Flores or Santa Elena there's an additional US$5 fee). Tikal Canopy Tour also offers hiking. ⊠ *Near entrance gate to Tikal park, about 40 minutes by car from Flores* ☎ *502/7926–4270* ⊕ *www.canopytikal.com* ⤳ *Q235.*

SHOPPING

Although most souvenirs here are similar to those found elsewhere in Guatemala, the beautiful wood carvings are unique to El Petén. More than 70 families in this small town dedicate themselves to this craft. Their wares are on display on the side of the highway right before the turnoff for the Camino Real and La Lancha hotels on the road to Tikal, and also in small shops in El Remate.

NORTH SHORE, LAKE PETÉN ITZÁ

8 miles (13 km) west of El Remate.

The small villages of San Pedro, San José, and San Andrés, on the northwest shore of Lake Petén Itzá, have beautiful views of the sparkling lake. Several upscale lodges and hotels have opened here, and the area is accessible via bus or car on an improved (but bumpy) dirt road from El Remate or Santa Elena, or in the clockwise direction from San Benito.

WHERE TO STAY

$$$$ ⛨ **Camino Real Tikal.** To experience the natural beauty of the jungles
RESORT   surrounding Lago Petén Itzá without sacrificing international-style hotel creature comforts, you could head to the Camino Real Tikal. **Pros:** largest international-style hotel in the Petén; beautiful setting. **Cons:** somewhat remote; rooms somewhat tired and dated; upgrading and renovations needed; lots of steps may pose problem for mobility-impaired guests. $ *Rooms from: Q1030* ⊠ *3 miles (5 km) west of El Remate, Lote 77, Parcelamiento Tayasal, San José* ☎ *502/7926–0204, 502/2410–5299 reservations* ⊕ *www.caminorealtikal.com.gt* ⤳ *72 rooms* ⦿ *Breakfast.*

$$$$ RESORT Fodor's Choice ★ [hotel] **La Lancha.** Francis Ford Coppola's Guatemalan lodging is done in exquisite taste, and it's the only one with air-conditioning. **Pros:** lovely lake views; excellent restaurant; air-conditioned rooms; all done in good taste. **Cons:** very expensive (for Guatemala); somewhat remote; lots of steep steps; you can hear your neighbors in the cheaper duplex units. [$] *Rooms from: Q1520* ✉ *8 miles (13 km) west of El Remate, San José* ☎ *502/7928–8331, 800/746–3743 in U.S. and Canada* 🌐 *www.coppolaresorts.com/lalancha* 🛏 *10 casitas* 🍴 *Breakfast.*

$$$$ B&B/INN Fodor's Choice ★ [hotel] **Ni'tun Lodge and Private Reserve.** After hiking through the jungle, you'll love returning to this charming cluster of cabins owned by a former coffee farmer across the lake from Flores. **Pros:** small, very personal lodge experience; excellent food; engaging owner. **Cons:** off the beaten path; expensive. [$] *Rooms from: Q1300* ✉ *near San Andrés, across Lake Petén Itzá northwest of Flores, San Andrés Xecul* ☎ *502/5201–0759* 🌐 *www.nitun.com* 🛏 *4 cabins* ⏲ *Closed late May–early June* 🍴 *Breakfast.*

OTHER MAYAN SITES IN EL PETÉN

Although Tikal is the most famous, El Petén has hundreds of archaeological sites, ranging from modest burial chambers to sprawling cities. The vast majority have not been explored, let alone restored. Within a few miles of Tikal are several easy-to-reach sites. Because they're in isolated areas, it's a good idea to go with a guide. If you have limited time, Yaxhá is the easiest to reach from Belize or from El Remate or Flores, and after Tikal it's one of the best sites to explore.

Some travelers stop over at Yaxhá, about 25 miles (43 km) by road from the Belize border at Melchor de Mencos, on their way to Tikal, though this requires an overnight in the Tikal area, as you won't have time to explore both Yaxhá and Tikal in one day. Many tour operators in Flores and El Remate offer day or overnight tours to Yaxhá, for around US$50–US$70, but at present there are few tour operators in Belize that do tours to Yaxhá. Ka'ana Resort and duPlooy's Lodge near San Ignacio do offer trips to Yaxhá as part of a multiday package. You may have to negotiate with a San Ignacio tour operator for a custom day tour. You also could rent a car in San Ignacio and do it on your own, or hire a taxi on the Melchor side of the border to take you to Yaxhá.

El Mirador in the Mirador Basin is potentially the most exciting Maya site in the Petén, rivaling Tikal. But at present to reach it requires a multiday trek by foot with mules or horses and is impractical to visit except for the most adventurous travelers in top physical condition.

⚠ **Mexican drug cartels, including the Zetas and others, are known to operate in the remote areas of El Petén south of the Mexican border, and they are said to own large tracts of land. Several major incidents (that is, murders of government officials and local citizens) have taken place here. Ask locally about safety before traveling to remote destinations.**

EXPLORING

TOP ATTRACTIONS

Ceibal. Upriver about 10 miles (17 km) from Sayaxché are the impressive ruins of Ceibal, frequently rendered "Seibal" in English. The site takes its name from the many canopylike ceiba trees, the national tree of Guatemala, in the area. Ceibal achieved prominence in ancient times serving as a tollgate collecting tribute from barges plying La Pasión river. Its archaeological attractions are several restored temples, including the only circular one known to exist. Here you will also find intricately carved stelae—dozens in all—some of the best preserved in the region. Interestingly, a number of anomalies were found in these monuments, which hint at a foreign influence, most likely from the Toltecs of central Mexico. Carvings on structures here show dates corresponding to about AD 900, and are some of the latest among Mayan ruins in Mesoamerica. Ceibal is now thought to have undergone two distinct periods of growth, one in the Late Pre-Classic period and another in the Late Classic period, the two interrupted by centuries of abandonment. The area is quite marshy, and rife with mosquitoes; lather up with insect repellent. There are buses from Santa Elena/Flores to Sayaxché, and from there you can get to Ceibal by boat on the Pasión River or by partly dirt road by taxi or car. Tour companies in Flores can also arrange trips to Ceibal. The Sayaché area is considered a center for Mexican drug cartels, and large farms and tracts of land are said to be owned by narcotraffickers. ⊠ *On the Río de la Pasión, Ceibal* 🖾 *Free* ☉ *Daily 6–6.*

El Mirador. El Mirador, once equal in size and splendor to Tikal, may eventually equal Tikal as a must-see Mayan ruin. It's just now being explored, but elaborate plans are being laid to establish a huge park four times the size of Tikal. Dr. Richard D. Hansen of the University of Idaho is director for the Mirador Basin Project, sponsored by the Foundation for Anthropological Research and Environmental Studies (FARES). The Mirador Basin contains the El Mirador site itself, four other known Mayan cities that probably were as large as Tikal (Nakbé, El Tintal, Xulnal, and Wakná), and many smaller but important sites—perhaps as many as 80 to 100 cities. The Mirador Basin is home to an incredible diversity of plant and animal life, including 200 species of birds, 40 kinds of animals (including several endangered ones, such as jaguars), 300 kinds of trees, and 2,000 different species of flora. It has been nominated as a UNESCO World Heritage Site. Currently, fewer than 2,500 visitors get to El Mirador annually, as it's a difficult trek requiring four to six days of hiking (round-trip). The jumping-off point for the trek is Carmelita Village, about 50 miles (84 km) north of Flores. There are no hotels in the Mirador Basin, and no roads except for dirt paths. Local tour companies in Flores and elsewhere can arrange treks. Expect to pay US$300 or more if in a group. For those with the budget, like actor Mel Gibson, you can visit by helicopter. ⊠ *40 miles (66 km) northwest of Tikal* ⊕ *www.miradorbasin.com.*

WORTH NOTING

Dos Pilas. Dos Pilas is about 7 miles (12 km) west of the northern end of Lake Petexbatún. The nearest town is Sayaxché. Dos Pilas was founded in AD 640 by nobles from Tikal who fled Tikal after it was conquered by Calakmul. Most impressive of the ancient structures found here are limestone staircases and stelae covered with carvings that recount the battles against other city-states in the region, including Tikal. Unlike most other Mayan cities, this one was surrounded by a defensive wall. Dos Pilas was abandoned the late 8th century AD. This is not an easy, or inexpensive, destination to reach. In Sayaxché, you may be able to organize transportation by boat and horseback. ⊠ *Dos Pilas, Sayaxché* ⌧ *Free* ☉ *Daily 6–6.*

El Zotz. El Zotz is where you'll find the remnants of a Mayan city guarded by bats and monkeys and a few park guards. On a clear day you can see the tallest of the ruins at Tikal from the top of El Diablo Temple or other mostly unexcavated mounds. The name, which means "the bat" in Ket'chi Maya, refers to a cave from which thousands of bats make a nightly exodus. Troops of hyperactive spider monkeys seem to have claimed this place for themselves, swinging through the treetops and scrambling after each other like children playing a game of tag. Unlike those in Tikal, however, these long-limbed creatures are not used to people and will shake branches and throw twigs and fruit to try to scare you away. During the rainy season the mosquitoes can be fierce, so bring your strongest repellent. A few tour operators in Flores arrange two-night treks to El Zotz for around US$200 per person. ⚠ **Some visitors have been robbed on guided treks from Tikal to El Zotz.** ⊠ *15 miles (24 km) west of Tikal* ⌧ *Free.*

Nakúm. The Late Classic ceremonial center of Nakúm lies deep within the forest, connected to Yaxhá via 10 miles (17 km) of jungle trails that are used for dry-season horseback expeditions, SUV trips, or hikes. A number of structures here have been excavated. You can't visit during the rainy season, as you'll sink into mud up to your ankles. Even during the dry season, a four-wheel-drive vehicle with high clearance is a good idea. Explorer Alfred Tozzer rediscovered Nakúm in 1909, and began to assign certain structures descriptive names, some of which may not be accurate. ⊠ *16 miles (26 km) east of Tikal and 10 miles (17 km) north of Yaxhá*

Punta de Chimino. Southwest of the town of Sayaxché is the remains of the fortress of Punta de Chimino, 2½ miles (4 km) north of Aguateca. It was the last residence of the area's besieged royal families as the area descended into chaos in the 10th century AD. The defenders dug several moats into the peninsula where the fort stood, turning it into an island. ⊠ *near Lago Petexbatún, Sayaxché.*

Uaxactún. The 4,000-year-old city of Uaxactún once rivaled Tikal's supremacy in the region. It was conquered by Tikal in the fourth century and lived in the shadow of that great city for centuries. Inscriptions show that Uaxactún existed longer than any other Mayan city, which may account for the wide variety of structures. Here, among the stelae and palaces, you'll find a Mayan astronomical observatory, thought to be the oldest in Mesoamerica. It is designated "Structure

8

E-VII-B." From the observatory, the sun lines up precisely on the solstices and equinoxes. As the excavated ruins here are much smaller and less impressive than at Tikal, you won't have to fight the crowds as you do at neighboring Tikal, leaving you free to enjoy the quiet and mystic air of the ruins. Although there are daily local buses from Santa Elena to the village of Uaxactún near the ruins, you'll probably want to arrange with a tour company in Flores to see the Mayan site. Some multinight tours combine a visit to El Zotz with one to Uaxactún. ⊠ *16 miles (24 km) north of Tikal, Uaxactún* ☎ *Q60* ⊗ *Daily 6–6.*

Yaxhá. Yaxhá is part of the Yaxhá-Nakúm-Naranjo Natural Monument. It is relatively easy to reach by car from the Belize border, with a guide tour from San Ignacio, or by a guided tour from Flores or El Remate (around US$50–US$70 for a day tour). From the Belize border it's about 25 miles (43 km) or an hour by car, on roads that are passable even in the rainy season. There is a visitor center and small museum here, along with restrooms. While much smaller than Tikal, and can be seen in about half a day, it has a lot of wildlife, including spider and howler monkeys. The ruins, built of an unusual light-toned limestone, give it a different feel than most other ruins in the region. Only rarely are there more than a handful of visitors at Yaxhá.

Overlooking a beautiful lake of the same name, the ruins of Yaxhá are divided into two sections of rectangular structures that form plazas and streets. ■TIP→ A guide is a good idea here, since it is not obvious what all the structures are. Here's what is known: the city was probably inhabited between the Pre-Classic and Classic periods, and at its peak contained 20,000 people. It was also an important ally of nearby Tikal. Only a portion of the estimated 500 structures are visible at present, the most famous of which is designated Templo 216, Yaxhá's highest edifice with splendid views of the adjoining lake and rain forest.

Lake Yaxhá—the name, pronounced *Yah-SHAH,* translates as "green waters"—surrounded by virgin rain forest, is a good bird-watching spot. In the middle of the lake sit the ruins of **Isla Topoxté,** a fortress dating from the Post-Classic period about AD 1000, and the site of one of the last strongholds against Spanish invaders. Ask the park staff here about transportation. Someone can take you if you pay for the boat's gas. Crocodiles inhabit the lake.

You can camp at Yaxhá, or stay at the solar-powered jungle lodge, **Camapmento Ecológico El Sombrero** (☎ *502/7861–1687*) about 1 mile (2 km) south of the Yaxhá ruins. ⊠ *29 miles (48 km) east of Flores, 19 miles (30 km) southeast of Tikal, about 6½ miles (11 km) off route CA 13, Melchor de Mencos* ⊕ *From the Belize border at Melchor de Mencos, go about 19 miles (32 km) on Route CA13 toward Ixlú and watch for a sign to Yaxhá. Turn right on a dirt road and go about 6½ miles (11 km) to Yaxha visitor center and the ruins.* ☎ *Q80* ⊗ *Daily 7–5.*

UNDERSTANDING BELIZE

FAST FACTS

Name: Officially changed from British Honduras to Belize in 1973

Capital: Belmopan City

Type of government: Parliamentary democracy

National anthem: "Land of the Free"

Population: 357,000 (2012 World Bank estimate)

National Tree: Mahogany (*Swietenia macrophilla*)

This prized tree has been heavily logged in Belize, and large specimens are found in only a few areas. The "big leaf" mahogany tree can grow more than 150 feet high and takes 80 years to reach maturity. The wood has a coppery red sheen, a tight, knot-free grain, and a single mature tree can be worth US$100,000 or more.

National Flower: Black Orchid (*Prosthechea cochleata*)

The name is deceiving. Only the lip of the flower is black, and the long, slender sepals and petals are yellow-green. These fragrant little flowers bloom year-round and can be found growing on trees in damp areas.

National Bird: Keel-Billed Toucan (*Ramphastos solfurantus*)

The toucan, with its huge canoe-shape beak and bright yellow cheeks, can be found in open areas all over the country and loves to eat fruit.

National Animal: Baird's Tapir (*Tapirello bairdii*)

Called the mountain cow by most Belizeans, the tapir is actually related to the primitive horse and rhinoceros. A beefy vegetarian, it can weigh up to 600 pounds and is often found in heavy bush, near rivers and streams.

National Motto: *Sub Umbra Florero*

"Under the Shade I Flourish" refers to the shade of the mahogany tree, which is on Belize's coat of arms and flag.

National Drink: Orange Fanta and **Belikin Beer** (unofficially, of course).

Did You Know?

More than 40% of Belize's land is protected as national parks or reserves.

Belize has the longest barrier reef in the Western and Northern hemispheres.

The two tallest buildings in Belize, one at Caracol and one at Xunantunich, date back more than 1,000 years.

Belize is thought to have the largest population of manatees in the world.

Belize is the only country in Central America with English as the official language.

Belize has fewer than 400 miles (640 km) of paved roads.

The names of two of the four major highways in Belize officially changed in 2012. Western Highway is now George Price Highway and Northern Highway is Philip Goldson Highway.

The expanse of Selva Maya (Maya Forest), which Belize shares with Guatemala and Mexico, covers some 9,600 square miles (25,000 square km), the largest block of tropical forest north of the Amazon Basin.

At the height of the Mayan civilization, Belize may have had a population approaching 1 million people, about three times the population of the country today.

Belize is the only country in Central America without a border on the Pacific Ocean.

A MAYAN PRIMER

Chronology

Traditionally, archaeologists have divided Mayan history into three main periods: Pre-Classic, Classic, and Post-Classic. Although some academics question the validity of such a uniform chronology, the traditional labels are still in use.

The **Pre-Classic** (circa 3,000 BC–AD 250) period is characterized by the influence of the Olmec, a civilization centered on the Gulf Coast of present-day Mexico. During this period cities began to grow, especially in the southern highlands of Guatemala and in Belize, and it's at this time that Belize's Cuello, Lamanai, Santa Rita, Cahal Pech, Pacbitun, and Altun Ha sites were first settled, along with El Mirador in Guatemala.

By the **Late Pre-Classic** (circa 300 BC–AD 250) period the Maya had developed an advanced mathematical system, an impressively precise calendar, and one of the world's five original writing systems. In Belize, Cerros (also called Cerro Maya) was established during the Late Pre-Classic period.

During the **Classic** (circa AD 250–900) period, Mayan artistic, intellectual, and architectural achievements literally reached for the stars. Vast city-states were crisscrossed by a large number of paved roadways, some of which still exist today. The great cities of Caracol (Belize), Palenque (Mexico), Tikal (Guatemala), and Quirigu (Guatemala) were just a few of the powerful centers that controlled the Classic Mayan world. In AD 562 Caracol—which at its height was the largest city-state in Belize, with a population of about 150,000—conquered Tikal. Other notable Classic period sites in Belize include Xunantunich, El Pilar, and Lubaantun.

The single largest unsolved mystery about the Maya is their rapid decline during the **Terminal Classic** (AD 800–900) period and the centuries following. Scholars have postulated that climate change, pandemic disease, extended drought, deforestation, stresses in the social structure, overpopulation, and changes in the trade routes could have been responsible. Rather than a single factor, several events taking place over time could well have been the cause.

The Maya of the **Post-Classic** (AD 900–early 1500s) period were heavily affected by growing powers in central Mexico. Architecture, ceramics, and carvings from this period show considerable outside influence. Although still dramatic, Post-Classic cities such as Chichén Itzá and Uxmal pale in comparison to their Classic predecessors. By the time the Spanish conquest reached the Yucatán, the Maya were scattered, feuding, and easy to conquer. Several sites in Belize, including Lamanai, were continuously occupied during this time, and even later.

Key Dates

Here are some key dates in the history of the Maya in Belize and in the El Petén area of Guatemala. Most of the dates are approximate, and some dates are disputed.

BC

3114	Date of the creation of the world, or 0.0.0.0.0 according to the Long Count calendar
3000	Early Olmec and Mayan civilizations thought to have begun
2500	Cuello established
2000	Santa Rita established
1500	Lamanai established
1000	Cahal Pech established
900	Olmec writing system developed; Caracol established
800	Tikal established
500	First Mayan calendars carved in stone
400–300	First written Mayan language
250	Altun Ha established
200	First monumental buildings erected at Tikal and El Mirador

AD

400–600 Tikal becomes leading city-state, with population of perhaps 200,000

553 Accession of Lord Water as Caracol ruler

562 Caracol conquers Tikal

599 Accession of Lord Smoke Ahau as Caracol ruler

618 Accession of Kan II as Caracol ruler

631 Caracol defeats Naranjo; Caracol's population is 150,000

700 Lubaantun established

800 Cahal Pech abandoned

895 Xunantunich abandoned

899 Tikal abandoned

900 Classic period of Mayan history ends

900–1500 Mayan civilization in decline, many cities abandoned

1000 Southern Belize Mayan centers mostly abandoned

1050 Caracol abandoned

1517 Spanish arrive in Yucatán and begin conquest of Maya

1517–1625 Diseases introduced from Europe cause death of majority of Maya

1524–25 Hernán Cortés passes through Belize en route to Honduras, after leading expeditions to conquer the Aztecs in Mexico

1546–1600s Maya in Belize rebel against Spanish

1695 Tikal ruins rediscovered by Spanish

1700s Lamanai continuously occupied over 3,000 years

1724 Spanish abolish *encomienda* system of forced Mayan labor

1839 John Lloyd Stephens and Frederick Catherwood visit Belize

1847 Caste Wars in Yucatán begin

1881 Early archaeological work begins at Tikal, by Alfred Maudslay

1894 Thomas Gann begins exploring Xunantunich and other Belize ruins

1926 Ruins of El Mirador, one of the earliest and largest Mayan cities, found in remote area of the Petén

1936 Caracol ruins rediscovered by a lumberman

1956 William Coe and others begin excavations at Tikal

1985 Drs. Arlen and Diane Chase begin excavations at Caracol, which continue to this day

1992 Rigoberta Menchu, a Maya from Guatemala, wins Nobel Peace Prize

2012 The time some predicted would be the end of the world, December 21, 2012, or 13.0.0.0.0 in the Long Count Mayan calendar passed as just another day

2013 The looting and export of Mesoamerican Mayan artifacts for illegal sale to collectors becomes an estimated $100-million-a-year business

MAYAN ARCHITECTURE

One look at the monumental architecture of the Maya, and you might feel transported to another world (perhaps that's why Tikal was used as the rebel base in the original 1977 *Star Wars*). The breathtaking structures are even more impressive when you consider that they were built 1,000 to 2,000 years ago or more, without iron tools, wheels, or pulleys. The following is a brief explanation of the architecture you see at a Mayan ruin.

Influences

Mayan architecture, even the great temples, may echo the design of the typical thatch hut ordinary Maya used for thousands of years. The rectangular huts had short walls made of a limestone mud and were topped by a steeply tilted two-sided thatch roof. Caves—ever-important Mayan ceremonial sites—were also influential. Many aboveground Mayan temples and other monumental structures have cave-like chambers, and the layout of Mayan cities probably reflected the Mayan cosmology, in which caves played a critical role.

Building Materials

With few exceptions, the large buildings in Mayan cities were constructed mostly from limestone, which was widely available in Belize and the Mexican Yucatán. Quarries were often established close to a building site so that workers didn't have to haul stone long distances. The Maya used limestone for mortar, stucco, and plaster. Limestone was crushed and burned in wood-fired kilns to make lime. A cement-like mortar was made by combining one part lime with one part of a white soil called *sahcab*, and then adding water.

The Maya also used wood, which was plentiful in Mesoamerica. In fact, some of the early temples were probably constructed of wood poles and thatch, much like the small houses of the Maya; unfortunately, these buildings are now lost.

Tools

The Maya were behind the curve with their tool technology. They didn't have iron tools, pulleys to move heavy weights, or wheels to build carts. They didn't have horses or other large animals to help them move materials. Instead, they used large numbers of laborers to tote and haul stones, mortar, and other building materials.

Obsidian, jade, flint, and other hard rocks were used to make axes, knives, and saws. The Maya had mason's kits to cut and finish limestone, and they had the equivalent of a plumb bob and other tools to align and level stones. The Maya were skilled stoneworkers, although the degree of finish varied from city to city.

City Layout

In most Mayan cities large plazas were surrounded by temples and large pyramids, probably used for religious ceremonies and other important public events. Paved causeways connected the plazas. Away from the city center were sprawls of "suburbs"—smaller stone buildings and traditional thatch huts.

Most cities had ball courts, and although the exact rules are unclear, players used a ball of natural rubber (rubber was discovered by the Olmecs) and scored points by getting the ball through a hoop or goalpost. "Sudden death" had a special meaning—the leader of the losing team was sometimes killed by decapitation.

The celebration of Belize's historic multiculturalism begins on its flag: the two young men—one black and the other white—are woodcutters standing beneath a logwood tree. Under them is a Latin inscription: *sub umbra floreat*—"In the shade of this tree we flourish."

BELIZE HISTORY

Anthropologists believe that humans from Asia crossed a land bridge, in what is now the Bering Strait in Alaska, into North America about 25,000 years ago. Gradually these Paleoindians, or "Old Indians," whose ancestors probably were Mongoloid peoples, made their way down the continent, establishing Native American or First Nation settlements in what is now the United States and Canada. Groups of them are thought to have reached Mesoamerica, which includes, besides Belize, much of central Mexico, Guatemala, Honduras, and Nicaragua, around 20,000 to 22,000 years ago.

These early peoples were hunter-gatherers. The Olmec civilization, considered the mother culture of later Mesoamerican civilizations including that of the Maya, arose in central and southern Mexico 3,000 to 4,000 years ago. The Olmecs developed the first writing system in the New World, dating from at least 900 BC. They also had sophisticated mathematics and created complex calendars. The Olmecs built irrigation systems to water their crops.

As long ago as around 3000 BC—the exact date is in question and has changed as archaeologists have made new discoveries—the Maya began to settle in small villages in Belize and elsewhere in the region. They developed an agriculture based on the cultivation of maize (corn), squash, and other fruits and vegetables. Some archeologists believe that the Maya—like other Indians in the region as well as in the South American Amazon—augmented soils with charcoal, pottery fragments, and organic matter to create *terra preta* (Portuguese for dark soil), very fertile earth that stood up to hard tropical rains. In Belize, small settlements were established as early as 2500 BC at Cuello in what is now Orange Walk District in northern Belize. Then, over the next 1,000 years or so, settlements arose at Santa Rita in Corozal and Lamanai in Orange Walk, and at Cahal Pech, Caracol, and elsewhere in Cayo District in western Belize. What would become the great city-states of the region, including Tikal in today's Petén region of Guatemala and Caracol in the Cayo, were first settled around 900 to 700 BC.

Several centuries before the time of Christ, several Mayan villages grew into sizable cities. The Maya began to construct large-scale stone buildings at El Mirador, Tikal and elsewhere. Eventually, Tikal, Caracol, and other urban centers each would have thousands of structures—palaces, temples, residences, monuments, ball courts, even prisons. Although the Maya never had the wheel, and thus no carts or wagons, they built paved streets and causeways, and they developed sophisticated crop irrigation systems.

At its height, in what is known as the Classic period (250 BC to AD 900), the Mayan civilization consisted of about 50 cities, much like ancient Greek city-states. Each had a population of 5,000 to 100,000 or more. Tikal, the premier city in the region, may have had 200,000 residents in and around the city during its heyday, and Caracol in Belize probably had nearly as many. The peak population of the Mayan civilization possibly reached 2 million or more, and as many as a million may have lived in Belize alone—more than three times the current population.

The Mayan culture put a heavy emphasis on religion, which was based on a pantheon of nature gods, including those of the sun, moon, and rain. The Mayan view of life was cyclical, and Mayan religion was based on accommodating human life to the cycles of the universe.

Contrary to what scholars long believed, however, Mayan society had many aspects beyond religion. Politics, the arts, business, and trade were all important and dynamic aspects of Mayan life.

Dynastic leaders waged brutal wars on rival city-states. Under its ruler Lord Smoke Ahau, Caracol, the largest city-state in Belize, conquered Tikal in AD 562, and less than a hundred years later conquered another large city, Naranjo (also in Guatemala).

The Maya developed sophisticated mathematics. They understood the concept of zero and used a base-20 numbering system. Astronomy was the basis of a complex Mayan calendar system involving an accurately determined solar year (18 months of 20 days, plus a five-day period), a sacred year of 260 days (13 cycles of 20 days), and a variety of longer cycles culminating in the Long Count, based on a zero date in 3114 BC, or 0.0.0.0.0—the date that the Maya believed was the beginning of the current cycle of the world.

The Mayan writing system is considered the most advanced of any developed in Mesoamerica. The Maya used more than 1,000 "glyphs," small pictures or signs, paired in columns that read from left to right and top to bottom. The glyphs represent syllables and, in some cases, entire words, that can be combined to form any word or concept. There is no Mayan alphabet. Mayan glyphs can represent either sounds or ideas, or both, making them difficult to accurately interpret. The unit of the writing system is the cartouche, a series of 3 to 50 glyphs, the equivalent of a word or sentence in a modern language.

As in most societies, it's likely that the large majority of the Maya spent much of their time simply trying to eke out a living. In each urban area the common people lived in simple thatch dwellings, similar to those seen in the region today. They practiced a slash-and-burn agriculture. Farmers cleared their small plots by burning the bush, then planting maize, squash, sunflowers, and other crops in the rich ash. After two or three years, when the soil was depleted, the plot was left fallow for several years before it could be planted again.

Beginning around AD 800, parts of the Mayan civilization in Belize and elsewhere in Mesoamerica began to decline. In most areas the decline didn't happen suddenly, but over decades and even centuries, and it took place at different times. For example, the cities in the Northern Lowlands of the Yucatán, such as Chichén Itzá, flourished for several more centuries after Tikal and Caracol were abandoned.

Scholars are still debating the reasons for the decline. Climatic change, lengthy droughts, overpopulation, depletion of arable land, social revolutions by the common people against the elites, epidemics, and the impact of extended periods of warfare all have been put forth as reasons. Earthquakes, hurricanes, and other natural disasters may have played a role at certain sites. It may well have been a combination of factors, or there may have been different causes in different regions.

Whatever the reasons, the Mayan civilization in Belize and elsewhere in Mesoamerica never regained its Classic period glory. By the time the Spanish arrived in the early 1500s only a few of the Mayan cities, mainly in the Highlands of Guatemala, were still thriving. Most of the great cities and trading centers of Belize and Guatemala, including Caracol and Tikal, had long been abandoned. Lamanai and a few other urban settlements were still inhabited.

Seeking gold and other plunder, the Spanish began their conquest of the Maya in the 1520s. Some Mayan states offered fierce resistance, and the last Mayan kingdom, in Mexico, was not vanquished until almost 1700. The Maya in Belize rebelled against the Spanish several times, but there was one enemy against which the Maya were defenseless: European disease. Smallpox, chicken pox, measles, flu, and other infectious diseases swept through the Mayan settlements. Scientists believe that within a century nearly 90% of the Maya had been wiped out by "imported" diseases.

Mayan resistance to European control continued from time to time. In 1847 Mayan Indians in the Yucatán rose up against Europeans in the bloody Caste Wars, which lasted until 1904. This had a major impact on Belize, as many Mexican Mestizos (persons of mixed Indian and European heritage) and Maya moved to northern Belize to escape the violence. Sarteneja, Orange Walk Town, and Ambergris Caye were among the areas at least partly settled by refugees from the Yucatán.

Much of the Mayan civilization was buried under the tropical jungles for centuries, and Westerners knew little about it. In the process of trying to convert the Maya to Christianity in the 16th century, the Spanish burned most of the codices, Mayan "books" made of deer hide or bleached fig-tree paper. Only in the last few decades have scholars made progress in deciphering Mayan glyphic writing.

In 1839 two British adventurers, John Lloyd Stephens and Frederick Catherwood, visited Central America, including Belize, and explored a number of the Mayan sites. Their books, especially *Incidents of Travel in Central America, Chiapas, and Yucatán,* with text by Stephens and illustrations by Catherwood, brought the attention of the world to the Mayan past.

In the late 1800s the first systematic archaeological excavations of Tikal and Mayan sites in Belize were begun. Alfred Maudslay, an Englishman, conducted excavations at Tikal in 1881–82, and Harvard's Peabody Museum did fieldwork there between 1895 and 1904. Sylvanus Morley, a well-known Maya expert, conducted work at Tikal at times between 1914 and 1928. In 1956 the University of Pennsylvania began the first large-scale excavation project at Tikal. In Belize, Thomas Gann, a British medical officer stationed in what was then British Honduras, carried out the first excavations of several major Belize Mayan sites, including Santa Rita, Xunantunich, Lubaantun, sites on Ambergris Caye, and others, starting in 1894. Since then, many university and museum teams, including ones from the University of Pennsylvania, the Royal Ontario Museum, Tulane University, the University of Texas, the University of California, and the University of Central Florida, have conducted extensive fieldwork in Belize. Drs. Diane and Arlen Chase, of the University of Central Florida, have been at work at the largest site in Belize, Caracol, since 1985.

About 30,000 Maya live in Belize today, according to the 2010 Belize Census, of which about 17,000 are Ketchi, 11,000 are Mopan, and 2,000 are Yucatec. In southern Belize they're predominantly Ketchi and Mopan Maya; in western Belize, Mopan Maya; and in northern Belize, Yucatec Maya. The largest concentration of Maya in Belize is in the small villages in Toledo District near Punta Gorda.

By some interpretations, the end of the world, or at least its current cycle, was supposed to have taken place on December 21, 2012, according to the Long Count calendar of the ancient Maya. A number of hotels and other tourism organizations in Belize, Guatemala, Mexico and elsewhere attempted to capitalize on this supposed apocalypse with tours and special lodging packages. However, other experts said that the Maya did not see this as the end of the world but rather as a transition from one age to another. In any event, the day passed like any other day.

Barry Bowen

When he died February 26, 2010, in the crash near San Pedro of the Cessna 206 he was piloting, Sir Barry Bowen not only was the most prominent and best-known businessman in Belize, whose products touched nearly every Belizean and every visitor to Belize, but he also was a central figure in the political and economic history of modern Belize and a key link to the British Honduras past.

Born September 19, 1945, in Belize City, Bowen connected in some way to nearly every major development in Belize. He owned the most storied (and also at times the most hated) business enterprise in the country's history, Belize Estate and Produce Company; he was a pioneer in the two industries that now dominate commerce in Belize, agriculture and tourism; he was a supporter, leader, and major financier of the most powerful political party in the country, the People's United Party, although he also had close friends and associates in the United Democratic Party; and he proved himself one of the toughest and most capable entrepreneurs in modern Belize, using a combination of savvy marketing, hard ball tactics, and government connections to make Belikin beer and Coca-Cola soft drinks his personal cash cows.

Bowen could trace his roots in Belize back to the middle of the 18th century, when the first Bowen, from England, disembarked from a British ship and joined the ragtag band of Baymen at an encampment at the mouth of the Belize River.

In 1978, just before independence, Barry Bowen bought Bowen and Bowen from his father. Bowen moved quickly to develop and exploit the opportunities he saw in the backwater of Belize. He developed the Coca-Cola franchise and turned Belikin, first brewed in the late 1960s, into the national drink of Belize.

Today, thanks in part to the virtual monopoly status granted by the Belize government to Bowen Brewing, Belikin controls nearly all of the beer market in Belize.

Barry Bowen seemingly never believed in the great potential in mass tourism that some others saw, preferring instead to invest in industries such as aquaculture. Although he owned valuable seafront property on Ambergris Caye, Belize's number one tourist destination, he didn't open a resort there. However, in 1988, he did develop a pioneering upscale jungle lodge, Chan Chich Lodge, on Gallon Jug Estate lands, formerly part of the Belize Estate and Produce Company, which controlled hundreds of thousands of prime acres in Orange Walk District. Built literally on top of a Mayan plaza, Chan Chich Lodge is widely considered among the top few jungle lodges in Central America, and one of the best in the world.

Barry Bowen's life was not without its controversies and contradictions. Although he actively supported many conservation causes, and was a friend and supporter of the Belize Zoo and its director Sharon Matola, he was an advocate of the construction of the Chalillo Dam, which Matola strongly opposed due to destruction of habitat for the Scarlet Macaw and other birds and animals.

Bowen also was criticized for building his jungle lodge on a Mayan site. Lord Smoking Shell, an ancient Mayan chief, will roll over in his grave, some said. In defense, Bowen claimed the location of the lodge protected the site from looters.

Admired or distrusted, envied or loved, Sir Barry was a one of a kind. Bold and full of life, ambitious and willing to take a risk, a man of vision and large plans, he was a multimillionaire who certainly achieved things in little Belize.

THE MANY CULTURES OF BELIZE

Belize is a rich gumbo of colors and languages. Creoles, also known as Kriols, once the majority, now make up only about a quarter of the population. Creoles in Belize are descendants of slaves brought from Jamaica to work in the logging industry. By the early 18th century, people of African descent came to outnumber those of British origin in Belize. The two groups united early in the country's history to defeat a common enemy, the Spanish. Most of the Creole population today is concentrated in Belize City and in the rural villages of Belize District such as Gales Point and Crooked Tree, although there are predominantly Creole villages elsewhere, including Monkey River and Placencia. English is the country's official language and taught in school, although an English dialect, Creole, is widely spoken, and there are now more native Spanish speakers in Belize than English speakers.

Mestizos are the fastest-growing group in Belize and make up about half the population. These are persons of mixed European and Mayan heritage, typically speaking Spanish as a first language and English as a second. Some migrated to Belize from Mexico during the Yucatán Caste Wars of the mid-19th century. More recently, many "Spanish" (as they're often called in Belize) have moved from Guatemala, El Salvador, Honduras, or elsewhere in Central America. According to the 2010 Belize Census, more than 33,000 residents of Belize were born in other Central American countries. Mestizos are concentrated in northern and western Belize.

Numbering close to a million at the height of the Mayan kingdoms, the Maya today constitute less than one-tenth of the Belize population of 357,000. There are concentrations of Yucatec Maya in Corozal and Orange Walk districts, Mopan Maya in Toledo and Cayo districts, and also Ketchi Maya in about 30 villages in Toledo. Most speak their Mayan dialect and either English or Spanish, or both.

About one in twenty Belizeans is a Garífuna. The Garinagu (the plural of Garífuna) are of mixed African and Carib Indian heritage. Most originally came to Belize from Honduras in the 1820s and 1830s. Dangriga and Punta Gorda are towns with large Garífuna populations, as are the villages of Seine Bight, Hopkins, and Barranco. Besides their own tongue—an Arawakan-based language with smatterings of West African words—many Garinagu speak English and Creole and sometimes Spanish.

Other groups include more than 11,000 Mennonites, who tend to live in their own communities such as Spanish Lookout, Blue Creek, Barton Creek, Shipyard, and Little Belize; and sizable groups of East Indians and Chinese, mostly from Taiwan and Hong Kong. Belize's original white populations were English, but today's "gringos" are mostly expats from the United States and Canada, with some from the United Kingdom and various Commonwealth countries, together numbering several thousand. All these groups find in this tiny country a tolerant and amiable home.

Whatever the background of its citizens, Belize's population is young. More than two out of five Belizeans are under 15 years of age, and the median age is just 22.

FLORA AND FAUNA

Belize is home to thousands of species of trees and flowers, hundreds of kinds of birds, butterflies, and moths. An amazing array of creatures makes its home in Belize. Many are not terribly difficult to see, thanks to their brilliant coloring. Others are likely to elude you completely. A rundown of some of the region's most attention-grabbing mammals, birds, reptiles, amphibians—even a few insects—is provided below. Also, we've listed a few of the more colorful or interesting plants and trees. Common names, in English and Spanish or Mayan, are given, so you can understand the local wild things lingo.

Africanized Honeybee (killer bee): African honeybees were accidentally released in Brazil in the 1950s, interbred with European honeybees (a subset of the genus *Apis*) and spread north, reaching Belize in the 1980s. Now, most honeybees in Belize are Africanized. While their sting is no worse than a regular bee, they are highly aggressive. Many livestock animals have been killed by Africanized bees in Belize, and in 2013 a four-year-old Mennonite child was stung to death. If attacked, try to protect your face and get inside a building.

Bat (*murciélago*): There are more than 80 species of bats in Belize, making them by far the most common mammal found in the country. Belize has three species of vampire bats.

Black orchid (clamshell orchid, cockleshell orchid): The national flower of Belize is the black orchid, now *Prosthechea cochleata* and formerly *Encyclia cochleata*. The very dark purple flower is unusual among orchids, as the flower is effectively upside down. It is pollinated not by bees but by a small fly.

Bukut (stinking toe): Howler monkeys love the leaves of the bukut, which grows to almost 100 feet (30 meters) in open fields and pastures. You can see bukut trees at Community Baboon Sanctuary, along the Hummingbird Highway, and elsewhere in Belize. In April and May they are loaded with salmon-pink flowers. The long brown seedpods also are eaten by monkeys and birds, but they have an unpleasant smell, like sweaty socks. Hence the common name, stinking toe.

Cacao (wild cacao, kakaw): Most prevalent in Toledo District, the wild cacao is a small tree that grows to about 32 feet (10 meters). Its fruit pods, which are directly on the trunk, contain seeds that are the source of chocolate and cocoa powder. The Toledo Cacao Growers' Association (TCGA) represents over 1,000 organic cacao growers in Southern Belize.

Caiman (*cocodrilo*): The spectacled caiman is a small crocodile that subsists mainly on fish. It's most active at night (its eyes glow red when illuminated by a flashlight), basking in the sun by day. It's distinguished from its American cousin by its sloping brow and smooth back scales.

Cashew (*marañon*): This tree, related to the mango, is about the size of a small apple tree, growing up to about 40 feet (12 meters), often in a serpentine fashion. In late spring and early summer it bears cashew apples, pear-shaped bright red or yellow pseudofruit. These can be eaten, though they have a somewhat unpleasant aftertaste, but a wonderful grape-like aroma. But the true fruit is the cashew nut, attached to the base of the cashew apple. The cashew nut shell contains a poisonous liquid. Before the nuts can be safely eaten they must be roasted twice. Crooked Tree village is the center of cashew cultivation in Belize, and cashew wine is also available here.

Ceiba (cotton tree, kapok, *yaaxche*): The national tree of Guatemala and the sacred tree of the ancient Maya, who cultivated it in their plazas, the ceiba (*say-ba*) is one of the giants of the bush, sometimes growing more than 230 feet (70 meters), rising out of the jungle canopy. It has a gray, cylindrical trunk supported by large buttresses at the ground and, high up, nearly horizontal branches.

Cohune palm (*corozo* palm): The cohune is one of the most important trees for the Maya in Belize. Its leaves are used to thatch the roofs of buildings, its nuts are used for oil or soap and as fuel for fires, the sweet heart is eaten, traditionally in Belize during Easter week, and the heart sap can be used to make a wine. It is often a marker for ancient Mayan sites now hidden by jungle. Its distinctive fluted shape and tall height (up to 100 feet or more than 30 meters) make it easy to spot.

Cougar (puma): Growing to 5 feet (1½ meters) in length, mountain lions are the largest unspotted cats in Central America. Rarely seen, they live in most habitats in the region and feed on vertebrates ranging from snakes to deer.

Crocodile (*lagarto*): Although often referred to by Belizeans as alligators, crocodiles reign supreme in this region. They are distinguished from the smaller caiman by their flat heads, narrow snouts, and spiky scales. Crocodiles seldom attack humans, preferring fish, birds, and the occasional small mammal. Both species are endangered and protected by international law.

Fer-de-lance (*barba amarilla*): One of the most dangerous of all pit vipers, the fer-de-lance has a host of names, such as tommygoff, in Belize. This aggressive snake grows up to 8 feet in length and is distinguished by the bright yellow patches on its head.

Flamboyant (flame tree, royal Poinciana, *guacamayo*): This is perhaps the most visually striking tree in Belize, at least May through July when it is covered in blazing blossoms of flame-color orange. Originally from Madagascar, the flamboyant is easily identified, even when not in bloom, because of its umbrella shape, much wider than it is tall.

Frog (*rana*): More than 30 species of frogs can be found in Belize. Most are nocturnal in an effort to avoid being eaten, but the brightly colored poison dart frogs—whose brilliant red, blue, and green coloration warns predators that they don't make a good meal—can be spotted during the day. Red-eyed leaf frogs are among the showiest of nocturnal species.

Howler monkey (*mono congo*): These chunky-bodied monkeys travel in troops of up to 20. A bit on the lethargic side, they eat leaves, fruits, and flowers. The deep, resounding howls of the males serve as communication among and between troops. Erroneously termed "baboons" by Belizeans, these dark-faced monkeys travel only from tree to tree, limiting their presence to dense jungle canopy.

Iguana: The largest lizards in Central America, these scaly creatures can grow to 10 feet. They are good swimmers, and will often plop into a body of water when threatened by a predator. Only young green iguanas are brightly colored; adult females are grayish, while adult males are olive (with orangish heads during mating season). They are considered a delicacy among Belizeans, who call them "bamboo chicken."

Jaguar (*tigre*): The largest feline in the Western Hemisphere grows up to 6 feet (2 meters) long and can weigh up to 250 pounds. Exceedingly rare, this nocturnal predator is most often spotted near the Cockscomb Basin Wildlife Sanctuary in Belize or near Chan Chich Lodge.

Leaf-cutter ant (*zompopa*): Called wee wee ants in Creole, leaf-cutter ants are the region's most commonly noticed ants. They are found in all lowland habitats. Columns of these industrious little guys, all carrying clippings of leaves, sometimes extend for several hundred yards from plants to the underground nest. The leaves are used to cultivate the fungus that they eat.

Macaw (*lapas*): The beautiful scarlet macaw is the only species of this bird found in Belize. Huge, raucous birds with long tails, macaws use their immense bills to rip apart fruits to get to the seeds. Their nests are in hollow trees. They are endangered because of poachers and deforestation.

Mahogany (*caoba*): The national tree of Belize appears on the Belize flag, and the country's motto, *Sub Umbra Florero* (Under The Shade I Flourish), refers to the mahogany tree. Mahogany was the mainstay of the Belize (then British Honduras) economy for almost two centuries, from the mid-1700s until the 1950s. Most of the largest trees—the mahogany can soar to over 150 feet (45 meters) and reach trunk widths of over 6 feet (2 meters)— were cut down and exported to Europe where they were made into fine furniture and railway carriages. Some large specimens remain in the Programme for Belize lands in Orange Walk District.

Manatee: An immense and gentle mammal, the manatee is often called the sea cow. Living exclusively in the water, particularly in shallow and sheltered areas, manatees are said to be the basis of myths about mermaids. Fairly scarce today, these vegetarians have been hunted for thousands of years for their tasty flesh; their image frequently appears in ancient Mayan art.

Morpho (*morfo*): This spectacular butterfly doesn't fail to astound first-time viewers. Easy to overlook when resting, their color is only apparent when they take flight. One species has brilliant-blue wings, while another is distinguished by its intense violet color. Adults feed on fallen fruit, never flowers.

Parrot (*loro*): A prerequisite of any tropical setting, there are five species of parrot in Central America. All are clad in green, which means they virtually disappear upon landing in the trees. Most have a splash of color or two on their head or wings.

Poisonwood (*che chem, chechem negro*): Avoid this low-growing small tree. Fairly common in Belize, it can be identified by the black, oily sap on the trunk. The bark, sap, and leaves of the poisonwood cause a reaction similar to poison ivy or poison oak. Fortunately, an antidote, the red gumbo limbo tree, usually grows next to or near the poisonwood. Rub a strip of gumbo limbo bark on the affected area, or boil the bark in water and apply with a sponge.

Scorpion (*escorpión*): *Centruroides gracilis* is the most common scorpion in Belize. It grows up to 6 inches in length. Its sting is poisonous, and painful— about like a wasp sting—but not serious or fatal except in the case of an allergic reaction. If you're stung, don't panic— wash the area with soap and water (the venom is water-soluble) and apply an icepack.

Sea turtle: Sea turtles on the coasts of Belize come in three varieties: green, hawksbill, and loggerhead. All have paddlelike flippers and have to surface to breathe.

Spider monkey (*mono colorado, mono araña*): These lanky, long-tailed monkeys hang out in groups of two to four. Their diet consists of ripe fruit, leaves, and flowers. Incredible aerialists, they can swing effortlessly through the trees using their long arms, legs, and prehensile tails.

Tapir (*danta*): The national animal of Belize is also known as the mountain cow. Like a small rhinoceros without the armor, it has a stout body, short legs, and small eyes. Completely vegetarian, it uses its prehensile snout for harvesting vegetation. The shy creature lives in forested areas near streams and lakes, where it can sometimes be spotted bathing.

Toucan (*tucán, tucancillo*): Recognizable to fans of Froot Loops cereal, the toucan is common in Belize. The keel-billed and chestnut-mandibled toucans can grow to 22 inches long. The smaller and stouter emerald toucanet and yellow-ear toucanet are among the most colorful. All eat fruit with their curved, multihued beaks.

A CREOLE PRIMER

The Creole language (also spelled Kriol) is associated with the Creole or black people of Belize, especially those around Belize City. But people all over Belize know the Creole language and speak it daily. You'll hear Creole spoken by Mennonite farmers, Chinese shopkeepers, and Hispanic tour guides. Creole was brought to Belize by African slaves and former slaves from Jamaica and elsewhere in the Caribbean. Creole words are primarily of English origin, with some words from several West African tongues, Spanish, Miskito (an indigenous language of Central America, spoken by some 200,000 people in Honduras and Nicaragua), and other languages.

Spoken in a lilting Caribbean accent and combined with a grammar and syntax with West African roots, the language, despite English word usage, is difficult for foreigners to understand. Plurals aren't used often in Creole. For some, knowing how to speak Creole is a test you have to pass before you can become a "real" Belizean. However, with the increasing number of Hispanic immigrants in Belize, it's heard less and less, while Spanish is heard more and more.

Here are a few Creole words and phrases. If you want to learn more, get the *Kriol-Inglish Dikshineri* (Paul Crosbie, Editor-in-Chief) published by the Belize Kriol Project and available in gift shops and bookstores in Belize.

Ah mi gat wahn gud guf taim: I had a really good time

Bashment: Party

Bwah: Boy

Chaaly prise: A large rat, after Sir Charles Price, an 18th-century Jamaican planter

Chinchi: A little bit

Dis da fi wi chikin: This is our chicken (well-known slogan of a Mennonite chicken company)

Dollah: A Belize dollar

Fowl caca white and tink eh lay egg: A chicken sees its white droppings and thinks it laid an egg (said of a self-important person)

Grind mean: Ground meat

Gyal: Girl

Humoch dis kaas?: How much is this?

Ih noh mata: It doesn't matter

Madda rass: Foolishness (literally, mother's ass)

Tiga maga but eh no sic: Tiger's skinny but he's not sick (that is, don't judge a book by its cover)

Waawa: Foolish

Wangla: Sesame seed or candy made from sesame seeds

Weh di beach deh?: Where's the beach?

Yerrisso: Gossip, from "Ah her so" (so I hear)

TRAVEL SMART BELIZE

GETTING HERE AND AROUND

▌ AIR TRAVEL

TO BELIZE

All international flights to Belize fly into the international airport (BZE) in Ladyville about 9 miles (15 km) from downtown Belize City. The airport has a 9,700-foot-long runway capable of handling all but the largest jets. The major U.S. departure gateways are Atlanta, with nonstop flights on Delta to Belize City (most flights are regional jets with one-class service, with service significantly reduced in summer and fall); Charlotte, with weekly nonstops on US Airways to Belize City; Houston, with service two or three times daily, depending on the time of year, on United (which has merged with Continental); and Miami and Dallas-Fort Worth with daily nonstop service from each city on American. One of the Miami flights is a code-share with British Airways. (As of this writing, American plans to merge with US Airways, and it is unclear how service to Belize may be impacted.) United also has a weekly nonstop from Newark. Delta has a nonstop, new in late 2013, from Los Angeles (LAX) weekly on Saturday. TACA flies to Belize City from several U.S. cities, but flights involve a change of planes in San Salvador, El Salvador. In the past there have been seasonal charter flights from Toronto, Canada, to Belize by Sunwing and other charter operators, but as of this writing there are no nonstop flights from Canada.

To Belize City it's roughly 2½ hours from Miami and Atlanta; 2½–3 hours from Dallas, Houston, and Charlotte; 4½ hours from Newark, and about 6 hours from Los Angeles.

Tropic Air, one of two Belizean airlines, offers twice-daily service between Belize City's international airport and Flores, Guatemala, with continuing service (often on a code-share with TAG, a Guatemalan airline) to and from Guatemala City. It also has daily (some flights may be only six days a week) service between Belize City and Cancún, Mexico, and San Pedro Sula and Roatán, Honduras. Maya Island Air, another Belizean airline, currently has domestic service only.

Airfares to Belize are often twice or more the cost of a ticket to Cancún or Cozumel, Mexico, so, if you have the time, it may pay to fly into the Yucatán and take a bus. From Cancún or Playa del Carmen a first-class or deluxe ADO bus costs US$25 or less, and takes five to six hours, to Chetumal, Mexico, a border town where you can transfer to a Belize bus to Belize City (US$6–$7) or take a water taxi to San Pedro, Ambergris Caye, or to Caye Caulker (US$35–$45).

WITHIN BELIZE

Domestic planes are single- or twin-engine island-hoppers and puddle-jumpers, such as Cessna Caravans. They typically carry 4 to 14 passengers. The carriers are Tropic Air and Maya Island Air, both of which fly to San Pedro on Ambergris Caye and Caye Caulker as well as Corozal Town, Dangriga, Placencia, and Punta Gorda. Tropic Air also has service between Belize City and Belmopan and San Ignacio, between Placencia and San Ignacio. For those going to certain remote inland resorts, Tropic Air can fly to Blancaneaux Lodge, Hidden Valley Inn, Lamanai Outpost, and Chan Chich Lodge. Maya Island Air also has service on demand to Savannah near Placencia, as well as charter flights to remote lodges and resorts. In addition, *as noted above,* Tropic Air has service to and from Flores, Guatemala, with continuing service to and from Guatemala City, to Cancún, Mexico, and San Pedro Sula and Roatán, Honduras.

Belize domestic flights on Maya Island and Tropic Air from and to the international airport are between BZ$250 and BZ$500 round-trip and about BZ$150 to BZ$400 round-trip between the municipal airstrip in Belize City and domestic destinations. A Belize Airports Authority Rider Fee of BZ$5 is added into the cost of tickets, and BZ$1.50 security fee if using the international airport.

Charter services such as Javier Flying Service and Cari Bee Air Service will take you almost anywhere for around BZ$400 per hour and up; Javier has flights to Chan Chich Lodge. Both Maya Island and Tropic also have charter services. Astrum Helicopters, based near Belize City, offers transfers, aerial property tours, and custom sightseeing and photography tours anywhere in Belize. Costs for up to six people in the Bell 206 helicopters are around BZ$2,000 an hour. Fixed rates apply for transfers to specific resorts, starting at BZ$2,500 for four persons.

You'll save 10% to 40% on flights within Belize by flying to and from the municipal airport near downtown Belize City, rather than to or from the international airport north of the city in Ladyville. If you're arriving at the international airport, a transfer by taxi to the municipal airport is BZ$50 (for up to four persons, not per person); transferring to the municipal airport makes more sense for families or groups traveling together. If you need to fly between the Belize City area and another part of the country, it's always at least a little cheaper to fly to or from municipal. As of this writing the Belize City municipal airstrip (TZA) is set for improvements in late 2013–14. Be aware that this airstrip is short, only a little over 1,700, suitable only for short-takeoff-and-landing aircraft, and sits right beside the sea. Landings and take-offs sometimes can be a thrill.

Air Contacts American Airlines ✉ *San Cas Plaza, Belize City* ☎ *800/433–7300 in U.S. and Canada, 223/2522 in Belize City* ⊕ *www.aa.com.* **Astrum Helicopters** ✉ *Cisco Base, Mile 3½ George Price Hwy., formerly Western Hwy., Western Suburbs, Belize City* ☎ *222/5100* ⊕ *www.astrumhelicopters.com.* **Cari Bee Air Service** ✉ *Belize City Municipal Airstrip, Marine Parade Harbor Front, Belize City* ☎ *224/4253.* **Delta Airlines** ✉ *Philip S.W. Goldson International Airport, Ladyville* ☎ *888/750–3284 in U.S. and Canada, 255/2010 in Belize* ⊕ *www.delta.com.* **Javier Flying Service** ✉ *Central Farm Airstrip, San Ignacio* ☎ *824/0460* ⊕ *www.javiersflyingservice.com.* **Maya Island Air** ✉ *Belize City Municipal Airstrip, Marine Parade Harbor Front, Belize City* ☎ *223/1140 reservations* ⊕ *www.mayaislandair.com.* **TACA** ✉ *41 Albert St., Commercial District, Belize City* ☎ *800/400–8222 in U.S., 501/227–7363 in Belize* ⊕ *www.taca.com.* **Tropic Air** ✉ *San Pedro Airstrip, San Pedro* ☎ *226/2012 Reservations in Belize, 800/422–3435 in U.S. and Canada* ⊕ *www.tropicair.com.* **US Airways** ✉ *Philip S. W. Goldson International Airport, Ladyville* ☎ *800/428–4322 in U.S. and Canada, 225/4091 in Belize* ⊕ *www.usairways.com.* **United Air Lines** ✉ *4792 Coney Dr., Whitfield Tower 1st Floor, Belize City* ☎ *800/226–3822 reservations, 822/1062 in Belize* ⊕ *www.united.com.*

Airlines and Airports Airline and Airport Links. Airline and Airport Links has links to many airlines and airports. ⊕ *www.airlineandairportlinks.com.*

AIRLINE SECURITY ISSUES

Transportation Security Administration ☎ *866/289–9673 in U.S.* ✉ *TSA-ContactCenter@dhs.gov* ⊕ *www.tsa.gov* ⊙ *Weekdays 8 am–11 pm Eastern Time, Weekends/Holidays: 9 am–8 pm Eastern Time.*

AIRPORTS

International flights arrive at the Philip Goldson International Airport (BZE) in Ladyville, 9 miles (15 km) north of Belize City, probably the world's only airport with a mahogany ceiling (it's in the original terminal building). Small domestic airports (mostly just landing strips with a one-room check-in) in Belize are at Belize City municipal (TZA), Belmopan (BCV), Corozal (CZH), Dangriga (DGA), Savannah (SVH), Placencia (PLJ), Punta Gorda (PND), San Pedro (SPR), Caye Caulker (CUK), Maya Flats near San Ignacio (MYF), and Sarteneja (SJX).

The future of a controversial new, privately funded international airport under construction near the north end of the Placencia peninsula is unclear. As of this writing, construction work has essentially stopped, and the airport remains unfinished.

Philip Goldson International Airport has security precautions similar to those in the United States; the domestic airstrips have limited security systems, but there has never been an airline hijacking in Belize. For international flights, arrive at the airport at least two hours before departure; for domestic flights, about half an hour. For connections from international flights to domestic flights, allow 45 minutes. In Belize, domestic airlines with more passengers than seats sometimes simply add another flight.

A new visitor identification system including fingerprint scanners was introduced in July 2013 by Belize immigration at Philip Goldson, paid for in part by the U.S. The government says it soon will be expanded for use for all 11 land and sea arrival points to Belize. Initially the system caused delays of up to two hours for arrival processing, but such delays probably will be greatly reduced as wrinkles are ironed out. The new system includes computer workstations, webcams, passport readers, and fingerprint scanners and will be managed through a central server at Immigration headquarters in Belmopan.

Contacts Belize Municipal Airstrip (TZE) ⌧ *On seafront off Princess Margaret Dr., Belize City Municipal Airstrip, Marine Parade Harbor Front, Belize City.* **Philip S. W. Goldson International Airport (BZE)** ⌧ *9 miles (15 km) north of Belize City center, off Northern Hwy., Ladyville* ☎ *225/2045* ⊕ *www.pgiabelize.com.*

▌ BOAT TRAVEL

Since Belize has about 200 miles (325 km) of mainland coast and some 400 islands in the Caribbean, water taxis, passenger ferries, and private boats are key.

FERRIES AND PRIVATE BOATS

A local ferry company, Coastal Xpress, provides scheduled boat transportation up and down the east side of Ambergris Caye.

Several private boats make daily runs from Dangriga to Tobacco Caye for BZ$35–BZ$50 per person one-way. They leave Dangriga around 9 or 9:30 am and return from Tobacco Caye later in the day. Check at the Riverside Café in Dangriga or ask your hotel on Tobacco Caye.

Information Coastal Xpress ⌧ *Beachfront, Amigos del Mar Dock, San Pedro* ☎ *226/2007* ✉ *coastalxpress@yahoo.com.* **Riverside Café** ⌧ *Riverside and Oak Sts., west side of North Stann Creek Bridge, Dangriga* ☎ *601/6390.*

WATER TAXIS

There are three main water-taxi companies, with fast boats that hold up to 50 to 100 passengers, connecting Belize City with San Pedro (Ambergris Caye) and Caye Caulker. They also connect San Pedro with Caye Caulker and these islands with Chetumal, Mexico.

Most scheduled water taxis allow two pieces of luggage per person, along with miscellaneous personal items. Bicycles and other larger items may be permitted, if there's space, but you may be charged extra. Life jackets are carried on board the boats but aren't handed out to passengers. Seas, especially in the south between Dangriga and Placencia and Puerto Cortes, and also between Punta Gorda and

Puerto Barrios, can be rough. Postpone your trip if the weather looks bad, or, in the case of private charters, if the boat offered looks unseaworthy or crowded.

The Belize water-taxi business is still in a state of flux, and schedules and rates are subject to change.

DEPARTURE POINTS

Caye Caulker Water Taxi boats and Water Jets International, also known as San Pedro Water Jets Express, leave from the Marine Terminal at 10 North Front Street near the Swing Bridge in Belize City; San Pedro Belize Express boats leave from the Brown Sugar dock at 111 North Front St. near the Tourism Village.

ARRIVAL POINTS

Caye Caulker Water Taxi boats arrive at the Main Public Pier on Front Street on Caye Caulker, and on San Pedro they arrive at the Texaco Marina; on Caye Caulker, San Pedro Belize Express boats arrive at the pier near the basketball court on Front Street, and in San Pedro they arrive at the pier on Black Coral Street on the east (sea) side of the island; on both Caye Caulker and Ambergris Caye the Water Jets International terminals are on the back (lagoon) side of the islands.

RIDE TIMES AND FARES

From Belize City it's a 45-minute ride to Caulker and 75 minutes to San Pedro. Going between Caulker and San Pedro takes about 30 minutes. Fares vary a little among companies. At press time, one-way fares between Belize City and Caye Caulker were BZ$24 on Water Jets International, BZ$20 on Caye Caulker Water Taxi Association, and BZ$20 on San Pedro Belize Express; one-way fares between Belize City and San Pedro were BZ$35 on Water Jets International, BZ$30 on Caye Caulker Water Taxi Association, and BZ$30 on San Pedro Belize Express. Round-trip rates are slightly discounted from two one-way tickets.

Two of these water-taxi companies, Water Jets International and San Pedro Belize Express, also have daily service between the Muelle Fiscal or municipal pier in Chetumal, Mexico, and San Pedro and Caye Caulker, a trip of about 90 minutes to San Pedro, for US$30–US$45 to San Pedro and US$35–US$50 to Caulker, or the equivalent in Mexican pesos, though sometimes in Chetumal you can negotiate a lower rate. Rates are usually highest on weekends. Off-season, during slow periods, the two Chetumal water taxis may alternate days, so there is only one boat a day. The fares do not include US$5 port fees in Mexico and an exit fee of US$18.75 (BZ$37.50) leaving Belize. You may also have to pay a 295 Mexican peso (about US$22 at current exchange rates) fee leaving Mexico, if you have not already paid it, and 295 pesos when you enter Mexico by boat.

Another company, Thunderbolt, has daily service between Corozal Town and San Pedro for BZ$45 one-way. The trip takes 90 minutes to two hours, depending on weather conditions and whether there is a stop in Sarteneja. In Corozal, the Thunderbolt leaves from the Reunion Pier in the center of town; it arrives in San Pedro at the dock on Black Coral Street on the back side of the island near the soccer field.

Information Caye Caulker Water Taxis Association ☒ *Marine Terminal, 12 N Front St., Commercial District, Belize City* ☎ *223/5752 in Belize City, 226/0922 in Caye Caulker* ⊕ *www.cayecaulkerwatertaxi. com.* **Requena's** ☒ *12 Front St., Punta Gorda* ☎ *722/2070* ✑ *watertaxi@btl.net* ⊕ *www.belizenet.com/requena.* **San Pedro Belize Express Water Taxi** ☒ *Brown Sugar Terminal, 111 North Front St., near Tourism Village, Commercial District, Belize City* ☎ *223/2225* ⊕ *www.belizewatertaxi.com.* **Water Jets International.** Also confusingly known as San Pedro Water Jets International, Water Jets Express, San Pedro Water Taxi, and San Pedro-Jet Express. ☒ *Angel Coral St., on back (lagoon) side of island near soccer field, San Pedro* ☎ *226/2194* ⊕ *www.sanpedrowatertaxi.com.*

REACHING REMOTE CAYES AND ATOLLS

To reach the more remote cayes and the atolls, you're basically left to your own devices, unless you're staying at a hotel where such transfers are arranged for you. The resorts on the atolls run their own boats, but these usually aren't available to the general public.

Information D-Express ✉ *Shell Dock, Placencia Village* ☎ *523/4045 Placencia BTIA office, 624/6509 D-Express cell in Belize* ✐ *info@placencia.com* ⊕ *www.belizeferry.com.*

TRAVEL TIMES FROM BELIZE CITY		
To	By Air	By Car or Bus
San Pedro	20 minutes	n/a
Caye Caulker	15 minutes	n/a
Corozal Town	1–2 hours (via San Pedro)	2–3 hours
San Ignacio	30 minutes	2–2½ hours
Placencia	50 minutes	3–3½ hours
Punta Gorda	1 hour	4–6 hours
Cancún, Mexico	1½ hours	8–11 hours

▮ BUS TRAVEL

There's frequent bus service on the Philip Goldson and George Price highways and to southern Belize via the Hummingbird and Southern highways. Elsewhere service is spotty. There's only limited municipal bus service in Belize City on several small local lines. Fares are BZ$1–BZ$2 depending on the route and the bus line.

Buses can get you just about anywhere cheaply (about BZ$2–BZ$30 for inter-town trips) and quickly. Expect to ride on old U.S. school buses or retired North American Greyhound buses. On some routes there are a few express buses, some with air-conditioning. These cost a few dollars more.

▮TIP→ Be prepared for tight squeezes—this can mean three people in a two-person seat—and watch for pickpockets. Drivers and their assistants (in Guatemala, cobradors or ayudantes, fare collectors, who call out the stops) are knowledgeable and helpful. They can direct you to the right bus, and tell you when and where to get off. To be sure you're not forgotten, try to sit near the driver.

Most buses on main routes run according to more-or-less reliable schedules; on less-traveled routes the schedules may not mean much. Buses operate mostly during daylight hours, but they run until around 9 pm on the western route between Belize City and San Ignacio. Published bus schedules are rare, and almost no bus lines have websites. Some lines post hand-written schedules in bus terminals. The Belize Tourism Board sometimes has schedules for popular routes. Also check online for the Belize Bus Blog (⊕ *www.belizebus. wordpress.com*), which has generally up-to-date information on Belize bus rates and schedules and also on other types of transportation in Belize. Buses in Belize accept only cash in U.S. or Belize dollars.

Inexpensive public buses, also of the converted school bus variety, criss-cross Guatemala, but they can be slow and extremely crowded, with a three-per-seat rule enforced. Popular destinations from Guatemala City, such as Santa Elena/Flores near Tikal, use Pullman buses, which are as well equipped as North American bus lines. Your hotel or INGUAT office can help you make arrangements. Fares on public buses in Guatemala are a bargain.

▮TIP→ In Guatemalan cities you pay the bus driver as you board. On intercity buses, fare collectors pass through the bus periodically. Buses follow loose schedules, sometimes waiting to leave until the bus fills up. On some routes the day's very last bus isn't always a sure thing. Schedules for Pullman buses are usually observed.

Reservations are usually not needed or expected in Belize or Guatemala, even for Pullman or express departures. The terminals in Belize City and some towns have ticket windows where you can pay in advance and get a reserved seat. If you board at other points, you pay the driver's assistant and take any available seat. Arrive at terminals about a half hour before departure.

Belize Companies James Bus Line ✉ *7 King St., Punta Gorda* ☎ *702/2049.*

Guatemala Companies Autobuses **del Norte** ✉ *Terminal de Buses, Guatemala* ☎ *502/2251-0610 in Guatemala City, 502/7924-8131 in Santa Elena, Guatemala* ⊕ *www.adnautobusesdelnorte.com.* **Fuente del Norte** ✉ *Terminal de Buses, Santa Elena, Guatemala* ☎ *502/7947-7070 in Guatemala, 223/0457 Marine Terminal in Belize City, 502/7926-2999 Terminal de Buses, Santa Elena* ⊕ *www.grupofuentedelnorte.com.* **Línea Dorada** ☎ *502/5983-1163 Línea Dorada in Santa Elena, Guatemala, 223/1200 Mundo Maya Travel, in Belize City* ✍ *mundomaya travels@yahoo.com* ⊕ *lineadorada.info.*

■ CAR TRAVEL

GASOLINE

Modern gas stations—Texaco, Uno, Sol, Puma, and other brands, some of them with convenience stores and 24-hour service—are in Belize City and most major towns and along major highways in Belize. In more remote areas, especially in the south, fill up the tank whenever you see a station. Unleaded gas costs around BZ$12 a U.S. gallon. Diesel fuel is slightly less. Most stations have attendants who pump gas for you. They don't expect a tip, though they are happy to accept it. Most stations now accept credit cards.

Prices at Guatemala's service stations aren't quite as high as in Belize. At most stations an attendant will pump the gas and make change. Plan to use cash, as credit cards sometimes aren't accepted.

PARKING

In Belize City, with its warren of narrow and one-way streets, downtown parking is often at a premium. For security, try to find a guarded, fenced parking lot, and don't leave your car on the street overnight. Elsewhere, except in some areas of San Ignacio and Orange Walk Town, there's plenty of free parking.

There are no parking meters in Belize. In most cities and towns parking rules are laxly enforced, although cars with license plates from another district of Belize or a foreign country may attract a ticket.

ROAD CONDITIONS

All four main roads in Belize—the George Price Highway (formerly Western Highway), Philip Goldson Highway (formerly Northern Highway), Southern Highway, and Hummingbird Highway—are completely paved. These two-lane roads are generally in good condition. The once horrendous Placencia Road is now completely paved. At this writing the road to Hopkins is scheduled for paving in late 2013 or 2014. The San Antonio Road from the Southern Highway near Punta Gorda to the Guatemala border is being upgraded and paved as of this writing. Signage is good along the main highways; large green signs direct you to major sights.

Elsewhere in Belize, expect fair to stupendously rough dirt, gravel, and limestone roads; a few unpaved roads, and occasionally stretches of even paved roads, may be impassable at times in the rainy season.

FROM/TO	ROUTE	DISTANCE
Belize City–Corozal Town	Northern Highway	99 miles (160 km)
Belize City–San Ignacio	Western Highway	72 miles (116 km)
Belize City–Placencia	Western, Hummingbird, and Southern highways	147 miles (237 km)
Belize City–Punta Gorda	Western, Hummingbird, and Southern highways	200 miles (323 km)
San Ignacio–Placencia	Western, Hummingbird, and Southern highways	113 miles (182 km)

Immense improvements have been made to Guatemala's ravaged roads. A highway from Río Dulce to Tikal has cut travel time along this popular route significantly. In the Petén, the road from Belize toward Tikal has a few short stretches near the border without pavement, but after that, both to Tikal and to Flores, it's paved and in excellent condition. Roads in remote areas are frequently unpaved, rife with potholes, and treacherously muddy in the rainy season. Four-wheel-drive vehicles are recommended for travel off the beaten path. In cities, expect narrow brick streets. Road signs are generally used to indicate large towns; smaller towns may not be so clearly marked. Look for intersections where people seem to be waiting for a bus—that's a good sign that there's an important turnoff nearby.

ROADSIDE EMERGENCIES

When renting a car, ask the agency what it does if your car breaks down in a remote area. Most agencies in Belize send a driver with a replacement vehicle or a mechanic to fix the car. For help in Guatemala, your best bet is to call the National or Tourist Police. In either country, consider renting a cell phone, or buy a cheap local cell phone or a local

SIM card for your own unlocked cell phone. *(⇨ Phones, under Communication in Essentials.)*

Emergency Services Belize Police ☎ *911 for police and other emergencies nationwide, 90 for police, fire, and ambulance in Belize City only.* **Guatemalan National Police.** *The local equivalent of 911 in Guatemala is 110 or 120.* ☎ *110 for emergencies, 120 for emergencies, 501/2421-2810 police.* **Guatemalan Tourist Police.** *POLITUR (Tourist Police) is a joint National Police and INGUAT tourism service.* ☎ *502/2421–2810 for 24-hour security information provided by INGUAT, 1/500 POLITUR, for emergencies.*

RULES OF THE ROAD

Driving in Belize and Guatemala is on the right. Seat belts are required, although the law is seldom enforced. There are few speed-limit signs, and speed limits are rarely enforced. However, as you approach villages and towns watch out for "sleeping policemen," a local name for speed bumps. The entire country of Belize has only about a dozen traffic lights, and only Belize City and downtown San Ignacio have anything approaching congestion. One unusual aspect of driving in Belize, likely a hold-over from British Honduras days when driving was on the left, is that vehicles turning left against traffic are not supposed to hold up cars behind them; instead, they are supposed to pull over to the right and wait for a break in traffic to turn.

Despite the relatively small number of private cars in Belize, traffic accidents are the nation's number one cause of death. Belizean drivers aren't always as skilled as they think they are, and drunk drivers can be a problem. Guatemala's narrow roads and highways mean you can be stuck motionless on the road for an hour while a construction crew stands around a hole in the ground. Always allow extra travel time for such unpredictable events, and bring along snacks and water. In both Belize and Guatemala, be prepared to stop for police traffic checks. Usually tourists in rental cars are checked only cursorily. Otherwise, if you observe the rules you follow at home, you'll likely do just fine. Just don't expect everyone else to follow them.

▌ RENTAL CARS

Belize City and the international airport in Ladyville have most major car-rental agencies as well as several local operators. At the international airport, a line of about 10 rental car offices is on the far side of the main parking lot across from the airport entrances. There also are car-rental agencies in Corozal Town, San Ignacio, Placencia, and Punta Gorda. Some Belize City car rental companies will deliver vehicles to other locations in Belize, but there is always a drop fee, ranging from around BZ$100 to BZ$300, depending on destination. Prices for car rentals vary, but all are high by U.S. standards (BZ$120–BZ$275 per day, plus 12.5% tax), and vehicles are often a few years old with quite a few miles. If renting from an agency at the international airport, there's a BZ$10 airport fee. Off-season, rates are a little lower. Weekly rates usually save you money over daily rates.

For serious safaris, a four-wheel drive vehicle is invaluable. But since unpaved roads, mudslides in rainy season, and a general off-the-beaten-path landscape are status quo here, all drivers will be comforted with a four-wheel-drive vehicle.

Car rental has never really caught on in Guatemala, which, given the narrowness of some roads, is just as well. If you do rent a car, opt for four-wheel drive, which will run around US$65 a day. Several international and local car-rental companies are based at the Flores airport.

In Belize and Guatemala, rental-car companies routinely accept driver's licenses from most other countries without question. Most car-rental agencies require a major credit card for a deposit, and some require you be over 25.

Most Belize agencies don't permit their vehicles to be taken into Guatemala or Mexico. Crystal in Belize City does permit its vehicles to be taken into Guatemala, as do a couple of the car-rental companies in San Ignacio, although without any insurance coverage while in Guatemala. There is no place to buy Guatemalan liability insurance at the Belize-Guatemala border.

On Belize's cayes you can't rent a car, but you can rent a golf cart, at prices not much less than renting a car. You'll need a driver's license and a credit card.

CAR-RENTAL INSURANCE

If you own a car, your personal auto insurance may cover a rental to some degree, though not all policies protect you abroad; always read your policy's fine print. If you don't have auto insurance, then seriously consider buying the collision- or loss-damage waiver (CDW or LDW) from the car-rental company, which eliminates your liability for damage to the car. Some credit cards offer CDW coverage, but it's usually supplemental to your own insurance and rarely covers SUVs, minivans, luxury models, and the like. American Express and some other credit/charge card companies offer a premium CDW plan for a flat fee, usually around US$20 per rental, not per day, that has more leeway than regular CDW plans, for example covering SUVs, trucks, and driving off paved roads. If your insurance coverage is secondary, you may still be liable for loss-of-use costs from the car-rental company. But no credit-card insurance is valid unless you use that card for *all* transactions, from reserving to paying the final bill. All companies exclude car rental in some countries, so be sure to find out about the destination to which you are traveling.

In Belize CDW insurance from car rental companies costs BZ$25–BZ$40 a day, and you may still be liable for the first BZ$1,000–BZ$4,000 in damages.

Major Agencies Budget. Offices at the international airport, on the Goldson Highway in Belize City, and in Placencia. ✉ *Mile 2½ Goldson Hwy., formerly Northern Hwy., Northern Suburbs, Belize City* ☎ *223/2435 in Belize* ✍ *reservations@budget-belize.com* ⊕ *www.budget-belize.com.* **Cayo Auto Rentals** ✉ *81 Benque Rd./George Price Hwy., San Ignacio* ☎ *824/2222* ⊕ *www.cayoautorentals.com.* **Crystal.** With offices at the international airport and on the Goldson Highway in Belize City, Crystal is the largest car rental company in Belize. It is one of the few rental companies in Belize that permits its vehicles to be taken into Guatemala. ✉ *Mile 5, Goldson Hwy., formerly Northern Hwy., Northern Suburbs, Belize City* ☎ *223/1600 in Belize, 800/777–7777 toll-free in Belize* ⊕ *www.crystal-belize.com.* **Hertz.** Offices at international airport, in Fort George area of Belize City, and an affiliated agency in Placencia. ✉ *Philip S. W. Goldson International Airport, Ladyville* ☎ *800/654–3001 in U.S. for international reservations, 225/3300 in Belize* ⊕ *www.carsbelize.com.*

∎ CRUISE SHIPS

About 700,000 cruise passengers visit Belize annually, all arriving on big ships that call on Belize City. Because of shallow water near shore, passengers are brought ashore in small boats called tenders. Although Carnival Cruise Lines agreed to build a new US$50 million cruise terminal in Belize City, construction has been indefinitely delayed. Norwegian Cruise Line (NCL) announced in August 2013 that, with Belize government permission, it has purchased what is called Harvest Caye about 3 miles off Placencia. NCL plans to invest a total of around US$50 million in a "floating" terminal there for its cruise ships, both using Harvest Caye as a private island destination and also as a site to tender in passengers to Placencia for tours of southern Belize. NCL says the terminal will open by 2015 and that it plans to eventually quadruple the number of passengers to visit Belize on the line. Speculation is that NCL will reduce or eliminate passengers to Belize City, where the shallow harbor requires all cruise ships to dock offshore and tender in passengers. Surveys and straw polls suggest that a large majority of Placencia and southern Belize citizens, along with most southern Belize hotel operators, don't approve of a cruise port in southern Belize.

On arrival in Belize City, most passengers take snorkel, cave tubing, or Mayan ruin tours, or just wander around the historic Fort George area, visiting the Tourist Village.

Cruise Lines Carnival Cruise Line ☎ *800/764–7419* ⊕ *www.carnival.com.* **Costa Cruises** ☎ *800/462–6782* ⊕ *www.costacruise.com.* **Holland America Line** ☎ *877/932–4259* ⊕ *www.hollandamerica.com.* **Norwegian Cruise Line** ☎ *866/234–7350* ⊕ *www.ncl.com.* **Princess Cruises** ☎ *800/774–6237* ⊕ *www.princess.com.* **Regent Seven Seas Cruises** ☎ *877/505–5370* ⊕ *www.rssc.com.* **Royal Caribbean International** ☎ *866/562–7625* ⊕ *www.royalcaribbean.com.* **Seabourn Cruise Line** ☎ *866/755–5619* ⊕ *www.seabourn.com.*

∎ SHUTTLES

Belize has some shuttle services, primarily between Belize City and San Ignacio, though shuttles also are available to Placencia, Chetumal, Mexico, and elsewhere. Most hotels and lodges in Cayo will arrange round-trip van transfers for guests to and from the international airport in Belize City for BZ$250–BZ$450 for up to four passengers. William's Shuttle in the Cayo offers van transfers to and from Belize City (rates depend on the number of passengers). Belize Shuttles in Belize City has both scheduled and on-demand shuttles between the international airport and San Ignacio, at BZ$70 per person for the scheduled shuttles and BZ$180 for a private shuttle for up to three persons and BZ$30 for additional persons. Belize Discounted Shuttles offers transfers from the international airport to San Ignacio for BZ$90 per person, to Placencia for BZ$150 per person, and Corozal for BZ$120 per person. Minimum of two persons in all cases, tax included. This shuttle company also offers tours to major visitor sites on the mainland from around BZ$100–BZ$220 per person. In the north, Belize VIP Transfers will whisk you across the border to Chetumal for around BZ$70 per person (not including the BZ$37.50 Belize exit fee).

San Juan Travel, Línea Dorada, and Fuente del Norte run daily vans or minibuses between Belize City and Flores, Guatemala, for BZ$50–BZ$60. These fares don't include exit fees of BZ$37.50 when leaving Belize by land.

Shuttles in Guatemala are private minivans that hold up to eight passengers. They're faster and more comfortable than public buses. Public minivans from the Belize border to Santa Elena near Flores cost around US$5; they're often packed. Taxi shuttles from the border to Tikal or Flores are around US$45–US$70 for up to four passengers, depending on your bargaining ability. Shuttles between Flores and Tikal charge a flat US$5 per person round-trip and run frequently, starting at 5 am from Flores.

Reservations are generally required for shuttle service in both Belize and Guatemala. Some may ask for payment up front; before obliging, be sure you're dealing with a reputable company.

Belize Companies Belize Discounted Shuttles ☎ 620/1474 in Belize, 616/283–0789 in U.S. ⊕ www.discountedbelizeshuttles andtours.com. **Belize VIP Transfers** ☎ 422/2725 ⊕ www.belizetransfers.com. **William's Shuttle** ✉ belizeshuttle@yahoo.com ⊕ www.parrot-nest.com/belize-shuttle.html.

Guatemala Companies
Fuente del Norte ☎ 502/7947–7070 ⊕ www.grupofuentedelnorte.com. **San Juan Travel** ☎ 502/7926–0042 in Santa Elena, Guatemala, 223/223–1200 Mundo Maya Travel, for tickets in Belize ✉ mundomayatravels@yahoo.com.

ESSENTIALS

■ ACCOMMODATIONS

Regardless of the kind of lodging, you'll usually stay at a small place, as only a few properties have more than 50 or 75 rooms, and most have fewer than 30; the owners often actively manage the property. Thus, Belize accommodations usually reflect the personalities of their owners, for better or worse.

APARTMENT AND HOUSE RENTALS

You can most easily find vacation rentals on Ambergris Caye. Marty Casado's Ambergris Caye website has a good selection of rental houses and condos. Vacation Rentals By Owner (VRBO) has scores of rentals on Ambergris Caye and elsewhere in Belize. There also are some vacation rental houses in Placencia and Hopkins and on Caye Caulker. *Individual chapters in this guide direct you to vacation rental sources.*

Information Ambergis Caye website ⊕ *www.ambergriscaye.com.* **Vacation Rentals By Owner (VRBO)** ⊕ *www.vrbo.com.*

BEACH HOTELS

Beach hotels range from a basic seaside cabin on Caye Caulker to a small, deluxe resort such as Hamanasi near Hopkins. On Ambergris Caye many resorts are "condotels"—low-rise condo complexes with individually owned units that are managed like a hotel.

JUNGLE LODGES

Jungle lodges are concentrated in the Cayo, but they are also in Toledo, Belize, and Orange Walk districts and can be found most anywhere except the cayes. Jungle lodges need not be spartan; nearly all have electricity (though the generator may shut down at 10 pm), an increasing number have swimming pools, and a few have air-conditioning. The typical lodge has a roof of bay-palm thatch and may remind you of a Mayan house gone upscale.

STAYING ON REMOTE CAYES

Lodging choices on remote cayes appeal to the diving and fishing crowd. Amenity levels vary greatly, from cabins with outdoor bathrooms to simple cottages with composting toilets to comfortable villas with air-conditioning.

TRADITIONAL HOTELS

Traditional hotels, usually found in larger towns, can be basic budget places or international-style hotels such as the Radisson Fort George in Belize City.

CANCELLATIONS

As most hotels have only a few rooms, a last-minute cancellation can have a big impact on the bottom line. Most properties have a sliding scale for cancellations, with full refunds (minus a small administrative fee) if you cancel 60 or 90 days or more in advance, with reduced refund rates for later cancellations, and often no refunds at all for cancellation 30 to 45 days out. Practices vary greatly, so check on them.

RATES

In the off-season—generally May to November, though dates vary by hotel—most properties discount rates by 20% to 40%. Although hotels have published rates, in the off-season at least you may also be able to negotiate a better rate, especially if you're staying more than one or two nights. ■TIP→ **Walk-in rates are usually lower than prebooked rates, and rooms booked direct on the Internet may be lower than those booked through agents.**

Most hotels allow children under a certain age to stay in their parents' room at no extra charge, but others charge for them as extra adults; find out the cutoff age for discounts.

All prices for Belize are in Belize dollars for a standard double room in high season with no meals included, including service charges and 9% hotel tax. There has been discussion of increasing the room tax rate to the same rate as the sales tax, 12.5%, but as of this writing no final action has been taken.

■ COMMUNICATIONS

INTERNET

Belize is relatively wired. DSL high-speed (though not always the "high speed" you may be accustomed to) Internet is available in most populated areas, and cable Internet is offered in Belize City, Placencia, San Pedro, and elsewhere. Relatively high-speed cell Internet is becoming popular around the country. In more remote areas, there's the option of satellite Internet. There are Internet cafés in San Pedro, Caye Caulker, Belize City, San Ignacio, Placencia, Hopkins, Corozal Town, Punta Gorda, and other areas. Rates are usually around BZ$10–BZ$20 an hour. Most offices of the main phone company, Belize Telemedia, Ltd., have computers with DSL Internet connections (BZ$10 per half hour). BTL also has Wi-Fi hot spots at the international airport (free) and elsewhere. Most hotels, lodges, and inns now offer free Wi-Fi access for guests.

CYBERCAFÉS AND INTENET CAFES

Cybercafés are now common in Belize City and in most towns and resort areas all over Belize. The problem is that these lightly capitalized businesses frequently are here today and gone tomorrow. Your best bet is just to scout the area where you're staying for an open Internet café. If you're visiting on a cruise ship, Click & Sip is inside the Tourism Village in Belize City. Rates vary, but typically you'll pay around BZ$5–BZ$10 for a half hour, BZ$8–BZ$15 for an hour. There is free Belize Telemedia Ltd. Wi-Fi at the international airport.

Cybercafés Cybercafes. Cybercafes lists more than 4,200 Internet cafés worldwide. ⊕ *www.cybercafes.com.*

INTERNET CAFÉS

Click & Sip Internet Café ⊠ *Fort St., in Tourism Village, Belize City* ☎ *223/1305.*

INTERNET AT ACCOMMODATIONS

Most mid-level and upscale hotels, and many budget ones, now provide Internet access, typically Wi-Fi, for your laptop, tablet computer, or Internet-enabled smartphone, and also a computer or two in the office or lobby, at no charge. A few hotel operators still charge a fee, up to BZ$30 a day. In towns and resort areas this is usually DSL, but with speeds of only 1 or 2 Mbps down or less. At jungle lodges and other remote properties, the access is usually via a satellite system, with very limited bandwidth. At these lodges you're usually asked to use the Internet for email only and not to upload or download large files. ■TIP→ If you're traveling with a laptop in Belize, be aware that the power supply may be uneven, and most hotels don't have built-in current stabilizers. At remote lodges power is often from fluctuating generators. Bring a surge protector and your own disks or memory sticks to save your work.

PHONES

CALLING WITHIN BELIZE

All Belizean numbers are seven digits. (In Guatemala there are eight digits.) The first digit in Belize is the district area code (2 for Belize District, 3 Orange Walk, 4 Corozal, 5 Stann Creek, 6 for mobile phones, 7 Toledo, and 8 Cayo). The second indicates the type of service (0 for prepaid services, 1 for mobile, 2 for regular landline). The final five digits are the phone number. Thus, a number such as 22x/xxxx means that it's a landline phone in Belize District.

To dial any number in Belize, local or long distance, you must dial all seven digits. When dialing from outside Belize, dial the international access code, the country code for Belize (501), and all seven digits. When calling from the United States, dial 011/501–xxx–xxxx.

Belize has a good nationwide phone system. There are pay phones on the street in the main towns. All take prepaid phone cards rather than coins. Local calls cost BZ25¢; calls to other districts, BZ$1. Dial 113 for directory assistance and 115 for operator assistance. For the correct local time, dial 121. You can get phone numbers in Belize on the website of Belize Telemedia Ltd.

CALLING OUTSIDE BELIZE

To call the United States, dial 001 or 10–10–199 plus the area code and number. You'll pay around BZ$1.50 a minute. Pay phones accept only prepaid BTL phone cards, available in shops at BTL offices in denominations from BZ$5 to BZ$75. BTL blocks many foreign calling cards and also attempts to block even computer-to-computer calls on Skype and similar services.

The country code is 1 for the United States and Canada, 502 for Guatemala, 52 for Mexico, 61 for Australia, 64 for New Zealand, and 44 for the United Kingdom.

RESOURCES

Belize Telemedia Ltd. ☎ *800/225–5285 toll-free in Belize, 223/2368 main number in Belize City* ⊕ *www.belizetelemedia.net.*

MOBILE PHONES

If you have a multiband cell or smartphone and your service provider uses the GSM 850/1900 digital system (like AT&T) you can use your phone in Belize on BTL's DigiCell system. You'll need a new SIM card (your provider may have to unlock your phone for you to use a different SIM card). The SIM card will cost about BZ$50, and you'll also need a prepaid phone card to pay for outgoing calls (incoming cell calls are free). Both items and also rental cell phones (starting

at BZ$10 a day or BZ$70 a week) are available at the BTL office at the international airport (near the rental car kiosks), at some BTL offices, and at a number of private shops and stores around Belize that are DigiCell distributors. A few car rental companies throw in a free cell phone with a vehicle rental.

Another option is a small BTL competitor, Smart!, which operates a nationwide cell-phone system that uses CDMA technology (like Verizon in the United States). At one of its offices—in Belize City, Corozal Town, Orange Walk Town, Belmopan City, San Ignacio, San Pedro, or Benque Viejo—you can reprogram your unlocked 800 MHz or 850 MHz CDMA phone for use in Belize. There's an activation fee of BZ$40, and you'll need to purchase a prepaid plan with per-minute rates for outgoing calls of BZ55¢ to BZ70¢ (incoming calls, text messages, and voice mail are free).

You may also be able to activate your own cell phone for use in Belize. Check with your service provider, but be aware that international roaming charges are high. Typically, you'll pay US$3 or more per minute to use your cell in Belize, even if you are calling local numbers.

Contacts BTL International Airport Office. The BTL office at the international airport, which rents cell phones and sells phone cards and SIM chips for cell phones to use in Belize, is at the far left end of the group of car rental offices across the main parking lot, as you face the line of offices. ☎ *225/4162 office at international airport, 800/225–5285 toll-free in Belize.* **Smart!.** Smart! also has other offices around Belize where you can purchase a cell phone or have your CDMA phone activated to work with a local number in Belize. ⊠ *Mile 2½ Goldson Hwy., formerly Northern Hwy., Northern Suburbs, Belize City* ☎ *280/1000 in Belize City* ✍ *customerservice@smart-bz.com* ⊕ *www.smart-bz.com.*

▌CUSTOMS AND DUTIES

At the international airport in Belize City it rarely takes more than 30 minutes to clear immigration and customs.

Duty-free allowances for visitors entering Belize include 1 liter of liquor and one carton of cigarettes per person. Customs officials may confiscate beer, including beer from Guatemala or Mexico, as Belize protects its domestic brewing industry. The exception is beer from countries in CARICOM, of which Belize is a member. ▌TIP➔ **When arriving by international air at Philip Goldson International Airport you can buy up to four bottles of spirits or wine at the duty-free shop in the arrival terminal near the baggage claim area. These won't be counted toward your regular import allowance.**

In theory, electronic and electrical appliances, cameras, jewelry, or other items of value must be declared at the point of entry, but unless these are new items you plan to leave in Belize, you probably will not be required to declare them. You should have no trouble bringing in a laptop for personal use.

Firearms of any type are prohibited, as are fresh fruits and vegetables. Although a couple of dozen food items, including meats, rice, beans, sugar, and peanuts, require an import license, grocery items in small amounts for personal use, in their original packages, are usually allowed.

To take home fresh seafood of any kind from Belize, you must first obtain a permit from the Fisheries Department. There's a 20-pound limit. It is illegal to export any Mayan artifact from Belize.

You may enter Guatemala duty-free with a camera, up to six rolls of film, any clothes and articles needed while traveling, 500 mg of tobacco, 3 liters of alcoholic beverages, two bottles of perfume, and 2 kg of candy. Unless you bring in a lot of merchandise, customs officers probably won't even check your luggage, although a laptop may be somewhat scrutinized.

LOCAL DO'S AND TABOOS

CUSTOMS OF THE COUNTRY

Patience and friendliness go a long way in Belize. Don't criticize local ways of doing things—there's usually a reason that may not be obvious to visitors—and, especially with officials, adopt a respectful attitude.

GREETINGS

Belizeans generally are incredibly kind and friendly. Greet folks with a "Good morning" before asking for directions, for a table in a restaurant, or when entering a store or museum, for example. It will set a positive tone and you'll be received much more warmly for having done so.

SIGHTSEEING

Don't take pictures inside churches. Do not take pictures of indigenous people without first asking their permission. Offering them a small sum as thanks is customary.

LANGUAGE

English is Belize's official language. Spanish is widely spoken especially in northern and western Belize. Several Mayan dialects and the Garifuna language are also spoken. Some Mennonite communities speak German. Creole, or Kriol, which uses versions of English words and a West African influenced grammar and syntax, is spoken as a first language by many Belizeans, especially around Belize City.

Around Tikal, wherever tourist traffic is heavy, you'll find a few English speakers; you'll have considerably less luck in places off the beaten path. In general, very little English is spoken in El Petén, and in some small villages in the region absolutely none. In addition, many Guatemalans will answer "yes" or "si" even if they don't understand your question, so as not to appear unkind or unhelpful. To minimize such confusion, try posing questions as "Where is so-and-so?" rather than asking "Is so-and-so this way?"

It's illegal to export most Mayan artifacts. If you buy any such goods, do so only at a well-established store, and keep the receipt. You may not take fruits or vegetables out of Guatemala.

Information in Belize Belize Fisheries ☎ 223/2623 Coastal Zone Management ⊕ www.agriculture.gov.bz.

U.S. Information U.S. Customs and Border Protection ☎ 877/227–5511 in U.S., 202/325–8000 for international callers ⊕ www.cbp.gov. **United States State Department** ☎ 202/647–4000 State Dept. main switchboard in Washington, 888/407–4747 emergency help for travelers who are calling from U.S., 877/487–2778 passport information, 202/501–4444 emergency help for travelers calling from outside U.S. ⊕ www.travel.state.gov.

▌ EATING OUT

For information on food-related health issues, see ⇨ *Health.*

MEALS AND MEALTIMES

You can eat well in Belize thanks to a gastronomic gumbo of Mexican, Caribbean, Mayan, Garífuna, English, and American dishes (on the American side, think fried chicken, pork chops, burgers, and T-bone steaks). On the coast and cayes, seafood—especially lobster, conch, snapper, and grouper—is fresh, relatively inexpensive, and delicious.

Try Creole specialties such as cow-foot soup (yes, made with real cows' feet), "boil up" (a stew of fish, potatoes, plantains, cassava and other vegetables, and eggs), and the ubiquitous "stew chicken" with rice and beans. Many Creole dishes are seasoned with red or black *recado*, a paste made from annatto seeds and other spices.

In border areas, enjoy Mestizo favorites such as *escabeche* (onion soup), *salbutes* (fried corn tortillas with chicken and a topping of tomatoes, onions, and peppers), or *garnaches* (fried tortillas with refried beans, cabbage, and cheese).

In Dangriga, Hopkins, and Punta Gorda or other Garífuna areas, try dishes such as *sere lasus* (fish soup with plantain balls) or cassava dumplings.

Breakfast is usually served from 7 to 9, lunch from 11 to 2, and dinner from 6 to 9. Few restaurants are open late. Remember, though, that small restaurants may open or close at the whim of the owner. Off-season, restaurants may close early if it looks as if there are no more guests coming, and some restaurants close completely for a month or two, usually in September and October. Unless otherwise noted, the restaurants listed in this guide are open daily for lunch and dinner.

▌TIP➡ **Other than at hotels, Belize restaurants are often closed on Sunday.**

RESERVATIONS AND DRESS

Reservations for meals are rarely needed in Belize or the Tikal area. The exceptions are for dinner at jungle lodges and at small restaurants where the owner or chef needs to know in advance how many people are dining that night. We mention reservations only when they're essential.

A couple of restaurants in Belize City have a dress code, which basically means that you can't wear shorts at dinner. We mention dress only when men are required to wear a jacket or a jacket and tie, which is nearly unheard of in Belize.

▌ ELECTRICITY

There's no need to bring a converter or adapter, as electrical current is 110 volts, the same as in the United States, and outlets take U.S.-style plugs. In a few remote areas lodges and hotels may generate their own electricity, and after the generators are turned off at night, power, if there's any, comes only from storage batteries.

■ EMERGENCIES

In an emergency, call 911 nationwide, or 90 in Belize City only. There are police stations in Belize City and in Belmopan City, in the towns of Benque Viejo, Corozal, Dangriga, Orange Walk, Punta Gorda, San Ignacio, and San Pedro, and in Placencia Village and a few other villages. Police try to respond quickly to emergencies, although lack of equipment, supplies, and training may sometimes reduce their effectiveness.

Police are generally polite, professional, and will do what they can to help. In Belize City and in most tourist areas, including Placencia and San Pedro, there are special tourist police whose job is to patrol areas where visitors are likely to go and to render any assistance they can, including providing directions.

There are checkpoints on most major highways in Belize, especially near border areas and around Belize City. Police officers may ask for your driver's license or passport; just as frequently, they will wave you through.

Most Belizeans are extremely solicitous of the welfare of visitors to the country. In an emergency, it's likely that bystanders or people in the area will gladly offer to help, usually going out of their way to render any assistance they can.

Your hotel can provide the names of nearby physicians and clinics. You can also go to the emergency room of public hospitals in Belize City and major towns. Don't worry about payment—in an emergency, you'll be treated regardless of your ability to pay, though after being treated you may be asked to pay what you can. Private hospitals (there are two in Belize City and one in San Ignacio) may ask for some guarantee of payment. ⇨ For more information, see Health, below.

Guatemala police, overwhelmed at times by the amount of crime—in 2012 there were more than 400 murders a month in Guatemala—may not be able to respond effectively to emergencies. For tourist

assistance in Guatemala, dial 1500 from any phone, or dial the equivalent of 911—either 120, 122, or 123. The good news is that the serious crime rate in both Belize and Guatemala has declined in recent years.

American Embassy Embassy of the United States in Belize ⊠ Floral Park Rd., Belmopan City ☎ 822/4011 during office hours weekdays, 610/5030 emergency number after office hours ✉ embbelize@state.gov ⊕ belize.usembassy.gov ⊗ Weekdays 8–noon, 1–5.

■ HEALTH

Many medicines requiring a doctor's prescription at home don't require one in Belize; drugstores often sell prescription antibiotics, sleeping aids, and painkillers. However, pharmacies generally have a very small inventory, and only the most commonly prescribed drugs are available. In Belize private physicians often own an associated pharmacy, so they sell you the medicine they prescribe. A few pharmacies are open 24 hours and deliver directly to hotel rooms. Most hotel proprietors will direct you to such services.

CRITTERS

Sand flies (also sometimes referred to as no-see-ums, or as sand fleas, which are a different insect) are common on many beaches, cayes, and in swampy areas. They can infect you with leishmaniasis, a disease that can cause the skin to develop sores that can leave scars. In rare cases, the visceral form of leishmaniasis, if untreated, can be fatal.

Use repellent containing at least a 30% concentration of DEET to help deter sand flies. Some say lathering on Avon's Skin So Soft or any oily lotion such as baby oil helps, too, as it drowns the little bugs.

The botfly or beefworm is one of the most unpleasant of Central American pests. Botfly eggs are deposited under your skin with the help of a mosquito, where one can grow into larva, a large living worm. To rid yourself of your unwanted pal, cover the larva's airhole in your skin with Vaseline, and after it suffocates you can remove it with a sterile knife. Or see your doctor. The good news is that unless you spend a lot of time in the bush in Belize, you are unlikely to encounter botflies.

Virtually all honeybees in Belize and Guatemala are Africanized. The sting of these killer bees is no worse than that of regular bees, but the hives are much more aggressive. Farm animals and pets frequently are killed by Africanized bees, and in 2013 a young Mennonite boy in northern Belize died after being stung hundreds of times in his backyard. If attacked by Africanized bees, try to get into a building, vehicle, or under water; protect your mouth, nose, and other orifices.

Scorpions are common in Belize and around Tikal. Their stings are painful, but not fatal. There are many venomous snakes in Belize and lowland Guatemala, including the notorious fer-de-lance and small but deadly coral snakes. Most visitors never even see a snake, but if bitten can go to medical centers for antivenom.

Crocodiles (called alligators by many Belizeans) are present in many lagoons and rivers, but very rarely are they known to attack humans.

Divers and snorkelers may experience "itchy itchy" or *pica pica*, a skin rash, in spring and early summer, when the tiny larvae of thimble jellyfish may get on the skin. Putting Vaseline or other greasy lotion on the skin before entering the water may help prevent the itch, and applying Benadryl, vinegar, or even Windex to the affected area may help stop the itch.

If you're a light sleeper, you might want to pack earplugs. Monkeys howling through the night and birds chirping at the crack of dawn are only charming on the first night of your nature excursion.

FOOD AND DRINK

Belize has a high standard of health and hygiene, so the major health risk is sunburn, not digestive distress. You can drink the water in Belize City, the Cayo, Placencia, on Ambergris Caye, and in most other areas you're likely to visit, though you may prefer the taste of bottled water. In remote villages, however, water may come from shallow wells or cisterns and may not be safe to drink.

On trips to Tikal or other areas in Guatemala, assume that the water isn't safe to drink. Bottled water—*agua mineral* or *agua pura* in Spanish—is available even at the smallest *tiendas* (stores) and is cheaper than in the U.S. or Canada. Eating contaminated fruit or vegetables or drinking contaminated water (even ice) could result in a case of Montezuma's revenge, or traveler's diarrhea. Also skip uncooked food and unpasteurized milk and milk products.

INFECTIOUS DISEASES

HIV/AIDS is an increasing concern in Central America. This is especially true in Belize, where the incidence on a per capita basis is the highest in the region.

According to the U.S. Centers for Disease Control and Prevention, there's a limited risk of malaria, hepatitis A and B, dengue fever, typhoid fever, and rabies in Central America. In most urban or easily accessible areas you need not worry. However, if you plan to spend a lot of time in the jungles, rain forests, or other remote regions, or if you want to stay for more than six weeks, check the CDC website.

In areas where malaria and dengue are prevalent, sleep under mosquito nets. If you're a real worrier, pack your own—it's the only way to be sure there are no tears. Although most hotels in Belize have screened or glassed windows, your room probably won't be completely mosquito-proof. Wear clothing that covers your arms and legs, apply repellent containing at least 30% DEET, and spray for flying insects in living and sleeping areas.

There's no vaccine for dengue, but you can take antimalarial pills; chloroquine (the commonly recommended antimalarial for Belize and Guatemala) is sold as Aralen in Central America. It must be started a week before entering an area with malaria risk. Malarone is prescribed as an alternative, and it can be started only two days before arrival in a risk area. Don't overstress about this: in Belize there are fewer than 1,000 reported cases of malaria a year, mostly in the far south, actually fewer cases than are reported in the United States. In Guatemala, El Petén is a risk area.

You should be up-to-date on shots for tetanus and hepatitis A and B. Children traveling to Central America should have current inoculations against measles, mumps, rubella, hepatitis, and polio.

Health Warnings United States Centers for Disease Control & Prevention (*CDC*) ☎ *800/232-4636* ⊕ *www.cdc.gov.* **World Health Organization** (*WHO*) ⊕ *www.who.int.*

MEDICAL INSURANCE AND ASSISTANCE

Consider buying trip insurance with medical-only coverage. Neither Medicare nor some private insurers cover medical expenses anywhere outside of the United States. Medical-only policies typically reimburse you for medical care (excluding that related to preexisting conditions) and hospitalization abroad, and provide for evacuation. You still have to pay the bills and await reimbursement from the insurer, though.

Another option is to sign up with a medical-evacuation assistance company. A membership in one of these companies gets you doctor referrals, emergency evacuation or repatriation, 24-hour hotlines for medical consultation, and other assistance. A few credit cards, such as American Express Platinum, include medical evacuation among their perks. International SOS Assistance Emergency and AirMed International provide evacuation services and medical referrals. MedjetAssist offers medical evacuation.

Medical Assistance Companies AirMed International ☎ *205/443-4840, 800/356-2161* ⊕ *www.airmed.com.* **MedjetAssist** ☎ *800/527-7478* ⊕ *www.medjetassist.com.*

Medical-Only Insurers International Medical Group ☎ *800/628-4664, 317/655-4500* ⊕ *www.imglobal.com.* **International SOS** ⊕ *www.internationalsos.com.* **Wallach & Company** ☎ *800/237-6615, 540/687-3172* ⊕ *www.wallach.com.*

▌ HOURS OF OPERATION

Belize is a laid-back place that requires a certain amount of flexibility when shopping or sightseeing. Small shops tend to open according to the whim of the owner, but generally operate 8–noon and 1–6. Larger stores and supermarkets in Belize City and in larger towns such as San Ignacio and San Pedro don't close for lunch.

On Friday some shops close early, and many are only open a half day on Saturday. On Sunday, Belize takes it easy: few shops are open, and many restaurants outside of hotels are closed. Most Mayan sites in Belize are open 8–5. Guatemala's Tikal ruins are open daily 6–6, with longer hours for those staying at lodges in the park.

HOLIDAYS

New Year's Day (January 1); Baron Bliss Day (officially March 9, but observation date may vary); Good Friday; Holy Saturday; Easter Monday; Labour Day (May 1); Sovereign's Day, also called Commonwealth Day (May 24); National Day (September 10); Independence Day (September 21); Columbus Day, also known as Pan-American Day (October 12); Garífuna Settlement Day (November 19); Christmas Day; Boxing Day (December 26).

■ MAIL AND SHIPPING

When sending mail to Central America, be sure to include the city or town and district, country name, and the words "Central America" in the address. Don't use the abbreviation "CA" or your mail may end up in California, USA. Belizean mail service is very good, except to and from remote villages, and the stamps, mostly of wildlife, are beautiful. An airmail letter from Belize City takes about a week to reach the United States, longer—sometimes several weeks—from other areas.

An airmail letter to the United States is BZ60¢, a postcard, BZ30¢; to Europe, BZ75¢ for a letter, BZ40¢ for a postcard. The post office in Belize City is open Monday–Thursday 8–5 and Friday 8–4:30.

EXPRESS SERVICES

If you have to send something fast, use FedEx or DHL Worldwide Express, which are expensive but do the job right. Both have offices in Belize City and agents elsewhere. In San Pedro, Mail Boxes Etc. can wrap and ship your packages.

Express Services DHL Worldwide Express ✉ *41 Hydes Ln., Belize City* ☎ *223/4350* ⊕ *www.dhl.com.* **FedEx** ✉ *6 Fort St., Fort George, Belize City* ☎ *223/1577* ⊕ *www.fedex.com.* **Mail Boxes Etc.** ✉ *Coconut Dr., San Pedro* ☎ *226/4770* ⊕ *www.mbe-belize.com.*

POST OFFICES

There are two post offices in Belize City (N. Front Street and Queen Square) as well as in Belmopan, Benque Viejo, Caye Caulker, Corozal Town, Dangriga, Independence, Ladyville, Orange Walk Town, Placencia, Punta Gorda, San Pedro, and San Ignacio. Mail service from Belize City to and from the United States and other countries is generally fast and reliable (airmail to and from the United States usually takes about seven days). To and from outlying towns and villages service is slower, and for remote villages may take weeks. For faster, though expensive, service use DHL and FedEx.

Post Office Main Post Office—Belize Postal Service ✉ *150 N. Front St., Belize City* ☎ *227/2201* ⊕ *www.belizepostalservice.gov. bz* ☉ *Mon.–Thurs. 8–noon and 1–5; Fri. 8–noon and 1–4:30; closed Sat. and Sun.*

■ MONEY

There are two ways of looking at the prices in Belize: Either it's one of the cheapest countries in the Caribbean or one of the most expensive countries in Central America. A good hotel room for two will cost you upward of BZ$250; a budget one, as little as BZ$40. A meal in one of the more expensive restaurants will cost BZ$50–BZ$75 for one, but you can eat the classic Creole dish of stew chicken and rice and beans for BZ$8. Prices are highest in Belize City, Ambergris Caye and the Placencia peninsula.

ITEM	AVERAGE COST IN BELIZE
Cup of Coffee	BZ$2
Glass of Wine	BZ$10–BZ$18
Glass of Beer	BZ$3–BZ$10
Sandwich	BZ$6–BZ$18
One-Mile Taxi Ride in Belize City	BZ$7
Museum Admission	BZ$10–BZ$20

Prices throughout this guide are given for adults. Substantially reduced fees are usually available for children, students, and senior citizens.

ATMS AND BANKS

Belize has three local banks: Heritage Bank ⊕ *www.heritageibt.com,* Atlantic Bank ⊕ *www.atlabank.com,* and Belize Bank ⊕ *www.belizebank.com*; and two international ones, First Caribbean International ⊕ *www.cibcfcib.com,* and ScotiaBank ⊕ *www.belize.scotiabank.com.* Hours vary, but are typically Monday–Thursday 8–2 and Friday 8–4. There is a branch of Atlantic Bank at the international airport, with longer hours. Belize Bank closed its branch at the international airport but still has an ATM there. All the banks have ATMs across the country that are open 24/7, though occasionally machines may run out of cash or are out of order.

Your own bank will probably charge a fee for using ATMs abroad; the foreign bank you use will also charge a fee. However, extracting funds as you need them is a safer option than carrying around a large amount of cash. That said, machines sometimes are down or out of money. As a backup, carry some U.S. currency, a credit card, and perhaps a few traveler's checks.

ATMs in Belize give cash in Belize dollars. There are ATMs in Belize City (including two at the international airport), Corozal Town, Orange Walk Town, San Pedro, Caye Caulker, Belmopan, San Ignacio, Spanish Lookout, Dangriga, Hopkins, Placencia, and Punta Gorda. Most ATMs in Belize have a BZ$500 daily limit. Belize Bank's 25 ATMs around the country take ATM cards issued outside Belize on the CIRRUS, MasterCard, PLUS, and Visa networks. Atlantic Bank's 15 ATMs also accept foreign cards on the CIRRUS, MasterCard, PLUS and Visa networks. First Caribbean International Bank's seven ATMs and ScotiaBank's 11 ATMs around the country also accept foreign-issued ATM cards. Heritage Bank has ATMs, but as of this writing they only accept ATM cards issued in Belize. Other bank offices you see in Belize City or San Pedro are likely international banks; they are set up to do business with individuals and companies outside of Belize and do not provide retail banking services in Belize.

In the Petén you can get cash in quetzales from ATMs in Flores and Santa Elena.

The biggest employer in Belize—the Belize government—pays most employees on the 14th or 15th of the month, and on those days in particular banks in Belize are jammed, with customer lines often snaking around the outside of the building. Banks are also usually busy on Friday.

You should have a four-digit PIN. ATM scams—where the ATM "eats" your card or your PIN is stolen—are rare in Belize but increasingly common in Guatemala. Most banks offer cash advances on credit cards issued by Visa and MasterCard for a fee ranging from BZ$10 to BZ$30.

BELIZE CITY

Banks Atlantic Bank ☒ *Main Office, Corner Freetown Rd. and Cleghorn St., Belize City* ☎ *223/4123* ⊕ *www.atlabank.com.* **Belize Bank** ☒ *Main Office, 60 Market Sq., Belize City* ☎ *227/7132* ⊕ *www.belizebank.com.* **First Caribbean International Bank** ☒ *21 Albert St., Belize City* ☎ *227/7212.* **Heritage Bank** ☒ *106 Princess Margaret Dr., Belize City* ☎ *223/5698.* **ScotiaBank** ☒ *4 Albert St., Belize City* ☎ *227/7027.*

AMBERGRIS CAYE

Banks Atlantic Bank. The Atlantic Bank San Pedro office is on Pescador Drive, but the ATM is on Barrier Reef Drive. ☒ *Pescador Dr. (Office), Barrier Reef Dr. (ATM), San Pedro* ☎ *226/2195.* **Belize Bank** ☒ *49 Barrier Reef Dr., San Pedro* ☎ *226/2482.* **Heritage Bank** ☒ *33 Barrier Reef Dr., San Pedro* ☎ *226/2136* ⊕ *www.heritageibt.com.* **ScotiaBank** ☒ *12 Coconut Dr., San Pedro* ☎ *226/3730.*

NORTHERN BELIZE

Banks Atlantic Bank ☒ *4th Ave. and 3rd St. N., Corozal* ☎ *422/3473.* **Atlantic Bank Orange Walk.** Also a second Atlantic Bank branch in Orange Walk Town on Belize-Corozal Rd. ☒ *47 Main St., Orange Walk Town* ☎ *322/1575.* **Belize Bank** ☒ *5th Ave. at 1st St. North, Corozal* ☎ *422/2087.* **ScotiaBank** ☒ *4th Ave. at 3rd St., Corozal* ☎ *422/2046.* **ScotiaBank Orange Walk** ☒ *Main St. and Park St., Orange Walk* ☎ *322/2194.*

THE CAYO

Banks Atlantic Bank ☒ *17 Burns Ave., San Ignacio* ☎ *824/2347.* **Belize Bank** ☒ *Constitution Dr., at Melhado Dr., Belmopan* ☎ *822/2303.* **First Caribbean International Bank** ☒ *Market Square, Belmopan* ☎ *822/2382.* **ScotiaBank** ☒ *Burns Ave., San Ignacio* ☎ *824/4191.*

THE SOUTHERN COAST

Banks Atlantic Bank ⊠ *Atlantic Bank, Main St., Placencia* ☎ *523/3431.* **Belize Bank** ⊠ *24 St. Vincent St., Dangriga* ☎ *522/2903* ⊠ *Placencia Point, Main St., Placencia* ☎ *523/3144.* **First Caribbean International Bank** ⊠ *1 Commerce St., Dangriga* ☎ *522/2015.* **Scotia-Bank** ⊠ *Main St., Placencia* ☎ *523/3277.*

THE DEEP SOUTH

Banks Belize Bank ⊠ *30 Main St., at Hospital St., Punta Gorda* ☎ *722/2324.* **Scotia-Bank** ⊠ *Prince and Main Sts., Punta Gorda* ☎ *722/0098.*

CREDIT CARDS

It's a good idea to inform your credit-card company (debit-card companies, too) before you travel, especially if you're going abroad and don't travel internationally very often. Otherwise, the credit-card company might put a hold on your card owing to unusual activity—not a good thing halfway through your trip.

Record all your credit-card numbers—as well as the phone numbers to call if your cards are lost or stolen—in a safe place, so you're prepared should something go wrong. Both MasterCard and Visa have general numbers you can call (collect if you're abroad) if your card is lost, but you're better off calling the number of your issuing bank, since Master-Card and Visa usually just transfer you to your bank; your bank's number is usually printed on your card.

In Belize, MasterCard and Visa are widely accepted, American Express less so, and Discover and Diner's hardly at all.

■TIP➔ Hotels, restaurants, shops, and tour operators in Belize sometimes levy a surcharge for credit-card use, usually 5% but ranging from 2% to 10%. This practice happily has become less common, but it still happens. If you use a credit card, ask if there's a surcharge. Most credit-card issuers now also charge an international exchange fee, usually 2% to 3%, even if the foreign purchase is denominated in U.S. dollars.

Reporting Lost Cards American Express ☎ *800/528–4800 in U.S., 954/473–2123 collect from abroad* ⊕ *www.americanexpress.com.* **Discover** ☎ *800/347–2683 in U.S., 801/902–3100 from abroad* ⊕ *www.discovercard.com.* **MasterCard** ☎ *800/627–8372 in U.S., 636/722–7111 collect from abroad including Belize* ⊕ *www.mastercard.com.* **Visa.** *Visa is the most widely accepted credit card in Central America.* ☎ *800/847–2911 in U.S., 303/967–1096 from abroad including Belize* ⊕ *www.visa.com.*

CURRENCY AND EXCHANGE

Because the U.S. dollar is gladly accepted everywhere in Belize, there's little need to exchange it. When paying in U.S. dollars, you may get change in Belize or U.S. currency, or in both.

The Belize dollar (BZ$) is pegged to the U.S. dollar at a rate of BZ$2 per US$1, and nearly all shops, stores, hotels, restaurants, and other businesses honor that exchange rate. Note, however, that moneychangers at Belize's Mexico and Guatemala borders operate on a free-market system and pay a rate depending on the demand for U.S. dollars, sometimes as high as BZ$2.15 to US$1. Banks (and ATMs) generally exchange at BZ$1.98 or less.

The best place to exchange Belize dollars for Mexican pesos is in Corozal, or at the Mexico-Belize border where the exchange rate is quite good. At the Guatemala border near Benque Viejo del Carmen, you can exchange Belize or U.S. dollars for quetzales—moneychangers will approach you on the Belize side and also on the Guatemala side. Usually the money changers on the Guatemala side offer better rates.

When leaving Belize, you can exchange Belizean currency back to U.S. dollars (up to US$100) at Atlantic Bank at the international airport. The Belize dollar is difficult if not impossible to exchange outside of Belize.

In Belize most hotel, tour, and car-rental prices are quoted in U.S. dollars, while most restaurant prices are in Belize dollars.

In this guide, all Belize prices are quoted in Belize dollars. Because misunderstandings can happen, if it's not clear, always ask which currency is being used.

TRAVELER'S CHECKS

Traveler's checks should be in U.S. dollars, and the American Express brand is preferred. Most hotels and travel operators accept traveler's checks, and some restaurants and gift shops do. However, even in Belize City and popular tourist areas such as San Pedro, clerks at groceries and other shops may be reluctant to accept traveler's checks or will have to get a supervisor's approval to accept them. Some places charge a small fee, around 1% or 2%, if you pay with a traveler's check. Most banks will cash them for a fee of 1% to 2%, but it may require a long wait in line. In all cases, you will need your passport in order to use or cash a traveler's check.

∎ PACKING

Pack light. Baggage carts are scarce at Central American airports, and international luggage limits are increasingly tight. Tropic Air and Maya Island Air officially have 70-pound (32-kilogram) weight limits for checked baggage. However, in practice the airlines in Belize rarely weigh luggage, and if you're a little over it's usually no problem. Occasionally, if the flight on the small Cessna or other airplane is full and there's a lot of luggage, some bags may be sent on the next flight, usually no more than an hour or two later.

Bring casual, comfortable, hand-washable clothing. T-shirts and shorts are acceptable near the beach and in tourist areas. More modest attire is appropriate in smaller towns, and the same long sleeves and pants will protect your skin from the ferocious sun and mosquitoes. Bring a hat to block the sun from your face and neck. If you're on a boat, you'll want a tight fitting cap or hat with chinstrap to keep it from being blown away.

If you're heading into the mountains or highlands, especially during the winter months, bring a light sweater, a jacket, and something warm to sleep in, as nights and early mornings can be chilly. Sturdy sneakers or hiking shoes or lightweight boots with rubber soles for wet or rocky surfaces are essential. A pair of sandals (preferably ones that can be worn in the water) are good, too.

Be sure to bring insect repellent, sunscreen, sunglasses, and an umbrella. Other handy items include tissues, a plastic water bottle, and a flashlight (for occasional power outages or use in areas without streetlights). A mosquito net for those roughing it is essential, but people staying in hotels or lodges—even budget-level ones—rarely need one. Snorkelers should consider bringing their own equipment, especially mask and snorkel, if there's room in the suitcase. Divers will save money—typically BZ$50 a day in rentals—by bringing their own equipment. Sand and high humidity are enemies of your camera equipment. To protect it, consider packing your gear in plastic ziplock bags. Also bring your own condoms and tampons. You won't find either easily or in familiar brands.

∎ PASSPORTS AND VISAS

To enter Belize, only a valid passport is necessary for citizens of the United States, European Union countries, Australia, Canada, CARICOM member states, Commonwealth realms, Great Britain, Switzerland, Hong Kong, Mexico, Costa Rica, Chile, Guatemala, New Zealand, Norway, Iceland, Tunisia, South Africa, and Venezuela; no visa is required. Nationals of most other countries require a visa and/or clearance by the immigration office. Check the Belize Tourist Board website for updates on visas. You can also check with the Belize Immigration and Nationality Department, the Embassy of Belize in Washington, DC, or other Belize embassies.

If upon arrival the customs official asks how long you expect to stay in Belize, give the longest period you might stay—you may be granted a stay for up to 30 days on the tourist stamp you'll receive for your passport on entry—otherwise, the official may endorse your passport with a shorter period.

You can renew your entry permit at immigration offices for a fee of BZ$50 per month for the first six months; after six months, it costs BZ$100 a month for up to six more months, at which time you may have to leave the country for 72 hours to start the process over (sometimes this rule isn't enforced). Note that renewals aren't guaranteed, but normally are routinely granted.

If you're young with a backpack and entering Belize by land from Mexico or Guatemala, there's a slight chance you'll be asked to prove you have enough money to cover your stay. You're supposed to have US$60 a day, though this requirement is rarely enforced. A credit card also may work.

Citizens of the United States, Canada, and most other Western countries do not need a visa when entering Guatemala from Belize.

Info in Belize Belize Immigration and Nationality Department ☎ *822/0284 in Belmopan* ⊕ *www.governmentofbelize.gov.bz.* **Belize Tourism Board** ✉ *64 Regent St., Belize City* ☎ *227/2420 in Belize, 800/624–0686 toll-free in U.S. and Canada* ✍ *info@ travelbelize.org* ⊕ *www.travelbelize.org.* **Belize Tourism Industry Association (BTIA)** ✉ *10 N. Park St., Belize City* ☎ *227/1144* ⊕ *www.btia.org.*

U.S. Passport Information U.S. Department of State ☎ *877/487–2778 passport information* ⊕ *www.state.gov.*

GENERAL REQUIREMENTS FOR BELIZE	
Passport	Must be valid for 3 months after date of arrival.
Visa	Not required for Americans, Canadians, and European Union citizens, among others; a tourist card good for up to 30 days is issued free upon arrival
Vaccinations	Yellow fever only if coming from an infected area such as parts of Africa
Driving	Valid driver's license from your home country
Departure Tax	By international air: US$39.25, usually included in the cost of your airline ticket; if not, it must be paid in U.S. dollars or by credit card. By land border into Mexico or Guatemala: US$18.75, payable in U.S. or Belize dollars. By water taxi or boat: usually US$18.75, payable in U.S. or Belize dollars

▌ RESTROOMS

You won't find many public restrooms in Belize, but hotels and restaurants usually have clean, modern facilities with American-style—indeed American-made—toilets. Hot-water showers in Belize often are the on-demand type, powered by butane gas.

Restrooms in Guatemala use Western-style toilets, although bathroom tissue generally shouldn't be flushed but discarded in a basket beside the toilet.

Find a Loo The Bathroom Diaries. The Bathroom Diaries is flush with unsanitized info on restrooms the world over—each one located, reviewed, and rated. Unfortunately, only one bathroom is listed in Belize. ⊕ *www.thebathroomdiaries.com.*

▌SAFETY

CRIME

There's considerable crime in Belize City, but it rarely involves visitors. When it does, Belize has a rapid justice system: the offender often gets a trial within hours or days and, if convicted, can be sent to prison ("the Hattieville Ramada") the same day. Tourist police patrol Fort George and other areas of Belize City where visitors convene. Police are particularly in evidence when cruise ships are in port. If you avoid walking around at night (except in well-lighted parts of the Fort George area), you should have no problems in Belize City.

Outside of Belize City, and possibly the rougher parts of Dangriga and Orange Walk Town, you'll find Belize to be safe and friendly. Petty theft, however, is common all over, so don't leave cameras, cell phones, and other valuables unguarded.

Thefts from budget hotel rooms occur occasionally. Given the hundreds of thousands of visitors to Belize, however, these incidents are isolated, and the vast majority of travelers never experience any crime in Belize.

The road from the Belize border toward Tikal has long been an area where armed robbers stopped buses and cars, and there also have been incidents at Tikal Park itself. In mid-2011 murderous attacks on Guatemalan farm workers and Guatemalan government officials in the Petén (including the decapitation of more than two-dozen workers on a farm southwest of Flores) allegedly by members of Mexico's Los Zetas drug cartel prompted the U.S. Embassy in Belize to "strongly recommend against" travel to Flores and Tikal, but that has since been lifted. Ask locally about crime conditions before traveling to Tikal.

If you are an American citizen, consider enrolling in the U.S. Statement Department's Smart Traveler Enrollment Program (⊕ travelregistration.state.gov/ibrs/ui), which makes it easier to locate you and your family in case of an emergency. Many other countries have similar programs.

CONCERNS FOR WOMEN

Many women travel alone or in small groups in Belize without any problems. Machismo is not as much a factor in the former British Honduras as it is in Latin countries in the region. Unfortunately, in the past Guatemala has been the site of some disturbing assaults on women. These have occurred on buses, usually late at night in remote areas. Women should avoid making such trips alone. A more common complaint is catcalling, which is typically more of an annoyance than a legitimate threat. Most women, locals and foreigners alike, try to brush it off. That said, however, women make up a large percentage of the travelers in Guatemala, and the vast majority have positive experiences.

SCAMS

Most Belizeans and Guatemalans are extremely honest and trustworthy. It's not uncommon for a vendor to chase you down if you accidentally leave without your change. That said, most organized scams arise with tours and packages, in which you're sold a ticket that turns out to be bogus. Arrange all travel through a legitimate agency, and always get a receipt. If a problem does arise, the Belize Tourism Board or INGUAT may be able to help mediate the conflict.

Advisories and Other Information
Transportation Security Administration
(TSA). ☎ 866/289-9673 ⊕ www.tsa.gov. **U.S. Department of State** ⊕ www.travel.state.gov.

▌TAXES

The hotel tax in Belize is 9%, and a 12.5% Goods and Services Tax (GST) is charged on meals, tours, and other purchases at the hotel, along with most other purchases in Belize including car rentals and tours. The GST is supposed to be included in the cost of meals, goods, and services, but some businesses add the tax on instead. There has been discussion by the government of raising the hotel tax, likely to the 12.5% GST rate, but as of this writing no final decision has been made.

When departing the country by international air, even on a short hop to Flores, Guatemala, you'll pay US$39.25 departure tax and fees. This must be paid in U.S. dollars or by credit card. However, most international airlines include the departure tax in the airline ticket price. Don't pay twice—check your airline to see if the tax is included.

When leaving Belize by land to either Guatemala or Mexico, there's a border exit fee of BZ$30, plus a conservation fee of BZ$7.50. This may be paid in either U.S. dollars or Belize dollars, but not by credit card. For departures by boat to Guatemala or Honduras, you'll also pay the BZ$7.50 conservation fee and the BZ$30 exit fee, in U.S. or Belize dollars. Those in transit through Belize, staying less than 24 hours, can avoid paying the BZ$7.50 conservation fee but have to fork out the other taxes and fees.

Some Guatemalan hotels and some tourist restaurants charge a 10% to 20% tourist tax, though others include the tax in the price. The Guatemala airport-departure tax is US$30, plus an almost US$3 security fee. Guatemalan border officials often charge a Q20 fee (about US$2.50) when entering Guatemala at Melchor de Mencos, though this is not really official; however, it's often easier just to pay the small amount than to raise a major fuss.

▍TIME

Belize and Guatemala time is the same as U.S. Central Standard Time. Daylight saving time is not observed. (Note that Mexico does observe daylight saving time.)

Time Zones Timeanddate.com
⊕ www.timeanddate.com/worldclock.

▍TIPPING

Belize restaurants rarely add a service charge, so in better restaurants tip 10%–15% of the total bill. At inexpensive places, leave small change or tip 10%.

Many hotels and resorts add a service charge, usually 10%, to bills, so at these places additional tipping isn't necessary. In general, Belizeans tend not to look for tips, though with increasing tourism this is changing. It's not customary to tip taxi drivers.

In Guatemala, restaurant bills do not typically include gratuities; 10% is customary. Bellhops and maids expect tips only in the expensive hotels. Guards who show you around ruins and locals who help you find hotels or give you little tours should also be tipped. Children will often charge a quetzal to let you take their photo.

TIPPING GUIDELINES FOR BELIZE	
Bartender	BZ$2–BZ$5 per round of drinks, or 10%-15% of the cost of the drinks
Bellhop	BZ$1–BZ$4 per bag, depending on the level of the hotel
Hotel Doorman	BZ$2–BZ$4 if he helps you get a cab
Hotel Maid	BZ$4–BZ$10 a day (either daily or at the end of your stay, in cash); nothing additional is required if a service charge is added to your bill, though some guests tip extra directly to the maid
Hotel Room-Service Waiter	BZ$2–BZ$5 per delivery, even if a service charge has been added
Porter at Airport	BZ$2 per bag
Taxi Driver	Not usually tipped, unless he or she carries your luggage or performs other extra services
Tour Guide	10% of the cost of the tour
Waiter	10%–15%, with 15% being the norm at high-end restaurants; nothing additional if a service charge is added to the bill
Fishing Guides	BZ$40–BZ$80 a day

■ TOURS

See also individual chapters for local operators. Note: Many of the recommended operators below, in addition to the categories they are listed under, offer multisport adventures and expeditions.

ARCHAEOLOGY

In Belize you can participate in a "dig" at a Mayan archaeological site, usually under the direction of a university archaeological team. Sessions run only a few weeks of the year, usually in spring or summer. Archaeological digs that accept volunteer workers are mostly in Orange Walk District. Archaeological programs start at around BZ$1,440 per person for a one-week volunteer session, and BZ$2,240 to BZ$3,500 for a two-week session. Some programs offer academic college credit. Prices don't include transportation to Belize or incidental personal expenses.

Road Scholar, a division of Elderhostel, offers a 14-day program in Belize, Guatemala, and Honduras on the history of the Maya, with insight into modern-day issues affecting their community, starting at around US$3,385 per person. It also offers a 10-day Kingdoms of the Maya program, new in 2014, in Belize, Mexico, Honduras, and Guatemala for US$5,399 per person, and a nine-night Mystery of the Maya Program in Belize and Guatemala that combines snorkeling and visiting Maya sites for US$2,839 per person. All the Road Scholar programs include accommodations, meals, guides, field trips, and in-country transportation, but not flights to and from Belize. The Maya Research Program, established in 1992, has two-week volunteer programs in the Blue Creek area of Orange Walk District, at US$1,750 (US$1,500 for students). The University of Texas Mesoamerican Archaeological Research Laboratory (MARL) accepts volunteers at its field station in the Rio Bravo Conservation area of Orange Walk District, located on Programme for Belize lands.

Volunteers (who pay a fee of US$645 to US$1,465 to participate, which covers room and board but not air fare to and from Belize) must commit for one to three weeks. The program usually runs from February to May, with other options in summer, some for a semester of academic credit. Volunteers live in a rustic dorm setting and learn the basics of field archaeology through lectures and hands-on experience.

Contacts Elderhostel ⊠ *11 Avenue de Lafayette, Boston, Massachusetts, USA* ☎ *800/454–5768* ⊕ *www.roadscholar. org.* **Maya Research Program** ⊠ *1910 East Southeast Loop 323, #296, Tyler, Texas, USA* ☎ *817/831–9011* ⊕ *www. mayaresearchprogram.org.* **Road Scholar** ⊠ *11 Avenue de Lafayette, Boston, Massachusetts, USA* ☎ *800/454–5768* ⊕ *www. roadscholar.org.* **University of Texas Mesoamerican Archaeological Research Laboratory (MARL)** ⊠ *J. J. Pickle Research Campus, Building 5, 10100 Burnet Rd., Austin, Texas, USA* ☎ *512/471–5946* ⊕ *www.utexas.edu/ cola/orgs/mesolab/.*

BIRD WATCHING

Nearly 600 species of birds have been spotted in Belize, and every year five or more additional species are found in the country. Birders flock to Belize to see exciting species such as the jabiru stork, the largest flying bird in the Western Hemisphere; the harpy eagle; the scarlet macaw; the keel-billed toucan, the national bird of Belize; 21 species of hummingbirds; and endangered or rare species such as the yellow-headed parrot, ocellated turkey, orange-breasted falcon, and chestnut-breasted heron. Birding hot spots in Belize include Crooked Tree Wildlife Sanctuary, the Mountain Pine Ridge, the area around Chan Chich Lodge at Gallon Jug, and the Cockscomb Basin.

When selecting a bird-watching tour, ask questions. What species might be seen? What are the guide's qualifications? Does the operator work to protect natural habitats? How large are the birding groups? What equipment is used? (In addition to binoculars and a birding guidebook, this should include a high-powered telescope, a recorder to record and play back bird calls, and a spotlight for night viewing.) Trips can cost from BZ$1,600 per person for a six-day/five-night birding trip, including guides, lodging, and some meals. On an à la carte basis, short birding hikes with a local guide cost from BZ$30 per person, though at some jungle lodges such as Chaa Creek local birding hikes are free.

Victor Emanuel Nature Tours (VENT) has 2014 tours to Chan Chich. Wildside Nature Tours has 14-day birding trips in 2014 that visit Crooked Tree, Cockscomb, Cayo, and Tikal, from US$3,900 per person, not including airfare.

Contacts Victor Emmanuel Nature Tours ✉ *2525 Wallingwood Dr., Suite 1003, Austin, Texas, USA* ☎ *800/328–8368, 512/328–5221 in U.S.* ⊕ *www.ventbird.com.* **Wildside Nature Tours** ✉ *241 Emerald Dr., Yardley, Pennsylvania, USA* ☎ *888/875–9453, 610/564–0941* ⊕ *www.wildsidenaturetours.com.*

CULTURE TOURS AND HOMESTAYS

Homestays and village guesthouse stays in Mayan villages in Toledo District are offered by Toledo Ecotourism Association and Maya Villages Homestay Program, local organizations in the Punta Gorda area. These stays are very inexpensive, typically less than BZ$100 per day including meals and activities, but accommodations are basic.

Contact Maya Villages Homestay Program ✉ *Dem's Dats Doin', General Delivery, Punta Gorda* ☎ *722/2470.* **Toledo Ecotourism Association (T.E.A.)** ✉ *TEA c/o BTIA Office, 46 Front St., Punta Gorda* ☎ *722/2531 BTIA Office* ✎ *reservations@teabelize.org* ⊕ *www.teabelize.org.*

FISHING

The best-known fishing lodges in Belize are high-end resorts catering to affluent anglers who, after a hard day on the water, expect ice-cold cocktails, equally icy air-conditioning, and Sealy Posturepedic mattresses. El Pescador on North Ambergris Caye, two lodges on Turneffe Atoll (Turneffe Flats and Turneffe Island Lodge), and several beach resorts in Placencia and Hopkins offer fishing with a touch of luxury—everything from guides to cold drinks included. Fishing travel companies like Rod & Reel Adventures typically book with fishing lodges.

If you want a less expensive fishing vacation, you can make your own arrangements for lodging and meals and hire your own local fishing guides in San Pedro, Placencia, Hopkins, Punta Gorda, and elsewhere. Destinations Belize in Placencia is a compromise between a total package and doing it all yourself. The owner, Mary Toy, can help you arrange moderate accommodations, some meals, and guides for light-tackle or fly-fishing day trips (or for longer periods). She also puts together moderately priced packages for fishing in Placencia and elsewhere in southern Belize.

Contact Desinations Belize ✉ *Placencia Village* ☎ *523/4018* ⊕ *www.destinationsbelize. com.* **Rod and Reel Adventures** ☎ *800/356– 6982 in U.S. and Canada, 541/349–0777* ⊕ *www.rodreeladventures.com.*

HORSEBACK RIDING

U.S. Based Equitours offers riding tour packages in the Cayo. A six-day, five-night trip is US$950 per person. There is a maximum 200-pound weight limit.

Contact Equitours ✉ *10 Stalnaker St., Dubois, Wyoming, USA* ☎ *800/545–0019* ⊕ *www.equitours.com.*

KAYAKING

There are two types of kayaking trips: base kayaking and expedition kayaking. On a base kayaking trip you have a home base—usually a caye—from which you take day trips (or longer). On an expedition-style trip you travel from island to island or up mainland rivers. Typically, base kayaking is easier, but expedition kayaking is more adventurous.

G Adventures (formerly GAP Adventures) has a weeklong island-hopping kayak trip, starting and ending in Placencia, for around BUS$1,650 per person, not including air fare to Belize. You paddle for two to four hours a day, with stops at several cayes. Typically, about 10 people are on the kayak trip.

Island Expeditions does complete expedition packages, several of which combine sea and river kayaking and base and expedition aspects.

Contact G Adventures ⊠ *19 Charlotte St., Toronto, Ontario, Canada* ☎ *888/800-4100, 416/260-0999* ⊕ *www.gadventures.com.* **Island Expeditions** ⊠ *4-1384 Portage Rd., Pemberton, British Columbia, Canada* ☎ *800/667-1630 in North America, 0800/404-9535 from the U.K., 604/894-2312* ⊕ *www.islandexpeditions.com.*

MULTISPORT

Multisport simply means that you can take part in a series of different activities—hiking, kayaking, cave tubing, birding, swimming, snorkeling.

Many Belize adventure trips include a bunch of different activities. For example, the eight-day Land of Belize trip offered by Adventure Center (US$1,050 per person not including meals) starts with a day in Belize City, then moves on to caving, biking, and hiking in the Cayo, followed by a visit to Tikal, and ending with snorkeling or diving off Caye Caulker. Adventure Life offers an 11-day Ultimate

Adventure tour, at US$2,499 per person, with jungle hiking, paddling, snorkeling, and visits to Mayan sites. Island Expeditions' 10-night Ultimate Adventure trip (US$2,499 per person, including taxes and government fees) combines sea kayaking, snorkeling, and optional diving at Glover's Atoll with a river trip on the Moho in Toledo District.

Contacts Adventure Center ⊠ *1311 63rd St., 2nd Floor, Emoryville, California, USA* ☎ *800/228-8747, 510/654-1879* ⊕ *www. adventurecenter.com.* **Adventure Life** ⊠ *712 W Spruce St., Suite 1, Missoula, Montana, USA* ☎ *800/344-6118, 406/406-541-2677* ⊕ *www.adventure-life.com.* **Island Expeditions** ☎ *604/452- 3212, 800/667-1630* ⊕ *www.islandexpeditions.com.*

PHOTO SAFARI

Nature Photography Adventure runs a "Secrets of the Maya" weeklong photo safari to Belize and Tikal. The company also has a "Wild Bunch" photo-safari trip to Belize and Guatemala, with an emphasis on remote caves. You have to be reasonably physically fit to join this trip. The 2014 trip is US$3,260–US$3,560 per person, not including air travel to Belize.

Contact Nature Photography Adventures ⊠ *P. O. Box 1900, Ava, Missouri, USA* ☎ *417/683-6881* ⊕ *www.naturephotographyadventures.com.*

SPECIAL INTEREST

International Zoological Expeditions has eight- to 10-day trips, usually with an educational component such as ethnobotanical walks or mapping an island. IZE's trips combine time inland at Blue Creek in Toledo and at South Water Caye.

Contact International Zoological Expeditions ⊠ *210 Washington St., Sherborne, Massachusetts, USA* ☎ *508/655-1461* ⊕ *www.izebelize.com.*

ONLINE RESOURCES

For information on Belize, your first stop should be the official site of the Belize Tourism Board at ⊕ *www.travelbelize.org*. Belize Explorer (⊕ *www.belizeexplorer. com*), formerly the ToucanTrail.com site operated by the BTB, now is a private site that provides information on budget hotels—those priced under US$70 double. The **Belize Tourism Industry Association** (⊕ *www.btia.org*) also provides visitor information, mainly through information offices and monthly publications for visitors in Placencia and Punta Gorda.

The Belize Forums (⊕ *www.belizeforum. com/belize*) is an active online community of Belize visitors and residents; many regulars are happy to answer questions, though occasionally discussions become heated. Also, Lan Sluder, the author of this guide and other books on Belize, has his own site called ⊕ *www.belizefirst.com*.

Belize Bus Blog (⊕ *belizebus.wordpress. com*) has detailed and comprehensive information on bus, water taxi, shuttle, and other transportation in Belize.

For destination-specific information, check out ⊕ *Ambergriscaye.com* for San Pedro; ⊕ *GoCayeCaulker.com*, and *CayeCaulker. org* for Caye Caulker; ⊕ *Belmopan CityOnline.com* for Belmopan; ⊕ *Belizex.com* for the Cayo district and elsewhere; ⊕ *Placencia.com* and *Destinations Belize.com* for Placencia; ⊕ *Southern Belize.com* for Punta Gorda and southern Belize; ⊕ *HopkinsBelize.com* and *Cometo Hopkins.com* for the Hopkins area; and ⊕ *NorthernBelize.com* and *Corozal.com* for northern Belize. There also are hundreds of personal blogs on living in and visiting Belize.

For information on Guatemala, contact that country's tourist board, INGUAT.

Contacts Belize Tourism Board (*BTB*) ⊠ *64 Regent St., Belize City* ☎ *227/2420, 800/624-0686 in U.S. and Canada* ⊕ *www. travelbelize.org* ⊗ *Mon.–Thurs. 8–5, Fri. 8–4.* **Belize Tourism Industry Association (BTIA)** ☎ *227/1144* ✑ *info@btia.org* ⊕ *www.btia.org.* **INGUAT.** INGUAT's websites are now in Spanish only. ☎ *502/2421–2800 general information, 1500 in Guatemala dial this number for tourist assistance* ✑ *info@inguat.gob.gt* ⊕ *www.visitguatemala.com.*

INDEX

PHOTO CREDITS

NOTES

NOTES

NOTES

Fodor's BELIZE

Publisher: Amanda D'Acierno, *Senior Vice President*

Editorial: Arabella Bowen, *Editor in Chief*; Linda Cabasin, *Editorial Director*

Design: Fabrizio La Rocca, *Vice President, Creative Director*; Tina Malancy, *Associate Art Director*; Chie Ushio, *Senior Designer*; Ann McBride, *Production Designer*

Photography: Melanie Marin, *Associate Director of Photography*; Jessica Parkhill and Jennifer Romains, *Researchers*

Maps: Rebecca Baer, *Senior Map Editor*; David Lindroth and Ed Jacobus, *Cartographers*

Production: Linda Schmidt, *Managing Editor*; Evangelos Vasilakis, *Associate Managing Editor*; Angela L. McLean, *Senior Production Manager*

Sales: Jacqueline Lebow, *Sales Director*

Marketing & Publicity: Heather Dalton, *Marketing Director*; Katherine Fleming, *Senior Publicist*

Business & Operations: Susan Livingston, *Vice President, Strategic Business Planning*; Sue Daulton, *Vice President, Operations*

Fodors.com: Megan Bell, *Executive Director, Revenue & Business Development*; Yasmin Marinaro, *Senior Director, Marketing & Partnerships*

Copyright © 2014 by Fodor's Travel, a division of Random House LLC.

Writer: Lan Sluder

Editor: Eric B. Wechter

Production Editor: Carolyn Roth

6th Edition

ISBN 978-0-8041-4169-7

ISSN 1559-081X

All details in this book are based on information supplied to us at press time. Always confirm information when it matters, especially if you're making a detour to visit a specific place. Fodor's expressly disclaims any liability, loss, or risk, personal or otherwise, that is incurred as a consequence of the use of any of the contents of this book.

SPECIAL SALES

This book is available at special discounts for bulk purchases for sales promotions or premiums. For more information, e-mail specialmarkets@randomhouse.com

PRINTED IN THE UNITED STATES OF AMERICA

10 9 8 7 6 5 4 3 2 1

ABOUT OUR WRITER

Belize First magazine founder **Lan Sluder** has been banging around Belize since 1991. In addition to authoring *Fodor's Belize* since the first edition, *Easy Belize,* and other books on the country, he's written about it for *Caribbean Travel & Life,* the *Bangkok Post,* and Canada's *Globe & Mail,* among other publications. His favorite parts of Belize? Sarteneja and Punta Gorda. His family, though, prefers Caye Caulker and Placencia.